Ireland's Empire

How did the Irish stay Irish? Why are Irish and Catholic still so often synonymous in the English-speaking world? *Ireland's Empire* is the first book to examine the complex relationship between Irish migrants and Roman Catholicism in the nineteenth century on a truly global basis. Drawing on more than 100 archives on five continents, Colin Barr traces the spread of Irish Roman Catholicism across the English-speaking world and explains how the Catholic Church became the vehicle for Irish diasporic identity in the United States, Australia, Canada, South Africa, New Zealand, Newfoundland, and India between 1829 and 1914. The world these Irish Catholic bishops, priests, nuns, and laity created endured long into the twentieth century, and its legacy is still present today.

Colin Barr is Senior Lecturer in history in the School of Divinity, History and Philosophy at the University of Aberdeen. He is the author of several books on Irish history, including *Paul Cullen, John Henry Newman, and the Catholic University of Ireland, 1845–1865* (2003) and *The European Culture Wars in Ireland: The Callan Schools Affair 1868–1881* (2010), and is co-editor of *Nation/Nazione: Irish Nationalism and the Italian Risorgimento* (2014), with Michele Finelli and Anne O'Connor, and *Religion and Greater Ireland: Christianity and Irish Global Networks, 1750–1950* (2015), with Hilary M. Carey.

Ireland's Empire

The Roman Catholic Church in the English-Speaking World, 1829–1914

Colin Barr

University of Aberdeen

CAMBRIDGE
UNIVERSITY PRESS

CAMBRIDGE
UNIVERSITY PRESS

University Printing House, Cambridge CB2 8BS, United Kingdom

One Liberty Plaza, 20th Floor, New York, NY 10006, USA

477 Williamstown Road, Port Melbourne, VIC 3207, Australia

314–321, 3rd Floor, Plot 3, Splendor Forum, Jasola District Centre,
New Delhi – 110025, India

79 Anson Road, #06–04/06, Singapore 079906

Cambridge University Press is part of the University of Cambridge.

It furthers the University's mission by disseminating knowledge in the pursuit of
education, learning, and research at the highest international levels of excellence.

www.cambridge.org
Information on this title: www.cambridge.org/9781107040922
DOI: 10.1017/9781139644327

First published 2020

A catalogue record for this publication is available from the British Library.

ISBN 978-1-107-04092-2 Hardback

For the archivists

Contents

Acknowledgements

This book began with a trip to Australia in 2004. I was coming to the end of four happy years in the Department of History at what was then the National University of Ireland, Maynooth, where I had been first a Government of Ireland Research Fellow in the Humanities and Social Sciences and then a contract lecturer. For much of that time, I had been working on a biography of Cardinal Paul Cullen of Dublin, a project that had grown out of my doctoral thesis and subsequent book on the origins, development, and ultimate failure of John Henry Newman's Catholic University of Ireland. Somewhere I had seen a reference to a diary kept by Cullen's nephew which had apparently survived in Sydney, so I made the long trip. Once there, I fell in love with Australia and resolved to learn more about its history. This led to compulsive prowling in what were then the city's many second-hand bookshops, and it was in one of these that I found John Molony's *The Roman Mould of the Australian Catholic Church*, published in 1969 by Melbourne University Press. I had never heard of it, and when I got home realized that few other people in the northern hemisphere had either. I was astonished to discover that Cullen, whose career I thought I knew well, had been central to the ecclesiastical and in some ways the secular history of Australia. I also soon learned that, while aspects of Molony's argument were controversial among Australian historians, there was no dispute at all about Cullen's importance. My first reaction was mortification. How did I not know this? Cullen is probably the best-documented Irishman of the nineteenth century, and I was familiar with the vast collections of his papers in Dublin and Rome. I knew that they were filled with letters from bishops, priests, nuns, and laypeople from all over the world, but I had not thought about why that might be or what it might mean. Molony made me wonder if Cullen might have been similarly influential elsewhere. To find out, I began an archival odyssey that has now lasted well over a decade and taken me to every corner of the globe.

This book is the result of that research. It draws on material found in 104 archives in 12 countries on 5 continents, the vast majority of which

I have visited personally. I have thus contracted an unusually large number of debts to the archivists, librarians, and diocesan and other administrators who welcomed me with unfailing kindness, professionalism, and
curiosity. I am grateful to them all without exception, including those
whose names I never knew or can no longer recall. It is, however,
a pleasure to be able to record my gratitude to Carol Anderson of the
Bathurst Repository of the Institute of Sisters of Mercy of Australia and
Papua New Guinea Archives; Donna Bailey, the archivist of the Diocese
of Sandhurst in Bendigo, Victoria; Jennifer Ballantine Perera, the director
of Gibraltar's magnificent Garrison Library; Wanita Bates, the archivist
for the Presentation Sisters of St John's, Newfoundland; Aidan Bellenger,
formerly the abbot of Downside Abbey in Somerset; Alberto Belletti, the
archivist of the North American College in Rome; David Bracken, the
archivist of the Diocese of Limerick; Damien Burke, the archivist of the
Irish Jesuits; Fr Christopher Francis Clarke, who kindly permitted me to
use the archives of the Discalced Carmelites in Dublin; Fr Kevin Clark,
the (now retired) archivist of the Diocese of Christchurch, who rescued
the archives after the devastating 2011 earthquake and then allowed me to
use them in their temporary store shortly afterwards; the late Bishop
Michael Coleman of Port Elizabeth, South Africa, who shared both his
knowledge and his archive; Alan Delozier, at Seton Hall University in
New Jersey; Gionni Di Gravio, the archivist of the University of
Newcastle, Australia; Chris Doan, the archivist of the Archdiocese of
San Francisco; the late and much lamented Larry Dohey, formerly the
archivist of the Archdiocese of St John's, Newfoundland; Brian Fahey of
the Diocese of Charleston, South Carolina; Kate Feighery, who has
helped to return the archives of the Archdiocese of New York to its proper
role in the story of the American Catholicism; Michael Foight, the Special
Collections and Digital Library Coordinator at the Falvey Memorial
Library, Villanova University; Richard Garcia of the Cathedral
Archives, Gibraltar; Pauline Garland and her successors and colleagues
at the archives of the Archdiocese of Sydney; the welcoming and hospi-
table Helena Glanville, who kindly hosted me in Port Elizabeth and
guided me through the nearly untouched (by historians) diocesan
archives; the similarly welcoming Jackie Grant, now retired from the
archives of the Diocese of Bathurst, Australia; Sr Elizabeth Hellwig OP
of the Dominican Archives in Sydney; Naomi Johnson of the archives of
the Archdiocese of Birmingham; Fr Thomas Kilbride, the rector of the
Royal Scots College in Salamanca; Marc Lerman, the former archivist of
the Archdiocese of Toronto; Jan Linley, who looks after the archives of
the Sisters of St Joseph of Peace in New Jersey; Ruth Long and her
colleagues at the Carmelite Centre, Gort Muire; Donna Maguire of the

Scottish Catholic Archives in Edinburgh; James McGuire, now retired from his role as chairman of the Irish Manuscripts Commission, who facilitated my access to the archives of the Archdiocese of Cashel; Áine McHugh, the archivist of the Loreto Sisters in Dublin; Mary McHugh, the archivist of the Archdiocese of Glasgow; Perry McIntyre, who in addition to her career as a scholar of Irish migration is also the archivist of St John's College in the University of Sydney; Fr Tom Murray of the Diocese of Ardagh and Clonmacnois; the estimable Rachel Naughton of the Melbourne Diocesan Historical Commission, upon whose labours most work on Catholic Victoria now rests; Odhran O'Brien of the Archdiocese of Perth; Fr Art O'Shea, the historian and archivist of the Diocese of Charlottetown, Prince Edward Island; Olivia Parkinson, the archivist at the Southern Administrative Centre of the Institute of Sisters of Mercy of Australia and Papua New Guinea in Alphington, Victoria; Anthony Pitaluga, the director of the Gibraltar National Archives; Tricia Pyne and Alison Foley at the Associated Archives, St Mary's Seminary and University, Baltimore; Richard Reid, formerly of the National Museum of Australia and now in retirement an independent researcher; Sr Assumpta Saunders RSM of Callan, Co. Kilkenny; Ken Scadden and the staff of the Marist Archives in Wellington, New Zealand; Rena Schergen, the archivist of the Archdiocese of St Louis; Robin Scott of the Archive Centre, Loreto College Ballarat; Fr Gerard Sharkey, the former vice rector of the Scots' College in Rome; Michael Taffe, the archivist of the Diocese of Ballarat; Karen White, formerly the archivist of the Archdiocese of Halifax; Kenneth White of the Archives and Records Center, Catholic Diocese of Pittsburgh; Maurice Whitehead of the Venerable English College in Rome; and, finally, Fr John Wisdom of the Falkland Islands, who kindly scanned important items from the archives of St Mary's parish in Port Stanley.

It is invidious to draw distinctions, but there are two archivists that I must nevertheless single out. The first is Julie Craig, now retired from the diocese of Maitland-Newcastle. Over several visits Julie gave me lifts, hosted me in her home, and granted me the run of her magnificent archive, probably the best-preserved Catholic archive in Australia. I could not have had a more productive and pleasant experience. Then there is Noelle Dowling, the archivist of the Archdiocese of Dublin. I never laugh so hard nor learn so much as when I go to see Noelle, and she oversees her great archive with professionalism, enthusiasm, and kindness. Both she and it are treasures. Finally, I am grateful to the staff at the many other archives and libraries that I have visited around the world, from the British Library to the Tasmanian Archive Service. This book is dedicated to you and to all the archivists and librarians who made it possible.

I have many other debts. In New Zealand, I was twice welcomed by Peter and Helen Field into their home in Christchurch, while Rory Sweetman both hosted me in Dunedin and gave me books from his own vast library. Clyde and Connie Lee always had a bed for me in Sydney, as did Brian and Ruth Barr in Ottawa, Matt O'Brien and Gina Casalegno in Pittsburgh, Peter Ludlow and his family in Antigonish, and Caroline McGregor in Boston and New Jersey. In Dublin, I could always count on Isabella and Adam Hanna and Tom and Rebecca Bartlett for company and accommodation. In Rome, Ciarán O'Carroll has been for many years a welcoming host at the Irish College, as were his predecessors Liam Bergin and John Fleming. Matteo Binasco kindly checked references for me at the Propaganda Fide and generally guided me around the Roman archives, while Luca Codignola and Matteo Sanfilippo provided sage advice and guidance. Kathleen Sprows Cummings of the University of Notre Dame has proved herself many times over a gracious host in both South Bend and Rome, and the emphasis on women religious in this book owes much to her example.

I owe an especially great debt to Hilary M. Carey. Hilary and I collaborated on the edited volume *Religion and Greater Ireland: Christianity and Irish Global Networks, 1750–1950*, which was published in 2015, and she arranged my visiting fellowship at the Humanities Research Institute at the University of Newcastle, Australia. Many of the themes of *Ireland's Empire* were first discussed with Hilary and, in particular, the concept of a spiritual Greater Ireland. When I reread our Introduction and Conclusion to *Religion and Greater Ireland*, I can no longer tell which words were hers and which were mine, and I hope she will excuse seeing some of her ideas here. She also read each chapter of this book, and her honesty and support have made it very much better. I am also grateful to the wider Carey family, who have over the years welcomed me into their homes in Newcastle, Sydney, and Bristol. It is a profound regret to me that I will not be able to give Bernard Carey a copy of this book. He is sorely missed.

Vincent Comerford in Ireland and Terrence Murphy in Nova Scotia also read each chapter as it was produced, often with very long gaps between, and they made the book much stronger with their suggestions, criticisms, and encouragement. I am also grateful to Vincent for our many tours around Ireland. John McGreevy graciously read the chapter on the United States, as did Gerard Horn the one on New Zealand. Carolyn Lambert, Patrick Mannion, and John FitzGerald helped me with the complexities of Newfoundland, while Peter Ludlow assisted with Canada as a whole. Leea Stroia lent her red pen and taught me about prepositions. Elizabeth Sullivan-Burton and Mary Carmichael graciously shared the research they conducted as undergraduates. I am grateful to them all, but, of course, the mistakes that remain are entirely my own.

This book would not have been possible without significant financial support. The Irish Research Council for the Humanities and Social Sciences (now the Irish Research Council) funded travel to South Africa, Australia, and New Zealand as part of the 'Correspondence of Paul Cullen' project, and I am grateful to the principal investigator Dáire Keogh and my fellow co-investigator Anne O'Connor for their help in launching this project. I am also grateful to Andrew Shields for his heroic work in deciphering and transcribing Cullen's outgoing letters. The first fruits of the project will soon appear when Anne's magisterial edition of Cullen's Italian letters is published by the Irish Manuscripts Commission, and I am grateful to her for sharing some of her work in advance of publication. The Social Sciences and Humanities Research Council of Canada supported the project 'Irish-Catholic Discourse and Social Mobility in Nineteenth-Century Halifax: The Exemplary Case of Holy Cross Cemetery', which funded significant research travel and the services of a postdoctoral researcher, Ben Thomas. I am grateful to the principal investigator Mark McGowan for inviting me to join the project. I have also enjoyed excellent institutional support, first at Maynooth, then in Florida, and, finally, in Aberdeen. I am especially grateful to Michael Dauphinais, formerly Dean of Faculty at Ave Maria University, and John Morrison, formerly Head of the School of Divinity, History and Philosophy at the University of Aberdeen, for their financial, professional, and personal encouragement. My colleagues in all three places have provided friendship, support, and constructive criticism, and I would like to thank Filipe Ribeiro de Meneses, Terrence Dooley, Georgina Laragy, Ian Speller, Paul Baxa, Jeff Hass, Michael Sugrue, Michael Brown, Alex Crawford, Andrew Dilley, Isabella Jackson, Rose Luminiello, Andrew Mackillop, Heidi Mehrkens, and Tom Weber. Thomas Bartlett in particular has been an invaluable friend and supporter, both before our time together in Aberdeen and since. I have also benefited greatly from conversations with friends and colleagues around the world, including Jill Bender, Ciara Breathnach, Seán Brosnahan, Michael De Nie, Doug Kanter, Joe Lee, Mark McGowan, Matt O'Brien, Oliver Rafferty, John Stenhouse, Paul Townend, Angela McCarthy, Tim McMahon, and James H. Murphy. My former doctoral supervisor, Eugenio Biagini, has remained a constant source of encouragement and support. He also arranged my tenure as a visiting fellow of

Sidney Sussex College, Cambridge, and I am most grateful to the master and fellows for welcoming me to the College in 2012. I am similarly grateful to the Humanities Research Institute at the University of Newcastle, Australia, where I was a visiting fellow in 2013.

A project of this length has inevitably produced various by-products along the way, and, consequently, parts of this book have appeared in preliminary or abbreviated form elsewhere. A truncated version of Chapter 4 appeared in *Religion and Greater Ireland: Christianity and Irish Global Networks, 1750–1950*, for example, while sections of Chapter 1 appeared in modified form in *The Irish College, Rome, and Its Worlds*, edited by Dáire Keogh and Albert McDonnell. Elements of the discussion of St Brigid's Missionary College in Chapter 6 of this book first appeared in the essay I co-wrote with Rose Luminiello for *Ireland in an Imperial World: Citizenship, Opportunism, and Subversion*, edited by Timothy G. McMahon, Michael De Nie, and Paul Townend, and I am grateful to Rose not only for collaborating on this project but for much else besides. I am also grateful to the several editors and publishers for their support, patience, and forbearance. I must also record my gratitude to Michael Watson and Liz Friend-Smith of Cambridge University Press. I will always be grateful to Michael for commissioning this book and then waiting patiently as I missed deadline after deadline. Liz in turn then inherited with good humour and greater patience a project that she must have doubted would ever see completion. To them and the rest of the staff at the Cambridge University Press I owe an enormous debt. I am also grateful to Linsey Hague, who at short notice made effective sense of a text that was put together over many years and in many formats, and in doing so saved me from many errors.

It only remains to thank my family, without whose love and support none of this would have been possible or worthwhile.

Abbreviations

AAB	Archives of the Archdiocese of Boston
AACT	Archives of the Archdiocese of Cape Town
AAH	Archives of the Archdiocese of Halifax
AANY	Archives of the Archdiocese of New York
AAQ	Archives de l'Archevêché de Québec
AAS	Archives of the Archdiocese of Sydney
AASF	Archives of the Archdiocese of San Francisco
AASMSU	Associated Archives, St Mary's Seminary and University, Baltimore
ABSI	Archivum Britannicum Societatis Iesu, London
AC	*Letters on the Go: The Correspondence of Suzanne Aubert*
ACAA	Archives of the Archdiocese of Adelaide
ACDA	Archives of the Catholic Diocese of Auckland
ACGA	Archives of the Archdiocese of Canberra-Goulburn
ACRSM	Archives of the Callan Sisters of Mercy, Co. Kilkenny
ACUA	The American Catholic Research Center and University Archives, The Catholic University of America
ADA	Antigonish Diocesan Archives, Nova Scotia
ADB	*Australian Dictionary of Biography*
ADC	Archives of the Diocese of Charlottetown
ADD	Archives of the Diocese of Dunedin
ADDB	Archives Diocésaines de Bathurst, New Brunswick
AHCA	All Hallows College Archive
ANPF	*Annals of the Propagation of the Faith*
APF	Archivio Storico di Propaganda Fide
ARCSJ	Archives of the Archdiocese of St John's, Newfoundland
ARDA	Ardagh & Clonmacnois Diocesan Archives
ARSMP	Sisters of Mercy Archive, Parramatta, New South Wales
ASIC	Archivio Storico dell'Istituto della Carità
ASMA	Archives of the Sisters of Mercy, Auckland
ASSP	Archivio Storico di San Paolo fuori le Mura (St Paul's Outside the Walls)

ASV	Archivio Segreto Vaticano
AVCAU	Venerable English College, Rome
BAA	Archives of the Archdiocese of Birmingham
BDA	Bathurst Diocesan Archives, New South Wales
BDAV	Ballarat Diocesan Archives, Victoria
CD	*The Cape Diary of Bishop Griffith, 1837–1839*
CDA	Archives of the Archdiocese of Cashel, Ireland
CHDA	Christchurch Diocesan Archives, New Zealand
CLD	Irish Province of the Order of Carmelites, Carmelite Library, Gort Muire, Dublin
CLHR	Cory Library for Historical Research, Grahamstown
CU	Rare Books and Manuscript Library, Columbia University, New York
CUL	Cambridge University Library
DAA	Downside Abbey Archives
DACI	Dominican Archives, Cabra, Ireland
DADL	Dominican Archives Dún Laoghaire, Ireland
DAS	Dominican Archives Strathfield, New South Wales
DCB	*Dictionary of Canadian Biography*
DDA	Dublin Diocesan Archives
DNZB	*Dictionary of New Zealand Biography*
FJ	*Freeman's Journal* (Sydney)
FLK	Franciscan Archives, Dún Mhuire, Killiney, Co. Dublin
HAA	Archives of the Archdiocese of Hobart
IJA	Irish Jesuit Archives, Dublin
IOR	India Office Records, British Library, London
KD	*Diary and Visitation Record of the Rt. Rev. Francis Patrick Kenrick*
KFC	*The Kenrick-Frenaye Correspondence*
LAB	Loreto Archives, Ballarat
LAC	Library and Archives Canada, Ottawa
LAD	Loreto Archives, Dublin
LDA	Limerick Diocesan Archives
MAW	Marist Archives, Wellington
MCA	Maynooth College Archive
MD	Diary of Patrick Francis Moran
MDHC	Melbourne Diocesan Historical Commission
MNDA	Maitland-Newcastle Diocesan Archives
MSCUN	Manuscripts and Special Collections, University of Nottingham
MUL	Melbourne University Library

MUN	Archives and Special Collections, Queen Elizabeth II Library, Memorial University of Newfoundland
NLNZ	National Library of New Zealand, Alexander Turnbull Library
NZT	*New Zealand Tablet*
OCDA	Archives of the Discalced Carmelites, Clarendon Street, Dublin
PAHRC	Philadelphia Archdiocesan Historical Research Center
PANS	Nova Scotia Archives, Halifax
PCGA	Presentation Convent, Galway, Archives
PDA	Pittsburgh Diocesan Archives
PEDA	Port Elizabeth Diocesan Archives, Eastern Cape
PICRA	Pontifical Irish College, Rome, Archives
PL	*The Letters of John Bede Polding*
SAA	Archives of the Archdiocese of Southwark, London
SCA	Scottish Catholic Archives, Historic Collections, University of Aberdeen
SCACH	Scottish Catholic Archives, Columba House, Edinburgh
SCR	Scots College Rome Archives
SJDA	Saint John Diocesan Archives, New Brunswick
SMFI	St Mary's Church Archives, Stanley, Falkland Islands
TAA	Toronto Archdiocesan Archives
TNA	The National Archives, Kew
UNDA	University of Notre Dame Archives
WAA	Wellington Archdiocesan Archives
WDA	Westminster Diocesan Archives, London
WL	*The Correspondence of Mother Vincent Whitty, 1839–1892*

Introduction

The Roman Catholic Church is the only truly global institution the world has ever known. It is centrally managed, rigidly hierarchical, and has offices everywhere. It is probably the planet's largest employer. It has its own legal system, its own state, and its own small army. Its leader is a global celebrity, Europe's last absolute monarch, and under certain circumstances claims to be infallible. Some 1.2 billion people profess its faith, about 16 per cent of the world's population, and every year tens of millions are educated in its schools, nursed in its hospitals, married in its churches, and buried in its cemeteries. From China to Chile, its buildings mark the landscape and its devotions console the afflicted. In the English-speaking world alone, there are today some 250 colleges and universities associated with the church in the United States, while the constitutions of three Canadian provinces guarantee public support for Catholic schools, which also educate nearly 20 per cent of Australian children, 8 per cent of New Zealanders, and 87,000 New Yorkers.[1] As many as one in six American hospital beds are provided by Catholic institutions, and one in ten in Australia. Despite its recent scandals, the Catholic Church matters.

In the English-speaking world, Catholicism has long been associated with the Irish. As the St Benedict's Young Men's Society of Sydney, Australia, boasted in 1861, 'in every clime, in the dark forests of America, beyond the Rocky Mountains, in the Islands of the Pacific Ocean, in the burning deserts of Africa, on the hot plains of Hindostan, in the wild bush of Australia, the priests of Ireland are to be found spreading and cultivating the holy religion of St. Patrick'.[2] In many places and for many people, Irish and Catholic became synonymous: as the

---

[1] See Australian Bureau of Statistics, 4221.0 – Schools, Australia 2017, available at www.abs.gov.au; www.nzceo.org.nz/catholic-schools-roll-report (consulted 20 August 2018); New York City Independent Budget Office 22 April 2014, available at www.ibo.nyc.ny.us/cgi-park2/2014/04/how-many-students-attend-nonpublic-k-12-schools-in-new-york-city (consulted 20 August 2018).

[2] *Freeman's Journal* (Sydney) [*FJ*], 8 May 1861.

index to James Jupp's 2004 study *The English in Australia* put it, for Catholics '*see also* Irish' and for the Irish '*see also* Catholics'.[3] This conflation remains true for many of the some 70 million people who today claim Irish ancestry; and despite the migration of millions of Italians, Germans, Croats, Poles, and many others, Catholicism in the anglosphere retains in many places a distinctively green hue. This has had several consequences, among them that the clerical sexual abuse crisis roiling the Catholic Church has at times seemed to be a largely Irish phenomenon; it has not gone unnoticed that what linked scandal-ridden places such as the eastern United States, Newfoundland, or Australia (and indeed Ireland itself) was a long-standing Irish ecclesiastical domination. This is neither entirely accurate – the scandals have crossed borders and ethnicities, as recent events in Germany, the Netherlands, and Chile have made clear – nor attributable to some mysterious flaw in the Irish character. Yet it is the case that the church that the Irish built has been particularly susceptible, in part because of the kind of church the Irish built: unaccountable power, social deference, and self-segregation have proved a fertile terrain for predators.

The conflation of Irish and Catholic dates back to the nineteenth century. In 1897, for example, Cardinal Patrick Francis Moran of Sydney marked the consecration of Melbourne's St Patrick's Cathedral with a celebration of what he called the 'marvellous expansion' of an 'Anglo-Celtic Empire' that had come to number some 200 Irish bishops, 16,000 Irish priests, and 20 million Irish Catholics. This empire far exceeded that of Britain, he boasted, because it followed the English language as it achieved 'an ever-widening and unique position among the languages of the world'. Everywhere English was spoken, 'through the Celtic Soldiers of the Cross, the Catholic Church extends her conquests'. The result, Moran concluded, was that the 'the sun never sets on the spiritual empire of St. Patrick's Apostolate', and 'the faith of Ireland's sons, like a golden chain, binds the whole English-speaking world to God'.[4]

Moran's audience would have recognized that he was echoing the language of Charles Wentworth Dilke, who had 'followed England round the world' and then written about it in his 1868 classic *Greater Britain*. 'Everywhere', Dilke recalled, 'I was in English-speaking, or in English-governed lands. If I remarked that climate, soil, manners of life, that mixture with other peoples had modified the blood, I saw, too, that in

---

[3] James Jupp, *The English in Australia* (Cambridge: Cambridge University Press, 2004), 214–15.

[4] *The Advocate* (Melbourne), 6 November 1897.

essentials the race was always one.' This left him with a 'conception, however imperfect, of the grandeur of our race, already girdling the earth, which is destined, perhaps, eventually to overspread'. The legacy of 'the England of Elizabeth' was not to be found in 'the Britain of Victoria', he concluded, 'but in half the habitable globe'. 'If two small islands are by courtesy styled "Great", America, Australia, India, must form a Greater Britain.'[5]

The Irish were quick to repurpose this concept. It helped that 'Greater Ireland' had a long pedigree: a handful of medieval sources described a *Hibernia major* far to the west, for example, while at least one twelfth-century Norse text referred to a Greater Ireland, or *Írland hið mikla*. Eager nationalists claimed that this proved not only that St Brendan had discovered North America, which was a long-cherished myth, but that the Irish were still there when the Vikings arrived.[6] Under Dilke's influence this slipped easily into assertions of a more modern 'Greater Ireland'. Shortly after *Greater Britain* appeared, for example, an Irish newspaper in South Australia pointedly observed that 'England' now had to 'take account of another Ireland beyond the Western waves, and another in that great Empire of the future beneath the Southern Cross'. 'Millions of Irishmen in America and Australia', it concluded, 'constituting a greater Ireland, still consider themselves part of the Irish nation, and think and plan and pray for the freedom and happiness of their traditionary fatherland.'[7] Five years later, another Australian newspaper delightedly reported on the celebrations of Daniel O'Connell's centenary, not only 'in almost every town and village throughout the Australias' but also in 'the greater Ireland across the Atlantic'.[8] By the turn of the century, the concept had become so deeply embedded that on the one hand James Joyce could have a character in *Ulysses* boast of the nationalist reinforcements waiting 'in our greater Ireland beyond the sea', while on the other the Irish Recruiting Council could claim 'that Greater Ireland, from Adelaide to Brisbane, from San Francisco to New York, is heart and soul behind the men in Flanders'.[9]

This Greater Ireland was widely assumed to be essentially Catholic. As the 'priests and laity of Dunedin' put it in 1889, 'as we are the devoted children of Rome, so it is our joy and pride, while duly fulfilling our duties

---

[5] Charles Wentworth Dilke, *Greater Britain: A Record of Travel in English-Speaking Countries during 1866 and 1867*, 2nd ed. (London: MacMillan and Co., 1869), vii–viii.
[6] See Hilary M. Carey and Colin Barr, 'Introduction', in Colin Barr and Hilary M. Carey (eds.), *Religion and Greater Ireland: Christianity and Irish Global Networks, 1750–1850* (Montreal and Kingston: McGill-Queen's University Press, 2015), 17.
[7] *The Irish Harp and Farmers' Herald* (Adelaide), 23 July 1870.   [8] *FJ*, 14 August 1875.
[9] James Joyce, *Ulysses*, Oxford World's Classics (Oxford: Oxford University Press, 1998), 316; *Woodville Examiner* (New Zealand), 26 June 1918.

as New Zealand colonists, to form a constituent part of the greater Ireland'.[10] Nearly forty years later, Laurence J. Kenny boasted to the American Catholic Historical Association that from 'Armagh to Baltimore, from Los Angeles to Auckland, from Melbourne to Manila, from Zanzibar to Sierra Leone, from the Cape of Good Hope to Riga, are, from the right hand of the chair of Peter, the sons of Innisfall are the heralds of the pure and true gospel: verily, their sound has gone forth to the ends of the earth.' Would America too, he wondered, convert and truly become '*Irland it Mikla*, a Greater Ireland'?[11]

Although Kenny's imagery was triumphalist, it was not fantastic: by the early twentieth century, Irish Catholics and their descendants in the English-speaking world very often had more in common with their coreligionists across the globe than with their neighbours across the street. They understood themselves to be members of a common cultural, religious, and in some cases political space and saw no contradiction between their identification as Irish and their status as Americans, South Africans, or Newfoundlanders. This was relatively simple in the republican United States, where the first Catholic newspaper (published in Charleston, South Carolina) printed the first amendment to the constitution on its masthead, but it was also true in the British world, where the bulk of the Irish and their descendants considered themselves both committed Irish patriots and contented citizens of Empire. In 1914, for example, the Galway-born archbishop of Melbourne, Thomas Carr, urged Irish Australians to fight 'for the mother country and the best balanced constitution in the world', which many thousands did, while his colleague Henry Cleary left his position as bishop of Auckland to serve as a chaplain for Irish New Zealanders on the Western Front and later accepted the Order of the British Empire.[12] In Canada, the nationalist Ancient Order of Hibernians not only backed the war effort of 'that great Empire' of which they boasted Canada was an integral part but denounced the opposition of their American brethren as anti-British.[13] As Mark McGowan has pointed out, for 'many Irish Catholics in Canada, constitutional Irish nationalism and fighting the war were two sides of the same coin', and his tag 'Imperial Irish' could equally well be applied to their coreligionists in Newfoundland, South Africa, New

---

[10] *Evening Star* (Dunedin), 8 October 1889.   [11] Quoted in Carey and Barr, 19.
[12] Quoted in T. P. Boland, *Thomas Carr: Archbishop of Melbourne* (St Lucia: Queensland University Press, 1997), 404.
[13] See Robert McLaughlin, *Irish Canadian Conflict and the Struggle for Irish Independence, 1912–1925* (Toronto: University of Toronto Press, 2013), 83–5.

Zealand, or Australia.[14] Fierce critics of Britain could be fiercely loyal to the British Empire.

Yet there is nothing intrinsically enduring about Irishness. Consider the fate of Irish Protestants, who also migrated in great numbers and who also insisted on their own membership in a Greater Ireland.[15] In parts of the United States, some Canadian provinces, and all of South Africa, they were a majority of Irish migrants, and they formed strong local majorities across Australia and New Zealand. Every American president with parents or grandparents born in Ireland was a Protestant, while as late as 1871 Irish Protestants and their descendants outnumbered Irish Catholics by two to one in Ontario.[16] Yet it is the descendants of the Catholic migrants who are most often thought of as Irish: John F. Kennedy's nearest relationship to Ireland was his great-great grandparents.[17]

Take the case of New Zealand, where around 45 per cent of Irish migrants in the nineteenth century belonged to one of the island's Protestant denominations.[18] They reached every level of society, from the Londonderry-born William Massey, prime minister from 1912 to 1925 and an enthusiastic Orangeman, to Rutherford Waddell, the Down-born Presbyterian minister, Dunedin social reformer, and tentative ecumenist. Orange Lodges were omnipresent, and the Orange Order enthusiastically played its part in political and sectarian conflict.[19] Yet like their coreligionists in Ontario, New South Wales, or South Africa, New Zealand's Irish Protestants abandoned their Irish identity with what Gerard Horn has aptly described as 'indecent haste'.[20] The Orange Order has effectively vanished, not only from New Zealand but everywhere except Northern Ireland and parts of Scotland. As Donald

---

[14] Mark G. McGowan, *The Imperial Irish: Canada's Irish Catholics Fight the Great War, 1914–1918* (Montreal and Kingston: McGill-Queen's University Press, 2017), 8.

[15] See, for example, Leigh-Ann Coffey, 'Drawing strength from past migratory experiences: The *Church of Ireland Gazette* and southern Protestant migration in the post-independence period', in Barr and Carey, *Greater Ireland*, 52–70.

[16] Both of Andrew Jackson's parents were born in Co. Antrim, James Buchanan's mother was born in Co. Donegal, and Woodrow Wilson's grandfather was born in Co. Down; Donald Harman Akenson, *The Irish in Ontario: A Study in Rural History* (Montreal and Kingston: McGill-Queen's University Press, 1984), 27–8.

[17] *Irish Independent*, 20 May 2011, 'US presidents with Irish heritage'.

[18] Alasdair Galbraith, 'Re-discovering Irish Protestant traditions in colonial New Zealand', in Brad Patterson (ed.), *Ulster-New Zealand Migration and Cultural Transfers* (Dublin: Four Courts Press, 2006), 32.

[19] Rory Sweetman, 'Towards a history of Orangeism in New Zealand', in Patterson, *Ulster-New Zealand Migration*, 155.

[20] Gerard Horn, '"A loyal united and happy people": Irish Protestant migration to Wellington province, 1840–1930: Aspects of migration, settlement, and community', unpublished PhD diss., Victoria University of Wellington, 2010, 14.

Akenson observed, Irish Protestants 'blended so quickly with the dominant culture in New Zealand that they are hard to trace', while Irish Catholics 'simply refused to go away'.[21] The same is true across the English-speaking world, where Irish Protestants first became Protestants and then simply Canadians or Australians or Europeans. The only exception is the American south, where 'Scotch-Irish' remains a recognizable identity. Irish Protestants vanished while Irish Catholics did not.

This phenomenon can be seen at every level. In the United States, for example, there are hundreds of 'Irish' gift shops that sell items ranging from '*Cead Mile Failte*' coffee mugs to 'Genuine Connemara Marble Rosary Beads'. Belleek china in the Northern Ireland firm's famous shamrock pattern can share a shop window with a selection of first communion gifts. The conflation of Irish and Catholic in such places is total and unselfconscious. The same is true of the symbolism associated with Glasgow Celtic football club or the 'Vatican Army' that supports New Zealand's Marist Rugby Football Federation. This would have gladdened the heart of Daniel O'Connell, but what accounts for the endurance of Irish Catholic identity in the English-speaking world?

The obvious answer is the Roman Catholic Church. Yet the Catholic Church in Greater Ireland was always comprised of more than just the Irish, both in the nineteenth century and later. In 1850, for example, one Irish bishop estimated that, while there were approximately one million Irish Catholics in the United States, there were also some 500,000 Germans and 200,000 French, while in the Canadian Maritimes the Irish were often in a minority even of anglophone Catholics.[22] Although the vast migration associated with the Great Famine and its aftermath was necessary to secure Irish control of their church, it was not sufficient. Power had to be seized.

This was because before the mid-1840s the Irish rarely held the ecclesiastical reins anywhere except Ireland itself. The Catholic Church in Australia was dominated by English Benedictines, New Zealand was under the control of the French Society of Mary, America was largely the preserve of French and German bishops, many associated with a French religious order, and India was contested by the Portuguese, the French, several other European nationalities, and a significant indigenous Catholic population. What French Canadians did not dominate

---

[21] Donald Harman Akenson, *Half the World from Home: Perspectives on the Irish in New Zealand 1860–1950* (Wellington: Victoria University Press, 1990), 198.

[22] Hugh J. Nolan, *The Most Reverend Francis Patrick Kenrick, Third Bishop of Philadelphia 1830–1851* (Philadelphia: American Catholic Historical Association of Philadelphia, 1948), 418.

in Canada, Scots did. Only South Africa and Newfoundland were wholly Irish missions. In each case, the incumbents fiercely resisted Irish incursions, and, in each case, they succumbed to a deliberate, ruthless, and organized Irish campaign to gain control of the church. Ireland's empire was planned. It was not acquired in a fit of absence of mind.

It was also largely the work of one man: Paul Cullen, rector of the Irish College in Rome (1832–49), archbishop of Armagh (1849–52), archbishop of Dublin (1852–78), and from 1866 Ireland's first cardinal. Working first on behalf of others, and then on his own account, Cullen systematically planted like-minded allies, former students, relatives, and Dublin diocesan priests in senior positions across the English-speaking world. These men in turn pursued policies and built institutions that made Catholicism's Greater Ireland possible, allowed it to cohere, and then helped it to thrive. What they created was the largest, most important, most enduring, and most historiographically convincing of all imperial networks. It was global in reach, ideologically coherent, centrally led, and its legacy can still be seen at any St Patrick's Day parade anywhere in the world.

It was also an example of what Tony Ballantyne has described as the 'horizontal linkages' that bound the constituent parts of the British Empire to one another. Ballantyne's point was that the traditional understanding of that empire as a series of largely discrete bilateral relationships (political, cultural, economic) between the metropole and the periphery did not fully capture the complexities of the British imperial world. People, information, goods, ideas, and armies also moved between colonies and not simply between the colonies and 'home'. He preferred the image of a spider's web or webs, arguing that if 'we conceive of the empire not as a single web but as a complex accumulation of overlapping webs, it is possible to envisage that certain locations, individuals or institutions in the supposed periphery might in fact be at the centre of complex networks themselves'.[23]

This was certainly true of Catholicism's Greater Ireland, where Rome largely replaced London as the metropole and Dublin assumed the vice-regal functions exercised in Britain's South Asian empire by Delhi. Indeed, Ireland served as the sort of alternative imperial 'nodal point' described by Thomas Metcalf, 'from which peoples, ideas, goods, and institutions – everything that enables an empire to exist – radiated outward'.[24] Yet it also reflects the fact that the Catholic Irish moved freely

---

[23] Tony Ballantyne, *Webs of Empire: Locating New Zealand's Colonial Past* (Wellington: Bridget Williams Books, 2012), 44.

[24] Thomas R. Metcalf, *Imperial Connections: India in the Indian Ocean Area, 1860–1920* (Berkeley: University of California Press, 2007), 1.

through the English-speaking world. Consider three Canadian examples: Philip Francis Little was born in 1824 in Prince Edward Island to Irish parents, moved to Newfoundland, became its first premier, then a judge, and retired to Ireland where he was active in Home Rule politics and where one of his sons featured in James Joyce's fiction and another fought in the civil war and then helped found Fianna Fáil; Timothy Warren Anglin was born in Cork, the son of an employee of the East India Company, before moving to New Brunswick where he edited a newspaper for Irish Catholics and entered provincial and then federal politics as the champion of Irish Catholics; Thomas D'Arcy McGee was born in Ireland, emigrated to the United States, returned to Ireland, rebelled, fled, edited a newspaper in Boston, moved to Montreal, became a Father of Canadian confederation, and was shot dead by a fellow Irishman in Ottawa. Irish Catholics moved in every direction: John Boyle O'Reilly rebelled with the Fenians, was transported to Australia, escaped to America, and became the editor of McGee's old newspaper, the Boston *Pilot*; John O'Shanassy migrated from Ireland to South Australia and then Victoria, where he became the second anglophone Catholic premier in the British Empire (Little was the first) and was knighted by both the queen and the pope. The same was true of tens of thousands of others who followed gold or jobs or family across the globe; if California or the Cape did not work out, Victoria or Otago might. They were served by a similarly mobile clergy: M. Ursula Frayne, for example, founded the Sisters of Mercy not only in Newfoundland but also in Western Australia and Victoria. Thomas Croke was the second bishop of Auckland before he became the patriotic archbishop of Cashel; one of his brothers was a prominent priest in northern California (where he co-owned the leading Catholic newspaper, *The Monitor*) and another made his career as a businessman in Ballarat, while one of their sisters was a nun in Co. Cork and another a nun in New South Wales.[25] Everywhere the Catholic Irish were bound together by thick webs of shared history, shared devotions, and shared institutions, including a global Irish Catholic press.

Yet this Irish spiritual empire was only possible because ecclesiastical power in the English-speaking world was centralized in the Sacred Congregation for the Propagation of the Faith, known as the Propaganda Fide or simply the Propaganda. Founded in 1622 to improve papal oversight of the mission to India, by the nineteenth century it had become what amounted to the pope's colonial office. As the English

---

[25] See 'Articles of co-partnership', 12 October 1880, Archives of the Archdiocese of San Francisco [AASF], Joseph Sadoc Alemany papers [AP], 1880/27.

convert John Henry Newman unhappily observed in 1863, 'the whole English-speaking Catholic population all over the world is under Propaganda, an arbitrary, military power'. It could appoint a bishop but also depose him, grant a marriage or refuse it, suspend a priest or absolve him, open a university or close it. It was, Newman fumed, 'our only court of appeal'.[26] Letters from across the world arrived in its splendid palace on the Piazza di Spagna, where they were opened, read, and summarized by a small group of bureaucrats known as *minutanti*. They were overseen by a secretary, who reported to the cardinal prefect, who in turn chaired the monthly meeting of a larger group of cardinals that decided everything from an episcopal appointment in Boston to a marriage dispensation in Ceylon to a liturgical dispute in Syria. Its decisions were then submitted to the pope for his approval before being put into formal language and communicated by the *minutante* responsible for the relevant region. The entire apparatus, including the semi-detached cardinals of the congregation, never amounted to more than twenty at any one time.

If the key to the church was the Propaganda, the key to the Propaganda was the cardinal prefect: the *minutanti* had influence, and the cardinals authority, but the cardinal prefect had power, which he might or might not share with his secretary. Only eight men held the office between 1826 and 1916 and only two during the greatest period of Irish ecclesiastical expansion before 1874. (More than forty ministers had responsibility for Britain's colonies in the same period.) The first was Giacomo Fransoni, an aristocratic papal diplomat who had served as the nuncio in Lisbon before his appointment in 1834. By all accounts gentle, well-liked, and attentive to detail, Fransoni was part of the conservative faction in the curia associated with the cardinal secretary of state Luigi Lambruschini, and in the late 1830s was their preferred candidate in the event of a papal election.[27] Yet he was also close to Gregory XVI, and his diplomatic skills are suggested by his ability to navigate the pope's frequent interventions in the congregation's affairs. In so far as he had an agenda, it was to ensure good ecclesiastical governance in the mission churches, by which he meant they should be well organized, well disciplined, and obedient to Rome. During his more than two

---

[26] Newman to William Monsell, 13 January 1863, *The Letters and Diaries of John Henry Newman*, edited by Charles Stephen Dessain et al., 32 vols. (Edinburgh and Oxford: Thomas Nelson and Oxford University Press, 1961–2008), 20: 391.

[27] See Christopher Dowd, *Rome in Australia: The Papacy and Conflict in the Australian Catholic Missions, 1834–1884*, 2 vols. (Leiden: Brill, 2008), 1: 82; Vincent Viaene, *Belgium and the Holy See from Gregory XVI to Pius IX (1831–1859), Catholic Revival, Society and Politics in 19th-Century Europe* (Leuven: Leuven University Press, 2001), 285.

decades in office, he was served by four secretaries, the last and most important of whom was Alessandro Barnabò.

Born to a noble family in Foligno in 1801, Barnabò was taken at the age of ten to France as hostage against the good behaviour of the region's nobility. While there, he was educated in a military school, which a later observer thought accounted 'for his prompt and energetic bodily movements and the quick decision on all matters brought before him'.[28] It may also have produced his formidable work ethic: he once boasted that he had read every letter written by the congregation.[29] On his return, he trained for the priesthood, studied law and philosophy in Rome, and was ordained in 1833. After parish work and a stint elsewhere in the curia, he joined the Propaganda in 1838, became secretary in 1847, and succeeded Fransoni in 1856.

In many ways, Alessandro Barnabò *was* the Propaganda. He read every paper, took every decision, and exercised an essentially despotic control until a few months before his death in early 1874. He was short, strong, temperamental, voluble, and did not suffer fools. While still secretary to the congregation he was reputed to have badly beaten two men who had tried to rob him 'just under the shadow of the Colosseum'. His frugality was widely remarked, as was his modesty: one Irish seminarian recalled that at the reception to mark his elevation to cardinal he kept his back to a pillar with his hands behind him 'to prevent the hand-kissing universal in Rome from all below to all above'.[30] Another Irish observer was impressed that his free time was apparently spent in a punishing round of confessions, retreats, and visits to schools and orphanages.[31] Nor was Barnabò much bothered by social niceties: he had a cruel sense of humour, which he applied widely, and was prepared to challenge the pope, sometimes furiously. As John Henry Newman revealingly complained, he was a 'mere clerk – to whom routine, and dispatch, are everything and gentleness, courteousness, frankness and consideration are words without meaning'.[32]

Yet the Propaganda was not simply a bureaucracy: it was also a school. Founded in 1627 by Urban VIII, the *Collegio Urbano* was located in the Palazzo di Propaganda Fide where it educated seminarians from mission territories. For many years, this was largely understood to mean the 'Oriental' churches in the lands under Ottoman control, but there was

---

[28] R. V. Howley, 'Cardinal Barnabò: A reminiscence', *Catholic World*, April 1903, 81. Howley was the clerical brother of Michael Howley, a future bishop of St John's, Newfoundland.

[29] Dowd, *Rome in Australia*, 1: 189.   [30] R. V. Howley, 'Barnabò', 81, 79.

[31] See Dowd, *Rome in Australia*, 1: 189–90.

[32] Newman to John Duke Coleridge, 26 April 1867, Newman, 23: 191.

always a smattering of other nationalities. Soon after the college reopened in 1814, and for reasons that are not entirely clear, it became an established choice for ambitious Irish families. Within a year or two, four of the college's twelve students were Irish and the authorities began to consider capping Irish numbers.[33] Among these early residents was Francis Patrick Kenrick, the first Propaganda graduate on the American mission, bishop of Philadelphia, archbishop of Baltimore, and the focus of Chapter 1 of this book.

Study in the Propaganda was uniquely advantageous. The co-location of the college with the congregation and the small number of students ensured an intimacy not only with the *minutanti* but also with the secretary and cardinal prefect. When the Newfoundlander Richard Howley arrived in 1855, for example, he found the building deserted until he was finally led to Cardinal Fransoni's study, where he was poring over papers with Barnabò.[34] The students mixed with the officials on a daily basis, seeing at first-hand how the church administered its far-flung domains. They also had the opportunity to forge relationships with both fellow students and potential patrons. Barnabò in particular took a close interest in the resident students, was relaxed in their company, and later followed and advanced their careers. In return, they were expected to keep the Propaganda apprised of developments on their mission. Students became watchers.

It was this confluence of intimate access and concentrated ecclesiastical power that equipped Paul Cullen with the vision, experience, and connections necessary to conceive and then execute the seizure or attempted seizure of the ecclesiastical hierarchies of every English-speaking country bar England itself. He learned how the Propaganda worked, gained the trust of its officials, and drove its agenda for nearly fifty years. With the Propaganda on your side, everything was possible.

Cullen's power and influence in Ireland have long been recognized. When he died in 1878, *The Times* remarked that for the previous twenty-six years 'No man in the kingdom has exercised a greater personal influence, or wielded more absolute power.'[35] Yet even in his own lifetime his reputation was that of a dour reactionary 'unacquainted', as Charles Gavan Duffy put it, 'with Ireland, unskilled in the principle of parliamentary government, and slow to comprehend or accept new ideas'.[36] Other

[33] Diary of Patrick Francis Moran, 21 June 1871, Archives of the Archdiocese of Sydney [AAS]. Moran often recorded information about Cullen's early life as part of his projected but uncompleted life of his uncle.

[34] R. V. Howley, 'Barnabò', 77.   [35] *The Times*, 25 October 1878.

[36] Charles Gavan Duffy, *My Life in Two Hemispheres*, 2 vols. (New York: Macmillan, 1898), 2: 90.

critics saw him as 'far more an Italian than an Irishman in spirit' and others again as a 'deadly foe of *Irish liberty*'.[37] In *A Portrait of the Artist as a Young Man*, James Joyce has the patriotic Mr Dedalus mock him as 'little old Paul Cullen! Another apple of God's eye!'[38] This reputation as an anti-nationalist became fixed, and has endured, but is not entirely accurate. Nor was it universal: in 1850, for example, the lord lieutenant of Ireland described Cullen as 'the most malignant enemy of the English'.[39] He was still calling him a 'viper' more than twenty years later.[40]

Historians have also agreed on Cullen's importance but on little else.[41] Joseph Lee probably came closest to catching his character when he described Cullen as a kind of Tammany Hall machine boss, a headmaster, or 'the pope's chief whip in Ireland'. He also emphasized Cullen's 'feline sensitivity for the levers of power in the Vatican', refusal to lead 'the Irish Church in a genuinely theocratic direction', and 'almost consistent common sense and moderation'.[42] Emmet Larkin credited him with sparking a devotional revolution through which 'the great mass of the Irish people became practising Catholics', while Australian historians have never doubted his importance in their country.[43] Yet the impression remains of a narrow and unimaginative bureaucrat, devoted to the papacy, to the church, and to his own obscure ends. Few have recognized that he was also the ruthless author of a carefully planned and meticulously executed global campaign, the consequences of which long survived his own death. Paul Cullen was the United Kingdom's most enduringly successful imperialist.

Cullen was born in Prospect, Co. Kildare, in 1803, and named after an uncle who had been shot by crown forces in the wake of the bloody rising of 1798. His own father had been spared only by the intercession of local

---

[37] James Macaulay, *Ireland in 1872: A Tour of Observation with Remarks on Irish Public Questions* (London: H. S. King and Co., 1873), vi–viii; quoted in John O'Leary, *Recollections of Fenians and Fenianism*, 2 vols. (London: Downey and Co., 1896), 2: 51. Emphasis in original.

[38] James Joyce, *A Portrait of the Artist as a Young Man*, edited by Kevin J. H. Demar (New York: Barnes and Noble, 2004), 33.

[39] Lord Clarendon to Lord John Russell, 5 January 1850, Bodleian Library, Clarendon deposit, Irish vol. 5.

[40] Clarendon to Odo Russell, 25 January 1869, in Noel Blakiston (ed.), *The Roman Question: Extracts from the Despatches of Odo Russell from Rome, 1858–1870*, new ed. (Wilmington, DE: Michael Glazier, 1980 [1932]), 358.

[41] See Colin Barr, '"An ambiguous awe": Paul Cullen and the historians', in Dáire Keogh and Albert McDonnell (eds.), *Cardinal Paul Cullen and His World* (Dublin: Four Courts Press, 2011), 414–34.

[42] Joseph Lee, *The Modernization of Irish Society, 1848–1989* (Dublin: Gill & Macmillan, 1989 [1973]), 49.

[43] Emmet Larkin, *The Historical Dimensions of Irish Catholicism* (Washington, DC: The Catholic University of America Press, 1987), 58.

Quakers, who testified to his political loyalty.[44] Partly as a consequence, the young Paul was sent to the Quaker boarding school at Ballitore, which had also once educated Edmund Burke. He then entered Carlow College in 1816 to train for the priesthood and moved four years later to the Urban College, where he became one of six Irishmen in residence out of a student body of only twenty.[45] Unlike the English and Scots, the Irish had no national college in which to reside: an Irish College had been established in Rome in 1628 but it had passed through various vicissitudes before being closed during the French occupation. Thus, while the Propaganda's English and Scottish students lived in their own ancient establishments, the Irish resided in the college itself. When everyone else went home, the Irish stayed and watched.

Cullen was struck by the incredible diversity of the Propaganda, reporting home that some were 'Turks, some Armenians, Persians, Caldeans [sic], Greeks, Egyptians, and Arabians'. When each spoke his own language, he marvelled, 'one would be led to imagine that he was in the town of Babylon & not in a Roman college'.[46] Cullen himself was a gifted linguist, and within six months he had acquired a working knowledge of Italian and set to work on Greek and Hebrew. He already had Latin and soon added French, but it was his mastery of Italian that mattered. Not only was it the language of the Propaganda and the holy see but relatively few in Rome could read or speak English. Neither Fransoni nor Barnabò did, for example, and only occasionally could a *minutante* or one of the other cardinals. This presented an enormous challenge to those who could not speak Italian. Even if they could write in French, which everyone understood, or in intelligible Latin, which surprisingly few did, there would inevitably be much of importance that the Propaganda could not read. As Newman grumbled, 'how is Propaganda to know anything about an English controversy since it talks Italian?'[47] The congregation's invariable solution was to ask an English-speaker to read English letters, translate English documents, and explain English-language controversies to them. That person needed to be available, trusted, and perfectly bilingual.

As early as April 1821, Cullen's superiors were 'well pleased with him' and were soon assessing him as possessing a 'superior talent'.[48] His four

---

[44] Desmond Bowen, *Paul Cardinal Cullen and the Shaping of Modern Irish Catholicism* (Dublin: Gill & Macmillan, 1983).
[45] Cullen to Hugh Cullen, 12 January [1821], Dublin Diocesan Archives [DDA], Cullen papers [CP].
[46] Ibid.   [47] Newman to Monsell, 13 January 1863.
[48] Maher to Margaret Cullen, 5 April 1821, DDA/CP; Christopher Korten, 'Converging worlds: Paul Cullen in the world of Mauro Cappellari', in Dáire Keogh and

gold medals in 1826 confirmed their opinion. In 1828, in front of an audience that included Pope Leo XII and two future popes, Cullen capped his academic career with a doctoral defence of 224 theses drawn from the whole of theology and ecclesiastical history. Leo's presence was a signal honour: as Cullen told his father, 'few Italians, less of any other nation, can boast of the Pope's presence on such an occasion; I believe no Irishman was ever honoured in this way.'[49] The performance cemented Cullen's reputation as the outstanding student of his generation, not simply in the Urban College but in Rome as a whole. As a fellow student noted, 'Paul is the object of praise and adulation.'[50] For its part, the Propaganda both published his defence and appointed him professor of Oriental Languages.[51]

Cullen's gifts had already drawn the attention of Mauro Cappellari, a Camaldolese monk and theologian who had been the cardinal prefect of the Propaganda since 1826. Following established Roman practice, Cappellari had from the late 1810s begun to gather around himself a small group of talented protégés. He shaped their thinking, encouraged their studies, and advanced their careers. Among them were Antonio Rosmini, who gained prominence as a controversial philosopher and founded the Institute of Charity, the Englishman Nicholas Wiseman, a future cardinal archbishop of Westminster, and from around 1828 Cullen himself. Three years later, Cappellari emerged as Gregory XVI from the extended papal conclave of 1830–1.[52]

Yet Cappellari's patronage also had more immediate consequences. In 1829, for example, Cullen's Irish bishop ordered him home to take up a chair in Carlow College. Cappellari produced a range of reasons why he could not possibly leave, including the lateness of the season, the dreadful Irish weather, and the young man's health. He also claimed that Cullen was crucial to the successful completion of the Propaganda's projected Hebrew Bible. Such favouritism was unusual: Cappellari's biographer Christopher Korten could only identify one other such instance.[53] The admiration was fully reciprocated: as Cullen wrote after the 'affable, kind and obliging' Cappellari's election, the new pope continued to treat his

---

Albert McDonnell (eds.), *Cardinal Paul Cullen and His World* (Dublin: Four Courts Press, 2011), 40.

[49] Cullen to Hugh Cullen, 25 January 1829, DDA/CP.   [50] Quoted in Korten, 41.

[51] Paul Cullen, *Publicam Disputationem de Theologia Universa et Historia Ecclesiastica* (Roma: Congregazione de Propagande Fide, 1828).

[52] See Alan J. Reinerman, *Austria and the Papacy in the Age of Metternich, Vol. 2: Revolution and Reaction, 1830–1838* (Washington, DC: Catholic University of America Press, 1989), 4–9.

[53] Korten, 43.

protégés 'with as much humility as if he were one of his own lowest subjects'.[54]

Cappellari's elevation also marked the apotheosis of the Propaganda within the Roman bureaucracy. This was signalled by the choice of Gregory as his regnal name – the last Gregory had founded the Propaganda Fide in 1622. Although Gregory XVI was by most measures a theological conservative, and certainly a political one, under him the Catholic Church began again to turn its attention to the extra-European world. Within the curia, that change was reflected in a rebalancing of power among the various congregations. Although the secretariat of state remained preeminent, the Propaganda could and did resist encroachments through the simple expedient of a direct appeal to the pope. Paul Cullen thus found himself at the centre of ecclesiastical power only a few years after his own ordination. He would remain there for the fifteen years of Gregory's reign, an intimate of the pope and trusted advisor on Irish affairs. By the time Gregory died in 1846, Cullen was embedded in the latter position. After he himself left Rome in early 1850, the role passed to his friend Tobias Kirby.

Gregory's most important intervention was his agreement in late 1831 that the young Irishman might make a suitable rector of the Irish College. Cullen previously had had little to do with the college, which had reopened only in 1826, and knew relatively little about it. He had been relieved when it was agreed that the Propaganda's existing Irish students would not be compelled to transfer to it; he knew he was 'better off' in the Urban College.[55] Yet he could hardly refuse the rectorship, and under his leadership and then that of Tobias Kirby the college became the Roman embassy of Ireland's spiritual empire and the principal training centre for its elite. It continued to fulfil both roles long into the twentieth century.

Of course, Gregory was not Cullen's only patron: he had a gift for friendship with Italians and forged close relationships with the two great cardinal prefects of the Propaganda, Giacomo Fransoni and Alessandro Barnabò. Fransoni trusted the younger man implicitly and seems to have regarded him paternally. When he died, he bequeathed Cullen his episcopal ring.[56] His relationship with his near-contemporary Barnabò was more one of equals: Cullen was already an established figure in the Propaganda when Barnabò joined the congregation and was an archbishop for several years before the Italian became cardinal prefect. Their alliance was forged in 1849, with their common experience of

---

[54] Cullen to Maher, 30 April 1831, DDA/CP.
[55] Cullen to Maher, 4 March 1826, DDA/CP.
[56] See Emmet Larkin, 'Paul Cullen: The great ultramontane', in Keogh and McDonnell, *Cardinal Paul Cullen*, 20.

Giuseppe Mazzini's short-lived and profoundly anti-clerical Roman Republic: Barnabò sheltered for a time in the Irish College, while Cullen temporarily oversaw the Urban College. Indeed their bond was so strong that Barnabò, then still a mere monsignor, was prepared to threaten resignation in order to ensure Cullen's translation to Dublin in 1852. Bystanders heard him shouting at Pius IX through a closed door.[57]

Rome's influence was also more than merely practical. The city shaped Cullen's ideas about theology, churchmanship, and politics, while giving him a love of Italian, a global outlook, and a model against which to measure everything from architecture to devotional practice. All of this he then transmitted to his protégés and through them across Greater Ireland. In particular, he learned to revere the papacy and situate all authority in the person of the pope. His doctoral defence, for example, drew on similar sources and lines of argument as those found in the book that had made Cappellari's own reputation, his 1799 vindication of papal authority *Il trionfo della Santa Sede*.[58] The papacy remained at the centre of Cullen's universe from a very early age until the day of his death.

Cullen also imbibed the wider political and theological currents then dominant in Rome. In politics, this meant an emphasis on stability, authority, and political deference that Vincent Viaene has described as 'transigent ultramontanism'. This combined an abhorrence of revolution and political violence with a pragmatic acceptance of the civil and religious liberties increasingly offered by constitutional regimes such as those in Belgium, the United Kingdom, and the United States.[59] In its most sophisticated form, this position was articulated by another of Gregory's protégé's, Antonio Rosmini. A close reader of Alexis de Tocqueville, Rosmini was among the first to recognize that the secular United States offered the church more freedom than it enjoyed in many nominally Catholic states.[60] Although he rejected popular democracy as tending to majoritarian tyranny and political corruption, Rosmini emphasized the church's hostility towards all forms of despotism and its insistence on the legal and even political equality of all citizens regardless of religion.[61] This was very well received in Gregory's Rome: shortly after the final volume of his *Filosofia della Politica* was published in 1838, for example, the pope approved the establishment of the Institute of Charity, while Cullen

---

[57] Moran diary, fragment dated '1852', AAS.   [58] Korten, 42.

[59] For a summary of transigent ultramontanism, see Viaene, 110–11.

[60] See Axel Körner, *America in Italy: The United States in the Political Thought and Imagination of the Risorgimento, 1763–1865* (Princeton: Princeton University Press, 2017), 103–8.

[61] See Giorgio Campanini, 'Antonio Rosmini and representative institutions', *Parliaments, Estates and Representation*, vol. 17, no. 1 (2010), 129–37.

sought Rosmini's advice on books to assign at the Irish College. 'Being completely blind in philosophical matters', he wrote in 1840, 'I feel myself naturally driven to take recourse to one who can safely guide on the correct path to the true sources of light.'[62]

Although Pius IX later rejected Rosmini's qualified support for the Risorgimento and placed many of his works on the Index of Prohibited Books, the Italian's influence can be detected throughout Greater Ireland. In part, this was because Rosmini gave philosophical and theological cover to Irish experience: Daniel O'Connell had built his career as an ally (critics said a creature) of the Catholic Church, but he was also an unabashed champion of political pluralism and parliamentary government.[63] To Cullen and his generation of bishops and clergy, he was the *beau idéal* of the Catholic politician, and they held him up as such to a receptive laity. This combination of Roman philosophy and Irish example helped lead Irish Catholicism in surprisingly liberal directions. Across the English-speaking world, for example, almost all Irish Catholic bishops and priests engaged in democratic debate and electoral politics, most came to use the term 'liberal' as praise and 'illiberal' as an insult, and many backed avowedly liberal parties. Cullen himself regularly voted for a Protestant Liberal as his member of parliament. This willingness not only to participate in the democratic process but to implicitly defend democratic pluralism was at odds both with Catholic practice elsewhere and with the edicts of Pius IX and several of his successors. It also had a profound effect on the political and social development of the United States and the settler dominions of the British Empire, where a very real and enduring sectarianism never degenerated into the bitter church–state conflicts that plagued much of Europe and South America. To a great extent, this was because the merits of political liberty and religious equality were recognized by Paul Cullen and his contemporaries more than a century before they were explicitly defended by the American theologian John Courtney Murray.[64] Joseph Lee rightly referred to Cullen as 'Paul the Prudent', but his pragmatism had its roots in the political thought of papal Rome in the late 1820s and 1830s.

Not every such influence endured. The emphasis placed on the thought of Alphonsus Liguori, for example, did not long survive the death of

---

[62] Cullen to Rosmini, 17 January 1840, Archivio Storico dell'Istituto della Carità [ASIC], Antonio Rosmini papers [RP], 647–648. Original in Italian.

[63] For O'Connell's impact on several generations of Italian Catholics, see Rosanna Marsala, 'Catholics in the Irish parliament: Daniel O'Connell and his influence in Italy', *Parliaments, Estates, and Representation*, vol. 34, no. 2 (2014), 167–81.

[64] See John Courtney Murray, *We Hold These Truths: Reflections on the American Proposition* (New York: Sheed & Ward, 1960).

Gregory XVI, who had canonized the eighteenth-century Italian theologian in 1839. Liguori's rejection of the puritanical rigourism of Jansenism had a profound impact on Cullen and his contemporaries, and several of the first generation of Irish colonial bishops published translations of his works.[65] These men largely preferred a moral theology that was significantly more relaxed, more humane, and much less troubled by sexuality than the neo-Jansenism dominant under Pius IX and his successors. In Philadelphia, Francis Kenrick went so far as to insist on a man's duty to provide his wife with sexual pleasure. Yet Pius' hostility effectively foreclosed for several generations any chance of a more forgiving approach to human sexual behaviour. In Ireland itself, Liguorian moral theology largely disappeared after Cullen's death in 1878, leaving the field to the enthusiastic puritanism of the national seminary at Maynooth. It lingered longer elsewhere in Greater Ireland, but eventually it faded there, too, and with similar consequences.

What Pius IX did not abandon was Gregory's emphasis on the authority of the pope, a project that concluded in the definition of papal infallibility at the First Vatican Council (1869–70). There, Cullen led an international phalanx of more than sixty pro-infallibility Irish bishops, gave several well-regarded Latin speeches in favour of the definition, and finally wrote the formulation that was ultimately accepted as dogma. As the disgusted Anglo-German aristocrat (and liberal Catholic) Lord Acton reported, Cullen had boasted to the council that 'Ireland has always believed in infallibility', citing in evidence the decrees of his own Synod of Thurles in 1850.[66] This was the culmination of a line of thinking that his mentor Gregory XVI had done so much to advance and in which Cullen himself passionately believed.

Across Greater Ireland, Irish bishops, priests, and nuns mediated these political, theological, and devotional preferences to largely (but rarely overwhelmingly) Irish Catholic populations. The result was an amalgam that was neither wholly Irish nor wholly Roman but rather Hiberno-Roman. It emphasized loyalty to both the papacy and to Ireland, encouraged Irish symbolism and Roman devotions, and insisted on communal cohesion and social separation, especially in education and matrimony. This is why Ireland's spiritual empire was more than a simple transplantation of the Catholicism of the island of Ireland, and why it is necessary to

---

[65] This was part of a wider Irish boom in Liguorian translations in the 1840s and 1850s. See Anne O'Connor, *Translation and Language in Nineteenth-Century Ireland: A European Perspective* (London: Palgrave Macmillan, 2017).

[66] Acton to Johann Joseph Ignaz von Döllinger, 21 May 1870, in Victor Conzemius (ed.), *Ignaz v Döllinger Briefwechsel mit Lord Acton, Vol. 2: 1869–1870* (Munich: C. H. Beck'sche Verlagsbuchhandlung, 1965), 572. Original in German.

look beyond mere ethnicity in identifying its scale and reach. For Cullen, it was necessary that the church be both Irish *and* Roman. This is why, for example, he helped replace Irish Franciscans in Newfoundland and Irish Dominicans in South Africa with more ideologically congenial Irishmen. It is also why some colonial Irish bishops, such as Robert Dunne of Brisbane or John Walsh of Toronto, rejected or resisted elements of Hiberno-Romanism, while others such as John Hughes of New York or James Goold of Melbourne largely conformed even as they remained wary of Cullen and his acolytes.

The representative figure of this Hiberno-Roman Catholicism was the same Patrick Francis Moran who had boasted of 'the spiritual empire of St. Patrick's Apostolate' in Melbourne. He was born in Ireland, educated at the Propaganda, and ordained for Dublin. He then served as vice rector of the Irish College, Cullen's secretary, editor of the *Irish Ecclesiastical Record*, and Roman agent for the Australian Irish bishops before being appointed a bishop in Ireland and then the first cardinal archbishop of Sydney, Australia. There he convened the first council of the Australasian church and founded a national seminary modelled on the Irish College. He also happened to be Cullen's nephew. Men like Moran, Francis Kenrick, and dozens of others spread Hiberno-Roman Catholicism to the farthest corners of the English-speaking world and then ensured that it was replicated through schools, seminaries, and effective social controls. In time it became normative, and the Catholic Church in Greater Ireland even now remains to a significant extent the product of the Rome of the 1820s, 1830s, and 1840s. This was only possible because of the concentration of ecclesiastical power in the Propaganda, and by Paul Cullen's influence within it.

The purpose of *Ireland's Empire* is to trace how this spiritual empire was created and with what consequences. To do so, it is necessary to focus on the bishops who in a hierarchical church were supreme in their own domain. They exercised a near-despotic power over both clergy and laity, and those who objected were faced with the choice of either leaving the church or appealing to Rome. To many the first was unappealing and for most the second was unavailing. This was most obviously the case with the ferocious campaigns against mixed marriages which invariably followed the appointment of a Hiberno-Roman bishop and which were often years in advance of practice in the church as a whole. (Roman hostility to mixed marriages was only codified by the decree *Ne Temere*, which was issued in 1908.) What the bishops imposed, the people largely accepted, even when what was at issue was whom they should marry, where, and under what conditions. What one bishop said to another, and what both said to the Propaganda, is therefore crucial in explaining not only how Hiberno-Roman Catholicism spread but also how Greater Ireland subsequently developed. It was bishops who set devotional and disciplinary priorities, established schools and oversaw what they taught, decided whom to recruit and where, and chose how much or how little emphasis to place on Irish history, culture, and identity. As the Australian historian Patrick O'Farrell pointed out when his own work was criticized for an overemphasis on clerical elites, 'I still view the Roman Catholic as, historically, a hierarchical and clerically controlled church, and make no apology for the continued substantial attention I have given to bishops and priests, their characters, politics and conflicts. This appears to me', he concluded, 'an appropriate reflection of historical reality, and I remain unmoved by suggestions that the contemporary role of the laity should be read back into the past.'[67] I agree, and although the ultimate goal of this book is to explain the endurance of Irish Catholic identity in the English-speaking world, its central argument is that that explanation is to be found in ecclesiastical politics, or rather in the consequences that flowed from ecclesiastical disputes.

The chapters that follow examine in turn each of the major centres of Irish ecclesiastical activity, starting with the United States and then the British dominions of Newfoundland, India, South Africa, Canada, Australia, and New Zealand. These geographically bounded chapters are then followed by a conclusion that seeks to draw together the social, moral, and intellectual consequences of Irish ecclesiastical success. Of course, neither Irish Catholics nor Hiberno-Roman Catholicism were limited to these countries. Throughout the book I have sought to draw attention to events in places as diverse as Scotland, Gibraltar, Trinidad, and the Falkland Islands, but the primary focus is on the jurisdictions that are treated here at chapter-length. This has left significant gaps. Much more could be said about Scotland, for example, where a determined Hiberno-Roman assault was repulsed in the late 1860s, while England has been omitted on the grounds that Cullen and his successors never challenged the powerful English church on its own terrain. Argentina, which received many Irish Catholic immigrants, is ignored entirely, as is the rest of Central and South America. The enormous Irish missionary presence in Asia and sub-Saharan Africa, meanwhile, is a largely twentieth-century phenomenon separate from that considered here, except in the specific cases of India and South Africa. There are numerous other lacunae: to take only the most obvious, it is impossible in a chapter or two to provide even a partial history of the activities of Catholic religious

---

[67] Quoted in Edmund Campion, 'Patrick O'Farrell: An extended memory', *Journal of Religious History*, vol. 31, no. 1 (March 2007), 21.

orders in any country, let alone one of the size of the United States, Canada, or Australia. Much is left out.

As a result, the focus is on the ecclesiastical politics associated with the Hiberno-Roman takeover of each national church and its immediate aftermath. In any successful empire there is a time of conquest, there are episodes of resistance, and then a long period of consolidation. The emphasis here is on the first two: how did the Irish come to control the Catholic Church in each of the countries discussed, how were they resisted, by whom, and with what effect? Consolidation is not ignored, but the bulk of attention is given to how Ireland's spiritual empire was built and not how it was then governed. Yet, in the end, what really mattered was not the machinations of bishops, or the behaviour of priests, or the recruitment of nuns but the lived experience of the millions of people who organized their lives and identities around the Catholic Church; and the reality is that, by 1914, Irish Catholics across the English-speaking world largely worshipped in the same way, read the same books, were educated by the same religious orders, observed the same social and sexual disciplines (especially surrounding marriage), and shared the same heroes, villains, and martyrs. They retained their identity long after sustained migration from Ireland ceased and today form Ireland's numerous diaspora. As one Newfoundland priest boasted in 1869, the 'Shamrock cannot be extirpated from the soil where it has taken root'.[68] This book is about why that is so.

[68] M. F. Howley, *Sermon Preached by the Rev. Doctor Howley in the Cathedral, St. John's, on the Feast of St. Patrick, 1869* (St John's: n.p., 1869), 22.

1   The United States

It all began with a row. In 1831, the newly appointed coadjutor bishop of Philadelphia, Francis Patrick Kenrick, came home one day to find that his furniture had been piled on the lawn and the locks had been changed on the house he shared with his elderly bishop, Henry Conwell. His offence, Conwell claimed, was to have opened a 'restaurant' in the house, kept boarders, and locked the bishop out of his own parlour. The newspapers reported it, local Protestants loved it, and Conwell boasted of it; but, to Kenrick, it was all simply one more cross to bear as he struggled to bring long-tempestuous Philadelphia to heel.[1]

For years, the Catholic Church in the city had been practically ungovernable. The problem was an ongoing and vicious conflict over whether bishops, priests, or the laity should control church property. This was a common issue across Greater Ireland (contrary to what some American historians have thought), with similar struggles erupting from Gibraltar to Halifax to Cape Town.[2] Its origins were straightforward: where the church was poorly organized, the legal climate inclement, priests few, and episcopal supervision distant or absent, it made sense to vest ecclesiastical property with the people who used and maintained it. Yet no bishop could long tolerate it in his territory, especially as many trustees thought that their influence should extend beyond temporalities to the selection, oversight, and payment of the parochial clergy. In Philadelphia, this problem was exacerbated by the presence of a string of

[1] There are two accounts, both by Conwell, of the duelling locksmiths. The first, which appears to have been written in Latin in 1832, contains the story of Kenrick's career as a restaurateur. It was translated and published in Martin I. J. Griffin, 'The Life of Bishop Conwell of Philadelphia', *Records of the American Catholic Historical Society*, vols. 24 (1913)–29(1918) at 29, no. 2, pp. 181–2 and 24, no. 3, at pp. 251–4. The second, which contains Kenrick's reply mentioned above, was privately printed by Conwell. It carries no title or date and is headed 'not published'. A copy may be consulted at the Philadelphia Archdiocesan Historical Research Center [PAHRC], St Mary's papers [SM], Box 1, Folder 8.

[2] See Patrick W. Carey, *People, Priests and Prelates: Ecclesiastical Democracy and the Tensions of Trusteeism* (Notre Dame, IN: University of Notre Dame Press, 1987).

strong-willed priests backed by stubborn trustees at the city's largest church. It was Conwell's struggles with the Rev. William Hogan, several of his successors, and the parishioners of St Mary's Church that opened the door to the appointment of Kenrick. It was a decision that would have enduring consequences for American Catholicism.

Francis Patrick Kenrick was born in 1796, the son of a scrivener and the nephew of a Dublin parish priest. After an initial education under his uncle's eye, and a period working for his father, Kenrick was sent in 1815 to the Urban College of the Propaganda Fide in Rome. There, the bookish Irishman was exposed to the liturgical grandeur and ultramontane theology of a revivified papacy that was slowly recovering from the serial catastrophes of the revolutionary and Napoleonic periods. Students like Kenrick emerged not only with a powerful *romanità* but also speaking the language of Rome both literally and figuratively: they knew who to speak to and how to speak to them. This gave them important advantages.

One of the consequences of this Roman education was an elevated view of the power of the papacy. To Kenrick, the pope enjoyed not only universal jurisdiction over the church but at least some degree of infallibility as well. Explaining his views on the 'the plentitude of his Spiritual powers' to his doubtful uncle Richard in 1823, Kenrick reminded him that 'You were educated at Maynooth and if I mistake not under French preceptors; I at Rome.'[3] This was an important distinction: the pre-revolutionary French church was largely Gallican in nature, emphasizing the independent power of the episcopate against the papacy and largely deferring to the state. These views were then transmitted to places such as Maynooth that hosted many French theologians fleeing the revolution; this is one reason why Cullen and his allies never trusted the national seminary, a distrust that was heartily reciprocated. Kenrick, by contrast, was a champion of papal authority, and his most important English-language work was *The Primacy of the Apostolic See Vindicated*, which first appeared in 1837. By 1855, it was in its fifth edition and dedicated to Pope Pius IX. Even allowing for the conventional pieties, Kenrick's protégé Michael O'Connor was right to observe that it was the papacy above all else for which Kenrick 'cherished special love and devotion'.[4]

To this extent, Kenrick's clerical biographer was entirely correct to argue that the 'influence of Irish thought' on Kenrick could be 'easily overestimated'. His Roman education, Hugh Nolan continued, 'led him

---

[3] Kenrick to Richard Kenrick, 3 March 1823, The American Catholic Research Center and University Archives, The Catholic University of America [ACUA], Francis Patrick Kenrick papers [FK].

[4] Michael O'Connor, *Archbishop Kenrick and His Work: A Lecture* (Philadelphia, PA: Catholic Standard, 1867), 7.

at times to differ vehemently from many of the native-trained Irish clergy, some of whom he thought leaned towards Gallicanism because of the French influence in their education'.[5] What Nolan overlooked was that Francis Kenrick was both Irish *and* Roman. To Kenrick, the first student of the Propaganda on the American mission, there was no meaningful distinction between the two; he was distant not from Ireland but from French-inflected theology. His lifelong point of reference was the Rome of Pius VII and his formative influence the Propaganda, not the pre-revolutionary network of Irish colleges that shaped men like Conwell, nor the Sulpician seminaries of North America and France, which provided the bulk of the American episcopate Kenrick joined in 1830, nor Maynooth or one of the other Irish seminaries. Kenrick was instead a Hiberno-Roman, the first of many who came to dominate Catholicism in the English-speaking world.

Kenrick's influence has been underestimated by historians. He receives only a handful of mostly passing mentions in both James Hennesey's *American Catholics* and John T. McGreevy's *Catholicism and American Freedom*, for example, and none at all in Jay Dolan's *The American Catholic Experience* or Kerby A. Miller's *Emigrants and Exiles*, which otherwise pays close attention to the Catholic Church and manages ten index entries for Paul Cullen.[6] Yet, intellectually and administratively, through his theological writings, synodical legislation, ecclesiastical patronage, and influence in Rome, Francis Kenrick shaped American Catholicism to an extent unmatched in the nineteenth century. Others such as John Hughes of New York or William Henry O'Connell of Boston had a greater impact on their own dioceses, but none matched Kenrick's on the American church as a whole. He put American Catholicism irrevocably on a new and ultramontane path strikingly similar to that later travelled by his fellow Hiberno-Romans throughout the English-speaking world. Writing shortly after Kenrick's death, Michael O'Connor hit upon an image that captured both his importance and the reason for his subsequent neglect. Kenrick's influence, O'Connor wrote, 'may be compared to the dew that falls at night'. Although its crucial moisture remained, he continued, 'it is itself lost sight of when the sun has arisen'.

---

[5] Nolan, *Kenrick*, 12–13.

[6] James Hennesey, *American Catholics: A History of the Roman Catholic Community in the United States* (New York: Oxford University Press, 1981); John T. McGreevy, *Catholicism and American Freedom: A History* (New York: W. W. Norton, 2003); Jay Dolan, *The American Catholic Experience: A History from Colonial Times to the Present* (New York: Doubleday, 1985); Kerby A. Miller, *Emigrants and Exiles: Ireland and the Irish Exodus to North America* (New York: Oxford University Press, 1985).

Yet it is to the dew that 'the earth is indebted for its fertility much more than to the heavy rain which falls down in torrents'.[7]

It was also Kenrick's misfortune to come to prominence in what remains an understudied period in the history of American Catholicism. Although both violent nativism and outstanding figures such as John England of Charleston have not lacked for attention, the 1830s and early 1840s have often been overlooked in favour of the colonial and early republican periods or the immigrant church of the later nineteenth and early twentieth centuries. The Irish story in particular is largely seen as beginning with the Great Famine. Yet, as David Noel Doyle has pointed out, by 1845 most of the major urban areas that would come to be particularly associated with Irish migration were already under Irish bishops. 'These bishops', he continued, 'in turn accelerated the creation of a distinct Irish-American culture that was urban and catholic.'[8] That culture has survived with exceptional and surprising vitality: as the American politician and public intellectual Daniel Patrick Moynihan observed in 1963, creating the edifice of institutional Catholicism was 'incomparably the most important thing [the Irish] have done in America'.[9] Kenrick was integral to this achievement.

Yet the Irish did not have the field to themselves: American Catholicism was always diverse and became more so as time passed. As a result, Irish Catholics faced the twofold challenge of preserving their own identity while absorbing that of others. They succeeded spectacularly, and the consequent 'greening' of American Catholicism can be illustrated by three brief examples: the archdiocese of Boston, the Sisters of Notre Dame de Namur, and the University of Notre Dame.

Consider Boston, by all appearances the most Irish and most Catholic city in the United States; but it was not always the most Irish Catholic. For most of the nineteenth century, Boston eluded the episcopal Irish, and, although two of its bishops during this period had Irish parents, they were educated in the French tradition and preferred Yankee society. They took little interest in Ireland or the Irish and stood aloof from their fellow Irishmen in the American episcopate. One result of this was that, as late as 1894, less than half of Boston-area priests (thirty-nine of ninety-seven) had been born in Ireland, which was very few for a major east coast city.

---

[7] Michael O'Connor, *Archbishop Kenrick and His Work: A Lecture* (Philadelphia, PA: Catholic Standard, 1867), 1.

[8] D. N. Doyle, 'The Irish in North America, 1776–1845', in W. E. Vaughan (ed.), *A New History of Ireland, Vol. 5: Ireland under the Union, 1801–1870* (Oxford: Oxford University Press, 1989), 714.

[9] Daniel Patrick Moynihan, 'The Irish', in Lee and Casey (eds.), *Making the Irish American: History and Heritage of the Irish in the United States* (New York: New York University Press, 2006), 483. The essay was originally published in 1963.

The city's bishops preferred American-born priests in their own 'Yankee Catholic' image and systematically favoured them.[10] This had important consequences, and it was probably no coincidence that the social and economic conditions of the Boston Irish lagged far behind their brethren elsewhere in the United States.[11] A similar phenomenon can be observed in the Scottish city of Glasgow, which also escaped Irish episcopal control despite a substantial Irish population and an abortive attempt to impose an Irish bishop in the mid-1860s.

Irish marginalization in Catholic Boston only ended with the appointment of William Henry O'Connell in 1907. The son of poor Irish immigrants, O'Connell entered the North American College in Rome in 1881 where, like so many before him, he made important contacts, absorbed the Roman atmosphere, and learned Italian. On his return, he quickly built a reputation as an orator and was much in demand in Boston's Irish enclaves. Perhaps because the Montreal-trained Archbishop John Joseph Williams was happy to get rid of him, in 1885 he found his way to the bottom of the archbishops' *terna* for the vacant rectorship of the North American College and became Rome's surprise choice. In 1901, O'Connell became bishop of Portland, Maine, and, six years later, archbishop of Boston. His thirty-seven-year episcopate overturned the Yankee Catholicism of his predecessors and ushered in an unabashedly Irish and Roman era. The title of James M. O'Toole's biography catches it well: *Militant and triumphant*.[12] Boston had become and would remain an Irish Catholic city.

The Sisters of Notre Dame de Namur, meanwhile, had been founded in Amiens, France, in 1804, before moving to Belgium not long after, where they concentrated on the education of poor children and later on teacher training. In 1840, a party of eight led by an English-speaking Belgian, Louise Van der Shrieck, came to Cincinnati at the invitation of the Irish-born John Baptist Purcell. Despite their francophone origins, the new community's first novice was the Donegal-born Susan McGroarty who, as Sister Julia, taught in Ohio and Massachusetts before becoming the superior in Philadelphia in 1860. She remained there for twenty-five years until elected provincial superior in 1886, a position she held until her death in 1901. During her tenure, she oversaw a near doubling of the community, most of whom were Irish-born or

---

[10] Donna Marwick, *Boston Priests, 1848–1910: A Study of Social and Intellectual Change* (Cambridge, MA: Harvard University Press, 1973), xi, 78–89.

[11] For a typically brisk and insightful discussion of the historiography of Boston Catholicism and its distinctiveness, see J. J. Lee's introduction to Lee and Casey, 11–14.

[12] James M. O'Toole, *Militant and Triumphant: William Henry O'Connell and the Catholic Church in Boston, 1859–1944* (Notre Dame, IN: University of Notre Dame Press, 1992).

Irish-American, and, by 1900, the Sisters of Notre Dame de Namur in the United States were an essentially Irish-American order.[13]

But perhaps the starkest example is the University of Notre Dame, where every Saturday, from early September through to late November, hundreds of thousands of American football fans cheer for the 'Fighting Irish'. Although there are hundreds of Catholic colleges and universities in the United States, only Notre Dame commands a national following among those who identify as Irish Catholic. The university itself is saturated in Irish imagery, from the student leprechaun who entertains the crowd at football games to a long-established interest in Irish Studies; but the university was founded in 1842 at the behest of a French bishop by French members of a French religious order, and its name remains L'Université de Notre Dame du Lac. By 1900, both the university and the Congregation of Holy Cross had become largely Irish in identity and personnel.[14]

None of this was inevitable. Although the Irish and their descendants always represented a substantial proportion of the Catholic population, and at times an overwhelming one, they were always part of a larger ethnic mosaic. They could not rely solely on weight of numbers to ensure their ecclesiastical dominance. There were and remained significant and widely distributed populations of German, French, and Spanish-speaking Catholics, and later large numbers of Italians, Poles, and others, and the country's larger cities still retain vibrant ethnic parishes representing some or all of these communities. Irish control was neither predestined nor inevitable. It was instead Francis Patrick Kenrick who ensured that the American church was Hiberno-Roman before the bulk of the Irish arrived and that that Hiberno-Romanism was robust enough to absorb the millions of non-Irish who followed them. As Michael O'Connor pointed out, not even 'the most enthusiastic admirer of Bishop Kenrick' would 'pretend for a moment that the vast increase of Catholicity was due to his labors'. It was, he admitted, 'Irish landlordism and English misgovernment' that 'dotted the hills and valleys of Pennsylvania, as of so many other States, with churches, and filled them with people'. 'But it was', O'Connor insisted, 'the work of Bishop Kenrick to have prepared the mould, in which the material of this growing Church was cast.'[15]

---

[13] The information for this paragraph is drawn from Kathleen Sprows Cummings, *New Women of the Old Faith: Gender and American Catholicism in the Progressive Era* (Chapel Hill, NC: University of North Carolina Press, 2009), 63–7.

[14] For the university's early history, see Robert E. Burns, *Being Catholic, Being American: The Notre Dame Story, 1842–1934* (Notre Dame, IN: University of Notre Dame Press, 1999).

[15] O'Connor, *Archbishop Kenrick*, 11.

None of this was obvious to the seven bishops gathered in Baltimore in 1829. They just wanted an effective solution to the problem of Philadelphia, which had reached an undeniable crisis point under the disastrous Conwell. Haughty and imperious by temperament, he did himself no favours by downplaying his own Irishness and refusing to engage with the ethnic issues so important to his clergy and people. By the mid-1820s, Conwell and two Irish Dominican priests had managed to elevate what was in essence a parochial squabble to the point that the president of the United States felt compelled to make enquiries of the papal government. As a consequence, Conwell was effectively sacked in August 1827 and offered the choice of resigning and returning to Ireland or retaining his title but not his authority in Roman exile. He chose the latter. Two years later, the Propaganda ordered the Dominicans to leave as well. Sensing an opportunity, Conwell left Rome in the middle of the night. When the papal authorities realized he was missing, they forbade him from travelling to the United States on pain of suspension. He went anyway.

Even before Conwell's escape, no one in Rome or America doubted that a solution had to be found for Philadelphia. Partly to achieve this, the bishops of the United States were summoned to Baltimore, the sole archiepiscopal see, for the first council of the Catholic Church in the United States. It was quickly decided to appoint a coadjutor bishop with full power and right of succession and to get Conwell to accept this in exchange for his public rehabilitation. The bishops were nearly unanimous in selecting the young Francis Kenrick, then based in Kentucky. Even Conwell, lurking uninvited around the margins, gave his approval. Rome accepted both Kenrick's nomination and Conwell's apparent acquiescence with alacrity.

Kenrick had been a rising star since his arrival in America in 1821. He had come to work in the French Sulpician Bishop Benedict Flaget's small seminary, and he was perfectly suited to a life of teaching, reading, writing, and translating theology and scripture. Left to his own devices, Kenrick would spend the entire day at his desk. Yet, in the Kentucky backwoods, he blossomed into a charismatic preacher and bare-knuckle pamphleteer, publishing both learned treatises on baptism and polemical exchanges with Protestant ministers.[16] Other bishops tried to poach him, Flaget wanted him as his own successor, and, by the time he travelled to Baltimore as Flaget's assistant, he was already marked as an inevitable future bishop.[17] His links to the Propaganda – which Archbishop James Whitfield of Baltimore stressed in his letter of recommendation to Rome –

---

[16] Kenrick to his mother, 1 August 1827, ACUA/KP.   [17] Nolan, *Kenrick*, 59.

did not hurt either.[18] Despite discussion of a handful of others, and Flaget's pleas, there was never any doubt of the nomination.[19] Pope Pius VIII confirmed the Propaganda's appointment on 31 January 1830, the news reached America in late April, and Kenrick was consecrated in Kentucky on 6 June.

His first task was to subdue Philadelphia. After several failed attempts to negotiate the capitulation of the trustees of St Mary's, Kenrick was forced by what he called their 'aggression on Episcopal authority' to interdict the church in April 1831.[20] Despite Conwell's behind-the-scenes encouragement of 'the suffering multitude', the trustees were unwilling to call Kenrick's bluff and go into open schism, and the church reopened on 28 May 1831.[21] Conwell was not so accommodating, and, after locking Kenrick out, he continued to do everything he could to undermine his coadjutor until his own death in 1842. Yet this was manageable, if undeniably frustrating. There was also no ethnic dimension: in the struggle against the Irish Conwell, the Irish Kenrick had enjoyed the support of his fellow bishops. That quickly dissipated, and, by late 1831, Archbishop Whitfield was complaining to Rome that Kenrick's 'ardent and enthusiastic spirit' tended to go 'beyond the bounds that prudence constitutes'.[22]

Distrust of Irish turbulence had been a constant in the hierarchy since at least the death of Archbishop John Carroll of Baltimore in 1815, and the subsequent period saw crises cascading into what Peter Guilday called a 'veritable epidemic of misrule'.[23] The dominant French bishops were in little doubt as to who was at fault: 'sacerdotes Hiberni', Archbishop Ambrose Maréchal of Baltimore told Rome in 1818, 'given over to intemperance or ambition' together with their 'tribesmen, whom they bind to themselves by innumerable arts.'[24] The poor Irish, the archbishop of Quebec reported two years later, were stirred up by ambitious 'Irish monks [moines Irlandais] and vagabonds' who wanted 'les premières places' in the American church

[18] Quoted in Nolan, *Kenrick*, 87–8.
[19] In mid-1832, Flaget could still remark that 'the void he left here behind him will never be filled up': Flaget to Martin Spalding, 18 June 1832, Filson Historical Society, Catholic diocese of Bardstown papers.
[20] Kenrick to 'The Pewholders of St. Mary's Church', 12 April 1831, PAHRC/SM/Box 1/Folder 8.
[21] Conwell to Archibald Randall, 13 May 1831, PAHRC/SM/Box 1/Folder 8. Randall was the secretary of the trustees.
[22] Whitfield to the Propaganda, 17 October 1831, quoted in Nolan, *Kenrick*, 132.
[23] Peter Guilday, *The Life and Times of John England, First Bishop of Charleston (1786–1842)*, 2 vols. (New York: The America Press, 1927), 1: 2.
[24] Maréchal's report to the Propaganda was printed, in its original Latin, in the *Catholic Historical Review*, vol. 1, no. 4 (January 1916), 439–53.

for themselves.[25] By 1820, as Guilday noted, 'the whole question seemed to have revolved itself into a struggle between the French and Irish elements in the country itself and abroad, particularly in Rome, for the control of the American Church'.[26]

This conflict informed the process of creating new dioceses to accommodate what was still a slowly growing Catholic population. The obvious first choice was Charleston, South Carolina, whose bishop was nearly 600 miles away in Baltimore. Partly as a result of this, the Catholic community both there and in Norfolk, Virginia, had been convulsed by internal conflicts, and, in Norfolk, some were even publicly flirting with the Old Catholics of Utrecht in the Netherlands.[27] Fearing schism, in 1819 the Propaganda informed Maréchal that new dioceses would be carved out of his own in the Carolinas and Georgia, which he had expected, and Virginia, which he had not.

Most likely acting on the advice of an Irish-born Charleston priest who had fallen foul of Maréchal and appealed in person to Rome, the Propaganda sought only the names of priests in Ireland for the new sees. The malcontents in the south had been Irish, just as in Philadelphia and elsewhere, and Maréchal was amazed when he discovered that yet more Irishmen was Rome's preferred solution. This was not, the archbishop insisted, because he was himself prejudiced but rather because Irish missionaries had been the 'croix' that he and his predecessors had had to bear. The Irish, he told Rome, simply could 'not live in peace', either with themselves or with 'missionaries from other nations'. He also pointed out that Irish priests and laity were making the lives of the three Irish-born bishops miserable and their dioceses ungovernable – sending more Irish bishops wouldn't help.[28] Although Maréchal tried to forestall an Irish appointment by despatching the American-born Jesuit Benedict Fenwick to Charleston and recommending him as its first bishop, he was too late: in June 1820, the Propaganda erected the sees of Charleston and Richmond and appointed Irishmen to head both. While Patrick Kelly stayed only two years in Virginia before gratefully returning to Ireland as bishop of Lismore, John England served more than twenty years in South Carolina and became one of the most important figures in the early American church and a significant one in American

---

[25] Joseph-Octave Plessis to Francesco Fontana, 6 September 1820. Quoted, in French, in Guilday, 1: 10. Plessis had been sent to the United States as apostolic delegate to report on the deteriorating situation.

[26] Guilday, 1: 11.

[27] Gerald P. Fogarty, S. J., *Commonwealth Catholicism: A History of the Catholic Church in Virginia* (Notre Dame, IN: University of Notre Dame Press, 2001), 44.

[28] Maréchal to Lorenzo Litti, 18 September 1819. Printed, in the original French, in Guilday, 1: 286.

history more generally. When Francis Kenrick eventually arrived in Philadelphia, he had an eager ally waiting in the south.

England was an energetic bishop, regularly travelling his vast diocese, launching the first American Catholic newspaper, the *United States Catholic Miscellany*, and establishing control over the previously fractious clergy and laity. He has been of interest to historians largely for his supposedly 'Americanizing' tendencies, and, as David Gleeson put it, 'he stoutly defended the compatibility of Roman Catholicism with American republicanism'.[29] But, although early, this was not unusual for an Irish Catholic bishop. Nor was it, as the late Peter D'Agostino suggested, limited to America.[30] The religious free market of the United States, United Kingdom, and British Empire made political pluralism attractive to a church that remained officially hostile to it. John England was among the first to realize this and to defend political and religious freedom as positive goods, but he was not alone in this insight.

But that is not to say that he was not in the vanguard of his church: many of the lessons that Antonio Rosmini drew from Tocqueville, for example, had already been articulated by England. They soon came to be shared across Greater Ireland. John England was also among the first to combine fervent American patriotism with an enduring love of Ireland: he saw no contradiction between loyalty to the United States and a firmly maintained Irish identity, whether in regular denunciations of British rule, support for Irish cultural and social organizations, the use of the Irish language, or keeping up a correspondence with Daniel O'Connell.[31] Although not all of England's enthusiasms were shared by his Irish successors, in his political posture and unabashed hybridity he was undeniably a trailblazer and his influence was enduring.

When England's fellow Irishman Francis Patrick Kenrick arrived in Philadelphia ten years later, there were eleven dioceses in the United States. Three (New York, Bardstown, Mobile) had French incumbents and New Orleans a francophone Belgian. The bishop of St Louis was a multilingual Neapolitan with strong French links. There were two American-born bishops, Edward Fenwick (a Dominican) in Cincinnati and Benedict Fenwick (a Jesuit) in Boston. Although apparently not closely related, both had been born in Maryland to long-established

---

[29] For example, Patrick W. Carey, *An Immigrant Bishop: John England's Adaptation of Irish Catholicism to American Republicanism* (New York: United States Catholic Historical Society, 1982); David T. Gleeson, *The Irish in the South, 1815–1877* (Chapel Hill, NC: University of North Carolina Press, 2001), 77.

[30] Peter R. D'Agostino, *Rome in America: Transnational Catholic Ideology from the Risorgimento to Fascism* (Chapel Hill: University of North Carolina Press, 2004), 44.

[31] Gleeson, 78.

Catholic families. Edward was educated in pre-revolutionary Belgium, Benedict entirely in the United States, where he became the protégé of Ambrose Maréchal. Maréchal's successor as archbishop of Baltimore was a French-educated Englishman, and the diocese of Richmond had been vacant since 1822. Kenrick and England were the only Irish and the only bishops without substantial connections to France. Yet there was more to this distribution than ethnic arithmetic: seven of the bishops were members of religious orders, one Jesuit, one Dominican, two Vincentians (the Congregation of the Mission, or Lazarists), and three Sulpicians. Only three, Kenrick, England, and Michael Portier of Mobile, Alabama, were secular priests. More importantly, the Sulpician bishops of Baltimore, New York, and Bardstown were members of a powerful network that had grown used to its control of the American church.

Sulpician dominance began with the appointment of Ambrose Maréchal as the third archbishop of Baltimore in 1817. Born and educated in France, he had fled from the revolution on the day of his ordination in 1792, one of the ten Sulpician priests and four clerical students to arrive between 1791 and 1795. Founded in Paris in 1642, the Sulpicians were dedicated to the education of the parochial clergy, and the appearance of so many saw the society almost instantly comprise nearly a third of the active priests in the entire United States. At the invitation of Archbishop John Carroll, the fugitives promptly opened the first American seminary near Baltimore. The lack of American vocations, however, caused the Sulpicians to disperse to other assignments, where their numbers and education distinguished them in the still tiny American church. That many became bishops was unsurprising.

The first was Benedict Flaget, who was appointed to Bardstown, Kentucky, in 1808. Maréchal was next and then John Dubois as the third bishop of New York in 1825. A well-connected Parisian (and school fellow of Robespierre), Dubois had also fled France in the early 1790s but did not join the Sulpicians until 1808. The same year he founded Mt St Mary's College in Emmitsburg, Maryland, which was intended to supply clerical students to the Sulpician seminary in Baltimore but wound up in competition with it for the handful of available vocations. Although the college was formally separated from the society in 1828, it continued in the Sulpician tradition.

To men like Flaget, Maréchal, and Dubois, the guiding model of ecclesiastical organization was, just as for Conwell, that of pre-revolutionary France or contemporary Quebec: a church ruled by educated, genteel bishops, respectfully distant from Rome and jealous of their prerogatives, dubious of theological innovations such as papal infallibility, socially accommodating, and politically quiescent. This was also the

formation of the numerous French missionary priests, largely concentrated in the lower Mississippi valley, who had been trained by the
Sulpicians in France.[32] The disorder of the 1810s and 1820s – brought,
the French thought, by the immigrant Irish – tried them deeply.
A polemical, political Irishman such as John England represented
a menace to be contained in distant Charleston. As the Sulpician archbishop of Baltimore declared flatly in mid-1829, 'experience has proved
that in general the Irish will not do'.[33] England in turn spent his episcopate butting heads with what he came to call 'the adepts of Saint
Sulpice'.[34]

The Sulpicians were right to worry, as John England's restless mind
quickly turned to the affairs of the wider American church. It was an
unlovely sight: in 1821, Maréchal described Philadelphia as being in
'complete confusion', while New York, since 1815 under the Irish
Dominican John Connolly, was experiencing 'grave disorders'.[35]
England's solution was to impose uniformity of discipline through the
mechanism of a national (technically, provincial) council which could
then be judged and approved by the Propaganda.[36] The American
French, however, had no intention of jeopardizing their power by acced-
ing to England's demands; Rome was a long way away, and they preferred
to keep it that way.

This was clear to England, and he badgered Maréchal relentlessly for
a council.[37] The archbishop's death in 1828 could have been a pretext, as
it was hard to argue for French bishops in perpetuity. Yet the Sulpicians
had been carefully preparing for the event, and not long before his death
Maréchal successfully arranged for an English-born member of the
society, James Whitfield, to be named as his successor. Whitfield had
been entirely educated in France, and, except for being a native English-
speaker, he was every bit a French Sulpician. It was a tactic that would be
emulated by other foreign religious orders under Irish pressure, most

---

[32] Michael Pasquier, *Fathers on the Frontier: French Missionaries and the Roman Catholic
Priesthood in the United States, 1789–1870* (Oxford: Oxford University Press, 2010).
[33] James Whitfield to Nicholas Wiseman, 12 June 1829, Archivium Venerabilis Collegii
Anglorum de Urbe (Venerable English College) [AVCAU], Scr. 69/12/111.
[34] England to John Hughes, 24 January 1837, Archives of the Archdiocese of New York
[AANY], Archbishop John Hughes Collection [JH], Box 2, Folder 20.
[35] [Ambrose Maréchal], *General Description of the Metropolitan Province of Baltimore in the
United States of America* (1821), quoted in Guilday, 2: 74. As Guilday points out, since
this document was intended for Roman eyes, Maréchal was careful to note that everything was going well in those dioceses lucky enough to have French bishops.
[36] At this stage, Baltimore was still the only archiepiscopal see, and therefore a national and
provincial synod effectively amounted to the same thing.
[37] Guilday, 2: 71.

notably some fifty years later by the French Marists of New Zealand (see Chapter 7).

For his part, England greeted Maréchal's death by complaining that he had not been invited to Whitfield's consecration. Only the two other Sulpicians, Flaget and Dubois, and the nearby Conwell, had been involved, and England thought that the discourtesy was simply a mask to avoid a gathering of the American hierarchy, which it probably was.[38] Undeterred, he immediately pushed his agenda on the new archbishop. 'There exists', Whitfield learned, 'every disposition to conform my mind to that of my brethren', but until they met it was 'impossible' to know 'what that *one mind* is'. He was 'distinctly of opinion, that we are every day increasing the evils of our state' by avoiding a council.[39] Whitfield was unmoved, and it was only the spiralling chaos of Philadelphia that forced his hand.

England was quick to seize the initiative. Writing to Whitfield in December 1828, he disclaimed having an agenda before setting one out at length. Six points were uppermost in his mind: creating a national seminary, at least in part to reduce the problem of vagabond priests; return of polemical fire against Protestants; proper Catholic education; an increase in the number of religious orders, especially of women; the creation of a Catholic press; and, finally, 'The laying down [of] general principles of discipline upon which we might enact our respective Diocesan statutes with as near an approach as possible to uniformity.' The last was the most important and the only one that he thought might be actually achieved.[40] England's agenda was for an American church in which priests and bishops alike could be held to fixed standards of behaviour and reported to Rome when they fell short. This was anathema to Whitfield and the French.

The long delayed first council of the American Catholic Church was duly convened in Baltimore in late September 1829. Other than sending Kenrick to Philadelphia and recommending Conwell's contingent pardon, the bishops did little of note. There was no appetite, for example, for England's suggestion that parish priests be given canonical status and thus protection from their bishops' whims. Most of the decrees were uncontentious: trustees were condemned and the ban on lay selection of parochial clergy reinforced, the need for Catholic schools stressed, and the Douay version of the Bible recommended. More significantly, Archbishop Whitfield was careless enough to permit a decree mandating

[38] England to Whitfield, 2 June 1828, Associated Archives, St Mary's Seminary and University, Baltimore [AASMSU], Whitfield papers [WP], 23 G1.
[39] Ibid.   [40] England to Whitfield, 26 December 1828, AASMSU/WP/23G2.

another provincial synod in three years' time. An unsatisfied England observed that the council had done useful work in regulating the clergy and 'very little else'.[41]

Whitfield himself had no desire to repeat the experiment. Nor was he eager to publish the council's decrees after Rome took its accustomed leisure to examine, modify, and approve them. By April 1831, England was complaining to a Baltimore Sulpician that not only had Whitfield still not published but he did not himself even have a copy.[42] By December, Bishop Dubois was astounded to find after a trip to Europe that the approved decrees had not been published in New York, despite explicit instructions to his Catholic newspaper, *The Truth Teller*. When he made enquiries, he was told that the exclusive copyright had been given to a printer in Baltimore, who seemed to be doing nothing with it. Even the Sulpician Dubois thought that this was a bit much.[43]

By June 1832, Whitfield had decided to indefinitely postpone the council that was due later that year. England was apoplectic, expressing to the archbishop his 'perfect dissent'. The previous council, he now claimed, had done 'great good' and prevented 'great evils' and more could be expected from its sequel.[44] He was not placated by Whitfield's assertion that he had unspecified 'good reasons', observing that Whitfield's refusal to call a council 'could convey that you had no respect for the opinion & judgment' of his fellow bishops. He knew that Whitfield thought him 'too agitating, too noisy & too fond of publishing', but that was no reason to avoid a council.[45]

Already planning a visit to Ireland to secure funds and, if possible, nuns and priests, England decided to take his case to Rome. While there, he told Whitfield in May 1833, the Propaganda had asked his opinion on a number of American matters, ranging from the proposed creation of a new diocese at Vincennes in Indiana to the recent vacancy in Cincinnati occasioned by the death of Edward Fenwick. To each query he recommended deferring a decision until the views of a provincial council could be learned. England found a ready audience in Rome: 'the Pope in particular', he told Whitfield, 'desired me to say, that if you did not see good results from the [last] council, he at least did & that it was his wish that we should meet as frequently as we could.' Indeed, Pope Gregory had 'thrice told' him that this wish would be formally conveyed to

---

[41] England to Judge Gaston, 7 November 1829, quoted in Guilday, 2: 127.
[42] England to Edward Damphoux, 19 April 1831, AASMSU/WP/23AU1.
[43] Dubois to Whitfield, 17 December 1831, AASMSU/WP/23F2.
[44] England to Whitfield, 13 June 1832, AASMSU/WP/23AD1.
[45] England to Whitfield, 4 January 1832, AASMSU/WP/23G4.

Whitfield.[46] It was a triumph: England, as one Roman observer reported back to Ireland, 'succeeds in all his affairs'.[47] Whitfield duly but reluctantly summoned the American bishops to Baltimore for October 1833.

The archbishop's consternation was amplified by the other achievement of England's European tour: a potential solution to America's chronic shortage of priests. From Ireland, England had informed Whitfield of his success in 'securing a good supply of candidates for orders & to suggest to you the utility of your acting on the same plan'. Ireland, he wrote, had 'a greater number of candidates for orders than the Irish Church requires'. At present, the Irish bishops selected the best, and the rest were left to fend for themselves, including some who would make excellent priests. Men whose families could not pay for their education were particularly overlooked. The authorities at Maynooth and Carlow had agreed that they would each year identify candidates for Charleston, receive them in England's name, and keep them in Ireland 'prosecuting their studies' until ready to depart for America.

Mindful of the long-established problem of dissolute or rebellious Irish priests crossing the Atlantic, England promised that he would not ordain any candidate who did not have the full endorsement of their college. Although he would naturally prefer those who could 'pay the expenses of his voyage & education', if none or not enough appeared he would subsidize both.[48] The plan worked well for Charleston, where 70 per cent of the priests who served between 1820 and 1880 were Irish or of Irish descent.[49] Whitfield did not even bother to reply – the last thing he wanted was more Irish priests.

England's success in Rome also underlined the importance of a physical presence in the Eternal City. At best a letter took several weeks to cross the Atlantic, and even a relatively simple correspondence could stretch out over several months. Being on the spot was optimal, as protocol insured a bishop's access to the Propaganda and the pope. Yet no bishop could stay in Rome forever, and in his absence an agent was necessary to receive correspondence, translate documents, explain circumstances, amplify successes, minimize failures, warn of danger, and thwart opponents. Not only did such an agent need to be trustworthy, he needed to have regular access to the Propaganda and the pope, be liked

[46] England to Whitfield, 14 May 1833, AASMSU/WP/23G5.

[47] Paul Cullen to John MacHale, 19 March 1833, in Bernard O'Reilly, *John MacHale, Archbishop of Tuam: His Life, Times, and Correspondence*, 2 vols. (New York: Fr. Pustet & Co., 1890), 1: 180–1. MacHale's private papers are lost, and O'Reilly's two-volume hagiography is now the primary source for the life of this important figure.

[48] England to Whitfield, 18 September 1832, AASMSU/WP/23AD3.   [49] Gleeson, 82.

and trusted by both, and speak and write fluent Italian. Luckily for John England, his new ally in Philadelphia knew just the man for the job.

Kenrick's first two years in Philadelphia had been focussed on the battle with Conwell and his own plans for the future of his diocese. He seems not to have taken any particular part in England's now decade-long campaign for regular councils, even if he almost certainly favoured them. He also had no a priori reason to be suspicious of the Sulpicians: Archbishop Whitfield had recommended him for Philadelphia, and his mentor Flaget was the longest serving of the Sulpician bishops. It was Whitfield's inability or unwillingness to make necessary decisions over episcopal vacancies and diocesan divisions that turned Kenrick's mind to Rome, and, on 4 July 1833, he wrote to the rector of the recently re-established Irish College in the city, Paul Cullen. They had known each other for years, overlapping as students in the Propaganda for two, but this letter marked a significant change in their relationship.

Almost as soon as he knew that he was likely to be sent to Philadelphia, Kenrick had sought the aid of his friend. Their first surviving letter, now preserved in Australia, suggests that Cullen had been considering the American mission and had asked for advice. Kenrick was enthusiastic: Cullen's native English and theological attainments would prove useful in the United States.[50] Writing again shortly before his consecration, Kenrick made an offer: come to America, 'aid in healing the wounds' of Philadelphia, and 'second my efforts to establish an Ecclesiastical Seminary'. 'O dear Paul', he lamented, 'What consolation if I had a bosom Friend into whose pure ears I could pour the distress of my Soul as often as I shall be tossed on the Sea of Episcopal solitude!'[51]

Cullen demurred. He lacked 'all the dispositions' necessary to be a missionary, but he did want to help: 'if I am not called to be a good missioner, I may at least in some humble situation cooperate to the advancement' of the Catholic faith. As far as Philadelphia was concerned, that meant he could provide Roman texts for Kenrick's mooted seminary, help Kenrick with the composition of his own theological works, and host Kenrick's protégés in the Irish College. By early 1831, two were already in residence – including Kenrick's ultimate successor as archbishop of Baltimore, Martin J. Spalding. Cullen hoped they would be the first of many.[52] Kenrick in turn sent the draft of his manual of dogmatic theology (of which more later) for a 'finishing stroke'. He could, Kenrick wrote,

---

[50] Kenrick to Cullen, 21 January 1830 (but not posted until 1 April 1830), AAS, Moran papers [MP], U2206. Moran kept this and a handful of other early letters from Kenrick as part of his long projected but never completed biography of Cullen.
[51] Kenrick to Cullen, 5 May 1830, AAS/MP/U2206.
[52] Cullen to Kenrick, 9 June 1831, AASMSU, Kenrick papers [KP], 28 R1.

'take every liberty which you would with your own productions'.[53] He also did not abandon hope that Cullen might be lured across the Atlantic, writing as late as September 1832 that 'A man of your character would realize all that I desire'.[54]

By mid-1833, his tone had changed. His chastisement of Cullen's poor correspondence habits (a lament of many throughout the 1830s) was pointed: 'Can you conceive', he wrote, 'that no advantage to Religion would arrive from frequent communications?' Kenrick thought 'great good would thence accrue', not simply for himself but for the American church. He drew Cullen's attention to the 'ludicrous' situation in Kentucky (where there was a question of the division of the diocese) and the ongoing episcopal vacancy in Cincinnati as instances of 'the necessity of such correspondence'. Cullen could 'easily perceive the advantages of familiar and confidential communications, which enable you to make opportune suggestions'.[55] Although Kenrick had not yet completely cast his lot with John England, he was anxious to secure a voice in Rome.

England had also recognized Cullen's potential. How much time they spent together in Rome is unclear, but Cullen undoubtedly watched the Corkman's progress sympathetically. By July 1833, when England was in Ireland on his way home, he was using Cullen as an intermediary to the pope.[56] By late September, he was comfortable enough to open his mind in advance of the second council of Baltimore. Writing from New York, he informed Cullen that 'In this city & in Baltimore things are as bad as ever.' Dubois was overseeing chaos in the 'finest city of the western world', a city of such riches that 'a man even ordinarily prudent' might harness its wealth to great effect; but instead 'with the great portion of his flock & of the public at large Doctor Dubois is looked upon as worse than crazy', and the diocese was nearly bankrupt. Baltimore was little better. In case there was any doubt where the fault lay, England spelled it out: 'The tricks & low cunning of some of those who for years have ruled the American Church have disgusted and alienated some of the most respectable & talented and wealthy members of the church itself.'[57]

Cullen had no hesitation in becoming the agent of what was emerging as the Irish faction of the American hierarchy. In early September 1833, he wrote Kenrick a 'long straggling letter' that demonstrated the great

[53] Kenrick to Cullen, 16 May 1832, AAS/MP/U2206.
[54] Kenrick to Cullen, 7 September 1832, Pontifical Irish College, Rome, Archives [PICRA], American Letters [AL], #3.
[55] Kenrick to Cullen, 4 July 1833, AAS/MP/U2206.
[56] England to Cullen, 20 July 1833, PICRA/AL/6.
[57] England to Cullen, 26 September 1833, PICRA/AL/10.

utility of a Roman agent. He began with a detailed account of England's visit to Rome. The bishop of Charleston, he reported, had made an excellent impression and 'fully persuaded the Pope that it is absolutely necessary for the interests of the Catholic Church in America to hold frequent councils there'. Since England's departure, Cullen continued, 'the Pope often spoke to me on the same subject, and he even went so far as to say that he would be happy that the American bishops meet as often as the Irish Prelates who regularly assemble once a year'. Sliding easily into his role as agent, Cullen had regularly met with the newly appointed secretary of the Propaganda, Angelo Mai (cardinal from 1838), 'to keep fresh in his memory' England's case. 'Indeed', he continued, 'I never let any opportunity pass in which I can promote the interests of religion in America, without doing it. I am as much interested in your success in the western hemisphere, as I am for the cause of religion in Ireland.'[58]

The second provincial council of Baltimore, however, turned out to be a disaster for the Irish. Kenrick informed Cullen that England was threatening to resign and leave America in frustration.[59] England himself sent a detailed report from Charleston, telling Cullen that 'a very general prejudice existed against me for what I had done in Rome'. He had had only three reliable allies: Kenrick, Michael Portier of Alabama, and the newly appointed bishop of Detroit, Frederick Rèsè. (The increasingly erratic Dubois flitted between the factions.)[60] Although a Frenchman, Portier was a secular priest, unaffiliated with the Sulpicians and a product of the *post*-revolutionary French church.[61] Rèsè was a Propaganda-educated German who often allied with the Irish until mental illness overtook him by 1837. 'It appeared to be fixed', England wrote a few days later, 'that whatever I would introduce should be negatived.' He urged Cullen to speak to the *minutanti* and to show his letters to the cardinal prefect.[62]

Rumours about the council reached Rome in early December 1833. Cullen was worried: 'complaints', he told Kenrick, 'will be certainly carried to Rome if they have not arrived against Dr England and those who agreed with him.' Although Cullen admitted he did not yet know the details of what had happened, he stressed the 'importance that these matters should be fairly represented'. Kenrick should consequently

---

[58] Cullen to Kenrick, 1 September [?1833], AASMSU/KP/28R2.

[59] Kenrick to Cullen, 16 November 1833, AAS/MP/U2206.

[60] England to Cullen, 15 December 1833, PICRA/AL/12.

[61] For Portier, see Oscar H. Lipscomb, 'The administration of Michael Portier, vicar apostolic of Alabama and the Floridas, 1825–1829 and the first bishop of Mobile, 1829–1859', unpublished Ph.D. diss., Catholic University of America, 1963.

[62] England to Cullen, 17 December 1833, PICRA/AL/13.

'write frequently to the Propaganda upon the wants of the American Church' and not give up on the policy of regular councils. Though they might 'not have an immediate effect, yet they will prepare the way for introducing a regular system into the ecclesiastical affairs of your adopted country'.[63]

Kenrick's detailed account arrived in January 1834. His primary goal was to ensure the chastisement of the 'rude' Archbishop Whitfield, but he also had other concerns. First, he was appalled that Flaget had appealed for yet another French Sulpician bishop in Bardstown, which already had both a bishop and, since 1817, a coadjutor bishop. 'Why', Kenrick asked, 'should three Bishops be in one Diocese?'[64] He simply could not see why yet another French Sulpician should be appointed. More importantly, John Dubois of New York had indicated that he was preparing to request a coadjutor. It was 'altogether necessary', Kenrick wrote, that he 'should have an Irish clergyman in whom he would repose implicit confidence'. He hoped that either Cullen himself or his young vice rector, Michael O'Connor, 'would volunteer' for the 'sacrifice' of being appointed to New York.[65]

The Irish bishops did not believe that the opposition they faced was the result of honest disagreement about policy. As England wrote in early January 1834, 'the good folk who have so long shut out the Irish from their proper place in the American church, have now French and Americans – Sulpicians and Jesuits, united & are likely to continue their operations with more powerful effect'.[66] Kenrick thought 'anti-Irish feeling' had marred the council, with England's 'proposal to supply this Country with Missionary Priests from Ireland' arousing particular opposition.[67] Writing in 1835, England spelled out the differences between Irish and French. 'The Irish', he told Michael O'Connor in Rome, 'are easily amalgamated with the Americans – their principles, their dispositions, their politics, their notions of government, their language, & their appearances become American very quickly, and they praise & prefer America to their oppressors at home.' The same was not true of the French: 'their language, manners, love of la belle France, their dress, air, carriage, notions, & mode of speaking of their religion, all – all are foreign.'[68] Kenrick lamented that the 'first Cities of the East' had bishops with 'imperfect English' which made them subjects of 'ridicule, rather than

---

[63] Cullen to Kenrick, 9 December 1833, AASMSU/KP/28 R3.
[64] Kenrick to Cullen, 14 January 1834, AAS/MP/U2206.   [65] Ibid.
[66] England to Cullen, 3 January 1834, PICRA/AL/15. The Jesuit was Bishop Fenwick of Boston, who was a loyal ally to the Sulpicians.
[67] Kenrick to Cullen 20 March 1834, PICRA/AL/19.
[68] England to O'Connor, 25 February 1835, PICRA/AL/37.

of edification'.[69] The solution was to try and ensure that future bishops be Irish. This had been the plan in Cincinnati, where, after much resistance, the Mallow-born John Baptist Purcell had been appointed. He was Kenrick's choice and consequently met with French resistance despite the fact that he was president of the formerly Sulpician Mt St Mary's. Some years later, John England told him that, even after his appointment, there had been a concerted attempt to substitute a Frenchman.[70] Whitfield and a number of others preferred a Jesuit.[71] Yet it was New York that would be the most important test of the success of this policy.

England emphatically supported John Power, a popular Irishman who had been the long-serving vicar general of the diocese, several times its administrator, founder of *The Truth Teller*, and leading figure in the Irish Emigrant Society; but Power was opposed by the French interest and thus by Whitfield who, according to England, was 'completely the tool of the Sulpicians, who have for a number of years created a government of faction & of intrigue, instead of an honest, open, strong administration'. Now those forces were deployed against Power. England feared an explosion, as the Catholics of New York were 'principally Irish and American in feeling & they see that in the administration of the American church, the whole action is Anti-Irish & Anti-American'. For the present that made them 'inert', not taking an active role, not giving any money, but not actively opposing episcopal authority either. Yet that could change, and England worried that the Sulpicians had a plan. As with Baltimore, they knew that appointing a Frenchman would be too provocative; but, instead, in order to 'shut out the man that the people wish', there was a movement 'to get an Irishman who has never been in the Diocese for coadjutor to Doctor Dubois'. Cullen was 'one of those in contemplation'. Yet if it was anyone other than Cullen, he concluded, 'the opposition will cease to be inert'. New York risked schism unless Paul Cullen or John Power became its next bishop.[72]

In the event, Dubois would not receive his coadjutor for another three years. In the meantime, the Irish had to navigate the wreckage the council

---

[69] Kenrick to Cullen 20 March 1834, PICRA/AL/19.

[70] England to Purcell, 1 July 1837, University of Notre Dame Archives [UNDA], Cincinnati papers, II-4-f. The only study of Purcell is M. A. McCann, *Archbishop Purcell and the Archdiocese of Cincinnati* (Washington, DC: Catholic University of America, 1918).

[71] This included the incumbent bishop, Edward Fenwick, who before his own death suggested only one name, the Irish Jesuit Peter Kenny, and Joseph Rosati of St Louis: see Fenwick to Whitfield, 22 August 1832 and Rosati to Whitfield, 14 February 1833, AASMSU/WP/23H6, 23S5.

[72] England to Cullen, 13 May 1834, PICRA/AL/22.

had made of their hopes. The first task was to ensure that Rome took the correct view of events. Writing to Kenrick in early February 1834, Cullen was able to report that he had passed 'the part of your letter which regarded Dr England to the Pope'. Gregory was 'very sorry' to hear what had happened and at a loss to understand 'why the other prelates sd be displeased with [England's] projects here in Rome', projects which he considered 'very reasonable and calculated to promote the interests of religion'. If England carried out his threat to resign Charleston, Cullen thought the pope would refuse. Less happily, he told Kenrick that his bid to block the third appointment to Bardstown was too late, as no one 'wrote against it from America'. What Rome did not know, Rome could not fix.[73]

This was not a mistake the Irish would make again. As a young John McCloskey (later the first American cardinal) noticed in 1835, 'the affairs of the American Church even to the minutest details' were 'very well known in the Eternal City'.[74] Nor did Kenrick abandon his faith in councils. In time, he thought they would 'establish order in the various Dioceses – would correct the discrepancies of rite – would strengthen legitimate authority, and take away occasion of schism – would, in a word, effectively advance the interests of Religion'.[75] This is an important point: to Hiberno-Romans like Kenrick and Cullen, councils were about control and uniformity, not the liberties of a particular national church. It was a mechanism for ensuring Roman authority and orthodox conformity, and from America to Australia securing a local majority of reliable Irish bishops was the preferred means of obtaining that end.

The council left England in despair, and he told Cullen in May 1834 that 'either I am totally unfit for an American Diocese, or the great body of my brethren have made sad mistakes'. The problem was that 'their minds & mine are cast in different moulds – and co-operation is out of the question'.[76] He was also increasingly tired and frustrated. As he wrote in late 1837, 'I have been much whipped & cursed for thinking to have my own way, and following my own notions, that I think it better to give it up.' He would focus on Charleston and 'have as little as I can do with any thing outside, so that they who have been so kind as to give me credit for intermeddling & intriguing will henceforth find me as quiet as they wish'.[77] In 1840, he informed Whitfield's successor that he had no

---

[73] Cullen to Kenrick, 1 February 1834, AASMSU/KP/28R4.

[74] McCloskey to John Power, '1835', Rare Books and Manuscript Library, Columbia University [CU], Henry Joseph Browne papers [BP], MS 1296, Series 1, Sub-series 1, Box 3, Folder 14.

[75] Kenrick to Cullen, 20 March 1834, PICRA/AL/19.

[76] England to Cullen, 13 May 1834, PICRA/AL/22.

[77] England to Hughes, 21 December 1837, CU/BP/MS 1296/1/1/1/5.

intention of speaking in that year's council of Baltimore. He would just be outvoted, so it 'would be a waste of time, a cause of dispute ... and an occasion of violation of charity & estrangement'. He would speak only when spoken to and 'act as I please for myself' while letting others do the same.[78] Although he never entirely withdrew from American ecclesiastical politics, and was certainly not reconciled to the Sulpicians (in 1837, he privately worried they were 'preparing the way for a schism'), England largely kept his word.[79]

Still, he had no intention of abandoning Kenrick entirely. Indeed, he sought to provide him with an important ally. When England arrived in Rome in late May 1834 to report on his first unsuccessful trip to Haiti as the pope's representative, he stayed as Cullen's guest in the Irish College and leaned heavily on Cullen's skill in navigating the papal bureaucracy. Cullen even postponed his first visit to Ireland in fifteen years because England 'may have need of me in getting through his business'. He would stay until 'we see his affairs settled' and then travel home with England.[80] In the event, England's affairs were not so easily settled, and Cullen ultimately set off alone on 30 June.

In his absence, England had an idea: why not arrange for Cullen to become his own coadjutor in Charleston? He could then concentrate on Haiti while securing Charleston attentive leadership and the Irish faction a powerfully connected addition. On 22 July 1834, England wrote to inform Archbishop Whitfield that, as it was necessary he return to Haiti, Rome might appoint a coadjutor to look after Charleston. In that event, he planned to nominate Paul Cullen as his first choice, a professor at Carlow, William Clancy, as his second, and the rector of the Irish College in Paris, Patrick MacSweeny, as his third.[81] This was a lie, as he admitted when he finally told Cullen of his plans on 1 August: he never mentioned 'any other names' in Rome.

When he raised the matter with the pope, he reported to Cullen, Gregory's first question was whether he had Cullen's consent. England assured him that he 'had no doubt of obtaining it'. It seems the pope did not believe him because a few days later England again told him that he could not manage without a coadjutor. 'I then said', England recalled, 'you were the person I looked for.' The pope, who had successfully kept Cullen in Rome since 1828, was 'evidently quite unprepared for this, & changed his manner at once'. A suspicious Gregory wanted to know if

[78] England to Eccleston, 7 February 1840, AASMSU, Eccleston papers [EP], 24T6.
[79] England to Hughes, 24 January 1837, AANY/HP/2/20.
[80] Cullen to Daniel Murray, 2 June 1834, Dublin Diocesan Archives [DDA], Murray papers [MP], 34/9.
[81] England to Whitfield, 22 July 1834, AASMSU/WP/23 G7.

Cullen was aware of the plan and was assured that it had been mentioned 'more than once'. England advised Cullen to settle the succession in the Irish College and plan for the journey to America.[82]

Gregory was right to be sceptical. Cullen had carefully avoided anything that might take him from Rome, from the presidency of Maynooth to the coadjutorship of New York, and he had no intention of accepting South Carolina. He did not have to try very hard to squash the idea: Gregory XVI had likely only consented because he had thought it was Cullen's desire to go to America. When he found it was not, he had no problem changing his mind. By mid-September, England was becoming concerned. He was waiting to set sail with his new coadjutor but had heard nothing from Cullen, who was still in Ireland, or from Rome, but he had 'heard reports that Doctor C. declines'. England had trouble believing this, 'after our conversations in Rome', but, if it were true, he would 'wish to know as soon as possible, that I might act accordingly'.[83] Cullen's explanation, when it finally came, does not survive. Yet other than a single brief letter, England did not write to him again for six months; and although the relationship was restored, it was never fully repaired.

Cullen's refusal left England stranded. In a panic, he approached William Clancy of Carlow College, the second man on the list he had disingenuously provided Whitfield. Clancy was unenthusiastic, England later admitted, having told him that 'he had many objections to leaving Ireland, and going to America'.[84] England should have listened because the appointment was a disaster: Clancy never settled in Charleston, the two men soon fell out, and by 1836 Clancy was begging Cullen to use 'your intimacy with the Pope & the authorities' to help him escape 'this wretched diocese'.[85] In 1837, England asked Rome to transfer Clancy to the first available vacant see anywhere else in the world.[86] The watching Sulpicians could be forgiven for a bit of *Schadenfreude* as they contemplated the spectacle.

By 1834, the factions in the American hierarchy were not yet in balance. The Irish had enjoyed some important successes, not least the clear requirement of triennial councils and, to a lesser extent, Purcell's appointment to Cincinnati. They could also take comfort from their growing influence at Rome, something manifested

[82] England to Cullen, 1 August 1834, PICRA/AL/28.
[83] England to Andrew Fitzgerald, 17 September 1834, PICRA/AL/31. Fitzgerald was the president of Carlow College, and England had asked him to find Cullen. He must have, as the letter survives in Cullen's papers in the Irish College.
[84] England to O'Connor, 7 March 1835, PICRA/AL/38.
[85] Clancy to Cullen, 23 November 1836, PICRA/AL/55.
[86] England to Eccleston, 27 February 1837, AASMSU/EP/24T3.

immediately after the council by the Propaganda's refusal to confirm a decree reintegrating Richmond into the archdiocese of Baltimore. Yet they had also experienced a number of reverses: the lopsided majorities at the council, the appointment in Bardstown, and England's disengagement from active politics. They also failed to end Sulpician dominance in Baltimore.

Just as he had been named by Archbishop Maréchal, James Whitfield hoped to designate his own successor in what was still America's sole archdiocese. 'If I should die', Whitfield instructed a fellow Sulpician in 1832, 'before I write for a coadjutor I desire that the Rev Mr Eccleston be proposed for my successor.'[87] The Propaganda acceded to the archbishop's wishes, and Samuel Eccleston was appointed coadjutor archbishop of Baltimore in a congregation held in January 1834.[88] By the end of the year, he was archbishop in his own right. Eccleston was an American-born Episcopalian, converted by the Sulpicians as a teenager when his Catholic stepfather consigned him to St Mary's. Ordained for the society in 1825, he was sent to France to complete his education before assignment to the seminary, where he quickly rose to be president.[89] Although it was impossible to claim that Eccleston was another of the 'foreign aristocracy' of which England often complained, he was every bit a Sulpician. He was also committed to resisting the relentless growth of Irish influence. With regular councils now an established feature of the American church, the question was who could command a majority.

Attention again turned to New York, where John Dubois' need had not gone away. As Eccleston admitted privately in 1837, 'The affairs of New York are more and more unmanageable.'[90] The only question was who should be appointed as his coadjutor: a Frenchman was out of the question, an anglophone Sulpician would be little better, Dubois was implacably opposed to John Power, the Sulpicians were implacably opposed to an appointee from Ireland, and the Irish of New York were insistent on an Irishman in general and Power in particular. As in 1834, various solutions were mooted: Dubois even proposed Kenrick. He wasn't interested, and it is not hard to imagine Archbishop Eccleston's reaction to the idea.[91]

---

[87] Whitfield to [?Telsier], 16 January 1832, AASMSU/WP/23D11b.
[88] See Cullen to Kenrick, 1 February 1834, AASMSU/KP/28R4.
[89] Thomas McCaffrey to James Stillinger, 8 May 1835, Pittsburgh Diocesan Archives [PDA], Monsignor A. A. Lambing Manuscript Collection [LC], 181.
[90] Eccleston to Fenwick, 24 February 1837, AASMSU, Baltimore Visitation Monastery Collection [BVM].
[91] Kenrick to Cullen, 23 July 1836, AAS/MP/U2206.

The most promising choice seemed to be one of Kenrick's parish priests, John Hughes, who although born in Ireland had emigrated with his family as a young man. Too poor to pursue a vocation, he had worked as a gardener at Mt St Mary's before Dubois finally admitted him as a student. He had stayed conspicuously loyal to Kenrick in Philadelphia, even as he maintained communications with the Sulpicians and other French bishops, usually in French. He was a formidable personality, pugnacious in person and print, and as early as 1833 copies of his polemics were circulating in Rome to general approval.[92] There was reason to hope that his appointment might please Dubois, Kenrick, the Irish of New York, Rome, and the Sulpicians. It did not. The problem was Kenrick. He had, he told Cullen, 'reason to think' that Hughes would not be acceptable to the New York clergy, who favoured Power, and did not see how Hughes could leave the Philadelphia parish that he had saddled with debt.[93] Yet he did not think Hughes unsuitable as a bishop: the year before he had enthusiastically recommended him as either his successor in Philadelphia or the first bishop of Pittsburgh.[94] In the complicated politics of the American hierarchy, the fates of New York, Philadelphia, and Pittsburgh had become entwined.

The diocese of Philadelphia was massive, encompassing all of Pennsylvania, Delaware, and parts of New Jersey and Ohio. Kenrick's meticulously recorded visitations demonstrate that, while he did his best to cover it all, the task was impossible. In 1835, he consequently asked the Propaganda to divide the diocese and erect a new see at Pittsburgh in far western Pennsylvania.[95] At first there seemed to be no problem: Cullen, for example, believed the pope 'without difficulty will accede to his request'.[96] Kenrick's first thought was to have himself translated and suggested Hughes as his successor. By early 1836, he had changed his mind: Conwell had publicly denounced Kenrick as an usurper and threatened to sue him. Kenrick now thought his departure would give the impression he 'was abandoning my post in despair' and asked Cullen to explain the situation to the Propaganda.[97] His alternative was that England be sent to New York ('in order to leave Dr Clancy at ease in Charleston'), Hughes to Pittsburgh, while he stayed in Philadelphia to

[92] Cullen to Kenrick, 1 September 1833, AASMSU/KP/28R2.
[93] Kenrick to Cullen, 23 July 1836, AAS/MP/U2206.
[94] *Diary and Visitation Record of the Rt. Rev. Francis Patrick Kenrick, Administrator and Bishop of Philadelphia, 1830–1851* (Philadelphia: Archdiocese of Philadelphia, 1916), 112–16. Hereafter *KD*. The diary was originally written in Latin.
[95] *KD*, 115.   [96] Cullen to Murray, 3 December 1835, DDA/MP/ 34/9.
[97] Kenrick to Hughes, 19 January 1837, CU/BP/MS 1296/1/1/1/9; Kenrick to Cullen, 23 July 1836, AAS/MP/U2206.

deal with Conwell.[98] This was unlikely to appeal to anybody, and the
Propaganda sought the advice of the American bishops, who were scheduled to meet in 1837. Cullen remained confident that the ultimate result
would be Philadelphia's division and Kenrick's removal to Pittsburgh.[99]

The delay inevitably led to rumours and hurt feelings. By at least
March 1836, it was widely known in America that Kenrick had asked
for the division of Philadelphia and the appointment of Hughes either
there or in Pittsburgh.[100] On 11 July, Hughes told a friend that his
appointment to the former 'seems to be confirmed'.[101] When nothing
happened, Hughes felt exposed. A visit by John England made matters
worse: he told Hughes that the whole business would be deferred until the
next provincial council because Kenrick had changed his mind about
Hughes' suitability. On 19 January 1837, he wrote his bishop a pained
letter, not trusting himself to raise the matter in person.[102] Kenrick did his
best to repair the damage: he informed Hughes that he had opposed his
appointment to New York only because he thought the Irish clergy there
would object. As for Pennsylvania, he had only agreed to await the verdict
of the council and had told Rome nothing 'that could derogate from the
high commendations I had given you'.[103]

Yet Hughes' intemperance had shaken Kenrick, and he told Cullen in
mid-February to withdraw his name for Pittsburgh. Cullen's subsequent
disapproving remarks about prospective bishops not showing humility or
'due respect towards their superiors' almost certainly referred to
Hughes.[104] In his place, Kenrick substituted three Irish-based priests,
including the vicar general of Dublin, William Meagher, and the future
titular archbishop of Calcutta, Patrick Carew.[105] Yet Kenrick knew it was
futile: there was little chance that the forthcoming council would agree, he
told Cullen, as the majority of the American hierarchy 'is totally averse to
Irish Clergymen thus imported'.[106]

He was right. Eccleston and his allies were alarmed by Kenrick's
growing influence in the Propaganda, largely because they knew that it
was becoming increasingly difficult to avoid Irish nominees to any vacancies that might occur. In existing sees, a living incumbent could expect to
exercise influence, and often named his own successor, but that was not

[98] Kenrick to Hughes, 19 January 1837, CU/BP/MS 1296/1/1/1/9.
[99] Cullen to Kenrick, 9 September 1836, AASMSU/KP/28R1.
[100] John McGirr to James Stillinger, 6 March 1836, PDA/LC/189.
[101] Hughes to Stillinger, 11 July 1836, PDA/LC/193.
[102] Hughes to Kenrick, 19 January 1837, CU/BP/MS 1296/1/1/1/9.
[103] Kenrick to Hughes, 19 January 1837, CU/BP/MS 1296/1/1/1/9.
[104] Cullen to Kenrick 17 April 1837, AASMSU/KP/28R10.
[105] Cullen to Kenrick, 17 April 1837, AASMSU/KP/28R10.
[106] Kenrick to Cullen, 14 February 1837, PICRA/AL/57.

the case in a new diocese. The suggestion of the ex-Sulpician bishop of Vincennes, Simon Bruté, that the forthcoming council create nine new dioceses thus represented a profound threat. New dioceses were evidently necessary, but the problem, as Eccleston admitted in February 1837, was that 'the project will be welcome to some of our colleagues'. So many new bishops, he continued, would 'require the introduction of episcopal candidates from Ireland'. In time, this would put the American church 'in the hands of those, who, having no experience of our wants or character, will be either mischievous or comparatively useless in proportion as they are more or less enterprising'. Kenrick, he told his ally Benedict Fenwick of Boston, 'has already sent me the names of three Irish ecclesiastics' for the proposed diocese of Pittsburgh. Eccleston's answer was that he would be happy to support any priest who 'had spent among us a sufficient time to know something about us and to be a little known by us'. Otherwise, 'I should rather delay the erection of any new See until we can find at home subjects who have afforded us sufficient guarantee of their competency.'[107]

These were effective arguments: Clancy's failure in Charleston allowed the archbishop to reprise the old Sulpician complaint about the incompetence of Irish bishops; it was hard to claim anti-Irish prejudice when the objection was not to Irishmen but to strangers; and 'home subjects' largely meant American-born products of the Sulpician or former Sulpician seminaries in Baltimore, Emmitsburg, France, or Montreal. From at least 1837, Samuel Eccleston's policy was to slow the administrative growth of the American Catholic Church as much as he could for as long as he could. Perhaps the pro-Irish mood of the Propaganda would dissipate in the meantime.

The great Irish victory of triennial councils thus proved at first to be Eccleston's great advantage: he still commanded a majority. For its part, Rome was committed to allowing the council to speak: it might not always concur, but it would always listen. After the long struggle to embed councils in the American church, it could hardly do otherwise. Thus the bishops had a great deal of work to do when they assembled in Baltimore in the spring of 1837. There was one immediate change: John England remained relatively quiet; and, perhaps as a result, there seems to have been much less open acrimony than in 1833. Both sides experienced setbacks: Eccleston accepted new dioceses in Iowa (Dubuque), Mississippi (Natchez), and Tennessee (Nashville), while Kenrick's plans for Pittsburgh were rejected. As the 'disappointed' Irishman diplomatically explained to one of his priests, his colleagues had 'concurred'

[107] Eccleston to Fenwick, 24 February 1837, AASMSU/BVM.

that a diocese was necessary 'but did not assent to my nominations'.[108] Hughes was recommended for New York despite Kenrick's new doubts about his temperament and England's continued preference for Power, while a Frenchman was nominated for Dubuque and an American-born Dominican for Nashville.[109]

The only Irish nominee – Thomas Heyden for Natchez – was a long-standing parish priest in south-western Pennsylvania. Although he had been in America for many years, he retained his links with Ireland, where he seems to have known the wider Cullen family. (Josephine Cullen, Paul Cullen's niece, was ultimately buried in his parish.)[110] Heyden was also close to both Power and Hughes and had been widely tipped for Pittsburgh in the event it went to neither Kenrick nor Hughes. His appointment to Mississippi seems to have come as an unwelcome surprise – as Hughes wrote in September 1837, 'What do you think of all this? You to the great desert and I to the great Babylon!'[111] Heyden refused, most likely in the hope of eventually getting Pittsburgh, and Natchez ultimately went to a Franco American Sulpician, John Joseph Mary Benedict Chanche, in 1840. The disastrous Clancy was offered the vicariate of Demerara in modern-day Guyana but refused to accept it for several years. Rome agreed to everything, accepting in each instance either the bishops' first choice or, when the Jesuits refused 'to have any of their men promoted', the next on the list.[112] Eccleston must have decided that councils were not so bad after all.

Yet success came at a price. Eccleston's arguments had been effective in blocking Irish appointments but could be turned against him. This became clear almost immediately when Benedict Fenwick proposed that an English-born but Canadian-based Sulpician (later Jesuit), John Larkin, become his coadjutor in Boston. Eccleston was understandably delighted but recognized the problem. Would not he be viewed 'in the same light as we all viewed the proposal of Bp. Kenrick to get a Bishop from Ireland for Pittsburgh?' Would it not embolden Kenrick and England to try again for Irishmen? Perhaps, Eccleston thought, they could make the case that Canada was quite nearby, and Larkin had 'more than once come among us to

---

[108] Kenrick to Heyden, 20 April 1837, PDA/LC/214.
[109] According to England, he was the only bishop to ultimately oppose Hughes' appointment. Not, he explained afterwards, because he thought him unworthy but because he was so committed to Power. See England to Hughes, 21 December 1837, CU/BP/MS1296/1/1/1/5.
[110] Cullen to Heyden, 31 January 1862, PDA/LC/949.
[111] Hughes to Heyden, 28 September 1837, PDA/LC/232.
[112] Cullen to Kenrick, 24 July 1837, AASMSU/KP/28 R11.

refresh his American spirits'.[113] Even he did not sound convinced, and Larkin remained in Montreal.

Kenrick's position was much worse. The refusal to erect Pittsburgh was a calculated and rather brutal insult, especially when Natchez and Dubuque were successful. Even the proposed appointment of Heyden could be construed as a refined snub – either he refused and thus compromised his future suitability for the episcopate or he accepted a distant, tiny, and impoverished diocese. Natchez itself had only 600 Catholics and the whole of Mississippi only two priests and not a single church.[114] By contrast, the city of Pittsburgh alone had some 8,000 Catholics and two churches.[115] The decision also left Kenrick badly exposed in Philadelphia. Conwell was neither dead nor quiet, and he still had the whole of his vast diocese to oversee alone. In 1833, Kenrick had estimated that it already contained 100,000 Catholics, and the number could only have risen subsequently.[116] As he lamented to Cullen in the immediate aftermath of the council, 'I wish the Pope would send you to us.'[117] Although Kenrick was, as Cullen reported to the archbishop of Dublin, 'obliged to abandon' his plan for the time being, he did not forget it.[118] For the next six years, the battle to create a diocese in Pittsburgh and place an Irishman of Kenrick's choice at its head was the primary conflict in the American church.

Yet the most important outcome of the third provincial council of Baltimore was undoubtedly the appointment of John Hughes, New York City's famous 'Dagger John'.[119] Hughes has unsurprisingly come to overshadow the other American Irish bishops of his generation: his gardener's cottage is preserved as a kind of shrine at Mt St Mary's, and he has even been pressed into service by American conservatives eager to attribute eventual Irish social integration to episcopal admonitions against sex and drink.[120] Hughes has also received much scholarly attention, although his policies in New York have at times wrongly been taken to be path-breaking, where they might be more accurately described as

---

[113] Eccleston to Fenwick, 7 December 1837, Archives of the Archdiocese of Boston [AAB], Fenwick papers [FP], 1.55.6.

[114] Randy J. Sparks, *Religion in Mississippi* (Jackson: Mississippi Historical Society, 2001), 203.

[115] *KD*, 114.   [116] Nolan, *Kenrick*, 140.

[117] Kenrick to Cullen, 13 June 1837, PICRA/AL/63.

[118] Cullen to Murray, 1 August 1837, DDA/MP/34/9.

[119] Hughes has only recently received a scholarly biography: John Loughery, *Dagger John: Archbishop John Hughes and the Making of Irish America* (Ithaca, NY: Three Hills – Cornell University Press, 2018).

[120] See William J. Stern, 'How Dagger John saved New York's Irish', *City Journal* (Spring 1997).

efficient emulation.[121] Yet his willingness to engage in public controversy, his robust and quotable pamphlets, and his uncompromising personality ensured his prominence. So too did the ever-growing importance
of New York, not least after the explosion of Irish emigration from the
mid-1840s. Neither his own people nor outside observers doubted who
was in charge of the Catholic Church in the era of mass emigration,
poverty, and riot portrayed in Martin Scorsese's *Gangs of New York*
(2002).

Hughes was something of an outlier among the episcopal Irish and
hard to place in the taxonomy of American Catholicism. Although he was
forced to work with substantial non-Irish Catholic populations
(principally German) in both Philadelphia and New York, Hughes was
unambiguously an Irishman: one of his earliest pamphlets was a sermon
marking Catholic emancipation dedicated to Daniel O'Connell.[122] Year
after year, he denounced English misrule and its consequences, which he
compared to African slavery.[123] Hughes encouraged the retention of Irish
identity, whether through the Ancient Order of Hibernians, the Irish
Emigrant Society, or the Emigrant Savings Bank. Yet he was also
a proud American, as eager as John England to reconcile republican
liberty with Catholicism.[124] As Hasia Diner noted, Hughes and the
institutions he established blended 'Catholic piety, love of the Irish homeland, and American patriotism'.[125] The other American Irish shared his
devotion to home and loyalty to the United States but none quite so
noisily.

Although educated by the Sulpicians, and fluent in French, he was not
their man. He happily criticized Gallicanism in print.[126] Yet he equally
had no experience of Rome or Roman theology: his first visit was as
a bishop, in 1840. He was impressed by 'the vestibule of Paradise' and
set himself to learning Italian, but he never felt the instinctive love of the

---

[121] For example, see Irene Whelan, 'Religious rivalry and the making of Irish-American identity', in Lee and Casey, 278.

[122] John Hughes, *A Sermon Preached in the Church of St. Augustine, in Philadelphia, on the 31st of May, 1829, at a Solemn, Religious Thanksgiving to Almighty God for the Emancipation of the Catholics of Great Britain and Ireland* (Philadelphia: Garden & Thompson, 1829).

[123] Ibid., 27.

[124] See, for example, John Hughes, *The Catholic Chapter in the History of the United States, a Lecture: Delivered in the Metropolitan Hall, before the Catholic Institute, on Monday Evening, March 8, 1852, for the Benefit of the House of Protection, under the Charge of the Sisters of Mercy* (New York: Edward Dunigan & Brother, 1852), esp. 8–9.

[125] Hasia R. Diner, '"The most Irish city in the Union": The era of the Great Migration, 1844–1877', in Ronald H. Bayor and Timothy J. Meagher (eds.), *The New York Irish* (Baltimore: Johns Hopkins University Press, 1996), 103.

[126] John Hughes, *The Church and the World, a Lecture: Delivered at the Chinese Museum, Philadelphia, on Thursday Evening, January 31, 1850* (New York: Edward Dunigan & Brother, 1850), 21.

Roman-trained.[127] Like the Hiberno-Roman bishops across Greater Ireland, he was a heated opponent of secular education, but unlike the Hiberno-Romans, and despite his iron grip on New York, he was careless in enforcing controls on marriage, even when neighbouring bishops complained.[128] In the feuding American hierarchy, his primary concern was to preserve his own freedom of action, especially after New York was raised to an archdiocese in 1850. He left little or no legacy outside the city, but New York itself still displays the scale of his achievement, from the bulk of St Patrick's Cathedral on Fifth Avenue to the vast parochial school system he effectively inaugurated. Echoing Emmet Larkin's famous claim for Paul Cullen, Hasia Diner credits him with 'making the Irish Catholics [of New York] a devout people'.[129]

Yet first he had to manage Dubois. The elderly bishop had required a coadjutor because he was widely considered unfit, and there was some hope that his failing health would prevent him from meddling; but, as Archbishop Eccleston told Hughes soon after his arrival, if Dubois got better and 'things remain as they are', it would be his 'duty' to acquaint Rome 'with the errors of his administration & the embarrassments of your position'.[130] Simon Bruté urged Hughes to show respect and charity to their increasingly paranoid 'unhappy brother'.[131] He tried, but there was little that could be done to placate the Frenchman, and the two men fought bitterly until Dubois' death in 1842. This was not the best start to running a diocese that already had, according to Hughes' somewhat optimistic assessment, some 200,000 Catholics, 56 priests, and 49 churches, and with the great Irish migration yet to come.[132] Still, Hughes did well, especially once he had full control: a seminary was founded, schools built, churches erected, priests and nuns recruited, and the social, financial, and political implications of the teeming Irish ultimately accommodated. His relationship with Kenrick was never entirely comfortable, although it became collegial, but he did not become an ally of Eccleston and the Sulpicians either. He was quick to use Cullen as his agent and, as an archbishop, sent him his 'love' and referred to him fondly as the 'Lion without [a] shaggy mane'.[133] In Rome he always stayed in the Irish College, and in Liverpool with

[127] Hughes to Margaret Rodrigue, 3 January, 20 January 1840, CU/BP/MS1296/1/1/2/18.
[128] James Roosevelt Bayley to Hughes, 29 January 1859, AANY/HP/2/14. Formerly Hughes' secretary, Bayley was now bishop of Newark. This is by no means the only such letter in Hughes' papers.
[129] Diner, 103.   [130] Eccleston to Hughes, 16 January 1839, AANY/HP/2/20.
[131] Bruté to Hughes, 29 March 1839, CU/BP/MS 1296/1/1/1/2.
[132] Hughes to the Leopoldine Society, 16 April 1840, CU/BP/MS1296/1/1/1/8.
[133] Hughes to William Walsh, February 1855, Archives of the Archdiocese of Halifax [AAH], William Walsh papers [WP].

Cullen's family.[134] Yet Hughes remained his own man: very Irish, proudly American, and deferential to Rome without being a Roman like Cullen, Kenrick, or Kenrick's new candidate for Pittsburgh, Michael O'Connor.

Unlike Hughes, O'Connor's career was quintessentially Hiberno-Roman. Born in 1810 in Cove, he was sent at the age of fourteen to the Urban College, where he mastered Italian, excelled academically, and, like Cullen before him, earned the patronage of the future Gregory XVI. According to Cullen, his doctoral defence had 'surpassed any thing that could be expected'.[135] Ordained in 1833, he found himself teaching sacred scripture at the Propaganda and living in the Irish College. At the pope's suggestion, he was soon deputizing for Cullen not only in the administration of the college but also in the management of American business.[136] Kenrick thought highly enough of him to suggest him for New York at the tender age of twenty-four. He decided to return home instead. But Roman success did not yet count for much in Ireland, and O'Connor languished as a convent chaplain. He set his sights on Maynooth, successfully soliciting letters of support from Rome, including from Cardinal Fransoni.[137] Cullen also did his best to support his protégé.[138] This probably did more harm than good, and O'Connor quickly realized that he had little chance of success. A visiting Kenrick saw his opening and 'induced me to go to Philadelphia', O'Connor reported to Cullen, 'which would not have been difficult though I had more prospects at Maynooth'.[139]

The lure of America was increased by Kenrick's offer of the rectorship of his nascent seminary. It was a good result for all concerned: Kenrick secured the most gifted and well regarded of the Roman Irish short of Cullen himself and O'Connor got a job. He also brought his younger brother James with him, launching him on a clerical career that would see him in turn a student in Rome, resident of the Irish College, rector of the Philadelphia seminary, administrator of the diocese of Pittsburgh, and first bishop of Omaha, Nebraska. Kenrick could also again begin to plan for Pittsburgh: after a few years in the United States, it would be difficult to argue that O'Connor was a stranger.

---

[134] Thomas Cullen to Kenrick, 13 June 1851, AASMSU/KP/28U5.
[135] Cullen to MacHale, 4 September 1832, O'Reilly, 1: 178–80.
[136] Cullen to Murray, 28 April 1834, DDA/MP/34/9.
[137] Henry A. Szarnicki, *Michael O'Connor: First Catholic Bishop of Pittsburgh, 1843–1860* (Pittsburgh: Wolfson Publishing, 1975), 21.
[138] Cullen to Murray, 'May' 1838, DDA/MP/34/9.
[139] O'Connor to Cullen, 1 October 1838, PICRA/AL.

Eccleston and his allies saw the danger and arranged for the fourth provincial council of Baltimore, held in May 1840, to mandate that only American citizens should be recommended as bishops. Although growing nativist sentiment made this prudent, it was aimed squarely at O'Connor, whom Kenrick nominated at the council. Yet a citizenship requirement could only delay Irish appointees, not block them: three years' residence was sufficient for naturalization. Nor did the decree necessarily bind Rome. Kenrick refused to budge and asked the Propaganda to intervene.[140] He also urged Cullen to use his influence to have the 'matter, so long deferred, finally terminated'.[141] There was little he could do: although sympathetic, the Propaganda was still unwilling to flatly overrule the American hierarchy. Undeterred, Kenrick sent O'Connor to Pittsburgh as parish priest with instructions to become an American citizen at the first opportunity.[142]

Kenrick's prospects soon brightened considerably with the surprise 1841 appointment of his younger brother Peter as coadjutor bishop of St Louis. Although the men were close, Peter was no clone of his brother. The most important difference was educational: financial difficulties had necessitated that he was educated in Maynooth, not Rome.[143] There, he was one of the four students who founded what became the Irish Vincentians, later the preferred male religious order of Hiberno-Roman bishops around the world. Ordained in 1833, he promptly departed to help run Kenrick's seminary in Philadelphia where he remained until 1839, when he went to Rome with a view to becoming a Jesuit. Francis Kenrick and O'Connor were both vehemently opposed and enlisted Cullen to dissuade him. He changed his mind at the last minute, on his way (in Cullen's company) to enter the novitiate. Cullen thought it 'most providential'.[144] Once home, he distinguished himself by drawing on earlier work by his brother to produce an important, early, and theologically innovative treatise denying the validity of Anglican orders.[145] The brothers were careful to send Cullen a copy to show in Rome, and the publication made the younger Kenrick's reputation as a theologian.[146]

---

[140] See Nolan, *Kenrick*, 256–7.   [141] Kenrick to Cullen, 23 June 1840, PICRA/AL/71.
[142] Szarnicki, 30.
[143] The difference may account for Peter's strong opposition to papal infallibility at the first Vatican Council, which enraged Cullen and would have shocked his brother.
[144] Cullen to Kenrick, 28 October 1839, AASMSU/KP/28R13.
[145] Peter Richard Kenrick, *The Validity of Anglican Ordinations Examined; Or, a Review of Certain Facts Regarding the Consecration of Matthew Parker, First Protestant Archbishop of Canterbury* (Philadelphia: Eugene Cumminskey, 1841). For its importance and place in the theological debates of the time, see Kenneth L. Parker and Daniel Handschy, 'Eucharistic sacrifice, American polemics, the Oxford Movement, and *Apostolicae Curae*', *Journal of Ecclesiastical History*, vol. 62, no. 3 (July 2011), 515–42.
[146] Cullen to Kenrick, 11 December 1841, AASMSU/KP/28S1.

Kenrick owed his appointment to the Italian-born bishop of St Louis, Joseph Rosati. Originally ordained for the Vincentians, Rosati had been an American bishop since 1822 and had been a largely reliable supporter of the French and Sulpicians. In the late 1830s, however, Rosati had grown closer to Francis Kenrick, and, in 1841, he was summoned to Rome to assume the ageing England's mission to Haiti. Like England, he believed that that role would require a coadjutor, recommended Peter Kenrick, and suggested that Rome compel him to accept. The Propaganda agreed, as did a reluctant Kenrick. Why Rosati chose him is unclear: most likely it was the younger man's Vincentian links combined with a desire to please his brother. Whatever the case, Rosati's intervention was the occasion of a powerful addition to the American Irish. That was only compounded when Rosati died unexpectedly in 1843, leaving Peter Kenrick as bishop of St Louis in his own right. He died in 1896.

Things were finally beginning to move in Kenrick's favour. Knowing that 'the problem of choosing' suitable bishops would be raised in the upcoming council, Peter Kenrick added his voice to the call for Irish ones.[147] As he pointed out to Purcell of Cincinnati, Eccleston's 'anti-Irish prejudices' had cost the American church bishops of the quality that had recently been appointed to Calcutta, Madras, Gibraltar, Nova Scotia, and the Cape of Good Hope. In future, he wrote, they should look to the talent 'at home'.[148] The council of 1843 thus saw dioceses recommended for Chicago, Little Rock, Hartford, Milwaukee, and Pittsburgh, as well as coadjutors for Boston and New York and a new bishop for Charleston. Four were American-born (Boston, Charleston, Hartford, and New York), three Irish (Chicago, Little Rock, and Pittsburgh), and one German in Wisconsin. None were French, and only John Bernard Fitzpatrick in Boston was obviously congenial to the Sulpicians, having been educated by them in Montreal and Paris.[149] The now American O'Connor was recommended for Pittsburgh, despite having recently announced his intention to become a Jesuit. He was already in Rome making the arrangements when the council's recommendations arrived, and he reluctantly acceded to its (and the pope's) wishes. Before he left, he secured at least three student places at the Urban College, thus ensuring a suitably trained clergy for his new diocese.[150] He then set out for

---

[147] Francis Kenrick to Peter Kenrick, 25 April 1843, *The Kenrick-Frenaye Correspondence*, 166. Hereafter *KFC*.

[148] Peter Kenrick to Purcell, 17 February 1843, UNDA/CP/II-4-h.

[149] See Thomas H. O'Connor, *Fitzpatrick's Boston, 1846–1866: John Bernard Fitzpatrick, Third Bishop of Boston* (Boston: Northeastern University Press, 1984).

[150] See M. Gibson to Stillinger, 25 October 1843/PDA/LC/393.

Ireland 'to select a few priests or students to accompany him to his mission'.[151]

O'Connor also needed nuns. Although the number of women religious in Ireland had been slowly growing from a mere 122 in 1800, by 1843 there were still less than 1,000 on the island. The great export market for Irish nuns was in its infancy, if that, and only a handful had yet left the country. Despite the recent creation and rapid success of the Sisters of Mercy, the Sisters of Charity, and the Irish branch of the Loreto Sisters, there was more than enough work at home and not yet enough women to do it. In this context, O'Connor's decision to approach the Sisters of Mercy was significant. Although Catherine McAuley had formally established the community in Dublin in 1831 (its origins went back to 1827), it had not expanded further than England during her lifetime. Although after her death in late 1841 a short-lived attempt was made to establish a community in Newfoundland (see Chapter 2), there was no particular reason for the women to consider missionary work, nor to choose the United States if they did.

O'Connor's decision to approach the Sisters of Mercy was almost certainly informed by Cullen. As the agent for the Irish bishops, he had assisted McAuley in the long process of getting the community's constitution approved in Rome and was consequently well known and highly regarded by them. More importantly, two of Cullen's cousins were members of the Mercy convent in Carlow. One, Cecilia Maher, was the mother superior, and it was Maher who allowed her predecessor, Frances Warde, to lead a group of seven volunteers to America. She was accompanied by Cullen's other cousin, Josephine Cullen, and a niece of the future Cardinal Wiseman of Westminster. Under Warde's formidable leadership, the sisters quickly established themselves in Pittsburgh and then spread rapidly throughout the United States. Without what soon became thousands of Mercy Sisters, the vast infrastructure of Ireland's spiritual empire would have been entirely impossible. Securing the erection of Pittsburgh and Michael O'Connor's appointment to lead it was an even greater triumph than Francis Kenrick knew.

Yet episcopal infighting was not Kenrick's sole occupation. He had a large and complicated diocese to run, Conwell to contain (until 1842), and escalating social and ethnic tensions to manage; but he also codified the organization and discipline of the diocese of Philadelphia, oversaw the creation of a suitable seminary, and personally produced the theological texts to be used there and elsewhere in the United States. All three had long-lasting implications for American Catholicism.

---

[151] Cullen to Kenrick, 17 August 1843, AASMSU/KP/28S3.

As soon as he arrived in Philadelphia, Kenrick began planning for a diocesan synod. Commonplace elsewhere, they were a novelty in the United States; only John England had held one prior to 1832. Although a gathering of the priests of the diocese, and a forum for discussion, it was not an exercise in ecclesiastical democracy: Kenrick wrote all of the decrees, and their purpose was to impose uniform practice and discipline. The council was thus a reflection of Kenrick's agenda for his diocese and, by extension, the American church. The first decree promulgated the first provincial council of Baltimore and insisted on the observation of its edicts. Others included a ringing denunciation of trusteeism and a requirement that no new church could be built, or orphanage or school opened, without the bishop's written permission. All church property was to be vested in the bishop's name. Other decrees involved the placement of baptismal fonts and the correct keeping of records, especially of marriage. The intent was to centre Catholic worship and devotional life in the parish under the watchful eye of the parish priest. The behaviour of priests, meanwhile, was carefully regulated (including an admonition about the age of their housekeepers), as was the treatment of the blessed sacrament. Taking direct aim at French practice, priests were forbidden to carry it on their person except when answering a sick call. Its exposition was limited to the Mass, with two exceptions: the feast of Corpus Christi and the Forty Hours Devotion, the latter an important popular devotion favoured throughout Greater Ireland.[152]

Kenrick followed up these decrees by insisting on the completion of a detailed annual questionnaire that, among other things, required every priest to note whether he kept proper registers of baptisms, marriages, and deaths, as well as the '*status animarum*', the detailed record of the Catholics of the parish or district. There were also pointed questions about the level of giving to both the prospective seminary and the 'Episcopal fund', and a full account of parish property and the activities of any charitable or social groups were also demanded. Priests were to submit the form and all parish records for inspection during one of Kenrick's regular visitations.[153]

The Philadelphia synod was also widely copied by other American dioceses and in the legislation of successive provincial councils, and in 1850 it informed the first plenary council of the Irish Church, held at Thurles, Co. Tipperary. In advance of that council, the new archbishop of Armagh and apostolic delegate, Paul Cullen, sought 'hints regarding our

---

[152] See Nolan, *Kenrick*, 138–48.
[153] A printed copy may be consulted in the Pittsburgh diocesan archives. It is undated but seems likely to come from the mid-1830s.

Synod' from Kenrick. 'You see so many of our poor people in America', he wrote, 'that you must know what their wants are, better than we do.'[154] It was Thurles that effectively embedded Tridentine Catholicism in Ireland and established the institutional context for what Emmet Larkin saw as Cullen's great achievement of 'making practicing Catholics of the Irish people in a generation'.[155] Two years later, the policies set out in Philadelphia in 1832 and adopted in Thurles in 1850 were absorbed into the decrees of the first plenary council of the United States, convened by the new archbishop of Baltimore and apostolic delegate, Francis Patrick Kenrick. In 1885, the new archbishop of Sydney and apostolic delegate, Cullen's nephew Patrick Francis Moran, convened the first plenary council of the Catholic Church in Australasia. Its avowed model was Thurles and thus, by extension, Philadelphia. Not all influences flowed from Ireland outwards.

However Philadelphia was organized on paper, it was moot without properly educated priests. As with all later Hiberno-Roman bishops, Kenrick was determined to build a seminary that conformed as closely as possible to what he had known in Rome. When Cullen refused to come and help, Kenrick begged him to provide the Roman books that were otherwise unobtainable in America. He responded with enthusiasm, collecting volumes from the Propaganda, obtaining more 'from some friends', and adding others from his own personal library.[156] For the next twenty years he was effectively Kenrick's bookseller, and few letters passed between Rome and Philadelphia that did not contain lists of titles requested or sent. These volumes formed both the necessary core of a Roman seminary education on the American east coast and the raw material for Kenrick's own theological publications. Cullen's stated goal was for his own Irish College to combat Gallicanism, teach 'Roman doctrine', and 'be the means of introducing Roman maxims into Ireland and uniting that Church more closely with the Holy See'.[157] Substitute 'America' for 'Ireland' and he could have been speaking for Kenrick.

Despite his undoubted commitment, Kenrick did not find it easy to build his seminary. He gave some early thought to encouraging the relocation of Mt St Mary's to Philadelphia, but the staff were happy in Emmitsburg and nothing came of it.[158] Forced to begin on a smaller

---

[154] Cullen to Kenrick, 5 July 1850, AASMSU/KP/28T2.
[155] Emmet Larkin, *The Historical Dimensions of Irish Catholicism* (Washington, DC: The Catholic University of America Press, 1984), 83.
[156] Cullen to Kenrick, 9 June 1831, AASMSU/KP/28R1.
[157] Cullen to Kenrick, 1 September 1833 and 9 December 1833, AASMSU/KP/28R2, 28R3. Emphasis in original.
[158] George E. O'Donnell, *St. Charles Seminary, Philadelphia: A History of the Theological Seminary of Saint Charles Borromeo, Overbrook, Philadelphia, Pennsylvania, 1832–1964,*

scale, by 1832 Kenrick had 'three young Irishmen studying Philosophy in my own house'.[159] By the end of the year there were five students, four of whom were Irish. The fifth was an American of Irish descent who had already been a student in the Propaganda.[160] At first, Kenrick handled the teaching himself. From 1834, he relied on his brother, Peter. In 1837, another Irish former Propaganda student, Edward Barron, joined them. A few years later the gentle, somewhat unworldly Redemptorist (the only man other than Kenrick to address Cullen as 'Paul') became a singularly inappropriate choice to head a mission to Liberia.[161] A Pennsylvania charter and Michael O'Connor both appeared in 1838. The few students were still mostly Irish: in 1839, Barron reported to Rome that three 'young natives' had just been admitted, 'but two of them were born in the land of Erin'.[162] The teaching staff was overburdened and within a few years scattered from St Louis to Monrovia. Money was also a problem. The Propaganda had none to spare (they sent books instead), despite Cullen's suggestion that Kenrick approach the pope directly.[163] Still, with the aid of a successful diocesan collection that raised some $5,400, Kenrick was able to open a new building in 1839. Rumour put its ultimate cost at $20,000. It was 'so magnificent', a German priest in Philadelphia acidly reported, 'that it might serve as a palace for the Grand Mogul'.[164] As a statement of intent it could not have been clearer.

A grand building and trusted professors needed books. Cullen's efforts had furnished an excellent and very Roman theological library (almost certainly the best in the country), but Kenrick knew that America was not Rome. At heart a theologian and a scholar, his 'wicked passion for writing' (scribendi malus amor) consumed his time and increased his debts, but it also produced the first sustained Catholic theological work written in the United States.[165] Kenrick's writing was intended for two distinct audiences. More popular works like his book on the papal primacy (which ultimately saw seven editions and a German translation) were written in English and aimed to explain Catholic beliefs and counter Protestant attacks. Yet his real interest was his manuals of theology: Kenrick recognized that the American church lacked theological textbooks suited to the

with a Chronological Record of Ordinations and Pictures of the Living Alumni (Philadelphia: American Catholic Historical Society, 1964), 10–11.

[159] Kenrick to Cullen, 7 September 1832, PICRA/AL/3.   [160] O'Donnell, 13–14.

[161] See Seán P. Farragher, *Edward Barron, 1801–1854: Unsung Hero of the Mission to Africa* (Dublin: Paraclete Press, 2004).

[162] Barron to Cullen, 7 October 1839, PICRA/AL.

[163] Cullen to Kenrick, 1 February 1834, AASMSU/KP/28R4.

[164] Quoted in O'Donnell, 25.

[165] Francis Kenrick to Peter Kenrick, 'The Seventh Day before the Ides of February', 1843, *KFC*, 161, 163.

peculiar conditions of a growing secular republic, and he set out to fill the gap.

He began what became the four volumes of his *Theologia Dogmatica* while a professor in Flaget's Kentucky seminary, it was well advanced by at least 1832, and in 1833 Cullen passed a partial draft to Angelo Mai at the Propaganda.[166] He offered suggestions himself, as did Kenrick's prize student and eventual successor, Martin Spalding.[167] The first volume appeared in print in 1838. Cullen was delighted, reported regularly on its good reception in Rome, and thought it 'desirable that several copies should be introduced into Ireland' in order to counteract the more Gallican texts in use there.[168] The work was completed in 1840, an astonishing achievement given its author's punishing episcopal schedule and other scholarly projects. Little known today, Kenrick's *Dogmatica* was primarily distinguished by its detailed attention to Protestant teachings and critiques of Catholic belief and for its unabashed support for papal infallibility.[169]

Even before the *Dogmatica* was complete, Kenrick had turned his attention to a manual of moral philosophy, which would be the first produced in the United States. Published in three volumes in Philadelphia up to 1843, Kenrick's *Theologia Moralis* was more successful than its predecessor. Today, it is primarily known for its treatment of slavery, which Kenrick reluctantly held to be legitimate, whatever caveats he placed around the actual treatment of the slaves themselves.[170] His reasoning was that, while enslaving a man was wrong (thus Gregory XVI's 1839 condemnation of the slave trade), American slaves had largely been born into bondage. Since slavery itself appeared to have scriptural sanction, the passage of time therefore legitimized American slavery, however odious. Although the discussion made up only a small part of the work, it has inevitably overshadowed it, not least because Kenrick's qualified defence later gave theological cover to Catholics who backed the Confederacy.[171]

The *Theologia Moralis* was also distinguished by its detailed knowledge and discussion of American civil law and for its use of non-Catholic (principally Anglican) texts where they agreed with or illuminated

---

[166] Cullen to Kenrick, 9 December 1833, AASMSU/KP/28R3.
[167] Nolan, *Kenrick*, 237.
[168] Cullen to Kenrick, 28 October 1839, AASMSU/KP/28R13.
[169] Nolan, *Kenrick*, 237–40.
[170] For the exclusive attention to slavery, see, for example, McGreevy, 53, or Angela F. Murphy, *American Slavery, Irish Freedom: Abolition, Immigrant Citizenship, and the Transatlantic Movement for Irish Repeal* (Baton Rouge: Louisiana State University Press, 2010), 82.
[171] For an example, see McGreevy, 86.

Catholic practices or beliefs. The latter was nearly unique in contemporary Catholic theology, and it is likely that Cullen – who regularly acquired secular and Anglican books for his own personal library – helped supply at least some to Kenrick.[172] Theologically, it was inspired by Alphonsus Liguori, whose more emollient influence can be detected in Kenrick's strikingly enthusiastic endorsement of sexual love. As Peter Gardella put it, Kenrick was the 'first American writer to prescribe orgasm' and to insist on a woman's right to sexual pleasure and a man's duty to provide it.[173] There was no need to lie back and think of Ireland. Even obscured by Latin and strictly limited to married couples, this was very advanced by any measure, especially in the English-speaking world. Yet it also accorded fully with the Liguorian moral theology then ascendant in Rome. Cullen thought the work 'most useful', urged its 'general circulation', and gave it to the pope.[174]

Kenrick always intended his work to be influential beyond Philadelphia. He carefully noted when it was taken up by other seminaries or bishops, remarking delightedly when John Hughes bought 15 copies or 100 were sent to New Orleans.[175] In 1843, the fifth provincial council of Baltimore enjoined Archbishop Eccleston to recommend it to all American seminaries, although as Kenrick's biographer dryly remarked, 'No record of this commendation has been found.'[176] Eccleston's lack of enthusiasm was unsurprising. In 1838, he had eagerly encouraged a French Sulpician to publish a catechism derived from an earlier French version. Convinced the Irish would be opposed, he decided to publish it solely in Baltimore.[177] Even so, by 1850 the *Theologia Moralis* was in use in most American seminaries.[178]

Its ultimate impact is hard to trace. It was well regarded in Europe and a clear influence on many of its American successors; but it was reprinted only once, in Belgium. Charles Curran is probably right that this had less to do with Kenrick's views on slavery or sex and more with the fact that as a secular priest he had no religious order to tend the flame or produce new editions.[179] Although moral theology is undoubtedly recherché, it is

---

[172] On several occasions while Kenrick was composing his moral theology, Cullen received shipments from Dublin containing 'the Best English writers against Deists and Infidels', as well as more secular works ranging from the complete Edmund Burke to Samuel Johnson. See Meyler to Cullen, 19 February 1838, 2 January 1839, PICRA/CP/405, 479.

[173] Peter Gardella, *Innocent Ecstasy: How Christianity Gave America an Ethic of Sexual Pleasure* (Oxford: Oxford University Press, 1985), 9.

[174] Cullen to Kenrick, 18 January 1845, AASMSU/KP/28S4.

[175] Francis Kenrick to Peter Kenrick, 22 February, 22 March 1844, *KFC*, 186, 207.

[176] Nolan, *Kenrick*, 244.   [177] Eccleston to Fenwick, 4 October 1838, AASMSU/BVM.

[178] Nolan, *Kenrick*, 244.

[179] Charles E. Curran, *The Origins of Moral Theology in the United States: Three Different Approaches* (Washington, DC: Georgetown University Press, 1997), 81–2.

important: manuals like Kenrick's were designed to help clergy understand what was and was not sinful, when, to what degree, and what to do about it. Although the social controls that so successfully preserved diasporic Irish Catholic identity had many aspects, the confessional was the most intimate; and despite its American focus and Latin prose, Francis Patrick Kenrick's *Theologia Moralis* is the clearest expression of the Hiberno-Roman approach to personal morality.

A numerous and well-educated clergy was the desiderata of all the American bishops of whatever faction. The problem was supply. In the United States, both native born and emigrant men had excellent chances of gainful employment and consequently of marriage, or at least better than in much of Europe. The crowded cities provided endless distractions and tended to loosen social bonds, at least until the church solidified its social controls. The situation was even more acute with women, who would ultimately be needed in much greater numbers. This was not just an American problem: the shortage of clergy was a constant across the English-speaking world. So too were its consequences, not least a global cohort of *vagabondi* priests, often drunk, sometimes worse, usually disputatious, and a constant source of episcopal frustration and public scandal; and, as Ambrose Maréchal and many others were quick to point out, they tended to be Irish.

Despite this, Ireland remained the obvious source: as John England had discovered in 1833, the island had an excess of vocations. For personal, financial, or spiritual reasons, many more young Irish men wanted to become priests or brothers (and Irish women nuns) than could be accommodated at home. Often the problem was money: a seminary education or conventual dowry cost much more than most Irish families could command, and Irish bishops reasonably preferred those who could support themselves. Although not followed up, England's idea of educating in Ireland missionary priests destined for America at American expense had been a good one. Certainly Cullen thought so, and in 1837 he reminded Archbishop Daniel Murray of Dublin that Ireland 'could supply a great abundance of [priests] if means could be found for their support and education'. This was better, he wrote, than the British colonies and United States being abandoned entirely 'or provided with missionaries who cannot speak a word of English'.[180]

He returned to the topic in 1840. In Ireland on a rare visit home, he had been asked by the Propaganda to see about obtaining 'some missionaries for the Indies'. This had proved impossible, he told his vice rector Tobias Kirby, not only because the seminaries had already been 'drained' by

---

[180] Cullen to Murray, 13 March 1837, DDA/MP/34/9.

foreign bishops but also because of an absolute shortage of candidates. Yet there were, he wrote, 'many students who wd enter a college for such a mission, but they have not the means to get through their studies'. He asked Kirby to stress to Cardinal Fransoni that 'if there were a college for the foreign missions in Ireland, it wd be well supplied with students'.[181] When the Rev. John Hand decided to start a missionary college in Dublin with just this in mind, he found powerful support and encouragement in Rome.

Ordained in 1835, Hand was an early member of the Irish Vincentians, teaching in their small school on Ussher's Quay in Dublin and living with the community in Castleknock. His enthusiasm for a missionary college seems to date from 1838 or 1839. Like England and Cullen, Hand thought that there were 'hundreds of young men' who wanted to be priests, 'cannot be provided for at home', and would be willing to 'cheer-fully devote' their lives to the foreign missions.[182] In 1840, he pitched his idea to Archbishop Murray, who cautiously agreed. The other Irish bishops did not. Most thought him mad, and his plan was flatly refused. Undaunted, he decided to try his luck in Rome. Cullen and Kirby actively supported him, introduced him to the officials in the Propaganda, and accompanied him on his visits. By February 1842, he was able to report that the Propaganda had approved of the college and would provide it with books.[183]

Writing to Murray in early 1842, Cullen reported on Hand's reception at the Propaganda. Cardinal Fransoni, he wrote, was 'desirous that such an establishment should be got up in Ireland, as otherwise it will be quite impossible to provide for the wants of the British Colonies'.[184] Fransoni would, Cullen continued a few months later, 'do every thing in his power to promote the interests of the projected missionary establishment'.[185] That was necessary: as Cullen remarked in 1842, nobody in Dublin thought Hand would succeed or that he was a 'fit person to manage a college'. The bishops did not like him, he wrote, and 'will not encourage him'. Yet Cullen was cautiously optimistic, despite his worries about anaemic fundraising.[186] In early 1843, he told Kenrick that 'no one can well conjecture how it is likely to succeed' before

[181] Cullen to Kirby, 15 August 1840, PICRA, New Kirby papers [NK], Carton 1, Folder 1, #10.
[182] Hand to the Bishops of Ireland, 30 December 1840, quoted in Kevin Condon, *The Missionary College of All Hallows, 1842–1891* (Dublin: All Hallows College, 1986), 21.
[183] The information for this paragraph is drawn from Condon, *All Hallows*, chaps. 1–3.
[184] Cullen to Murray, 19 February 1842, DDA/MP/34/9.
[185] Cullen to Murray, 10 June 1842, DDA/MP/34/9.
[186] Cullen to Kirby, 27 July [1842], PICRA/KP/106.

dropping a heavy hint about how the 'want of priests must be a great obstacle in your way'.[187]

All Hallows proved a remarkable success, opening in the Dublin suburb of Drumcondra on All Saints Day 1842. As Bartholomew Woodlock recalled many years later, he, John Hand, and one other priest 'said Mass on a little cabinet in the drawing room of the old house with one student ... and with a borrowed Chalice & borrowed vestments'.[188] All Hallows' model was that of a matchmaking service: colonial or American bishops provided partly or wholly subsidized places for seminarians willing to commit to their diocese. The cost was low, £20 per annum at first only slowly rising to £25 in 1861 (of which the recruiting bishop was expected to pay £15) and £56 from 1912 until the 1950s.[189] For those still too poor, many bishops were prepared to pay the entire sum.

In time, All Hallows College became an integral part of the American clerical supply chain, but not immediately: some were no more willing to take priests from Dublin in 1842 than they had been when John England had first proposed the systematic recruitment of Irish priests nearly a decade before. Bishops such as the American-born Richard Pius Miles of Nashville and the French Sulpician John Chanche in Natchez, for example, peremptorily refused Hand's repeated offers; Miles reported that he intended to train his priests 'in my own Seminary at home'.[190] Their wariness was not entirely unwarranted, and in time many non-Irish bishops came to rue their decision to fill their ranks with All Hallows graduates. As the hard-pressed John Murdoch of Glasgow explained in 1862 to the rector of the Scots' College in Spain, 'I would to Heaven that I had never been under the necessity of bringing labourers from the other side of the channel.'[191]

Yet the Irish were eager customers. When he succeeded Miles in Nashville, for example, the Kilkenny-born James Whelan wasted no time in asking for 'Irish students for our Missions in Tennessee, where their services are needed very much'.[192] The Propaganda-trained Martin Spalding told the college's president in 1854 that he needed 'some priests of talent' for Louisville where there were 'about ten thousand Irish

---

[187] Cullen to Kenrick, 21 January 1843, AASMSU/KP/28S2.

[188] Woodlock to James Murray, 23 November 1892, Maitland-Newcastle diocesan archives [MNDA], Murray papers, 3/1/1810/2/8.

[189] Condon, *All Hallows*, 162, 165.

[190] See Miles to Hand, 31 January 1844 and Chanche to Hand, 26 March 1844, All Hallows College Archive [AHCA], NAS.2, NAT. 1.

[191] John Murdoch to John Cameron, 2 April 1862, Royal Scots College, Salamanca, 64/1/19.

[192] Whelan to 'President of All Hallows College [Bartholomew Woodlock]', 14 March 1861, AHCA/NAS.3.

Catholics'.[193] Without the college, it would have been impossible to supply enough parish clergy for the rapidly growing country. As the Corkman John Quinlan of Mobile wrote within weeks of being appointed to succeed the Frenchmen Michael Portier, 'God Bless All Hallows'. It was, he continued, 'the pride of the Green Isle', and he took four of its students with him to Alabama.[194] They were not alone: between 1842 and 1891, nearly half (652) of the some 1,500 Irish men that All Hallows sent on the missions went to America.[195] Many more followed in the twentieth century.

All Hallows also served a previously unappreciated role in the 'greening' of American Catholicism. Not only did the more flexible or desperate foreign-born bishops begin to recruit from Drumcondra, some began to use it as a finishing school for their foreign-born priests. Jean-Marie Odin of Galveston (and later New Orleans), for example, scoured France for likely recruits but then educated them at All Hallows, largely to learn English.[196] The Catalan Thaddeus Amat of Los Angeles recruited both Spanish and Irish priests for the college, the latter because the 'number of Americans are on the increase in my Diocese, so I feel obliged to increase also the number of Irish students'. He requested an initial batch of ten 'besides those I may send from Spain'.[197] A decade later, he sent another five Spaniards 'for the purpose of finishing their studies, learning the English language, and in a special manner form themselves for the Ministry'.[198] Although language-training was no doubt the primary attraction, these men and others like them were exposed to both Ireland and a Hiberno-Roman seminary education before entering on their American career.

By 1845, the Irish-American bishops could be quietly confident, despite serious nativist violence in Philadelphia and elsewhere the year before. Their leader was no longer isolated, the administrative chaos of the preceding thirty years had subsided, and Irishmen ruled in the biggest cities and most important sees, save those of Baltimore, Boston, and New Orleans. Seminaries to compete with the Sulpicians had been founded and were slowly growing, and a new and seemingly limitless source of

---

[193] Spalding to Woodlock, 25 July 1854, AHCA/LOU.1.
[194] Quinlan to Woodlock, 1 October 1860, AHCA/MOB.1.
[195] Derived from the 'Matricula: 1842–91' published in Condon, *All Hallows*, and analysed by Mary Carmichael (nee Schmidt) for an unpublished assignment completed at Ave Maria University in 2010. I am grateful to Mrs Carmichael for permission to use her research.
[196] Odin to Woodlock, 30 June 1860, 3 January 1861, AHCA/Gal. 3.
[197] Amat to Dowley, 23 June 1860, AHCA/MLA.3. Both Amat and Dowley were Vincentians, and Amat seems to have used Dowley as his Irish agent.
[198] Amat to 'President of All Hallows', 18 October 1870, AHCA/MLA.16.

Irish clergy was taking shape in Dublin. All of this was achieved before the successive waves of Irish migrants fleeing the Famine and its consequent dislocations began to arrive on American shores.

The new order became even clearer in the wake of the sixth provincial council of Baltimore, held in 1846. As usual, Cullen helped prepare the ground in Rome. John Hughes, for example, sought his aid in dividing New York and establishing new dioceses at Albany and Buffalo. Cullen 'immediately translated' his letter into Italian, 'and brought it and the map of the State of N. York with the proposed divisions marked on it to the Propaganda'.[199] The result was that Hughes' coadjutor, John McCloskey, was sent to Albany and John Timon, an American-born Vincentian of Irish descent, was appointed to Buffalo. McCloskey was already marked as a star, having been sent to Rome in the 1830s where he later recalled that Cullen had 'acted as a most kind Father & Patron'.[200] For his part, Timon was very highly regarded by Kenrick, who had long lobbied for his promotion.[201] The French-born bishop of New Orleans had unsuccessfully sought him for his coadjutor in 1844, specifically because he would appeal to Irish and American Catholics, 'the principal support of the ecclesiastical authority' in the still very French city.[202] Before recommending Timon for Buffalo, Hughes had first suggested him as McCloskey's replacement as coadjutor in New York. According to Peter Kenrick, Hughes thought the appointment 'would be pleasing to the Irish' without provoking nativist angst.[203] Yet most importantly of all, St Louis was unexpectedly elevated to become the second archdiocese in the United States.

Baltimore's status as the lone American archdiocese had long been anomalous.[204] Even before the Famine migration, there were more than enough Catholics (perhaps 400,000, although Catholics claimed a million) in the vast country to justify several ecclesiastical provinces. The delay was again the result of Eccleston's fear of the Irish. As early as 1840, he admitted privately that his opposition to a new archdiocese was driven solely by dread of the 'influences to which the measure would subject our Eastern Disciples', by which he seems to have meant his correspondent, Benedict Fenwick of Boston. He would 'make every reasonable exertion to have it postponed'.[205] By 1846, he could delay

---

[199] Cullen to Hughes, 13 March 1846, CU/BP/MS1296/1/1/1/3.

[200] Diary of Patrick Francis Moran [MD], 10 November 1875, AAS/MP/T1208.

[201] See Kenrick to Cullen, 7 December 1846, PICRA/AL/112.

[202] Blanc to Fenwick, 10 January 1844, AAB/FP/1.14.5. In French.

[203] Peter Kenrick to Richard Kenrick, 9 July 1846, quoted in Nolan, *Kenrick*, 358.

[204] Oregon City in the far west was raised to an archdiocese in 1846, but for some time it looked more to Canada and Quebec than to the American east coast.

[205] Eccleston to Fenwick, 10 February, 1840, AAB/FP/1.55.8.

no longer, although it is striking that the council did not suggest the elevation of any particular place. Most assumed New York or New Orleans had the best claim, while the western bishops pleaded distance in urging a province of their own.[206]

Rome kept the decrees of the sixth provincial council for nearly a year, raising suspicions that the Sulpician bishops were engaged in behind-the-scenes lobbying, which indeed they were.[207] They were not the only ones: nobody had expected St Louis to be named in July 1847, and Francis Kenrick was widely suspected of having manipulated Rome to secure his brother's promotion.[208] He would only admit to having answered a direct question from Cardinal Fransoni about which western city was most suitable, but it was likely that that suggestion combined with Cullen's influence was enough.[209]

The elevation of St Louis and Peter Kenrick by Roman fiat made it clear where power now lay. Cullen was bombarded with letters, from the Irish vicar general of Chicago asking him to use his 'powerful influence' to secure an Irish bishop, to Bishop Purcell of Cincinnati seeking his 'zealous influence' in resolving the vacant coadjutorship in Louisville.[210] The appointment in late 1848 of Kenrick's protégé Martin Spalding to the latter only confirmed how things stood. Yet the real fight was for Baltimore, where the Kenricks were convinced that Eccleston wanted to name his own coadjutor, just as Maréchal and Whitfield had done before him; but now they could turn his long-established policy against him: 'you might', Francis told his brother, 'write [to Rome] to say that a point of such importance ought to wait the judgment of the Council before it is decided.'[211] The question was duly postponed to the seventh provincial council in 1849, which duly failed to agree on a candidate.

That council did recommend the erection of a further three ecclesiastical provinces of New York, New Orleans, and Cincinnati, as well as the creation of a diocese in Savannah, Georgia, where the first bishop was Kenrick's vicar general, the Dublin-born Francis Gartland. After some delay occasioned by the trauma of Mazzini's republic, Rome agreed to everything.[212] The Irish victory was capped by the death of Archbishop Samuel Eccleston in April 1851. A search of his papers revealed that he had wanted the Sulpician John Chanche of Natchez to succeed him, but

---

[206] Nolan, *Kenrick*, 360.
[207] Purcell to Hughes, 16 May 1847, CU/BP/MS1296/1/1/1/13.
[208] Nolan, *Kenrick*, 361.
[209] Francis Kenrick to Peter Kenrick, 24 May 1848, *KFC*, 279.
[210] J. A. Kinsella to Cullen, 3 June 1848, Purcell to Cullen, 14 June 1848, PICRA/AL/ 125, 126.
[211] Francis Kenrick to Peter Kenrick, 1 June 1848, *KFC*, xxx.
[212] Cullen to Kenrick, 5 July 1850, AASMSU/KP/28T2.

the three bishops present at his funeral instead agreed to recommend John Timon of Buffalo.[213] This was unsurprising, as those bishops were Francis Kenrick, Michael O'Connor, and the newly appointed John McGill of Richmond. The last had been born in Philadelphia to Irish parents and was a keen supporter of Kenrick. Although McGill apparently 'hesitated', O'Connor convinced him.[214] Peter Kenrick and, more tentatively, Purcell agreed.[215] Cullen too was enthusiastic, remarking approvingly that Timon was 'very orthodox on education questions'.[216] Among the Irish only John Hughes expressed any doubts, telling Rome that Timon would be too hard to replace and expressing a more general reluctance to translate bishops between American sees.[217] He qualified this, however, by telling Francis Kenrick that, if an existing bishop was to be appointed, it should be Kenrick himself.[218] Ignatius Reynolds of Charleston had already come to the same conclusion.[219]

This was not the Hiberno-Romans' first choice. A vacancy in Buffalo would be easier to fill than one in the larger and more important Philadelphia, and Kenrick seems to have been genuinely reluctant to make the move. As Michael O'Connor explained to Cullen's successor at the Irish College, Tobias Kirby, the question was one of status: Philadelphia 'is a place of far greater importance than Balt[imore]', he wrote, '[b]ut if we are to have a Cardinal or even a primate Bp K[enrick] in Balt[imore] is the man'.[220] The decision assumed an added significance in light of the upcoming first plenary council of the United States, scheduled for 1852. Just as Cullen's appointment to Armagh in late 1849 carried with it a commission as apostolic delegate with authority to convene what became the Synod of Thurles, the Propaganda decided that the new archbishop of Baltimore would also be apostolic delegate for the plenary council. The writing was on the wall when Hughes learned that the Propaganda was 'inclined' to a translation, not a fresh appointment.[221] In the end, Kenrick's elevation was predictable: Cullen's private view that he was 'one of the best Bishops in the world' was widely shared in Rome, and there is little doubt that Kirby and the

---

[213] Francis Kenrick to Hughes, 13 May 1851, CU/BP/MS1296/1/1/1/9; Francis Kenrick to Peter Kenrick, 26 April 1851, *KFC*, 316.

[214] Francis Kenrick to Peter Kenrick, 15 May 1851, *KFC*, 317.

[215] Nolan, *Kenrick*, 423.

[216] Cullen to Bernard Smith, 30 July 1851, Archivio Storico di San Paolo fuori le Mura (St Paul's Outside the Walls) [ASSP], Bernard Smith papers [SP], 1851/7/30.

[217] Hughes to Fransoni, 17 May 1851, CU/BP/MS1296/1/1/1/8.

[218] Hughes to Kenrick, 'St John's Day' 1851, AASMSU/KP/29H10.

[219] Francis Kenrick to Peter Kenrick, 15 May 1851, *KFC*, 317.

[220] O'Connor to Kirby, 13 August [1851], [transcript], PDA, O'Connor papers [OP], Box 260, ff. 7.

[221] Smith to Hughes, 24 June 1851, CU/BP/MS1296/1/1/3/1.

other Roman Irish were encouraging.[222] The secretary of the Propaganda ordered the news conveyed to Kenrick via the Irish College, and Cullen was 'literally charmed' when he heard.[223] Others were less enthusiastic: as the Sulpician John Chanche wryly observed, 'Four Irish Archbishops in the country – well – it will all turn out as it ought I hope in the end.'[224]

Francis Patrick Kenrick was now the effective leader of a church that had grown by his estimation to some 1.8 million people. By no means all of them were Irish or of Irish descent, but by 1850 Kenrick thought about a million were, many recently arrived. Yet he also reported half a million Germans, 200,000 French, and some 30,000 Spanish-speaking Catholics. The clergy had grown to about 800, of whom Kenrick believed only some 300 were Irish.[225] Whatever the numbers, the Irish had effectively seized control of the commanding heights of a hierarchical church. The first plenary council confirmed this: Francis Kenrick chaired it, Peter Kenrick wrote its agenda, and John Timon presented it with a revised catechism.[226] Its decrees almost completely absorbed those of Philadelphia. The struggle begun by John England in 1820 and joined by Francis Kenrick ten years later was over. The Irish had won.

Of course not everything went Kenrick's way. Rome refused, for example, to make Baltimore the primatial see of the American church, but only because the Propaganda was opposed to erecting new primatial sees anywhere.[227] At John Hughes' suggestion, they ultimately granted Baltimore a 'nominal' precedence.[228] In Pennsylvania, Michael O'Connor became increasingly unstable, leaving Pittsburgh to become the first bishop of Erie before moving back to Pittsburgh. In 1856, he seems to have suffered a breakdown and was diagnosed with what his doctors told him was the potential for 'a softening of the brain'.[229] This led him to go on a lengthy world tour, leaving his brother James in charge in Pittsburgh until he finally joined the Jesuits. More importantly, each ecclesiastical province went its own way, albeit within the limits imposed by the plenary council of Baltimore. In 1854, Kenrick supported the archbishop of New Orleans' proposal that episcopal vacancies be decided solely by the bishops of the relevant province.[230] He also backed

[222] Cullen to Kirby, 7 May 1845, PICRA/NK/1/1/27.
[223] See Francis Kenrick to Peter Kenrick, 19 September 1851, *KFC*, 319; Kirby to Kenrick, 'Octave of the Assumption' 1852, AASMSU/KP/30I7.
[224] Chanche to Blanc, 11 October 1851, UNDA, Archdiocese of New Orleans papers.
[225] Nolan, *Kenrick*, 418.
[226] Francis Kenrick to Peter Kenrick, 'Feast of the Holy Name', 1852, *KFC*, 325–6.
[227] Smith to Hughes, 22 May 1858, CU/BP/MS1296/1/1/3/1.
[228] Smith to Hughes, 17 July 1858, CU/BP/MS1296/1/1/3/1.
[229] Kenrick to Heyden, 16 September 1859, PDA/LC/814.
[230] Kenrick to Hughes, 25 September 1854, CU/BP/MS1296/1/1/1/9.

a suggestion that existing bishops should lose the right to name their own coadjutor.[231] By 1858, Hughes was optimistic that the Irish system of parish priests nominating episcopal candidates would soon be introduced into the United States.[232] All of this had the effect of decentralizing power within the United States, even as more and more power devolved to Rome.

None of this stopped the Kenricks working to fill vacant sees with their preferred candidates; and if not all were Irish, many were. By 1853, they were often involving Hughes in their discussions.[233] When Chicago became vacant that year, for example, Francis Kenrick's first choice was the Mayo-born Anthony O'Regan, formerly the president of St Jarlath's College, Tuam. When O'Regan declined, Kenrick's next thought was the Maynooth-born James Duggan. His other suggestions for a city closely divided between Irish and German Catholics were a Tobias Mullen, a Patrick Reilly, and a John McCaffrey.[234] O'Regan ultimately accepted and Duggan eventually succeeded him. When Duggan resigned in 1880, he was replaced by the Tipperary-born Patrick Feehan, who had been bishop of Nashville. His successor was Edward Quigley, an Irish Canadian educated at the Propaganda. He died in 1915. In Charleston, the American-born Ignatius Reynolds was succeeded in 1857 by the Irish-born Patrick Lynch, whom John England had sent in 1834 as one of the diocese's first two students at the Urban College, where he was placed under Cullen's watchful eye. Typically for a future Hiberno-Roman bishop, he excelled academically, winning almost every available prize before being chosen to give an address in Hebrew before Gregory XVI. (He also led his class in Arabic.) When he returned to America in 1840, he stopped first in Philadelphia to see Kenrick.[235]

This pattern repeated itself across the United States. Two years after Lynch was appointed in Charleston, the successor to the Frenchman Michael Portier of Mobile was the Corkman John Quinlan. In Nashville, the American-born Richard Miles was followed by the Irish-born James Whelan in 1860 and then Patrick Feehan in 1865. When the Catalan Dominican Joseph Alemany decided to divide distant San Francisco in 1859, he gave Rome only Irish names for the new diocese of Grass Valley. His first choice was James Croke, the brother of the future bishop of Auckland and archbishop of Cashel.[236] His second choice and

---

[231] Francis Kenrick to Peter Kenrick, 1 October 1854, *KFC*, 375–6.

[232] Hughes to Heyden, 31 August 1858, PDA/LC.

[233] See Francis Kenrick to Hughes, 7 January 1853, CU/BP/MS1296/1/1/1/9.

[234] Francis Kenrick to Peter Kenrick, 14 March 1854, *KFC*, 365.

[235] David C. R. Heisser and Stephen J. White, Sr., *Patrick N. Lynch: Third Catholic Bishop of Charleston* (Columbia: University of South Carolina Press, 2015), 20, 24–5.

[236] See John B. McGloin, *California's First Archbishop: The Life of Joseph Sadoc Alemany, 1814–1888* (New York: Herder & Herder, 1966), 174.

the ultimate appointee was a product of All Hallows, Eugene O'Connell.[237] Almost inevitably, Cullen performed his consecration.[238] When Cullen's former secretary George Conroy visited Grass Valley in 1878, he reported delightedly that 'nearly all the priests of this diocese are from All Hallows'.[239] A few years before that, Alemany had begged Cullen's help in securing 'a little colony of Christian Brothers' to prevent the children of the growing number of Irish emigrants from falling into 'indifference or infidelity'.[240] When Alemany finally retired in 1884, his successor was a Canadian-born and Propaganda-educated Irishman, Patrick William Riordan.

Of the fourteen dioceses eventually carved out of Peter Kenrick's St Louis, the first bishops of eight were Irish-born. Even in Philadelphia, Kenrick had preferred the brother of the Irish Archbishop Purcell of Cincinnati as his successor to the Bohemian-born Redemptorist and future saint John Neumann. As the *New Zealand Tablet* boasted in 1888, 'Our Irish-American prelates are easily known by their names. They are Right Revs. McQuaid of Rochester, Ryan of Buffalo, Harkins of Providence, McMahon of Hartford, McNeirny of Albany, Kain of Wheeling, McCloskey of Louisville, Gallagher of Galveston, Cosgrove of Davenport and Healy of Portland.' Four of the archbishops, the paper continued, had Irish parents.[241]

Perhaps more importantly, the ascendancy of Kenrick and the Irish saw ever-deepening links with Rome. In early 1854, Pius IX privately urged the American bishops 'to open a college in Rome for American students'. The Kenricks and O'Connor were immediately enthusiastic. John Hughes was not.[242] His objection, according to Kenrick, was that 'Propaganda students lack training for the missions'. Other bishops simply thought they could not afford it.[243] By the end of 1854, only seven had made a financial contribution and Peter Kenrick had failed to convince his own provincial council to support the idea.[244] Rome did not give up, instructing Francis Kenrick to consult the entire hierarchy.[245] From the beginning, the project was Roman, driven particularly by Alessandro

---

[237] See John T. Dwyer, *Condemned to the Mines: The Life of Eugene O'Connell, 1815–1891: Pioneer Bishop of Northern California and Nevada* (New York: Vantage Press, 1976).
[238] See O'Connell to William Fortune, 'Spy Wednesday' 1870, Sacramento diocesan archives, O'Connell papers.
[239] Conroy to his family, 20 April 1878, Ardagh & Clonmacnois Diocesan Archives [ARDA], Conroy papers, 20.
[240] Alemany to Cullen, 15 June 1858, DDA/CP/319/1/II/24.
[241] *New Zealand Tablet* [*NZT*], 3 February 1888.
[242] Francis Kenrick to Peter Kenrick, 21 January 1854, *KFC*, 362.
[243] Francis Kenrick to Peter Kenrick, 15 December 1854, *KFC*, 385.
[244] Francis Kenrick to Peter Kenrick, 30 November 1854, *KFC*, 392–3.
[245] Kenrick to Hughes, 2 April 1855, CU/BP/ MS1296/1/1/1/9.

Barnabò, the already powerful secretary of the Propaganda who became cardinal prefect in 1856. By late 1855, Hughes was promising Barnabò that the American church could find some sixty students who would yield an annual income of around $9,000.[246] Other bishops promised $250 towards fittings.[247] Yet although O'Connor went to Rome in 1857 hoping to advance the cause, nothing happened.

The lack of enthusiasm had two distinct elements. First was the very real question of money. The bishops had many calls on their resources and often substantial building projects of their own. Buying, outfitting, and running a Roman college seemed an extravagance. In 1858, Barnabò eased matters by agreeing that the Propaganda would purchase the land and buildings.[248] This did not eliminate the need for American contributions but substantially reduced it. Even so, in 1858 Hughes tried to delay his promised subvention to help pay for St Patrick's Cathedral: his Roman agent strongly advised him against incurring Barnabò's wrath.[249] The cardinal prefect, Francis Kenrick noted later, 'speaks frequently of the money to be contributed for the College at Rome'.[250] He was also prepared to order a plenary council to secure it.[251] In 1859, the province of New York duly contributed $17,674, of which $5,770 came from Hughes.[252]

More than money, many feared the consequences of a Roman seminary. Writing to his agent, Hughes remarked that it was 'unfortunate' that the prospective college had been represented 'as the channel of future ecclesiastical preferment in this country'. This was a 'great and unmerited slight' to those, like Hughes himself, who had been educated in the United States. Worse, he thought that the few Americans who had been educated in Rome had been unimpressive.[253] He could say this without fear of its finding its way back to Kenrick because the cautious Hughes had, since 1855, preferred as his Roman agent Bernard Smith, who had lost his job as vice rector at the Irish College to what he called 'dirty nepotism' and had consequently fallen out with Cullen and Kirby.[254] His job remained the same, however: putting Hughes' letters before the Propaganda 'in an Italian dress'.[255] Hughes was not alone in his fears:

---

[246] Hughes to Barnabò, 29 December 1855, AANY/HP/1/8.
[247] David Bacon to Hughes, 20 December 1855, AANY/HP/2/14.
[248] Smith to Hughes, 19 July 1858, AANY/HP/3/7.
[249] Smith to Hughes, 11 September 1858, CU/BP/MS1296/1/1/3/1.
[250] Francis Kenrick to Peter Kenrick, 4 March 1859, KFC, 419.
[251] Francis Kenrick to Peter Kenrick, 19 January 1859, KFC, 417.
[252] Smith to Hughes, 22 December 1859, AANY/HP/3/7.
[253] Hughes to Smith, 23 December 1858, CU/BP/MS1296/1/1/3/12.
[254] Smith to Hughes, [Summer 1855], CU/BP/MS1296/1/1/3/1. Cullen's nephew Patrick Moran had been given Smith's job.
[255] Smith to Hughes, 26 April 1861, CU/BP/MS1296/1/1/3/1.

Thomas Heyden, the Irishman who in 1837 had declined Natchez and remained a parish priest, was 'disgusted with these Propagandists – seeing the undue influence they have at Rome, that I am forced to be ungenerous towards the American Roman College'. 'If such are the men Rome produces for this country', he told Hughes, 'then, I say, the *fewer* there are the *better*.'[256] Hughes agreed but doubted that anything could be done. 'As you say', he told Heyden, '*Propagandists* have it nearly all their own way.'[257] Yet that did not stop Hughes, who had a sense of humour, putting Heyden third when Rome asked for a list of possible rectors.[258]

With Barnabò pushing, there was no doubt that a college would be erected. Uncompromising in New York, the slightest hint of Roman displeasure terrified Hughes.[259] Rome was in any event quick to dispel fears that the college would 'not be American', although an initial decision to dress the students all in green probably did not help.[260] (A helpful Barnabò had thought it would be the favourite colour of what he assumed would be mostly Irish students.)[261] Smith also assured Hughes that his fears were without foundation.[262] The question was who would run the college. Kenrick and Timon preferred the Vincentians but knew that 'the Americans will want one of their own as Rector'.[263] Some went even further and urged Barnabò to close the college to the Irish-born.[264] Rumours that the Propaganda had agreed to limit admission to 'pure Americans' spooked the American Irish but proved to be unfounded.[265]

Prudently, Rome asked the five archbishops for names. Kenrick suggested George McCloskey, while Hughes named George's brother William, a professor at Mt St Mary's.[266] In December 1859, Rome chose the latter, probably to please Hughes.[267] The college itself had already opened on 8 December, the Feast of the Immaculate Conception, with Bernard Smith its temporary rector. Barnabò closely supervised it, and its students were under his eye at the

---

[256] Heyden to Hughes, n.d. [1859], AANY/HP/3/13. Emphasis in original.
[257] Hughes to Heyden, 30 August 1859, PDA/LC. Emphasis in original.
[258] Hughes to Barnabò, 23 September 1859, AANY/HP/1/8.
[259] See Smith to Hughes, 4 March, 1 May 1858, AANY/HP/3/7. Hughes had heard a rumour that the secretary of the Propaganda, Gaetano Bedini, was unhappy with him. Smith had to send multiple assurances that it wasn't true.
[260] Francis Kenrick to Peter Kenrick, 4 March 1859, *KFC*, 419.
[261] Robert F. McNamara, *The American College in Rome, 1856–1955* (Rochester, NY: The Christopher Press, 1956), 61.
[262] Smith to Hughes, 22 January 1859, CU/BP/MS1296/1/1/3/1.
[263] Francis Kenrick to Peter Kenrick, 4 March 1859, *KFC*, 419.
[264] Smith to Hughes, 2 June 1860, AANY/HP/3/7.
[265] O'Connor to Smith, 19 May 1860 [transcript], PDA/OP/260, ff. 7.
[266] Francis Kenrick to Peter Kenrick, 14 July 1859, *KFC*, 422.
[267] Hughes to William McCloskey, 19 December 1859, AANY/HP/1/27.

Propaganda.[268] Kenrick and his allies were delighted, while Hughes promised McCloskey he would always pay to keep seven students in Rome.[269] The North American College quickly became what its opponents had feared: the recognized path to an American mitre. Of the first thirteen students, three died young, and three of the survivors became archbishops.[270] More importantly, the college ensured that the future elite of the American church shared the love of papal Rome that had shaped the first generation of American Hiberno-Romans.

Much has been made of the shift towards Rome exemplified by the establishment of the North American College, and it has been seen by some historians to be the most important development in nineteenth-century American Catholicism, overshadowing the steady march of the Irish. The late Peter D'Agostino, for example, emphasized the role of Rome and the Roman Question in binding American Catholicism together. 'Rome', he wrote, 'not Jerusalem, Washington, Baltimore, or Dublin, was the center of the American Catholic world from 1848 to 1940.' Papal Rome made possible, he continued, 'whatever unity existed among disparate American Catholic classes, ethnic groups, and regions'.[271] John McGreevy quoted Martin Spalding's 1866 boast to Cullen after the second plenary council of Baltimore – 'We are Roman to the heart' – to make a similar point.[272] This is undoubtedly true but tends in both cases to overlook the fact that it was Irish bishops who made this possible. Spalding, after all, was trained in Rome under Cullen's supervision – as were the first promoter of the council, Patrick Lynch of Charleston, and its secretary, James Corcoran, who had accompanied Lynch to Rome in 1834.[273] After Kenrick's elevation to Baltimore, a solid majority of American bishops either self-identified as Irish or had been trained in Rome or both. This pattern continued long into the twentieth century.

As the American church turned more and more to Rome, it also turned steadily greener. This was most obvious in episcopal appointments, but it pervaded the institution at every level. In part, this was the inevitable result of massive Irish migration: the Famine-era migrants were regularly replenished, with perhaps 4 million arriving before 1900, of whom some 2.3 million left Ireland after 1860. Yet it was also the result of a conscious plan to establish Irish control at every level from the convent to the parish to the episcopal residence. This was reinforced by a steady supply of trained personnel from home, whether from All Hallows or other Irish

---

[268] David Bacon to Hughes, 31 December 1859, CU/BP/MS1296/1/1/2/2. Bacon was the bishop of Portland, Maine, and was writing from Rome.
[269] Hughes to McCloskey, 30 March 1860, AANY/HP/1/27.   [270] McNamara, 64.
[271] D'Agostino, 4.   [272] McGreevy, 26–7.   [273] Heisser and White, 20.

seminaries. Carlow, for example, sent 466 young Irish priests to America up to 1922, while between 1885 and 1914 St Brigid's Missionary College in Callan, Co. Kilkenny, despatched at least 120 Irish women to become nuns.[274]

The Irish were also able to absorb or marginalize other ethnic groups. This was true not only of those who had arrived at roughly the same time, such as the Germans, but also those who came after, most notably the Italians. The primary means of achieving this was the ethnic parish. The idea was to allow a non-Irish ethnic group to have its own parish (or if numbers required, parishes), with a priest of its own nationality, and then to leave them alone. Masters in their own house, they were of little importance more widely. As Michael O'Connor advised Bishop Bayley of Newark, the 'only way to manage Germans' was 'to put them in a position where they cannot annoy you, and then let them do what they please'.[275] Hughes did the same in New York.[276] Tolerance did have its limits, however: Hughes threatened to interdict the leading German parish if it did not abandon its separate cemetery, while John Timon's first task in Buffalo was to crush the rebellious trustees of the city's German parish.[277] Chicago experienced enduring tensions between the two groups. Yet, by and large, it suited everybody, and by 1912 there were some 1,600 ethnic parishes.[278]

The Catholic Church in the United States never became solely an Irish or Hiberno-Roman preserve. America was too vast, too varied, and too complex for that. There were and remained factions, some ethnic, some not, that rose and fell in influence. Not all the Irish were Romans, and not all the Romans Irish. Some, including some bishops, were neither Irish nor Roman. Different ethnic groups arrived, some in great numbers, and claimed their place. More so than anywhere else in the English-speaking world, religious orders carved out positions of real influence and power, often independent of local bishops. By no means all were Irish, or Irish-influenced, although many were. A few were relatively hostile or indifferent (within the bounds of their faith) to the Romanization of the American church. Yet the events of the 1830s and 1840s were transformative and

---

[274] See 'Carlow College Ordained Students 1793–1993'. Figures compiled by Mary Carmichael.

[275] O'Connor to Bayley, no date [?1855], Seton Hall University Library, Bayley papers, 1.37, Folder 3.

[276] Jay P. Dolan, *The Immigrant Church: New York's Irish and German Catholics, 1815–1865* (Baltimore: Johns Hopkins University Press, 1975), 72.

[277] Dolan, *Immigrant Church*, 89–90; Paul E. Lubienecki, 'John Timon – Buffalo's first bishop: His forgotten struggle to assimilate Catholics in western New York', *New York History Review* (August, 2010).

[278] Lee, 'Introduction', in Lee and Casey, 27.

ensured an enduring bond between Ireland and America and Irish and American Catholicism. As Patrick Francis Moran (Cullen's nephew, and later the first cardinal archbishop of Sydney) confided to his diary after an 1875 meeting with Cullen and Cardinal McCloskey of New York, 'It is a very important matter that the union of the American & Irish Churches shd be cemented as far as possible. Their material power & strength will serve as a prop to us; & we can contribute a great deal of spiritual life & energy to them.'[279]

[279] Moran diary, 9 November 1875, AAS.

2   Newfoundland

In her memoir *Reels, Rock and Rosaries*, the musician, broadcaster, and journalist Marjorie Doyle recalled 'wriggling through childhood under a heavy Irish shroud'. Doyle's Newfoundland was a world where schoolchildren celebrated the 100th birthday of an Irish nun with a chorus of *The Rose of Tralee*, where learning that the pope was not Irish was startling, and where St Patrick's Day was a welcome break from both the Lenten fast and the long winter. It was a place where only 'close sociological examination' could tell if the Newfoundland-born nuns who taught her in the 1960s 'were more Irish or more Newfoundland'. Writing many years later, Doyle wondered about the Irishness that still pervaded her speech and shaped her identity; that sparked anger when she passed a government building named for a sixteenth-century English adventurer who had both explored Newfoundland and brutalized Ireland. Yet both sides of her family had lived on the island for so many generations 'that surely we are Newfoundlanders'. Was she even, Doyle wondered, Irish?[1]

Her dilemma is understandable: Newfoundland was and remains strikingly Irish. It is the only foreign place to enjoy an Irish name – *Talamh an Éisc*, Land of the Fish – that is not simply a translation of the English original. St John's in particular feels, sounds, and looks very much like a colder Ireland. Newfoundland's history is also distinct from that of the country it did not join until 1949, and Newfoundlanders are quick to assert this. Just as Orcadians speak of taking the ferry 'to Scotland', Newfoundlanders often travel 'to Canada'. From 1855 until bankruptcy brought a return to British rule in 1934, Newfoundland was a self-governing colony and then (from 1907) a Dominion, constitutionally the equal of Canada, Australia, New Zealand, and South Africa. It was also the only jurisdiction in the English-speaking world above a municipality in which Irish Catholics comprised a majority of the population, albeit transiently. The consequent fusion of Irish and

---

[1] Marjorie Doyle, *Reels, Rock and Rosaries: Confessions of a Newfoundland Musician* (Lawrencetown Beach, NS: Pottersfield Press, 2005), 18–31.

Catholic identities was perhaps more complete and longer lasting than anywhere else in Greater Ireland.

In comparison with its sister Dominions, Newfoundland has received only glancing attention. There are numerous reasons for this: a small population; isolation; a dysfunctional state; the absence of a university before 1949; absorption into Canada. To make matters worse, the material records of the nineteenth and early twentieth centuries were poorly preserved. There was no public archive act until 1959, no public archive until 1960, and no comprehensive catalogue of it until the 1970s. Compounding the dearth of public records, individual Newfoundlanders, as John Greene complained, 'have historically shown an aversion to preserving written records'.[2] There are almost no private papers for the era's leading politicians; prominent Irish Catholics such as Philip Francis Little and John Kent have left almost no archival trace, despite being the colony's first premiers.[3] The result was a late and thin historiography: D. W. Prowse's 1895 *History of Newfoundland* stood virtually unrivalled until the late 1960s, and even today remains influential.[4] In Wayne Johnston's fiction, for example, it becomes 'The Book', capable of exercising an unsettling, even lethal influence.[5]

The apparent paucity of sources also impacted the study of Newfoundland Catholicism. Most of the church's early records were destroyed by fire in 1846, including the bulk of Bishop Michael Anthony Fleming's papers. The archdiocesan archives preserve small holdings for his immediate successors down to 1893, but these are nothing like complete. There is a large collection from the episcopate of Michael Howley, the first native-born bishop and subsequently the first archbishop of St John's, but while useful the papers are comparatively unrevealing. His surviving diaries, for example, mostly amount to a relentless if entirely understandable reflection on the weather. The archives of the religious orders that played such an important role in the island's history are largely unavailable, where they exist at all. As a result, the only single-volume account of Catholicism in this most Catholic of Britain's worlds remains Howley's own *Ecclesiastical History of*

---

[2] John P. Greene, *Between Damnation and Starvation: Priests and Merchants in Newfoundland Politics, 1745–1855* (Montreal and Kingston: McGill-Queen's University Press, 1999), 4.

[3] There is a small collection of Little's papers preserved at the National Library of Ireland, but these are largely limited to his 1854 mission to London to secure responsible government.

[4] D. W. Prowse, *The History of Newfoundland, from the English, Colonial, and Foreign Records* (London: Macmillan & Co., 1895). For its enduring influence, see Jerry Bannister, 'Whigs and nationalists: The legacy of Judge Prowse's History of Newfoundland', *Acadiensis*, vol. 32, no. 1 (Autumn 2002).

[5] Wayne Johnston, *The Colony of Unrequited Dreams* (Toronto: Knopf Canada, 1998).

Newfoundland, published in 1888.[6] Although far above the normal standard of contemporary clerical history, it was nonetheless careful, reverent, and ended with Fleming's death in 1850. Yet recent years have seen a great deal of progress, with the publication of important document collections, essays, and articles, as well as several book-length surveys of the period.[7] Newfoundland-Irish Catholicism has also been the subject of two important but as yet unpublished doctoral dissertations by John FitzGerald and Carolyn Lambert, as well as Patrick Mannion's recent comparative study of the Irish in Newfoundland, Nova Scotia, and Maine.[8] While Newfoundland's history still remains significantly understudied, it has come into much clearer focus.

Although Newfoundland claims to be England's oldest colony, its development was haphazard and slow. The focus was entirely on the rich migratory cod fishery and as a result settlement was long discouraged. It was not until the 1760s that the island's naval administration took on most of the characteristics of a civilian government, and in 1764 the permanent population was still only some 16,000. Before the arrival of the Irish Franciscan James O'Donel in 1784, Catholic practice had been formally proscribed, intermittently persecuted, frequently harassed, and provided by a handful of mostly transient priests. At first merely a prefect apostolic (a rank below that of bishop but above a parish priest), O'Donel faced rebarbative clergy and hostile naval governors. By the early 1790s, he had stabilized the situation, with three mostly reliable priests and several chapels. In 1796, he was appointed vicar apostolic, the first anglophone bishop in British North America. O'Donel's tenure was marked by enthusiastic loyalism and a concomitant opposition to any manifestation of Irish unrest; in 1805, the latter earned a £50 gratuity from the governor.[9] He returned to Ireland in 1807 and died of shock four

---

[6] M. F. Howley, *The Ecclesiastical History of Newfoundland* (Boston: Doyle and Whittle, 1888).

[7] In addition to the works cited elsewhere in this chapter, see Raymond J. Lahey, 'Catholicism and colonial policy in Newfoundland, 1779–1845' in Terrence Murphy and Gerald Stortz (eds.), *Creed and Culture: The Place of English-Speaking Catholics in Canadian Society, 1750–1930* (Montreal and Kingston: McGill-Queen's University Press, 1993); Luca Codignola, *The Coldest Harbour of the Land: Simon Stock and Lord Baltimore's Colony in Newfoundland, 1621–1649* (Montreal and Kingston: McGill-Queen's University Press, 1988).

[8] John Edward FitzGerald, 'Conflict and culture in Irish-Newfoundland Roman Catholicism, 1829–1850', unpublished PhD diss., University of Ottawa, 1997; Carolyn Lambert, 'Far from the homes of their fathers: Irish Catholics in St. John's, Newfoundland, 1840–86', unpublished PhD diss., Memorial University of Newfoundland, 2010; Patrick Mannion, *A Land of Dreams: Ethnicity, Nationalism and the Irish in Newfoundland, Nova Scotia, and Maine, 1880–1923* (Montreal and Kingston: McGill-Queen's University Press, 2018).

[9] FitzGerald, 44.

years later when his chair caught fire.[10] O'Donel was followed by two further Irish Franciscans, Patrick Lambert and Lambert's nephew Thomas Scallan. All three had been trained in continental Europe and shared their generation's faith in social and political quiescence.[11] Scallan in particular enjoyed almost preternaturally good relations with both power and Protestants.[12] This changed with the appointment in 1829 of Michael Anthony Fleming as coadjutor vicar apostolic with right of succession.

Fleming, who had first come to Newfoundland in 1820 at Scallan's behest, was also a Franciscan but of an entirely different type: educated in Ireland, politically assertive, socially aggressive, and religiously unapologetic.[13] He was also noisily Irish. Fleming found a colony that was finely balanced between mostly English Protestants (Anglicans and Methodists) and almost entirely Irish Catholics. By 1827, there were 30,928 Catholics and 28,212 Protestants living on the island, with the Catholics concentrated in the city of St John's (10,214 Catholics to 4,951 Protestants) or nearby on the Avalon Peninsula.[14] As John Mannion has pointed out, Irish migration was unusually concentrated not only in its destination but also in its origins, with most coming from a small area of the south-east in counties Wexford, Waterford, Kilkenny, and Tipperary.[15] Fleming's hometown of Carrick-on-Suir was a particular centre. Also unusually, there was very little Irish Protestant migration, perhaps no more than 5 per cent of the Irish total.[16] Indeed, the origins of the Protestant population were almost as concentrated as the Catholics, with most coming from the English West Country. The rough religious balance on the island as a whole and the Catholic domination of St John's would continue throughout Fleming's life and beyond, although by 1845 Protestants had become and would remain a slight majority in the province while remaining a substantial minority in the capital.

Fleming's first task on becoming vicar apostolic in his own right in 1830 was to secure control of his church. Like Francis Kenrick in Philadelphia,

[10] In Collaboration, 'O'Donel, James Louis', *Dictionary of Canadian Biography* [*DCB*]. The *DCB* is online at www.biographi.ca.

[11] The surviving correspondence of the early bishops and many of their priests has been published in Cyril J. Byrne (ed.), *Gentlemen-Bishops and Faction Fighters* (St John's: Jesperson Press, 1984).

[12] Greene, 51–4.

[13] See Martin Anthony Fleming to Scallan, 7 October 1820, Franciscan Archives, Dún Mhuire [FLK], Box 36, E60/72.

[14] Gertrude Gunn, *The Political History of Newfoundland, 1832–1864* (Toronto: University of Toronto Press, 1966), 206.

[15] See John Mannion, 'Tracing the Irish: A geographical guide', *Newfoundland Ancestor*, vol. 9, no. 1 (May 1993).

[16] FitzGerald, 32.

he was confronted by assertive lay trustees; unlike Kenrick, he was also challenged by a colourful and largely ungovernable clergy. The latter had plagued Scallan who publicly excommunicated one priest for serial disobedience and expelled another for persisting in his habit of smuggling boys into the episcopal residence.[17] Fleming's solution was to recruit an entirely new clergy in Ireland. They were to be as free as possible from any connection to the island, and no Newfoundlander need apply. This policy of *transo attachi* was informed by the vicious factionalism of Newfoundland's Irish who were divided on roughly provincial lines of Leinster v. Munster, or even Wexford v. Waterford.[18] As Fleming explained to a Roman correspondent in 1842, it was 'not uncommon' for two priests 'to struggle to displace each other upon the Altar and even to exchange blows'.[19] Fleming ultimately imported thirty-two priests, with a strong preference for men from Co. Kilkenny, and John FitzGerald is surely right to see his blanket prohibition of native clergy as crucial in the development of Newfoundland Catholicism.[20]

Fleming challenged the status quo on every level: politically, he abandoned his predecessors' policy of conciliation in favour of confrontation, unabashedly embraced O'Connellite nationalism, and behaved as if Newfoundland were a part of Ireland; ecclesiastically, he reversed their ecumenism, and set out to break the power of the laity, remarking in 1842 that they 'should be kept entirely at bay' lest small concessions grow to a 'monstrous power'; and, socially, he condemned everything from intemperance to mixed marriages to Sunday labour.[21] All of this appalled the political, social, and economic elites of St John's, both Catholic and Protestant, who had grown comfortable with loyal and undemanding bishops.

Fleming's initial target was those he referred to as '*questi Cattolici liberali*', usually of some wealth or social standing, who had been close to Scallan and his predecessors and supporters of their policy of social integration.[22] Fleming's newly imported Irish clergy, and especially his vicar general Edward Troy, called them 'Mad Dogs' and sought their political, economic, and spiritual destruction. Troy's tactics included defamatory newspaper articles, economic blockade, mob violence, and denial of the sacraments to 'Mad Dogs' and their families. What began as a struggle for dominance within the church soon became conflated with

---

[17] Ibid., 69–70.   [18] Ibid., 46–7.
[19] Fleming to Charles Januarius Acton, 26 September 1842, Propaganda Fide Archives [APF], Scritt. Riferite nei congressi, America Settenrionale, Canada, Nuova Brettagna, Labrador, Terra Nova [AS], vol. 5, ff. 280–1.
[20] FitzGerald, 99.   [21] Fleming to Walsh, 22 November 1842, quoted in Greene, 59.
[22] Howley, *Newfoundland*, 229.

the charged political landscape as the island grappled with the consequences of the self-government that was granted in 1832.

Historians have tended to ascribe the consequent explosion of what Sean Cadigan called 'the blood sport of narrow sectarianism' to Fleming's assertiveness.[23] Gertrude Gunn, for example, saw Newfoundland in the 1830s and 1840s as an 'embittered little Ireland' that had received an assembly far too soon, and with far too wide a franchise, with the result that 'clerical direction and coercion, and mob violence and intimidation, ensured a united Catholic vote and a Catholic-dominated House'.[24] There is some truth to this, in that a continuation of Scallan's policies might have delayed, but could not have prevented, the assertion of Irish Catholic power that demography and the advent of electoral politics made inevitable. As Philip Gosse noticed in 1827, Newfoundland Protestants had long felt 'an habitual dread of the Irish as a class'; neither Fleming nor representative government created sectarian divisions, although both amplified them.[25]

Nor was Fleming a simple sectarian in his politics, choosing to ally himself with a religiously diverse group of mostly Irish-born reformers that had coalesced in the early 1820s in opposition to the heavy-handed justice often meted out to the poorer classes. Most of the leaders of what became the Reform or Liberal party were Irish Catholics but also included a smattering of liberal Protestants, including the Whiggish Scottish doctor William Carson. Fleming was particularly close to a kinship group radiating from the Waterford merchant Patrick Morris, and Morris' charismatic and ruthless nephew John Kent quickly became the dominant figure in the party, a position consolidated by his 1834 marriage to Fleming's sister. In the 1832 election, the bishop publicly endorsed Kent, Carson, and the English Protestant William Thomas in St John's against the 'Mad Dog' Irish Catholic Patrick Kough. Kent and Thomas were returned, but so was Kough; Carson had to wait for a bitter 1833 by-election against another 'Mad Dog'. Fleming and his successor J. T. Mullock became the effective leaders of the Liberal party, and while day-to-day decisions were left to the politicians real power lay in the episcopal palace. As the speaker of the House of Assembly declared on the hustings in 1857, 'My friends, they say the Bishop is your Governor;

---

[23] Sean Cadigan, *Newfoundland and Labrador: A History* (Toronto: University of Toronto Press, 2009), 111.
[24] Gunn, 182–3.
[25] Edmund Gosse, *The Naturalist of the Sea-shore: The Life of Philip Henry Gosse* (London: William Heinemann, 1896), 43.

well, what if he is! Is he not a good one, and who has a better right to govern you?'[26]

The colony's elites saw only danger and demagoguery, something the behaviour of Fleming, Troy, and Kent did little to dispel. 'Protestants went in mortal fear', Edmund Gosse wrote of his father's decision to leave in 1834, and 'Newfoundland was fast becoming a most unpleasant place to live in.'[27] Philip Gosse himself looked forward to Canada, where one could 'climb to the top of the tallest tree in the forest and shout "Irishman!" at the top of our voice, without fear'.[28] That fear was given shape in 1835 when Henry Winton, the English Protestant proprietor of the *Daily Ledger*, was set upon outside Carbonear and had his ears cut off. Winton and the *Ledger* had been in open war with Fleming since 1832, and Protestants naturally blamed Irish Catholics for the assault. Nothing was proved, but Catholic ditties about 'Croppy Winton' and gloating leaders in the Catholic press aggravated tensions.[29] (The affair was cited as far afield as New South Wales as an instance of Catholic aggression.)[30] The governor's suggestion that the franchise be immediately reduced was ignored, and in 1836 a united Catholic vote abetted by some Methodists secured a commanding majority in the Assembly; nine of the eleven Liberal seats were held by Irish Catholics, all four of the Conservative seats by Protestants.[31] The election was invalidated on a technicality, and the 1837 rerun produced an even larger Liberal majority.[32]

The commitment of the clergy to the Liberal cause confirmed long-standing Protestant anxieties about the consequences of granting democracy to the priest-ridden Irish. Fleming himself encouraged the association with Ireland, raising funds for Daniel O'Connell as early as 1829, and using him as his conduit to parliament and the British government.[33] In 1838, he described O'Connell (the 'Day Star' of Irish freedom) as 'the advocate of the oppressed throughout the world'.[34] He regularly attacked British misrule in Ireland, which he contrasted unfavourably with colonial

---

[26] Quoted in Frederick Jones, 'Mullock, John Thomas', in *DCB*. The speaker was Ambrose Shea.

[27] Gosse, 81–2.   [28] Ibid., 43.

[29] Patrick O'Flaherty, 'Winton, Henry David', in *DCB*. For an analysis of the text of 'Croppy Winton', see G. M. Story, '"A tune beyond us as we are": Reflections on Newfoundland song and ballad', *Newfoundland Studies* 4, 2 (1998), 129–44 at 134–5.

[30] See *The Colonist* (Sydney), 22 September 1833.

[31] Sir Henry Prescott to Lord Aberdeen, 16 February 1835, The National Archives [TNA], CO194/90/ff. 56–9.

[32] See the tables published by Gunn, 194–5.

[33] See Archives of the Archdiocese of St John's [ARCSJ], Fleming papers [FP], 103/20/2.

[34] Quoted in Philip McCann, 'Bishop Fleming and the politicization of Irish Roman Catholics in Newfoundland, 1830–1850', in Terrence Murphy and Cyril J. Byrne

freedoms.[35] It is little wonder that Fleming became the focus of the fears of Newfoundland's Protestants, successive governors, and the Colonial Office. As the newly arrived governor observed in early 1835, 'We have unfortunately an illiterate and vulgar Roman Catholic Bishop whose dependent clergy, being principally of his own choice, too closely resemble him in character.'[36]

The only solution was to remove the bishop, which could only be done by Rome. The problem was that the United Kingdom lacked formal diplomatic relations with the Holy See, and despite the presence of an unofficial envoy in Rome the foreign office did not understand the intricacies of papal politics. The British approached the cardinal secretary of state, who was sympathetic – removing an awkward bishop from a colonial backwater was a small price to pay for London's favour. Yet under Gregory XVI real power lay in the Propaganda, and they had different interests and concerns. Thus the first attempt to have Fleming sacked was thwarted in late 1834, when he nearly simultaneously received a warning from the undersecretary of state and a letter of support from Cardinal Fransoni.[37] Three subsequent attempts over the next decade met with similar results, although the pope warned Fleming off politics (and suspended Troy) in 1838, and as late as 1841 Rome remained worried by what it called the 'high complaints against your political interference in the colonial government of Newfoundland'.[38] The colonial office came to suspect that 'the Pope secretly enjoys the power of keeping a whole English colony in a ferment', while Fleming told the Propaganda that the British 'despairing of being able to stab Religion in Ireland are solicitous to cramp it in the Colonies in order to plant upon its ruins the symbols of their own adulterous creed'.[39] With apparently no other option, the decision was taken in 1842 to suspend the constitution, truncate the franchise, and merge the elected assembly and appointed legislative council, thus effectively abandoning representative government.

Yet politics did not consume all of Fleming's attention. On assuming control in St John's, he sought to assert his authority over the Benevolent Irish Society (BIS), which had been founded in 1806 by both Catholic and Protestant Irishmen with the support of Bishop O'Donel. Avowedly

(eds.), *Religion and Identity: The Experience of Irish and Scottish Catholics in Atlantic Canada* (St John's: Jesperson Press, 1987), 86.

[35] See, for example, Fleming's St Patrick's Day toast, 'Ireland as she ought to be', published in St John's in 1832.

[36] Prescott to Aberdeen, 16 February 1835.   [37] FitzGerald, 169.

[38] FitzGerald, 248; Antonio DeLuca to Fleming, 25 May 1841, ARCSJ/FP/103/17/1.

[39] Note by James Stephen, 30 January 1838, quoted in FitzGerald, 247; Fleming to Fransoni, 27 December 1842, ARCSJ/FP/103/17/6.

non-sectarian, the BIS did not have a Catholic president until Patrick Morris in 1822.[40] Its original function was the relief of impoverished Irish, but in 1826 it opened the 'Orphan Asylum School' (OAS) with financial support from both the Catholic and the Anglican bishops, and it quickly became the primary provider of education to the poor Irish. To Fleming's horror, Scallan was untroubled that the OAS was non-denominational and omitted religious instruction despite the fact that its students were almost entirely Catholic. In 1834, Fleming tried to provide after-hours instruction on school grounds but was thwarted by his 'Mad Dog' opponents on the BIS executive.[41] He consequently purged both his Catholic opponents and any vestige of Protestant involvement, and the BIS became in practice purely Catholic. Although an Irish Protestant could notionally still join, Michael Howley observed in the late 1880s, 'such is not likely ever to occur'.[42]

Seeking both education for girls and a more compliant provider of education for boys, Fleming set out for Ireland in early 1833. On 20 June, he appeared unannounced at the Presentation convent in Galway, told the sisters of the 'hundreds' of poor children in St John's who were 'exposed to a perverted and anti-Catholic education', and promised them a convent, a school, and the annual interest on £1,500.[43] The women agreed on the condition that they could return after six years at Fleming's expense, and four sisters sailed with him to Newfoundland under the leadership of M. Bernard Kirwan.[44] Despite never letting them 'forget that we are nuns and he our Superior', the community flourished – even if they required 'all the fervour of our devotions to keep us warm'.[45] They soon opened a school targeted at poor children in a temporary building, moving to better quarters soon after and again in 1843 at a cost of some £4,000. In 1844, Fleming claimed the average daily attendance had long exceeded 1,000.[46]

In 1842, the Presentations were joined by a small group of Sisters of Mercy whom Fleming had recruited in Dublin. The initial party of three included a Newfoundlander sent to Ireland for her novitiate and two Irish

---

[40] Howley, *Newfoundland*, 227.
[41] Noel A. Veitch, 'The contribution of the Benevolent Irish Society to education in Newfoundland from 1823 to 1875', unpublished M.Ed. thesis, Saint Francis Xavier University, 1965, 34, 49–51.
[42] Howley, *Newfoundland*, 228.
[43] Fleming to 'Revd. Mother', 17 July 1833, Presentation Convent Galway Archives [PCGA]. The recipient was most likely M. John Power.
[44] M. John Power to Fleming, 22 July 1833, PCGA.
[45] M. Xaverius Lynch to 'Ann', 6 January 1834, M. Magdalene O'Shaughnessy to M. Augustine, 21 November 1833, Presentation Congregation Archives, St John's.
[46] Howley, *Newfoundland*, 291.

women. In St John's, they were joined by a local whom Fleming quickly professed. In 1843, they opened a school for wealthier girls; but the community quickly collapsed after Fleming clashed with the strong-willed M. Ursula Frayne.[47] The Irish nuns returned home, and Frayne went on to found the Mercy communities in Western Australia and later Victoria (see Chapter 6).[48] From this point on, the Sisters of Mercy in Ireland 'did not look upon the Establishment in Newfoundland as belonging to our Institute', and felt no obligation towards it.[49] The Newfoundlanders remained as the lone members until M. Francis Creedon's niece joined in 1850. The school remained open, and by 1844 had around fifty students.[50] The Newfoundland Sisters of Mercy are thus distinctive in Greater Ireland as being an essentially indigenous (if still Irish) foundation from the beginning.

The challenges of providing education were soon eased by the denominational peculiarities of Newfoundland politics. Just as the island was the first jurisdiction to elect an Irish Catholic government, it was also the first in the English-speaking world to embrace state-funded Catholic education. Everywhere else in Greater Ireland it was the majority Protestant population (local or national) that opposed denominational education as truckling to Catholic obscurantism. The irony is that in Newfoundland it was evangelical Protestants who insisted on a system beyond even the wildest Catholic hopes.[51]

In 1836, the colony's first Education Act appropriated £2,100 per annum to education, with £300 specifically allocated to the OAS, which still formally denied it was a Catholic school, and £100 to the Presentation convent, which most certainly did not. Established Protestant schools attracted similar sums. Yet the bulk of the grant was allocated to new local school boards, which were enjoined to include the clergy of all denominations among their number. Neither religious instruction nor sectarian texts were permitted. The model was Ireland's national school system, and indeed an 1838 amendment allocated £150 to centrally purchase texts used there. Fleming was not enthusiastic, but followed the Irish bishops in tolerating it. Yet sectarian prejudice ensured

---

[47] See Kathrine E. Bellamy, *Weavers of the Tapestry* (St John's: Flanker Press, 2006), 66–71.

[48] See Anne McLay, *Women Out of Their Sphere: A History of the Sisters of Mercy in Western Australia* (Northbridge, WA: Vanguard Press, 1992).

[49] M. Vincent Whitty to Mullock, 25 January 1854, in *The Correspondence of Mother Vincent Whitty, 1839–1892*, compiled by Anne Hetherington and Pauline Smoothy (St Lucia: University of Queensland Press, 2011), 103.

[50] Bellamy, 82.

[51] See Philip McCann, 'The politics of denominational education in nineteenth century Newfoundland', in William A. McKim (ed.), *The Vexed Question: Denominational Education in a Secular Age* (St John's: Breakwaters Books, 1998), 36–7.

that only 18 of the 117 positions on the nine boards were filled by Catholics, and several Protestant-dominated boards immediately imposed the Authorised Version of the Bible.[52] The Catholic reaction was entirely predictable.

After the amalgamation of the legislature, Protestants pressed their newfound advantage in an effort to extend and embed denominationalism. Only denominational schools could ensure authentically Protestant texts, and a safely Protestant environment; there were simply too many Catholics to risk sharing a classroom. More importantly, the relatively large number of poor Protestants made a purely voluntary system financially impossible. The evangelical Protestant Richard Barnes carried the day by claiming that neither Catholics nor Protestants could assent to undenominational education without either abandoning or attenuating their faith, an argument Catholic bishops across Greater Ireland would regularly make for at least the next seventy-five years.[53] The Catholics warily acquiesced, and a new Education Act passed in May 1843. The grant was raised to £5,100, and the island was divided into educational districts, and each district further divided between Catholic and Protestant. Funds were allocated based on population, at both the district and the denominational level; the Catholics of St John's, for example, received £930 of the district's £1,250 grant. Linked plans to establish a Protestant and a Catholic academy in St John's faltered when the legislation required that the board of governors of the Protestant college be Protestant and include the Anglican bishop but made no similar provision for the Catholic college. Worse, the principals of both were required to be graduates of Oxford, Cambridge, or Trinity College, Dublin, which for all practical purposes meant a Protestant. Fleming was having none of that and the idea was abandoned.[54] Denominationalism however became a fixed principle of Newfoundland education, and legislation in 1851 and 1852 further embedded it.[55] The system remained in place until the 1990s.

As important as education was to Fleming, his overriding priority was his great construction project, the cathedral of St John the Baptist. For years, Fleming sought a grant of land from the government on which to build, and in 1838 he finally secured a commanding site above the city. His ambition was to erect a cathedral larger than any in Ireland or North America as a visible testament to the power and permanence of Irish

---

[52] Ibid., 32–3.   [53] Ibid., 36.

[54] Petition to the Newfoundland House of Assembly on a Bill for Education, 11 February 1843, ARCSJ/FP/103/23.

[55] Frederick W. Rowe, *The Development of Education in Newfoundland* (Toronto: The Ryerson Press, 1964), 63–6.

Catholicism on the island. Stone was imported in bulk from Ireland, and Fleming could be found cutting and loading it himself, including in the winter. Even the collapse of his London bank and the loss of some £4,700 could not stop him, and he instituted the tradition of an annual donation of a day's catch to help make up the shortfall. Most of the work was done by volunteers, many of the supplies were donated, and in 1841 the cornerstone was laid in a great ceremony after a procession that included a portrait of Daniel O'Connell.[56] Construction continued throughout the 1840s, absorbing all the men, money, and material Newfoundland Catholicism could provide.

The scale and cost of the cathedral also point to an important difference between the first generation of colonial bishops and the later Hiberno-Romans. The former expended enormous resources to build large cathedrals in places such as Cape Town, Sydney, and St John's. The latter preferred smaller-scale projects, and rarely undertook expensive prestige buildings. As Cullen's protégé James Murray observed during a trip to the western United States in 1889, 'both their churches and schools are on a magnificent scale', but if 'they had spent the same amount of money on smaller churches and schools and increased their numbers, it would be better'.[57] Fleming would not have agreed, and although the cathedral was not finished during his lifetime it is his monument, looming over St John's at the centre of a complex that contains schools, offices, and two convents.

This overwhelming need for money led Fleming into an unnecessary and ultimately counterproductive conflict with Paul Cullen and the Irish College. Instead of using Cullen as his agent, Fleming spent much of the 1830s and 1840s trying to recoup funds that he preferred to spend on the cathedral. In 1833, Archbishop Daniel Murray of Dublin had forwarded a £500 bequest to found 'a burse for Newfoundland' at the Irish College.[58] Cullen duly purchased some property and applied the income to the burse. In 1837, Fleming demanded the funds be returned to him, as they had 'been sent to Rome without any authority, and without his consent'. Cullen explained his case to the Propaganda, which referred the matter to Murray.[59] It seems that Fleming was ultimately unable to retrieve the funds, and the dispute may go some way to explain his wariness of the Irish College. Certainly he preferred to stay at the Franciscan St Isidore's when in Rome, and none of his surviving correspondence indicates any contact between him and the college, save

---

[56] FitzGerald, 301.   [57] Murray to Patrick Hand, 8 February 1889, MNDA/MP/E.1.42.
[58] Murray to Cullen, 1 August 1833, DDA/MP/34/9.
[59] Cullen to Murray, 3 June 1837, DDA/MP/34/9.

a single letter from Cullen concerned with Nova Scotia.[60] Given the relentless pressure placed on his position by the British government, he could have used the help.

Fleming's challenges were exacerbated in 1846 by a disastrous fire that destroyed much of St John's, including the Presentation convent and school. The decision of successive governors to allocate public funds to help rebuild Anglican but not Catholic buildings raised tensions, and Fleming was forced to set out for Europe to search for money, teachers, and his own successor. The need for each was acute, as the diocese was broke, its schools inadequate, and Fleming himself ailing. His first task was to provide for the Benevolent Irish Society's Orphan Asylum School, which he had long pressed to become more Catholic in character.[61] After failing to obtain the Christian Brothers, Fleming secured the services of four Irish Franciscan brothers who, on arrival in St John's in September 1847, promptly took over the school. Perhaps more importantly, he asked the Propaganda to appoint the Irish Franciscan J. T. Mullock as his coadjutor with right of succession. Mullock was a good choice: the father guardian of the Franciscan convent in Dublin since 1843, his knowledge of Italian had been useful in his role as Fleming's European agent. He also fulfilled Fleming's desire for an outsider untainted by family or other links who would nevertheless continue Franciscan rule. As for Rome, his suitability was no doubt enhanced by his 1847 translation of Alphonsus Liguori's *History of Heresies*.[62] Although he lacked Fleming's rough charisma, Mullock proved to be a bishop in his image.

Before this request could be acted upon, Rome made clear what could happen in the absence of a local agent. In November 1847, Pius IX unexpectedly erected Newfoundland into a diocese and placed it under the ecclesiastical province of Quebec. Fleming was aghast, but it was not the first time the idea had been mooted. The long-serving Joseph Signay of Quebec was a French bishop of the old school, distrustful of ultramontanism, resistant to calls for disciplinary or liturgical uniformity, and deferential to the province's British rulers. By contrast, the second bishop of Montreal, Ignace Bourget, was a keen ultramontane and enthusiastic advocate for an ecclesiastical province. Signay was reluctant: like the American Sulpicians, he knew that whatever his personal status a provincial council could impose its will. In 1840, Bourget urged

[60] See, for example, Fleming to Troy, 29 May 1837, ARCSJ/FP/103/16/8.
[61] Veitch, 75.
[62] J. T. Mullock, *The History of Heresies, Their Refutation, and the Triumph of the Church, Translated from the Italian of St. Alphonsus M. Liguori*, 2 vols. (Dublin: James Duffy, 1847).

Fleming to sign and personally convey an appeal to Rome for an eccle-siastical province to include Newfoundland.[63] Fleming unsurprisingly demurred. To Rome, he gave as his primary reason Quebec's distance. Privately, he recalled in 1843, his 'paramount' concern was that the church in Quebec was 'under the immediate control of the Protestant British Government' upon whom it depended for much of its income. Placing all of British North America under Quebec's 'Spiritual control', he wrote, 'would have the effect of strengthening their claim upon that Government for even more accession of pay'.[64] This was unfair to Bourget, but Fleming had reason to worry about what pressure the British could bring to bear via the compliant Signay.

The question re-emerged in 1843. This time Fleming feared the plan was to combine 'the North American British Provinces under one Spiritual Ruler an Archbishop at Montreal'. He and the newly appointed William Walsh of Nova Scotia (see Chapter 5) opposed their own inclu-sion, and Fleming provided Walsh with a copy of his earlier letter to the Propaganda. In May 1844, Bourget finally succeeded in securing Rome's approval for a province but there was no mention of Newfoundland. Despite this success, Fleming remained exposed: with no agent, he had no advance warning of the renewed threat, no one to point out that Quebec was a long way away, and no one to suggest that the first bishop of Newfoundland be consulted. He instead found himself in the unenvi-able position of forcing Rome to admit error.

Fleming again founded his argument on geography, although just in case he reminded the Propaganda that Newfoundland was Irish and Quebec French. He had never been there, he wrote, and he was too old and ill, and the journey too dangerous, to try now. It was easier and safer to reach Europe. Even more astonishing, he wrote, was the 'passing over' of New Brunswick, Prince Edward Island, 'and the two Dioceses of Nova Scotia, all in the vicinity of Canada', whereas 'the remote Island of Newfoundland' was separated from Quebec 'by a thousand miles of ocean'. Surely they had just misread the map?[65] Despite his disingenuous assessment of the dangers of sea travel, Fleming's case was strong, and by early 1848 Mullock at least was confident that Rome would reverse its decision.[66] It duly did in late 1850, although Fleming did not live to see

[63] The vicars apostolic of Nova Scotia and Prince Edward Island were approached at the same time on Bourget's behalf by Michael Power, later the first bishop of Toronto. See Mark McGowan, *Michael Power: The Struggle to Build the Catholic Church on the Canadian Frontier* (Montreal and Kingston: McGill-Queen's University Press, 2005), 113.

[64] Fleming to Walsh, 8 September 1843, ARCSJ/FP/103/10/2.

[65] Fleming to Fransoni, 25 November 1847, ARCSJ/FP/103/28/2.

[66] Mullock to P. B. Geoghegan, 16 March 1848, Archives of the Archdiocese of Adelaide [ACAA], Geoghegan papers [GP], Series 20, Box 2, Folder 2.

it.[67] Fleming's evasion of Quebec mirrored his successors' determination to resist later schemes for union with any portion of the Canadian church; Mullock was no more interested in joining the ecclesiastical province of Halifax in 1852 than Fleming had been to be placed under Quebec in 1847. Newfoundland's bishops were just as keen as other Newfoundlanders to keep their distance.

In the meantime, the confusion nearly derailed Fleming's plans. Mullock had been lingering in Rome since arriving with Fleming's letter of nomination just as the Propaganda's long vacation began. Once the *minutanti* returned, there was concern about continuing the Franciscan succession and some scruple about whether Archbishop Signay should be consulted as Newfoundland's new metropolitan.[68] Neither was insuperable, and Mullock was consecrated in late December 1847. Even then, Cardinal Fransoni didn't tell him about Quebec. The news came from Fleming (who had it from Signay), and the new bishop promptly delivered to the Propaganda an Italian translation of Fleming's protest and two detailed maps.[69] That job done, Mullock set out for Newfoundland. He knew nothing about it, he told a Franciscan friend in Australia, except that it had about 90,000 Catholics (far too many), two convents, four Franciscans (not counting the two bishops), and one very big and expensive church.[70]

Mullock was immediately forced to confront the highly politicized and sectarian landscape of Newfoundland. The establishment in 1848 of responsible governments in Nova Scotia and Canada (then the modern provinces of Ontario and Quebec) had led to demands for the same concession in Newfoundland. This was inevitably opposed by the governor and the conservative and merchant interest. The governor informed the Colonial Office that Fleming, Kent, and their allies simply wanted to 'withdraw all influence' from Protestants 'and place themselves, the Roman Catholics, in full possession of every place of emolument throughout the entire Colony'.[71] The 1848 election for the restored Assembly – Mullock's first – saw the return of ten Liberals, which meant nine Catholics and the Presbyterian Robert Parsons. The four St John's seats were uncontested. Despite the 'experimental silence' of the clergy, Protestants again claimed that the majority had been 'returned by the influence of the R. C. Clergy, though a majority of the population are Protestant'.[72]

[67] FitzGerald, 394 n114.   [68] Raymond J. Lahey, 'Fleming, Michael Anthony', in *DCB*.
[69] FitzGerald, 401.   [70] Mullock to Geoghegan, 16 March 1848, ACAA.
[71] Le Marchant to Grey, 22 May 1848, quoted in Gunn, 115.
[72] Gunn, 115, paraphrasing the *Ledger* of 17 November 1848; draft of a letter to an unidentified newspaper, J. T. Mullock, n.d. [1848], ARCSJ, Mullock papers [MP], 104/1/40.

In reply, Mullock flatly denied that clerical influence had been responsible for the outcome of the election, pointing out that in Harbour Grace the parish priest had unsuccessfully encouraged sympathetic Protestants to run, while St John's had simply elected 'known and tried friends of the people', one of whom was a Protestant. As for the bishops, Fleming had been 'confined to his room', and Mullock himself had taken no part, 'being unacquainted with either the persons or the parties' standing. Yet he was very clear that he was not ruling out future involvement. 'Let me not', he wrote, 'be understood to condemn interference of clergy at elections': priests paid taxes and were subject to the law; 'St. Paul claimed his Roman citizenship'; and a 'priest by his ordination does not forfeit the privilege of a British subject'. Mullock's point was clear: the church enjoyed a legitimate interest in politics, but had chosen not to exercise it. Yet there was no reason it should not do so in future.[73] Mullock of course had to be mindful of Rome's regularly reiterated prohibitions of priestly meddling in politics. The solution was to differentiate between the altar and everywhere else. As he warned one of his priests in 1856, 'I have no objection that a priest may express his private opinion as he pleases but the Altar of God is set aside for prayer, instruction & the Sacrifice ... & therefore I will never tolerate anything worldly or political in such circumstances.'[74] It was a fine point, and not likely to be appreciated by his opponents.

Both the Colonial Office and the average Protestant took it for granted that even if the priests didn't control the party, they certainly controlled its voters; and since Fleming's time they knew that the bishop controlled the priests. Their suspicions were confirmed when Mullock threw himself into the campaign for responsible government. From Halifax, Archbishop Walsh excitedly told him 'Now is the day, and now is the hour!' He also drew the inevitable comparison to O'Connell, remarking that 'the same would have been true for our poor, dear and never to be forgotten Ireland, if the Great Daniel were inter vivos'.[75] The campaign's success left no doubt as to where power lay in the Catholic community. A nervous John Kent went out of his way to promise that he would follow Mullock's advice to 'organise a liberal club in order to ensure something like unity of action' at the upcoming election. Worried that he had angered the bishop and lost his political support, Kent grovelled. Telling Mullock of his long-standing 'anxiety' to 'stand well with your Lordship', Kent promised 'to do nothing that might in any way be construed into a slight for your person, your high ecclesiastical status or

[73] Ibid.   [74] Mullock to Fr Condon, 7 June 1856, ARCSJ/MP/104/1/10.
[75] Walsh to Mullock, 2 March 1854, ARCSJ/MP/104/1/8.

for your Lordship's opinions'.[76] In May 1855, the Liberals returned seventeen members out of thirty (including the six from St John's, all unopposed), and Philip Francis Little became premier. Kent succeeded him three years later. With the advent of responsible government and apparently reliable Liberal majorities, Mullock became habituated to power.

Yet politics did not prove an easy game. In 1861, Mullock's lingering distrust of Kent broke into the open over the linked issues of colonial transport and poor relief. Mullock was furious when Kent sought to bring the distribution of government support under the control of individual members of the Assembly and set out to 'crush the scheme'. While he was undoubtedly opposed to the opportunity for corruption and to the failure to test for need, his primary worry was the threat to clerical power. Kent and his supporters had thought, Mullock explained privately, 'to destroy the influence of the priests by getting the people to call on the members [of the Assembly] instead of them for relief or rather bribery'. 'We have', he lamented, 'a miserable set of beggars in the Govt. & the Protestant opposition party are just as bad.'[77] An abject climbdown earned Kent a letter of approval from Mullock, which he used to save his government. The governor soon dismissed it anyway on frankly anti-Catholic grounds – in London, the undersecretary of state thought it 'somewhat in the nature of a *coup d'etat*' – and the resulting election displayed both the scale and the limitations of episcopal power.[78]

Mullock made his position clear, praising Kent's government, warning Catholics of Protestant tyranny and urging them to defer to their clergy.[79] Sectarian passions led to rioting, at least one death, and a tentative Protestant majority, and Mullock spoke darkly of 'a war of extermination' being waged against Catholics. The opening of the Assembly in heavily Catholic St John's was met by riots that were only quelled when Mullock summoned the mob to the cathedral, exposed the blessed sacrament, made them kneel, and demanded their good behaviour. Even so, sporadic violence continued for days, and the Anglican bishop was stoned and Anglican buildings attacked.[80] This naturally enraged Protestants and was too stark an exhibition of power even for many Catholics. Walsh's successor in Halifax feared things would 'end disastrously', and warned

---

[76] Kent to Mullock, 20 February 1855, ARCSJ/MP/104/1/9.
[77] Mullock to Sweeny, 9 February 1861, Archives of the diocese of Saint John [SJDA], Sweeny papers [SP], 1370.
[78] Note by Chichester Fortescue on Alexander Bannerman to Duke of Newcastle, 14 March 1861, TNA/CO/194/165/ff. 145–6.
[79] Letter to the editor, *The Record*, 21 March 1861.
[80] Frederick Jones, 'Mullock, John Thomas', in *DCB*.

the bishop of Chatham, New Brunswick, that 'If you interfere in politics
you will never forgive yourself.'[81] Newfoundland's governor allowed
himself the wistful hope that the bishop might 'fall in with Garibaldi' on
a post-election trip to Rome.[82] A chastened Mullock was forced to limit
his political interventions to more private fora, and the Liberal party
ceased to be the sole repository of Catholic votes, but the bishop remained
the most powerful individual in the colony.

Despite such setbacks and occasional embarrassments, from a Catholic
perspective Newfoundland was in many ways Greater Ireland's ideal
polity. The rough religious balance ensured that sectarian tensions were
never too far from the surface but also that Catholics had real political
power. In Newfoundland, this developed into a carefully balanced and
enduring confessional spoils system with everything from schools to assembly seats considered Catholic or Protestant. This was clearest in the area of
education, a universal flashpoint that unfailingly drew the Catholic hierarchy into politics from New York to New South Wales. Newfoundland's
compromises in the 1830s and 1840s had settled the issue to Catholic
satisfaction and consequently removed it from political debate. As Mullock
wrote in an 1857 pastoral letter, 'The justice of our government leaves the
education of Catholics to Catholics, and of Protestants to their respective
congregations, furnishing equally to all, according to population, a portion
of the taxes which all pay, and not vainly endeavouring to combine in an
impossible union persons of a different belief.'[83] With their most important
issue secure, Mullock and his successors could afford to indulge their
taste – or otherwise – for overt political meddling.

Yet Mullock was not solely concerned with politics. He also proved
to be an attentive and ambitious bishop. He encouraged both the
Sisters of Mercy and the Presentation Sisters, for example, with
the latter expanding to Harbour Grace in 1851, and then Carbonear
the following year, opening schools in both. In St John's, their rebuilt
convent opened in 1854 at a final cost of some £7,000. The Mercies
were less successful, largely because the initial failure had given
Newfoundland a bad name in Ireland. Yet they still grew slowly
from their near annihilation under Fleming, and by 1855 there were
three professed sisters to do the teaching and one lay sister to do the
chores. They were able to open an orphanage in 1854, a boarding
school in 1859, and a new convent at Burin in 1861. By 1855,
Mullock could boast to Archbishop Hughes in New York that the

---

[81] Connolly to Rogers, 22 May 1861, Archives Diocésaines de Bathurst [ADDB], Rogers
papers [RP], 1/3 (F2652).
[82] Quoted in Gunn, 174.   [83] 'Pastoral Letter', 22 February 1857, ARCSJ/MP/104/1/41.

diocese had '30 priests ... 5 Presentation convents, 1 Convent of Sisters of Mercy, Catholics about 65,000 or 70,000, Chapels 62'.[84]

It also had the cathedral, which in 1855 was finally ready for consecration. Fundraising for the massive building remained a challenge, with Mullock despatching both priests and himself to the far corners of the colony to ask 'the people to give us a day's fishing'.[85] He needed the money: John Hogan's 'The Dead Christ', for example, is the Irish sculptor's masterpiece, but it cost Mullock £350.[86] The consecration was a very Irish affair, despite the presence of Colin MacKinnon of Arichat in Nova Scotia and Armand-François-Marie de Charbonnel, the Sulpician bishop of Toronto: the BIS presented an address and hosted a celebratory banquet; of the twenty-four priests in attendance, all but one had an Irish surname, and he was secretary to the Scottish MacKinnon; the Mass of Dedication was celebrated by Bishop Connolly of New Brunswick, and the sermon delivered by Archbishop Hughes of New York.[87] Hughes' presence at the consecration, Mullock wrote when inviting him, would 'be hailed by thousands of Irishmen and their children'.[88] He even had Hughes' sermon printed in Dublin.[89] Hughes also laid the cornerstone for St Patrick's parish church in the west end of St John's, which was designed by the Irish architect J. J. McCarthy, who was also responsible for the cathedrals in Armagh and Monaghan, and the chapel at Maynooth.

Immediately after the consecration, Mullock set out for Rome with 'Maps (coloured) the Census and every other public document I thought would be useful'.[90] His aim was to secure approval for a new diocese at Harbour Grace, the centre of the important and religiously mixed area around Conception Bay on the Avalon Peninsula. Yet even an Italian speaker such as Mullock needed an agent, and he was no more willing than Fleming to use the Irish College. The source of this reluctance is unclear: the dispute over burses had been settled; the Irish of Nova Scotia and New Brunswick eagerly sought Cullen and Kirby's help (see Chapter 5); several Newfoundland seminarians were at the Irish College, including John Kent's nephew; and Mullock himself was prepared to seek

---

[84] 1855 'Memorandum' in Mullock's hand, quoted in Mary James Dinn, *Foundation of the Presentation Congregation in Newfoundland* (St John's: n.p., 1975), 19.

[85] Mullock to Hughes, 11 June 1855, CU/BP/MS1296/1/1/2/14.

[86] Mullock to Hughes, 1 May 1856, CU/BP/MS1296/1/1/2/14.

[87] John B. Ashley, 'The consecration of the cathedral in 1855', in John F. Wallis, et al. (eds.), *The Basilica-Cathedral of St. John the Baptist, St. John's, Newfoundland, 1855–1980* (St John's: The basilica parish, 1980), 48–53.

[88] Mullock to Hughes, 11 June 1855, CU/BP/MS1296/1/1/2/14.

[89] Mullock to Hughes, 19 April 1856, CU/BP/MS1296/1/1/2/14.

[90] Mullock to Hughes, 1 April 1856, CU/BP/MS1296/1/1/2/14.

Cullen's assistance in securing additional Sisters of Mercy.[91] He cannot
have been unaware of the utility of an agent or the effectiveness of the Irish
College. The most likely explanation lay in the politics of the Irish
Franciscan province in which Cullen had been meddling.[92] Whatever
the reason, Mullock made life much harder for himself.

Pius IX was initially opposed, telling Mullock that North America
already had too many dioceses. Mullock eventually changed his mind,
and the matter was referred to the Propaganda. As one congregation after
another passed without a decision, Mullock grew increasingly frustrated.
'It would be tedious', he told John Hughes, 'to tell you all the visiting,
fighting, writing, arguing etc etc etc I had to go thro' to have the matter
accomplished.' But Mullock was glad he went: had he not, he would still
be waiting on a decision 'or I would have had a Coadjutor instead of an
Independent Bishop'. This would have been the worst of both worlds: still
responsible for the entire island, but with a potential rival who could never
'feel the interest in providing priests, Chapels or schools that a principal
does'.[93] In the end he got his way, and the Propaganda agreed to the
creation of the diocese of Harbour Grace.[94]

Mullock also secured the appointment of his sole choice for the new
see, John Dalton. Only thirty-five years old, the Tipperary-born Dalton
was the nephew of the long-serving Franciscan Charles Dalton. After
joining his uncle in Newfoundland in 1839, he was sent to study in
Rome the following year. He resided in the Irish College, where he
enjoyed the bursary that Fleming had tried so hard to recover. Dalton
was 'a most excellent young man', Cullen wrote in 1844, 'pious, docile,
obedient'. Perhaps as a peace offering, Cullen noted that although the
Newfoundland funds did not cover Dalton's costs, he was happy to waive
the balance 'for the good of religion'.[95] Dalton was ordained in Rome in
1849, returned to Newfoundland and his uncle's parish in Carbonear,
and soon succeeded him as parish priest.

Still things did not proceed smoothly. The problem was again the lack
of a Roman agent. By April 1856, Mullock complained that he had heard
nothing from the Propaganda, which he compared unfavourably to the
'British court of Chancery'. (This was only three years after Dickens had
immortalized the court in *Bleak House's* Jarndyce v Jarndyce.) Between

---

[91] Kirby to Kent, 19 April 1853, ARCSJ/MP/104/1/7; Cullen to Mullock, 21 January 1854,
ARCSJ/MP/104/1/8.

[92] See Bonaventure MacLaughlin to Mullock, 16 February 1854, ARCSJ/MP/104/1/8.

[93] Mullock to Hughes, 1 April 1856, CU/BP/MS1296/1/1/2/14.

[94] For a rambling, pious, but not entirely useless history of the diocese, see R. J. Connolly,
A History of the Roman Catholic Church in Harbour Grace (St John's: Creative publishers,
1986).

[95] Cullen to Fleming, 4 October 1844, ARCSJ/FP/103–10/3.

Cardinal Fransoni 'dying & Barnabò overworked & the minutanti amusing themselves the Missions are going to the bad'.[96] The bulls finally appeared in May but only because Mullock had written again to the Propaganda. It turned out they had been sitting unnoticed on somebody's desk. Despite all the frustrations, Mullock was delighted that he could now leave the 'rough work' to Dalton.[97] Dalton himself promptly set out for Ireland in search of priests.[98]

Mullock was now free to concentrate on the educational and ecclesiastical infrastructure of St John's. His primary challenge was to secure the necessary clergy. The 1854 departure of three of the four Franciscan brothers had left the OAS foundering and the need acute. Mullock was unable to secure clerical reinforcements, and the Franciscans were replaced with lay teachers. By 1856, Mullock had decided to establish 'a School & small seminary in S. John's as I find it will be more & more difficult every year to procure students from Ireland'. The problem, he explained to Hughes, was the attractions of America and Australia had 'turned the attention of the youth of Ireland to secular pursuits'. Even those who wanted to become priests preferred 'the States to the English Colonies and it is hard to blame them'.[99] St Bonaventure's College opened in temporary quarters in late 1856 with a handful of students. Two years later, it moved to a new building near the cathedral.[100]

Mullock's unwillingness to entrust St Bonaventure's to the secular clergy led to a mistake that would haunt both him and his successor. He selected for its president Enrico Carfagnini, a young Italian Franciscan who had been lecturing in theology and philosophy at St Isidore's in Rome. Mullock distrusted the Irish Franciscans as 'but relaxed secular priests', and seems to have hoped to build a more observant community around Carfagnini.[101] He was bitterly disappointed as Carfagnini 'soon became lazy and discontented' and left Newfoundland when he was unable to find a more remunerative position because 'he scarcely spoke English and like most Italians knew nothing of Greek, science or French'. The experience soured Mullock on friars, and he flatly told the Irish provincial that 'If a Franciscan comes here it is to make money and live a life of ease.'[102] Needy bishops were tempted when a 'strolling friar turns

[96] Mullock to Hughes, 19 April 1856, CU/BP/MS1296/1/1/2/14.
[97] Mullock to Hughes, 14 May 1856, CU/BP/MS1296/1/1/2/14.
[98] C. B. Lyons to Cullen, 30 August 1857, DDA, Cullen papers [CP], 339/5/III/4. Lyons was Cullen's secretary.
[99] Mullock to Hughes, 1 April 1856, CU/BP/MS1296/1/1/2/14.
[100] See J. B. Darcy, *Noble to Our View: The Saga of St. Bonaventure's College, St. John's: The First 150 Years, 1856–2006* (St John's: Creative Publishers, 2007).
[101] Mullock to Dardis, 4 February, 29 September 1857, FLK/36/E60/114, 115.
[102] Mullock to M. A. Kavanagh, 23 February 1865, FLK/36/E60/118.

up', and 'if he be neither a *public* drunkard or a debaucher' he would be taken on until a diocesan priest could be supplied 'or until he gets discontented and goes elsewhere to repeat the same scene with his pockets full of dollars'. Irish ones were particularly bad, he wrote, and generally had '3 or 4 Irish busy-bodies to go round their gullible countrymen to get up a collection'. Foreshadowing future scandals, Mullock observed that the afflicted 'bishop is often glad to get rid of him quietly without being *publicly* obliged to say *why*'.[103] Such *vagabondi* ensured that Mullock could no longer risk a convent of Irish Franciscans, as it would simply become 'a *refugium peccatorum* [refuge of sinners] for the Irish province'.[104] As for Carfagnini, Mullock suspended his faculties and expelled him from the diocese. The Italian then 'tried all the N. American provinces and was found useless', he told the provincial, before a desperate Dalton gave him refuge in Harbour Grace where he 'thought of nothing but money'.[105] Yet Mullock seems not to have told Dalton, or indeed anybody other than the Irish provincial, why he had dismissed Carfagnini.

Mullock never resolved the problem of clerical supply. When he began his episcopate, he had twenty-four priests serving a Catholic population of some 47,000. When he died twenty-one years later, there were thirty-five serving nearly 60,000. Mullock had little to offer, and no access to the networks of supply that might have overcome Newfoundland's limited appeal. Few if any priests came from All Hallows during his tenure, for example. He did encourage a handful of native vocations, including the brothers Michael and Richard Howley, but by 1890 only one of the six native Newfoundlanders active in St John's had been born before 1868.[106]

Mullock has not done well by historians. Gertrude Gunn portrayed him as an unfailing if inept champion of sectarianism, while Patrick O'Flaherty described him as 'another intractable Catholic bishop', not as intelligent or charismatic as Fleming but 'more irascible and outspoken'.[107] Yet as Carolyn Lambert has pointed out there was rather more to even his political career than simple sectarianism, although it is difficult to portray the events of 1861 as other than disastrous. Like Fleming, he worked very hard in often difficult conditions, telling John

[103] Mullock to Kavanagh, 19 July 1865, ARCSJ/MP/104/1/19. Emphasis in original.
[104] Mullock to Kavanagh, n.d. [1865], ARCSJ/MP/104/1/19. Emphasis in original.
[105] Mullock to Kavanagh, 19 July 1865, 23 February 1865, ARCSJ/MP/104/1/19, FLK/36/E60/118.
[106] Lambert, 'Far from the homes of their fathers', 100.
[107] Patrick O'Flaherty, *Lost Country: The Rise and Fall of Newfoundland 1843–1933* (St John's: Long Beach Press, 2005), 36.

Hughes in 1856, for example, that he could not come to New York because he was 'obliged to be in Placentia Bay boating from one cove to another'.[108] He took great pride in the achievements of his church, achievements that he always understood to belong to the Irish. Where Louis XIV had failed to plant Catholicism in Newfoundland, Mullock wrote in 1860, 'the poor persecuted Irish fishermen succeeded, and the proud monument of his or his children's faith – the Cathedral – crowns the culminating point of the capital of the island'.[109] When he invited John Hughes to consecrate that cathedral, Mullock truthfully promised him 'the most Catholic & Irish City on this side of the Atlantic'.[110]

For nearly forty years, Fleming and then Mullock had built a distinctively Irish but not Hiberno-Roman church in Newfoundland. They had both kept Cullen and the Irish College at arm's length, often at some cost to themselves. Yet Mullock's death in March 1869 and then John Dalton's in early May ended that distance. Everyone involved expected that Cullen would choose their successors. As the administrator of St John's admitted in July 1869, 'Cardinal Cullen we are told will manage the business'.[111] They did not know that Newfoundland was very far down Cullen's list of priorities.

For a start, there were several colonial vacancies to consider. In particular, the Irish believed that New Zealand needed three new bishops, an opinion not at all shared by the French Marists who had long dominated that church. The Vatican Council, the vacant archdiocese of Armagh, and yet another attempt to have the Fenians condemned by Rome also consumed Cullen's time and attention. St John's became something of an afterthought and Harbour Grace fell through the cracks entirely. Still, in February 1870 Cullen solicited advice from his secretary George Conroy, whom he hoped would soon be the next archbishop of Armagh. According to Conroy, the only possible Newfoundlander was the Roman-educated Michael Howley, 'a very clever man, possessed of great talents, and eloquent to a remarkable degree'. As 'a native of the island' he would be very popular, Conroy thought, but 'unless experience has given him more steadiness than he had when I knew him' it would be too much of a risk to appoint him 'for the present'. He wondered instead if Canon Thomas Power of Dublin 'might suit St. John's'.[112]

[108] Mullock to Hughes, 18 July 1856, AANY/HP/3/3.
[109] J. T. Mullock, *Two Lectures on Newfoundland, Delivered at St. Bonaventure's College, January 25, and February 1, 1860* (St John's: John Mullaly, at the Office of the Metropolitan Record, 1860), 26.
[110] Mullock to Hughes, 10 July 1853, AANY/HP/3/3.
[111] Edward O'Keeffe to Rogers, 5 July 1869, ADDB/RP/1/11.
[112] Conroy to Cullen, 25 February 1870, DDA/CP/321/7/4/20.

Born in 1830 at Rosbercon, near New Ross, Co. Wexford, Power was educated at Carlow College, where he earned a first-class University of London BA by examination and seems to have at least intended to sit the MA exam.[113] He was recommended to Cullen in 1852 as a suitable candidate for Dublin, and his intellectual gifts earned him a place at the Irish College, which he entered in 1853.[114] He was ordained a year later, and returned to Ireland in Cullen's company in 1855 to take up a prison chaplaincy. In 1859, he became the first rector of Holy Cross College, Clonliffe, which Cullen had built as a Roman counterweight to a supposedly Gallican Maynooth. Power was only the third choice, after it was decided to retain Patrick Moran in Rome and a second nomination miscarried. Kirby then suggested him on the somewhat underwhelming grounds that 'We were all very much edified with his piety here.'[115]

Paul Cullen was the centre of Power's ecclesiastical and perhaps personal universe. When he sat down in 1882 to draft an account of the key moments of his own life, the first entries were Cullen's translation to Dublin in 1852 and his subsequent enthronement.[116] In his diary, Power carefully noted every meeting he had or letter he received from Cullen, and he was in the habit of celebrating Mass for Cullen to mark his birthday.[117] When the 'sad Telegram' arrived in October 1878 announcing Cullen's death, Power immediately ordered a collection to honour 'the memory of our great and beloved Cardinal' and to mark his own 'lifelong indebtedness to the large-hearted and most saintly Archbishop of Dublin'. Cullen, Power wrote, had been Newfoundland's 'ever vigilant protector'.[118]

Yet Cullen had originally intended to send Power to New Zealand, something Power himself only became aware of in June 1869 when he heard a rumour that Cullen had nominated him for Auckland.[119] By November, it was correctly rumoured in Ireland that Cullen instead wanted him appointed coadjutor bishop of Wellington.[120] In a striking example of the interconnectedness of Greater Ireland, in late March 1870

---

[113] R. W. Rothman to Power, 7 May 1852, ARCSJ, Thomas Power papers [PP], 105/1/2.

[114] James Walshe to Cullen, 6 July 1852, DDA/CP/325/4/II/42.

[115] Richard Sherry, *Holy Cross College, Clonliffe, Dublin, 1859–1959* (Dublin: Holy Cross College, 1959), 48.

[116] 'Memorandum of the Life of Bishop Power to 1870', 29 August 1882, ARCSJ/PP/ 105/ 1/2.

[117] Diary of Thomas Power, ARCSJ/PP/105/2/2.

[118] Power Diary, 25 October 1878; Power to O'Reilly, 13 January 1879, DDA/CP/44/I/VII/ 14. This is a cutting of a public letter printed in an unknown newspaper.

[119] Power Diary, 22 November 1877. This is a long autobiographical entry, in which Power notes that on 14 June 1869 'it was proposed to me to go to Auckland New Zealand'.

[120] See Lillian G. Keys, *Philip Viard: Bishop of Wellington* (Christchurch: Pegasus Press, 1968), 218.

the *Wellington Independent* reported that the *Charleston Herald* of South Carolina had revealed that 'the celebrated Dr Power' had told the local bishop that he had been offered Wellington.[121] As we shall see in Chapter 7, the incumbent Marists fought hard and were ultimately successful in preventing this. In fact, when Conroy first suggested Power for St John's in February 1870, it was because Wellington was now 'doubtful'.[122] There seems to have been no great enthusiasm for the idea; three days after he recommended Power, Conroy was wondering if his friend John Cameron 'now in Nova Scotia would make a good Bp for Newfoundland'; but Cameron was a Scot, and on balance an 'Irishman would be better'.[123] There also appears to have been a sense in Dublin that it was time for Power to move on, not least because his vice rector at Clonliffe was Cullen's nephew, Michael Verdon, and Cullen's relatives often experienced rapid and if necessary ruthless promotion. Yet with Rome consumed by the council, things moved slowly; 'Newfoundland, New Zealand in status quo idem Armagh', Cullen complained in early February.[124] He left Power's name with the Propaganda when he went home for Easter.

When he came back, Power had been selected.[125] Conroy was pleased: the appointment was a 'happy solution of the question as to whether regulars or seculars are to rule the Church' in Newfoundland.[126] The Franciscans unsurprisingly disagreed: the Irish Franciscan bishop of Adelaide, Laurence Sheil, lamented that despite their hard work St John's 'is gone from the Irish Province'.[127] Meanwhile, a 'grateful' Power headed for Rome.[128] He was consecrated in the Irish College by Cullen on 12 June, took his seat in the Vatican Council the next day, and 'on the 18th June voted for the Infallibility of the Pope'.[129] Cullen immediately appointed Verdon as his replacement.[130]

Harbour Grace was different, and to the astonishment of everybody its new bishop was to be Enrico Carfagnini. How this came about is unclear: Cullen told Tobias Kirby in early 1871 that he did not know who had

---

121 *Wellington Independent*, 31 March 1870. See also Michael O'Meeghan, *Steadfast in Hope: The Story of the Catholic Archdiocese of Wellington, 1850–2000* (Palmerston North: Dunmore Press, 2003), 101–2.
122 Conroy to Cullen, 25 February 1870, DDA/CP/321/7/4/20.
123 Conroy to Cullen, 28 February 1870, DDA/CP/321/7/4/20.
124 Cullen to Conroy, 'St Agatha's Day' [5 February] 1870, ARDA/CP/1870 5/2.
125 Cullen to Conroy, 7 May 1870, ARDA/CP/1870 7/5.
126 Conroy to Cullen, 13 May [1870], DDA/CP/321/7/4/38.
127 Sheil to Reville, 5 May 1870, ACAA, Sheil papers [SP], Series 36, Box 1, Folder 8. This is a copy of the original, which appears to be held elsewhere.
128 Conroy to Cullen, 13 May [1870], DDA/CP/321/7/4/38.
129 Power Diary, 22 November 1877.
130 Cullen to McCabe, 23 May 1870, DDA/CP/40/4.

recommended Carfagnini, or why the decision had been made. 'I was at home at Easter when this Bishop was appointed', he wrote, 'so I had nothing to say to the matter.'[131] Carfagnini had made himself useful in Harbour Grace, but on Dalton's death had fallen into a dispute about money and returned to Italy. It appears he owed his nomination to a single letter from a Newfoundland priest named Bernard Duffy, who praised the Italian's work at St Bonaventure's and in the construction of the Harbour Grace cathedral, but omitted his suspension and expulsion by Mullock.[132] (Duffy was rewarded with the parish of Brigus, where he lived with his niece and employed his nephew as curate.)[133] With no one to ask, and no other information, the Propaganda made the appointment. In a mere five years, Carfagnini had risen from *vagabondi* to bishop.

Neither man had much chance to enjoy Rome. Cullen was keen that Power depart quickly, as he had received letters from St John's that gave a 'deplorable picture' of the state of affairs in the absence of a bishop: among other things, the episcopal palace had apparently been 'converted into a drinking club'. The chief offender appeared to be Richard Howley, the Roman educated but drunkard brother of Michael. 'Dr Power', Cullen continued, 'will have no bed of roses.' He hoped that if Power could take with him 'two good priests' and make the entire Newfoundland clergy go on a retreat 'he might get things into working order'.[134]

The new bishop arrived in St John's in early September. He was delighted by his reception, marvelling to Cullen that 'nothing could surpass the enthusiasm of the people'. They were the 'best dressed people I have ever seen', ate meat every day, and were 'prepared to do everything for Pastors and Nuns'. The cathedral was vast, and the convents and episcopal palace superior to anything in Ireland. Power quickly realized the social and political importance of his position, receiving visits from numerous politicians, the Anglican bishop, and a representative of the governor. He was also largely pleased with the clergy, with only six of twenty-six 'not models'. (The dissolute Richard Howley was quietly encouraged to continue his career in the United States.)[135] Yet Power did not forget home: when meeting each of his priests, he ensured that they toasted 'the health of our own Cardinal'.[136]

[131] Cullen to Kirby, 15 January 1871, PICRA/NK/3/3/55.
[132] Hans Rollmann and Matteo Sanfilippo, 'Carfagnini, Enrico', in *DCB*.
[133] Power to Cullen, 19 March 1873, DDA/CP/335/1/8.
[134] Cullen to Conroy, 3 June 1870, ARDA/CP.
[135] Power to Cullen, 'Feast of St. Columbanus' DDA/CP/321/7/2/49.
[136] Power to Cullen, 14 September 1870, DDA/CP/321/7/2/24.

Power's first concern was to provide for the isolated and more ethnically diverse west coast, which had been badly neglected by a parish priest whose primary interest had been pecuniary. He asked Cullen to secure Roman approval for a prefect apostolic for 'that abandoned country' and suggested Thomas Sears, a Nova Scotia priest originally from Co. Kerry, who was already on loan to the region.[137] When Power himself visited the coast in 1871, he was greeted with such enthusiasm that 'in a short time the whole circuit of the bay was decorated with flags of all colours & guns were fired off from all directions'. This nearly proved disastrous, an accompanying Michael Howley recalled, as in the excitement 'The Bp ran a great risk of having his head blown off with every step.'[138] St George's became a vicariate in 1892 and Newfoundland's third diocese in 1904.

In St John's, Power immediately began the magnificent liturgical celebrations for which he became known. Writing in December 1870, he boasted to Cullen that the cathedral was filled to capacity for the Triduum of the Immaculate Conception: 'Protestants came in great numbers – & they hear all about Blessed Peter's Primacy, & Pius IX, & the Immaculate Mother.'[139] A week later he held a collection for the pope ('Pius the Great') and a protest at the Italian seizure of Rome.[140] He forwarded the £1,000 raised to Dublin. Cullen was delighted, remarking that Power 'will do a great deal of good, at all events he has commenced well by asserting the Pope's rights'.[141] The subventions continued, with £725 sent to Rome in 1877, for example.[142]

As with all Hiberno-Roman bishops, grand liturgies and papalism were accompanied by a concern for education and a desire to impose social controls. Almost as soon as he arrived in Newfoundland, Power 'manifested his anxiety for the welfare and religious advancement of the Catholic young men' and as a result founded the St Joseph's Society, which soon merged with the existing Catholic Institute to form the St Joseph's Catholic Institute. It had a library and a reading room and required its members to approach the sacraments on specified occasions.[143] On 8 December 1873, the entire diocese was consecrated

---

[137] Power to Cullen, 27 October 1870, DDA/CP/321/7/2/38.
[138] Diary of M. F. Howley, 1871–1883, ARCSJ, Howley papers [HP], 106/12/2.
[139] Power to Cullen, 7 October 1870, DDA/CP/321/7/2/52.
[140] Power to Cullen, 27 October 1870, DDA/CP/321/7/2/38.
[141] Cullen to Kirby, 15 January 1871, PICRA/NK/3/3/55.
[142] Kirby to Power, 20 December 1877, ARCSJ/PP/105/1/6.
[143] 'Rules and constitutions of St. Joseph's Catholic Institute' (*Newfoundlander* Office, 1872). A copy may be consulted at the Centre for Newfoundland Studies, Memorial University of Newfoundland.

to the sacred heart.[144] Two years later, Power succeeded where Fleming and Mullock had failed, securing Irish Christian Brothers for St Bonaventure's College. They soon took over the BIS's schools, replacing the existing OAS building with the purpose-built St Patrick's Hall.[145] In time, the brothers also opened several orphanages, including the now-infamous Mt Cashel. The Sisters of Mercy expanded as well, both within St John's and to isolated Burin on the south coast.

An already distinctively Irish church became yet more so. Power worked closely, for example, with the BIS as they planned the celebrations of the centenary of Daniel O'Connell's birth in August 1875. These included speeches, food, dancing, and a parade led by the BIS but including Mechanics' Society, the Phoenix and Cathedral Volunteer Fire Brigades, the Total Abstinence and Juvenile Benefit Societies, the Star of the Sea Association, and the St Joseph's Catholic Institute.[146] In 1880, Power threw himself into a campaign to relieve Irish poverty, ultimately securing some £2,000, which he sent directly to Dublin.[147] St Patrick's Day celebrations were a fixture of Catholic life. But it was education that mattered most, and that was now wholly in the hands of Irish orders.

Power's greatest challenge was his fellow bishop. Given his history, there was little reason to suppose that Carfagnini would prove to be anything other than a disaster, but he quickly exceeded all expectations. In Harbour Grace, one Irish nun wrote, the appointment was 'like a thunderbolt on all when the report was first spread that he got the Mitre. Not one could believe it.'[148] The diocesan administrator promptly appealed to Kirby, but other letters – apparently organized by Carfagnini – had also arrived, and having made the appointment the Propaganda decided to let things stand.[149] Most alarmed were the Presentation nuns who had established a convent and school in Harbour Grace in 1851. Among them was M. Xaverius Lynch, one of the pioneers who had come to Newfoundland in 1831 and now mother superior. Fortunately for her community, she was also the sister of James Lynch, one of the founders of the Irish Vincentians and later Cullen's spectacularly unsuccessful choice for the western district of Scotland and

[144] *Newfoundlander*, 9 December 1873.   [145] Veitch, 93–4.

[146] *Centenary Volume: Benevolent Irish Society, St. John's Newfoundland* (Cork: n.p., 1906), 218–20.

[147] Mannion, 'The Irish diaspora in comparative perspective: St. John's, Newfoundland, Halifax, Nova Scotia, and Portland, Maine, 1880–1923', unpublished PhD diss., University of Toronto', 149–50.

[148] M. Xaverius Lynch to James Lynch, 27 October 1870, DDA/CP/321/1/4/46(2)b.

[149] Kirby to [?Moran], 13 December [1870], DDA/CP/64/15/6(2).

then coadjutor bishop of Kildare and Leighlin. In writing to her brother, Lynch knew she was writing to Cullen.

Even before Carfagnini had arrived, Lynch was sending her brother information that the nuns 'should wish very much to have the Cardinal acquainted with'. The Italian, she wrote, had been the sole 'promoter' of the testimonials he had received on leaving Harbour Grace, and which had been used in Rome to discredit reports of his unpopularity there. He had been in the habit of extorting money from parishioners and intimidating his servants, and 'In fact I would never end if I were to tell you all the queer stories that every man, woman and even the very children have about him.' He hardly spoke English, and was altogether unsuitable 'to govern a flock composed of Irish or the descendents of Irish'. It was little wonder that the people were 'ready to rebel at getting such a Pastor'. The 'only hope we have now', Lynch concluded, 'is that when everything is known at Rome he may be removed ... oh do pray for us and get the Cardinal to use all the influence he has for us to get him removed from us.'[150]

In St John's, there was consternation because Carfagnini's appointment had been accompanied by a decision to detach two parishes and give them to Harbour Grace. To Cullen, Power reported that he had advised his priests that complaining was futile, but 'They reply no: we will write to Cardinal Cullen & get him to revoke the sentence.' He hopefully left the matter in Cullen's 'keeping'. As for his relations with Carfagnini, Power thought there could be 'no peace – only a *strict neutrality*'.[151] If Carfagnini himself was in any doubt about his likely reception he was quickly disillusioned. In Harbour Grace itself there was little enthusiasm at his arrival, and the Presentations did not illuminate their convent in welcome. His reception in the two new parishes was 'chilling'. Worse, Power had visited the same parishes a few weeks before and had found seven miles of road 'decorated with arches & filled with demonstrative crowds'. There was little wonder that Carfagnini might have 'felt sore about it', and according to Power he 'concocted' for the newspapers a wholly false account of an enthusiastic reception.[152] He also set out to stamp his authority on the diocese and exact revenge, starting with the nuns.

The sisters, Carfagnini told Lynch, 'had become the instrument of discord' in Harbour Grace. He demanded that they promise in writing to 'perform my will', 'never again fall into errors of similar nature', never keep anything from him, and 'not rely for support on the influence of

---

[150] M. Xaverius Lynch to James Lynch, 27 October 1870, DDA/CP/321/1/4/46(2)a.
[151] Power to Cullen, 27 October 1870, DDA/CP/321/7/2/38. Emphasis in original.
[152] Power to Cullen, 7 December 1870, DDA/CP/321/7/2/52.

others'.[153] He followed this up with an aggressive visitation, in which he lined the nuns up, made them kiss his pectoral cross, and then questioned them individually, in some cases for hours. Resistance was met with fury and 'Neapolitan excitement'.[154] He assigned an Italian confessor and placed an effective interdict on the convent. Cullen was appalled, telling Kirby that Carfagnini was likely to 'occasion a schism unless the Propaganda interfere'. He arranged for a portion of Lynch's letter to be translated and given to the Propaganda.[155]

Carfagnini was summoned to Rome and denied everything. There was little chance that nuns would be sustained against the word of a bishop, and they were not. The Propaganda asked Cullen to have Bishop Lynch instruct the sisters to show 'obedience and respect towards their bishop'; Lynch wrote 'a very strong letter' to his sister; and she in turn promised that her community 'was resolved to do all in their power to keep on terms of peace and submission'.[156] Cullen dismissed the matter. Carfagnini did not know how to deal with either nuns or Irish, he wrote, but it was 'not my affair'.[157] The wonder is that their appeal reached as far as it did.

Yet Carfagnini now knew that the sisters were peculiarly well connected, and this made him cautious. As Lynch reported in June 1873, since his return from Rome he had not interfered with the convent, entered it, or held a visitation.[158] He instead turned his attention to those who supported it. The struggle took on an increasingly ethnic cast as Carfagnini began to import Italian Franciscans and drive out Irish priests who showed sympathy to the nuns. He also attacked the local Benevolent Irish Society, which he held to be insufficiently deferential. He claimed authority to dissolve it, excommunicated its members, and suspended two Irish priests who were associated with it. He then reconstituted the society with members prepared to pledge their loyalty to him. The two priests fled to Dublin, and Cullen urged the Propaganda to call Carfagnini 'to a strict account for his absurdity'. 'The poor Irish fishermen are very good', he sighed, 'and it is a sad thing to persecute them.'[159] In St John's, Power had to defuse the rage of the local BIS by promising

[153] Carfagnini to 'Revd Mother' [M. Xaverius Lynch], 'Friday Evening' [1870], DDA/CP/321/7/2/59.
[154] M. Xaverius Lynch, undated memorandum of Carfagnini's visitation to the Harbour Grace convent, probably November or December 1870, DDA/CP/41/4/V/6.
[155] Cullen to Kirby, 15 January 1871, PICRA/NK/3/3/55.
[156] Cullen to Kirby, 3 September 1872, PICRA/KP/27/227; Lynch to Cullen, 10 March 1873, DDA/CP/335/4/I/64.
[157] Cullen to Kirby, 3 September 1872, PICRA/KP/27/227.
[158] 'Rev. Mother and her community' to Propaganda, 12 June 1873, DDA/CP/335/8/4/1.
[159] Cullen to an unknown correspondent, 23 April 1874, DDA/CP. The recipient was most likely Tobias Kirby.

that the matter had 'been sent to the highest ecclesiastical tribunal for solution'.[160]

By late 1875, the Propaganda had had enough and they summoned both bishops to Rome. The accident-prone Power made a poor impression, not least by staying in a luxury hotel while Carfagnini lodged at St Isidore's. On 16 December, the congregation decided that Carfagnini would be sent back to Harbour Grace, but only to 'maintain the Episcopal authority'. After a decent interval he would be translated elsewhere. Patrick Moran, who was on the spot representing Cullen and assisting his old friend Power, didn't believe a word of it ('*A questo pero non ci credo per niente*').[161] The problem was that the balance of power in the Propaganda had changed with Alessandro Barnabò's death in early 1874. His successor was Alessandro Franchi, a papal diplomat with no previous experience of the Propaganda. To him, Cullen was just another cardinal, albeit a dangerously influential one. As Moran put it, Franchi 'retains a little of his old diplomatic character in his new Missionary post', having told Moran before the meeting that it was settled that Carfagnini would be removed, 'However, non respondit eventus.' Moran thought Franchi had put Power's statements about Harbour Grace 'in quarantine', and Power hadn't helped matters by being poorly prepared and unable to speak either Italian or French.[162]

In an attempt to retrieve the situation, Moran submitted a 'short but very strong Memorandum' in Cullen's name. After conversations with various officials, it emerged that Power had undersold his case while Carfagnini had gone on the offensive against Power's rule in St John's. The Propaganda had come to the conclusion that if one bishop were to be censured so should the other. Moran did at least extract a renewed assurance that Carfagnini's return would be short-lived and he would in the meantime be urged to act with 'kindness towards the Irish'.[163] The only positive was a declaration that the Conception Bay BIS was not an ecclesiastical society, and thus Carfagnini had had no right to dissolve it.[164] Franchi had achieved his aim: Cullen's hold over the Propaganda had been broken, and seen to be broken. The implications were quickly absorbed from Ontario to New Zealand.

In Newfoundland, there was now open war. As one St John's lawyer wrote to Cullen, on a recent visit to the city Carfagnini had 'attempted to spread into the Flock of St John's the disorders that infect the Harbour

---

[160] Power to Morris, 17 April 1874, quoted in *Centenary Volume: Benevolent Irish Society, St. John's Newfoundland*, 216.
[161] Moran to Cullen, 16 December 1875, DDA/CP/40/6/II/46.   [162] Ibid.
[163] Moran to Cullen, 18 December 1875, DDA/CP/40/6/II/47.
[164] *Centenary Volume: Benevolent Irish Society, St. John's Newfoundland*, 216.

Grace Church'.[165] In 1877, George Conroy reported that to avoid meeting the bishops had travelled by separate steamers to the consecration of the new archbishop of Halifax and while there had 'scandalized all by their want of charity'. The priests and laity were as divided, and Conroy worried the ultimate result would be 'a fight and bloodshed'. By this stage even Cullenites like Conroy thought Power had handled things poorly: 'I fear both Bps are to blame', he wrote, 'but Dr Carfagnini most of all.'[166]

Conroy was in Halifax in his capacity as apostolic delegate to Canada, the story of which properly belongs to Chapter 5. Although Newfoundland was not his assignment he agreed to become involved at Power's request, and much to his pleasure.[167] It was a thankless task: Conroy's old friend John Cameron of Antigonish, Nova Scotia, for example, did not envy him 'his mission to the refractory belligerents of Newfoundland'.[168] As Power's original invitation miscarried (or was diplomatically lost), Conroy was unable to deal with Newfoundland until he had finished with Canada.[169] He finally arrived in St John's in the early summer of 1878, and promptly fell gravely ill. Power immediately informed Cullen by telegraph.[170] In late July, he reported Conroy was doing much better, but Cullen still wanted the Propaganda to order him home immediately.[171]

Power meticulously recorded the course of Conroy's illness in his diary: very serious through the first half of July, then steady improvement through early August; but then, on 4 August,

I visited the Delegate [Conroy] – found him in good spirits. At 12 spent some time with him. He was wonderful well – at 2 was with him – read & talked until 3. He was never more buoyant. At 4 went to dinner. Dr Carfagnini visited the Delegate – after his departure the Nun in attendance noted a change in his Excellency – at 5 ½ doctors were sent for – Symptoms became alarming – he recd Extreme Unction – & to our unutterable consternation & grief he died about 6pm!![172]

Although no allegation was ever made, Power's suspicion shines through the entry, and there is an oral tradition in St John's that

[165] G. Conroy to Cullen, 27 July 1876, DDA/CP/322/7/I/9. Conroy was a partner in the St John's firm Boone & Conroy. It is unclear if he was related to Bishop Conroy.
[166] Conroy to Cullen, 21 May 1877, DDA/CP/329/1/IV/10.
[167] Power to Cullen, 5 September 1877, DDA/CP/329/2/I/26.
[168] Cameron to E. A. Tascherau, 3 June 1878, Antigonish Diocesan Archives [ADA], Fonds 3, series 1, sub series 1. This is a copy of the original held in the Archives of the Archdiocese of Quebec.
[169] Conroy to Power, 29 November 1877, ARCSJ/PP/105/1/6.
[170] Cullen to Kirby, n.d. [July 1878], PICRA/NK/5/1/47.
[171] Cullen to Kirby, 2 August 1878, PICRA/NK/5/1/50.
[172] Power diary, 4 August 1878.

Carfagnini had somehow murdered Conroy, who he knew to be a Cullenite and friend of Power.[173] However fantastical, it was a sign of how far relations between Carfagnini and the Irish had fallen, and what the Italian was thought capable of. There is also the sneaking suspicion that he just might have done it. At all events, Power accompanied the body back to Ireland, but not before delivering a eulogy that focussed more on Cullen's virtues than Conroy's life.[174] As for Carfagnini, he picked fresh fights with the BIS and the Presentations, and the Propaganda finally forced him to resign. As a consolation he was made bishop of Gallipoli in Italy in 1880, ultimately dying in 1898 as an archbishop.[175] It is astonishing that no one has based a novel on his life.

Thomas Power continued on in St John's until his death in 1893. He kept a much lower profile than either of his predecessors or his successor, but was perhaps not quite as politically inert as Hans Rollmann has suggested.[176] Although his only substantive public intervention came in 1878, when he defended the conduct of Irish Catholics involved in a sectarian riot, his surviving diaries suggest regular private meetings with politicians.[177] He was also prepared to both vote for and support as premier the Anglican ex-Conservative Charles Bennett, although at first only in aid of his peculiar anti-confederation alliance of Protestant merchants and Catholics worried about the fate of home rule in an expanded Canada. The obituary in the St John's *Evening Herald* caught Power well, remarking on his 'exalted views of ecclesiastical discipline and decorum', the magnificent music and liturgy of the cathedral, and his training by 'one of the foremost church dignitaries of the day, the late Cardinal Cullen'.[178] He would have been satisfied with that.

Power's successor was Michael Francis Howley, who had been first considered for the job in 1870. Born in St John's in 1843 to prosperous Irish parents, his education was typical of the second generation of Hiberno-Roman bishops across Greater Ireland: a local education (in Howley's case at St Bonaventure's) followed by the Propaganda and the Irish College. He inevitably adored Rome, eagerly copying in his journal everything from ancient inscriptions to Italian poetry to the 'Song of the Zouaves for Pius IX'.[179] After ordination in 1868, his connections earned him an immediate posting as secretary to the newly appointed

---

[173] In conversation with the author, the then-archivist of the archdiocese of St John's recalled being told the story by an elderly priest.

[174] *The Morning Chronicle*, 'August' 1878.   [175] Rollmann and Sanfilippo, 'Carfagnini'.

[176] Hans Rollmann, 'Power, Thomas Joseph', in *DCB*.

[177] See, for example, Power to Sir John Glover, 22 January 1878, ARCSJ/PP/105/1/19.

[178] *The Evening Herald*, 5 December 1893.

[179] M. F. Howley, Journal for 1864, ARCSJ/HP/106/12a/1.

administrator of the western district of Scotland. After a visit home in 1869, Howley returned to Rome for the Vatican Council where he was recruited by Power. In Newfoundland, he proved to be an active, indeed too active, priest. On his appointment as prefect apostolic at St George's in 1886, for example, an Irish Christian Brother observed that neither Power nor the Sisters of Mercy were sorry to see him go: the bishop apparently thought him 'a little tart and busy', while the mother superior 'found him a little inconvenient in the planning and regulating of her new orphanage'.[180] Howley threw himself into life on the west coast, importing Sisters of Mercy from Rhode Island and becoming the spokesman for local opposition to British concessions to French treaty claims.[181] In 1892, St George's became a vicariate and Howley the first Newfoundland-born bishop.[182]

Howley is now primarily remembered as a Newfoundland nationalist. In addition to his *Ecclesiastical History*, he published scholarly studies of the journeys of Cabot and Cartier, investigated Newfoundland place names, and produced a volume of poetry. His rousingly patriotic 'The Flag of Newfoundland' (1903) was promptly set to music and is still performed. Unlike Power, he took an overt interest in politics; like Power, and more willingly than Fleming or Mullock, he was prepared to cross confessional lines to secure what he understood to be the best interests of Newfoundland in general and Catholics in particular. Howley was, for example, 'deeply grateful to God' for the electoral success of the patrician Methodist Robert Bond, for which he 'had no scruple in having the prayers of the Church offered up in sincere thanksgiving', and he was happy to urge that Bond thwart the Irish Catholic populist Edward Morris.[183] Yet at the same time he successfully claimed the right to select the 'Catholic' members of the executive council, whom he believed 'should have the full confidence of the Head of the Denomination to which they belong'.[184] He also bitterly attacked the self-publicizing Labrador doctor Wilfred Grenfell and denounced William Coaker's Fishermen's Protective Union on the grounds it was a secret society likely

---

[180] Fleming to Holland, 20 January 1886, quoted in Bellamy, 175.
[181] For the whole complicated issue, see Frederic F. Thompson, *The French Shore Problem in Newfoundland* (Toronto: Toronto University Press, 1961).
[182] Barbara A. Crosbie, 'Howley, Michael Francis', in *DCB*.
[183] Howley to Bond, 16 November, 28 November 1900, Archives and Special Collections, Queen Elizabeth II Library, Memorial University of Newfoundland [MUN], Bond papers [BP], Coll-237, 3.19.009.
[184] Howley to Bond, 16 November, MUN/BP. For more on the political climate in which Bond and Howley were operating, see S. J. R. Noel's *Politics in Newfoundland* (Toronto: University of Toronto Press, 1971).

to diminish clerical influence.[185] Howley was first and foremost
a Catholic bishop, and not simply what Sean Cadigan described as 'a
member of St. John's non-sectarian nationalist intelligentsia'.[186]

In fact, Michael Howley held four distinct identities with no difficulty
or apparent contradiction: he was Catholic; he was Irish; he was
a Newfoundlander; and he was a citizen of the British Empire. His
Catholicism was of course unquestioned, and between Irish and
Newfoundlander he made no material distinction.[187] He drew, for example, a direct comparison between Ireland's struggle for home rule and
Newfoundland's attempts to gain full control of its territory along the
French Shore, and he also spoke Irish and was interested in his family's
heritage.[188] As early as 1869, he gave a St Patrick's day sermon in which
he decried Ireland's 'centuries of oppression' and boasted of its spiritual
empire.[189]

Howley was also loyal to the British Empire, but not necessarily to the
United Kingdom, let alone to England. While he helped establish the
Catholic Cadet Corps in 1896, for example, he offered only tepid support
to the war in South Africa, remarking that the supposed sufferings of
British subjects in the Transvaal were mild compared to the continuing
denial of Irish self-determination.[190] Yet in 1914 he embraced the imperial war effort and urged Catholics to enlist. In both his conditional loyalty
to the Empire and enthusiasm for the Great War, Howley was typical of
his brethren. Throughout Greater Ireland, the aggressively Anglophobic
Irish republicanism of Melbourne's pugnacious Daniel Mannix was the
exception, Howley's imperial loyalty the rule; and just as the American
bishops' discovery of the benefits of constitutional liberty fed their
American patriotism, so the freedoms Irish Catholics enjoyed in
Britain's empire allowed Irish nationalism and Imperial patriotism to
comfortably coexist.

The elevation of St John's to an archdiocese in 1904 finally guaranteed
the island's ecclesiastical independence, and under Howley
Newfoundland Catholicism began to slowly indigenize. Shortly before
he was appointed, none of the priests serving in St John's itself had been
born on the island, and only 41 per cent of the twenty-eight in the diocese
as a whole. By 1911, 63 per cent of priests in the city and 66 per cent in the

---

[185] Among other things, he accused Grenfell of selling children and being an incompetent
surgeon. See ARCSJ/HP/106/23/7. For his attitude to the FPU, Crosbie, 'Howley'.
[186] Cadigan, 155.
[187] Carolyn Lambert, 'This sacred feeling: Patriotism, nation-building and the Catholic
Church in Newfoundland, 1850–1914', in Colin Barr and Hilary M. Carey (eds.),
Religion and Greater Ireland: Christianity and Irish Global Networks, 1750–1850
(Montreal and Kingston: McGill-Queen's University Press, 2015).
[188] Ibid.   [189] Howley, *Sermon*, 22.   [190] Lambert, 'This sacred feeling'.

diocese were Newfoundlanders. Yet this does not necessarily imply a decline in Irish influence; Patrick Mannion's analysis of the education of the nineteen priests serving St John's city between 1881 and 1921, for example, reveals that six were trained in Ireland, seven in Rome, two elsewhere in Europe, and only four in Canada. Lacking a native seminary, St John's made an unusual (although not unique) arrangement to send local seminarians directly to All Hallows for training.[191] Many of the Irish-born also followed that route, with at least thirty-two priests departing Drumcondra for Newfoundland by 1892. Carlow College sent a further thirteen to St John's and one each to St George's and Harbour Grace before 1922.[192]

Administratively, the two eastern dioceses of St John's and Harbour Grace continued to look to Ireland. As one priest recalled in 1902 in answer to a query about his devotional and administrative practice, 'As far as I know and believe the custom was that the Diocese was considered all along as if it were a branch of the Irish Church.'[193] On the west coast, geography and demography dictated that St George's began to draw closer to Canada. Howley's successor there was the Cape Breton–born Neil McNeil, who eventually became archbishop of Vancouver and then Toronto. He was succeeded by an Irish Newfoundlander.[194] Throughout Newfoundland, social barriers were high and impermeable, and social controls meticulously enforced. Behind these barriers was a Catholic community that was and remained the most Irish in Ireland's Empire. As the Canadian columnist Rex Murphy remarked, remembering the pervasive religiosity of his childhood, Newfoundland 'in the 1950s could have been certain parts of Ireland in the 1920s'.[195]

---

[191] Mannion, 'The Irish diaspora in comparative perspective', 146–8. At least two New Zealand seminarians were sent to All Hallows in the 1910s.

[192] Figures compiled by Mary Carmichael.

[193] J. Conroy to Howley, 4 December 1902, ARCSJ/HP/106/24/8.

[194] Mark McGowan, '"Pregnant with perils": Canadian Catholicism and its relation to the Catholic Churches of Newfoundland, 1840–1949', *Newfoundland and Labrador Studies*, vol. 28, no. 2 (Fall 2013), 193–218, at 203.

[195] Rex Murphy, 'How Trudeau's trendy "pro-choice" secularism became the left's new religion', *National Post*, 24 May 2014.

3 India

When Thomas Babington Macaulay arrived in Madras in 1834, he was surprised to discover that his 'half-caste' servant was a Catholic.[1] Despite Macaulay's apprehensions, they got on well. Not only could he 'speak the native languages' but he could also 'dispute a charge, bully a negligent bearer, arrange a bed, and make a curry'. 'His name, which I never hear without laughing, is Peter Prim.'[2] As Macaulay had discovered, Catholicism was native to India. Its earliest adherents claimed descent from the apostle Thomas, who was said to have made converts among the Jews of the Malabar Coast before finding martyrdom in AD 74. More likely, the community was the result of Nestorian missionary activity emanating from Baghdad in the sixth century or earlier. The St Thomas Christians – as they are now known – retained both their theology and their Syriac liturgy in relative isolation until the Portuguese arrived in the early sixteenth century.[3] They sought to bring them to the Latin rite and Roman communion, never completely succeeded, and instead built their own community at Goa and other possessions along the western coast. In 1553, Goa became a diocese and five years later an archdiocese. A series of agreements with Rome ensured the ecclesiastical supremacy of the Portuguese crown, a right that came to be known as the *padroado*, and by the nineteenth century there were four 'Portuguese' dioceses in India. Yet the relationship was never an easy one, and papal displeasure at Lisbon's waning evangelical enthusiasm contributed first to the establishment of the Propaganda Fide in 1622 and

---

[1] Throughout this chapter, I have chosen to use the nineteenth-century English names of Indian cities.

[2] Quoted in George Otto Trevelyan, *The Life and Letters of Lord Macaulay*, 2 vols., new ed. (London: Longmans, Green, & Co., 1878), 1: 372.

[3] There is an older but still useful history of the St Thomas Christians from the sixteenth century onwards: L. W. Brown, *The Indian Christians of St. Thomas: An Account of the Ancient Syrian Church of Malabar* (Cambridge: Cambridge University Press, 1956).

then to the creation of an entirely separate series of missions in India. By 1834, there were also four vicariates answerable to Rome.[4]

The situation was further complicated by the residual presence of the French in Pondicherry, where a bishop (but not a vicar apostolic) had long been based with responsibility for both the French enclaves and French missionary activity across southern India. There was also a long-standing Italian clerical presence in Bombay and Kerala associated with the Discalced Carmelites, and Jesuits of various nationalities were active in both the south and the far north. There were Portuguese and Spanish Augustinians in Calcutta and French and then Italian Capuchins in Madras. By 1857, this patchwork served some 801,858 Catholics across British India, of whom 16,000 were European soldiers.[5] The native Catholics were roughly grouped into the St Thomas Christians (or Syrians), Portuguese (or Goanese), and mostly Tamil converts of the various French missionary campaigns. Many smaller groups were scattered across the subcontinent.[6] As the Irish vicar general of Madras put it, 'The Catholic body in India includes persons of all classes and conditions – European, East Indian, and native; the great bulk, however, especially in Southern India, is made up of native cultivators, a miserable, ill-used class.' By 1857, they were served by 16 bishops and 736 priests, 397 of whom were of the Syrian rite.[7]

The peculiar example of the Begum Sombre illustrates the stunning variety of Indian Catholicism. Her real name was Farazan or Farazana, and she was a Muslim courtesan of uncertain origins.[8] Around 1765, she found herself in the household of Walter Reinhardt, a German Catholic brigand who had sold his services to most of the rulers of northern India.[9] He eventually settled at Sardhana, to the north of Delhi, where he turned a feudal land grant into a small state. Farazan somehow emerged as Sardhana's ruler, which she remained for more than sixty years under the name Begum Sombre, artfully avoiding British annexation and amassing great wealth. She was an enthusiastic patron of the Catholic Church,

---

[4] For a summary, see Thomas Anchukandam, *The First Synod of Pondicherry 1844: A Study Based on Archival Sources* (Bangalore: Kristu Jyoti Publications, 1994), 10–15.

[5] *Madras Catholic Directory*, quoted in Stephen Fennelly, *Relations of the Catholic Church in India with the Honourable the East India Company's Government* (Dublin: James Duffy, 1857), 4.

[6] There is a useful contemporary survey, with estimated populations, in the *Annals of the Propagation of the Faith*, vol. 1 (July 1839–November 1840) (London, 1840), 139–46. Hereafter *ANPF*.

[7] Fennelly, 4–5.

[8] The most recent study of this fascinating figure is by the late Susan Keay, *Farazana: The Woman Who Saved an Empire* (London: I.B.Tauris, 2014).

[9] Michael H. Fisher, *The Inordinately Strange Life of Dyce Sombre: Victorian Anglo-Indian MP and Chancery 'Lunatic'* (London: C. Hurst & Co., 2010), 14.

building what an astonished Irish Jesuit described as a 'splendid cathedral' 210 feet long, 165 feet wide, with a dome 100 feet high. Its pulpit
was made from a single marble slab.[10] In 1835, she gave Pope Gregory
XVI $70,000, and he in turn erected Sardhana into a vicariate and
elevated the improbably named Julius Caesar Scotti, her Italian
Capuchin chaplain, to the rank of bishop. His sole congregation was the
Begum and her servants.[11] On her death, she left another vast sum, this
time to the Irish vicar apostolic of Calcutta who dispersed it throughout
India to support seminary education; Bombay's share alone was 31,800
rupees (about £3,700).[12] Yet the Begum also gave the archbishop of
Canterbury £5,000, built an Anglican chapel, and endowed the
Anglican Bishop's College in Calcutta.[13] Although there is no reason to
doubt the Begum's private faith, her openhanded ecumenism was likely
part of a strategy to keep out of British clutches. If so, she was only partly
successful: Sardhana was annexed soon after her death. Still, Nicholas
Wiseman (the future cardinal archbishop of Westminster) pronounced
a funeral oration for her in Rome, and her first biographer was an Irish
missionary priest stationed in Sardhana.[14]

Indian Catholicism is not particularly well served by scholarship, especially in English and especially as it relates to the Irish.[15] Stephen Neill's
encyclopaedic history of Christianity on the subcontinent, for example,
gives ample space to the Catholics, but it misses or misunderstands much
about the Irish, even sending Archbishop Patrick Carew of Calcutta to his
grave some seven years prematurely.[16] The better informed works of the
clerical historians Thomas Anchukandam and George Kottuppallil stand
out for their rarity, and it is probably significant that it was thought useful
to translate Christopher Becker's 1920s volumes on Catholic missions in

[10] Edward Sinnott to John Ginnovan, [June] 1836, in Kevin Laheen, 'The Letters of an
Irish Brother, Edward Sinnott, S.J., from Calcutta, 1834–37', *Collectanea Hibernica*, nos.
46 & 47 (2004–5), 155–97 at 183.
[11] Cullen to Murray, 5 June 1835, DDA/MP/ 34/9; Sinnott to Ginnovan, [June] 1836,
Laheen, 80. Although Sinnott does not give the man's name, he was almost certainly
Scotti, an Italian Capuchin formerly on the mission to Tibet.
[12] Robert St. Leger to Pietro d'Alcantara, 20 June 1838, Archives of the Discalced
Carmelites, Clarendon Street [OCDA], Whelan papers [WP]. I am grateful to
Dr Andrew Mackillop for providing the conversion to sterling.
[13] Josiah Bateman, *The Life of the Right. Rev. Daniel Wilson, D.D., Late Lord Bishop of
Calcutta and Metropolitan of India*, 2 vols. (London: John Murray, 1860), 2: 105, 420.
For the donation to Canterbury, Stephen Neill, *A History of Christianity in India,
1707–1858* (Cambridge: Cambridge University Press, 1985), 285.
[14] William Keegan, *An Account of the Begum Sombre and Her Family* (Sirdhana: 1889).
[15] There is an important study in German based on a Roman doctoral dissertation:
Nikolaus Kowalsky, 'Die Errichtung der Apostolischen Vikariate in Indien 1834–1838
nach den Akten des Propaganda Archivs', Pontifica Universitá Urbaniana, 1950.
[16] Neill, 302.

north-east India as recently as 1989.[17] None of them dealt with the Irish except in passing. Kenneth Ballhatchet on the other hand did give the Irish of Madras extended treatment in his meticulously researched and posthumously published *Class, Caste, and Catholicism in India*, but his primary interest was the complex interactions suggested by his title. On the Irish experience in Calcutta, Bombay, or Hyderabad, he was largely silent. Even in Madras, his focus was on early conflicts and not the long period of consolidation that followed. Barry Crosbie meanwhile devoted a chapter of his study of Irish networks in India to religion, which unsurprisingly gave significant attention to the Irish Catholic Church, but this was not his primary focus, and like many scholars he did not exploit the full range of material available, particularly in Ireland.[18] Important archives such as those of the Discalced Carmelites and the Loreto Sisters, for example, have been almost uniformly overlooked, and as a result the story of Irish Catholicism in India remains largely untold.

In any event, the Irish came very late to the subcontinent and were at no time a dominant component of the Catholic population, not even of the European or Eurasian Catholic population. India is thus unique in Catholicism's Greater Ireland: not a settler colony, but with settled Catholics; never Irish, but with a substantial Irish ecclesiastical history. Although Irish influence was ultimately transient except in Madras and the south-east, the interactions of the British state and the Irish church in the religious kaleidoscope of colonial India reward sustained attention. The East India Company and then the Raj had to cope with a substantial and diverse Catholic community, mostly but by no means only in the south, with complex and shifting allegiances and radically different approaches to everything from liturgy to the perennially fraught issue of caste. To manage, the British colluded with Irish priests, bishops, and nuns, and although both Irish and Indian historians have often claimed otherwise, in India the Irish were unambiguously agents of empire. For every Irish nationalist or radical who called for Indian freedom or drew comparisons between Ireland and India, there were dozens of Irish priests

---

[17] Thomas Anchukandam, *Catholic Revival in India in the 19th century: Role of Mgr. Clément Bonnard (1796–1861)*, Vol. 1: *Up to the General Division of the Indian Missions (1845)* and Vol. 2: *From the General Division of the Indian Missions to the Death of Mgr. Bonnard* (Bangalore: Kristu Jyoti Publications, 1996, 2006); George Kottuppallil, *The History of the Catholic Missions in Central Bengal, 1855–1886* (Shillong: Vendrame Institute, 1988); Christopher Becker, *Early History of the Catholic Missions in Northeast India (1598–1890)* and *History of the Catholic Missions in Northeast India (1890–1915)* (Shillong: Vendrame Institute, 1980, 1989).

[18] Barry Crosbie, *Irish Imperial Networks: Migration, Social Communication and Exchange in Nineteenth-Century India* (Cambridge: Cambridge University Press, 2012).

and nuns, hundreds of Irish civil servants, and thousands of Irish soldiers who uncomplainingly played their part in maintaining British rule.

When it came to religion, the East India Company's priority was stability. Its officers understood the danger of religious conflict and worked assiduously to ameliorate or avoid it. As Penelope Carson has demonstrated, the company was both determinedly secular and conscientiously respectful of native religious practice.[19] As a scandalized Irish Jesuit reported from Calcutta in 1837, the 'many' Hindu and Muslim feasts were observed as government holidays but only Christmas among the Christian ones.[20] The company particularly distrusted Protestant missionaries, whose proselytizing activities were seen as potentially destabilizing. So far as it could, it discouraged their presence. Catholics were a different matter. This was not because the company was fond of papists but rather because Catholicism was largely considered an indigenous faith. Local priests were encouraged (a seminary was established at company expense in Bombay in 1828) and European ones tolerated on the grounds that, if they attempted to make converts, it was usually among other Europeans.[21] Problems arose, however, when different groups of priests and their parishioners fought among themselves, usually but not always on the pretext of conflicting loyalties to Rome or Lisbon. These long-standing conflicts became acute in Calcutta and Madras in the early 1830s and Bombay after 1840.

Although the company was inevitably dragged into ecclesiastical affairs by intra-Catholic rivalries, its overriding interest was to provide adequate spiritual support to its troops. As Thomas Bartlett put it, 'almost from the beginning of British involvement in India, the archetypal Irishman on the sub-continent was neither missionary nor merchant, neither doctor nor administrator, but soldier'.[22] By 1850, some 40 per cent of the combined armies of crown and company were Irish, and around half of those in the East India Company's army.[23] While not invariably Catholic, the bulk were. British rule in India thus depended in large part on the morale of existing Irish troops and the ability to recruit more. A refusal to provide or facilitate suitable chaplains was an unnecessary risk and not one the company or later

---

[19] Penelope Carson, *The East India Company and Religion, 1698–1858* (Woodbridge: The Boydell Press, 2012).

[20] Edward Sinnott to Robert Haly, 8 July 1837, Laheen, 194–5.

[21] Kenneth Ballhatchet, *Caste, Class and Catholicism in India 1789–1914* (Richmond: Curzon, 1998), 14–15.

[22] Thomas Bartlett, 'The Irish soldier in India, 1750–1947', in Michael Holmes and Denis Holman (eds.), *Ireland and India: Connections, Comparisons, Contrasts* (Dublin: Folens, 1997), 12.

[23] Ibid., 15.

the crown was minded to take. The Irish became adept at putting pressure on precisely this point.

Still, the catalyst for the first Irish ecclesiastical incursion into India was not soldiers but squabbling priests and embarrassed laity. In 1832, a mostly civilian group of Calcutta Catholics complained to Rome of the very public feuding of the Augustinian friars in the city. Their petition was for 'British' priests who knew or were prepared to learn local languages.[24] The Propaganda's first choice was the coadjutor vicar apostolic of the London district, Robert Gradwell, but he died without accepting in 1833.[25] It was then decided to send three British Jesuits to Calcutta, where, as Paul Cullen put it, 'religion is in a very bad state on account of the improper conduct of some Spanish friars'.[26] Ultimately, the party consisted of nine priests (seven Jesuits and two secular priests who had been studying at the Propaganda College) and a lay brother.[27] It was headed by the vice provincial of the Irish Jesuits, Robert St. Leger and included his brother John, also a priest, and an Irish lay brother, Edward Sinnott. The others were a mixture of English, French, and Scots. At the same time, Rome created the vicariate of Bengal and appointed St. Leger vicar apostolic. Exceptionally, he was not raised to episcopal rank, although this was due to Jesuit opposition to such promotions rather than deference to Portuguese sensitivities.[28]

St. Leger and his companions finally arrived on 2 October 1834. The situation was as bad as they had feared: one priest, a Portuguese who had been 'persecuted' by the Augustinians, welcomed the new vicar apostolic. The remainder denied that his authority applied to 'the Goanese or Portuguese priests of Bengal'. The appearance of a further papal rescript in 1835 did not alter their view 'that the Pope had no power or right to constitute in India a new spiritual head without the consent of the King of Portugal'.[29] This was the crux of the problem faced by all of the first generation of Irish vicars apostolic: the Goanese church flatly denied that the pope or the Propaganda Fide had any authority in India independent of the Portuguese crown. To complicate matters, between 1828 and 1834 Portugal was embroiled in a civil war to determine exactly who would

---

[24] Manuscript Account of the Jesuit Mission in Calcutta, no date, Archivum Britannicum Societatis Iesu [ABSI], India 1802–1911/4.

[25] See J. B. Polding to L. B. Barber, 26 March 1832, in Sisters of the Good Samaritan (eds.), *The Letters of John Bede Polding*, 3 vols. (Sydney: Sisters of the Good Samaritan, 1994), 1: 26. Hereafter *PL*.

[26] Cullen to Murray, 17 December 1833, DDA/MP/34/9. The friars seem to have been a mix of Spanish and Portuguese in origin.

[27] Cullen to F. Kenrick, 18 May 1834, AASMSU/KP/28-R5.

[28] Anchukandam, *Catholic Revival*, 1: 148.   [29] Jesuit Mission in Calcutta, ABSI.

wear that crown. When the war finally ended, the decision of the victors to seize church property completely ruptured relations with Rome.

This obviously placed the new vicar apostolic in a difficult position: how to control clergy or laity when large sections of both denied your right to do so? Yet it was also awkward for the East India Company state: who owned the buildings and property of a particular church? The local bishop, who might be loyal to Rome (or Goa), or the congregation who denied that he had any claim on it? The company's solution was to allow the local majority to decide. If a congregation wanted to move to Goa, it could; if Rome, that was fine as well. The courts restricted themselves to ascertaining and enforcing that choice. This made the laity both assertive and powerful. If they were dissatisfied with one bishop, they could always threaten to move to another.

To the eyes of the newly arrived Irish Jesuits this had provoked not only chaos but irreligion. Their official record claimed that the Catholic population of Calcutta had halved under the Augustinians (from 20,000 to 10,000) and that the 'Goanese priests never instructed the people' with the result that many had 'joined the ranks of the Protestants'.[30] There was certainly ample religious choice. As Brother Sinnott observed, there 'is no nation or religion who has not members in the city'.[31] Although Sinnott set himself to learning Bengali (a sort of defective Latin, he thought), taught in a newly established school that admitted both native and European children, and urged an Irish colleague to come and 'spread the odour of your good example among these naked blacks', the emphasis of the mission quickly became the Irish soldiers.[32]

That is not to say that civilian Catholics were ignored. Sinnott, for example, proudly recounted the 'escape' of three young Irish children from their Protestant guardian, the two boys into St. Leger's care and the girl into that of a 'good Irish lady'.[33] The Jesuits also worked hard to provide suitable schooling. The collegiate school that eventually became the College of St Francis Xavier, for example, was opened in 1835, and by 1840 it had some ninety-three boys, of whom thirty-nine were boarding.[34] At least in its early years, it welcomed both Catholics and Protestants, educating them together with little attention to ethnicity or caste.

Although he tried to put a brave face on it for Rome, St. Leger's time in Calcutta was difficult.[35] To Archbishop Daniel Murray of Dublin, he

[30] Ibid. [31] Sinnott to Bartholomew Esmonde, 21 December 1834, Laheen, 173.
[32] Sinnott to John Ginnovan, [June] 1836, ibid., 182.
[33] Sinnott to Alexander Kyan, 20 July 1836, Laheen, 177–8.
[34] Chadwick to Glover, 8 May 1840, ABSI/India/1802–1911/39.
[35] See Cullen to Murray, 5 June and 3 December 1835, DDA/MP/34/9.

revealed the extent of the challenge: the 'Augustinian Friars of Goa' continued to resist him, he wrote, and had appealed to Lisbon. They owned all but three of the churches in Bengal, thus controlling much of the mission's revenue. It was, St. Leger admitted, 'injurious to the progress of religion'. Still, he was optimistic that the bulk of the people now acknowledged his authority and 'religion is becoming more respected'. In particular, he was pleased to report that 'several observances, heretofore too much forgotten, [are] now beginning to be revived'.[36] As elsewhere, the Irish saw themselves as the agents of orthodoxy.

St. Leger's greatest success came with the government, which in 1835 publicly recognized that he exercised 'Spiritual Jurisdiction' in the presidency. Lord William Bentinck and his government promised St. Leger 'such support and countenance in the exercise' of that jurisdiction as was 'not inconsistent with the most perfect freedom of conscience in all who live under British Dominion, and with existing rights of property'.[37] The last was a significant caveat: they were not going to seize the Augustinian churches. Still, St. Leger was now the authorized voice of Bengal Catholicism and the sole source of chaplains. As C. A. Bayly has pointed out, the East India Company, like all other European colonizers, craved 'authoritative pronouncements on religion'.[38] In this case, the company state had chosen to support the Irish and Rome. It was quite open about why, expressing 'great satisfaction' to see the Catholic Church in Bengal 'in the hands of a born subject of the British Crown'.[39]

Although St. Leger admitted that this was a 'substantial benefit', it did not put Catholics on an equal footing.[40] When the sympathetic Bentinck departed not long after recognizing his status, for example, St. Leger found that his interim successor had different ideas about the utility of chaplains; he was not amused by Sir Charles Metcalfe's suggestion that a chaplain at Fort William could be funded by halving the salary of the one at DumDum. As he complained to Bentinck, Protestant chaplains already enjoyed 'ample pensions' while the Catholics 'receive next to nothing'.[41] This was a recurring grievance, and not just in India. The

---

[36] R. St. Leger to Murray, 20 November 1835, DDA/MP/34/9.
[37] See H. T. Prinsep to R. St. Leger, 26 January 1835, reproduced in *Address of the Right Rev. Daniel O'Connor, D.D. Vicar Apostolic of Madras to the Clergy and People of the See of Meliapore* (Madras: Printed at the Courier Press, 1838), 13–14.
[38] C. A. Bayly, *The Birth of the Modern World, 1780–1914: Global Connections and Comparisons* (London: Wiley-Blackwells, 2004), 340.
[39] Prinsep to St. Leger, 26 January 1835, *Address of the Right Rev. Daniel O'Connor*, 13–14.
[40] St. Leger to Lord William Bentinck, 12 March 1835, Manuscripts and Special Collections, University of Nottingham [MSCUN], Portland Wellbeck Collection, PwJf2030.
[41] St. Leger to Bentinck, 15 September 1835, MSCUN/PwJ2031.

army had come to tolerate Catholic chaplains, even welcome them, but it did not yet want to pay them, or at least not very much.

St. Leger was also able to attract at least a few more Jesuits, although never as many as were wanted. Yet even among the society there was dissension, as the English members resented their Irish superior, whom they claimed neither interacted with nor even spoke to them.[42] A small number of secular priests also found their way to Bengal, including at least one trained in the Irish College and Propaganda, Thomas Oliffe. He would go on to become coadjutor vicar apostolic of Bengal in 1843 and then vicar apostolic of the newly created vicariates of eastern Bengal (modern Dhaka in Bangladesh) in 1850 and then western Bengal in 1855. Oliffe was joined by the German Henry Backhaus, also Propaganda-educated, who spent nine years in Calcutta before moving on to a lengthy career in Australia, where he is still remembered.[43]

Despite these reinforcements and undoubted success in securing government recognition, St. Leger's position in Calcutta slowly deteriorated. The Augustinians never relented and from 1836 found their resistance buttressed by the advent of a claimant to the 'Portuguese' diocese of São Tomé (then usually called Meliapore), some 25 miles south of Madras. Under the terms of the *padroado*, the Portuguese crown had the right of appointment to the four Indian dioceses, but the nominee could only become a bishop once confirmed by the pope. Political unrest in Portugal had left most of the *padroado* sees vacant (Meliapore and Cochin since 1827, Goa since 1831) and under the rule of so-called episcopal governors. These were essentially priests given the authority but not the status of bishops by Lisbon. Although Antonio Texeira's claim to be *bishop* of Meliapore was primarily a problem for the Irish vicar apostolic of Madras, it made St. Leger's life difficult as Texeira also claimed authority in Bengal. The emboldened Augustinians thus began a new series of lawsuits to recover what property St. Leger had secured. 'They act', St. Leger complained to the Italian vicar apostolic of Bombay, 'in the name of the self-created & self-styled Bishop of Meliapore.'[44] Or as Cullen put it, 'a Portuguese friar got himself appointed bishop of Calcutta by the Queen of Portugal and is now making war on Mr St. Leger'.[45] Complaints about the Irish began to flow to the Propaganda, although Cullen later reported that St. Leger's 'friends in Calcutta say that he has been very harshly dealt

[42] Francis Chadwick to Glover, 24 November 1834, ABSI/India/1802–1911/8.
[43] M. J. Nolan, *The Enterprising Life of Dr Henry Backhaus: Bendigo Pioneer* (Bendigo: The Author, 2008).
[44] St. Leger to d'Alcantara, 20 June 1838, OCDA/WP.
[45] Cullen to Murray, 13 March 1837, DDA/MP/34/9.

with'.[46] For their part, the Jesuits had lost interest in the mission, and the departure of St. Leger and his brother in June 1838 marked the end of the Irish Jesuit presence in Bengal.[47]

The Propaganda turned to Cullen for advice, and he in turn suggested that Daniel Murray of Dublin be consulted.[48] This was typical: until his own promotion to the archdiocese of Armagh in late 1849, Cullen rarely acted on his own account and was happy to work on behalf of more senior men such as Murray or Francis Kenrick. In many ways a modernizer in Dublin, Murray was nevertheless a bishop of the older generation, like Henry Conwell in Philadelphia or Thomas Scallan in Newfoundland, and his suggestions for foreign missions tended to be priests in his own image. Often they belonged to religious orders, such as the Dominicans Patrick Griffith in Cape Town and John Hynes in Corfu and then Guyana, the Franciscan Henry Hughes in Gibraltar, or the Discalced Carmelite John Francis Whelan in Bombay.

The Propaganda welcomed Murray's involvement. As Calcutta was the 'principal city of India' and the home of a particularly learned Anglican bishop, St. Leger's replacement would need to not only be a man of 'great prudence, learning, and respectability' but also like Jesuits and get along with the government.[49] Murray thought that William Walsh, the incumbent of the important parish of Kingstown (now Dún Laoghaire), might fit the bill, but before his letter reached Rome news arrived from Calcutta that reduced the sense of urgency. It emerged that, on the instructions of the general of the Society of Jesus, St. Leger had asked Jean-Louis Taberd, the long-serving vicar apostolic of Cochin in French Indochina, to administer Calcutta until his replacement arrived. Taberd was in the city to oversee the publication of a Chinese dictionary and was expected to stay at least a year. A delighted Rome was happy to appoint him interim vicar apostolic and take its time about a permanent replacement.

This however was only temporary, and Cullen remained confident that Walsh would be appointed. It was 'now admitted' in Rome, he told Murray, 'that the vicars apostolic in the British possessions must be English subjects'. Taberd, he pointedly remarked, 'is a Frenchman'.[50] He also does not seem to have made himself especially popular. The laity were disappointed that their bishop was not 'of British origin', while the remaining Jesuits thought Taberd 'extremely pettish, jealous & exacting – coarse & insulting [in] his behaviour & language to his priests & to

[46] Cullen to Murray, 2 March 1839, DDA/MP/34/9.
[47] Cullen to Murray, 23 June 1838, DDA/MP/34/9.   [48] Ibid.
[49] Cullen to Murray, 23 June 1838, DDA/MP/34/9.
[50] Cullen to Murray, 25 August 1838, DDA/MP/34/9.

seculars'.[51] Nor were they pleased to be required to pay the bishop 100 rupees a month 'for his whim'.[52] Things got much worse when Taberd died unexpectedly in late July 1840. Custom dictated that the administration of the vicariate fell to the oldest European priest, in this case the lone Portuguese who had welcomed St. Leger in 1834. The Jesuits were appalled. 'We expect', one wrote, 'to be suspended.'[53] They were, occasioning what was described as 'a violent division in the Catholic community'.[54] Irish secular priests such as Thomas Oliffe fared little better, and everybody was anxious that Rome send a new bishop as soon as possible. There was no time to fetch William Walsh out of Ireland. A solution had to be found in India, and the Propaganda turned to Madras.

It was the obvious choice: the southern presidency was and would long remain the centre of Irish ecclesiastical activity in India; and, unlike Bengal, it had a substantial indigenous Catholic population in both the city and its hinterland. Since the mid-eighteenth century the mission had been entrusted to Capuchins dependent on Pondicherry and thus ultimately loyal to the Propaganda and Rome. The Portuguese bishops at nearby Meliapore, however, did not fully accept the Capuchins' right to be there, which resulted in a long-running conflict between the French and the Portuguese, with the British flitting between the sides largely on the basis of events in Europe. Although the French monks were eventually replaced by Italians, the feud with Meliapore continued. There was also the large British garrison to consider, where as early as 1819 Bishop Pietro d'Alcantara of Bombay had been approached by Irish soldiers seeking an English-speaking priest.[55]

By 1831, the situation was untenable. In one of the first acts of his pontificate, Gregory XVI convened a congregation of the Propaganda to discuss Madras. It was decided that the Capuchins would have to be replaced or radically reformed and agreed that a British priest should be sent as vicar apostolic.[56] The first thought was again of England, and by late 1832 the Benedictine John Bede Polding had reluctantly accepted. He promptly changed his mind, having worked himself up into 'a state of utmost agitation' and 'dread of the dangers to be encountered'.[57] He withdrew, consented again in early 1833,

---

[51] Cullen to Murray, 2 March 1839, DDA/MP/34/9; Chadwick to Glover, 16 March 1840, ABSI/India/1802–1911/38

[52] Chadwick to Glover 16 March 1840.

[53] Chadwick to Glover, 12 September 1840, ABSI/India 1802–1911/40.

[54] Jesuit Mission in Calcutta, ABSI.   [55] Ballhatchet, 93.   [56] Ibid., 97.

[57] Polding to T. J. Brown, 12 October 1832, PL, 1: 27.

and then refused on health grounds.[58] In early 1834, he agreed to go to Australia.

Rome's global shift towards the Irish began with this failure to find Englishmen prepared to accept difficult missionary assignments; except for a handful in Australia, the Propaganda for many years did not appoint another English candidate. As Cullen explained to Murray in late 1833, it was now the Propaganda's intention to 'get some good Irish priests' to go to India, 'where there are many good Catholics of Irish or English descent, entirely abandoned'.[59] Both Murray and James Doyle, the politically prominent bishop of Kildare and Leighlin, recommended Daniel O'Connor, an Irish Augustinian and former schoolfellow of Doyle. Rome agreed in April 1834, anticipating 'happy results' in Madras.[60] Even more optimistically, the Propaganda 'promised to find a sufficient number of priests to accompany him'.[61] In the event, however, O'Connor's departure was delayed for nearly a year by the twofold problem of a lack of willing companions and a lack of money. Humid and fractious Madras was not the most attractive of missionary opportunities, and a parsimonious Propaganda refused to subsidize the journey on the grounds that Madras was a rich mission and should pay its own way. They eventually agreed that O'Connor could borrow what he needed. Passage for the new bishop and his party of 'four priests, one Deacon, three Catechists and one Servant' came to £630 of the available £704. There would, he complained, be very little left 'of the *loan* from Propaganda on my arrival at Madras.'[62]

O'Connor also footed the bill for an extended stop in London, where he prudently chose to visit as many officials and politicians as possible. He managed interviews with the Duke of Wellington, Sir Robert Peel, the speaker of the House of Commons, the chancellor of the exchequer, and most of the court of directors. He was particularly pleased by his conversation with Sir John Hobhouse, the newly appointed president of the board of control, who promised that any previous hint of bigotry at the board would cease and Catholics would be treated with 'the utmost liberality'.[63] Thus fortified, O'Connor and his companions set out on what turned out to be a ninety-five-day journey to Madras. They arrived on 20 August 1835, minus a catechist who had died off the coast of Brazil.

[58] See Polding to Brown, 25 February 1833, *PL*, 1: 28–9; Anchukandam, *Pondicherry*, 16.

[59] Cullen to Murray, 17 December 1833, DDA/MP/34/9.

[60] Cullen to Murray, 10 April 1834, DDA/MP/34/9.

[61] Cullen to F. Kenrick, 18 May 1834, AASMSU/KP/28-R5.

[62] O'Connor to Murray, 7 May 1835, DDA/MP/34/11/2. Emphasis in original.

[63] Ibid. Although Hobhouse's diaries are in the British Library, there is unfortunately a gap for this period.

The new bishop was met by 'overjoyed' people, wary Capuchins, and a weary Bishop d'Alcantara, who had been forced to make the long journey from Bombay.[64]

O'Connor knew that his position was dependent on British support, and as in London he was delighted by his reception in official circles. 'Nothing', he gushed to Murray, 'could equal the kindness of the Government.' The governor invited him to dinner, as did the members of the council, the commander in chief (the Irish Anglican Sir William Robert O'Callaghan), the chief justice, various military officers, and 'several of the Catholic and Protestant Gentry'. The chief secretary to the government, Henry Charnier, was so kind it was as if Providence had 'raised him up' just to help Catholics. He hosted O'Connor at his residence for a month and introduced him 'to all the wealth and respectability of the surrounding country'. More importantly, Charnier acquainted him with 'the particulars of the disputes and property of the Mission' and 'instructed me how I was to address the Government, and procure its approbation and assurance of support' in 'getting possession of the funds of the Mission'. These tutorials helped O'Connor secure not only the money held in trust by the government but also 500 rupees to repair his cathedral church in Madras. The chaplain at Fort St George saw his salary raised from 35 to 150 rupees a month, and a promise was made that 50 rupees per month 'per mission will be allocated for a British clergyman at every British station' in the presidency.[65] O'Connor's success was capped in January 1837, when the Madras government publicly recognized him 'as the Official Superior through whom all communication on matters connected with the Roman Catholic religion and with the Church of that religion at Madras are to be made'.[66] As in Calcutta, the company had definitively chosen to support the Irish and co-opt them into the administration of their state.

Although O'Connor's embrace of the government was pragmatic, it was also ideological. His generation of bishops believed in political deference. So long as Catholicism was not actively oppressed, they were happy to adopt a non-confrontational and even collaborative approach to the state. Newfoundland's Scallan was an extreme instance of this, but he was hardly unique. Murray, for example, was a consistent and increasingly lonely supporter of British initiatives in Ireland. He was a regular guest at

---

[64] O'Connor to Murray, 12 February 1836, DDA/MP/34/11/4.   [65] Ibid.

[66] Quoted in 'India Ecclesiastical 2 July 1839', India Office Records, British Library [IOR], IOR/E/4/759, 960–4.

Dublin Castle, whereas Cullen (who succeeded him in 1852) waited some fifteen years to make his first, reluctant, visit.[67] Their loyalty was often reciprocated: Murray sat on several government boards and was nominated to the Irish Privy Council, while in Madras the governor praised O'Connor 'in the highest terms' to the papal authorities.[68] Their successors would be less accommodating.

O'Connor quickly crushed the Capuchins; one was expelled on the grounds that as he spoke neither English nor Tamil he was 'useless'.[69] Privately, he wrote that the Italian was a 'loquacious, contentious satirical man, who never wanted the British clergy to come here and has rendered himself odious to the people'. It was worth the £130 it had cost to get rid of him.[70] The rest drifted away. The Portuguese, however, were less easily dealt with, and O'Connor's initial attempt to secure control of the *padroado* churches in the city failed when the episcopal governor of Meliapore flatly referred everything to Lisbon. When he died in 1836, O'Connor claimed authority over Meliapore itself. The government's reaction was simply to observe that it was preferable that those with spiritual authority be British rather than foreign-born.[71] Soon, however, O'Connor met a more substantial opponent in Antonio Texeira, who, as we have seen, arrived claiming not the title of episcopal governor, but bishop. An archbishop was appointed to Goa at the same time, and both appointments marked Lisbon's attempt to resume control of imperial affairs after the conclusion of the civil war. That they would annoy Rome was an added benefit for the new and anti-clerical liberal government, which must have known that there was no chance of their being confirmed by the pope.

The Irish greeted the appointment with fury. O'Connor's vicar general P. E. Moriarty secretly attended Texeira's installation and subsequently described it publicly as 'a most audacious and Schismatical usurpation of the Episcopal Chair'. Texeira was not a bishop, he continued, and had 'no authority in Meliapore or any other Church'. His goal was to 'bring to British India the spiritual disorders of Portugal, where the people are the victims of a Government which has set itself up against the Spiritual authority of the Supreme Pontiff'. O'Connor meanwhile set about trying to gain control of the Madras churches through the courts.[72]

---

[67] For Murray's relationship to the government in the 1840s, see Donal Kerr, *Peel, Priests, and Politics: Sir Robert Peel's Administration and the Roman Catholic Church in Ireland, 1841–46* (Oxford: Oxford University Press, 1984).

[68] Cullen to Murray, 20 January 1838, DDA/MP/34/9.   [69] See Ballhatchet, 102.

[70] O'Connor to Murray, 12 February 1836, DDA/MP/34/11/4.   [71] Ballhatchet, 100.

[72] P.E. Moriarty to the Catholics of Madras, 6 October 1836, in IOR/F/4/1751/1403, 41–43.

Texeira was not without local support. One local critic, for example, complained to the government of O'Connor's 'scandalous proceedings' and exploitation of his monopoly on communications, remarking that it had 'been the occasion of introducing such a spirit of disunion and discord' among the company's Catholic subjects.[73] The Madras government was unmoved, and in 1839 its support for O'Connor was definitively confirmed by the government of India. O'Connor, they wrote, 'is a British Subject of character and education who holds a commission direct from the Pope'. His conduct in Madras had been 'very beneficent to the troops', and Calcutta felt 'no hesitation' in approving Madras' decision to recognize his authority. Texeira, by contrast, was 'a Portuguese, holding authority from the Portuguese Government only, and not from the Pope, and whose foreign allegiance and language, are alike unfavourable to the exercise of spiritual jurisdiction over our Roman Catholic subjects.'[74] Even in the more relaxed 1830s, such official enthusiasm for papal authority must count as unusual.

Texeira's already slim chance of support was fatally undermined by the promulgation in April 1838 of the papal brief *Multa Praeclare*. This marked Gregory XVI's final loss of patience with Portuguese behaviour, both in India and in Portugal itself. It effectively suppressed three of the four *padroado* sees (including Meliapore), while Goa was denied any metropolitan rights. Throughout India, Goanese churches, clergy, and laity were subjected to their local ordinary. The archbishop-elect of Goa promptly claimed that the document was either a forgery or had been obtained from the pope by trickery. In either case, he insisted, it had no validity without the assent of the queen of Portugal.[75]

Although Texeira remained an irritant, O'Connor quickly found himself with more serious problems. First and foremost, there was a shortage of clergy. If only, he complained to Murray, he had 'about sixteen Irish priests' to place at the various military stations and about 'eight Irish students' (and 'the same number of East Indian and Native students') for a seminary. Madras could then be 'one of the most flourishing missions in the church of God'. Yet O'Connor knew that, even with a British salary to offer, he could neither find nor pay the passage for so many. Instead, he urged Murray 'to procure two steady, intelligent and good Priests from Old Ireland' to provide for at least a few posts.[76]

The dearth of available priests and seminarians was of course a common problem throughout Greater Ireland, as was the related

[73] J.M. Pereyra to Government, 1 March 1838, IOR/F/4/1751/1403.
[74] 'India Ecclesiastical 2 July 1839', IOR/E/4/759, 960–4.
[75] Anchukandam, *Catholic Revival*, 1: 271–2.
[76] O'Connor to Murray, 9 January 1837, DDA/MP/34/11/6/1/(1).

problem of their quality. Madras was no different, and by early 1836 O'Connor was complaining that his primary burden was his own clergy. Of those who had come with him from Ireland, one had left after making himself 'very disagreeable' and another had been sent to a distant mission after giving 'much trouble'. He had only one 'efficient' priest, his vicar general Moriarty.[77] All this provided a useful pretext for an opponent far more formidable than Texeira to involve itself in the affairs of Madras.

Although they shared a common loyalty to Rome and animosity towards Meliapore, O'Connor had almost immediately clashed with the French in Pondicherry. The mission there had long been headed by a bishop but was not itself a vicariate. Its remit, although poorly defined, was understood to extend beyond France's residual territorial possessions to encompass the traditional French mission in what is now Tamil Nadu. O'Connor, however, claimed that the entirety of the mission, including the territorial enclaves, came under his authority. The French did not agree, not least because Bishop Louis-Charles-Auguste Hébert had already petitioned Rome for the erection of Pondicherry into a vicariate. This was granted as the Coromandel Coast in 1836, and the news reached India in 1837.[78] That put an end to O'Connor's claim to Pondicherry, but it did not prevent him from asserting the right to appoint chaplains to British posts within the new vicariate's boundaries. He further provoked Hébert and his successor Clément Bonnard by ordaining what Thomas Anchukandam calls native 'deserters' from their seminary; O'Connor did not share the French distrust of Tamil suitability for priesthood or their insistence that European priests must at all times outnumber the natives. His concern was to provide clergy for the substantial native population, freeing what Irish priests he had for the soldiers and European civilians. O'Connor ignored their letters of complaint, the French appealed to Rome, and the Propaganda ordered him to desist from ordaining further Pondicherry seminarians.[79] The British meanwhile added fuel to the fire by insisting that all priests in the Madras presidency report baptisms, marriages, and deaths to the government via O'Connor. Although undoubtedly genuine in part, French complaints about the conduct of the Irish priests should be seen in this context.

O'Connor also struggled to navigate the cultural and social preferences of his native flock. In Madras itself, there were two distinct groups: the low-caste Parias in the Parchery district and the Fisher caste in Rayapuram. The latter had particularly good relations with the British because of their crucial role in ferrying people and cargo from ships

[77] O'Connor to Murray, 12 February 1836, DDA/MP/34/11/4.
[78] Anchukandam, *Catholic Revival*, 1: 149.   [79] Ibid., 1: 257, 1: 159–60.

standing offshore. Each had their own church and their own social and liturgical preferences. Complaints about the Irish ranged from an unwontedly spartan taste in church decoration and dislike of display to insensitivity to caste distinction. All were carefully packaged and sent on to Rome by Bonnard.[80] As Cullen put it, 'a French bishop' had complained about O'Connor 'having prohibited processions which were customary in Madras, and having the crucifix removed from the pulpit'.[81] To Cullen and the Irish, these allegations were self-evidently political and easily ignored.

The question of caste was more complex. The Irish view was that it was a Hindu custom and should not apply to Catholics. The only distinction O'Connor was prepared to make was between those in European and native dress (but not between Europeans and natives as such). They were allocated separate sections in Madras' churches. This infuriated higher-status members of the congregation, who could find themselves next to low-status worshippers. A brief attempt to further divide the high and low castes (creating three sections) was quickly abandoned, and some eighty high-caste families defected to the *padroado*.[82] It is difficult to see what O'Connor might have done differently, as division infuriated lower-caste worshippers, who might defect, while not dividing infuriated high-caste worshippers, who did. No wonder O'Connor preferred the Irish soldiers. His solution was to create something like an American ethnic parish, albeit on a massive scale: the Irish would minister to the Europeans and control the vicariate, while the natives could within reason do as they chose in their own churches but not share power. This is what lay behind his enthusiasm for native clergy. By contrast, the French were willing to defer to local preferences even as they doubted native suitability to minister to local communities.

French complaints had their effect, and the Propaganda demanded an explanation.[83] O'Connor felt this as a 'deep wound to my heart' and a poor return 'for almost superhuman labour'.[84] He was also ill-prepared to defend himself, not least because he was unable to write in Latin. 'I am told', Cullen informed Daniel Murray, 'that [the Propaganda] scarcely understand the greater part of his letters.' This was a recurring problem with Irish missionaries, and Cullen urged that care should be taken to appoint bishops 'who could correspond in an intelligible manner with Rome'.[85] 'The French Missionaries', he sighed,

---

[80] See, for example, Bonnard to Fransoni, 31 December 1836, APF/SC/vol. 5/f. 923.
[81] Cullen to Murray, 13 March 1837, DDA/MP/34/9.   [82] Ballhatchet, 103–5.
[83] Cullen to Murray, 13 March 1837, DDA/MP/34/9.
[84] O'Connor to Murray, 6 April 1837, DDA/MP/34/11/7/1/(1).
[85] Cullen to Murray, 16 December 1837, DDA/MP/34/9.

'are wonderful at writing letters, and they generally give such good accounts of themselves and their duties that they easily obtain whatever they want.' By contrast, the Irish 'though in many instances most zealous and deserving find great difficulties in managing their affairs, either because they don't write at all, or write very little'.[86] It was such failures that drew Cullen ever further into the affairs of the global Irish.

O'Connor's health was also failing, and in late 1837 he asked Rome for a coadjutor.[87] He claimed to have suffered several 'attacks of paralysis', but in fact he was already heading for the full-scale mental breakdown that ultimately required that he be escorted home under strict supervision.[88] Rome had to act quickly, and although Cullen briefly wondered about sending the failed Bishop Clancy of Charleston, the Propaganda again threw the choice on Murray.[89] He recommended Patrick Carew, whom Francis Kenrick had unsuccessfully nominated for Pittsburgh the year before. A professor at Maynooth, Carew had published several books, including a meticulously documented ecclesiastical history of Ireland to 1200.[90] Cullen was delighted: there would be no problem about the comprehensibility of his Latin, and he suggested that Carew stop in Rome so as 'to become acquainted with the people and their manner of doing business'.[91] It was good advice, as Carew faced the same problems as O'Connor, not least the Propaganda's refusal to pay his passage.[92] He eventually arrived in early 1839, boasting to Cullen that he had converted thirteen Protestants on the voyage.[93] Although the now frankly unbalanced O'Connor resisted the new arrangements, he finally resigned in April 1840 leaving Carew in sole charge.[94] Given the challenges, Cullen's unwontedly charitable verdict on O'Connor is probably the right one: 'Perhaps he went astray in some smaller matters but it appears in general he is a most excellent missionary and vicar apostolic.'[95]

At first, Carew's policy was much the same, mixing public expressions of loyalty to the crown with pointed requests for money. Madras was broke: the 1,300 students in the free school were costing some 150 rupees a month, 24 new children had been consigned to the orphanage, and there

---

[86] Cullen to Murray, 20 January 1838, DDA/MP/34/9.
[87] Cullen to Murray, 2 December 1837, DDA/MP/34/9.
[88] Cullen to Murray, 1 February 1838, DDA/MP/ 34/9; for the gravity of O'Connor's condition, see Carew to Cullen 20 October, 1840, PICRA/CUL/620.
[89] Cullen to Murray, 2 December 1837, DDA/MP/34/9.
[90] P. J. Carew, *An Ecclesiastical History of Ireland, from the Introduction of Christianity into that Country to the Commencement of the Thirteenth Century* (Dublin: John Coyne, 1835).
[91] Cullen to Murray, 20 January 1838, DDA/MP/34/9.
[92] Cullen to Murray, 'May' 1838, DDA/MP/ 34/9.
[93] Cullen to Murray, 30 April 1839, DDA/MP/34/9.
[94] See William Kelly to Cullen, 'March' 1840, PICRA/CUL/589.
[95] Cullen to Murray, 20 January 1838, DDA/MP/34/9.

were still 3,000 rupees owing on the cathedral. The government had refused to provide any funds for the school, despite it being open 'to children of every persuasion'. Debts had reached nearly 25,000 rupees. Worse, although eleven Irish priests had been recruited, he had no means to provide for them.[96] There were also the usual thunderous denunciations of Meliapore and defiant *padroado* priests.[97]

Carew was only just settling in when the call came from Calcutta. Jean-Louis Taberd's death in July 1840 had thrown the church there into chaos, and the remaining Jesuits wrote to London and Rome requesting that a new vicar apostolic be appointed immediately.[98] The Propaganda was in a quandary. Although Carew had only just taken full control in Madras, Calcutta was the seat of the government of India. The decision to translate him was taken relatively quickly, with the news reaching the delighted Jesuits in early 1841.[99]

Carew's influence was quickly felt. He launched an assault on the local Protestant schools and 'all Catholic parents who support them', and denounced an undenominational Christian school that St. Leger had championed.[100] Carew was, an approving Jesuit reported to Rome, 'the terror of Protestants'.[101] The *Bengal Catholic Expositor* became conspicuously Irish, replacing didactic lectures on theology and news from London with biographical sketches of Daniel O'Connell and accounts of Father Mathew's temperance campaign. Carew also encouraged an existing plan to import a colony of Irish nuns, for which the Jesuits had raised some 12,000 rupees in just a few weeks from 'Catholics, Protestants & Hindoos even'.[102] (Such ecumenism should not be overstated: the *Calcutta Christian Observer* published a lengthy tirade against Protestants contributing to the foundation of a 'Romish Nunnery'.)[103] The impetus for the convent appears to have been lay, with the delightfully named 'Ladies of the Nun-Committee' providing funds to send the Roman-trained German Henry Backhaus to Ireland to recruit a community with a view to opening a girls' school. After failing to secure Ursulines in Cork, Backhaus managed to extract six volunteers from Teresa Ball, the

---

[96] See the lengthy pastoral letter reprinted in the *Bengal Catholic Expositor*, 30 May 1840.
[97] See Carew's circular letter dated 8 October 1839, published in the *Bengal Catholic Expositor*, 4 April 1840.
[98] Chadwick to Glover, 12 September 1840, ABSI/India/1802–1911/40.
[99] Chadwick to Glover, 13 March 1841, ABSI/India/1802–1911/46.
[100] Unknown Jesuit to Fr Jenkins, '1842', ABSI/India/1802–1911/53; Neill, 283–4.
[101] Quoted in Crosbie, 157.
[102] Chadwick to Glover, 8 May 1840, ABSI/India/1802–1911/39.
[103] 'Protestant subscriptions to popish institutions', *The Calcutta Christian Observer*, vol. 1 (January–December 1840), 462.

foundress of the Irish Loreto Sisters.[104] A further three sisters left Ireland in mid-1842.[105] Their school quickly had more than sixty students.[106] Carew also managed to recruit the Irish Christian Brothers to manage a companion school for boys, which opened in 1848. Even the English Jesuits were delighted by the 'wonders' Carew was doing, although they soon changed their mind.[107]

His first task was to obtain more clergy. Those that he had were a diverse, almost random assemblage. At the 1842 opening of the chapel at the Loreto convent, for example, there were two Irish priests, two Italians, a Greek, an 'Arabian', a Goanese, a Chinese, a German, and 'a native of Bengal'.[108] Carew preferred Irishmen and sent one of his priests on the first of several unsuccessful recruitment trips. Cullen tried to help, suggesting that two students at the Irish College might be induced to go to Calcutta: 'There is no place more good could be done', he told Kirby.[109] Few came, and Carew was reduced to asking Rome to order the Irish bishops to promise preference in the assignment of parishes at home to any young seminarian prepared to commit to a fixed number of years on the mission. He was 'anxious that the church of India should be indebted for its restoration to its former glory to the ministry of Ireland' and hoped that Murray and the other bishops would agree to his plan.[110] Nothing came of it.

Carew also pursued a more confrontational line with the government. While still in Madras, he had engaged in a very public row over the related issues of chaplains' stipends and the provision of properly Catholic books in place of the Book of Common Prayer and the Authorized Version of the Bible. Sensing the government's weak point, he warned that, if justice were not done, he would appeal to the clergy of Ireland 'to dissuade their countrymen from engaging in the military service of India'. The East India Company, he warned, 'would not succeed in raising a single regiment in Catholic Ireland'.[111] These threats earned placatory replies from the governor general and the court of directors, and the doubling of at least one chaplain's stipend, but little substantive change. Carew was not mollified and continued to complain of the 'hostility of a powerful Government which supports and fosters Protestantism in every

[104] See Backhaus to M. Teresa Ball, 23 August 1841, Loreto Archives Dublin [LAD], TB/IND/4/1.
[105] Cullen to Kirby, 13 July 1842, PICRA/KP/102.   [106] Nolan, *Backhaus*, 21.
[107] Unknown Jesuit to 'Rev. and Dear Father', 'Wit Tuesday' [1842], ABSI/India/1802–1911/58.
[108] See Nolan, *Backhaus*, 25.   [109] Cullen to Kirby, 13 July 1842, PICRA/KP/102.
[110] Carew to Murray, 9 February 1844, DDA/MP/34/11/13.
[111] Quoted in Ballhatchet, 107.

shape, whilst it unceasingly thwarts the progress of Catholicity'.[112] The first generation of missionary bishops had been grateful for toleration and respect, but their successors demanded equality.

Carew's other challenge was Goa. In 1842, sustained negotiations began between Rome and Lisbon, and in early 1843 a tentative agreement was reached with the pope for the first time in many years appointing bishops to Portuguese dioceses. Relations, however, remained tense as Lisbon asserted its own right of appointment across the subcontinent, including in British territory. Rome's claim that this was impossible due to British objections was scuttled when the Portuguese unexpectedly produced an assurance that the British were happy for their ancient ally to resume its traditional rights. A disgusted Cullen thought this a 'great perfidy on the part of England'.[113] The result was that, in April 1843, Lisbon nominated José Maria da Silva Torres as archbishop of Goa. Before he confirmed the appointment, and presumably to keep the balance between *padroado* and Propaganda, Gregory XVI also elevated Carew. India now had two archbishops.

Although Silva Torres' appointment had Rome's reluctant blessing, the peace did not last. The new archbishop acted as if the *padroado* had been fully restored and the vicars apostolic did not exist. As the *Madras Catholic Expositor* put it in mid-1844, 'We knew that the new Archbishop *might* prove a bad man – and that however fair his promises may have been, he *might* be unscrupulous enough to violate them. Unfortunately for himself, and for those in whose eyes Schism has its charms, our worst fears have been realised.'[114] Carew's successor in Madras was even blunter: Silva Torres was a 'hypocrite and a renegade', an arch-schismatic, and an arch-heretic. 'The cloven foot', John Fennelly announced, 'is broadly exhibited.'[115] Papal admonitions in 1845 and 1847 had no effect, and Carew was left to lament the 'schismatical ruinous rebellion' that had forced him to go 'deeply into debt in order to establish Priests & churches, wheresoever I thought he could do harm'. Although *padroado* priests retaliated by filing suit to recover church property in Calcutta, Carew remained confident: 'Thanks to God', he told Murray, 'so far I have out-generalled him spiritually and temporally.'[116] Anxious to avoid another break with Lisbon, Rome finally promoted and recalled Silva Torres at the end of 1848. In 1851, he was appointed coadjutor archbishop of Braga, the premier Portuguese see.

[112] Carew to Murray, 5 September 1845, DDA/MP/34/11/18/1.
[113] Cullen to Murray, 12 April 1843, DDA/MP/34/9.
[114] *Madras Catholic Expositor*, vol. 4, no. 4 (June 1844), 121. Emphasis in original.
[115] Letter from John Fennelly to the *Madras Examiner*, 6 May 1844.
[116] Carew to Murray, 5 February 1846, DDA/MP/34/11/21.

Nowhere was the Goanese threat more acute than Bombay. Although the island had passed to England in 1661 as part of the dowry of Catherine of Braganza, its Catholics remained or seemed to remain under the authority of Goa. Many saw themselves as Goanese. The ambiguity resulted in a long struggle for control between the archbishops of Goa and a community of Italian Discalced Carmelites answerable to the Propaganda. In 1786, the British declared that the former's authority should be recognized, Goa sought to remove the Carmelites, the Carmelites resisted, and the British reversed themselves in 1791. The Carmelites then sought to remove the Goanese, the Goanese resisted, and in 1794 the British split the difference, awarding two of Bombay's four churches to the Carmelites and two to Goa. There matters largely rested, although the British slowly drew closer to the Italian Carmelite vicar apostolic Pietro d'Alcantara, who had first arrived in 1792. They paid him a stipend and grudgingly supported his seminary until his death in 1840. His successor was another Italian Carmelite, the ineffectual Luigi Fortini. He proved incapable of coping with the feuding provoked by *Multa Praeclare* and promptly sought a coadjutor. The Propaganda turned to Ireland but in an effort to soften the blow decided that the new bishop should also be a Discalced Carmelite. Rome asked Murray to recommend a member of the Irish community, and he suggested John Francis Whelan, its provincial.[117] Rome agreed, and Whelan was consecrated on 3 July 1842.

Following a now well-worn path, Whelan travelled via London, where he collected letters of introduction, Paris, where he claimed Bombay's subsidy from the Propagation of the Faith, and Rome, where Tobias Kirby explained the workings of the Propaganda. His arrival in March 1843 was, he wrote, 'hailed with delight by the laity of the Island', while the governor was kind and attentive.[118] Then reality intruded: Whelan had not expected 'to find a perfect state of Church government', but he did not expect things to be as bad as they were. The Italian Carmelites were 'inexperienced and untutored' and the bishop was 'timid and narrow minded', while of the two large British military posts in the presidency outwith Bombay itself, Poona had no priest and Belgaum only a native 'who can do nothing but say Mass'.[119] Educating the native clergy, Fortini told him, 'wd be bad for the Italians', and the only English-language schools were effectively Protestant. The European

---

[117] Whelan Diary, 5 April 1842, in the Annals of the Irish Province of Discalced Carmelites, 607. This is a typescript document, and a copy may be consulted at the Carmelite Library, Gort Muire, Dublin [CLD].
[118] Whelan to Fr Gannon, 18 June 1843, Annals/CLD/612.
[119] Whelan to Murray, 30 April 1843, DDA/MP/34/11/10.

and native students who attended them, he told a Roman correspondent, 'come out either half indifferent Catholics or whole Protestants'.[120]

Whelan's suggestion that two Irish priests be recruited was 'received coolly', he thought, because the bishop and 'the Italian Fathers fear the Mission will come into the hands of Irishmen'.[121] Whelan and the priest he had brought from Ireland were forced to act as military chaplains, surviving only on what the British were prepared to pay. It is little wonder that within a month he asked to be relieved. Denied, Whelan then suggested that Fortini be removed and the vicariate made a diocese. The Propaganda instead advised him to 'coax' Fortini into giving him control. 'The fact', Whelan raged, 'is the Bp here will not be coaxed, he is determinedly opposed to the Irish.'[122] To make matters worse, Silva Torres soon appeared in the city, ordaining and preaching and carrying on as if neither Whelan nor Fortini existed. Whelan worried that it presaged the restoration of the *padroado*, which would leave the vicariate with only the churches on the island of Bombay itself. In that event, he told Murray, there would be no need for a second bishop. He sounded almost hopeful.[123]

Although they shared a religious order and hostility to Goa, Fortini and Whelan could not work together. Whelan thought the Italians grasping and incompetent and stressed that in India 'an English subject is the only one to whom the People will look up, or who can treat of Catholic affairs with the Government'. 'Therefore', he told Rome, 'the Bishop must be English or Irish; Foreigners will not answer.'[124] For his part, Fortini believed the Irish ignored the natives and that Whelan was dangerously close to the government. (He had impressed the authorities by his heroic efforts to comfort soldiers dying of cholera.) Both men wanted to resign.[125] Rome was worried, and the Irish Carmelite Francis Nicholson reported troubling conversations at the Propaganda. 'The affairs of Bombay', he wrote in April 1844, 'are going from bad to worse.'[126] By late July, Cullen was urging Murray to support Whelan 'as things were going on badly there before his arrival'.[127] By August, it was correctly reported in Rome that Whelan would leave Bombay on health grounds.[128] Crucially, he did not resign and remained coadjutor vicar apostolic with right of succession.

---

[120] Whelan to Charles Acton, 18 June 1843, Archivio Segreto Vaticano [ASV], Spogli Acton, vol. 4, f. 160.
[121] Whelan to Murray, 30 September 1843, DDA/MP/34/11/11.   [122] Ibid.   [123] Ibid.
[124] Whelan to Acton, 18 June 1843.   [125] Ballhatchet, 63–4.
[126] Nicholson to Raymund, 13 April 1844, Annals/CLD/614.
[127] Cullen to Murray, 27 July 1844, DDA/MP/40/4.
[128] Nicholson to Raymund, 24 August 1844/Annals/CLD/614.

With Whelan back in Ireland this did not matter for several years, but within days of Fortini's death in early 1848 some 11,000 'British' Catholics had signed a petition asking for Whelan's return and for 'priests who could speak English'.[129] They asked Cullen to present it to the pope.[130] Whelan was amenable, and by April Cullen told him that Pius IX was delighted by his willingness to go back to Bombay.[131] This time he was better prepared, securing Loreto Sisters for a convent, two free places at All Hallows, and money from Rome for his passage. Although unable to find any secular priests, he successfully approached Robert St. Leger (now Jesuit provincial) for two Irish Jesuits. On 16 May, he sang the Requiem High Mass at the Dublin pro-cathedral for the first anniversary of the death of Daniel O'Connell.[132]

Whelan reached Bombay on 5 November, revelling in the irony that his landing coincided with the Anglican bishop preaching on the continuing dangers of popish plots. 'At the moment his Congregation was thus piously engaged', he told Murray, 'a Salute from the Battery of "Fifteen Guns" *ordered by Government* announced the arrival of three Nuns, two priests and their Bishop.'[133] It was probably his only happy moment in India. What he found was chaos 'beyond description'. 'The wholesale plunder made after the Bishop's death by the Italian Friars', he wrote, 'obliged the English Party to have all the Church Property placed in the hands of Government.' He would have to appeal to the courts for its return.[134] He promptly sacked as vicar general Michael Antony, a particularly tempestuous Italian who Fortini had failed to control, and replaced him with Patrick Sheehan, one of the two Irish Jesuits. He also appointed Bombay's first vicar general for the native communities. Whelan then stripped Antony of his parish, provoking ferocious resistance on the part of its lay trustees. They appealed to the government, which tried very hard not to notice. The trustees also refused to unlock the doors of the church and presbytery and, when Whelan ordered them broken down, launched a lawsuit.[135]

With the bulk of the mission's funds sequestered and awaiting adjudication, and in the absence of any assistance from the Italian Carmelites, Whelan was forced to rely wholly on a government allowance of 200 rupees a month.[136] He gave the Jesuits the two military chaplaincies available on

---

[129] Cullen to Whelan, 18 June 1848, OCDA/WP.
[130] 'Bombay Catholics' to Murray, 15 January 1848, DDA/MP. This is a covering letter advising that the petition had been sent directly to Cullen.
[131] Cullen to Whelan, 18 June 1848, OCDA/WP.
[132] Whelan Diary, April–May 1848, CLD.
[133] Whelan to Murray, 15 November 1848, DDA/MP/34/11/27. Emphasis in original.
[134] Whelan to Murray, 15 November 1848, DDA/MP/34/11/27.   [135] Ballhatchet, 67.
[136] J. G. Lumsden to Whelan, 30 January 1849, OCDA/WP.

the island, which more or less provided for their needs, but all three Irishmen were forced to sleep in what he called the 'cells of the Native Seminarists' because the 'Italians would allow us no other'. The heat, Whelan complained, was 'unsufferable'. He eventually gained possession of the bishop's house and secured a government bungalow for one of the Jesuits. The other had had enough, resigning as vicar general and fleeing to the British post at Belgaum.[137] He would, he wrote, prefer anything to Bombay – 'I would sooner go to Purgatory than go back there again'.[138] Whelan also had to deal with the Goanese, launching a ferocious pastoral letter denying Goa's authority outwith Portuguese territory and demanding 'submissive obedience' to himself as the pope's representative.[139] It is unlikely anybody listened, although it was carefully translated into Portuguese. The only bright spot was his relationship with the government.

There was certainly a pent-up demand for chaplains. In early January 1849, a petition for an Irish priest was received from the station at Poona, some 90 miles south-east of Bombay. Almost all of the 279 signatories had an Irish surname.[140] At Belgaum, some 300 miles south near the border with Goa, a Scottish officer, Captain Charles Forbes Gordon, led appeals for a chaplain. Gordon thought the soldiers would rejoice to have a priest 'who will understand their characters'. 'The Irish Catholic soldiers are', he told Whelan, 'the best Catholics in India' and he offered 50 rupees a month for a salary.[141] Yet even in Belgaum things were not straightforward. On arrival, the Jesuit Sheehan discovered a long-serving native priest who did not wish to resign or share his house, and he was forced to lodge with the Gordons.[142] To clear Sheehan's path, Whelan offered Fr Maralino Antao the post of assistant chaplain at Kolapoor on 30 rupees a month, but Antao asked to be allowed to continue in Belgaum until he could apply to the East India Company for a long-service pension.[143] Whelan dithered and Sheehan began to panic: the monsoon was coming and Mrs Gordon wanted her house back.[144] By June, it was agreed that Antao could have a six-month leave of absence with Sheehan his stand-in.[145] At least the soldiers were 'pleased with their new chaplain'.[146]

---

[137] Whelan to St. Leger, 31 August 1849, OCDA/WP.
[138] Sheehan to Whelan, 9 June 1849, OCDA/WP.
[139] Pastoral Letter, 12 February 1849, OCDA/WP.
[140] A petition of the Roman Catholics of Poona to Whelan, 11 January 1849, OCDA/WP.
[141] Charles Forbes Gordon to Whelan, 8 February [1849], OCDA/WP.
[142] Sheehan to Whelan, 22 April 1849, OCDA/WP.
[143] Antao to Whelan, 26 May 1849, OCDA/WP.
[144] Sheehan to Whelan, 20 May 1849, OCDA/WP.
[145] Sheehan to Whelan, 9 June 1849, OCDA/WP.
[146] Sheehan to Whelan, 22 April 1849, OCDA/WP.

Whelan also fell out with the remaining Jesuit, Alexander Kyan, which seems to have been easy to do. Kyan, for example, entered into a vicious row with the Loreto Sisters for harbouring a Mrs Fleming who had fled from her husband. In increasingly hysterical letters, he demanded they expel her and 'treat her as a heathen & a publican'. 'For the sake of the children confined to your care', he raged, 'let not the house be any longer contaminated with her presence.'[147] By mid-June, Kyan and Whelan were barely speaking.[148] The underlying issue appears to have been the Jesuits' hope to use Bombay as an 'asylum' for members of the society forced to flee the Italian revolutions, which had been St. Leger's reason for sending Sheehan and Kyan in the first place.[149] The state of the vicariate made this impossible, and it seems that Kyan at least did not enjoy being relegated to chaplaincy duties.

Unable to procure priests in Ireland, Whelan turned to Madras. John Fennelly, who had replaced Carew in 1841, sent two: Richard Joseph Murphy and James Corry. This was not generosity: he liked neither, telling Whelan that they were both spendthrifts. He was appalled when Murphy spent 500 rupees on black suits, for example, 'a luxury which he was never allowed to enjoy in this vicariate'. Murphy's defence that this was how Irish priests dressed in Bombay cut no ice with Fennelly, and he recommended that neither be paid more than 50 rupees a month. It was hardly a ringing endorsement, but Whelan had no choice. Worse, their passage cost some 400 rupees he did not have.[150] Corry was sent to Poona, where he reported there were some 2,200 Catholics (2,000 European, the rest Tamil 'camp-followers'), 2,000 Protestants, and 2,000 'Goanese Schismatics'.[151] Murphy went to Fort Bombay to effectively replace Kyan.[152] He also became Whelan's vicar general, although whether by choice or by default is unclear.

Whelan was assailed from all sides, not least his own. Sheehan, for example, complained that he was treating the Jesuits very badly, himself very badly, and 'his vicariate very badly'. He drew Murray's attention to what he said was Whelan's excessive consumption of brandy, which he thought accounted for 'a violence of temper which is intolerable'. He also claimed to have seen Whelan drunk in public, 'making a fool of himself' as 'freemasons and profligates were chuckling with delight'. 'He has',

---

[147] Kyan to 'Dear Mother', 10 May 1849, OCDA/WP. There are many similar letters in Whelan's papers, obviously forwarded by the convent.
[148] See Whelan to Kyan, 15 June 1849, Kyan to Whelan, 15 June 1849, OCDA/WP.
[149] St. Leger to Whelan, no date [1849], OCDA/WP.
[150] Fennelly to Whelan, 7 March, 2 May 1849, OCDA/WP.
[151] Corry to Whelan, 20 December 1849, OCDA/WP.
[152] Corry to Murphy, 2 October 1849, OCDA/WP.

Sheehan concluded, 'lost caste.'[153] It is difficult to know what to make of these charges. Both Jesuits seem to have been frustrated by the failure of their refuge scheme and annoyed to have been reduced to insecure and poorly paid work as chaplains. Whelan also caught Kyan lying about his contacts with St. Leger in Dublin.[154] Nor is there anything in the bishop's surviving correspondence or that of the two Irish secular priests that suggest such conduct. Indeed Corry, admittedly writing to Whelan, blamed him only for 'excessive meekness & forbearance'.[155] Still, the charges were very specific.

The Loreto nuns were no more impressed. Within days of landing they were complaining about their accommodation, the consequent need to delay opening their school, and the fact that without a cloister they were still forced to wear 'secular dress'. 'All I can do is pray', M. Philomena Frizelle told Teresa Ball, 'for our wishes weigh lightly with the Bishop.'[156] Whelan soon made matters worse by sacking Frizelle as mother superior. Her replacement seems to have been grossly unsuitable: Kyan thought her an unbalanced plotter, while Whelan's successor found her a nuisance and ultimately sent her home.[157] Whelan also forced the women to dismiss the male servant who guarded their property, and within days they had suffered several break-ins and significant vandalism.[158] Soon Frizelle was completely broken: rain was pouring through their windows, the schoolroom was too small to teach in, the school itself was too far from the centre, and Whelan was disinterested in their plight. Everything was 'confusion and complaint', she told Ball, and she wanted to go home.[159]

From their strongholds on the Malabar Coast, the Italian Carmelites also denounced Whelan, whom they called 'Monsignor Villano'. They claimed that he was ruining the mission out of nationalism, replacing beloved Italian priests with Irishmen interested only in the European Catholics.[160] There was some truth to this: as elsewhere, the Irish bishops in India concentrated their resources on their Irish flock. Yet in India at least they sought to compensate by providing native clergy drawn from the communities they would serve. This resulted in an early enthusiasm for native seminarians and native ordinations. Whelan seems to have been

---

[153] Sheehan to Murray, 7 May 1849, DDA/WP/ 34/11/28.
[154] See Whelan to St. Leger, 31 August 1849, OCDA/WP.
[155] Corry to Whelan, 16 May 1849, OCDA/WP.
[156] Frizelle to Ball, 14 November 1848, LAD/TB/IND/1/6.
[157] Kyan to Ball, 13 January 1849, Anastasius Hartmann to Ball, 20 August 1850, LAD/TB/IND/3/1, 2/4.
[158] Frizelle to Ball, 28 June 1849, LAD/TB/IND/1/10.
[159] Frizelle to Ball, 20 May 1849, LAD/TB/IND/1/8.   [160] See Ballhatchet, 69.

particularly sympathetic, appointing a native vicar general and ordering Marathi sermons in the cathedral.[161] Nor were the Carmelites on particularly strong ground in denouncing Whelan's administration: Bombay had been consistently chaotic under the Italians, and Whelan's clashes with the lay trustees were hardly unique. Yet whatever the truth of the various accusations, they arrived at a dangerous time for the Irish: the pope and the Propaganda were in exile in Gaeta, while Cullen remained in Rome at the Irish College. He was in no position to interfere on Whelan's behalf and may not even have known of the Italians' complaints.

On 28 November 1849, Whelan received orders from the Propaganda requiring him to report to Rome.[162] Before he left, he had the pleasure of sending Fr Murphy to tell the visiting but uninvited Carmelite bishops of Kerala and Mangalore that neither they nor their meddling were welcome in Bombay and they would not be permitted to celebrate Mass there.[163] When he reached Rome, Whelan proved to be unwilling to save his position and soon resigned, much to the delight of the Loreto Sisters.[164] He retired to Ireland, where the Carmelites gave him a £150 annuity; Cullen later employed him as what amounted to an auxiliary bishop in Dublin. His replacement in Bombay was the Swiss Capuchin Anastasius Hartmann, who since 1845 had been vicar apostolic of Patna, in north-east India.

Hartmann had a mixed relationship with the Irish. On the one hand, he sacked Murphy as vicar general, refused to give him a new assignment, and ignored a petition from some 300 'British Catholics' asking for a 'British' priest. Subsequent enquiries were met, Murphy claimed, with Hartmann refusing the 'turbulent Irish' and slamming the door in their faces. With such a 'superlatively anti-Irish bishop' Murphy decided to return home.[165] Kyan and Sheehan had already left, and by early 1851 the *Bombay Catholic Standard and Military Chronicle* was complaining bitterly about Hartmann's disregard of the 'British community of Bombay'.[166] The Loreto nuns, however, were delighted with their new bishop, whom they thought had 'done wonders', while Hartmann himself not only asked for more Irish women but also unsuccessfully petitioned both Rome and Cullen for

---

[161] See Pastoral Letter, 12 February 1849, OCDA/WP.   [162] Whelan diary, CLD/631.
[163] For an account of the interview, see Murphy to Whelan, 31 December 1849, OCDA/WP.
[164] For example, Frizelle to Ball, 25 June 1850, LAD/TB/IND/1/15.
[165] Murphy to Whelan, 15 October 1850, OCDA/WP.
[166] *Bombay Catholic Standard and Military Chronicle*, 20 January 1851.

Irish Christian Brothers.[167] Yet at all events the Irish presence in Bombay had been swept away, leaving only the Loreto nuns and Fr Corry at Poona. Hartmann meanwhile left Bombay in 1856 and was replaced by a German Jesuit. The society retained power in the city until the 1950s.

Irish control lasted longer in Calcutta, but not much. Under Carew, the church there had a distinctly Irish feel, not least because his enthusiastic assertions of episcopal supremacy eventually drove the Jesuits out.[168] Irish news was prominent in the Catholic press and Irish chaplains ubiquitous among the troops. The city's Catholic schools were run by Irish religious orders, and Carew managed to recruit at least nine students from All Hallows.[169] In 1846, he was able to raise £5,000 for Irish famine relief in just a few weeks.[170] Yet all this depended on the archbishop himself. His rule became increasingly abrasive, and he quarrelled with both the Loreto Sisters and his own coadjutor Thomas Oliffe.[171] By 1852, Cullen wondered if Oliffe should be sent to Corfu as 'he is not fond of India and Dr. Carew does not admire him'.[172] Recruitment remained difficult, not helped by the activities of Carew's emissary who, in at least one instance, adopted a Maynooth seminarian for Calcutta despite warnings of 'his total lack of ecclesiastical spirit' and tendency to drink. He had the man ordained deacon and then cut all contact with him for months. As the dean of students at Maynooth noted dryly, such conduct 'appeared very strange to all of us here'.[173] It can only have hurt Calcutta's chances in what remained a highly competitive market for missionary priests.

In 1855, Carew fell seriously ill. Cullen tried to arrange an appointment to an Irish diocese 'to save his life', but he was too late.[174] He felt Carew's loss, remarking that 'It is singular how the best among the Bishops are the first to fall 'tho', he added coldly, 'some of the poor ones are also picked down occasionally.'[175] Although Cullen remained interested in Indian affairs, and especially the provision of chaplains for the Irish soldiers, Carew's death marked the end of his involvement in the ecclesiastical

[167] Frizelle to Ball, 25 June 1850, LAD/TB/IND/1/15; Hartmann to Ball, 16 April 1850, LAD/TB/IND/2/1; Cullen to T. C. Loughnane, 10 November 1855, DDA, Cullen Letter-book [LB] 1/92.
[168] Neill, 301; Crosbie, 158–9.
[169] Derived from the 'Matricula: 1842-'91' published in Condon, All Hallows, and analysed by Mary Carmichael.
[170] Carew to Murray, 5 February 1846, DDA/MP/34/11/21.
[171] See Carew to Murray, 5 September 1845, DDA/MP/34/11/18/(1).
[172] Cullen to Smith, 17 June 1852, ASSP/SP/Irlanda.
[173] Gaffney to Cullen, 28 November 1853, DDA/CP/325/8/155.
[174] Cullen to Kirby, [1855], PICRA/NK/ 2/1/93.
[175] Cullen to Kirby, 22 December 1855, PICRA/NK/2/1/94.

politics of the subcontinent. When Oliffe died in 1859, Cullen raised no objections to the introduction of the Belgian Jesuits, and the society went on to provide every bishop and archbishop of Calcutta until 1986. Although the Loreto Sisters and the Christian Brothers remained, many of the Irish priests left. Few new ones came: a mere three from All Hallows, for example, and none at all from Carlow. It was only in Madras that Irish influence endured.

Carew's translation meant that, for the third time in six years, Rome needed to find a new bishop for the southern presidency. At Daniel Murray's suggestion, the Propaganda chose another Maynooth product, its bursar John Fennelly. Described by Clément Bonnard as 'fine structured' and uncommunicative, Fennelly was from what became a prominent clerical family; his brother succeeded him in Madras, and his first cousin was the tempestuous and litigious Fr Robert O'Keeffe.[176] Fennelly began by recruiting in Ireland, securing four seminarians and a group of Presentation Sisters from Co. Kildare who promptly established a girls' school in the Georgetown district of Madras. They continued to bring women directly from Ireland, from the three who took the veil in a grand ceremony in 1844 to the nine who came from St Brigid's Missionary College before 1914.[177] In 1844, they were joined by three Irish Presentation Brothers who founded a boys' school.[178] The existing orphanage also continued to grow, and in Fennelly's first two years in Madras the soldiers contributed £550 and the European civilians £527, while £274 came from the 'East Indian community' for the 'maintenance of orphans of their own class'.[179] Although Fennelly bitterly complained that there was never enough money for education, the children of European Catholics at least were well provided for.

The ongoing shortage of clergy was his most significant challenge. Not long after he arrived at Madras, for example, Fennelly had fallen out with Carew over the suspicion that he was poaching priests for Calcutta. (Cullen was forced to mediate.)[180] In fact, Fennelly was relatively successful in securing clergy, at least compared to his brethren, largely

---

[176] See Anchukandam, Catholic Revival, 1: 187; for the extraordinary O'Keeffe, see Barr, *The European Culture Wars in Ireland: The Callan Schools Affair, 1868–81* (Dublin: University College Dublin Press, 2010).

[177] *Madras Catholic Expositor*, vol. 4, no. 5, July 1844, 193–8; Register of Aspirants/ ACRSM.

[178] The Presentation Brothers were an offshoot of the Irish Christian Brothers. They chose to follow the stricter rule of the Presentation Sisters and to live under the authority of the local bishop. See Tom O'Donoghue, *Catholic Teaching Brothers: Their Life in the English-Speaking World* (New York: Palgrave Macmillan, 2010), 36.

[179] *Madras Catholic Expositor*, vol. 4, no. 1, March 1844, 10.

[180] Ambrose Macaulay, *Dr Russell of Maynooth* (London: Darton, Longman and Todd, 1983), 236.

because of his close links to Maynooth. There was always a steady trickle of priests and seminarians. Fennelly's brother Stephen, for example, arrived in 1844 in the company of another priest and four clerical students.[181] More than twenty more came from All Hallows before 1891.[182] Although things were always tight, Fennelly could afford to send the unsatisfactory Fathers Murphy and Corry to Bombay, and after Carew's death Madras became the unquestioned destination for Irish clergy interested in the Indian mission. As one Irish priest reported on returning home after eight years there, traditional practices were finally 'yielding to the determination of Irishmen'.[183]

Fennelly knew that such an emphasis on Ireland and Irish personnel risked antagonizing the native population and to a degree sought to ameliorate it. He encouraged his priests to wear native dress and urged them to conform 'so far as religion will permit to the customs of this strange people, making ourselves all to all'.[184] Even a largely hostile French-led visitation in 1868 noted that at least three Irish priests in Madras devoted themselves to the native population.[185] This was more attention than the Irish paid to the Xhosa, Māori, or Mi'kmaq, but accommodation had its limits and Fennelly was implacably hostile to caste distinctions among Catholics. He was appalled when a new church in Pondicherry was built with a three-foot-high interior wall to separate high and low, for example.[186] It was the endurance of caste identities and prejudices that made Fennelly warier than his predecessors of native clergy; and, with Roman encouragement, he chose instead to recruit Irish missionaries who were prepared to learn native languages.[187]

When John Fennelly died in 1868, his brother Stephen was the obvious successor. He continued his brother's policies and looked to Ireland for clergy, not least from Maynooth.[188] His successor was John Colgan, an Irishman who had arrived with him in 1844. Colgan became Madras' first archbishop when the Indian hierarchy was created in 1886, and by 1908 was feted as far away as New Zealand as the 'oldest Bishop in the British Empire'.[189] When he died in 1911, he was commemorated in the *Irish Monthly* as one of 'Ireland's great men' who had 'belonged to that famous band of Irishmen who have ruled in Church or State, with conspicuous ability, vast provinces of the British Empire'.[190] Yet after nearly seventy-

---

[181] *Madras Catholic Expositor*, vol. 4, no. 1, March 1844, 14.
[182] Analysed by Mary Carmichael.   [183] Quoted in Ballhatchet, 108.
[184] Nathaniel O'Donnell to Woodlock, '1849', quoted in Crosbie, 157.
[185] Ballhatchet, 109.   [186] Ibid., 108.   [187] Ibid., 109.   [188] Macaulay, *Russell*, 236.
[189] *NZT*, 7 May 1908.
[190] J. J. L. Ratton, 'The bishop's cash-chest: A true story', *The Irish Monthly* (1911), quoted in Joseph Lennon, *Irish Orientalism: A Literary and Intellectual History* (Syracuse: Syracuse University Press, 2004), 177.

five years of Irish domination in Madras, his successor was a Dutch member of the English Mill Hill Missionaries. John Colgan was the last Irish bishop in colonial India.

This however was in the future; in the 1840s, there were still thoughts of expansion. When Ceylon unexpectedly fell vacant in 1842, for example, Carew and Fennelly agreed on the necessity of appointing an Irishman.[191] A transiting French priest had reported from Colombo that the Goanese clergy there were indolent and corrupt and the Irish soldiers badly neglected.[192] Thus primed, Rome selected Charles Russell, the scholarly professor of ecclesiastical history at Maynooth. Both the Goanese and Russell were horrified, and Russell spent months trying to get his appointment rescinded. Although Cullen thought it 'desirable' that there should be an Irish vicar apostolic in Ceylon allied to Carew and Fennelly, he reluctantly helped Russell escape.[193] Soon the restoration of relations with Lisbon had made further Irish appointments impossible, but as late as 1850 the vicar apostolic of heavily Tamil Jaffna was still seeking Irish teachers for his schools.[194]

The Irish could still expand by division, and in 1845 Fennelly successfully lobbied Rome to place a bishop at Hyderabad, some 650 kilometres north-west of Madras.[195] The choice was another Irishman, Daniel Murphy. Although he was appointed at the end of 1845 and consecrated the following year, he did not arrive in India until the middle of 1847. The reason as usual was the need to secure priests. Cullen thought three students at the Irish College might go, including the future bishop of Auckland and archbishop of Cashel, Thomas Croke. He did not, and Cullen found it necessary to warn another correspondent never to mention the names of potential recruits 'lest their friends sd throw obstacles in their way'.[196] India, and particularly central India, was simply not attractive. As Cullen put it when soliciting Italian recruits from Antonio Rosmini's Institute of Charity, Hyderabad had around two million people, 'some pagan, some Muslim', 6,000 Catholics, three priests, and no money. Any volunteer would have to pay his own way, although Cullen did

---

[191] See Cullen to Murray, 1 December 1842, DDA/MP/31/9/96.
[192] Macaulay, *Russell*, 40–1.
[193] Cullen to Murray, 1 December 1842, DDA/MP/31/9/96. For Russell's intensive man-oeuvrings, see Macaulay, *Russell*, 43–50.
[194] Joseph Maria Bettachini to Murray, 15 January 1850, DDA/MP/34/11/31.
[195] Until Hyderabad was erected as a vicariate in its own right in 1851, Murphy was technically Fennelly's coadjutor in Madras.
[196] Cullen to Dixon, 18 April 1847, Cardinal Tomás Ó Fiaich Memorial Library and Archive, Dixon papers, Irish College Rome file, Box 1.

promise that '*I pagani*' were easy to convert.[197] The prospect does not appear to have tempted the Rosminians, but Murphy did manage to secure the young Irish College student Matthew Quinn, who in 1865 became the first bishop of Bathurst, New South Wales. He also managed to obtain five students from Carlow and three from All Hallows.[198] This was just about enough to provide chaplaincy services across his vast territory, but little more.

Murphy proved to be an active bishop. Among other achievements, he built a cathedral, learned to speak Urdu and Tamil, and claimed to have converted seven Protestants during one of his sea voyages.[199] As Hyderabad was under a Muslim ruler, he set himself to learning Arabic and studying the Quran, and in later years boasted of an exchange with a 'leading Mahomedan' who had 'made a fierce attack on the Bible'. Murphy replied with English citations from the Quran; and, when his interlocutor demanded them in Arabic, he was 'quite confounded' when Murphy obliged.[200] He was a regular visitor to Rome and London, seeking priests and political support. At one point he used the English Catholic historian and MP Sir John Acton to facilitate his access to ministers.[201] The perpetual shortage of priests prompted him to turn to the newly established missionary seminary in Milan for help, and in 1855 Hyderabad received two of its first five graduates. Murphy was delighted with their quality, not least because they were sent 'out to the missions only after an apprenticeship of at least two years'.[202] By 1864, however, he was exhausted, telling friends in Rome that he would 'never return to India'.[203] In 1865, he was appointed to Hobart, Tasmania, where he eventually became an archbishop and served until 1907. His replacement in Hyderabad was one of the Milanese missionaries.

As Irish interest in India's ecclesiastical politics faded, attention turned to forcing the British state to provide chaplains on an equitable basis. One of the first opportunities came in 1852, when a parliamentary select committee was established to investigate Indian affairs. As the Catholic Liberal MP J. D. Fitzgerald told Cullen, 'the present opportunity of

---

[197] Cullen to Antonio Rosmini, 17 April 1847, ASIC/RP/1058–1059, f. 794. Original in Italian.
[198] Analysed by Mary Carmichael.
[199] For the last, Murphy to Cullen, 15 January 1853, DDA/CP/325/5/II/122.
[200] Moran diary, 12, 15 May 1889, AAS. Moran was visiting Murphy and had clearly been asking about his experiences in India.
[201] See Grant to Acton, 17 February 1860, Cambridge University Library [CUL], Acton papers, Add. 8119(2)/G132.
[202] Quoted in Neil, 300. This group eventually became the Pontifical Institute for Foreign Missions.
[203] Moran to Cullen, 20 May 1864, DDA/CP/40/4.

bringing before Parliament and the public the position of the Catholics of British India should not be neglected'.[204] Working to instructions from Cullen, Fitzgerald secured Irish clerical witnesses from Calcutta, Madras, and the erstwhile Bishop Whelan of Bombay. They all testified to the unequal treatment of Catholic chaplains and the general lack of support given to the Catholic Church by the East India Company state. Catholics, they argued, should be treated on the same basis as everybody else and enjoy government largesse in proportion to their numbers.[205] Although the committee reported in 1853, nothing much was done before the Crimean War diverted political attention.

Appeals continued to arrive in London, from Bombay in 1853 and 1854, for example, and from the Irish vicars apostolic as a group in 1856. The English bishops added their voice with Thomas Grant of Southwark insisting in November 1855 that the salary of Catholic chaplains ought to 'be fairly proportioned to the scale and style of living of the Protestant chaplains'.[206] In 1856, the government of India announced that it would pay a fixed stipend to Catholic chaplains in place of the ad hoc and variable salaries previously offered. If they were expecting praise, they were quickly disillusioned. In a lengthy pamphlet, Stephen Fennelly of Madras denounced British parsimony root and branch. The government, he wrote, supplied 'no aid' for the 785,858 native Catholics, despite generously providing for Hindu and Muslim religious institutions and directly or indirectly supporting the Church of England and Church of Scotland. As for the 'British-born Catholics', if they had 'had to trust to the Company's Government for a provision of their spiritual wants, they would not have a Catholic priest in India at the moment'. The government never built Catholic churches, never paid the passage for Catholic priests, either to India or within it, refused to pay for seminarians, and gave nothing to bishops, bar a derisory 200 rupees a year (raised to 400 in 1856) paid to four of the seventeen Indian bishops. This was not, Fennelly thundered, the 'way that Government provides for its Protestant servants'.

In Poonamallee, for example, the Protestant chaplain received a salary of 6,000 rupees and allowances amounting to another 1,179 rupees a year. The Catholic chaplain received 1,200. In Bangalore, where there were three Protestant chaplains and only one Catholic, the former received 19,413 rupees a year versus 1,800 for the Catholic. In Madras,

---

[204] Fitzgerald to Cullen, 29 April 1853, DDA/CP/325/6/17.
[205] See the Report from the House of Commons Select Committee on Indian Territories (1853).
[206] Quoted in A. E. Medlycott, 'Catholic army chaplains: An historical statement of their case', *The Tablet*, 17 February 1883.

the Anglican establishment cost some 100,000 rupees, the two Church of Scotland ministers 20,811, while the sole Catholic priest at Fort St George was paid 1,200 rupees a year. Fennelly calculated that, on average, a Catholic priest was paid only a sixth of what a Protestant chaplain earned. Nor did they receive paid holidays, sick leave, or a pension. 'Catholics', Fennelly insisted, 'contribute in proportion to their numbers to all the expenses of the state; they pay taxes like every other class, and one would expect them to receive at the hands of a Christian government at least as much consideration as the pagan or Mohomedan.'[207] Except for the 'Mohomedan', it was an argument that would not have sounded out of place in Dublin or Dunedin.

Fennelly seems to have written his pamphlet before the great rebellion began in earnest; but, as soon as news of its severity reached Europe, Cullen sensed an opportunity in England's difficulty. In early July, just days after the massacre at Cawnpore, he indirectly prompted the Cork MP William Fagan to give notice of his intention to ask a parliamentary question about why a soldier in India received five shillings a month for sending his child to a Protestant school but nothing if he chose a Catholic one. The message was received and understood, and the president of the board of control promptly appeared at Fagan's London home to 'beg' that the question not be asked in the 'present state of affairs'. Vernon Smith, Cullen learned, promised to investigate and absolutely end any hint of difference between Catholic and Protestant children.[208]

Cullen kept up the pressure, telling Grant of Southwark on 14 July that the 'moment is most opportune' and that he should insist on chaplains for the troops 'and a few allowances for the education of Catholic children'.[209] He was equally blunt to William Monsell, the leading Irish Catholic member of the government: 'It has occurred to me that the present would be a favourable opportunity to obtain some spiritual advantage for our troops in India' who 'have to suffer a great deal from the want of chaplains.' He asked Monsell to speak to the minister of war and the company authorities: 'I am confident that they would not refuse to listen to the claims of the Catholic soldiers at this critical moment.'[210] In early August, Vernon Smith met Fagan and Grant about a quid pro quo for Catholic support for military recruitment.[211] This was easily reached through a promise to provide as many chaplains as necessary

---

[207] Fennelly, 5–10.
[208] A. C. O'Dwyer to Cullen, 8 July 1857, DDA/CP/339/8/I/3. Cullen made suggestions to O'Dwyer, O'Dwyer passed them to Fagan, and O'Dwyer then reported back to Cullen.
[209] Cullen to Grant, 14 July 1857, DDA/LB1/361.
[210] Cullen to Monsell, 14 July 1857, DDA/LB2/54.
[211] O'Dwyer to Cullen, 1 August 1857, DDA/CP/339/8/I12/(I).

and treat them equally, and there was anyway a limit to how far Grant and other English Catholics were prepared to push the government in wartime. This was less true in Ireland, where newspapers such as the *Cork Examiner* complained regularly throughout the latter part of 1857 about the company's neglect of the religious needs of the 'Irish soldier, who fights and bleeds in their cause'.[212] As for Cullen, he was entirely unsympathetic to Britain's plight, remarking coldly in early August that the 'news from India is very bad. Those who promoted revolutions are likely to suffer from revolutions.'[213] India was Britain's comeuppance for its support of Italian nationalism.[214]

Cullen continued to take a close interest in events, urging the government to make more concessions and supply more chaplains. By late January 1858, he had come to the conclusion that the 'East India Company should be deprived of its powers'. 'After that', he told the Catholic MP George Bowyer, 'a grant ought to be asked for in favour of purely Catholic schools and orphanages, for a purely Catholic college, and a large number of Chaplains'.[215] This should not, however, be on any terms: Cullen was jealous of diocesan authority and insisted that chaplains should be under the local bishop and not attached to a regiment. Citing Fennelly's experience in Madras, he pointed out to Cardinal Wiseman of Westminster that the salary paid to a chaplain often supported an entire mission.[216] Cullen wanted them to work with the army, not for it.

Indian tragedy could also be domesticated, as Cullen demonstrated in his 1858 Lenten pastoral. He expressed horror at the fate of civilians, warned against vengeance, deplored the destruction of convents, churches, and the Begum Sombre's magnificent cathedral, and linked the rebellion's savagery to Islam, Hinduism, and atheism. Yet his real target was Protestant England, and he recounted in fine detail every inequality visited upon the Catholic Church in India. Cullen linked these to the failure of the Protestant churches to convert the natives: 'All the patronage of the State, all the zealous exertions of the missionary societies, all the contributions of England, all the millions of Bibles that were scattered over the land, could not fertilise the teaching of Protestantism, nor give efficacy to the words of its preachers.' Making the comparison with Ireland explicit, he drew a line between the 'godless'

---

[212] *Cork Examiner*, 7 September, 14 October 1857, quoted in Crosbie, 143.

[213] Cullen to Miley, 4 August 1857, DDA/CP/40/4.

[214] See Colin Barr, 'Paul Cullen, Italy and the Irish Catholic Imagination', in Colin Barr, Michele Finelli, and Anne O'Connor (eds.), *Nation/Nazione: Irish Nationalism and the Italian Risorgimento* (Dublin: University College Dublin Press, 2014).

[215] Cullen to Bowyer, 30 January 1858, DDA/CP/30/1.

[216] Cullen to Wiseman, 1 May 1858, Westminster Diocesan Archives [WDA], Wiseman papers, W3/35/10.

Irish Queen's Colleges and the government schools in India that replaced the faith of their native students not with Christianity but with atheism. He pointed to proselytizing military orphanages and observed that everywhere the work of 'Protestant missionaries is to pull down that which has been built up, to pervert poor Catholics, and to prevent the spread of Catholic truth'. In India, those missionaries were the 'dregs of society' just as were those who presently 'infest several parts of Ireland'.[217] Had the Catholic Church been allowed a free hand, Cullen implied, the rebellion would never have happened.

Whatever Cullen's complaints, the transition from company to crown saw the Irish secure much of what they had demanded; and, if the state did not provide equally or adequately for Catholic institutions, that was true almost everywhere in the Empire bar Newfoundland. Chaplains were better paid, and complaints slowly decreased in frequency. With their religious grievances largely addressed, and without a significant civilian population, the interests of the Irish in India were identical with the state. Indeed, Irish Catholics there consistently referred to themselves as 'British'. This was true of the petitioning 'British Catholics' of Bombay and Calcutta, who were mostly Irish, or the perennial requests for 'British priests' when what was meant was 'Irish'. Even Bishop O'Connor of Madras used the word 'British' to describe his wholly Irish clergy. This was unimaginable elsewhere in Greater Ireland; even in the Cape Colony, Irish Catholics became European or white, not British. The reality was that the Irish were in India as conquerors, whether armed or otherwise, and it is unsurprising that they identified with the imperial power even before the trauma of 1857.

In ecclesiastical terms, however, the Irish experience in India was one of near-total failure. Irish bishops and priests had been driven from Calcutta and Bombay and even Hyderabad, leaving only their Madras redoubt, and then only until 1911. Their sole enduring success was embedding the principle that Catholic soldiers should be provided with chaplains and that those chaplains should be treated with something approaching parity with their Protestant peers. Consider Rudyard Kipling's great novel *Kim*, published in 1901. When the young Kimball O'Hara is serendipitously caught by his father's Irish regiment, his interrogators are the dour and intolerant Anglican chaplain, the Rev. Bennett, and the portly and sympathetic Catholic chaplain, Father Victor. As Kim's father had been a freemason, his fate seemed to be a Protestant education at the military

---

[217] 'On the Church in India', in Patrick Francis Moran, *The Writings of Cardinal Cullen*, 3 vols. (Dublin: Browne & Nolan, 1882), 1: 542–4, 546–8. Cullen no doubt had the mostly English missionaries of the Society for Irish Church Missions in mind. See Miriam Moffitt, *The Society for Irish Church Missions to the Roman Catholics, 1849–1950* (Manchester: Manchester University Press, 2010).

orphanage. Yet, through the machinations of Fr Victor, Kim is sent instead to 'St. Xavier's in Partibus, Lucknow', departing with the priest's earnest instruction to tell the authorities there that he is a Catholic. There is no hint of bigotry or disadvantage, and *Kim* is a perfect illustration of Irish Catholicism's greatest success in India, except for two things: Father Victor was an Englishman and Kim became a British spy.

4   South Africa

The Irish in general and the Catholic Irish in particular are the lost tribe of southern Africa. Writing in 1991, Donald Akenson claimed that the 'Irish in South Africa were not a coherent ethnic group' because they raised no 'great memorials to themselves' and lacked the 'self-celebration' so notable in the American Irish. Excepting a few 'admirable fugitive pieces', Akenson continued, there is 'almost no historiographical tradition for the Irish in South Africa'.[1] For Donal McCracken, this lacuna was the result both of the country's long academic isolation and of the sense within South African academia that the study of a small English-speaking white ethnic group lacked 'historical relevancy'.[2] This remains the case: modern writing on the Irish in colonial South Africa can fit comfortably on a very small shelf. Other than Akenson's short book, what little there is is for the most part concerned with transient nationalists and pro-Boers such as John MacBride and the future Sinn Féin leader Arthur Griffith, exotics like the Fenian, police informer, militia commander, doctor, and newspaper editor Alfred Aylward, or the Irish bandits of the Transvaal goldfields.[3] Of the settled Irish there is almost nothing. What exceptions there are are largely associated with the wider McCracken family, including the three volumes of *Southern African-Irish Studies* published in Durban in the 1990s, J. L. McCracken's biography of the Ulster liberal and Cape Colony politician William Porter, Eileen McCracken's essays on Aylward and Arthur Griffith and her unpublished doctoral thesis on the Cape's demographics, and Donal McCracken's studies of the Irish pro-Boers. Yet these are the exceptions that prove the rule; and, the

---

[1] Donald Harman Akenson, *Occasional Papers on the Irish in South Africa* (Grahamstown: Institute of Social and Economic Research, Rhodes University, 1991), 42.

[2] Donal P. McCracken, 'Irish settlement and identity in South Africa before 1910', *Irish Historical Studies*, vol. 28, no. 110 (November 1992), 134–49, at 134.

[3] See, for example, Donal P. McCracken, *The Irish Pro-Boers, 1877–1902* (Johannesburg: Perskor, 1989); Ken Smith, *Alfred Aylward: The Tireless Agitator* (Johannesburg: AD. Donker, 1983); Charles Van Onselen, *Masked Raiders: Irish Banditry in Southern Africa, 1880–1899* (Cape Town: Zebra Press, 2010). There is a particularly full literature concerned with Aylward.

Porter biography aside, they tend to confirm Akenson's view that the history of the Irish in southern Africa before 1875 is *'terra incognita'*.[4]

In fact, the Irish seem to be little better represented after 1875. Classic single-volume histories by scholars such as Eric Walker and C. W. de Kiewiet omitted them entirely, for example, and they are equally invisible in more recent scholarship such as Vivian Bickford-Smith's 1995 *Ethnic Pride and Racial Prejudice in Victorian Cape Town*.[5] There, the only explicit mentions of Irish people *as Irish* are a quotation from a bigoted letter to the editor signed 'Ulster Irishman' and a handful of references to a group of Irish labourers imported into the Cape Town docks in the early 1880s.[6] To Bickford-Smith, the Irish either did not exist in Cape Town or did not exist as a distinct ethnic group. Instead, they were subsumed into the larger categories of 'English' or 'White'.

In discussing the racially tinged campaigns of the municipal 'clean party' in the early 1880s, for example, Bickford-Smith identified what he called a 'mobilisation of English ethnicity in the city'. This 'Englishness', he continued, 'could potentially assimilate all White English speakers, including the numerous Capetonians from Scotland and even those Dutch speakers who had become sufficiently Anglicised'.[7] The Irish are not mentioned, but those that lived in the city must presumably have assimilated along with their Scottish and even Dutch neighbours. Although Noel Ignatiev famously, if unconvincingly, claimed that the American Irish chose to become white, late Victorian Cape Town must surely be the first modern example of the Catholic Irish choosing to become English.

The apparent absence of the Irish from the Cape (and from South Africa) is all the more implausible given that evidence of their presence was all around. In Cape Town itself, for example, consider the Cape Town Irish Volunteer Rifles, founded in 1885, or the enduringly ecumenical Cape Town Irish Association, the first chairman of which was the proprietor of the *Cape Times*, the Limerick-born former Church of Ireland priest Frederick St. Leger.[8] The city also had an Irish Town district

---

[4] Akenson, *South Africa*, 72.

[5] Eric A. Walker, *A History of South Africa* (London: Longmans, Green & Co., 1935[1928]), C. W. de Kiewiet, *A History of South Africa: Social and Economic* (Oxford: Oxford University Press, 1975 [1941]). Although now outdated, these texts set the tone and agenda for South African history for many decades.

[6] Vivian Bickford-Smith, *Ethnic Pride and Racial Prejudice in Victorian Cape Town: Group Identity and Social Practice, 1875–1902* (Cambridge: Cambridge University Press, 1995). For 'Ulster Irishman', see 71 – the writer took the view that the Malays were lazy; for the dock labourers, see 84, 90, 128, 179.

[7] Ibid., 39.

[8] The Cape Town Irish Volunteer Rifles was a short-lived unit founded in 1885 under the command of one Thomas O'Reilly. It was absorbed into a larger unit in 1891. For

(centred on a Kildare Street), populated largely by the workers of a nearby brewery. Irish cabbies employed by the Hibernia Omnibus Company dominated the trade in mid-Victorian Cape Town.[9] Cecil Rhodes not only hosted touring Home Rule politicians but made an extraordinary £10,000 contribution himself; presumably he hoped to be rewarded with Irish votes.[10] Both the Cape and Natal had Irish-born premiers.[11] St Patrick's Day celebrations were widespread and well attended throughout the colony: in 1871, for example, a 'standing room'–only congregation at the Catholic cathedral in Cape Town (a 'large proportion' of whom were Protestant) observed vespers, benediction, and the exposition of the blessed sacrament conducted by priests named O'Haire, McMahon, and O'Reilly. They were edified by a lecture on St Patrick and entertained by the music of the Catholic members of the 86th (Royal County Down) Regiment and the singing of the students of the Catholic St Joseph's Academy.[12] Even the shebeen, the ubiquitous informal bars of the townships, suggests an Irish influence.

This is not to say that the Irish were anything like a large or dominant segment of the population, even of the European population. For the Irish, southern Africa was by far the least congenial of the settler colonies. As one Cape Town newspaper complained in 1876, the Irish 'labouring classes' would not come to the colony in any numbers because they 'know nothing about it beyond having a dim idea that it is associated with Kaffir wars'; but they did 'know all about America and Australia, or think they do, having heard them talked about from their infancy by those who had friends there'.[13] As late as 1897, a visiting James Bryce noted 'hardly any Irish immigration'.[14] Still, some Irish did come, although, as Donald Akenson pointed out, precise numbers are hard to establish before 1875. It is clear that the settled population was low, although there was always a large military presence, many of whom would have been accompanied by family: in the 1840s, for example, Harriet Ward recalled the soldiers' wives on a troopship caught in a storm who 'called on the Virgin

St. Leger, see Gerald Shaw, *Some Beginnings: The* Cape Times *1876–1910* (Oxford: Oxford University Press, 1975), 7.

[9] McCracken, 'Irish settlement', 142–3.

[10] See Robert I. Rotberg, *The Founder: Cecil Rhodes and the Pursuit of Power* (New York: Oxford University Press, 1988), 230–3. The money was to be paid in two parts. It is unclear if Charles Stewart Parnell and his party ever received the second £5,000.

[11] Sir Thomas Upington in the Cape (1884–6), Albert Hime in Natal (1899–1903).

[12] *The Standard and Mail*, 19 March 1871, quoted in James O'Haire, *Recollections of Twelve Years' Residence (as a Missionary Priest) Viz: From July 1863 to June 1875 in the Western District of the Cape of Good Hope, South Africa, Selected Chiefly from his Diary* (Dublin: Cooke, Keating & Co., [1876]), 544–6.

[13] *Capetown Daily News*, 2 February 1876, quoted in O'Haire, 47.

[14] James Bryce, *Impressions of South Africa* (London: Macmillan & Co., 1897), 478.

and their favourite saints to help them in their peril'.[15] Some of these individuals or families would have stayed after their service ended or the regiment moved. There was a small group from Ireland among the famous 1820 settlers in the Eastern Cape, and some 6,500 Irish came out as assisted emigrants between 1823 and 1873, with perhaps another 8,500 by 1900.[16] When the Irish priest James O'Haire began his travels into the Western Cape hinterland in the early 1860s, he was surprised by the number of Irishmen he found who had been living for many years in near-total isolation.[17] By 1891, a rough estimate suggests that there were 14,000 Cape residents of Irish birth or extraction, from a total 'white' population of 376,000, of which 130,000 identified with one of the constituent parts of the United Kingdom. The Irish were thus 3.7 per cent of the European population but 10.9 per cent of those from the British Isles.[18] This proportion seems to have held relatively steady: by 1926, Akenson estimated the some 59,000 Irish represented 3.5 per cent of whites.[19] Had this population been evenly scattered across the vast breadth of the Cape Colony, its relative absence in the historiography might be easier to understand. But it was not: the Irish were heavily urbanized, with 85 per cent living in towns by 1891.[20] While the Irish were clearly what Donal McCracken described as 'a minority of a minority', in places like Cape Town, Port Elizabeth, or Grahamstown, they must have been an important and visible minority.[21] In 1856, for example, the newly appointed Bishop Patrick Moran estimated that there were 1,700 mostly Irish Catholics in Port Elizabeth and another 450 in Grahamstown.[22] By 1874, a newly arrived priest reported that there were about 4,000 mostly Irish Catholics in the Eastern Cape as a whole.[23] When he arrived in 1863, James O'Haire thought that there were about 6,000 Irish in Cape Town proper; by 1868, perhaps 3,500 of them were Catholic.[24]

---

[15] Harriet Ward, *Five Years in Kaffirland; with Sketches of the Late War in that Country, to the Conclusion of the Peace. Written on the Spot*, 2nd ed., 2 vols. (London: Henry Colburn, 1848), 1: 16.

[16] Akenson, *South Africa*, 53.

[17] O'Haire, 355. There are many other examples in the book.

[18] Akenson, *South Africa*, 42; See also McCracken, 'Irish settlement', 135.

[19] Akenson, *South Africa*, 68.   [20] McCracken, 'Irish settlement', 142.

[21] Donal P. McCracken, 'Preface', in Donal P. McCracken (ed.), *The Irish in Southern Africa*, vol. 2 (Durban: Ireland and Southern Africa Project, 1992), 5.

[22] Moran to [Andrew O'Connell], 13 October 1856, Port Elizabeth Diocesan Archives [PEDA], Moran papers, PM/Doc/162/PM/1. The letter is addressed to 'My Dear Dean' but this is almost certainly O'Connell.

[23] E. Coghlan to Fr. Jones, SJ, 8 July 1874, ABSI, Zambesi Mission papers [ZM], #1. Coghlan – a secular priest – had just arrived in the Eastern Cape.

[24] O'Haire, 37; Kathleen Boner, 'The Irish Dominicans and education in the Western Cape (1863–1892)', unpublished MA thesis, University of South Africa, 1976, 14–15.

The Irish are not the only population to have been sent for ethnic reassignment. In his examination of the Scots in South Africa, John Mackenzie took Bickford-Smith to task for the 'rather transparent let-out' of simply defining all British Isles settlers as 'English'.[25] As Mackenzie correctly observed, the United Kingdom is too often seen as 'some kind of undifferentiated whole' and that, consequently, the 'metropole needs to be deconstructed as much as the periphery'. Only if that were done would it be possible to 'understand the complex of forces that were brought to bear upon southern Africa and its peoples'.[26] The result was a detailed study that emphasized the endurance of a distinctly Scottish identity and culture well into the twentieth century. That there has been no equivalent attention paid to the South African Irish is ironic, as Mackenzie himself took as a model the recent historiography of the global Irish diaspora, which he praised as 'subtle, suggestive and sophisticated'.[27]

This Irish elusiveness can be attributed both to their relatively small numbers and to the reluctance of South African scholars to consider the history of whites in general and non-Afrikaners in particular. As Saul Dubow has pointed out, 'Important dimensions of South African history risk being occluded or lost if the role of whites is viewed too narrowly in terms of settler colonialism and exploitation, and if resistance to apartheid becomes our only frame of historical reference'.[28] In the case of the Irish, this problem seems to be more acute as a result of two peculiarities in the pattern of their migration and settlement in southern Africa: a majority were Protestant and a high proportion of the total Irish immigrant pool were either prosperous or highly skilled or both.

As so often in Ireland itself, it was the question of religion that was paramount. In the Cape, only some 44 per cent of Irish immigrants were Roman Catholics.[29] It was relatively simple for Irish Anglicans or Presbyterians of a secure social or economic standing to comfortably blend with their English, Scottish, or even Dutch neighbours. As Mackenzie pointed out, the Calvinist Scots often found more religious and cultural common ground with the Afrikaners than they did with English Anglicans, and it is not difficult to imagine Ulster Presbyterians making a similar discovery.[30] It is equally easy to imagine prosperous Irish Anglicans like Frederick St. Leger blending easily with their social and

---

[25] John M. Mackenzie with Nigel R. Dalziel, *The Scots in South Africa: Ethnicity, Identity, Gender and Race, 1772–1914* (Manchester: Manchester University Press, 2007), 267.
[26] Ibid., 268.   [27] Ibid., 4.
[28] Saul Dubow, *A Commonwealth of Knowledge: Science, Sensibility, and White South Africa 1820–2000* (Oxford: Oxford University Press, 2006), 10.
[29] Akenson, *South Africa*, 41. This remained relatively constant: in 1926, 43.4 per cent of those who self-identified as Irish also indicated that they were Catholics (Ibid., 70).
[30] Mackenzie, 242.

denominational peers; Vivian Bickford-Smith, for example, described St. Leger without mentioning his ethnic origins, despite St. Leger's role in founding the Cape Town Irish Association.[31] It is also suggestive that Bickford-Smith almost invariably omitted the Roman Catholic Church when he considered the behaviour of the various Cape Town denominations, for example when he gives the number of white and non-white congregants for all churches *except* the Catholic, or his similar failure to discuss Catholic practice when noting the racial segregation of seats and then services and, finally, church buildings on the part of the Dutch Reformed, Methodist, and Anglican communities.[32] As Donal McCracken observed, 'assimilation into white society' was easier where 'the immigrant Irish population had a high preponderance of Protestants and held a position of status in colonial society'.[33]

South African Catholics were in a different position: their church obsessively discouraged institutional and matrimonial mixing, either with native Africans or with Protestant Europeans. As elsewhere, this tendency became more pronounced as the Catholic Church in the Cape became more established and, subsequently, more Hiberno-Roman. The best way, then, to approach the history of the Irish in southern Africa, at least as a distinct ethnic group with an enduring identity, is through the Roman Catholic Church. And the Cape Catholics were largely Irish: in the early 1920s, a young Denis Hurley, the future long-serving archbishop of Durban, supposedly answered 'Irish' when his teacher asked his religion.[34] John Mackenzie has noted that, while there were 'of course' some Scottish Catholics, 'they do not show up well in the record' and probably blended with their Irish co-religionists.[35] The same seems to have been true of English Catholics. There were exceptions, such as an English convert named Goldie who worked in the engineering department of the Cape government, or the Scottish-born historian and politician Alexander Wilmot, who among other things wrote a biography of the Irish Catholic bishop J. D. Ricards and an early history of the Cape Colony itself.[36] Yet despite individual outliers, isolated communities such as the Catholic soldiers of the British German Legion in Kaffraria,

---

[31] Bickford-Smith, 46.   [32] Ibid., 34, 25.   [33] McCracken, 'Irish settlement', 145.

[34] Paddy Kearney, *Guardian of the Light: Denis Hurley: Renewing the Church, Opposing Apartheid* (New York: Continuum, 2009), 12.

[35] Mackenzie, 174.

[36] Goldie seems to have been converted by Bishop Grant of Southwark: Thomas Grimley to Grant, 14 December 1861, Archives of the Archdiocese of Southwark [SAA], Grant papers [GP]; Alexander Wilmot, *The Life and Times of the Right Rev. James David Ricards, Bishop of Retimo, in partibus infidelium, and Vicar-Apostolic of the Eastern Districts of the Cape Colony* (Cape Town: The Salesian Institute, 1908). Wilmot's daughter entered the Port Elizabeth convent of the Irish Dominicans in 1900.

the colony of Filipino fishermen at Kalk Bay, and a smattering of high-profile converts such as F. C. Kolbe and Rebecca Schreiner, the mother of the campaigning novelist Olive Schreiner, it is nevertheless the case that the great majority of Catholics were Irish, even if the majority of the Irish were not Catholic. As Bishop Grimley of Cape Town boasted to Archbishop Cullen's secretary in 1862, 'If you were to remove from this colony the Irish Catholic element, our holy faith would be ... utterly unknown.'[37] This association was exacerbated by the reluctance or inability of the Irish bishops to engage in missionary activities, choosing instead to concentrate their limited resources on what they called 'the children of the household'.[38] As one French missionary complained, Irish priests only cared about 'their exiled fellow-country-men' with the result that the 'Cape of Good Hope has been lost to the Church by the Irish'.[39]

It is unfortunate that even less has been written on South African Catholicism than on the South African Irish. For the nineteenth-century Cape, there are no scholarly diocesan histories, only one contemporary episcopal biography, no modern ones, and a handful of hagiographical or institutional studies, mostly compiled by amateur historians. The growing literature concerned with missionary activity in the Cape largely omits the Catholics, most likely because the Cape Catholics largely omitted missionary activity. The only single-volume history of the Catholic Church in South Africa as a whole is now more than fifty years old. Written by W. E. Brown, a convert English-born Scottish priest who retired to South Africa, it is useful but also pious, incomplete, and poorly organized, which is understandable as Brown did not live to finish it.[40] There are also a small number of published primary texts and a handful of professional historical studies, including J. B. Brain's volumes on the Catholic Church in Natal and the Transvaal, Philippe Denis' social history of the Dominican friars across southern Africa, and Kathleen Boner's study of the Irish Dominican sisters in South Africa.[41] Finally, there is F. B. Doyle's

---

[37] Grimley to George Conroy, 20 January 1862, in O'Haire, 474.

[38] See Marcel Dischl, *Transkei for Christ: A History of the Catholic Church in the Transkeian territories* (N.P.: The Author, 1982), xii. This self-published book represents almost the entirety of what has been produced on the Catholic Church in the borderlands between the Cape and Natal.

[39] Quoted in Oliver Rafferty, *Violence, Politics and Catholicism in Ireland* (Dublin: Four Courts Press, 2016), 57.

[40] W. E. Brown, *The Catholic Church in South Africa*, edited by Michael Derrick (New York: P. J. Kennedy & Sons, 1960).

[41] J. B. Brain, *Catholic Beginnings in Natal and Beyond* (Durban: T. W. Griggs & Co., 1975); J. B. Brain, *Catholics in Natal II* (Durban: Archdiocese of Durban, 1982); J. B. Brain, *The Catholic Church in the Transvaal* (Johannesburg: Missionary Oblates of Mary Immaculate, 1991); Philippe Denis, *The Dominican Friars in Southern Africa: A Social*

short, derivative, and error-prone contribution to *A History of Irish Catholicism.*[42]

Natal has been the primary focus of what scholarship there is, partly because of Brain's work, partly because the church there was dominated by the Oblates of Mary Immaculate, who took a close interest in their own history, but more particularly because of the almost gravitational attraction of the idiosyncratic Austrian Trappists at Mariannhill: a 1979 bibliography of Catholic South Africa found only six publications related specifically to the Cape, all but one ephemeral, while Mariannhill earned eleven items, mostly book length, and several in German.[43] Interest has not waned, and the mission has been the subject of a deservedly prize-winning novel by Michael Cawood Green.[44] Yet the constituent parts of colonial South Africa were both politically and ecclesiastically distinct, and the unchallenged Oblate dominance of Natal largely limited Irish interest to the Cape Colony – although, just like the New Zealand Marists, the Natal Oblates would themselves come to take on a distinctly green hue: Archbishop Denis Hurley, for example, was the son of an Irish lighthouse keeper and was trained by the Oblates in Ireland.

The Cape Colony was, in any event, the oldest, largest, wealthiest, and most important of the British possessions in southern Africa, at least until the growth of the Rand and the final absorption of the Transvaal in the wake of the South African War of 1899–1902. By contrast, colonial Natal was tiny, with only some 47,000 white inhabitants in 1891, of whom perhaps 1,000 were first-generation resident Irish.[45] As for the future Transvaal and Orange Free State, as late as 1870 the Oblate Bishop Marie-Jean-François Allard of Natal estimated that there were only 600–800 Catholics between them, 'mostly Irish'.[46] It was the Cape of

History (1577–1990) (Leiden: Brill, 1998), Kathleen Boner, *Dominican Women: A Time to Speak* (Pietermaritzburg: Cluster Publications, 2000).

[42] Francis B. Doyle, 'South Africa', in Patrick J. Corish (ed.), *A History of Irish Catholicism*, vol. 6, fascicle 4 (Dublin: Gill & Macmillan, 1971). Doyle's contribution was derived from an earlier unpublished master's thesis: F. B. Doyle, 'The Irish contribution to the Catholic Church in South Africa, 1820–1900', unpublished MA thesis, National University of Ireland, 1963. Both seem heavily dependent on Brown.

[43] See Paul Michael Meyer (ed.), *The Roman Catholic Church in South Africa, A Select Bibliography* (Cape Town: University of Cape Town Libraries, 1979).

[44] Michael Cawood Green, *For the Sake of Silence* (London: Quartet Books Limited, 2010). The book was first published in South Africa in 2008 and was awarded the 2009 Olive Schreiner Prize.

[45] McCracken, 'Irish settlement', 135.

[46] Allard to an unknown correspondent, 30 December 1870, quoted in O'Haire, 501. Given that there is no reason for O'Haire to have had access to Allard's private correspondence, this letter was likely a public one, probably to the Propagation of the Faith at Lyon.

Good Hope that was at the centre of Irish ecclesiastical interest, and, for all practical purposes, the Cape was an Irish mission from the beginning: before the 1837 appointment of the Irish Dominican Patrick Griffith as vicar apostolic, Catholicism was at best a marginal presence there. During the long years of Dutch rule, formal Catholic practice was proscribed, even if individual Catholics did pass through or even spend time in the colony. The first period of British military control (1795–1802) relaxed things somewhat, and the short rule of the Batavian Republic (1802–6) was officially religiously neutral; that extended to the authorities permitting Mass to be said in Cape Town Castle.[47] Rome despatched three Dutch priests and appointed one of them, Joannes Lansink, prefect apostolic. For the Catholic Church, the permanent return of the British in 1806 was a regression; the priests were expelled and Lansink died on the way home. No further action was taken until 1818, when an English Benedictine monk, Edward Bede Slater, was appointed vicar apostolic of the Cape of Good Hope. As the British refused him permission to reside there, he was sent instead to Mauritius, where he died in 1832.[48] Slater did delegate an Irish priest for Cape Town, Patrick Scully, who secured from the colonial government £75 per annum and land to build a chapel; he left in 1824, his successors a Dutch secular priest and another English Benedictine. Both had departed by 1835. Other than a transient Spanish Dominican, there was no priest in the colony until the arrival of Griffith.[49]

The absence of an institutional Catholic Church did not imply the absence of Catholics. Cape Town itself had a modest Catholic population, for example, and there were Catholics among both the 1820 settlers in the Eastern Cape and the soliders of the various regiments assigned to the colony.[50] Within the British administration, the colonial secretary, Lt. Col. Christopher Bird, was both Catholic and had a Jesuit brother, a fact publicly seized upon by William Parker, a disgruntled Irish Protestant settler who blamed Bird for assigning him poor-quality land.[51] In 1821, Bird was dismissed in a power struggle with the authoritarian governor: he blamed religious prejudice; the governor heatedly denied it.[52] Bird remained in Cape Town, a pillar of the small Catholic community, and his son would eventually help the first French Oblates in Natal learn English.[53] In the 1830s, critics of the lieutenant governor of the Eastern

---

[47] Walker, *South Africa*, 143.   [48] Brown, *South Africa*, 6–7.   [49] Ibid., 9, 23.
[50] McCracken, *Irish in Southern Africa*, 2: 17.
[51] Robert Ross, *Status and Respectability in the Cape Colony, 1750–1870: A Tragedy of Manners* (Cambridge: Cambridge University Press, 1999), 105.
[52] Ibid., and Anthony Kendal Millar, *Plantagenet in South Africa: Lord Charles Somerset* (Cape Town: Oxford University Press, 1965), 189.
[53] Brain, *Natal*, 113.

Province, Andries Stockenström, sought to undermine him by falsely claiming he had converted to Rome, and some of those who set out on the Great Trek were partly impelled by rumours that the Boers would be forced into Catholicism.[54] Although some sectarianism had an Irish tinge – the first Orange Lodge opened in Cape Town in 1852 – overt anti-Catholicism was largely limited to the Dutch population. In 1843, for example, the newly built village of Burghersdorp refused to permit a Catholic church, and, as late as 1864, Father O'Haire was cursed in Dutch and had dung thrown at him when he tried to establish a mission at Malmesbury.[55] Yet this was not the whole story: the small Catholic (and Irish) population, the relative absence of priests, and the high social standing of some of the laity minimized tensions, especially in urban areas. In 1828, for example, the committee that founded the South African College included a layman who, in the absence of Catholic clergy, was appointed to speak for Catholic interests.[56] Of all the challenges Bishop Griffith faced when he arrived in Cape Town, sectarian prejudice was far down his list.

The Irish Mission

The decision to appoint a resident vicar apostolic to the Cape was an early instance of Roman interest in Africa. In part, this was a result of the growing European involvement with the continent and the concomitant activity of Protestant missionaries. More particularly, it was a product of the general missionary enthusiasm of Gregory XVI's pontificate. The Cape of Good Hope was the first African vicariate of the era – the second was the Two Guineas (roughly the west coast north of Portuguese Angola), which was erected in 1842, with Egypt following in 1844.[57] The Cape was a logical place to start, both because the British would now admit and possibly even support a vicar apostolic with minimal restrictions and because the abortive earlier attempt meant that the area was on the minds of the *minutanti*. By 1836, Propaganda had resolved to send a bishop, if one could be found and the means arranged to support him, and any priests he might convince to travel with him.

The choice of an Irishman was natural but not inevitable. A British citizen was necessary in order to secure both government permission and government money, and Ireland was the obvious place to look, although it

---

[54] Walker, *South Africa*, 207.   [55] Ross, 106; O'Haire, 122–3.

[56] Eric A. Walker, *The South African College and the University of Cape Town* (Cape Town: Cape Times, 1929), 12.

[57] See Adrian Hastings, *The Church in Africa, 1450–1950* (Oxford: Oxford University Press, 1994), 248.

is worth remembering that it was at this time that the Propaganda was recruiting English Benedictines for the Australian mission. As in India, the Propaganda chose to seek the advice of Archbishop Daniel Murray of Dublin. Unlike in India, however, there were no French or Portuguese seeking to protect their own interests: the question was simply finding a suitable, willing candidate and providing for his needs as well as possible.

Following the lead of W. E. Brown, it has been assumed by South African historians that Griffith was appointed as a result of the representations of one John Brady, an Irish priest based in Mauritius who called at the Cape in 1837 on his way back to Europe. According to this narrative, Brady (who would later become the disastrous and duplicitous first bishop of Perth in Western Australia) was appalled by what he found in Cape Town and brought back with him an appeal signed by the leading Catholics of the colony, including Lt. Col. Bird, several soldiers, and the vice-consul of France. It was on foot of this that Rome began the process that concluded with Griffith's appointment.[58] This is wrong: Brady did indeed carry such a petition to Rome in 1837, but the Propaganda had already resolved to take action, a decision that was also in advance of a mid-April 1836 request from the Benedictines on Mauritius. As early as February of that year, there seems to have been a search underway in Rome and Dublin for an appropriate candidate.[59] By July, the Propaganda had privately announced its firm intention to set up the Cape vicariate and asked Murray to approach the British government. By late August, they had settled on Patrick Griffith, a Limerick-born Dominican based in Dublin who Murray had first suggested as a possible vicar apostolic for Madagascar.[60] Still, no announcement would be made until it was known what if any official support might be available.[61] Finally, in July 1837, the vicariate was formally created and Griffith appointed.[62] The delay was attributable to Roman anxiety: all Cardinal Fransoni's 'fears', Cullen informed Murray, 'were regarding the means of support'.[63] The Propaganda hoped, he continued, that 'when

---

[58] Brown, *South Africa*, 8. Repeated by J. B. Brain in 'The Irish influence on the Roman Catholic Church in South Africa', in Donal P. McCracken (ed.), *The Irish in Southern Africa, 1795–1910*, vol. 2 (Durban: Ireland and Southern Africa Project, 1992), 121–31, at 122.

[59] See Denis, 69–70. Denis' claim that the Cape vicariate 'resulted from an initiative of the English Benedictines' cannot be sustained.

[60] Propaganda to Murray, 28 July 1836, DDA/MP/31/5/42; Murray to Cullen, 24 August 1836, PICRA/CP/292. For Madagascar, Murray to Propaganda [Draft], 6 February 1836, DDA/MP/31/4/174.

[61] Cullen to Murray, 20 October 1836, DDA/MP/34/9.

[62] Propaganda to Murray, 11 July 1837, DDA/MP/31/5/107.

[63] Cullen to Murray, 1 August 1837, DDA/MP/34/9.

the mission is once established the Colony will be able to do something for itself'.

It was a largely forlorn hope: Griffith arrived in Cape Town on 14 April 1838 with little more than £60 in passage money and the promise of £200 per annum from the government. He brought with him two priests (one Dominican, one Franciscan, both Irish), a clerical student, several family members, and two servants.[64] As in India, the £200 was a chaplain's salary, not a bishop's. As Joy Brain has pointed out, this had significant consequences for what would become the Western District: Griffith identified himself primarily as a chaplain, which meant he concentrated his attention on the military and those who presented themselves at his Cape Town church.[65] He did relatively little to seek out existing Catholics and even less to make new ones.[66]

Griffith's situation was certainly challenging. On arrival, he found perhaps 500 Catholics in Cape Town, no school, no priests, a chapel ruined by floods in 1837, and a conflict over lay trusteeship similar to that roiling Philadelphia. He took decisive action against the church wardens, telling Murray 'I *un*wardened them the first night of my landing here', and took possession of a room in the barracks that had been temporarily set aside for Catholic worship. When that space proved unsuitable, he was given the run of the complex to find one that was. Griffith was welcomed by the official Cape, both military and civilian.[67] This was no surprise: Cape Town was garrisoned by an Irish unit, the 27th (Inniskilling) Regiment of Foot, comprised, according to Griffith, of 'mostly Irish Catholics'.[68]

It was also the needs of the military that drove Griffith's early decision to travel to the Eastern Cape; on arriving in Cape Town, he had found a petition from the Catholics of the area – many of them soldiers – begging for a chaplain.[69] He took with him the Irish Franciscan Daniel Burke, intending to leave him in Grahamstown as the sole resident priest. Since 1820, that town had been the centre of British settlement in the turbulent region and an important garrison. The Cape government offered £100 for travel expenses and promised to recommend to the Colonial Office that a chaplain's salary be paid to Burke.[70] It was a revealing journey: in Port Elizabeth, Griffith met Irish soldiers stationed at Fort Beaufort who

---

[64] Ibid.   [65] Brown, *South Africa*, 9.   [66] Brain, 'Irish influence', 122–3.

[67] Griffith to Murray, 22 April 1838, printed in *The Cape Diary of Bishop Griffith, 1837–1839*, edited by J. B. Brain (Cape Town: South African Catholic Bishops Conference, 1988), 101–5. Hereafter *CD*.

[68] Griffith to an unknown correspondent, 25 May 1838, quoted in *CD*, 105.

[69] Griffith to Murray, 22 April 1838, in *CD*, 104.

[70] John Bell to Griffith, 10 May 1838, printed in *CD*, 109. Bell was the colonial secretary and was acting on behalf of the governor.

claimed to have been there eight years without a priest, accosted a 'red-haired man' on the docks and discovered he was from Co. Galway (after Burke spoke to him in Irish, the man offered himself as a servant), and learned about the local 'degenerate Caffers' and the threatening 'Zoolas'.[71] Port Elizabeth reminded the bishop of Cobh; and, despite assurances that it contained no Catholics, he soon had a congregation above thirty, largely Irish.[72] In Grahamstown, he met the leading citizens, including the governor and the lieutenant governor, and inspected the ground set aside for a chapel. Before returning to Cape Town, he continued his tour of the Eastern Province, finding both Catholics and Irish wherever he went, not least among the soldiers. He left Burke with a temporary chapel rented at £8 per annum and some £60 raised from various sources.[73]

As Griffith settled in Cape Town, he slowly formed a better picture of his new flock. He upgraded their numbers from his initial estimate of 500 up to 2,000, military and civilian, and took steps to provide services to the surrounding communities, beginning with Simonstown (not yet a great naval base) and then Stellenbosch, where he noted the presence of a relative of Daniel O'Connell, whom he referred to as 'the Great Dan'.[74] His immediate concern was with what he described as 'the religious laxity and indifference which have so long existed'.[75] Problems ranged from issues of ecclesiastical governance, such as the dispute over the lay wardens, to the many lapsed Catholics he met, to the apparent preference for a double hanging above religious services.[76]

Heavily reliant on this small and imperfectly committed community for support, money was and would remain an issue, even if matters improved after his first collection brought in a mere £1.13.9d.[77] The cost of living was high, and Griffith lacked everything from suitable vestments to prayer books to a spare chalice.[78] The government did at least pay his own and some of his priests' salaries, a concession that lasted until 1875 in the Cape and 1869 in Natal.[79] Although this brought much needed financial relief, it also imposed obligations. It effectively ruled out any extensive missionary activity, had Griffith been of a mind to attempt any, which he was not; the government would baulk at its chaplains spending months at a time in the bush, let alone at a distant mission station, and Griffith

---

[71] 7 July 1838, *CD*, 122–3. These entries were written up several days later when Griffith was at Uitenhage.
[72] Ibid., 1838, *CD*, 127.   [73] 5 August 1838, *CD*.   [74] 28 May 1838, *CD*, 106.
[75] Griffith to unknown correspondent, *CD*, 106.   [76] Ibid., 108.
[77] Griffith to Murray, 22 April 1838, in *CD*, 103.   [78] 31 May 1838, *CD*, 107.
[79] *CD*, 9.

himself was under the impression that there were no Catholics living more than 30 miles beyond Cape Town itself.[80]

Griffith's first act was to open denominational schools: his Mercantile and Classical Academy offered a daunting curriculum and promised prospective Protestant parents that there would be no proselytism, while his sister opened what J. B. Brain described as 'a more modest school for girls at the same time'.[81] The teaching in the boys' school was handled by Griffith himself, by George Corcoran, the other Irish Dominican who had travelled with him, and by a small group associated with St Peter's College in Wexford, including its professor of Latin, Aidan Devereux. This party of three – two priests and a deacon who was quickly ordained – had arrived in Cape Town not long after the bishop.[82]

The men did not remain there long: in 1838, the newly ordained Thomas Murphy was sent to Grahamstown, which was just as well as Burke died shortly after his arrival; Corcoran went to Port Elizabeth in 1841; and Devereux, although he was the driving force at the school, was assigned the following year to George, midway between Cape Town and Grahamstown. In each place, they ministered to the military and sought to organize the local Catholics into parish life, while imposing as much social and liturgical discipline as possible. They also began to build: Murphy's solid and forbidding St Patrick's church in Grahamstown, for example, was erected largely by the free labour of the Inniskillings.

It soon became apparent that the Cape Colony was far too large for one man to oversee, even if he only had responsibility for a handful of priests. In 1847, Griffith sent Thomas Murphy to Europe to seek Roman approval for a division of the vicariate. He was quickly successful: Propaganda created a new Eastern District and appointed Aidan Devereux vicar apostolic. What role Cullen played is unclear, largely because any letters sent home by Murphy do not seem to survive. It is likely that he gave him every assistance and even more likely that he supported the appointment of Devereux, whom he had known for more than fifteen years.[83] Although there is no direct evidence for the tradition that Devereux was at one time vice-rector of the Irish College, he had, like Cullen, spent the bulk of his career in education and seems to have preferred Roman models to those still prevalent in Ireland.[84] In 1836,

---

[80] Griffith to Murray, 22 April 1838, in *CD*, 104.   [81] Brain, 'Irish influence', 124–5.

[82] For the school and the Wexford group, see Brown, 31–3.

[83] The first surviving letter is Devereux to Cullen, 17 September 1833, PICRA/CP/108.

[84] It appears that the origin of the idea that Devereux had been vice-rector (and a close companion of Mauro Cappellari before his elevation) was Wilmot, 40. It has been repeated by subsequent historians, e.g. Brown, 31, Francis L. Coleman with Tony Farnell, *St. Aidan's College Grahamstown* (Grahamstown: Institute of Social and Economic Research, Rhodes University, 1980), 2, and Denis, 79.

for example, he told Cullen that what the Irish church needed was Roman-educated priests in order to stamp out both theological rigorism and disregard for papal authority.[85]

There was little for Devereux to control in his new territory. He had four priests, including himself, and churches at Grahamstown, Fort Beaufort, and Port Elizabeth. There was the embryo of a girls' school in Grahamstown and a more established boys' school in Port Elizabeth, which the Dominican Corcoran had built with assistance from the Lyon-based Society for the Propagation of the Faith.[86] Worse, the region had just endured one of its periodic bouts of warfare.[87] It was little surprise that Devereux headed for Europe as soon as he was consecrated.

Devereux's first task was to increase his numbers: this meant priests but also the religious who would be necessary if a serious attempt were to be made at denominational schooling. Of the former, he secured three Flemish priests, an Irish clerical student, and two schoolmasters intending to study for the priesthood. The Irish student was J. D. Ricards, yet another product of St Peter's in Wexford. He was ordained in 1851 and became the third vicar apostolic of the Eastern District twenty years later. The rest made little impression: neither of the teachers became priests, one of the Flemings was promptly sent north into what soon became the Orange Free State, while the other two ministered to the British Army and resident Catholics in relative obscurity in places such as Graaff-Reinet. When they died, Devereux's uncompromisingly Hiberno-Roman successor did not replace them with new Dutch-speaking clergy.[88]

The new bishop had greater success in securing religious. Although he had obtained from Cardinal Fransoni a circular letter recommending the mission to any interested community, how he found his way to the newly founded Assumptionist Sisters of Paris is unclear. His own sister and cousin were among the first group to travel to Grahamstown, but both were postulants and they do not seem to have been in Paris prior to the Assumptionists' commitment to the Cape, although it is possible that they had pre-existing contacts with the community.[89] In any event,

---

[85] Devereux to Cullen, 13 September 1836, PICRA/MP/298.

[86] Moran to O'Connell, 13 October 1856, PEDA/MP/ PM/Doc/162/PM/1.

[87] The Seventh Frontier War (1846–7), or the 'war of the axe'.

[88] Brown, 46–7, 49. One of the schoolmasters, Jeremiah O'Riley, would become the father of a future bishop of Cape Town.

[89] Sister M. Stanislaus was Devereux's cousin, and Sister M. Regis his sister. The latter later withdrew from religious life. *The Reminiscences of Amelia de Henningsen (Notre Mère)*, edited by Margaret Young (Cape Town: Maskew Miller Longman for Rhodes University, 1989), n1 181. In her otherwise very well-researched introduction, Young (herself an Assumption sister) does not give any indication of how Devereux and Paris came into contact, or if the link was his family.

Devereux's promise of schools and hardship secured three professed sisters and three novices (including his family) but more importantly the extraordinary Amelia de Henningsen as the first superior.[90] The Belgian-born de Henningsen was partly raised in England, where she received an excellent and privileged education. An efficient, driven woman, she is still remembered in Grahamstown as 'Notre Mère'.[91] The choice of a French order was unsurprising: mid-century France was the centre of an extra-ordinary effusion of both popular religion and new religious orders and institutions, including the influential Society for the Propagation of the Faith. Although the French empire would absorb many, there were religious to spare, not only for the Cape but also for places such as New Zealand where de Henningsen's near-contemporary Suzanne Aubert also built an enduring community almost from scratch. Coincidentally, the boat that took de Henningsen and her companions to Africa was also carrying Bishop Jean Baptiste Pompallier and a party of Irish Sisters of Mercy to Auckland.[92] In the absence of a willing Irish order, the Assumptionists would do nicely – not least because, of the original seven, three were Irish, one English, and one a Belgian partly raised in England; only two were actually French.[93]

Having secured at least some assistance, Devereux now had to find a way to pay for it. The natural solution was to turn to the Propagation of the Faith, which he duly did. The organization had been supporting Bishop Griffith since the inception of his mission, giving 13,000 francs in 1839–40, rising to 28,000 francs by 1845.[94] Although the reasons are unclear, it was Devereux who was the undoubted winner in the necessary reassessment of the society's commitments to the Cape. In 1849, the new Eastern District was awarded 26,000 francs (a little more than £1,000), while Griffith and the Western District saw their support slashed to 12,960 francs.[95] This disparity would endure until the late 1860s.

Devereux's final task in Rome was to divide his own newly divided vicariate. He knew he could not possibly assume responsibility for Natal, which had been formally annexed to the Cape Colony in 1845, with

---

[90] De Henningsen's memory of Devereux's pitch and the decision to accept it may be found in Young, *Amelia de Henningsen*, 107–9. There is no evidence to support F. B. Doyle's bizarre assertion that de Henningsen was herself Irish: see Doyle, 'South Africa', 12.

[91] There is an early biography of de Henningsen, which, although typically hagiographical, is still useful: Alban O'Riley, *Notre Mère: A Record of the Life of Sœur M. Gertrude du S. Sacrement, Foundress of the First Community of Nuns in South Africa* (London: Burns Oates & Washbourne, 1922).

[92] Young, *Amelia de Henningsen*, 21.

[93] A fact that rather puts the lie to W. E. Brown's observation that only de Henningsen spoke good English. Brown, 45.

[94] *ANPF*, 1: 342.   [95] *ANPF*, vol. 9 (1849), 206.

steady increases in territory thereafter; he could barely cope with the Eastern Cape. Griffith had ignored the area entirely, and Devereux sought the Propaganda's approval for a final disposition of the region. He pointed out that, between Durban and Pietermaritzburg, there was both a British regiment with many Catholics and at least 200 Catholic civilians, many of them Irish, none with access to the sacraments. He also reminded the Propaganda that there was extensive Protestant missionary activity in the area, urged that a religious order be assigned, and suggested either the Jesuits or the Holy Ghost Fathers.[96] His reason was simple: an order could afford to both staff and pay for the mission. Neither was interested, and Devereux continued to press through Cullen until the Propaganda approached the French Oblates of Mary Immaculate instead.[97] After some hesitation, they accepted and the new vicariate was formally erected in October 1850.[98] There was never any question of an Irish order (or an Irish province) undertaking the mission, and it is difficult to imagine one that could in 1849 or 1850.

Free of Natal, and possessed of at least some money, priests, and nuns, Devereux could turn to the practical business of running his vast territory. His first task was to establish the Assumption sisters in Grahamstown. The bishop gave them a house to live in, and there was already a small school, run by a wealthy convert who was prepared to turn it over to the sisters. The plan was to open two girls' schools, one fee-paying the other free. The former would support both the latter and the nuns themselves. It immediately attracted some fifty students, thirty of whom were Protestants drawn by the rigorous curriculum and by the sisters' European training. The poor school also did well, with 156 students in the first year, fifty-six of whom were Protestants.[99] All seem to have been European.

The sisters themselves had a difficult time adjusting. A number left; Paris was pressing, not least about the inability or unwillingness to implement the full rigour of the community rule in colonial conditions; an abortive attempt was made to establish a new community in Cape Town; Devereux sent the two original French sisters home as unsuitable for the mission; and de Henningsen was eventually ordered to return to France. She refused, and both Devereux and his successor backed her. The community was left with de Henningsen, the remaining Irish sisters, and two locals who had joined since 1849. Over the next several years, attempts were made to regularize their ecclesiastical status, with the

---

[96] Brain, *Natal*, 14–15.
[97] Cullen to Fransoni, 26 September 1849, APF/SC/Irlanda/vol. 30/ff. 214–15. Original in Italian.
[98] Brain, *Natal*, 26–7.   [99] Young, *Amelia de Henningsen*, 29–30.

preferred choice being to join the Sisters of Mercy. Negotiations proceeded at intervals throughout the 1850s, but the plan faltered when the Mercies decided that they were unwilling to expand into Africa.[100] The women instead became the Missionary Sisters of the Assumption, their French origins increasingly vestigial, and, in 1933, they expanded into Ireland and now sponsor a grammar school at Ballynahinch, Co. Down.

Devereux also took steps to provide education to boys. He had already purchased some land and imported the two schoolmasters and Ricards. The latter was given the responsibility of erecting a small school, which became known as 'Little St Aidan's', or 'Ricards' School'. Built by immigrants from Wexford, the school building was one long room with a second, smaller one for Ricards to live in. Unlike its successor St Aidan's College, little is known about Little St Aidan's, although it does seem to have enjoyed some success. What is clear is that the school was aimed at the more prosperous frontier families who might be attracted by a classical education for their sons. Like the girls' schools, it was open to Protestants and appears to have attracted at least a few.[101] Devereux hoped it might eventually become the nucleus of a South African seminary.

Devereux did well with his limited resources. As a hostile observer noted of Grahamstown in 1852, 'The Catholics are steadily progressing in numbers and make, I verily believe, more *genuine* converts among the coloured classes than any other sect.'[102] By Devereux's death in 1854, he had established two girls' schools and a boys' school in Grahamstown, a convent, new churches at Cradock and King William's Town, and even a newspaper, *The Cape Colonist* (later simply *The Colonist*), edited by Ricards. This was especially impressive in the context of the eighth frontier war (1850–3), which at times directly threatened Grahamstown. It was also impressive in comparison to what Griffith was able to achieve in a much larger and more stable Cape Town.

Devereux's unexpected death presented a new challenge to the vicariate. Although Ricards was appointed administrator, none of the local priests was a suitable replacement, on grounds of either temperament or age, and Rome inevitably turned to Cullen. It was surprisingly difficult to locate a willing candidate: the Eastern District was vast, underpopulated, poor, distant, and subject to unpredictable outbreaks of violence. There was nothing to attract an ambitious Irish cleric with prospects at home. In

---

[100] Ibid., 36–46.
[101] Coleman, 5–7. The establishment in 1855 of the Anglican St Andrew's College would have drawn away most of the Protestant students.
[102] Alfred W. Cole, *The Cape and the Kaffirs: Notes of Five Years' Residence in South Africa* (London: Richard Bentley, 1852), 155. Emphasis in original.

late January 1855, for example, Cullen nominated Edward McCabe, then the administrator of the pro-cathedral parish in Dublin, but he declined to deviate from a path that would eventually see him Cullen's successor.[103] Other names seem to have been suggested, including Bernard Smith, still vice-rector of the Irish College.[104]

Cullen finally settled on a Dublin priest, Patrick Francis Moran. Despite the name, he was no relation of either Cullen or the other Moran. Born in 1823, Moran came from large farming stock in Co. Carlow and had been educated by the Vincentians at Ussher's Quay (where he was taught by James Lynch, later of Glasgow) and then at St Peter's College in Wexford, where Devereux had been briefly his teacher and Ricards his schoolmate, and then again by the Vincentians at Castleknock. Unusually for a Cullenite, Moran also spent six years at Maynooth before his ordination for Dublin in 1847 or 1848. He then served as a curate in several Dublin parishes, including at Irishtown under Andrew O'Connell, the head of the Propagation of the Faith's Irish committee.[105] It is probably this connection that led to Cullen recommending Moran's appointment in early January 1856, despite his startlingly young age of thirty-three.[106] As Cullen told Kirby, 'He is very young, but an excellent man.'[107] For his part, Moran always held Cullen to be his *beau ideal* of an Irish Catholic bishop: the archives of the diocese of Dunedin, for example, contain an extraordinary thirteen-page handwritten poem commemorating the death of 'the Cardinal Prince of Hibernia', a 'Patriot Prelate' who watched over Ireland 'wisely and with fatherly care' even as he 'clasped' his heart to Rome. At one point, Cullen is imagined returning to life and gazing fondly at the poet. It was probably written by Moran.[108]

Yet Moran did not arrive in the Cape until late 1856. In the meantime, Ricards managed as best he could. He had to deal with de Henningsen's continuing problems with Paris, with the resistance of several of his older colleagues to his supposedly lax oversight of the nuns, and with Bishop Griffith, who sought to impose his will on the vicariate. By early 1856,

---

[103] C. J. Woods, 'McCabe, Edward', *Dictionary of Irish Biography*, 5: 748.

[104] Cullen to Kirby, 3 September 1855, PICRA/NK/II/I/68. Cullen was seeking confirmation of a rumour that Smith had accepted the appointment.

[105] For Moran's background, see Hugh Laracy, 'The life and context of Bishop Patrick Moran', unpublished MA thesis, Victoria University of Wellington, 1964.

[106] Cullen to Kirby, 11 January 1856, PICRA/NK/II/I/98.

[107] Cullen to Kirby, 5 April 1856, PICRA/NK/II/I/113.

[108] 'The Grave of Ireland's First Cardinal', Archives of the Diocese of Dunedin [ADD], Moran papers. The poem is written in a formal hand, with substantial corrections in Moran's handwriting. Although authorship cannot be definitively established, it seems highly likely that it was written by Moran.

relations had broken down completely. Griffith was annoyed by Ricards' refusal to force de Henningsen to conform and infuriated by his adherence to what he called Devereux's 'Irish notions'.[109] 'Nor Wexford, nor Thurles, nor the whole Irish Church', Griffith told him, 'is to regulate the discipline of these Vicariates', but rather the 'general Law of the Church.'[110] As the context was Ricards' apparent willingness to follow Devereux's practice of solemnizing mixed marriages under certain circumstances, it is not possible to read this as a case of the traditional Griffith clashing with a Hiberno-Roman Ricards; but it is nevertheless suggestive of Griffith's wider attitudes and policy in Cape Town.

In many ways, Griffith did not behave as an Irish bishop, or at least not as Irish bishops elsewhere in Greater Ireland behaved after 1850. He was himself proudly Irish – and often homesick – but his ecclesiastical reference point was neither Ireland nor even papal Rome, although he was familiar with both. Like Daniel Murray of Dublin, he was of an older generation of Irish priests: refined, undemonstrative in his faith, comfortable in lay society, and with Protestants, educated on the continent (Lisbon in Griffith's case, Salamanca in Murray's), and disposed to defer to the civil authorities.[111] His membership of the transnational Order of Preachers further broadened his view. As his attack on Ricards indicates, Griffith was dismissive of what he saw as peculiarly Irish habits and practices; in this he might be seen as the more authentically ultramontane, although there is no evidence beyond Griffith's own complaints for any laxity on the part of either Devereux or Ricards. Such laxity was in any event unlikely given Devereux's long relationship with Cullen and preference for Roman discipline and formation and Ricards' easy relations with the undeniably Hiberno-Roman Moran. Griffith's record in Cape Town suggests a man doing his best in challenging circumstances, but he displayed none of the drive, enthusiasm, or efficiency of his Hiberno-Roman successors.

Griffith's enduring problems were personnel and money. Since 1852, government support for clerical and episcopal salaries had been fixed at £1,000 per annum, but this was divided between the two vicariates; it was not enough to pay for schools or buildings. The funds from the Propagation of the Faith helped, but, when not absorbed by Cape Town's cathedral, they were largely used to seed local missions, usually by building a small church. The vicariate was always short of money,

---

[109] Griffith to Ricards, 29 May 1856, 20 March 1856, J. D. Ricards papers [RP], PG/JR/365/JR/1, PEDA/RP/PG/JR/499/PG/1.

[110] Griffith to Ricards, 29 January 1856, PEDA/RP/PG/JR/358/JR/1.

[111] Griffith entered the Dominican novitiate in Lisbon in 1816 before moving to Rome. Denis, 72.

especially after the Propagation of the Faith reduced its grant after 1848. It was also short of priests: after his initial party and the subsequent group from Wexford, Griffith never again attracted more than one man at a time, and not many in total. Fourteen letters appealing to All Hallows in Dublin resulted in nothing, probably because the All Hallows model was that the missionary bishop paid the expenses of his prospective subject, and Griffith apparently never felt able to expend the necessary funds.[112] Nor were the Dominicans much help. Unlike New South Wales, which was explicitly confided to the English Benedictines, or Newfoundland, which was supported by the Irish Franciscans, the Cape was not a Dominican mission as such, but merely headed by a friar. The order was under no obligation to it, and seems to have taken little interest in it. Other than Corcoran, the only Dominican sent to the Western Cape was a Dutchman, Pieter van Ewijk, who Griffith secured directly from the Master of the Order of Preachers on an 1852 European recruiting trip. Van Ewijk was not a success: he barely spoke English, although that did not prevent Griffith making him the sole pastor of Cape Town between 1854 and his return to Europe in 1857.[113]

Griffith was no more successful in securing nuns. From the beginning of the mission, Devereux had urged the importation of religious in order to provide female education. Griffith came to agree, but reluctantly: as he confided privately in 1840, he had hoped that a convent 'would be the last and most distant matter to which I would have to apply myself'.[114] His attempts to secure either Sisters of Mercy or a group of Assumption sisters were unsuccessful and seem desultory, although his courtship of the latter did much to disrupt relations between Paris and Grahamstown. These shortages had consequences for Catholic education in Cape Town. Despite its initial success, the Mercantile and Classical Academy petered out: all Griffith's coadjutor found when he arrived in 1861 was a 'not respectable' free school with some sixty students and one teacher. Girls' education was no better: in 1861, the school had some fifty pupils, exactly the same number as in 1840, despite a significant increase in the city's Catholic population.[115] Socially, there is little evidence of lay activity or organizations, or of the bishop's interest in either – although a St Vincent de Paul Society was founded in 1856 by what Griffith called 'a few pious lay men'.[116]

---

[112] Ibid., 80.   [113] Ibid., 86–7.
[114] Griffith to an unknown correspondent, 19 November 1840, quoted in Ibid., 81.
[115] Denis, 80–1.
[116] Griffith to Thomas Grant, 2 October 1856, SAA/GP. See also Wilmot, 47. The ubiquitous Wilmot was the first treasurer.

Griffith's primary achievement was the Cape Town cathedral, which is still in use. The original tender was for £5,000 but, on examination, building to the original plans was estimated to cost at least £20,000. A reduction in scale was ordered and a new estimate of £7,000 agreed. Although the foundations were laid in October 1841, it was not completed until 1851 at an ultimate cost of a substantial £10,377 3s 6d. This money was largely secured from the Propagation of the Faith's annual grant, special collections, fundraising sermons (including one by a transiting John Bede Polding of Sydney), and donations from around the world, including from Patrick Carew in Calcutta. Despite repeated appeals, the government contributed almost nothing.[117] The cathedral absorbed all of the vicariate's money and most of Griffith's attention. To put this into perspective, supporting a student at All Hallows in the 1840s would have cost £10 per annum, or £20 if the vicariate wished to completely subsidize him.[118] It is perhaps symbolic that Griffith's cathedral was dedicated not to an Irish saint but rather to St Mary of the Flight into Egypt. In fact, this was the primary dedication of the entire vicariate before its division; St Patrick was only the secondary patron, something that surprised Ricards when he looked into the matter in the late 1870s.[119]

Although the cathedral itself was completed with a minimum of debt, it drained the vicariate; Griffith had no money for other activities and was constantly in debt himself. By 1853, he admitted to the Oblate bishop of Natal that he was 'broke'.[120] This was a problem not only for Cape Town but also for the Eastern District as Griffith had spent the £580 that the Propagation of the Faith had asked him to hold in trust in anticipation of a new bishop for the Eastern Cape.[121] Moran was forced to repeatedly dun him for this money, but he was never able or willing to pay it. Worse, Moran had to supply further sums: in 1859, for example, Griffith thanked him for £30 'which secured me from the Bailiffs for the month'.[122] In 1860, Griffith declined to collect the Peter's Pence for the embattled pope, telling Moran that it had only been with 'great difficulty' that he had 'scraped together £100' during Pius' exile from

---

[117] See Brown, 33–4, and Christian Frantz, 'A history of St. Mary's Cathedral Parish', available online at www.stmaryscathedral.org.za/cathedralhistory.pdf. Consulted 7 November 2011.

[118] Condon, *All Hallows*, 162.

[119] See Ricards to the priests of the vicariate, 22 February 1879, Cory Library for Historical Research, Rhodes University [CLHR], PR3823.

[120] Quoted in Brown, 35.

[121] Thomas Heptonstall to Griffith, 1 June 1854, PEDA/RP/TH/PG/209/JR11. It is unclear how this letter, which does not seem to be a copy, wound up in Port Elizabeth.

[122] Griffith to Moran, 'Vigil of Pentecost' 1859, PEDA/MP/PG/PM/225/PM/1.

Rome in 1849.[123] By contrast, the Eastern District managed an immediate £83 (sent via Cullen) and a steady stream thereafter.[124]

The Hiberno-Roman Church

The arrival of Patrick Francis Moran in the autumn of 1856 changed South African Catholicism for good. In the Eastern Cape, he oversaw both rapid growth and a new, less compromising and more demanding relationship with the government. He was also unapologetically and unambiguously Irish. What he found was scanty enough: six nuns at Grahamstown teaching eighty-three students and caring for twelve orphans from the most recent frontier war, four free schools without teachers and overseen solely by priests, both 'miserably lodged', and 2,500 Catholic civilians and 4,000 Catholic 'soldiers on [the] Frontier & in lonely graves'.[125] He had only eight priests, five of whom told him that they wanted to return home. At least one was a drunkard. Most lived in 'hovels', without servants.[126] There were some positives, including the nearly finished church at Port Elizabeth, the 'same in size and design as that of Celbridge' in Co. Kildare.[127] Once settled in Grahamstown, Moran began to make immediate changes: he sent Ricards on a European recruiting mission, established a mission at Graaff-Reinet at a cost of some £1,200, assumed editorial control of *The Colonist*, sought to secure state aid for the Catholic soldiers of the British German Legion in British Kaffraria, and picked a series of fights with the government on a variety of other issues.[128] Moran was also formidably hard-working: Wilmot claimed a not unusual day began with Mass in Alice at 7 a.m., followed by a 15-mile ride to Fort Beaufort, Mass and a sermon there at 11 a.m., and then the long ride home to Grahamstown, arriving about 10 p.m.[129]

Moran understood the power of the press, and, as he would in Dunedin with the *New Zealand Tablet*, he used *The Colonist* as his personal platform

---

[123] Griffith to Moran, 12 May 1860, PEDA/MP/PG/PM/228/PM/1.

[124] See Cullen to Moran, 2 July 1860, PEDA/MP/CC/PM/270/PM/1. Receipt was acknowledged by Tobias Kirby: Kirby to Moran, '1860', PEDA/MP/JK/PM/268/PM/1.

[125] Diocesan Chronicle, PEDA. This handwritten diary, largely in Ricards' hand but with additions and corrections by Moran, is contained in a box labelled 'vol. xxv/vol. xxxvi', with no further file numbers. This entry is undated but is probably from the autumn of 1856.

[126] Moran to Cullen, 15 May 1860, DDA/MP/333/1/20. In this lengthy letter, Moran recounted for Cullen the history of the vicariate since his own arrival.

[127] Moran to [O'Connell], 13 October 1856, PEDA/MP/PM/Doc/162/PM/1.

[128] Moran to Cullen, 15 May 1860, DDA/CP/333/1/20. British Kaffraria consisted of the land between the Kei River and the Natal frontier. It was annexed to the Cape in 1865 and was also known as the Transkei or Transkeian territories.

[129] Wilmot, 50.

from which to engage government and society. If the newspaper under Ricards' editorship was notable, as Francis Doyle claimed, for its 'tolerant approach to those of other religious denominations', it was anything but under Moran.[130] In February 1857, for example, it published a lengthy lecture that he had given in Dublin on the doctrine of the Immaculate Conception as a riposte to criticisms made by the Anglican bishop of Cape Town.[131] Two weeks later, *The Colonist* used the occasion of the opening of the secular Grey Institute school in Port Elizabeth to launch a stinging attack on mixed education.[132] In a lengthy leader that was almost certainly written by Moran, the paper denounced undenominational schooling as the source of 'all the anarchy, rebellions, revolutions, and many other fearful crimes, for which the 19th century ... must be forever memorable'. Mixed education was unacceptable, and 'infidels' were its most 'strenuous advocates'. If only, he continued, 'statesmen divested themselves of hatred and jealousy' towards the Catholic Church, it would be possible to provide government funding to each denomination to manage the education of its own children. In the meantime, the project met with the bishop's 'unmitigated' disapproval.[133]

Moran's most pressing problem was the German troops who began to arrive in late 1856. Their presence was one of the more peculiar quirks of empire. The British German Legion had been raised during the Crimean War but never saw combat. As many could not return home, it was decided to offer the men the chance to go to turbulent British Kaffraria as 'military settlers'. Those that agreed would remain under military discipline for a fixed period, but it was hoped that they would stay after their service ended; about 2,300 soldiers and 550 women and children accepted.[134] Although the exact numbers are unclear, many of them were Catholic. Some became prominent, including Colonel Francis Xavier Schermbrücker who edited the *Kaffrarian Post* and eventually served in the Cape Parliament.[135] *The Colonist* promptly drew attention to the situation, complaining that the military authorities had refused to make any monies available to build an adequate church in the territory's capital,

---

[130] Doyle, 'South Africa', 12.   [131] *The Colonist*, 7 February 1857.

[132] The Grey Institute was established by the governor, Sir George Grey, at the urging of a number of Port Elizabeth citizens led by John Paterson. Grey provided land that would serve as the school's endowment. He sponsored a similar school a year or two earlier in Bloemfontein. Both still exist: Grey High School in Port Elizabeth and Grey College in Bloemfontein.

[133] *The Colonist*, 14 February 1857. Given the tone, and its similarity to later articles in the *NZT*, there is no doubt that this was written by Moran.

[134] See C. C. Bayley, *Mercenaries for the Crimea: The German, Swiss, and Italian Legions in British Service, 1854–1856* (Montreal and Kingston: McGill-Queen's University Press, 1977), 124–9.

[135] Dischl, 49.

King William's Town. As a result of this 'miserably parsimonious and cruel policy of the Government toward its Roman Catholic soldiers', some 300 to 400 people had been obliged to hear Mass outside for lack of space in the small existing chapel. In a pointed departure from Griffith's self-identification as a chaplain, *The Colonist* insisted that Moran's first duty was to 'the Roman Catholic colonists and their children', not to the British Army. It was unreasonable, the paper continued, that the 'alms of the Faithful' of the Eastern Cape should supply what should be provided by the state, not least when the vicariate was still unable to meet the 'essential religious wants' of many Catholic civilians. Nevertheless, *The Colonist* reported that Moran had provided £100 to enlarge the church at King William's Town.[136]

Moran had a point, and his aggressive approach provoked a response. At his insistence, the eminently tolerant Sir George Grey issued orders to 'discontinue the practice of requiring the attendance' of Catholic soldiers at Protestant services.[137] Grey also promised to ascertain the number of Catholics and approach the War Office with a request for a chaplain if they proved to be numerous.[138] Several months later, the commander of the Legion formally requested a chaplain, and the Cape government offered £100, a cottage, and five acres of glebe land – and a warning that the stipend could not be guaranteed in future.[139] In 1859, Moran asked to send a chaplain to Frankfort and received permission on similar terms, and with a similar warning.[140]

Moran was not satisfied with this minimal provision: he had to supply the priest, and an uncertain £100 and a house was not enough for one to live on. In practice, the vicariate and the civilian congregation would be obliged to pay the bulk of the costs and Frankfort did not get its chaplain. For Moran, this was an obvious injustice: the army met the full expense of its Church of England chaplains, who received £250, lodging, servants, and forage for their horses. 'The manner in which the Catholic soldiers in Her Majesty's service are treated is not only shameful', he complained to Bishop Grant of Southwark in 1860, 'but highly

---

[136] *The Colonist*, 31 January 1857.

[137] This was within the power of the governor, who was commander-in-chief of military forces in the Cape, Natal, and British Kaffraria. It was not within his gift to authorize the indefinite payment of a chaplain, as that power remained with London.

[138] Major Bates to Moran, 15 June 1857, PEDA/MP/COL/PM/486/COL/1. Bates was military secretary to Grey.

[139] Bates to Moran, 23 November 1857, PEDA/MP/COL/PM/491/COL/1.

[140] J. M. Maclean to Moran, 11 June 1859, PEDA/MP/COL/PM/497/COL/1. Now a very small town, Frankfort is due north of King William's Town in what is presently the Eastern Cape Province. There is also a Frankfort in the former Orange Free State.

criminal.' 'The Catholic soldiers', he continued, 'are treated as an inferior and degraded race.'[141]

A few months later, Moran complained that the army was clogging the colony's churches with soldiers while refusing to compensate the congregations who had built and sustained them. Nor did it contribute, with the exception of the chaplain at King William's Town, to the expenses of the priests who attended sick or dying soldiers, either in the field or in hospital. For Moran it was simple bigotry: 'When I contrast the treatment of Catholics in the British Army with that of Protestants I am amazed how any Catholic can be found so besotted as to enlist into such a service.'[142] Yet the army was not the only offender. When a Cape prison refused Catholic priests access on Sundays, citing an inconvenient clash with Protestant services, Moran exploded: 'I am under the impression', he wrote with heavy irony, 'that Catholics and Protestants are equal before the law.' There could be no excuse for excluding priests: 'surely your services do not occupy the entire Sunday – or am I to infer that it is quite uncertain at what hour the Protestant chaplain, who is a paid official, may think fit to hold service on Sundays?'[143] This was not the sort of language that Cape officials were accustomed to hearing from Catholic bishops.

The military and colonial authorities were not the only target of Moran's restless energy. Although he had no intention of supplanting the Oblates in Natal, Moran took a close interest in the increasingly chaotic affairs of the Western District. Ageing and beset with financial troubles, Griffith had become increasingly ineffective and seems to have been willing to accept a coadjutor by late 1857. As in the Eastern District, however, the problem was finding a suitable candidate willing to come to the Cape: Griffith's choice promptly declined the honour, leaving him to 'suppose between Barnabò and Dr Cullen some one will be made out to come here'.[144] The reality, however, was that the Cape was too marginal a mission to hold either Cullen's or Rome's attention in the absence of a crisis or actual vacancy, and nothing was done.

The situation changed in early 1860, when Moran reported that Griffith had suffered 'a very serious attack of paralysis' and had 'completely lost the use of speech'. It was, he suggested, 'but the beginning of an

---

[141] Moran to Grant, 16 June 1860, SAA/GP. Bishop Thomas Grant was responsible for coordinating Catholic chaplains in the British armed forces. For Grant, see Michael Clifton, *The Quiet Negotiator: Bishop Grant of Southwark* (The Author: n.p., n.d.). This self-published work is useful in sketching Grant's activities in securing chaplains in the Empire.

[142] Moran to Grant, 15 December 1860, SAA/GP.

[143] Moran to Henry Hutton, 23 November 1858, PEDA/MP/PM/HH(2)/373/PM1. Hutton appears to have been a prison governor.

[144] Griffith to Moran, 26 November 1857, PEDA/MP/PG/PM/218/PM/1.

end' and a coadjutor was now urgently needed. Unlike many Hiberno-Roman bishops, however, Moran did not have a personal relationship with Cullen and felt unable to baldly ask for his help with such a delicate matter. Instead, he asked his former parish priest, Andrew O'Connell, to 'announce' Griffith's illness to Cullen. The archbishop, Moran confidently wrote, would then 'do everything he can for the South African Missions'.[145] O'Connell raised the issue personally, Cullen asked him if he knew 'of any one fit for the important mission', and O'Connell recommended Thomas Grimley, a canon of the pro-cathedral in Dublin. Cullen concurred: if Grimley agreed, he would give his name to Rome.[146] Grimley did, and Cullen sent his recommendation and a translation of Moran's letter to the Propaganda.[147]

Grimley's background was strikingly similar to Moran: both were educated by the Vincentians at Ussher's Quay and Castleknock before proceeding to Maynooth. As Grimley himself put it, 'It is a strange coincidence that two class fellows in School and College … should be destined to be cast together' in a distant land.[148] It might have been a coincidence, but it was not a surprise: the early Vincentians produced a disproportionate number of bishops, despite the lay domination of Castleknock College.[149] Products of the first fifteen years of the college's history included archbishops of Madras, Philadelphia, Chicago, and Toronto, as well as bishops of a number of colonial and Irish sees.[150] Cullen was an early supporter, both of the order and Castleknock, and the Vincentians' parish missions were a crucial component of his reformation of Irish Catholicism, while Castleknock itself was committed both educationally and architecturally to what its historian called 'the greater Romanisation of the Irish Church'.[151] Indeed, Castleknock explains the otherwise surprising presence of Maynooth in the backgrounds of Moran, Grimley, and Grimley's successor in Cape Town John Leonard: Cullen despised Maynooth but trusted the Vincentians. It also helped that all three men had passed through the national seminary before Cullen's return to Ireland. Later Cullenite products of Castleknock, such as his

---

[145] Moran to O'Connell, 14 March 1860, DDA/CP/331/1/15.

[146] O'Connell to Moran, 4 May 1860, PEDA/MP/AOC/PM/PROP/IRE.

[147] O'Connell to Moran, 4 June 1860, PEDA/MP/AOC/PM/PROP/IRE. 'I will translate at least the principle part of [your letter] and send it to the Propaganda which I am sure will like it very much': Cullen to Moran, 2 July 1860, PEDA/MP/CC/PM/270/PM/1.

[148] Grimley to Moran, 2 January 1861, PEDA/MP/TG/PM/239/PM/1.

[149] James H. Murphy, '"Nursery of Saints": St. Vincent's ecclesiastical seminary, 1835–60', in James H. Murphy (ed.), *Nos Autem: Castleknock College & Its Contribution* (Dublin: Gill & Macmillan, n.d.), 12.

[150] Stephen Fennelly of Madras, Patrick Feehan of Chicago, Patrick Ryan of Philadelphia, and John Lynch of Toronto. All were students before 1850. See Ibid., 14.

[151] Ibid.

nephew Michael Verdon (Moran's eventual successor in New Zealand), attended Holy Cross College Clonliffe or the Irish College in Rome.[152]

Although no direct evidence survives, it is probable that Moran and O'Connell planned Grimley's nomination and likely that they at least indirectly confirmed his willingness to accept an appointment to the Cape.[153] Cullen was unlikely to object, not least because it was so difficult to find a willing and suitable candidate. Grimley was also a good choice: born in Skerries, Co. Dublin in 1821, he was ordained in 1846 and subsequently enjoyed a meteoric clerical career. He was first appointed curate at Balbriggan and then, in 1851, parish priest of St Paul's in Dublin, where he opened an 'ecclesiastical academy' on Arran Quay which purportedly played some role in the education of upwards of 200 future missionary priests.[154] In 1856, Cullen appointed him to a canonry. He also had experience that was pertinent to his future career in the Cape: he was both chaplain to the soldiers of the Dublin garrison and secretary of St Mary's School for Deaf Girls, run by the Dominican Sisters of Cabra.[155] Still, he was not Bishop Griffith's choice.

Griffith was ill and genuinely wanted a coadjutor, although his health was not quite as bad as Moran represented – even if as late as June 1860 he still had difficulty speaking.[156] Though Moran was forced to admit this, he insisted that there was 'no hope of his ultimate recovery'.[157] Moran also correctly guessed that Griffith had nominated 'some of the priests there [Cape Town]' and wrote to warn O'Connell and thus Cullen.[158] He need not have worried: Griffith had no influence and Grimley's appointment came as a complete surprise to him. He knew nothing about his new coadjutor, other than that he was presumably a 'favourite' of the archbishop of Dublin.[159] Griffith took the slight with outward equanimity, telling Moran that he was sure Grimley was a good man and he would let 'him do as he likes, so that he leaves me quiet'.[160]

[152] Two of Cullen's nephews actually became Vincentians. See Matthew Russell, 'Another batch of letters', The Irish Ecclesiastical Record, 4th series, vol. 3 (January–June 1898), 353.

[153] Moran's letters to O'Connell do not survive unless they were passed on to Cullen. O'Connell's letters to Moran do survive but they are almost wholly illegible.

[154] Paddy Halpin, 'A Skerries bishop', Time & Tide: Skerries Historical Society, vol. 1 (1998), 63–4. Although amateurish and deferential, this article is the only modern publication of which I am aware that is solely concerned with Grimley.

[155] See the obituary for Grimley in The Standard & Mail, 31 January 1871.

[156] Griffith to Moran, 9 June 1860, PEDA/MP/PG/PM/229/PM/1.

[157] Moran to Grant, 15 December 1860, SAA/GP.

[158] Moran to O'Connell, 13 July 1860, DDA/CP/333/1/28. As with Moran's earlier letter to O'Connell, this one also found its way into Cullen's papers.

[159] Griffith to Moran, 11 August 1860, PEDA/MP/PG/PM/231/PM/1.

[160] Griffith to Moran, 17 August 1860, PEDA/MP/PG/PM/232/PM/1.

Although the appointment seems never to have been in doubt, Rome still moved at its usual speed. The appointment was finalized in December 1860, and, after being consecrated by Cullen in February 1861, Grimley immediately set off for the Cape via London, Paris, and Rome.[161] In London, he called at the Colonial Office, where he was given a friendly reception but no money, while in Paris he secured £200 and a painting of the crucifixion from Napoleon III.[162] In Rome, where he stayed at the Irish College, Cardinal Barnabò gave him two free places at the Urban College and a library of devotional literature.[163] What he did not find anywhere were priests or seminarians prepared to accompany him to the Cape, although he does seem to have adopted at least a handful of students at All Hallows.[164]

On arriving in Cape Town, Grimley promptly fell out with the elderly Griffith, who despite his protestations was unwilling to cede control. Griffith, Grimley told his friend and eventual successor John Leonard, was 'determined to stay in Cape Town'. 'I had views of my own', he lamented, 'beautiful castles in the air.'[165] By August, Griffith had appealed to Moran to come to Cape Town to settle the dispute. As well as being 'startled' by this, Grimley was perplexed. He told Moran that Griffith had accepted an offer of financial support and the continuing and sole use of his house and had in turn promised 'not to interfere for the future'. He asked his old schoolmate's advice, wondering aloud whether it might not be a good idea to get the bishop to formally resign.[166] Griffith eventually subsided and died in 1862. His opposition seems to have been less ideological and more a difficulty in adjusting to the energy and ambition of his putative deputy – although Grimley was privately amused by the comparison at least one newspaper made between the late bishop and his 'intemperate successor'.[167]

Grimley's unsurprising first concern was education. Even before he departed, he approached an Irish clerical friend with the idea of founding a college or seminary in Cape Town.[168] When he finally got to Cape

---

[161] Cullen to Grimley, 17 December 1860, Archives of the Archdiocese of Cape Town [AACT], Thomas Grimley papers [GP], Box 13; Grimley to Moran, 4 February 1861, PEDA/MP/TG/PM/240/PM/1.

[162] Grimley to O'Haire, 19 February 1861, in O'Haire, 6–7.

[163] Grimley to O'Haire, 20 March 1861, in O'Haire, 8.

[164] See Bartholomew Woodlock to Grimley, 4 September 1861, AACT/GP/Box 13.

[165] Grimley to Leonard, 16 August 1861, AACT, John Leonard papers [LP], Box 18.

[166] Grimley to Moran, 23 August 1861, PEDA/MP/TG/PM/242/PM/1.

[167] Grimley to Moran, 21 June 1862, PEDA/MP/TG/PM/245/PM/1. The offending newspaper was apparently Saul Soloman's Cape Argus. Grimley blamed 'the Secret Societies' for the attack.

[168] Patrick Dunne to Grimley, 16 February 1861, AACT/GP/Box 13. Dunne declined to come on the mission, although he held out the possibility of joining if a college was in fact launched.

Town, he was appalled, telling Moran 'What grieves me most is the state of education.'[169] By August, he was 'striving to get two Male Schools established'.[170] He launched a special collection to 'open two schools on a respectable basis', which quickly drew some £300.[171] By December, that sum had risen to £428 and he had purchased land in the city for a new boys' school.[172] By May 1862, Grimley privately boasted of opening 'our sixth Catholic school in Cape Town'. 'That', he wrote, 'is not bad.'[173] With the boys seemingly provided for, Grimley's attention turned to the girls. He needed nuns.

Fortunately, he knew where to look: the Dominican Sisters of Cabra in north Dublin. Grimley was acquainted with the sisters' work with deaf education and was friendly with several of the women.[174] By at least August 1861, he was appealing directly for a colony of sisters to join him in Cape Town, and he hoped that his friend Dympna Kinsella would be selected to head the mission. 'You have a glorious future before you', he told her, 'We will do all in our power to make you happy.' He promised to get the convent ready, have 'grapes and figs' waiting, and to buy them a 'beautiful goat'.[175] He was very clear on his plans, explaining to the mother superior, Cullen's cousin Catherine de Ricci Maher, that their first task would be to open a 'school for the young infidels, and thus gain them to God'.[176] As he put it to Kinsella, in Cape Town there were at least 140 Catholic girls 'to bring up in the fear and love of our God', and he was sure that many Protestants and 'infidels' would soon send their children too.[177]

Cabra was willing in principle: the community had recently begun to expand outwith Ireland, with missions in both Lisbon and New Orleans. It also had ample personnel, but problems of finance and canonical status resulted in several years of delay. Grimley was not above begging, telling Maher 'If you let them come I believe that hundreds of little infidels will attend the Schools and thus would be gained for Jesus Christ.'[178] Securing the women was central to Grimley's plans: as he told Leonard, 'The Nuns would really do immense good in this City. I do not know any place they are

---

[169] Grimley to Moran, 30 July 1861, PEDA/MP/TG/PM/241/PM/1.
[170] Grimley to Moran, 23 August 1861, PEDA/MP/TG/PM/242/PM/1.
[171] Grimley to O'Haire, 16 October 1861, in O'Haire, 10.
[172] Grimley to Leonard, 19 December 1861, AACT/LP/Box 18.
[173] Grimley to Leonard, 21 May 1862, AACT/LP/Box 18.
[174] Máire M. Kealy, *Dominican Education in Ireland 1820–1930* (Dublin: Irish Academic Press, 2007), 47, 49–50.
[175] Grimley to Kinsella, 18 October 1862, Dominican Archives, Cabra [DACI], COPA/I4b. For the goat, Boner, *Dominican Women*, 44.
[176] Grimley to Maher, 18 October 1862, DACI/COPA/I4b.
[177] Grimley to Kinsella, 'Feast of St. Dympna' 1862, DACI/COPA/I4b.
[178] Boner, *Dominican Women*, 36–7.

so much wanted.'[179] Grimley was able to raise some £205 in Cape Town, although he carefully instructed Leonard only to tell the prioress if the nuns had departed: he was expecting Cabra to make a substantial contribution, and he did not want her deducting the sum.[180] By 1862, Cullen was able to clear the way by securing the necessary dispensations and, the following year, four choir sisters and two lay sisters under Kinsella's leadership finally set out from Cabra.[181] On arrival in Cape Town, the women were enthusiastically 'greeted by hundreds of Irish exiles', before being ceremoniously led by Grimley to their new home.[182] Less sympathetic observers only saw more 'low Irish Catholic immigrants'.[183]

Within months of the Dominicans' arrival they opened St Bridget's poor mission school, which quickly attracted some 100 children. This was soon augmented by a fee-paying school for young ladies and then an adult Sunday school.[184] In 1865, they added a fee-paying infants' school.[185] Four more sisters arrived in 1866, largely to open a school for what Grimley called 'the little female blacks'.[186] Soon they began to recruit, as Kathleen Boner put it, 'Local girls of good family, preferably Irish.' The first novice was originally from Tipperary.[187] The community and its operations continued to grow: a new convent and girls' school were opened in the Cape Town suburb of Wynberg in 1871, for example, and convents and schools followed in Woodstock (1898) and Rondebosch (1905), while Kinsella's private tutoring of deaf children became the Grimley Institute in 1874 and survives today as the Dominican-Grimley School in Cape Town.[188] Kinsella continued to oversee the community until her death in 1903, and her era and its assumptions continued to control conventual life for many years.[189]

Grimley was delighted with the sisters, but their success was not the end of his problems: 'I have now thanks to God made provision for the little girls', he wrote, but 'what am I to do for the boys?'[190] His six boys'

---

[179] Grimley to Leonard, 19 December 1861, AACT/LP/Box 18.
[180] Grimley to Leonard, n.d. [1863], AACT/LP/Box 18.
[181] This was largely to ensure that the sisters remained subject to diocesan authority and to secure them exemptions from certain fasts and other disciplines that were thought unsuitable in the Cape climate.
[182] Quoted in Boner, *Dominican Women*, 43.
[183] *Cape Argus*, 16 January 1864. This letter to the editor is quoted in Boner, *Dominican Women*, 43.
[184] Grimley to Leonard, 16 October 1863, AACT/LP/Box 18.
[185] Boner, *Dominican Women*, 47.
[186] Grimley to Maher, 10 February 1865, DACI/COPA/I4b.
[187] Boner, *Dominican Women*, 51.
[188] Ibid., 55. For the opening of the school, see *The Standard & Mail*, 22 September 1874.
[189] Boner, *Dominican Women*, 60–1.
[190] Grimley to Leonard, 16 October 1863, AACT/LP/Box 18.

schools were a start, but he could not provide adequate teachers. One of the attractions of nuns was their low cost, and Grimley needed male religious in a vicariate that had to rely on its own resources and a meagre £400 per annum from the Propagation of the Faith.[191] As late as 1866, the Cape superintendent general of education found, in Grimley's words, 'the "Lord Bishop" enthroned ... sitting on his chair ... hearing a class of Geography'.[192] He approached the Christian Brothers without success and then floated the idea of bringing out a 'few virtuous talented young lads from Ireland' who would be willing to join an 'Institute similar to the Christian Brothers' in order to 'give a Christian education to our little boys'.[193] Grimley was unsurprisingly unable to attract young Irishmen, who could just join the brothers at home, but he was able to find at least some locals. As he told Leonard in early 1864, 'I have two in harness.'[194] Grimley also approached the French Marist Brothers and the Italian Passionist Fathers, and, while the latter seem not to have been interested, the Marists were.[195] By mid-1866, it was agreed that five brothers would be sent from France. To Grimley's delight, the government was prepared to offer £30 towards travel expenses.[196] Every little bit helped: he had been forced to borrow some £2,500 to establish the brothers.[197] They arrived in 1867, and, despite illness and insufficient accommodation, they were able to open their school the following year in the presence of the governor, who donated £20 to mark the occasion.[198] The Marists filled the niche for an elite Catholic boys' school in Cape Town, and the brothers eventually spread to Port Elizabeth (1879), Uitenhage (1884), and Johannesburg (1889).[199]

Grimley also began to make up for the many years of little or no clerical education: after Castleknock 'refused to take lads who have no friends in Ireland', he sent two students to Terenure College, recently founded in Dublin by the Carmelites.[200] In early 1865, he sent three more, 'two for the Church – one of them nearly a black, but a most excellent lad'.[201]

[191] Grimley to Leonard, 19 April 1863, AACT/LP/Box 18.
[192] Grimley to Leonard, 9 July 1866, AACT/LP/Box 18.
[193] Grimley to Leonard, 16 October 1863, AACT/LP/Box 18.
[194] Grimley to Leonard, 18 February 1864, AACT/LP/Box 18.
[195] Grimley to Leonard, 22 August 1864, AACT/LP/Box 18.
[196] Grimley to Leonard, 9 July 1866, AACT/LP/Box 18.
[197] Grimley to O'Haire, 11 February 1868, in O'Haire, 364.
[198] Grimley to O'Haire, 25 August 1868, in O'Haire, 368–9. See also Brown, 70.
[199] Brain, *Transvaal*, 92.
[200] Grimley to Leonard, 18 February 1864, AACT/LP/Box 18. For Terenure, see Fergus D'Arcy, *Terenure College 1860–2010: A History* (Dublin: Terenure College, 2009).
[201] Grimley to Leonard, 12 January 1865, AACT/LP/Box 18.

'I am forming', he wrote, 'a Cape Corps in Ireland.'[202] By 1866, at least six students at Terenure were sponsored by the vicariate.[203] Grimley also had older clerical students, including two at All Hallows and four at the Propaganda who were doing 'poor old Ireland great credit'.[204] By 1866, he also had two students studying in Holland, although it is not clear if these were Dutchmen or Irish sent to learn the language.[205]

Like other Hiberno-Roman bishops, Grimley took clerical formation seriously. Unable to afford his own seminary, he preferred that the brighter students attend the Propaganda: 'I am very anxious', he wrote, 'to get very good students into that magnificent Institution', and he urged Leonard to keep an eye out for 'holy lads' of 'humble parentage'. It was intelligence that mattered, not background: 'a stupid priest on this mission would be no use'. He sent his own protégés to Rome, including two he had first taught at the 'little school on Arran Quay'. It was important to Grimley to both have men 'of my own training' with him in Cape Town and educate 'the majority of the [vicariate's] priests' in Rome;[206] but not all students could handle the Propaganda, either intellectually or financially, and All Hallows provided at least twelve students to the Cape by 1891.[207] Still, it was for many years Roman-trained Irish priests who dominated in the Western Cape.

With only limited success in attracting male religious and a growing but still small supply of priests, Grimley was forced to turn to the state to fully provide for the educational needs of his flock. This proved challenging and revealed an important difference of emphasis between Grimley and Moran. The educational system of the Cape in 1861 is best described as an ad hoc despotism: it provided for limited state aid under certain conditions at what amounted to the sole discretion of the cultivated and tolerant Langham Dale, the newly appointed superintendent general for education.[208] If Dale agreed, up to £75 per annum could be obtained for what Moran called a 'full set of schools' for boys, girls, and infants. The problem was that such aid was given not to a denomination as such, although they were termed mission schools, but rather to provide education in underserved areas. As Moran complained in late 1861, he had

---

[202] Grimley to Leonard, 10 February 1865, AACT/LP/Box 18.
[203] 'Record of examination results held in Terenure College, 1866', AACT, Box 13.
[204] Grimley to Leonard, 14 December 1865, AACT, AACT/LP/Box 18.
[205] Grimley to Leonard, 14 May 1866, AACT/LP/Box 18.
[206] Grimley to Leonard, 18 March 1867, AACT/LP/Box 18.
[207] Mary Carmichael's analysis gives nine to the 'Cape Mission', one each to the 'Cape Mission, Eastern District' and 'Cape Mission, Western District', and one to the 'Cape Province'.
[208] Ernst G. Malherbe, *Education in South Africa (1652–1922)* (Cape Town: Juta & Co., 1925), 133.

been refused support for two schools on the grounds that there were already grant-aided Protestant schools in the same area. His reaction was predictable: 'What is it to us how many Protestant schools there are? We want and demand Catholic schools.'[209]

To Moran, there was no point in dealing with the government. As he told Grimley, 'We have hitherto contrived to do without their aid, and unless aid be given on our own terms, will continue to live without them for the time [to] come.'[210] By contrast, Grimley was willing to see what might be had through negotiation and political agitation, and, in late 1861, he gave lengthy testimony to the Cape government's commission on education.[211] This was prudent: the Watermeyer Commission had been charged with proposing reforms to the Cape's educational system, and it was dominated by Langham Dale.[212] And, as Grimley soon discovered, Dale's hostility to a state system made him an important ally.[213] By late 1862, Grimley reported that Dale seemed 'most anxious that we should have our share of the educational grants'.[214]

While the committee deliberated, Grimley kept up the pressure. He organized a petition demanding denominational education and prevailed upon Moran to do the same in the east. Although he complied, Moran was convinced it would be 'perfectly useless' because of the Cape's 'tyrant Western majority'. He thought it possible that Grimley might secure a 'small grant' because 'it would be spent in Capetown and its vicinity', but there was no chance of 'justice' for the frontier.[215] Moran's predisposition to distrust the state had become intertwined with the long-standing grievances of the Eastern Cape, and he remained a convinced and noisy secessionist until his departure for New Zealand.[216] Grimley was more accommodating but no less committed. As he told Moran, 'I will agitate until I get justice.'[217]

Living in Cape Town, Grimley was able to form an accurate idea of what was politically obtainable. After meeting the colonial secretary in mid-1862, for example, he told Moran that the petition was indeed pointless, as there was 'no chance, at present, of getting our share of the educational grant'. Grimley wanted full denominational education, but as

[209] Moran to Grimley, 15 October 1861, AACT/GP/Box 13.   [210] Ibid.
[211] Grimley to Leonard, 19 December 1861, AACT/LP/ Box 18. For the Watermeyer Commission, which reported in 1863, see Malherbe, 94–5.
[212] Walker, South African College, 34.   [213] Malherbe, 111.
[214] Grimley to Moran, 15 October 1861, PEDA/MP/TG/PF/249/PM1.
[215] Moran to Grimley, 7 July 1862, AACT/GP Box 13.
[216] Although it concludes in 1854 with the granting of representative government, Basil A. Le Cordeur's The Politics of Eastern Cape Separatism 1820–1854 (Cape Town: Oxford University Press, 1981) is a useful summary of the secession movement.
[217] Grimley to Moran, 13 July 1862, PEDA/TG/PM/245/PM/1.

there was 'not the most remote chance of it in the Cape Colony', he would take 'the half-loaf as I cannot secure the whole one'.[218] Although such realism was anathema to the combative Moran, it was similar to Cullen's policy in Ireland after 1850: accept the possible while loudly demanding full satisfaction of Catholic 'rights' as a matter of justice.

By early 1863, Grimley had learned Watermeyer's recommendations privately from Langham Dale. What was proposed, and largely contained in the Education Act of 1865, was to create 'undenominational' public schools, which would be supported on a '£-for-£' basis by the government. Money raised locally would be matched up to £200 for 'first class' schools (with primary and secondary provision), £75 for 'second class' (primary only), and £30 for 'third class' schools, which largely catered for poor whites and 'coloureds' in rural areas. Although these schools would be locally managed, and in part locally funded, they were subject to government inspection; and, although there was provision for religious instruction, the right of withdrawal was guaranteed.[219] The ethos of each school would be a matter for its sponsor. Although this was not ideal, Grimley thought it a 'boon, and certainly a great improvement'.[220] The 1865 Act also continued to provide for outright grants to mission schools: these could range up to £75 but could be applied only to teachers' salaries.[221] This was not especially generous: in the Eastern Cape, Moran was forced to pay £70 per annum per teacher.[222] The grants were made at what amounted to the sympathetic Dale's sole discretion. For all intents and purposes, the mission schools, which could cater to native, coloured, or even European populations, were denominational, and, by 1866, Grimley was prepared to declare the Cape's educational system 'far superior to the National System in Ireland'.[223] As he told M. de Ricci Maher in Cabra, 'Bigotry will soon disappear and Catholicity will yet flourish in the Cape Colony.'[224]

Moran was not so sure. As he told Grimley in 1866, the problem was finding the money to build the schools and suitably trained Catholics to teach in them: 'The times are bad, the Catholics few and poor, and teachers are not to be found for the money we can afford to pay.'[225] He was also so short of clergy that Cullen even tried to source him a 'good

[218] Ibid.   [219] Malherbe, 95.
[220] Grimley to Moran, 1 January 1863, PEDA/MP/TG/PM/250/PM/1.
[221] Malherbe, 96.   [222] Moran to Cullen, 15 May 1860, DDA/CP/333/1/20.
[223] Grimley to Leonard, 9 July 1866, AACT/LP/Box 18.
[224] Grimley to Maher, 12 July 1866, DACI/COPA/I4b.
[225] Moran to Grimley, 25 September 1866, AACT/GP/Box 13.

priest' from Maynooth. 'He is', Cullen told the president, 'in great want.'[226] Yet Moran was committed to Catholic education, warning his flock that they would be 'doubly criminal' if they not only failed to patronize Catholic schools but added 'the crime of sending your children to non-Catholic schools'.[227] By then, he had the two girls' schools in Grahamstown run by the Assumptionists (which now boasted 'four very fine pianos' and a guitar) and two boys' schools in the same town: St Patrick's free school, staffed by two teachers with experience in Ireland's national schools, and a new St Aidan's designed to lure the town's 'respectable' Catholic children away from Protestant schools and transform them into 'thorough and enthusiastic Catholics'.[228] Moran also hoped that in time it would produce local vocations to the priesthood, although by 1868 at least it had yet to do so.[229]

The problem was how to provide for the girls, who, in rapidly growing Port Elizabeth, were served only by a small free school overseen by apparently untrained laywomen.[230] Like Grimley, Moran turned to Ireland for nuns. In 1867, he made a personal appeal to the Dominican community at Sion Hill, Blackrock, Co. Dublin. The Sion Hill Dominicans had split from Cabra in 1836 and relations between the two remained strained. How Moran found his way to Blackrock is unclear: probably he was aware that the sisters were open to missionary expansion, and indeed they found themselves forced to decide between the Eastern Cape and San Francisco. They chose Africa, and in October 1867 six sisters sailed with Moran on the aptly named *Celt*. Their passage and other expenses cost the community some £700 – Moran could not afford to help and was able to provide only an unsuitably small house in Port Elizabeth.[231] At least the sisters were greeted with enthusiasm: as one wrote home, 'the poor Irish Catholics distinguish themselves by crying with joy at seeing us'.[232]

Within months, they had opened two schools: St Mary's, which was fee-paying and had a small boarding element, and St Joseph's, which was free and aimed at the poor, both white and native. Within a year, it had 269 students.[233] The sisters continued to grow in Port Elizabeth, assuming responsibility for two more Catholic schools in 1895, both focussed on the children of Irish immigrants; in 1898, they added a 'coloured'

---

[226] Cullen to Charles Russell, 14 April 1864, Russell Library, Maynooth College Archive, Charles Russell papers, 10/17/10.
[227] 'Lenten Pastoral, Feast of St. Agatha, 1860'. There is a copy in Moran's papers in Dunedin.
[228] Moran to Cullen, 16 May 1860, DDA/CP/333/1/20.
[229] Moran to Grimley, 10 June 1868, AACT/GP/Box 13.
[230] Moran to Cullen, 16 May 1860, DDA/CP/333/1/20.
[231] Boner, *Dominican Women*, 69, 75.   [232] Quoted in Ibid., 72.   [233] Ibid., 78–9.

school which endured until 1973, when it was destroyed by the Group Areas Act.[234] In 1887, they expanded to Uitenhage, opening both schools and a convent. The sisters maintained their links with Ireland and with Sion Hill, which they relied on for recruitment. There were a few local vocations (the first in 1874), usually but not always of Irish extraction, but for many years they were the exception.[235]

By 1870, both the Eastern and the Western District possessed a full range of schools, overseen by a combination of laity and male and female religious. Given the poverty of both, it was a remarkable achievement but not enough on its own: as elsewhere, it was necessary to consolidate the gains of the first generation of Hiberno-Roman bishops when death, age, illness, or transfer created a vacancy. In the Cape, these happened nearly simultaneously. First, in 1870, Patrick Moran was translated to the newly created see of Dunedin, in New Zealand. Rome had been considering that step for some time and finally made its decision in early 1870. They had not, however, decided who should replace him in the Cape. Moran himself seems to have considered suggesting an amalgamation of the two vicariates, although he did not pursue the idea.[236] With the Vatican Council in session it was possible for the Propaganda to hear in person from all concerned, and from Cullen. Moran, who had previously declined to attend on grounds of poverty, left for Rome in early May.[237] In July, he met there with Grimley and Allard of Natal to recommend a successor. Their unanimous choice was J. D. Ricards: as Grimley confided to his diary, he was the 'only person we could recommend for the high office'.[238] With Allard's consent there was no possible opposition, and Cullen informed him of his promotion in early 1871.[239]

Ricards now oversaw a vicariate containing a mere five priests, all Irish – their surnames Murphy, O'Connell, Fagan, O'Brien, and Farrelly.[240] Ricards proved to be both ambitious and successful: by 1879, there were twenty-one priests serving some 5,300 Catholics.[241] He was also committed to expanding the church's physical infrastructure, for example the expensive (£4,500) new church at King William's Town.[242] His success did not go unnoticed in Ireland, and in 1876 he was forced to appeal to Cullen to block his translation to the diocese of

---

[234] Ibid., 82.   [235] Ibid., 77.
[236] Grimley to McMahon, 1 February 1870, AACT/GP/Box 18.
[237] Thomas Murphy to Ricards, 3 May 1870, PEDA/RP/TM/JR/706/TM/1.
[238] Grimley Diary, 6 July 1870, AACT/GP/Box 12.
[239] Cullen to Ricards, 19 February 1871, in Wilmot, 87–8.   [240] Wilmot, 89.
[241] J. D. Ricards, *The Catholic Church and the Kaffir: A Brief Sketch of the Progress of Catholicity in South Africa, and the Prospects of Extensive Catholic Mission on the Point of Being Founded for the Natives of British Kaffraria* (London: Burns & Oates, [1879]), 5–6.
[242] Ricards to Leonard, 26 August 1876, AACT/LP/Box 30.

Ferns in his native Wexford.[243] Despite having spent his entire career at the Cape, Ricards proved to be a typical Hiberno-Roman bishop: one of his first acts as vicar apostolic, for example, was to give a series of public lectures on education, which, if more temperate than Moran's, nonetheless hit all the same notes. He denounced mixed and secular education, pointed to its deleterious effects in Ireland, and quoted Cullen as his authority.[244]

Whatever his own inclinations, Ricards was forced by circumstance to be flexible. In 1875, for example, he handed over St Aidan's to the English Jesuits. His first choice had been the Irish Jesuit province, but they declined after lengthy negotiations.[245] Ricards and his predecessors had already spent some £6,000 on the school and had still been unable to transform it into the desired seminary; he hoped the Jesuits could do better.[246] They paid £500 for the building and grounds but that money was spent on their own passage and on the school itself.[247] They also secured from Ricards a £200 annual subsidy until the college was self-supporting.[248] When the Jesuits arrived, the local 'St Patrick's Society' greeted them at the jetty.[249] It also seems to have been Ricards who first suggested what became the society's famous Zambesi mission.[250] In addition to the Jesuits, Ricards was able to convince the Marist Brothers to expand from Cape Town to Port Elizabeth and Uitenhage, and he actively sought a German-speaking priest for Kaffraria.[251]

In 1877, Ricards obtained for King William's Town a colony of six German Dominican sisters, but only after he failed over several years to secure an Irish community.[252] Quite how this came about is unclear: the intermediary was a German merchant in Port Elizabeth, and there is some suggestion that the government might have encouraged the scheme as a way of meeting the needs of the military settlers, but there is no certainty.[253] Although Ricards at first financially supported the

---

[243] Cullen to Ricards, 15 March 1876, in Wilmot, 100–1. Ricards had been placed first on the *terna* by the parish priests of the diocese.

[244] J. D. Ricards, 'Popular education: A lecture delivered by the Right Rev. Dr. Ricards, R. C. bishop, and vicar apostolic of the Eastern Province of the Cape Colony, in St. Augustine's Hall, Port Elizabeth, and in the Albany Hall, Graham's Town, June, 1872' (Port Elizabeth: Richards, Impey & Co., 1872).

[245] See Ricards to Peter Gallwey, 31 October 1874, ABSI/ZM/3.   [246] Ibid.

[247] Memorandum of understanding between Ricards and Peter Galloway [sic] SJ, 20 September 1875, CLHR/PR3797.

[248] Ricards to Gallwey, 31 October 1874.   [249] Wilmot, 98.

[250] See Ricards to Gallwey, 13 July 1876, ABSI/ZM/17. In this letter, Ricards suggested that a Jesuit mission into the lake country in central Africa, and the Zambesi mission began the following year.

[251] Ricards to Leonard, 26 August 1876, AACT/LP/Box 30.   [252] Wilmot, 97.

[253] Brown, 102–3.

community through his prolific speaking and pamphleteering, the school they established was soon self-sufficient. The sisters opened a deaf school and a native school in 1885 and, in 1891, an industrial school for Africans. In 1883, they built a school in East London and the following year a convent and then a native school in Graaff-Reinet.[254] Despite the sisters' German origins, they greened rapidly with many recruits coming directly from Ireland. When they expanded into Natal in 1889, three of the four pioneers were Irish.[255] In 1890, five sisters under Mother Patrick Cosgrave followed the Jesuits into what is now Zimbabwe, and in 1892 they opened the first Catholic school in what is now Harare. By the late 1890s, these women had become an independent congregation and were primarily concerned with hospitals. They too began to import postulants directly from Ireland.[256]

Ricards' most famous decision neatly demonstrates both his preference for Ireland and the Irish and his willingness to adapt when necessary. Since at least 1875, Ricards had had the idea of importing Trappist monks into the Eastern Cape with a view to beginning native evangelization.[257] That this was wholly contrary to the Trappists' normal pattern of stability, silence, and manual labour did not trouble Ricards, and quite why he became fixated on the monks is unclear: perhaps he thought them best suited to inculcate habits of labour and industry among the Xhosa, a concern among frontier missionaries since the late 1840s.[258] More likely he was simply familiar with the Irish foundation at Mt Melleray in Co. Waterford, and it seems he approached them first.[259] Unsuccessful in Ireland, Ricards turned to the continent. By 1878, he thought he had secured the agreement of the French Trappists at Aiguebelle and solicited Cullen's help in getting Rome to apply pressure so they would be allowed to go.[260] Frustrated again, Ricards finally found a surprise volunteer in the abbot of the community of Maria-Stern, in what is now Bosnia. In 1880, Franz Pfanner and thirty-one other monks

---

[254] Ibid., 103.

[255] Brain, *Natal II*, 97. The Irish were Mary Gabriel Foley, Mary Joseph Ryan, and Columba O'Sullivan. It is suggestive that the Augsburg/King William's Town community is almost wholly absent from Kathleen Boner's book on Dominican women in South Africa. Although Cabra and Sion Hill have long since reconciled, it seems Augsburg remains outside the pale.

[256] See the excellent chronology on the website of the Dominican Missionary Sisters, the group that split from King William's Town: www.dominicanmissionarysisters.org/index .php?page=our-story-2. Accessed 8 December 2011.

[257] Ricards to James O'Brien, 3 December 1875, in Wilmot, 107.

[258] For this idea, see Richard Price, *Making Empire: Colonial Encounters and the Creation of Imperial Rule in Nineteenth-Century Africa* (Cambridge: Cambridge University Press, 2008), 139.

[259] Dischl, 84.   [260] Cullen to Ricards, 21 August 1878, in Wilmot, 125–6.

arrived in the Eastern Cape. Their new home was called Dunbrody, named by Ricards after the ancient Cistercian foundation in Co. Wexford. It was a disaster: the site was unsuitable, the bishop and abbot were incompatible, and the experiment was doomed. In 1882, the community moved to Natal and established Mariannhill, while Dunbrody was transferred to the Jesuits. Although fictional, Michael Cawood Green's narrative of the mutual incomprehension between the Trappists and the 'very Irish Bishop Ricards' captures the situation perfectly.[261]

Although Ricards did everything he could to secure an Irish successor, here too he was forced to compromise. In failing health since at least the mid-1880s, by 1890 he began to seek a coadjutor. He seems to have had two primary goals: to select an Irishman and to prevent the vicariate falling into the hands of a religious order. The latter threat was real: one correspondent of the English Jesuits hopefully suggested as early as 1874 that if the supply of priests from Ireland ran short – as he thought it would – 'the whole vicariate will fall into the Jesuits' hands'.[262] Ricards consequently commissioned William Fortune, president of All Hallows since 1866, to identify a 'proper selection' in Ireland. As always with the Cape, this proved difficult. Fortune eventually recommended the president of Holy Cross College Clonliffe, Bartholomew Fitzpatrick. He was eminently suitable: Moran (Cullen's nephew) had recommended him as a possible successor for Kirby at the Irish College, and his uncle was the long-serving abbot of Mt Melleray, which would appeal to the Trappist-fixated Ricards.[263] 'With him as your Coadjutor', Fortune wrote, 'the Vicariate is secured forever to the Secular Clergy.'[264] He also obtained the reluctant consent of Archbishop William Walsh of Dublin, who agreed not to raise objections at Rome.[265] For reasons that remain unclear, the appointment did not occur; probably Fitzpatrick, who does not seem to have been consulted in advance, simply did not want to go to the Cape.[266]

Thwarted in Ireland, Ricards was forced to look closer to home. He ultimately recommended Pietro Strobino, an Italian-born priest who he had recruited some ten years earlier. After the appointment was

[261] Green, *For the Sake of Silence*, 109–11. The scene is the reception of the monks at Algoa Bay and Ricards' speech marking the occasion.

[262] E. Coghlan to a Fr. Jones, SJ, 1 November 1874, ABSI/ZM/7. Although a secular priest of the vicariate, Coghlan was close to the English Jesuits and encouraged them to accept Ricards' offer.

[263] Sherry, *Clonliffe*, 80.

[264] Fortune to Ricards, 17 April 1890, PEDA/RP/WF/JR/680/JR/2.

[265] Fortune to Ricards, n.d. [1890], PEDA/RP/WF/JR/681/JR/2. From the context, this letter must date later than 17 April.

[266] W. E. Brown seems to have been unaware of the attempts to find an Irish coadjutor, noting that Ricards only gave Strobino's name to the Propaganda. This is true but not the whole story. See Brown, *South Africa*, 121.

confirmed in 1891, Ricards essentially retired, playing little role in the administration of the vicariate except for an occasionally obstructive one.[267] He died in 1893. Although he suffered from poor health himself, Strobino proved to be an eager reformer; among other things, he arranged for the removal of the prioresses of three Eastern Cape convents and was a disciplinarian with his clergy.[268] In 1896, he was given an Irish coadjutor, Hugh McSherry, a protégé of Cardinal Michael Logue of Armagh. Strobino died later the same year, and the vicariate (and later diocese of Port Elizabeth) subsequently remained firmly in Irish hands: McSherry lived until 1940 and was followed by the Corkman James Colbert, whose successor Hugh Boyle was born in Antrim. He was succeeded in 1955 by the South African–born but Irish-educated Ernest Green. Green tried to break the Irish stranglehold, for example by ordaining a few local (white) men, something his predecessors had largely refused to do, preferring priests both born and educated in Ireland. Local tradition in Port Elizabeth suggests that Green finally resigned in despair at Irish resistance to this policy.[269] His successor, John Patrick Murphy, was born in Mayo. He retired in 1986. Strobino proved to be only a brief interlude: the Eastern District and the subsequent diocese of Port Elizabeth remained the most emphatically Irish in southern Africa.[270]

Not long after Patrick Moran's 1870 departure for New Zealand, another vacancy occurred in the Cape. This one was unexpected: shortly after his return from Rome, Thomas Grimley died. He had served slightly less than ten years and had no obvious replacement. Moran observed that it would be 'hard to find a successor'.[271] In Cape Town, there seems to have been two possible candidates: the vicar general, a protégé of Griffith's named McMahon, and James O'Haire, the energetic and self-promoting sometime parish priest of Malmesbury. It seems likely that Grimley's own choice would have been his friend John Leonard, by 1871 the parish priest of Chapelizod in Dublin. Throughout the 1860s, Leonard had served as the bishop's confidant and outlet: 'writing to you', Grimley told him in 1864, 'is a sort of holiday for me'.[272] Leonard had made himself prominent as an opponent of the placement of Catholic children in the Royal Hibernian School for military orphans in the Phoenix Park, and, as Grimley noted as early as 1861, 'Many an eye

---

[267] Ibid.   [268] Ibid., 122–3.
[269] The late Bishop Michael Coleman of Port Elizabeth, in conversation with the author, August 2009.
[270] There is an interesting and well-illustrated commemorative history of the vicariate/ diocese: Helena Glanville, *Growing in Faith: A Historical Sketch of the Diocese of Port Elizabeth 1847–2007* (Port Elizabeth: n.p., n.d.).
[271] Moran to Laurence Forde, 11 May 1871, PICRA/FP.
[272] Grimley to Leonard, 25 October 1864, AACT/LP/Box 18.

will mark your footsteps.'[273] As the school was in his parish, he remained involved in the issue until his promotion and had regular dealings with Cullen as a result.[274] He also served as Grimley's Dublin agent, a role for which Grimley sought him recognition in Rome.[275] In 1869, he offered Leonard charge of the cathedral or any other parish he might wish in an unsuccessful attempt to lure him to Cape Town.[276]

With Grimley dead, however, Leonard was not the inevitable candidate, and no appointment was made until late 1872. In fact, Leonard was not the first choice: despite or perhaps because of his ill-health, a Fr Ryan of the pro-cathedral in Dublin was nominated in early August.[277] But, as so often with the Cape, the care and attention that Cullen gave to episcopal appointments elsewhere was lacking: Ryan was fiercely opposed by Moran of Dunedin, who for unknown reasons thought him 'so very objectionable'. This surprised Dublin, and, when Cullen learned of Moran's opposition, he telegraphed Rome 'at once to have all steps suspended'.[278] Cullen's influence proved decisive and, by late September, Leonard was appointed. He appears to have been slightly reluctant, although this was probably pro forma; in November, he went out of his way to tell McMahon in Cape Town that Cullen had 'advised' him to submit to the wishes of the Holy See.[279] He was duly consecrated by Cullen at the Cabra convent.

John Leonard proved to be an effective bishop. He needed to be: the vicariate was more than £2,000 in debt.[280] As soon as his appointment was announced, he wrote repeatedly to Cape Town to find out exactly how many priests there were and how many Protestant and Catholic schools.[281] This was an early manifestation of what seems to have been the primary attribute of his tenure: detailed attention to both clerical and lay discipline and conduct. He was also an effective fundraiser, retiring Grimley's debt and, by 1880, securing more than £16,000 above the normal collections. Leonard continued Grimley's focus on education, telling Ricards in 1874 that he soon hoped to open another poor school

---

[273] Grimley to Leonard, 19 December 1861, AACT/LP/Box 18.

[274] For example, see Cullen to Leonard, 6 June and 16 July 1871, AACT/LP/Box 30.

[275] Grimley to Leonard, 8 June 1865, AACT/LP/Box 18. Grimley was frustrated when Rome failed to grant the mark of respect he thought was deserved: see Grimley to Leonard, 20 March 1866, AACT/LP/Box 18.

[276] Grimley to Leonard, 5 June 1869, AACT/LP/Box 18.

[277] Kirby to Cullen, 7 August 1872, DDA/CP/45/1. I have been unable to discover Ryan's first name. According to Kirby, Pius IX made the point that the Cape had an excellent climate.

[278] Forde to Moran, 22 August 1872, ADD/MP.

[279] Leonard to McMahon, 8 November 1878, AACT/MP/Box 38.

[280] Brown, *South Africa*, 91.

[281] Leonard to McMahon, 22 October 1872, AACT/LP/Box 38.

in Cape Town and after that to provide schools to each district in the vicariate. If Catholics then continued to send their children to Protestant schools, he wrote, 'it will be their own fault'.[282] Leonard also imported a group of Sisters of Nazareth into the Cape. Founded (or re-founded) by French émigrés in London, the community seems to have contained a substantial number of Irish. Leonard needed them to take over St Brigid's orphanage, which was run by the Dominican sisters who had neither the resources nor the interest in maintaining it. When they arrived, the Dominicans hosted them to an 'Irish tea'.[283]

In the mid-1880s, Leonard's health began to fail, and, in 1886, he recommended that John Rooney be appointed his coadjutor. Born in Edenderry in the King's County and ordained for Dublin in 1867, Rooney was yet another product of the Arran Quay school and the Propaganda. He had come to the Cape in Grimley's later years, becoming the parish priest first of Oudtshoorn and then Simonstown, the latter in succession to another Arran Quay and Propaganda man, Patrick Dunne.[284] His selection was bitterly opposed by some of the Cape Town priests, who demanded a say in the process. Leonard squashed that notion.[285] Leonard lived until 1908, and Rooney until 1926, although he retired in 1924 and was replaced by the second native-born South African bishop, Bernard O'Riley. (The first was the Oblate David O'Leary for the Transvaal in 1925.) O'Riley was the son of one of the Irish schoolmasters imported by Devereux in 1850. He resigned in 1932. His successor was the first non-Irishman and the first member of a religious order to become vicar apostolic in the Cape, the German-born Pallottine Franziskus Xaver Hennemann. He resigned in 1949 and was replaced by Owen McCann, whose father was Irish and mother Irish-Australian. McCann became the first archbishop of Cape Town in 1951 and South Africa's first cardinal in 1965. He retired in 1984 and died ten years later.

Yet securing the episcopal succession was always the means and not the end for the Hiberno-Romans, and the early Irish bishops faced challenges beyond the establishment of schools and the importation of religious. If nothing else, there was never enough money: in 1863, for example, the Propagation of the Faith gave the Eastern District some £700 and the Western a mere £400 per annum, although that had equalized by 1868.[286] In Cape Town, Grimley struggled with Griffith's debts,

---

[282] Leonard to Ricards, 7 March 1874, PEDA/LP/JL/JR/685/JR/2.
[283] Anonymous, *The Centenary of the Congregation of the Poor Sisters of Nazareth, Cape Town, 1882–1982* (Cape Town: Salesian Institute, 1982), 5.
[284] Brown, *South Africa*, 64.   [285] Ibid., 97–8.
[286] Grimley to Leonard, 18 March 1864, AACT/LP/Box 18; O'Connell to Grimley, 5 June 1868, AACT/GP/Box 13.

including a substantial legal claim against the vicariate.[287] He also had to deal with heavy outward migration, mostly to New Zealand. 'Some of my best Catholics are emigrating', he lamented in 1864, 'throwing back this Mission to its infancy.'[288] Worse, what little public money the church received for clerical salaries came under sustained political attack in the mid-1860s. Since 1852, the amount the Cape government granted per year to religious denominations was fixed at £16,060.[289] Also fixed was its distribution under what was known as 'Schedule C': the Dutch Reformed Church received £8,812, the Church of England £4,702, and the Catholics £1,000, while the Methodists received less than £700 and the Lutherans and the Church of Scotland less than £250 each.[290] Grimley regularly railed at the disparity and particularly at the consequent wealth of the Anglicans: 'Gray the Protestant bishop', he complained in 1864, 'has cash to any amount. It is most difficult with three or four hundred pounds to cope with thousands.'[291] From at least 1867, attempts were made to either repeal Schedule C or redistribute the monies on the basis of population. (The opposition to Schedule C was less anti-Catholic than anti-Anglican, or simply voluntaryist.) It was eventually eliminated in 1875, and the churches were thrown wholly on their own resources. The same year, both the Eastern District and the laity of Port Elizabeth were nearly bankrupted by their half-built Catholic Hall, which had already cost some £12,000 before a property crash rendered it worth a mere £3,700.[292] As late as St Patrick's Day 1890, Ricards was forced to issue a special appeal to balance his budget and retire some of his crushing debts.[293]

Another challenge was the imposition of order, not least on the clergy. As Grimley complained in 1862, his predecessor had given his priests 'unlimited faculties, and no printed or special Rules for their guidance'.[294] They also seem to have been left to their own devices liturgically, and Grimley was forced to insist that all his priests use only

---

[287] The vicariate was sued by a man named Begley who claimed he was owed £1,500 (later £900), something Grimley disputed. See Grimley to O'Haire, 18 March 1862, in O'Haire, 11, and Grimley to Moran, 1 May 1862, PEDA/MP/TG/PM/243/PM/1.

[288] Grimley to Leonard, 25 October 1864, AACT/LP/Box 18. The emigrants were given free passage and a promise of land in New Zealand, where wages were believed to be higher. In October 1864, as many as 700 Catholics departed Cape Town.

[289] Under Ordinance No. 3, 1852, quoted in Statutes of the Cape of Good Hope, 1872–86, 1358.

[290] Cape of Good Hope, Debates in the Legislative Council, 25 June 1867, vol. 1, 135.

[291] Grimley to Leonard, 18 March 1864, AACT/LP/Box 18.   [292] Wilmot, 114–15.

[293] Ricards to the Laity of the vicariate, 'St Patrick's Day' [17 March] 1890, CLHR/PR3823. The appeal worked: the budget was balanced and £390 was applied to the accumulated debt.

[294] Grimley to Moran, 9 September 1862, PEDA/MP/G/PM/248/PM/1.

the Roman rite.[295] Moran too asserted himself: one of his early decisions was that no convert could be accepted 'without express permission of the Bishop'. He also kept a careful note of every dispensation granted, from exemptions from the Lenten fast to the exceedingly rare mixed marriages.[296] On arriving in Cape Town, Leonard cracked down on his priests' financial activities and curtailed their independence.[297] The bishops not only imposed uniformity on their priests but agreed it between themselves: Grimley, for example, was pleased to discover that neither vicariate solemnized mixed marriages contracted before Protestant ministers.[298] Ireland was usually the model: in 1878, for example, Ricards and Leonard were discomfited to discover that at Mass they had been sitting on the 'wrong' side of the altar because that was where they had seen Cullen sit.[299] As elsewhere in Greater Ireland, devotional and liturgical conformity was a key desiderata of the Hiberno-Roman bishops: as Grimley wrote in 1862, 'uniformity of discipline is so desirable'.[300]

Uniformity was also imposed on the laity, not least to keep them institutionally, sexually, and socially separate from Protestants. As elsewhere, this was achieved through compulsion, persuasion, and denominational segregation. The primary threat was withdrawal of sacraments, which had both spiritual and social consequences, and the circumstance in which this threat was most often made and carried out was the education of children. In 1874, for example, John Leonard decreed that Catholic children attending Protestant schools could not receive communion, and their parents no sacraments at all. In 1883, he told a woman who had sent her child to such a school that she was consequently 'so cruel a mother' that he had no choice but to 'deprive' her of the sacraments. She submitted.[301] In 1859, Moran bluntly refused his blessing to a Catholic woman who had been offered employment as a teacher in Port Elizabeth's undenominational Grey Institute.[302]

---

[295] Grimley to Leonard, 18 March 1867, AACT/LP/Box 18.

[296] 'Bp. Moran's notebook', bound volume, PEDA/MP. There is no file number.

[297] Brown, *South Africa*, 92–3.

[298] Grimley to Moran, 15 October 1862, PEDA/MP/TG/PM/249/PM1.

[299] Leonard to Ricards, 17 July 1878, PEDA/RP/JL/JR/674/JR/2. The question was whether to sit on the 'gospel' or 'epistle' side: bishops sat on the gospel, vicars apostolic on the epistle. None of the Irish Cape bishops had realized and had simply copied Cullen.

[300] Grimley to Moran, 15 October 1862, PEDA/MP/TG/PM/249/PM1.

[301] Leonard to Schillinth, 19 July 1883, quoted in Boner, 'Irish Dominicans', 17.

[302] Moran to Sarah Acton, 1 October 1859, PEDA/MP/PM/SA/873/PM/3. At issue was whether Acton could teach the Bible, which Moran pointed out was impossible because the church had 'nothing to say' to the school 'in consequence of the erroneous principle on which' it was based. This had the effect of preventing her employment, as reading the Bible was part of a teacher's responsibilities.

This self-segregation required a full range of institutions and not simply schools and orphanages. Cape Town and Port Elizabeth both had a Young Men's Society and Societies of St Vincent de Paul, and both vicariates raised (after Griffith's death) the annual Peter's Pence. Grimley built a Catholic Hall in Cape Town, and the city had two Catholic mutual societies by the mid-1860s; in 1859, Moran opened the inevitably named St Patrick's Mutual Benefit Society in Grahamstown.[303] As well as providing safely Catholic groups and spaces, the Cape bishops sought to shape behaviour. Moran, for example, often preached against dances and the 'contemptible' people who attended them in an effort to fit in with society.[304]

Yet institutions and episcopal threats were not themselves sufficient to maintain order in what was ultimately a voluntary organization; willing conformity was necessary. The Irish bishops in the Cape turned to what they knew in order to achieve it: missions. In describing his famous 'devotional revolution' thesis, Emmet Larkin drew particular attention to the growth of parish missions, pointing out that, by 1860, one had been held in almost every Irish parish. These emphasized preaching, lectures, and magnificently staged liturgies complete with carefully planned music and lashings of candles and incense. The missions drew people back to the church and the gains were then consolidated by parish and diocesan groups ranging from the temperance societies to the Society of St Vincent de Paul.[305] This was all familiar to Moran, Grimley, and Leonard, who, before coming to the Cape, were not only priests in Cullen's Dublin but also closely linked to the Vincentians, the religious order most closely associated with the Irish missions. It is no surprise that they exported the model to the Cape. In 1861, for example, Moran thanked Grimley for personally giving a mission in the Eastern District. 'Even after your departure', he wrote, 'a great many people who had absented themselves from their religious duties for years come to the Sacraments.'[306]

Ireland remained the inescapable model for Cape Catholicism. This was represented symbolically, as with the ubiquitous dedication of schools, parishes, mutual societies, and even choirs to St Patrick and other Irish saints; at one point the diocese of Port Elizabeth had no fewer than seven parishes named for Patrick.[307] Irish symbols permeated

---

[303] Grimley to Leonard, 17 November 1863, AACT/LP/Box 18; O'Haire, 45; see 'Rules of the Grahamstown St. Patrick's Catholic Mutual Benefit Society' (Grahamstown: Journal Office, 1890).

[304] Moran to Grimley, 11 December 1865, AACT/GP/Box 13.

[305] Larkin, *Historical Dimensions*, 78.

[306] Moran to Grimley, 15 October 1861, AACT/GP/Box 13.

[307] The late Bishop Michael Coleman of Port Elizabeth, in conversation with the author. August 2009.

the church at every level: in 1870, for example, Grimley obtained from the Marquis of Bute money for a new bell for the Cape Town cathedral. It was cast in Dublin and featured a carving of Mary on one side and on the other 'an Irish harp, wolf-dog, and round tower – encircled in a wreath of shamrocks – with the words "Erin-go-bragh" underneath'.[308] As Bishop Grimley wrote when he dedicated the first church in Namaqualand to St Columbanus, 'Hurrah for old Ireland!'[309]

Despite the overwhelming Irishness of Cape Catholicism, it was not unaffected by wider concerns, either international or domestic. The Cullenite bishops shared, for example, their patron's terror of secret societies: Grimley anticipated 'much mischief from the Secret Societies', while *The Colonist* thought that 'For centuries, secret societies have been the curse of Europe.'[310] Here too the Hiberno-Roman bishops marked a change from their predecessors; Grimley's campaign against the Odd Fellows was complicated by the fact that Griffith had never condemned them.[311] For Grimley, it was enough that Cullen had once told him that it was impossible to absolve an active Odd Fellow, and both Grimley and Moran consequently denied the sacraments to Catholic members.[312] Cape Catholics were also exposed to and interested in such burning issues as the fate of the Papal States and the doctrine of papal infallibility. O'Haire, for example, incorporated a discourse on the temporal power into his visits to even the smallest settlements; in 1866, he toured the south coast with a lecture entitled 'How the Pope became a King'. In Mossel Bay, he managed to earn £12 from it, after expenses.[313] In 1860, Moran dedicated much of his Lenten pastoral to the evils of the Risorgimento, and, when he returned from Europe in 1867, he immediately delivered a public lecture on the papal supremacy.[314] In early 1870, the two vicariates combined to send (via Cullen) an address and £310 to the embattled pope.[315] Moran and Grimley were enthusiastic supporters of infallibility at the Vatican Council, and Grimley planned but did not deliver a speech in support of it.[316]

---

[308] *Standard and Mail*, 15 December 1870, quoted in O'Haire, 433–4.
[309] Grimley to Leonard, 13 October 1865, AACT/LP/Box 18.
[310] Grimley to Moran, 1 July 1862, PEDA/MP/TG/PM/246/PM/1; *The Colonist*, 24 January 1857.
[311] Grimley to Moran, 1 July 1862, PEDA/MP/TG/PM/246/PM/1.
[312] Grimley to Moran, 1 May 1862, PEDA/MP/TG/PM/243/PM/1.
[313] In tiny Fraserburg in the Karoo desert, for example, O'Haire completed an eleven-day visit with a lecture on the temporal power: see O'Haire, 257–8. For Mossel Bay, 251–2.
[314] 'Lenten Pastoral, Feast of St. Agatha, 1860'. Moran's speech was reported in the *Great Eastern*, 5 December 1867.
[315] Wilmot, 87.
[316] 'Diary of Bishop Thomas Grimley at the Vatican Council, 1869–70', AACT/Box 12.

The Cape, however, was not Europe, and it was not like the other settler colonies. Not only were the settlers as a whole outnumbered by the non-European inhabitants but those from the British Isles were substantially outnumbered by those of Dutch descent, and the Irish represented only some 10 per cent of those from the British Isles and the Catholics only some 44 per cent of them. Like all settlers, the Irish Catholics were forced to confront and adapt to this reality. It seems that they did so largely by ignoring the vast non-European population: at no point in the history of the Cape before 1910 was there any sustained success in spreading Catholicism beyond its Irish (or at least European) base. Kathleen Boner has pointed out that, in 1868, there were only some fifty 'coloured' Catholics in the Western Cape, the majority of whom were a group of Filipino fishermen living at Kalk Bay on the Cape peninsula; by 1891, that number was 257, of whom 180 were Filipino.[317] There were practical reasons for this failure: the church simply did not have either the money or the personnel to expand much beyond its own flock. As Moran put it in 1860, his first responsibility was 'to provide for those who had the faith, and for their children. It would have been sheer insanity and highly criminal to leave these inadequately provided for and go in search of natives amongst whom, perhaps, no good could be done.'[318] He was as good as his word: there was no missionary activity in the Eastern Cape until after his departure.

Yet Moran was not necessarily representative, and he appears to have been suspicious of all attempts to evangelize indigenous peoples; in New Zealand, for example, one of his first acts was to halt almost all missionary work among the Māori. By contrast, Grimley was an enthusiast for conversions in general and native conversions in particular. Yet Cape Town was not the frontier, and the 'coloured' population of the Western Cape was not as feared as were the Xhosa or the Zulu. Nevertheless, within weeks of arriving in Cape Town, Grimley was privately boasting of having baptized 'four young Africans'.[319] As he told Leonard in 1863, nothing could compare 'to the happiness of admitting the heathen or the heretic into the bosom of our holy faith'.[320] Grimley took practical steps as well, opening in early 1864 what he called 'our school for little blacks'. Although it had at first only three students, Grimley was sanguine: St Paul's school in Dublin had started with that number too. He recruited two women to teach for free, a saving that allowed him to provide

[317] Boner, 'Irish Dominicans', 14–15.
[318] Moran to Cullen, 15 July 1860, DDA/CP/333/1/20.
[319] Grimley to Leonard, 16 August 1861, AACT/LP/Box 18.
[320] Grimley to Leonard, 16 October 1863, AACT/LP/Box 18.

lunch.[321] Within a month, there were more than fifty students, 'some of them little Mahometans'.[322] He also encouraged his priests, telling O'Haire that his primary duty at Malmesbury would be to open a 'school for coloured children': 'You must gather them around yourself; become all to all for their salvation.'[323] When O'Haire duly opened the school, Grimley was thrilled: 'Get in the coloured children – the natives! the natives!'[324] He was also pleased to show his successes to the public, telling O'Haire in mid-1864 that 'I have the blacks, at least eleven of them, walking in procession. They edify the whole congregation, and gratify all the blacks who crowd to see the procession.'[325] Grimley was undoubtedly enthusiastic, but he was equally undoubtedly ineffectual.

There seem to have been several reasons for this, and they apply across the Cape. First, neither vicariate had enough money for its own needs, nor did either possess an adequate number of priests and religious. As Marcel Dischl observed of the Eastern Cape, 'The bishops had just enough priests to cater for the white Catholics; there was no chance to start with real missionary work among the indigenous people.'[326] This was equally true in the west. Priests or seminarians who wanted to engage in native missions were discouraged: in 1877, for example, Leonard told a Western Cape student at Rome that he could not undertake such a mission on ordination. If he really wanted to work with 'the blacks of South Africa', he could in his spare time give some attention to the coloured population in and around Cape Town.[327] The lack of funds also put the Catholics at both an absolute and a competitive disadvantage: as Grimley complained, the Protestant churches had what seemed to him almost unlimited resources; the Anglican bishop had 'parsons, schoolmasters etc to spread in every hole and corner'.[328] There was some truth to this: in government support alone, the Church of England enjoyed an almost five-to-one advantage. As they struggled to open, fund, and staff schools and churches in Cape Town and elsewhere, Grimley and his successors simply could not afford more than relatively token attempts at evangelization.

Within the bounds of the era, there does not seem to have been much active racism. Bishop Griffith did at first accept the settlers' contemptuous views of the natives, but he quickly modified his opinions. By 1840, he

---

[321] Grimley to O'Haire, 29 February 1864, in O'Haire, 126.
[322] Grimley to Leonard, 18 March 1864, AACT/LP/Box 18.
[323] Grimley to O'Haire, 2 March 1864, in O'Haire, 128.
[324] Grimley to O'Haire, 6 April 1864, in O'Haire, 134.
[325] Grimley to O'Haire, 26 May 1864, in O'Haire, 145.   [326] Dischl, 49.
[327] Leonard to John O'Reilly, 5 July 1877, AACT/LP/Box 32.
[328] Grimley to Leonard, 18 March 1864, AACT/LP/Box 18.

was lamenting his financial inability to open schools for native children and criticizing the 'boorish Dutch' for not allowing 'children of colour to be educated with them in the same schools'. He also had vague hopes of a seminary to train African priests.[329] Grimley was an enthusiastic evangelist and seems for his day to have been relatively colour-blind, while Ricards imported the Trappists specifically to convert the frontier. He also gave a surprisingly nuanced account of indigenous religion and customs in his 1879 book *The Catholic Church and the Kaffir*, although his recommendation was the conventional one of breaking the power of the Xhosa chiefs. Of course, Africans were not seen as equals: O'Haire, for example, observed that he always travelled with two dogs that watched over him at night and warned him 'upon the approach of jackals, wild cats, natives, baboons, or anything objectionable'.[330] There was no Catholic equivalent of the Xhosa Presbyterian minister Tiyo Soga, who died in 1871;[331] and Moran appears to have adopted frontier attitudes almost in their entirety, whether those related to the possibility of authentic conversion among the Xhosa or the duplicity of Cape Town politicians.[332] Still, under his editorship, *The Colonist* delivered a stinging assault on phrenology, already much in vogue to explain supposed African inferiority.[333] Well into the twentieth century, Port Elizabeth, the most Irish of all the vicariates and dioceses, distinguished itself by its continuing disinterest in its surroundings. Ultimately, the Irish Catholic Church in the Cape both failed to make inroads with the indigenous population and seems to have been little troubled by that fact, at least after the 1880s. The great Irish missionary movement in sub-Saharan Africa only emerged after the Great War and then was largely focussed on west Africa and Kenya.[334] The Kiltegan Fathers, for example, were only founded in 1932.

Changing Catholic practice largely coincided with changes in the Cape itself, in particular the increasing racial segregation of Cape Town from the early 1880s. This was partly driven by a depression, which saw demands that 'white' labour be substituted for African.[335] This quickly became a campaign to ensure educational segregation, something that was supported by, among others, the Irish Anglican Frederick St. Leger.[336] As Cape Town became more racially conscious, so too did the Catholic Church, or at least lay Catholics. As Saul Dubow has pointed out, for example, the publications of Alexander Wilmot became

---

[329] *CD*, 201.   [330] O'Haire, 260.   [331] Dubow, 111.

[332] Richard Price has noted a 'closing of the missionary mind' in the Eastern Cape beginning in the 1850s. One aspect of this was an increasing suspicion that the Xhosa might not be capable of real conversion. See Price, 141.

[333] *The Colonist*, 28 February 1857.   [334] Hastings, 581.   [335] Bickford-Smith, 107.

[336] Ibid., 140.

increasingly 'anti-black' over time.[337] By 1893, the Marists' school ceased to accept non-white students, although it was one of the last in Cape Town to do so.[338] It was the same elsewhere in southern Africa: in 1897, Bishop Jolivet of Natal admitted to Rome that he permitted the operation of separate schools for whites and blacks but insisted that 'coloureds' were usually admitted to white schools and argued that he was seeking to break down community preference for a colour-bar.[339] Still, and unlike almost all other denominations, what non-white converts there were were not segregated at worship either in the Cape or in Natal.[340]

The Catholic Church did not face the racial complexities of the Cape anywhere else in the settler empire, not even in New Zealand. Those complexities did, however, inform another difference between the Cape and the rest of Greater Ireland: sectarianism was less of a force there than in any of the other regions discussed in this book. It is hard, for example, to imagine another late nineteenth-century Irish Catholic colonial bishop participating, as John Rooney of Cape Town did, in an avowedly non-sectarian Irish Association in company with a lapsed Anglican priest and an Irish émigré rabbi.[341] Even Newfoundland's Michael Howley might have drawn the line at that. The reason, as Donal McCracken pointed out, is simple: sectarian fervour 'was ameliorated by the intimacy of colonial society and by common dangers far more immediate than the threat of Rome or the Orange menace'.[342] From the moment of Griffith's arrival, the institutional Catholic Church was welcomed by the state. It was also funded by the state, even if not on grounds of equality; and whatever Moran's complaints, what legal disabilities existed were swept away by 1868, leaving, in Grimley's words, not 'a vestige of inferiority, as far as Catholics are concerned'.[343]

On a social level, there also seems to have been more acceptance of Catholics than elsewhere in the Anglo world. Even when there was conflict, it was increasingly marginal. When Grimley was humiliated and spat upon by a Dutch lay preacher in Namaqualand, for example, the local Dutch community publicly apologized.[344] As Robert Ross has observed, 'Anti-Catholic prejudice survived, but decreasingly as the century wore on.'[345] This was

---

[337] Dubow, 137.   [338] Bickford-Smith, 143.   [339] Brown, *South Africa*, 168–9.

[340] Ibid., 204.

[341] Shaw, 7. In addition to St. Leger and Rooney, the Cape Town Rabbi A. P. Bender was a member.

[342] McCracken, 'Irish settlement', 140.

[343] Grimley to O'Haire, 25 August 1868, in O'Haire, 368–9.

[344] See O'Haire, 353, quoting from an otherwise undated 1867 number of the *Cape Standard*. Namaqualand is the coastal region in what is now the Northern Cape Province.

[345] Ross, 105–6.

particularly clear in the normally explosive realm of education. In the 1867 debate on Schedule C, for example, the old Eastern Cape separatist (and Methodist) Robert Godlonton noted that, before coming to the legislative council that morning, he had observed a 'large number of young urchins as they came out of a school kept by the Roman Catholics'. His view was that the Catholic Church had earned its subsidy by taking such children 'out of the streets' and not only caring for them but teaching them 'lessons which might not be only to their own interest, but also to that of the colony'.[346] Langham Dale's public praise was even more fulsome: the Catholic schools were 'the ornament of our three chief towns', he wrote, and their construction a result of the 'rule of an *Episcopus* backed by the love and admiration of the congregation'. It is little wonder that Leonard quoted this in a fundraising letter for a monument to Grimley; Dale himself gave £5.[347]

As the century wore on, the small anglophone society of the Cape, and especially Cape Town, accepted and to a point absorbed the Catholic Church: important events such as the opening of the Marists' school were attended by the governor or other officials, as were high-profile lectures on explicitly religious topics.[348] Grimley even accepted an invitation to give a lecture on Father Mathew on behalf of the Methodist temperance campaign and in the Methodist Hall.[349] On the frontier, the sense of a common threat no doubt made other differences seem less important to the small European population. This is not to say that there were not tensions. Moran's political activism, for example, raised temperatures in Grahamstown: in 1869, 'Fair Play' complained to a local newspaper about the bishop ordering, with 'true Paddy precipitancy', that all Catholics should vote for a favoured candidate and urged that true Protestants should vote for his opponent. Yet even here the Cape was different: that candidate was an Anglican, and the aggrieved letter writer hoped that 'the little flirtation between St. George and St. Patrick may not end in a more tender and close alliance'.[350]

The Cape Irish can indeed be seen as having become, in Vivian Bickford-Smith's terms, 'white'; but it does not necessarily follow that they also lost their Irish identity and became 'English', or at least not immediately. In 1887, for example, Ricards forbade children in the

---

[346] *Cape of Good Hope, Debates in the Legislative Council*, 25 June 1867, vol. 1, 135.

[347] John Leonard, circular Letter in support of the erection of a monument to Bishop Thomas Grimley, 5 January 1877, AACT/LP. Dale's comments originally appeared in a pamphlet he wrote entitled 'Ecclesiastical topics'.

[348] For example, O'Haire reports that the governor attended his own lecture in St Mary's Cathedral on the subject of inspiration in scripture. See O'Haire, 178.

[349] O'Haire, 102.   [350] *The Journal* (Grahamstown), 17 February 1869.

Catholic schools from celebrating Queen Victoria's golden jubilee on the grounds of British cruelty towards Ireland, while touring Home Rule politicians were always able to count on a warm welcome at the Cape.[351] Still, when the South African War broke out, the wholly Irish episcopate in the Cape firmly supported the British cause. The Dutch convert priest F. C. Kolbe, for example, was forced by episcopal pressure to temporarily resign as editor of *South African Catholic Magazine* because of his pacifistic stand.[352] Whatever their social integration, the Irish retained a firm control of the Catholic Church in the Cape, and the Catholic Church kept firm control of Irish Catholics.

In South Africa more widely, the country was slowly divided up into vicariates and prefectures and entrusted to religious orders. With the exception of the Irish Franciscans, who were given charge of Kokstad in the Transkei in 1935, none of these were Irish.[353] Still, over time, many of Irish descent rose to prominence in the various religious orders of South Africa, particularly among the Oblates: David O'Leary was appointed vicar apostolic in the Transvaal in 1925, while Denis Hurley's 1946 appointment to Natal was met by ferocious French resistance within the Oblates, resistance that at points flirted with outright rebellion.[354] Irish religious also began to spread through the country, including the Irish Christian Brothers who opened the still elite St Patrick's College in Kimberly in the late 1890s. When the South African hierarchy was established in 1951, those of Irish descent were well represented, including in two of the three archdioceses (Cape Town and Durban) and the diocese of Johannesburg.[355] Archbishop Hurley and Cardinal Owen McCann became prominent internal opponents of the apartheid regime. Although South Africa and the Cape of Good Hope both developed in their own fashion, the Cape at least was without doubt a participant in the global Irish and Cullenite expansion of the nineteenth century. As Thomas Grimley melodramatically wrote not long after he arrived in Cape Town, 'When I look around me, and see what Ireland has done for South Africa, I cannot refrain from exclaiming: "Poor Ireland! God has destined you for the conversion of the world."'[356]

---

[351] Brown, *South Africa*, 320.

[352] Frederick Hale, 'A Catholic voice against British imperialism: F C Kolbe's opposition to the Second Anglo-Boer War', *Religion and Theology*, vol. 4, no. 1–3 (1997), 94–108, at 102.

[353] Dischl, 46–8.   [354] Kearney, 55.

[355] See the useful 'episcopal genealogy' at the rear of 'Fr Agathangelus' (ed.), *The Catholic Church and Southern Africa: A Series of Essays Published to Commemorate the Establishment of the Hierarchy in South Africa* (Cape Town: The Catholic Archdiocese of Cape Town, 1951).

[356] Grimley to Conroy, 20 January 1862, in O'Haire, 474.

5   Canada

Visitors to the Roman Catholic cathedral in Antigonish, Nova Scotia, are bid '*Failte Do Àrd-Eaglais Naoimh Ninian*'. The language is Scots Gaelic, and the sign is a reminder that Canadian Catholic history is more than a simple binary of French and English. In the Maritime provinces of Nova Scotia, New Brunswick, and Prince Edward Island, for example, the Catholic population in the nineteenth century consisted of French-speaking Acadians, the descendants of settlers who had first arrived in the region in the early seventeenth century; converts, some of very long standing, among the indigenous Mi'kmaq; mostly Gaelic-speaking Scots, largely highlanders and islanders, the first of whom began arriving in the 1750s; American loyalists and their descendants; and what was at first a small but soon rapidly growing number of Irish.

This diversity has not always been fully appreciated by Canadian historians. The late John S. Moir's influential description of English-speaking Catholics as a 'double-minority', for example, is largely applicable only to Lower and Upper Canada (from 1867, Quebec and Ontario).[1] This is also true for the large and convincing literature that stresses the distinctive development of Catholicism in Toronto.[2] The vast historiography of Catholic Quebec is almost entirely distinct, not least because it is largely in French. There is no English Catholic (or English-language) equivalent of Léon Pouliot's five-volume life of Archbishop Ignace Bourget of Montreal, for example, nor is there a single study in English that successfully covers the entire country: despite its title, Roberto Perin's *Rome in Canada* is largely and lovingly concerned with the francophone church, while Terence J. Fay's attempt at a balance

---

[1] John S. Moir, 'The problem of a double minority: Some reflections on the development of the English-speaking Catholic Church in Canada in the nineteenth century', *Histoire sociale/Social History*, vol. 7 (1971), 53–67.

[2] In particular, Brian P. Clarke, *Piety and Nationalism: Lay Voluntary Associations and the Creation of an Irish-Catholic Community in Toronto, 1850–1895* (Montreal and Kingston: McGill-Queen's University Press, 1993); Mark G. McGowan, *The Waning of the Green: Catholics, the Irish, and Identity in Toronto, 1887–1922* (Montreal and Kingston: McGill-Queen's University Press, 1999).

between English and French in his book *A History of Canadian Catholics* comes at the expense of the Maritimes. They are in turn served by a historiography that is at once sophisticated, alert to differences, and unapologetically provincial. The Prairies and Western Canada meanwhile have seen a handful of studies on subjects as diverse as the Oblates of Mary Immaculate in British Columbia and the Manitoba Schools Crisis, the latter attractive largely for its national implications, but the region still remains significantly underexplored.[3] Even Terrence Murphy and Gerald Stortz's excellent collaborative volume on English-speaking Catholics hardly ventures west of Manitoba.[4] Indeed, across Canada, much of the best recent work is to be found not in monographs or biographies but in a handful of collaborative volumes and in journals such as *Acadiensis* and the Canadian Catholic Historical Association's *Historical Studies*.[5]

Canada's intense regionalism has also had its effect on the Irish. One of the most influential studies of Irish Canada, for example, is Donald Akenson's *The Irish in Ontario*, but what was true of Ontario was not necessarily so of Prince Edward Island or Saskatchewan. The relative weight of Irish Catholic and Irish Protestant migration is a case in point. Between 1815 and 1845, some 450,000 Irish people migrated to what became Canada, at least two-thirds of whom were Protestant. This inevitably led to sectarian tensions and has rightly been identified as the primary driver of Ontario's distinctively accommodative variant of Irish Catholicism. Yet, although Irish Protestant migration was significant elsewhere in Canada, this vast and enduring imbalance was unique to Upper Canada, where, as late as 1871, Irish Protestants still outnumbered Irish Catholics by around two to one.[6] Everywhere else, Catholics either were a majority of the Irish by 1850 or had never been a minority in the first place. Studies of the Irish in other provinces do exist but are often either amateurish or obscurely published, although here too there are a handful of excellent collaborative volumes.[7] Important figures such as

---

[3] For example, Vincent J. McNally, *The Lord's Distant Vineyard: A History of the Oblates and the Catholic Community in British Columbia* (Edmonton: University of Alberta Press, 2000); Manoly R. Lupol, *The Roman Catholic Church and the North-west School Question* (Toronto: University of Toronto Press, 1974); Paul Crunican, *Priests and Politicians: Manitoba Schools and the Election of 1896* (Toronto: University of Toronto Press, 1974).

[4] Murphy and Stortz, *Creed and Culture*.

[5] For example, Terrence Murphy and Cyril J. Byrne's edited collection *Religion and Identity*.

[6] See Akenson, *Irish in Ontario*, chap. 1.

[7] For example, Brendan O'Grady, *Exiles and Islanders: The Irish Settlers of Prince Edward Island* (Montreal and Kingston: McGill-Queen's University Press, 2004), which tends to the antiquarian, or the largely excellent essays in Peter Toner's almost unobtainable volume *New Ireland Remembered: Historical Essays on the Irish in New Brunswick* (Fredericton, NB: New Ireland Press, 1988). In addition to Toner, David A. Wilson's

Thomas D'Arcy McGee and subjects such as transatlantic landlordism or Irish Catholic participation in the Great War have also been examined, but there is as yet no national study along the lines of Patrick O'Farrell's *The Irish in Australia*.[8]

Both Canadian Catholicism and the Catholic Irish must therefore be approached on a regional basis, if only to avoid the trap of treating the experience of any one region as normative. By 1900, the Canadian Catholic Church consisted of four distinct components, which Roberto Perin called 'Maritime, French Canadian, Ontario Irish, and Oblate Missionary'.[9] This chapter focusses on the first and, to a lesser extent, on the third, as reflecting the limits of Irish ecclesiastical interest in Canada. That is not to say that there were not Irish in Quebec, where there were in fact many, or among the Oblates, where there were some, but they enjoyed relatively little influence in their own right. In the Atlantic provinces and Upper Canada/Ontario, the Irish became masters in their own house, albeit at different times, under different conditions, and with different outcomes.

The Triple Minority: Atlantic Canada

It was in the Maritimes that the Irish first carved out an ecclesiastical sphere independent of vast, Catholic, and francophone Quebec; Irish dominance of Ontario, the Prairies, and the west came later. The four provinces (Cape Breton was a province in its own right between 1784 and 1820) had steadily anglicized since the 1750s, not least because of the brutal expulsion of the Acadians in 1755, and by 1800 the total population had reached nearly 80,000. Most spoke English and had emigrated from the British Isles, with the Catholic portion coming largely from Scotland or Ireland. The Irish thus not only had to fight off what they still called 'Canada', by which they meant the francophone establishment centred on what is now the province of Quebec, but also had to contain the Scots, marginalize the remaining Acadians, and settle their own internal differences.

two edited volumes are especially useful: *The Orange Order in Canada* (Dublin: Four Courts Press, 2007) and *Irish Nationalism in Canada* (Montreal and Kingston: McGill-Queen's University Press, 2009).

[8] For example, Catherine Anne Wilson, *A New Lease on Life: Landlords, Tenants, and Immigrants in Ireland and Canada* (Montreal and Kingston: McGill-Queen's University Press, 1994); Mark G. McGowan, *The Imperial Irish: Canada's Irish Catholics Fight the Great War* (Montreal and Kingston: McGill-Queen's University Press, 2017).

[9] Roberto Perin, *Rome in Canada: The Vatican and Canadian Affairs in the Late Victorian Age* (Toronto: University of Toronto Press, 1990), 14.

The historical reliance on Quebec for all of British North America meant that ecclesiastical organization came late to the region. Although the first Anglican bishop was appointed to Nova Scotia in 1787, there was no Catholic equivalent until 1817 when the Irishman Edmund Burke was appointed vicar apostolic and consecrated the following year. This was the first division of the vast diocese of Quebec, and it thus marked the beginning of what would eventually become a distinct anglophone church. In the short term, however, the practical consequences were limited: British North America's ecclesiastical infrastructure remained largely francophone and largely in Quebec, as did its wealth and most of its personnel. Burke himself had been educated in Paris, and, after a decade in Ireland, he became a popular professor at the Séminaire de Quebec, then a pastor near the city, and finally a missionary in the contested country around Detroit. In 1801, the bishop of Quebec had sent him to Halifax as his vicar general. There, Burke found a growing Irish population, largely from Newfoundland, who had been organized by James Jones, an Irish Capuchin who had been given responsibility for the entire region as 'superior of the missions' in 1787. Jones left in 1800 and was succeeded by an Irish Dominican, also named Edmund Burke, who was appointed vicar general before himself leaving just a year later. The second Burke quickly recognized that Nova Scotia was too diverse and too distant to be ruled from Quebec, and in 1815 he travelled to Europe under the pretext of ill health to campaign for the erection of a new vicariate.[10] In a neat foreshadowing of what was to come, among the reasons he advanced to Rome was that Bishop Joseph-Octave Plessis was too old and too ill to properly oversee his vast diocese. In fact, Plessis had made several visits to the region, was in rude health, and was anyway ten years younger than Burke himself, but this was beside the point.[11]

Even before his appointment as vicar apostolic, Burke faced a number of challenges, including an assertive laity and a hostile Anglican establishment. The entire region also had far too few priests, many of very poor quality. His predecessors had been tormented by *vagabondi* such as the Irishman William Phelan, a habitual embezzler who charged for communion, scoffed at suspensions, and supplemented

[10] Luca Codignola, 'The policy of Rome towards the English-speaking Catholics in British North America, 1750–1830', in Murphy and Stortz, *Creed and Culture*, 100–25, at 111.

[11] See Terrence Murphy, 'Language, ethnicity, and region: Rome and the struggle for dominance of the Canadian Catholic Church, 1785–1930', in Matteo Binasco (ed.), *Rome and Irish Catholicism in the Atlantic World, 1622–1908* (London: Palgrave Macmillan, 2019), 73–91. For Plessis' attention to the Maritimes, see John Jennings, *Bishop Joseph-Octave Plessis and Roman Catholics in Early 19th Century New Brunswick* (Saint John: Diocese of Saint John, 1998).

his income through fishing.[12] Others were drunk, sexually incontinent, crooked, or simply insubordinate.[13] As elsewhere, this was an enduring problem: between 1827 and 1831, for example, at least four priests were expelled from the province for bad behaviour, while in 1842 the vicar apostolic of the northern district of Scotland despatched a habitual drunkard who 'cannot be trusted alone' to Nova Scotia or, as he put it, 'any where but here'.[14] Yet Burke could also draw on a handful of effective Scottish priests who had largely followed their migrating countrymen, a small number of émigré Frenchmen, and a slow but steady trickle of more competent Irishmen and Canadians; but, most importantly, after 1818 he could do as he wished without reference to Quebec.

Nova Scotia was not the only place that chafed at being ruled by distant Canadians. Catholics in Prince Edward Island, New Brunswick, and Cape Breton Island all felt themselves to be neglected, particularly in the provision of priests. So did English-speakers in Upper Canada, which had been growing in population and importance since the conclusion of the American War of Independence. In 1819, an attempt to secure a fresh division of Quebec saw Alexander MacDonnell and Angus Bernard MacEachern appointed vicars apostolic of Upper Canada and the provinces of New Brunswick and Prince Edward Island, respectively. The plan miscarried after the newly elevated bishop of Quebec took fright at the prospect of so many anglophones, and the men were demoted to vicars general with episcopal rank. As MacEachern grumbled to a Roman correspondent later that year, as a mere vicar general 'his hands were bound'. This was unfortunate, he continued, because 'our people being the same in these Provinces require a different management from the Canadians'.[15] He was also annoyed that Cape Breton had been excluded from his jurisdiction, pointing out to the rector of the Scots College in Rome that the Catholic population there was largely comprised of 'Highlanders and Acadian French', the former having been established on the island in 1790 by his own brother and now numbering some 500 'Highland Catholic families'.[16]

---

[12] For Phelan, see Terrence Murphy, 'James Jones and the establishment of Roman Catholic church government in the Maritime provinces', *CCHA Study Sessions*, vol. 48 (1981), 26–42.

[13] Terrence Murphy, 'The emergence of Maritime Catholicism', *Acadiensis*, vol. 13, no. 2 (Spring, 1984), 36.

[14] Fraser to MacDonald, 28 December 1831, SCR/12/119; James Kyle to Andrew Scott, 15 January 1842, University of Aberdeen Library Special Collections, Scottish Catholic Archives Historic Collection [SCA], Oban Letters [OL], 1/38/3.

[15] MacEachern to Paul MacPherson, 9 November 1819, Scots College Rome Archives [SCR], 12/104.

[16] MacEachern to MacPherson, 20 August 1819, SCR/12/103.

The shortage of priests was a particular frustration. The Scottish bishops believed that Quebec was programmatically refusing to supply them, either by direct provision or through adequately subsidized places at the Séminaire de Québec. As MacEachern put it in 1824, 'No effort was ever made by any Bp in Canada to raise Clergymen for our Highlanders, who have been emigrating this way since the year 1771.'[17] Three years later, after Quebec had refused yet another request for priests, he raged that successive bishops and their coadjutors knew 'nothing about these vast regions' and had never set foot there. 'Why then', he wondered, 'are we kept hanging after men who never cared about us, more than they did, or do about the Hottentots, or the Siberians?'[18] His colleague William Fraser, who after a long interregnum had finally succeeded Burke in 1827, complained that Scotsmen were not admitted to the Séminaire except at 'an exorbitant rate'. Those who did enter, he continued with heavy irony, often found themselves first 'sent to a French settlement' before an eventual return to Lower Canada, 'the land of promise, flowing with milk and honey'.[19]

The consequent shortage was acute. As MacEachern pointed out in 1828, he had only two priests despite nearly half of Prince Edward Island's some 22,000 inhabitants being Catholic.[20] In Upper Canada, MacDonnell had only 'about a dozen Priests' and an uncertain £750 a year from the government to provide for what he rather optimistically estimated were 40,000–50,000 Catholics.[21] The situation in Nova Scotia was slightly better, and in his short episcopate Burke had managed to ordain a handful of local men, all apparently without significant qualifications. Even so, his successor Fraser still complained in 1831 that he had a mere fifteen priests for a Catholic population approaching 50,000.[22]

The obvious solution was to train candidates locally, and as early as 1819 Burke, MacEachern, and MacDonnell had discussed establishing an anglophone seminary in the Maritimes.[23] Burke's death in 1820 ended these early hopes, although by 1828 Fraser was using a small government grant to support 'a little seminary for young candidates for the church' in Antigonish. Even this was made harder by Quebec, which took more than two years and several requests to authorize the transfer of his preferred

[17] MacEachern to MacPherson, 8 July 1824, SCR/12/106.
[18] MacEachern to Bernard Donald MacDonald, '1827', SCR/12/110.
[19] Fraser to MacDonald, 8 October 1828, SCR/12/112.
[20] MacEachern to MacDonald, 6 May 1828, SCR/12/111.
[21] See Thomas Weld to Nicholas Wiseman, 19 May 1829, Archivium Venerabilis Collegii Anglorum de Urbe [AVCAU], Scr. 63/3/1.
[22] William Fraser to Ranald MacDonald, 28 December 1831, SCR/12/119.
[23] MacEachern to MacPherson, 9 November 1819, SCR/12/104.

rector.[24] Nor did it help that rural Antigonish was far from the province's political and economic centre. In May 1833, MacEachern followed Fraser's lead and founded St Andrew's College in Charlottetown partly in the hope of generating local vocations.[25] MacEachern was its first president, his eventual successor Bernard Donald MacDonald vice president, and Fraser a trustee.[26] The hope in both cases was that local seminaries would not only supply their needs and protect them against Canadian indifference but also reduce their reliance on 'every adventitious Priest' who offered himself to the mission. As MacEachern wrote in 1821, 'the clergy ought to be raised in the country, as then the habits of the land, and the natural amor Patria would dictate to them the necessity of subordination'.[27]

The Scottish bishops also had to find priests able to communicate in Gaelic, something their Irish clergy could rarely do. This mattered, because the region contained a number of Gaelic-speaking Presbyterian ministers who were more than happy to pick up the slack. Of the two Irishmen recruited to Nova Scotia by William Fraser in the late 1820s, for example, one apparently spoke 'no Celtic of any kind' while the other, who did, needed 'some superior who can curb his vehement temper'.[28] Fraser himself complained that 'our countrymen in Cape Breton' were 'sadly off, for want of Scotch priests'. They were, he continued, attended only occasionally by '*Eirinich* [Irish] who are but indifferently acquainted with the Gaelic language and consequently obliged to confess by means of an interpreter'.[29] Nearly fifteen years later, he denied a place to two Irish allies fleeing inclusion in the new diocese of Halifax because their lack of Gaelic rendered them 'useless'.[30]

The problems of inadequate and unsuitable clergy were exacerbated by administrative dysfunction. Edmund Burke's death in November 1820 left the Maritime provinces without an independent episcopal authority, a situation that was compounded by the extremely long interregnum which followed it. The entire process was a hopeless muddle: Burke had hoped to be succeeded by an Irishman and had nominated two before his death, both of whom declined; Archbishops John Thomas Troy and Daniel Murray of Dublin also wanted another Irishman, as did Thomas

---

[24] Angus Anthony Johnston, *A History of the Catholic Church in Eastern Nova Scotia*, 2 vols. (Antigonish, NS: St Francis Xavier University Press, 1971), 2: 89–90.
[25] Fraser to MacDonald, 8 October 1828, SCR/12/112.
[26] See the Minutes of St Andrew's College, Charlottetown, 1833–62, Archives of the Diocese of Charlottetown [ADC], Bernard Donald MacDonald papers [BM].
[27] MacEachern to MacPherson, 5 July 1821, SCR/12/105.
[28] MacEachern to MacDonald, 14 October 1830, ADC/BM.
[29] Fraser to MacDonald, 28 December 1831, SCR/12/119. Emphasis in original.
[30] See Fraser to Dollard, 8 August 1845, SJDA, William Dollard papers [DP], P/458.

Scallan of Newfoundland; MacEachern, MacDonnell, and the Scottish vicars apostolic preferred a fellow Scot; Quebec hoped to suppress the vicariate entirely and return Nova Scotia to Canadian control. All made their voices heard in Rome. In mid-1824, the Propaganda finally appointed a priest of the diocese of Cork, who promptly declined. The frustrated cardinals then turned to the Scots' nominee, William Fraser. He was duly confirmed as vicar apostolic of Nova Scotia in late 1824, although a comedy of errors delayed his consecration until mid-1827.[31]

Fraser was an obvious choice, a Gaelic-speaker who had been educated at the Royal Scots College in Valladolid before returning to Scotland where he had oversight of several missions and, from 1814, the highland seminary at Lismore. Two of his cousins were bishops. Fraser himself had been first suggested for a mitre in 1819, when he was one of several candidates proposed for the vacant western district of Scotland. In 1822, he migrated to Nova Scotia, where his brother had already settled the district that came to be known as 'Fraser's Grant'. Two years later, he was given the mission at Antigonish in the heart of Gaelic Nova Scotia but only after a vicious campaign to displace the incumbent Irish priest.[32] He proved to be an active and influential pastor who was unafraid to assert ecclesiastical and secular leadership and often behaved more like a clan chief than a Catholic prelate. In the 1824 provincial election, for example, he threw his influence behind the candidacy of John Young, who, although a Presbyterian, was also a Scot and a friend. Unaccustomed voters from outlying districts were led to the poll by their priests accompanied by pipers. Young's defeated opponent complained of 'priestly terrorism', while others, including several Protestants, publicly defended Fraser's conduct.[33] More than a decade later, Young was still urging that a vote for him was a vote 'for the Bishop'.[34] Despite his activism, or perhaps because of it, Fraser was widely respected. When his mooted elevation became public, the governor was happy to endorse it, as was the Colonial Office.[35]

Fraser was emphatically a Scottish bishop for a Scottish people, and in eastern Nova Scotia and Cape Breton he was in his element. As vicar

---

[31] The best account of the process is in Johnston, *Eastern Nova Scotia*, 1: 506–18.
[32] See Peter Ludlow, '"Disturbed by the Irish howl": Irish and Scottish Roman Catholics in Nova Scotia, 1844–1860', *Historical Studies*, vol. 81 (2015), 32–55, at 39.
[33] Brian Cuthbertson, *Johnny Bluenose at the Polls: Early Nova Scotian Election Battles 1758–1848* (Halifax: Formac Publishing, 1994), 262–3; Petition to the House of Assembly, [?November] 1824, Nova Scotia Archives [PANS], RG5, Misc. A, Series P, vol. 2, 60. For the response, see Petition to the House of Assembly, 2 March 1825, PANS/RG5/Misc. A/Series P/vol. 3/12.
[34] Cuthbertson, 266.
[35] Lord Bathurst to Sir James Knight, 7 December 1825, PANS/RG61/vol. 65/56.

apostolic, however, his responsibility was much wider. From the beginning he showed little interest in Halifax and its growing Irish population. He was similarly disinterested in the Acadians and Catholic Mi'kmaq, although he dutifully provided for them as best he could. Fraser's distaste for Halifax was magnified by the long-standing conflict there between successive priests and an assertive laity. As in Philadelphia, Gibraltar, or Bombay, Halifax's lay trustees (known locally as wardens) asserted their right to control church revenue and property and at times claimed a say in clerical appointments and conduct. They had made James Jones' life miserable, digging up bodies he had buried, burying others without his consent, and even threatening him with arrest.[36] The second Edmund Burke had been able to impose some order, but, as Terrence Murphy has pointed out, the conflict merely went dormant.[37] The power vacuum that followed Burke's death revivified it.

In 1827, Fraser moved to quell this 'demon of discord' by appointing as his vicar general an Irishman, John Loughnan, who had been educated by Burke in Halifax and then ordained after his death in Boston.[38] He proved to be unsuitable, being tactless, grasping, self-regarding, and prone to picking fights.[39] He quickly fell out with the city's middle-class elite, themselves mostly Irish, partly because of his temperament and partly because he went far out of his way to forbid mixed marriages.[40] Fraser, however, trusted him and hoped he would be his successor, claiming that this proved his own 'impartiality despite of *national prejudices*'.[41] Loughnan remained the sole priest in Nova Scotia's largest city until 1838, when Fraser asked Daniel Murray of Dublin to provide two more to serve the city's some 6,000 Catholics, 'all Irish or [of] descent'.[42] In response, Murray despatched the Franciscan Lawrence Joseph Dease and the diocesan priest Richard Baptist O'Brien. Dease appears to have been yet another of the wandering friars of whom Cullen and others were so suspicious, but O'Brien was an altogether more significant character. He was, as Murray wrote, undeniably 'a very clever and well informed young

---

[36] See Terrence Murphy, 'Priests, people and polity: Trusteeism in the first Catholic congregation at Halifax, 1785–1801', in Murphy and Byrne, *Religion and Identity*, 68–80.

[37] Ibid., 77.

[38] Fraser to John Carroll, [1827], quoted in Johnston, *Eastern Nova Scotia*, 2: 77.

[39] See Johnston, *Eastern Nova Scotia*, 2: 80–1.

[40] Terrence Murphy, 'Trusteeism in Atlantic Canada: The struggle for leadership among the Irish Catholics of Halifax, St. John's, and Saint John, 1780–1850', in Murphy and Stortz, *Creed and Culture*, 131–2.

[41] Fraser to [?Daniel Murray], 26 April 1842, PICRA/CUL/NC/4/1842. Emphasis in original. This letter was presumably forwarded to Cullen by Murray.

[42] Fraser to Murray, 20 July 1838, in [Hugh O'Reilly], *The Letters of Hibernicus, Extracts from the Pamphlet Entitled 'A Report on the Committee of St. Mary's Parish, Halifax, N.S.', and a Review of the Same* (Pictou: n.p., 1842), 115.

Man', but in Halifax he proved also to be a committed self-promoter, gifted preacher, and enthusiastic politician.[43] Several years after he left Nova Scotia, for example, he famously organized a pro-O'Connell protest in Limerick that resulted in a serious assault on the advanced nationalist leader William Smith O'Brien, and in the late 1860s he became a leading clerical advocate of home rule.[44] He was also a modestly successful novelist. There was never any chance of such men getting along with Loughnan when they finally arrived in Halifax in late 1839, and they did not.

Writing to Cullen in June 1841, Murray set the scene. Dease and O'Brien's 'reception was so cold and their visit so apparently unwelcome', he reported, that they at first planned to re-embark and travel to the United States instead. Only the earnest entreaties of the 'Catholic People' changed their minds. Once settled in the city, Murray continued, and 'notwithstanding the total want of cooperation on the part of the Parish Priest', they had succeeded splendidly. They even founded a school, St Mary's College, that had 'already acquired so much repute that the Legislature has conferred on it the rank of a University'. Although he was careful to note that Fraser himself 'was a good easy man', Murray pointed out that he nevertheless resided 'two hundred miles from Halifax and seems quite happy among his Highlanders without troubling himself much about the Capital'. As a result, the city was left to the tender mercies of Loughnan, who lacked both energy and education. If this was not bad enough, there were rumours that Fraser planned to recommend the Irishman as his coadjutor. If this happened, Murray wrote, it 'would be one of the heaviest blows that could be inflicted on religion in Nova Scotia'. He wanted Cullen's help in securing a suitable Irish alternative, or at least 'any but Mr Loughnan'.[45]

This was not the first complaint to arrive in Rome. In 1840, John England of Charleston had stopped briefly in Halifax en route to Europe where, in the words of a later Roman summary, 'he heard the appeals and complaints made by his fellow Irishmen' who claimed that Fraser was too old, too partial to his fellow Scots, and too attached to living in his 'obscure village'.[46] Religion was suffering. England duly reported all this to Murray, who passed it to the Propaganda. At roughly

---

[43] Murray to Cullen, 10 June 1841, PICRA/CUL/651.
[44] David A. Wilson, *Thomas D'Arcy McGee, Vol. 1: Passion, Reason, and Politics, 1825–1857* (Montreal and Kingston: McGill-Queen's University Press, 2008), 101–2.
[45] Murray to Cullen, 10 June 1841, PICRA/CUL/651.
[46] This is an extract from Antonio DeLuca's 'Report on Nova Scotia' of 15 July 1844 on the situation in Nova Scotia, which is extensively printed in translation in vol. 2 of Johnston, *Eastern Nova Scotia*. The Italian original is at APF, *Acta* (1844), vol. 207, ff. 234–47.

the same time, Rome received a similar report from Jacques Merle (in religion Vincent de Paul), the founder of a Trappist monastery at Tracadie in eastern Nova Scotia.[47] He told the Propaganda bluntly that, despite being holy and having 'good intentions', Fraser was an incompetent administrator who urgently needed a coadjutor. The congregation was sufficiently alarmed to write to the bishop of Quebec, Joseph Signay, who disclaimed all knowledge of the situation, and the Propaganda graduate Colin MacKinnon, who loyally supported his bishop after showing him the letter.[48] In early 1842, the cardinals decided on a compromise: Nova Scotia would be elevated from vicariate to diocese but Fraser would be sent an Irish coadjutor. Their choice was William Walsh of Kingstown, near Dublin.

The Irish were delighted – as Kirby told the new bishop, 'the good Dr. Cullen worked hard to get you into harness' – but the whole plan was nearly wrecked by the over-eager Halifax Irish.[49] As Cullen explained to Murray in early April 1842, Lawrence Dease had appeared in Rome to complain about Fraser and Loughnan.[50] The proximate cause was the desire of the Irishmen and their lay allies to build a second parish in Halifax with Dease as its pastor. Loughnan had objected both to the presumption and to the dilution of his revenue, Fraser had backed him, and Dease had announced his intention to leave in a huff. A lay petition asking Fraser to retain him was 'committed to the flames', while Loughnan excommunicated the signatories of another asking Dease to approach the Irish bishops for help in securing Fraser an Irish coadjutor.[51] Although Loughnan and Fraser derided their opponents as mere 'purse-proud pedlars and butchers', they included men such as Lawrence O'Connor Doyle, the province's leading Catholic, and Michael Tobin, a member of the house of assembly and son of one of Nova Scotia's wealthiest men.[52] Doyle, in particular, was a substantial figure: famously witty and notably devout, he had been instrumental in securing Catholic political emancipation before becoming one of the province's leading Reform politicians. As an early biographer recalled, Doyle's 'politics were

---

[47] For Merle and the Trappist foundation, see A. Muriel Kinnear, 'The Trappist monks at Tracadie, Nova Scotia', *Report of the Annual Meeting, Canadian Catholic Historical Association*, vol. 9, no. 1 (1930), 97–105.

[48] Johnston, *Eastern Nova Scotia*, 2: 181, 186–7.

[49] Kirby to Walsh, 14 April 1842, AAH/WP.

[50] Cullen to Murray, 4 April 1842, DDA/MP/34/9.

[51] Fraser to Michael Tobin, 20 November 1841, in *Letters of Hibernicus*, 121.

[52] Fraser to Signay, 13 September 1842, Archives of the Archdiocese of Québec [AAQ], Nouvelle Ecosse [NE] VII/126. The jibe about butchers was aimed at Tobin's father, who had made his money in that trade. I am grateful to Professor Terrence Murphy for sharing with me his notes from Québec.

Liberal first, last, and all the time'.[53] Loughnan and Fraser were now in very public conflict with much of the city's Catholic population and almost all of its leaders.

Dease's mission was further proof of the chaos in Halifax, and thus of Fraser's incompetence; to this extent it strengthened Cullen's hand. Yet it also alerted Fraser and his allies to the danger of a Roman intervention and gave them time to prepare a response. Loughnan even took the extraordinary step of writing directly to Murray, hinting 'at matters of great importance to this vicariate' and urging him to apply directly to Fraser for 'further information'.[54] In Rome, Fraser's friends at the Scots College anticipated Dease's arrival by alleging that he and O'Brien had deliberately set out to undermine episcopal authority. This worried Cullen. As he diplomatically explained to Murray, 'perhaps when the other side of the question will have been heard, the case may have a different appearance'. He consequently urged him to provide 'accurate information on the state of affairs', as without it the Propaganda 'will not know what to do'. 'Nova Scotia is so far off', he reminded the archbishop, 'that it is with difficulty they can expect to get accurate information direct from that country.' Until they did, Walsh's appointment was on hold.[55]

Murray promptly defended Dease as 'unexceptionable' and O'Brien as a 'person of solid piety, excellent talents, close application, and of course considerable acquirements'. Given the situation in Halifax, he grumbled, it was unsurprising that their 'exertions to give a new impulse to the cause of Religion should have excited jealousy'.[56] A few days later, he reported that the visiting Michael Anthony Fleming of Newfoundland was thrilled with Walsh's appointment, which he was sure 'could hardly fail to gain heaven for me'. As for Fraser, Murray continued, Fleming's view was that he was a 'good man, but can hardly be induced to go beyond the limits of his farm'.[57] This was exactly the kind of information that Cullen was looking for, and he promptly translated Murray's letters on 'the affairs of Halifax'. He was confident that they 'would have the effect of inducing the Propaganda to settle all that business without further delay', and by mid-April they had.[58]

[53] George Mullane, 'A sketch of Lawrence O'Connor Doyle, a member of the house of assembly in the thirties and forties', *Collections of the Nova Scotia Historical Society*, vol. 17 (1913), 151–95, at 157.

[54] Loughnan to Murray, 2 June 1842, PICRA/CUL/NC/4/1842/15. In this letter, Loughnan refers to an earlier one he had written six months previously.

[55] Cullen to Murray, 4 March 1842, DDA/MP/34/9.

[56] Murray to Cullen, 19 March 1842, PICRA/CUL/720.

[57] Murray to Cullen, 22 March 1842, PICRA/CUL/721.

[58] Cullen to Murray, 4 April 1842, DDA/MP/34/9.

The appointment of William Walsh was a turning point for Canadian Catholicism. Prior to it the church in British North America outwith Newfoundland was run by, for, and from Quebec. Those anglophone bishops who had preceded Walsh – Burke and Fraser in Nova Scotia, MacDonnell in Kingston, MacEachern and MacDonald in Prince Edward Island, and Michael Power in Toronto – were generally peripheral figures chosen for what were then generally peripheral places. Often they were personally, canonically, or financially dependent on Quebec, and even those with experience of Europe largely lacked it of Rome.

Walsh was different. He was born in Waterford in 1804, where he attended St John's College and then Maynooth before being ordained for Dublin in 1828. His reputation there was excellent. Murray thought him 'a good and ready Preacher; a pious, active and well informed Priest, [and] a mild, modest and conciliatory Gentleman.' In 1838, he had nominated him for Calcutta, but the scheme had miscarried when circumstances made a local appointment necessary (see Chapter 3). This had had nothing to do with Walsh's suitability, and in 1842 Murray thought that it would 'be difficult to make a better' choice for Nova Scotia.[59] Walsh was also close to Tobias Kirby, who had been in his class at St John's College, and it was through Kirby that Cullen came to know him.[60] Together they advocated Walsh's appointment, bucked up his courage, and fought his battles in Rome.

Yet Walsh's Roman links were not simply personal. He was very aware of ecclesiastical, theological, and liturgical developments there and sought to emulate them. One important manifestation of this was his interest in Alphonsus Liguori, which he shared with men such as Kenrick in Philadelphia, Mullock in St John's, and Cullen himself. Indeed, at the time of his appointment Walsh was translating 'many' of Liguori's works, a fact Cullen singled out for the Propaganda in his Italian summary of Murray's letter of recommendation.[61] The influence of the milder Liguorian moral theology was soon apparent in Halifax, where, among other things, Walsh bitterly criticized Loughnan for 'ruling the unfortunate people here with a rod of iron'. He was also infuriated when Loughnan mocked his first cycle of Easter services, insisting to Fraser that the ceremonies had strictly conformed to Roman practice.[62]

[59] Murray to Cullen, 19 March 1842, PICRA/CUL/720.
[60] In 1851, Walsh described him as 'my dear old friend and Class fellow': Walsh to John Hughes, 12 February 1851, AANY/HP/Box 3/Folder 9.
[61] Murray to Cullen, 19 March 1842, PICRA/CUL/720; Italian extract of Murray to Cullen, 19 March 1842, APF/SC/AS/vol. 5/ff. 73–4.
[62] Walsh to Fraser, 'Holy Saturday', 1843, AAH/WP.

Under Walsh, the church in Nova Scotia strove to be as Roman as possible. As he remarked to a neighbouring bishop in 1844, no one could be 'more anxious than I am and always have been, for the maintenance of Church Discipline and the suitable celebration of the mysteries of our religion, and the faithful administration of the Sacraments'.[63] He emphasized liturgical display, celebrated Pontifical High Mass every week, and acquired a magnificent processional cross; one of his most telling complaints about Fraser was that 'He scarcely ever wears the insignia of his rank, and he cannot even bear the ceremonies of the Church.'[64] Like other bishops across Greater Ireland, Walsh purchased a wide variety of books and sacred art, some of very high quality and much of it acquired in Rome. Pride of place was given to Gregory XVI's gift of a relic of the Roman martyr St Cornelia.[65] Despite having no direct Roman experience, Rome was and remained Walsh's lodestar.

Walsh also never ceased to think of himself as Irish. He patronized Irish societies, encouraged Irish symbolism, and referred to Daniel O'Connell as the 'Great Daniel'.[66] He erected an arch of green boughs before his episcopal throne and regularly spoke at celebrations of St Patrick's Day.[67] He was also an enthusiastic supporter of Irish causes, from sending money to alleviate the Famine, to encouraging collections for the Catholic University of Ireland, to boycotting the funeral of the lieutenant governor in protest of the Ecclesiastical Titles Act.[68]

Word of Walsh's appointment reached Nova Scotia in late April 1842. Fraser was appalled: he had known of Dease's mission, and taken steps to counter it, but it had not occurred to him that he would be sent a coadjutor without consultation. He had heard nothing from Rome, and even now the news came from reports published in Irish newspapers. He immediately wrote to Murray, whom Bishop Fleming (who had arrived on the same ship as the reports) had identified as the ultimate source of the appointment. He furiously disputed what he took to be a series of lies, among them that he had asked for a coadjutor in general and for Walsh in particular, that he was ailing, and that he was seventy-five years old. How could Murray have said, as Fleming had reported him to have done, 'that I had applied to the court of Rome for a Coadjutor, which I *never did*, much less for Revd Mr Walsh, whom I *never heard of*?' As for his supposed

[63] Walsh to Dollard, [?30] September 1844, SJDA/DP/416.
[64] Walsh to the Propaganda, 18 January 1843, quoted in Ludlow, 'Disturbed by the Irish howl', 41.
[65] See Terrence Murphy, 'Transformation and Triumphalism: The Irish Catholics of Halifax, 1839–1858', *Historical Studies*, vol. 81 (2015), 56–81, at 64.
[66] Walsh to Mullock, 2 March 1854, ARCSJ/MP/104/1/8.
[67] Murphy, 'Transformation', 64.
[68] Walsh to James Roosevelt Bayley, 26 March 1852, AANY/HP/Box 4/Folder 5.

age, it was 'a palpable falsehood'. 'My mother', he continued with heavy irony, 'must have possessed uncommon procreative powers if she brought me to the world in the thirteenth year of her age.' In fact she was now eighty-three and still living, while he was a hale and hearty sixty-three.[69] Months later he was still raging, telling a friend shortly after meeting Walsh for the first time that 'it was lucky for him and the batch of some Irish Bishops ... that I had them not entwined in my iron grasp; they would feel whether I was confined by infirmity in my bed of sickness, and seventy six years of age.'[70]

Fraser was yet another victim of the increasingly habitual Irish tactic of exaggerating or misrepresenting the physical, moral, or mental capacity of their opponents. Thus John Dubois of New York was 'worse than crazy', Patrick Griffith of Cape Town was paralyzed, John Gray of Glasgow 'was entirely and irretrievably incompetent', the Benedictines of New South Wales were priapic drunkards, and Jean Baptiste Pompallier of Auckland seduced nuns.[71] This gave the Irish a fearsome reputation within their church: as a francophone priest on Cape Breton complained, 'no crime frightens an Irish Catholic. He makes the sign of the cross with calumny in his mouth and hell in his heart.'[72] Fraser was lucky only to have had twelve years added to his age. It was often the case, however, that there was a germ of truth to the charges: Dubois had grown increasingly erratic, Griffith had had a minor stroke, Gray had bouts of amnesia, some Sydney Benedictines were dissolute, and although Pompallier was hardly a seducer, he did have a long-standing problem with drink. For his part, Fraser hardly left Antigonish, rarely wrote letters, and paid little attention to any but his highlanders. It was not unreasonable to attribute this to age, illness, or a lack of energy.

That it was the Halifax Irish who were the source of the stories about Fraser is beyond question. It is also clear that Cullen deployed these during his campaign to secure Walsh's appointment. Whether he believed them or not is unknown; he certainly did not disbelieve them. Nor did the Propaganda, which at the time of Walsh's appointment had only the testimony of Murray, England, Merle, and Cullen on which to base their assessment of Fraser's fitness; Signay had refused to comment and Colin MacKinnon was too obviously loyal. This was enough to account

---

[69] Fraser to Murray, 26 April 1842, PICRA/CUL/NC/4/1842. Emphasis in original. Like most of Fraser's letters, Murray forwarded it to Cullen to deploy in the Propaganda.
[70] Fraser to William McDonald, 23 December 1842, TAA/M/AE2013.
[71] For Gray, see James Lynch to Cullen, 16 March 1867, DDA/CP/334/4/5.
[72] J. B. Miranda to C. F. Cazeau, 22 May 1842, from an English translation and transcription of the French original in the Archives of the Archdiocese of Québec, AAQ/N.E./VI-167. I am grateful to Dr Peter Ludlow for drawing my attention to this remark and providing me with a copy of the letter.

for the decision to appoint a coadjutor. What is harder to explain is why Fraser was allowed to learn his fate from the newspapers; indeed, just a few weeks before the news arrived he had received a letter from the cardinal prefect that had given no hint that an appointment was even contemplated. This only aggravated his sense of injustice. As he furiously asked the Propaganda, 'in any court, before pronouncing judgment, is it not right that both parties be heard?' He would, he continued, 'hold no communication with Monsignor Walsh whatsoever until the formal and due notice of election is sent to me'.[73] Three years later, Fraser was still complaining that had he 'been entrusted with the grand *secret* from the beginning there would have been no annoyance, and no public scandal to religion'.[74]

Despite the Irish College's well-earned reputation for cruelty, this seems to have been a genuine mistake. There was an obvious advantage in keeping Fraser ignorant of the possibility of a coadjutor being appointed, but there was no point in humiliating him after it was done. Ironically, the source of the confusion was the delay caused by Fraser's countermeasures against Dease. The timeline makes this clear: Gregory XVI approved Walsh's appointment in early January, Murray was told in early March, Dease arrived in Rome not long after, and Walsh learned his fate about the same time. In the meantime, rumours of his appointment had spread in Ireland where they soon became public knowledge, despite a warning from Cullen that everything was now uncertain.[75] Walsh's elevation was not finalized in Rome until mid-April, the Irish newspapers arrived in Halifax a few days later, and he was consecrated on 1 May. Walsh then wrote to Fraser for the first time on 4 May, only realizing after the fact that 'He may have painfully heard the news long before that reached him.'[76] The Irish accepted that this was unfortunate; Walsh thought it 'most curious', Murray dryly described it as 'somewhat surprising', and Kirby was startled to find that Cardinal Fransoni 'seemed to make very little of it'.[77]

Whatever the reasons, Walsh had been left in a terrible position. As he retrospectively complained to Cullen, the manner of his appointment might as well have been 'calculated to irritate and inflame' Fraser, 'as it

---

[73] Fraser to Fransoni, 24 May 1842, quoted in Johnston, *Eastern Nova Scotia*, 2: 191.

[74] Fraser to [?Fransoni], 14 March 1845, APF/SC/AS/vol. 5/ff. 677–8. Emphasis in original. This letter was most likely written to Fransoni, although it is possible that the recipient was Cardinal Acton.

[75] Johnston, *Eastern Nova Scotia*, 2: 188; Cullen to Murray, 4 March 1842, DDA/MP/34/9; Murray to Cullen, 19 March 1842, PICRA/CUL/720.

[76] Walsh to Murray, 2 June 1842, DDA/MP/39/1/111.

[77] Walsh to Murray 22 June 1842, DDA/MP/31/9/112; Murray to Walsh, 25 June 1842, Kirby to Walsh, 7 July 1842, AAH/WP.

actually did to the highest pitch'; but, although Fraser had indeed been humiliated, Walsh grumbled, he had at least been promoted from the 'comparatively dependent state of a Vicar Apostolic to the dignity a Diocesan Bishop'. By contrast, Rome had sent him out 'unarmed and defenceless' against Fraser's wrath.[78] It did not take him long to realize what he was facing, and within weeks of his consecration Walsh had confided to Murray that his appointment was 'so singular', and the situation in Halifax so 'deplorable', that it was unreasonable to expect that the 'Enemy of all good will be idle, or that he will not raise up obstacles and annoyances to obstruct my path.'[79]

Those obstacles soon revealed themselves. Writing in late June, Walsh noted that Fraser appeared resolved to ignore his letter. 'This is certainly neither courteous', he told Murray, 'nor cheering.' Fraser had also encouraged his clergy to draft a letter of their own to the Propaganda deploring the appointment, blaming it on a fractious minority in Halifax, and insisting that they would not recognize Walsh until Rome had explained itself.[80] Twenty-one of the vicariate's twenty-three priests signed, thirteen of whom also had the courage to put their names to what Walsh called a 'Hostile Manifesto', warning among other things that 'many – very many difficulties will meet you on your arrival among us'.[81] It was clear, Walsh wrote, 'that the Bishop & his friends had determined on having a Coadjutor of their own choice'.[82]

These letters require some explication. It is striking, for example, that of the twenty-one priests who wrote to the Propaganda, fully eleven were Irish or of Irish descent, while six were Scots, three Canadian, two French, and one a German.[83] This is relatively easy to explain: Fraser remained their bishop and refusing to support him was dangerous. The possibilities for coercion, or at least coordination, were such that Walsh even wondered if the signatures were genuine, 'or whether they have been freely given'.[84] There was probably something to this: the intemperate Hugh O'Reilly, for example, later recalled that Loughnan had explicitly instructed him 'to espouse Dr Fraser's case or rather to defend the episcopal dignity'.[85] Further indirect evidence can be found in the fact that only thirteen were prepared to take the more serious step of addressing Walsh directly. Of these, A. A. Johnston calculated that six were

---

[78] Walsh to Cullen, 30 June 1843, PICRA/CUL/807(1).
[79] Walsh to Murray, 2 June 1842, DDA/39/1/111.
[80] Johnston, *Eastern Nova Scotia*, 2: 191–2.
[81] Priests of Nova Scotia to Walsh, 28 May 1842, APF/SC/AS/vol. 5/ff. 69–70.
[82] Walsh to Murray, 22 June 1842, DDA/MP/31/9/112.
[83] Johnston, *Eastern Nova Scotia*, 2: 191.
[84] Walsh to Murray, 22 June 1842, DDA/MP/31/9/112.
[85] O'Reilly to Dollard, 24 October 1844, SJDA/DP/457.

Irish, a further six Scots, and one a Frenchman.[86] This probably better reflects Fraser's real strength, which was clearly uniform among the Scots, all of whom signed both letters, but much less sure among the Irish and francophone clergy.

Nevertheless, the six Irish signatories complicate the traditional understanding of the dispute between Walsh and Fraser as a simple Scots vs Irish; not only was Loughnan an Irishman but so too were some of Fraser's most vociferous supporters. The most prominent of these was O'Reilly, who published a series of invective-laden letters in the Pictou *Observer* under the transparent pseudonym 'Hibernicus'. There, he assailed the 'Irish Schismaticks of Halifax' at great length, predicted their damnation, and compared them unfavourably to Pharisees, condemned criminals, and the inhabitants of Sodom and Gomorrah. Their motivation was 'national prejudice' and their methods were slur, slander, and rebellion, while O'Reilly declared himself to have taken 'Scotland for his client' and dedicated *The Letters of Hibernicus* (published in late 1842) to the president of the Highland Society of Nova Scotia.[87]

O'Reilly was a curious episcopal champion, not least because by the time he wrote the Hibernicus letters he was clearly unbalanced, if not actually unhinged. Yet it is likely that he was telling the truth when he later claimed that Loughnan had commissioned his intervention: his letters seem very well informed and, in at least one case, reproduce private correspondence that could only have come from the bishop or his vicar general.[88] The most likely explanation is that neither Fraser nor Loughnan expected the tide of invective that O'Reilly actually produced. He certainly touched a nerve: Walsh bitterly complained of the 'very offensive and disrespectful discourse' that he had been subjected to and alleged that in Pictou O'Reilly had 'attacked the Irish people, and actually mimicked on the altar the manner in which they peeled the potatoes in Ireland with their fingers!'[89] Beneath all the insults, sneers, and repetition, however, there was a not entirely unreasonable argument.

O'Reilly's overriding concern was to prove that the opposition to Fraser was driven 'solely on account of his being a Scotchman by birth' while insisting that it was limited only to a handful of politically motivated and economically self-interested Irishmen in Halifax.[90] The Irish elsewhere in the province were delighted with their bishop, admired Loughnan, and deplored the attacks upon them. O'Reilly even caused the Irish Catholics of New Glasgow (not a numerous

[86] Johnston, *Eastern Nova Scotia*, 2: 192.   [87] *Letters of Hibernicus*, 2.
[88] Murray to Fraser, 26 May 1839, in *Letters of Hibernicus*, 67.
[89] Walsh to Fraser, [n.d., but likely late 1842], AAH/WP.   [90] *Letters of Hibernicus*, 2.

tribe) to declare that they 'never knew kinder men or better Priests at home or abroad than the Scotch Priests' of Nova Scotia.[91] This was the same point that Fraser was making with the clerical letter to the Propaganda: the protests that had led to Walsh's appointment were only about ethnicity and only involved Halifax.

The Letters of Hibernicus also sought to situate the conflict within a global pattern of lay defiance. For O'Reilly, the problem was not simply that the Irish hated the Scots but that they sought to overthrow episcopal authority. By appointing Walsh, he argued, the Propaganda had unwittingly aided what he called 'the Haligonian Gibraltar Junta'.[92] The Halifax Irish were thus in the same class 'as the ecclesiastical insurgents in Gibraltar last year, who were excommunicated by the Pope himself'.[93] This was clever, as there were undeniable similarities between the British territory and Nova Scotia, and if Rome could be convinced that the situations were analogous it might even be possible to overturn Walsh's appointment.

It is easy to see why the comparison attracted O'Reilly. Like Walsh, Bishop Henry Hughes of Gibraltar owed his elevation to the complaints of disgruntled laity and the influence of Archbishop Murray. In the case of Gibraltar, regular appeals from the Irish population had in 1835 led the Propaganda to despatch an Irish priest and two Irish Christian Brothers to the territory. Disagreements with the powerful lay trustees (known as the Junta of Elders) led to multiple appeals to Rome and Dublin and the brothers' departure after only two years, while the remaining Irish priest continued to grumble that the Junta was comprised of 'the worst kind of Masons, a sort of sacrilegious kind of group'.[94] In 1839, the Propaganda imposed an Irish vicar apostolic and ordered the departure of his long-standing Spanish predecessor, Juan Bautista Zino. The first Zino and the Junta knew of it was when a letter arrived from Rome announcing the appointment of Hughes.[95]

Relations between Hughes and the Junta quickly faltered and then failed over issues such as the sanctioning of mixed marriages, control of church property, Masonic symbolism, and Hughes' removal of the vicariate's Spanish and Genoese clergy. There was a bitter dispute with the governor, a violent incident involving Irish soldiers acting on the bishop's orders, and finally a high-profile court case (ultimately decided by the Privy Council) culminating in February 1842 with Hughes'

---

[91] Ibid., iv–v.   [92] Ibid., 158.   [93] Ibid., 4.
[94] See E. G. Archer and A. A. Traverso, *Education in Gibraltar, 1704–2004* (Gibraltar: Gibraltar Books, n.d.), 19–25; quoted in Charles Caruana, *The Rock under a Cloud* (Cambridge: Silent Books, 1989), 58.
[95] Caruana, 61.

imprisonment for contempt of court.[96] He appealed to Rome, Cullen and Murray took his side, and the Propaganda duly denounced the Junta's 'pertinacious disobedience', usurpation of episcopal authority, and appeal to the courts 'for the sake of making war on their holy pastor'.[97]

Although O'Reilly's appeal to the precedent of Gibraltar was not without irony – it was the imposed Irish bishop who was supported by the Propaganda – it bore enough similarity to the situation in Halifax to be useful. (Newfoundland's Fleming made the same comparison, albeit from a different perspective.)[98] There was even the helpful example of Murray and Cullen supporting the bishop against his rebellious laity. More importantly, it also illustrates the interconnected nature of Catholicism's Greater Ireland, where even the most parochial understood their affairs in a global context.

Walsh finally arrived in Halifax in mid-October 1842. His first impression was relatively positive, telling a friend that while the 'abuses are certainly very great' they could be solved with 'time and patience'.[99] He knew that he needed to soothe Fraser and set out for Antigonish. He even took Loughnan with him.[100] For his part, Fraser paid Walsh 'every attention in my power, which was more than he had reason to expect from the arbitrary manner in which he was forced upon me'.[101] He asked Walsh to look after the capital on his behalf, although Loughnan would remain as vicar general. Back in Halifax, the trustees even agreed to hand over the church's property and revenue, abruptly ending more than fifty years of lay control.[102] It all seemed very hopeful.

The reality was different. The problem was that Walsh had no actual power; his authority from Fraser was informal and contingent. He was indeed a bishop but not the diocesan bishop, while Loughnan exercised Fraser's authority. Walsh nevertheless resolved to act as if he were in charge, buying a 'barn' in the city's north end to serve as a temporary church, attempting to supply priests to underserved outlying areas, paying the salary arrears of another (a neat dig at Loughnan), and boasting to

[96] The best account of the legal aspects of the affair is John Restano, *Justice So Requiring: The Emergence and Development of a Legal System in Gibraltar* (Gibraltar: Calpe Press, 2012), chap. 32. For the dispute with the governor and official Gibraltar, see T. J. Finlayson, *Gibraltar, Military Fortress or Commercial Colony* (Gibraltar: Gibraltar Books, 2011), chap. 8.

[97] Quoted in W. H. Rule, *Memoir of a Mission to Gibraltar and Spain, with Collateral Notices of Events Favouring Religious Liberty, and of the Decline of Romish Power in That Country, from the Beginning of This Century, to the Year 1842* (London: John Mason, 1844), 308–9.

[98] Fleming to Walsh, 22 November 1842, PICRA/NC/4/1842/37.

[99] Walsh to William Hamilton, 18 October 1842, DDA, Hamilton papers [HP]/36/5/29.

[100] Walsh to Fraser, 21 October 1842, AAH/WP.

[101] Fraser to William McDonald, 23 December 1842, TAA/M/AE2013.

[102] Murphy, 'Transformation', 61.

Fraser that lay conduct was rapidly improving and 'numbers are returning to their duty'.[103] Loughnan meanwhile carried on as if nothing had changed, countermanded Walsh's orders, denied him access to funds, and barred him from living in the parochial house.

By early March 1843, their relationship had utterly collapsed, with Walsh bitterly complaining to Fraser that Loughnan had treated him with *'open indignity and contempt'* from the moment they returned from Antigonish. He was a man 'without principles, without honour, *without truth'*, and if Fraser were to 'permit him much longer to continue his present career, it *will infallibly end* in his own ruin, and bring scandal to the Church, a renewed religious war in Halifax, and goodness knows what annoyance, grief and pain to yourself'. It had been a 'cruelty' for Fraser to ask him to administer Halifax while refusing to support him.[104] He demanded that Loughnan be removed, blamed the ongoing troubles throughout the province on 'a few turbulent, undisciplined Clergymen' who had 'never felt the firm exercise of Episcopal Authority', claimed they were in reality not Fraser's friends but his 'bitterest enemies', and heatedly defended 'the people' from any blame.[105]

Walsh also appealed to Rome, where Kirby had anticipated him by providing the Propaganda with a 'short statement in Italian of the affairs in Halifax'.[106] Both Kirby and Cullen – who 'interested himself a good deal' – haunted the Propaganda, and by late May they had secured an important victory: Fraser would be told to withdraw Loughnan, leaving Halifax 'entirely' under Walsh's jurisdiction. Kirby also offered encouragement, counselled patience, and above all warned against 'any premature act of untimely zeal' that could be used against him.[107] By mid-July, Cullen was able to report that the Propaganda now contemplated dividing Nova Scotia in two and giving 'Halifax and its vicinity to Dr Walsh'.[108]

This was not a new idea. Fraser had first proposed a division along national lines in May 1842, largely in an attempt to forestall Walsh's appointment.[109] In March 1843, Walsh had himself suggested division

---

[103] Walsh to Fraser, n.d. [1842], AAH/WP. Based on internal evidence the most likely date is late November or early December 1842.

[104] Walsh to Fraser, 27 March 1843, AAH/WP. Emphasis in original.

[105] Walsh to Fraser, 29 April 1843, AAH/WP.

[106] Kirby to Walsh, 17 March 1843, AAH/WP.

[107] Kirby to Walsh, 23 May 1843, AAH/WP.

[108] Cullen to Murray, 11 July 1843, DDA/MP/34/9.

[109] See Johnston, *Eastern Nova Scotia*, 2: 205–6. The sympathetic Johnston was slightly disingenuous in drawing his reader's attention to the fact that Fraser had 'made this suggestion before he had learned that Rome had given him a coadjutor'. In fact, Fraser had known this since the rumours arrived in Nova Scotia in mid-April, and his proposal was in part an attempt to meet that problem.

as one of several options but only for the lifetime of the two bishops. Yet the driving force appears to have been the Propaganda-trained Colin MacKinnon, now based near Antigonish where he was a confidant of Fraser. MacKinnon was convinced that only a division that left Fraser with his Scots and Walsh in Halifax could resolve the situation. He recognized that peace could not be restored so long as an Irishman stood to inherit the entire diocese. As he told Walsh bluntly in April 1843, a division would liberate 'our Caledonians' from the fear that 'they would fall under what they are pleased to call Irish yokes'.[110] He told the Propaganda much the same.[111]

This was easier said than done, as Walsh and Fraser agreed only at the most basic level that separation was desirable. As Walsh put it with heavy irony, 'God knows the Diocese is large enough for the untiring zeal of two Bishops.'[112] The problem was that Fraser insisted on retaining Cape Breton and three mainland counties with large Scottish populations, something Walsh opposed on the grounds that it left Fraser with some two-thirds of the province's Catholics. It also failed to solve the problem of his incompetence and inertia. MacKinnon kept at it, consoling with Walsh about Loughnan (MacKinnon's primary rival for preferment), urging his own schemes on the Propaganda, and helping Fraser craft his proposals. It was a tribute to MacKinnon's tact that he managed to retain the trust of all parties. Walsh was so pleased with the 'warm' support of 'the good Dr McKinnon', for example, that he forwarded his letters to the Irish College and the Propaganda.[113]

Fraser did not wait patiently. He had already decided to ignore the congregation's instruction to remove Loughnan, ordering his vicar general to 'hold fast'.[114] He also arranged to send Rome meticulous reports detailing 'the conduct of Dr Walsh'. 'Let nothing be advanced', he warned Loughnan, 'but what can be substantiated.'[115] Loughnan himself retaliated by suspending Walsh's chaplain, Thomas Louis Connolly, on the pretext that he had never received the appropriate faculties from Fraser. Walsh's protestation that Fraser had explicitly accepted Connolly's presence was true but beside the point.[116] He was unsurprisingly furious, complaining to an Irish friend that Loughnan was 'as bad a

[110] Quoted in Johnston, *Eastern Nova Scotia*, 2: 206.
[111] Johnston, *Eastern Nova Scotia*, 2: 211.
[112] Walsh to Fraser, 29 April 1843, AAH/WP.
[113] Walsh to Cullen, 30 June 1843, PICRA/CUL/807(1). See MacKinnon to Walsh, 22 March 1843, PICRA/CUL/NC/4/1843/14, MacKinnon to Walsh, 12 April, 26 May 1843, 26 October 1844, APF/SC/AS/vol. 5/ff. 328–9, 330–1, 332–3.
[114] Fraser to Loughnan, 22 July 1843, AAH/008–4-17/19.
[115] Fraser to Loughnan, 24 July 1843, AAH/008–4-17/18.
[116] Walsh to Fraser, 24 July 1843, AAH/WP.

specimen of a wicked priest as you would desire to know', while 'a greater calamity was never inflicted on the people' than Fraser's appointment as their bishop.[117]

He was similarly scathing in his letters to the Propaganda. Fraser's 'whole course', he told Fransoni in late July 1843, 'has been one of insincerity, tergiversation, and inconstancy'.[118] Several weeks later, Walsh turned to the calamitous state of those parts of the diocese under Fraser's direct control. In the Scottish heartland of Cape Breton and eastern Nova Scotia, he wrote, 'the state of religion, the spiritual desolation of the people, the number who have fallen away altogether, the violent & scandalous conduct of the Clergy is most deplorable and most shocking'. 'I grieve to say', he continued, 'that the people have not had shepherds, but Wolves and Wolves who did not take the trouble to put on the sheep's clothing.' It was all Fraser's fault, and nothing would change until Rome intervened.[119]

This too was a recurring Hiberno-Roman theme: their ecclesiastical rivals were invariably weak, distracted, diffident, incompetent, or indolent. Replacing them was necessary for the good of religion; souls were at risk. Similar allegations were made from New York to New South Wales, and Cullen himself used the same strategy to remake the Irish hierarchy after 1850.[120] Yet the key to the technique's enduring success was that the allegations almost always contained a grain of truth, and sometimes much more.

This was certainly the case in Nova Scotia, where it was clear that Fraser had lost control of his clergy. James Drummond of Sydney, for example, went to war with his own parishioners partly for political reasons and partly because they had requested an additional priest for the large district. Walsh complained of his 'cursing and excommunicating' those who disagreed with him.[121] At an election in Arichat, Jean Baptiste Maranda backed the Protestant opponent of James McKeagney, the brother of Maranda's clerical neighbour Patrick McKeagney.[122] The McKeagneys blamed Maranda for their defeat, while Maranda in turn allegedly stopped using the English language 'unless it be to abuse the Irish'. As one disgruntled parishioner complained to Bishop Dollard of New Brunswick in early 1844, Fraser had listened 'very kindly' to their

[117] Walsh to Hamilton, 28 August 1843, DDA/HP/36/6/4.
[118] Walsh to Fransoni, 29 July 1843, APF/SC/AS/vol. 5/ff. 398–403.
[119] Walsh to Fransoni, 28 August 1843, PICRA/CUL/NC/4/1843/38(1).
[120] See Emmet Larkin, *The Making of the Roman Catholic Church in Ireland, 1850–1860* (Chapel Hill: University of North Carolina Press, 1980).
[121] Walsh to Fraser, 29 April 1843, AAH/WP. In the early 1850s, Drummond provoked a similar row in Guysborough. See Johnston, *Eastern Nova Scotia*, 2: 252.
[122] Cuthbertson, 282–4.

complaints but had done nothing: 'he is an excellent man but he has no energy.'[123] Even the sympathetic A. A. Johnston admitted Fraser was 'not eminently successful as an administrator', although he attributed this to an excessively trusting nature.[124] The reality was that Fraser was temperamentally unsuited to the episcopate and grew increasingly unwilling to exercise its functions. The inevitable result was indiscipline and drift.

The contrast with Halifax was stark. Indeed, Walsh's achievements were astonishing, especially considering Loughnan's ongoing obstructionism. As he put it in late August 1843, 'I have been rather active.'[125] The most obvious manifestation of this was the creation of the city's Holy Cross Cemetery, which was built in three bursts between July and September 1843.[126] Walsh organized everything down to the last detail, joined the processions of several thousand volunteers from cathedral to cemetery, and personally oversaw the works. Irish symbolism was omnipresent: the Charitable Irish Society led the first procession, there were toasts to 'old Ireland', and a holy well on the Irish model was prominent in the design.[127] The most notable achievement was the rapid erection of the chapel, and the half-myth of its completion in a single day still enjoys a modest place in provincial folklore. Walsh was hugely proud of it, boasting to Cullen that the 'Catholics of Halifax are a noble people'.[128] A few weeks later the blessing of the burial ground and consecration of the chapel supplied the pretext for a splendid liturgical display far grander than anything seen before in the city, or indeed in the Maritimes as a whole. As Terrence Murphy has pointed out, the entire project was not only a declaration of ultramontane intent but a demonstration of the unity, sobriety, and respectability of the capital's some 7,000 mostly Irish Catholics.[129] As Walsh put it after the erection of the chapel, 'we have had another grand demonstration of Catholic unity and zeal in Halifax, which consoled me very much'.[130]

---

[123] Andrew Madden to Dollard, 1 January 1844, SJDA/DP/456–1.
[124] Angus Anthony Johnston, 'A Scottish bishop in New Scotland: The right reverend William Fraser, second vicar apostolic of Nova Scotia, first bishop of Halifax and first bishop of Arichat', *The Innes Review*, vol. 6, no. 2 (1955), 107–24, at 121.
[125] Walsh to Hamilton, 28 August 1843, DDA/HP/36/6/4.
[126] Holy Cross Cemetery was recently the subject of an important research project supported by the Social Sciences and Humanities Research Council of Canada. Much of this research was published in a special volume of *Historical Studies*, edited by Mark McGowan and Michael Vance: *Historical Studies*, vol. 81 (2015), 'Irish Catholic Halifax: From the Napoleonic Wars to the Great War'.
[127] Quoted in Terrence Murphy, '"Religion walked forth in all her majesty": The opening of Holy Cross Cemetery and the transformation of Halifax Catholicism', *Journal of the Royal Nova Scotia Historical Society*, vol. 18 (2015), 77–88.
[128] Walsh to Cullen, 2 September 1843, PICRA/CUL/NC/4/1843/39.
[129] Murphy, 'Religion walked forth'.
[130] Walsh to Hamilton, 28 August 1843, DDA/HP/36/6/4.

Holy Cross was not Walsh's only achievement. Among other things, he created a new temperance society (Loughnan had run the existing one), took direct control of St Mary's College, and established St Patrick's parish in Halifax's north end, where he erected both a school and a church.[131] With support from the Propagation of the Faith he also launched a diocesan newspaper, *The Cross*, and built a close relationship with *The Register*, an unapologetically nationalistic Irish Catholic paper under O'Brien's effective control. Together they helped to spread his message of energy, authority, and Irish pride. He wrote most of the articles in *The Cross* and distributed it widely, including to Daniel Murray in Dublin and the Irish College in Rome.[132] Among the laity Walsh's energy quickly earned the support not only of the elite figures such as Tobin and O'Connor Doyle but also of the bulk of the Catholic population.[133] Supportive meetings were organized and then reported in loving detail in *The Cross*. In early November 1843, for example, 'the Catholics of the Parish and District of Windsor' (almost all of whom had Irish surnames) declared their 'abhorrence of the works of those who endeavour to calumniate and obstruct his Lordship'.[134] He even dined with the lieutenant governor once a month.[135] Although Loughnan and his allies were irreconcilable, others sensed which way the wind was blowing: the frustrated Irish of Arichat, for example, sent Walsh their petition for redress against Jean Baptiste Maranda in the expectation that 'he may soon [be] invested with some powers from Rome that will authorize him to take our case in to consideration'.[136]

Word that the Propaganda had finally resolved to divide the diocese arrived in Halifax in December 1843, although they were frustratingly vague about when or exactly how. Walsh was sure that when the news did become public it would give 'unbounded joy to thousands', although he also thought that it would 'consign many, very many thousands to despair'.[137] Fraser, who appears to have heard only in mid-January, immediately ordered Loughnan to try and find out what Walsh knew.[138] He also issued a pastoral letter on 9 February 1845 in which he flatly denied that he had received orders to recall Loughan, instructed the laity to obey him, and insisted that there was only one bishop of Halifax.[139]

[131] For a comprehensive account of Walsh's early achievements, see Murphy, 'Transformation', 61–4.
[132] See, for example, Kirby to Walsh, 1 May 1847, AAH/WP.
[133] Murphy, 'Transformation', 62.   [134] *The Cross*, 17 December 1843.
[135] Walsh to Hamilton, 26 December 1843, DDA/HP/36/6/6.
[136] Andrew Madden to Dollard, 1 January 1844, SJDA/DP/456–1.
[137] Walsh to Hamilton, 26 December 1843, DDA/HP/36/6/6.
[138] Fraser to Loughnan, 22 January 1844, AAH/008-4-17.
[139] Johnston, *Eastern Nova Scotia*, 2: 204–5.

There was nothing for Walsh to do but set out for Rome, telling Fraser that he hoped that 'the wisdom of the Holy See will secure some peaceful arrangement of our unfortunate misunderstandings'.[140] The ball was now firmly in the Propaganda's court.

The outcome was surprisingly finely balanced. Canadian historians have noticed this but have not explained how the isolated and habitually uncommunicative Fraser was able to mount such an effective fight against the combined might of Murray and the Irish College. To Cullen's consternation, for example, Fraser managed to secure the support of Bishop Signay of Quebec, who despite residing 'at least a thousand miles from Halifax has interfered also against Dr. Walsh'.[141] This was almost certainly a by-product of Fraser's visit to Quebec in early July 1843, his only absence from the Maritimes in his nearly twenty-five years as a bishop. The pretext was the consecration of William Dollard as the first bishop of New Brunswick, but it is difficult to see Fraser's journey as anything other than a search for allies. To secure them, however, he needed something to trade, and it seems likely that he offered his support for Ignace Bourget's revivified dream of a single ecclesiastical province; he joined seven other bishops there in signing a letter requesting one.[142] This was a significant change: he had opposed the idea in 1842 but five years later told the rector of the Scots College in Rome that he had always been in favour 'for reasons which I need not explain'.[143] As Walsh later bitterly recalled, years of Canadian complaints 'over the shortcomings, neglect &c of poor Dr Fraser' were suddenly forgotten, and the moment he 'swallowed that Archiepiscopal Memorial he was transformed into a second St. Charles Borromeo'.[144]

Although undeniably useful, Signay's influence was not sufficient to account for Fraser's success in Rome. Much more important was the support of Charles Januarius Acton, a Cambridge-educated Anglo-Italian aristocrat who had served as governor of Bologna in the late 1820s before returning to Rome where he rose steadily through the curial ranks until he was created cardinal in 1842 and given a seat on the Propaganda. In this new role, Acton sought to establish himself as the protector of *British* Catholic interests and immediately wrote to both the Scottish and the Canadian bishops to express what Joseph Signay called his '*disposition à seuvier les interets dela religion dans les Colonies Britanniques, et en particulier dans colle du Canada*'.[145] The Scots were particularly quick to avail

---

[140] Walsh to Fraser, 26 February 1844, AAH/WP.
[141] Cullen to Murray, 8 June 1844, DDA/MP/34/9.
[142] For the bare facts of Fraser's trip, see Johnston, *Eastern Nova Scotia*, 2: 203.
[143] Johnston, 'A Scottish bishop', 119; Fraser to Grant, 10 November 1847, SCR/16/91C.
[144] Walsh to Dollard, 7 November 1850, SJDA/DP/443.
[145] Signay to Acton, 22 April 1842, APF/SC/AS/vol. 5/ff. 99–100.

themselves of his services. Andrew Scott of the Western District, for example, complained of the difficulty of expressing his needs 'so as to be understood by Italians' and asked Acton to represent him at the Propaganda, while James Kyle of the Northern District was delighted to have 'a protector, so well acquainted with the circumstances of our country, so intelligent, so zealous & so powerful'.[146] Fraser also took up Acton's invitation, sending the cardinal in late May 1842 a detailed summary of events in Halifax. He claimed the vicariate's problems were solely due to Irish resistance to episcopal authority, complained about Walsh's appointment, and insisted that, had 'the affair been left to me, it would have been settled before now, with out noise, disturbance or scandal'.[147] Although Acton's replies do not survive, Fraser must have been encouraged enough to continue to send him complaints about Walsh.[148]

Why Acton decided to involve himself directly is unclear. Before mid-1844, he appears to have remained neutral: Walsh never sensed any threat, kept the cardinal updated on events in Nova Scotia, shared his plans for the division of the diocese, and was open in his complaints about Fraser. As late as June 1844, his letters to Acton took it for granted that he would be given Halifax.[149] Although it is possible that Walsh's presumption may have irritated the cardinal, the more likely explanation is that Acton understood Fraser's agony as simply another iteration of English Catholicism's eternal struggle with the Irish. English cardinals knew what to do about that. At all events, he was a powerful ally; as a worried Cullen put it in early July, Walsh's enemies 'had gained Cardinal Acton'.[150]

Acton's support also carried with it that of two influential *minutanti*, Antonio De Luca and Giambattista Palma. Both spoke English, both were Anglophiles (De Luca was a 'constant reader of the London Tablet'), and both were in Acton's orbit.[151] De Luca had even co-founded the high-profile journal *Annali delle Scienze Religiose* with Acton in 1835 and had served as Michael Anthony Fleming of Newfoundland's Roman agent since at least 1837.[152] Palma was murdered in Rome in late

---

[146] Scott to Acton, 7 February 1842, Kyle to Acton, 12 February 1842, ASV/Spogli Acton/vol. 4/ff. 62–3, 76.

[147] Fraser to Acton, 31 May 1842, APF/SC/AS/vol. 5/ff. 109–112.

[148] See, for example, Fraser to Loughnan, 24 July 1843, AAH/008–4-17/18.

[149] See Walsh to Acton, 13 July 1843, 12 June 1844, APF/SC/AS/vol. 5/ff. 394–5, 722–4.

[150] Cullen to Murray, 6 July 1844, DDA/MP/32/1.

[151] De Luca to Fleming, 25 May 1841, ARCSJ/FP/103/17/1. For Palma, see Christopher Dowd, *Rome in Australia: The Papacy and Conflict in the Australian Catholic Missions, 1834–1884*, 2 vols. (Leiden: Brill, 2008), 1: 118–19.

[152] For De Luca's links with Acton, see C. Michael Shea, *Newman's Early Roman Catholic Legacy, 1845–1854* (Oxford: Oxford University Press, 2017), 35 f. 15. For his

1848, an event which helped precipitate Pius IX's flight from the city, but De Luca's political skills were later rewarded with appointments as nuncio in Bavaria and then Austria before becoming a cardinal (and member of the Propaganda) in 1863. Their support for Fraser mattered, because it was De Luca who prepared the crucial *ponenze*, the formal report that explained the complex situation to the busy cardinals, and Palma who managed the congregation's agenda and kept its minutes. For the first time since he became involved in colonial affairs, Cullen had a serious fight on his hands.

With Acton, Palma, and De Luca in the field, Cullen could not control the flow of information to the Propaganda. Cardinal Fransoni trusted him implicitly, and he had important allies among the *minutanti*, but none of them were committed to Walsh; Cullen would have to convince the entire congregation of the merits of his complicated case. As he reported to Daniel Murray in early June 1844, 'the Cardinal Prefect finds it difficult to determine what is to be done'. Walsh had submitted his allegations against Loughnan and Fraser – all carefully translated and explained by Cullen or Kirby – but the men had 'endeavoured to turn the tables' and 'sent a number of allegations against Dr. Walsh'.

Fraser's advice to the Propaganda was absolutely clear: according to Cullen, he claimed that Walsh lacked the 'prudence' necessary in a bishop and, while the diocese should indeed be divided, 'Dr Walsh is not a fit person to govern it or a part of it.' Cullen anxiously urged Murray to write promptly to the Propaganda about 'the state of things in Halifax'. It would be better, he continued, 'not to mention I have written on the matter'.[153] Although Murray's reply came 'just in time' for the congregation's meeting, Cullen worried it might not be enough. Walsh's 'enemies in Halifax', he wrote, had been moving 'heaven and earth against him since he left that city'.[154] Their effectiveness soon became apparent.

The Propaganda was presented with De Luca's *ponenza* at a congregation on 15 July 1844. The dispute was essentially ethnic in nature, De Luca wrote, with the 'mild, cold and reflective' Scots unable to live easily alongside the 'vivacious and thoughtless' Irish. The 'two nationalities' were consequently 'anxious' to avoid each other, which accounted for the dominance of the Scots on Cape Breton and the eastern mainland and of the Irish in Halifax. This antipathy extended to the church, he continued, with the Irish 'inclined to complain should the bishop be a Scot, and the Scots if he be Irish'. De Luca acknowledged that Irish complaints against

relationship with Fleming, see Fleming to Acton, 26 September 1842, APF/SC/AS/vol. 5/ff. 280–1.
[153] Cullen to Murray, 8 June 1844, DDA/MP/34/9.
[154] Cullen to Muray, 6 July 1844, DDA/MP/32/1.

Fraser had not all been unreasonable – he lived far away, he was over-strict – but blamed the conflict squarely on Dease, O'Brien, and a few 'rich citizens'. Loughnan was chastised for being overly fond of money but was otherwise spared. Walsh was not: although he was forced by 'justice' to admit that the Irishman had behaved prudently 'at first', De Luca insisted that under O'Brien's influence he had soon contracted an unreasonable aversion towards Loughnan. It was Walsh's 'repeated, public invectives' against him that had pushed Halifax into unrest and rebellion. According to De Luca it had merely been a suggestion that Fraser should remove Loughnan, and his pastoral letter of 9 February had been an entirely reasonable assertion of episcopal authority. The report was a complete vindication of the Scotsman's position, drawn largely from his own letters and those of his allies.[155] As Cullen remarked after-wards, the allegations against Walsh 'induced the Cardinals to believe that there must have been something very imprudent in his conduct'.[156]

The Propaganda consequently decided to divide the diocese along the lines Fraser had suggested, with the exact boundaries to be determined by an unspecified neighbouring bishop. More importantly, that bishop would also be solicited for a private opinion on the wisdom of appointing Walsh to the newly created diocese of Halifax.[157] In the meantime, Walsh should await his fate in Europe. Fraser had won, despite the Irish College, despite Murray, and despite Walsh's own presence in Rome. The reason was simple: the cardinals had no reason to disbelieve De Luca. They had charged him with reading, absorbing, and explaining all the relevant correspondence, he had done so, and there was no suggestion that he was anything other than neutral. Cullen was not present at the meeting, almost certainly did not see the *ponenza* before it was presented, and had no means of influencing the congregation's deliberations. By contrast, Acton was a member of the Propaganda, had probably arranged De Luca's assignment, and could vouch for Fraser. He had outplayed Cullen at his own game.

Yet the Irish did not give up. As Kirby reported a few days after the congregation, Cullen was 'engaged in working hard for poor Dr. Walsh'. He had even postponed what was to have been only his third visit home since 1820.[158] Cullen had one final card to play: he could see Gregory XVI at will. In late July, he reported to Murray that he had visited the

---

[155] The bulk of De Luca's report was published in translation by Johnston in *Eastern Nova Scotia*, 2: chaps. 8–9. The original is in the Propaganda Fide archives, *Acta* (1844), vol. 207, ff. 234–47.

[156] Cullen to Murray, 27 July 1844, DDA/CP/40/4.

[157] APF/*Acta* 1844/vol. 207/ff. 226–7.

[158] Kirby to Murray, 20 July 1844, DDA/MP/40/4.

pope, shown him the archbishop's letters, and expressed his own opinion that 'no prudence and no virtue would have conciliated' Walsh's enemies.[159] Gregory, Cullen reported, decided to 'take the matter into his own hands, and he has ordered the cardinals to propose a new arrangement of the controversy'. He was confident that there would consequently be 'no difficulty in dividing the diocese of Halifax immediately, and sending Dr Walsh back without delay'.[160] Cardinal Fransoni was already sympathetic.[161] On 2 September 1844, the chastened cardinals duly divided the diocese, giving Cape Breton and three eastern mainland counties to Fraser and leaving Walsh with the rest of the province.[162] Gregory confirmed the decision a few weeks later.[163]

The Irish were ecstatic. 'You perceive', Kirby told Walsh, 'that tho' Rome appears sometimes tardy in its movements, it gets in the right when the proper moment arrives. O Felix Roma!'[164] Murray 'rejoiced' at Walsh's 'triumph', telling Cullen that it would 'give a new impulse to the progress of Religion in Halifax'.[165] Fraser's Roman supporters were understandably less delighted. Giambattista Palma, for example, caused the minutes to reflect that Walsh had been assigned to Antigonish and Fraser to Halifax, an error that was only discovered when Cullen enquired as to why it was taking so long to draw up the brief for Walsh's appointment; he blamed it on Palma being 'displeased at Dr Walsh's success'.[166] Indeed, Walsh had already noticed the *minutante*'s animosity, reporting to Cullen in early September that he had been supplying 'two Canadians' at Paris with information about the case to be transmitted back to Halifax.[167] Palma's behaviour did have an effect, as, without the correct briefs, Walsh had no authority and could not risk returning, but it ultimately amounted to little more than a show of pique. Acton on the other hand graciously accepted defeat, asking Cullen to introduce an Irish friend to the pope and then inviting him to dinner.[168]

Cullen had had to work hard to secure this result. As he complained in October 1844, there had been a 'deep laid conspiracy against poor

---

[159] Cullen to Murray, 27 July 1844, DDA/CP/40/4.
[160] Cullen to Murray, 26 July 1844, DDA/CP/40/4. On his appointment to Dublin, Cullen extracted all the letters dealing with Gregory's intervention from Murray's archives and placed them in his own papers.
[161] Cullen to Murray, 27 July 1844, DDA/CP/40/4.
[162] Cullen to Murray, 22 September 1844, DDA/CP/40/4.
[163] Johnston, *Eastern Nova Scotia*, 2: 213.
[164] Kirby to Walsh, n.d. [1844], AAH/WP. The letter most likely dates from August or September 1844.
[165] Murray to Cullen, 7 September 1844, PICRA/CUL/943.
[166] Cullen to Murray, 5 October 1844, DDA/MP/34/9.
[167] Walsh to Cullen, 18 September 1844, PICRA/CUL/944.
[168] Acton to Cullen, 7, 17 November 1844, PICRA/CUL/NC/4/1844/52, 53.

Dr. Walsh'.[169] But his efforts also had an important long-term consequence: they taught the small and observant world of the curia that there was little point in challenging the Irish if the pope was willing to intervene on their behalf against the resolutions of a full congregation. So long as Cullen avoided England itself – which he scrupulously did – he could dominate the Propaganda's decision-making in the English-speaking world. Cardinal Fransoni was already an ally and patron and his successor Alessandro Barnabò even more so. The other cardinals challenged him only warily and the *minutanti* dared not challenge him at all. This power survived the death of Gregory in 1846 and his own departure for Ireland in 1850. Ironically, it was seriously challenged only once between 1844 and 1874, when in the mid-1860s a combination of deft politicking, luck, and an incompetent Irish bishop helped repel a Hiberno-Roman attempt on Scotland itself.

Indeed, the lessons of the 1840s were very much in the minds of the besieged Scots of the mid-1860s. As one explained to a colleague in 1867, the goal of Cullen's Irish was 'very clear, they wish to do the same thing in Scotland as some years ago they did in Nova Scotia'. There, he continued, 'by dint of misrepresentations and intrigues they laboured & succeeded after ... insinuating themselves into missions that the Scots had founded to get the native clergy superseded, the Irish Bishop promoted into an ArBp, and to leave no room ... for any one who could speak to the poor people'. 'This is plainly', he concluded, 'what they mean by Scotland.'[170] Their solution was also familiar: disrupt Cullen's monopoly on information, denounce the imprudent Irish interloper, and appeal for English support.[171] That it worked in 1867 did nothing to change the implications of its failure in 1844.

The immediate consequence of Cullen's victory was that William Walsh was now free to return to Halifax, and he promptly began to plan his 'holy campaign in Nova Scotia'. The Propaganda supplied him with suitably Roman books, the Propagation of the Faith gave him money, and he recruited five priests in Ireland.[172] He also found two seminarians to send to Rome and accelerated his search for nuns.[173] The latter proved difficult, as the Sisters of Mercy refused to send a colony despite his long links with the community. 'It is mortifying enough to reflect', he told a

---

[169] Cullen to Fleming, 3 October 1844, ARCSJ/FP/103–10/3.
[170] James Kyle to John Strain, 29 May 1867, SCA, Eastern District Papers [ED], ED3/37/16.
[171] See Colin Barr, '"Imperium in Imperio": Irish Episcopal Imperialism in the Nineteenth-Century', *The English Historical Review*, vol. 123, no. 502 (2008), 611–50 at 636–43.
[172] Kirby to Walsh, n.d. [1844], AAH/WP; Walsh to Dollard, [?30] September 1844, SJDA/DP/416; Johnston, *Eastern Nova Scotia*, 2: 219.
[173] Walsh to Cullen, n.d. [1844], PICRA/CUL/1020(1).

friend, 'that there is hardly a priest in Ireland who did and suffered more for those good people at Baggot St than myself, and yet the veriest strangers can get Communities from them, whilst old friends are forgotten.'[174] This was unfair: in 1844, the Sisters of Mercy had only just begun their overseas expansion and memories of the failure in Newfoundland were fresh enough to render nearby Nova Scotia unappealing. In the event, Walsh did not secure nuns until 1849, and then from America and not Ireland.

Walsh's other problem was the new diocesan boundaries. Cullen had not succeeded in overturning Fraser's request that his diocese – now called Arichat – should include the three mainland counties closest to Cape Breton. Walsh had long complained that this would leave Fraser some two-thirds of the province, two-thirds its Catholic population, and two-thirds of its clergy; even MacKinnon had suggested keeping only the heavily Scottish districts around Antigonish within the new diocese.[175] Walsh responded to this setback by painting Halifax bright green. Not only did he bring the five Irish priests home with him, he ordained another four Irish-born men on arrival. At the same time, Fraser's allies fled: Walsh gleefully reported that Loughnan 'had sold one of his houses [and] his horse & had given notice that he wd officiate no longer as being in a strange Diocese'; after a lengthy world tour, he settled at North Sydney in Cape Breton.[176] Fraser's favourite John Quinan evacuated himself to Tracadie with Edmund Burke's crozier in his bag, while Hugh O'Reilly had to beg to be admitted to New Brunswick after Fraser denied him sanctuary, ostensibly because of his lack of Gaelic.[177] He was only able to stay in Pictou once it became clear that the town would remain under Fraser's authority. Walsh's campaign was so successful that, within weeks of his return to Nova Scotia, only two Scottish-descended priests were left in his diocese.[178]

Walsh also re-examined his friendships, arranging on Cullen's advice for Richard O'Brien to be lured home by the prospect of a better job.[179] O'Brien, Cullen told Daniel Murray, was a 'violent politician' and 'a hot and independent young man'.[180] He was also a rival for the affections of the city's Irish Catholic laity. The backlash was ferocious, with O'Brien's

[174] Walsh to Hamilton, 13 February 1845, DDA/HP/36/7/5.
[175] Johnston, *Eastern Nova Scotia*, 2: 208–11.
[176] Walsh to Thomas Griffiths, n.d. [1845], WDA, Wiseman papers, W/1/2; Johnston, *Eastern Nova Scotia*, 2: 243–4.
[177] Walsh to Dollard, 20 October 1850, SJDA/DP/447; O'Reilly to Dollard, 24 October 1844, SJDA/DP/457.
[178] Johnston, *Eastern Nova Scotia*, 2: 219.
[179] Walsh to Cullen, n.d. [1844], PICRA/CUL/1020(1).
[180] Cullen to Murray, 22 September 1844, DDA/CP/40/4.

supporters indulging in 'monstrous calumnies', threats of violence, and accusations of toadying to the government, but Walsh's authority was only enhanced when he successfully weathered the storm.[181] With O'Brien gone, Walsh moved to establish full control over his clergy, inaugurating regular clerical conferences to inculcate good practice.[182] In Halifax itself, he ensured compliance by creating 'a very pleasant clerical society' in his own home and under his personal supervision.[183] He soon felt able to boast that the 'assertion of Ecclesiastical authority in Halifax is complete and triumphant: The Church of God is ruled on Church principles, and not one of the Laity dares to meddle in the slightest degree with the affairs of the Sanctuary.'[184]

One of the apparent paradoxes of Hiberno-Roman Catholicism is that the neutering of lay power almost invariably coincided with a flourishing of lay activity and observance. This is less paradoxical, however, than it might at first appear: as Brian Clarke has pointed out, ultramontane bishops of all nationalities encouraged lay *activism* but feared lay *initiative*.[185] In Halifax, this manifested in a great effusion of lay organizations, from the St Patrick's Temperance Society to the Catholic Literary Institute, all founded and run under clerical supervision. Walsh particularly favoured the local committee of the Propagation of the Faith, chaired its meetings, and urged that branches be established across the diocese.[186] Terrence Murphy has calculated that, in all, at least a dozen lay societies were established by 1850, collectively amounting to what he described as a 'metamorphosis in the institutional and spiritual life of Halifax Catholics'.[187] Ireland and Irish identity were often in the foreground. A report in *The Cross* on an 1846 meeting of the Catechistical Society, for example, quickly became a tribute to the generosity of the 'Exiles of Erin in Nova Scotia'.[188]

Yet Walsh could not build his model Hiberno-Roman diocese without nuns. Thwarted in Ireland, he turned his attention to New York, where he could rely on the support of its bishop, John Hughes. Their friendship apparently dated to a 'tour' of the United States the men undertook together in late 1847, and it must have been at this time that Walsh also came to know Hughes' sister Angela, a leading member of the Sisters of Charity in New York.[189] They too became friends, and, when she fell seriously ill in early 1848, Walsh suggested she spend the summer in Halifax and promised to send his vicar general to collect her if

---

[181] See Murphy, 'Transformation', 65–6.   [182] Ibid., 68.
[183] Walsh to Dollard, 6 April 1846, SJDA/DP/426.   [184] Ibid.   [185] Clarke, 3.
[186] *The Cross*, 25 September 1847.   [187] Murphy, 'Transformation', 71–3.
[188] *The Cross*, 14 March 1846.   [189] Hughes to Walsh, 26 November 1847, AAH/WP.

necessary.[190] He also invited Hughes, asking him to dedicate the new St Patrick's parish church. 'If you have a drop of *Irish blood* in your veins', he teased, 'you won't refuse *St. Patrick's invitation*.'[191] It was the Hughes siblings who facilitated the expansion of the Sisters of Charity to Halifax, with four arriving from New York in May 1849 under the leadership of the Irish-born Rosanna McCann. They immediately opened a poor school with some 200 pupils, a number that soon doubled. They also began taking in orphans.[192]

Within weeks the women were joined by a party of five Religious of the Sacred Heart, also from New York and also prompted by Hughes, who quickly had some forty girls in their own more elite school.[193] Walsh soon boasted that there were already 'six Protestants attending the School, one of whom is a Boarder'.[194] He was delighted with both communities, telling Hughes of 'the immense and almost miraculous change they have already wrought in our children'.[195] By Walsh's death in 1858, there were fourteen Sisters of Charity, nine of whom had joined in Halifax, and by the 1860s they had expanded to New Brunswick and western Nova Scotia, ultimately founding more than 100 missions across the region, including numerous schools, several hospitals, and the women's college that eventually developed into Mount Saint Vincent University.[196] The Religious of the Sacred Heart grew more slowly, but their school in Halifax remains one of the most exclusive in the province. In addition to the educational and other social services these women provided to all levels of Catholic society, the sodalities and Marian devotions they encouraged did much to inculcate Hiberno-Roman Catholicism in generations of Haligonians and Maritimers.[197]

Walsh's triumph had firmly established Hiberno-Romanism in the region's largest city, but Prince Edward Island, New Brunswick, and the new diocese of Arichat remained under the control of bishops who were at best indifferent to his priorities and over whose actions he had no control. Two were Scottish. As a result, Walsh needed to extend his influence and fight off a watchful and rapacious Quebec. To do that he

---

[190] Walsh to Hughes 17 February 1848, CU/BP/MS1296/Series 1/Sub-series 1/Box 3/ Folder 5.
[191] Walsh to Hughes, 9 May 1848, AANY/HP/Box 3/Folder 9. Emphasis in original.
[192] 'Sister Maura', *The Sisters of Charity of Halifax* (Toronto: Ryerson Press, 1956), 3–4.
[193] Murphy, 'Transformation', 69.
[194] Walsh to Dollard, 7 November 1850, SJDA/DP/443.
[195] Walsh to Hughes, 3 September 1849, CU/BP/MS1296/Series 1/Sub-series 1/Box 3/ Folder 5.
[196] See Marianna O'Gallagher, 'The Sisters of Charity of Halifax: The early and middle years', *CCHA Study Sessions*, vol. 47 (1980), 57–68.
[197] Murphy, 'Transformation', 70.

needed to control his neighbourhood, and from the late 1840s he and his successors set out to do exactly that.

Scottish dominance had never faltered in tiny Prince Edward Island, despite several pre-Famine waves of primarily Catholic Irish migration. The largest of these began in 1830 at the behest of the Island-born but Scottish-descended priest John MacDonald, who was then serving in a Glasgow parish.[198] In that year, MacDonald invited his mostly Irish parishioners to return with him to Prince Edward Island, where he promised to settle them on his family estate. The success of this venture began a chain migration, largely but not exclusively from Co. Monaghan, which did not end until 1848.[199] Several thousand ultimately emigrated, with most settling together on a handful of rural 'lots'.[200] They joined thousands more who came by other channels and spread more widely across the Island. By the early 1860s, Catholics comprised some 45 per cent of the population.

Intensive Irish Catholic migration inevitably led to sectarian tensions, especially over education. This was particularly acute from the late 1850s, but as early as 1847 there was a fatal riot with at least some sectarian overtones.[201] Political life began to divide along denominational lines, and by the early 1860s almost all Catholics voted for the Liberals, who counted a number of Irish Catholics among their leaders, while almost all Protestants voted Conservative.[202] As the bishop of the day complained in 1862, the Conservative government 'wages war in the Protestant & Tory papers of the Island unceasingly against the Catholics'.[203] The Island's idiosyncratic system of leasehold tenure further exacerbated tensions, with an Irish-style Tenant League emerging in the mid-1860s with substantial Catholic support. There was even a Fenian scare whipped up by a 'half-witted schoolteacher', the delightfully named Leland H. 'Rufus' Stumbles.[204]

Yet the steady greening of Island Catholicism did not reach the episcopacy. Under the long-serving Angus MacEachern there was no doubt of the church's fundamentally Scottish character. When he established St

---

[198] It was MacDonald's father who in 1772 had settled the first wave of Scottish Catholic migrants as tenants.

[199] O'Grady, 142–50.

[200] See Peter McGuigan, 'From Wexford and Monaghan: The Lot 22 Irish', *The Abegweit Review*, Winter 1985, 61–84, at 66.

[201] See O'Grady, chap. 9.

[202] Ian Ross Robertson, *The Tenant League of Prince Edward Island: Leasehold Tenure in the New World* (Toronto: University of Toronto Press, 1996), 5.

[203] Peter McIntyre to Sweeny, 21 October 1862, SJDA, Sweeny papers [SP]/1497.

[204] See Edward MacDonald, 'Who's afraid of the Fenians? The Fenian scare on Prince Edward Island, 1865–1867', *Acadiensis*, vol. 38, no. 1 (Winter/Spring 2009), 33–51.

Andrew's College in 1833, for example, its trustees were named MacDonald, MacDonald, Brennan, and MacDonald.[205] He worked well with successive governments (at least after the mid-1810s), which he thought 'vastly kind to us', and railed against the indifference and aggression of Quebec.[206] As he explained in 1826, the Catholics were clustered 'at both extremes of the colony', were often mixed with Protestants, and, despite having 'no voice or vote in the Legislature, we find no inconvenience from that preclusion'.[207] Following Scottish practice, MacEachern encouraged his priests to eschew provoking displays, whether political, architectural, or sartorial. Many in Quebec and among the French clergy in the Maritimes interpreted this as something between slovenliness and heterodoxy, and, as in India, it became a recurring ground of complaint. As late as 1839, for example, one complained bitterly that the new bishop of Charlottetown had refused to compel his clergy to button their cassocks at a party.[208]

The erection in 1829 of a single diocese for Prince Edward Island, New Brunswick, and the Îles de la Madeleine had given a measure of protection from Quebec, but its bishops had not reconciled themselves to the loss. Shortly before MacEachern died, for example, there were rumours of an attempt to impose a French coadjutor on him; Fraser blamed his death on the shock. Quebec then tried to fill the vacancy with Antoine Gagnon, an Island priest primarily distinguished for his impartial contempt for both the Irish and the Scots. (He referred to one Irish colleague as a 'galopin irlandais', or Irish urchin.) The Propaganda was unimpressed by the submission of only one name for their consideration, told Quebec to mind its own business, and ultimately selected MacEachern's preferred choice Bernard Donald MacDonald instead.[209] The reluctant MacDonald proved to be almost preternaturally passive, and he seems to have been even less communicative than Fraser.[210] His long tenure was primarily distinguished by the cession of New Brunswick in 1842 and by a nasty row with the importer of the Monaghan Irish, his cousin John MacDonald. In the late 1850s, he accidentally became the catalyst for decades of sectarian unrest over educational

---

[205] Minutes of St Andrew's College, CDA/BM.
[206] MacEachern to MacPherson, 20 August 1819, SCR/12/103.
[207] MacEachern to Aeneas MacDonald, 12 December 1826, SCR/12/109.
[208] See Ronnie Gilles LeBlanc, 'Antoine Gagnon and the mitre: A model of relations between *Canadien*, Scottish and Irish clergy in the early Maritime church', in Murphy and Byrne, *Religion and Identity*, 98–113, at 108.
[209] See LeBlanc, 'Antoine Gagnon'.
[210] MacDonald's letters books appear to be intact at the Charlottetown diocesan archives but contain almost no letters other than those related to the bitter struggle with his cousin.

policy.[211] Typically, both he and Edward Whelan, the province's leading Catholic politician, attempted to cool tensions by urging that religion be excluded entirely from the schools. To Whelan, it was 'improper and worse than useless to connect religious with secular training'.[212] Although by no means hostile to the Irish, MacDonald was not especially encouraging, and when he died in late 1859 only five of his seventeen priests were Irish or of Irish extraction, despite the likelihood that they already comprised a majority of his flock.[213]

MacDonald was succeeded in 1860 by Peter McIntyre, whose parents had emigrated from Scotland with Angus MacEachern and in whose home the bishop had often said Mass.[214] The dynamic McIntyre quickly asserted his control over clergy and laity alike, pursued a more confrontational policy with the government, and regularly demanded state funding for Catholic schools. The Island's system, he complained, was 'virtually Protestant, and unjust to Catholics', and he insisted on the same protections enjoyed by religious minorities in Quebec and Ontario.[215] Like several of his colleagues, including the archbishop of Halifax, he supported confederation (and the Conservatives who advocated it) in hopes that it would bring with it denominational schooling, but, when it did not, he unsuccessfully ordered Catholic legislators to oppose the entire deal.[216] The issue did not lose its political heat until the early 1880s.

McIntyre was also a builder, erecting among other things some twenty-five churches, eight convents, a hospital, an episcopal palace, and a comprehensive school system.[217] He was particularly committed to

[211] See Ian Ross Robertson, 'The Bible question in Prince Edward Island from 1856 to 1860', in P. A. Buckner and David Frank (eds.), *The Acadiensis Reader, Vol. 1: Atlantic Canada before Confederation* (Fredericton, NB: Acadiensis Press, 1985), 261–83, at 264–7.

[212] Peter McCourt, *Biographical Sketch of the Honorable Edward Whelan, Together with a Compilation of his Principal Speeches* (Charlottetown: The Author, 1888), 143.

[213] For a list of the Prince Edward Island clergy at MacDonald's death, see Art O'Shea, *A Century Plus Forty: An Historical Review of the Diocese of Charlottetown, 1829–1969* (The Author, 2009), 45; for biographical information on the Island's priests, see Art O'Shea, *Priests and Bishops Who Served in the Diocese of Charlottetown, 1829–1996* (The Author, 1996).

[214] See G. Edward MacDonald, 'McINTYRE, PETER', in *DCB*.

[215] Pastoral Letter to the clergy and laity of the diocese of Charlottetown, 22 December 1873, copy in the CDA.

[216] Francis W. P. Bolger, *Prince Edward Island and Confederation, 1863–1873* (Charlottetown: St Dunstan's University Press, 1964), 285–6.

[217] Edward MacDonald, *The History of St. Dunstan's University, 1855–1956* (Charlottetown: Board of Governors of St Dunstan's University and Prince Edward Island Museum and Historical Foundation, 1989), 73. See also Heidi MacDonald, 'Developing a strong Roman Catholic social order in the late Nineteenth-Century Prince Edward Island', *Canadian Catholic Historical Association, Historical Studies*, vol. 69 (2003), 34–51.

St Dunstan's College, which his predecessor had opened in 1855 as a combination seminary and higher school. He patronized it, rebuilt it, and the 1863 election largely turned on his demand that the province fund it.[218] McIntyre was also a reliable ultramontane, regularly visiting Rome and enthusiastically supporting papal infallibility. Yet his model was Quebec, where he had been almost entirely educated and where he continued to send most of his clerical students. (The future Archbishop Cornelius O'Brien of Halifax, whom McIntyre sent to the Propaganda in 1864, was a conspicuous exception.) He also turned to the province for religious, convincing the Congrégation de Notre-Dame in Montreal to establish a convent in 1857, for example, and importing the Soeurs de Charité de Sainte-Marie (the Grey Nuns) from the same city to open a hospital in 1878.[219] He also welcomed the Irish Christian Brothers in 1870, but, much to the relief of later generations of diocesan lawyers, they remained less than a decade.[220]

Island historians have tended to portray McIntyre's relations with his Irish flock as reasonably good, despite his being unambiguously a Scot.[221] This was no doubt facilitated by the effect of decades of Protestant hostility towards all Catholics, not simply Irish ones. It is also clear, however, that McIntyre was wary of arousing Irish national feeling. In 1886, for example, he was furious when an Irish priest appeared to raise money for Monaghan's cathedral. When he persisted despite being refused permission to collect, McIntyre felt compelled to issue a public prohibition. This, he complained to the man's Irish bishop, had 'sown the seeds of ill feeling between the bishop and his people, who imagine that their countryman has been severely dealt with'.[222] Shortly afterwards, he sent the pope an account of his silver jubilee via Kirby and the Irish College and then advertised that he had done so.[223]

Irish interest quickened as McIntyre aged. Complaints that he excluded 'from the ranks of the clergy "*young men of Irish blood*"' began to flow to Archbishop O'Brien, a former protégé whom McIntyre had backed for Halifax against fierce opposition from his neighbours.[224] He furiously reminded O'Brien that the Irish had stood by him through years of bitter persecution and insisted that the very idea that he had turned

---

[218] MacDonald, *St. Dunstan's*, chap. 4.
[219] See Carmel MacDonald, 'An era of consolidation', in Michael F. Hennessey (ed.), *The Catholic Church in Prince Edward Island, 1720–1979* (Charlottetown: The Roman Catholic Episcopal Corporation, 1979), 68–9.
[220] O'Grady, 194.   [221] MacDonald, 'McIntyre', *DCB*.
[222] McIntyre to James Donnelly, 13 December 1886, CDA, McIntyre Papers [MP].
[223] McIntyre to the Clergy of Charlottetown, 31 January 1887 [printed circular], CDA/MP.
[224] McIntyre to O'Brien, 'February' 1890, CDA/MP; John Cameron to John Sweeny, 9 May 1882, SJDA/SP/1401. Emphasis in original.

away 'postulants for the priesthood because of their Irish blood' grieved him 'to the heart'.[225] He could not explain what the archbishop apparently called 'the great scarcity of Priests of Irish descent' but was adamant that 'it cannot be attributed to a want of sympathy on my part towards that people'. If 'dissatisfaction invades the breasts of Irishmen', he wrote, 'before God I feel that I am not by any means responsible'.[226] The real issue was that it was widely known that he needed a coadjutor and scarcely less widely known that his choice was the rector of St Dunstan's, James Charles MacDonald, whom he had known 'from his boyhood'.[227] Despite ferocious opposition, he got his way and MacDonald was consecrated in the summer of 1890. McIntyre died the following year. One of his last acts was to send a donation of £15 10s 6d to Longford 'for the relief of Irish distress'.[228]

Although MacDonald's appointment quieted Irish complaints for a time, the threat remained. In 1901, for example, he opposed a suggestion to create a diocese for the Acadian population of New Brunswick on the grounds that it 'would establish a precedent that must inevitably carry with it a fund of trouble for the future'. 'If nationality be introduced into the affairs of religion,' he continued, 'the result will be confusion and race hatred where order and charity should obtain, and the peace and concord of the church in the Maritime Provinces would give way to faction and strife.'[229] It is difficult to think that he did not have the Irish in mind.

MacDonald's fears were soon realized. In late 1907, 'We, the native-born clergy of Irish extraction' issued an astonishing manifesto. They claimed that 21,992 of the Island's 45,796 Catholics were Irish, 'nearly double that of the Acadian, and triple that of the Scotch'. Despite this, there were only eleven Irish priests against twenty-five Scots in the diocese. This was, they wrote, directly 'owing to the fact that the bishops and the first priests were of the nationality of the minority, and that they not only cultivated vocations among that nationality, but by every special means induced their own kinfolk to enter the priesthood'. Those Irish that did persist were badly treated, were rarely sent to study at the Propaganda (seven Scots against two Irish), and were denied favourable postings even in 'unmistakably Irish parishes'. The bishop had even given his imprimatur to an ecclesiastical history of the diocese that was 'grossly insulting to

[225] McIntyre to O'Brien, 'February' 1890, CDA/MP.
[226] McIntyre to O'Brien, 24 February 1890, CDA/MP.
[227] McIntyre to O'Brien, 26 February 1890, CDA/MP.
[228] McIntyre to Bartholomew Woodlock, 20 March 1891, ARDA, Bartholomew Woodlock papers.
[229] MacDonald to Diomede Falconio, 2 December 1901, CDA, James Charles MacDonald papers [JMP]. Now the papal nuncio, Falconio had previously served as Enrico Carfagnini's right-hand man in Harbour Grace.

our Irish Catholics'. They had long turned the other cheek, and hesitated 'to raise the cry of nationality at all', but the position of Irish priests in Prince Edward Island had become 'simply intolerable'.[230]

MacDonald's reply was robust. He told the apostolic delegate in Ottawa that the Irish had ignored the Îles de la Madeleine, which contained 5,000 mostly francophone Catholics, counted every Irishman on the Island as a Catholic, and likely undercounted the Scots. He preferred a private census conducted under McIntyre in 1890, which gave 18,203 Irish Catholics, 16,633 Acadians, and 11,737 Scots. Since then, he insisted, only the Acadian population had shown significant growth, and it was likely that they were now in a majority in the diocese. The supposed eleven Irish priests were actually fourteen, and three more had recently died prematurely. Of the twenty-five Scots, more than half were elderly survivors of the era of Scottish majority. Among younger priests, there was a rough balance. He flatly denied that Irish vocations were discouraged, that Irish priests were discriminated against, or that the Irish laity were disgruntled. Most simply wished to be ministered to by 'pious and exemplary priests without regard to their nationality' and had only been stirred up by Irish priests sowing 'amongst them the seeds of national prejudice'. The whole thing, he concluded, was a deliberate attempt to deceive both the apostolic delegate and the local hierarchy.[231]

This was true but irrelevant. Continuing Scottish domination was clearly untenable, and, as MacDonald's health slowly declined, the struggle to succeed him intensified. The 1912 appointment to Antigonish (as Arichat was renamed in 1886) of his formidable vicar general, James Morrison, removed the only plausible Scottish candidate, and in 1913 Rome appointed the Irish New Brunswicker Henry Joseph O'Leary.[232] O'Leary had already enjoyed a meteoric career: born in 1879, he was educated at the largely francophone St Joseph's College in Memramcook and then in Montreal, ordained in 1901, and then sent to Rome for advanced study and in 1909 appointed the Roman agent for the Maritime hierarchy.[233] After just seven years on the Island he was appointed the third bishop (and second archbishop) of Edmonton, where he earned the nickname 'The Builder'. His appointment to Charlottetown represented the definitive end of Scottish domination,

---

[230] 'The Irish Priests of Prince Edward Island' to MacDonald, 1 November 1907, ADA, Cameron papers [CP]/Fonds 3/Series 2/Sub series 1.

[231] MacDonald to Donatus Sbarretti, n.d., copy in CDA, James Morrison papers. This letter likely dates either to late 1907 or to early 1908.

[232] For Morrison, see Peter Ludlow, *The Canny Scot: Archbishop James Morrison of Antigonish* (Montreal and Kingston: McGill-Queen's University Press, 2015).

[233] For the Roman appointment, see Thomas F. Barry to Henry J. O'Leary, 7 March 1909, CDA/JMP.

just as his arrival in Alberta was a watershed in the decline of French Oblate dominance in the Prairies. He died in 1938.

Yet Prince Edward Island was only ever a sideshow. Irish attention was more closely focussed on the other 'Scottish' diocese, William Fraser's Arichat. This is not to say that there was ever any hope of imposing an Irish bishop on an overwhelmingly Scottish population. Rather, William Walsh and his successors wanted to ensure that the church there conformed as nearly as possible to their own visions of ecclesiastical best practice. This began almost immediately after Nova Scotia's division in 1845. On the face of it everything was peaceful: Walsh boasted to friends of his 'very good understanding' with Fraser, while MacDonald, Fraser, and Walsh himself made each other honorary vicars general.[234] In 1847, Walsh even paid Fraser a visit, a courtesy Fraser returned the following year.[235]

Yet this was all on the surface: Walsh remained determined to address Arichat, both for its own sake and to preserve Irish gains against a rapacious Quebec. Fraser's increasing (and genuine) ill health gave him the opportunity he needed. In September 1847, Fraser privately raised the possibility of asking for a coadjutor, telling the rector of the Scots College in Rome that the only suitable candidates were Colin MacKinnon and John Loughnan.[236] Although Loughnan appears to have been optimistic – Walsh later remarked acidly on his supposed purchase of episcopal regalia during a visit to Rome – there was never any serious chance of his appointment.[237] MacKinnon was an entirely different matter. Walsh had been impressed with his tact during the fight with Fraser, remarking to Kirby afterwards that he had been 'a fast friend of reconciliation and peace'.[238] He was also an effective self-promoter, carefully eschewing outward signs of ambition while reminding Rome of his achievements at every opportunity.[239] He was also adept at playing both sides: in late October 1844, for example, he reminded Walsh that neither Fraser nor Loughnan knew that they were in contact and hoped that Walsh would keep it that way.[240] It was no surprise that the 'young, amiable, learned, alumnus of the Propaganda' was already being spoken

---

[234] Walsh to Hamilton, 'Good Friday' 1847, DDA/HP/37/1/7; Walsh to Dollard, 21 July 1847, SJDA/DP/431.

[235] Johnston, *Eastern Nova Scotia*, 2: 224.

[236] Fraser to Grant, 10 September 1847, SCR/16/90.

[237] Walsh to Dollard, 20 October 1850, SJDA/DP/447.

[238] Walsh to Kirby, 27 December 1845, quoted in Ludlow, 'Disturbed by the Irish howl', 42.

[239] The diplomatic A. A. Johnston hinted strongly at this trait, see Johnston, *Eastern Nova Scotia*, 2: 218, 225.

[240] MacKinnon to Walsh, 26 October 1844, APF/SC/AS/vol. 5/ff. 332–3.

of as a possible coadjutor to Fraser.[241] Walsh was certainly thrilled with the prospect, which is perhaps why Fraser quietly dropped the idea.

By 1850, however, Walsh's steady complaints and Fraser's increasingly obvious incapacity had forced Rome to act; a diocese with nearly 50,000 Catholics (some 70 per cent of the province's total) could not be left to drift indefinitely. In mid-July, the Propaganda ordered Fraser to hold an election for a coadjutor and advise on the result. When he finally did so, MacKinnon won all but a handful of votes. Walsh was ecstatic: he had already told Kirby that he was '*the* man, the *only* man for the crisis'.[242] Fraser himself responded by doing absolutely nothing. He did not comment on the result, or inform Rome, and Walsh grew increasingly anxious as months passed with no word of MacKinnon's appointment.[243] He urged Kirby to investigate and encouraged Bishop Dollard of New Brunswick to write as well.[244] Although Kirby assured him that he looked on MacKinnon 'already as Bishop', the Propaganda was loath to act on the grounds that 'it was better to tolerate for a while some inconveniences than to proclaim war against the pious old man who is now probably on his last legs'.[245] They would do nothing until Fraser 'either goes to heaven or gives human consent'.[246] William Fraser finally died on 4 October 1851, and Colin MacKinnon was confirmed as his successor the following month.

This was an enormous relief to the Scottish Catholics of Nova Scotia, who had long worried that Fraser would have an Irish successor. MacKinnon himself had warned Walsh of this as early as 1843. As one young Scot studying at the Propaganda told his father, he no longer needed to fear that 'the future Bishop would be an Irishman'. Instead, he continued, he 'will be neither *orange* nor *green*' but acceptable to all.[247] For Walsh and the Irish, MacKinnon was also the best possible choice: an efficient, educated Scot who seemed to share their ecclesiastical vision. The Propaganda had the pleasure of promoting a trusted former student and assiduous correspondent. Everybody was happy, except perhaps John Loughnan.

MacKinnon quickly proved to be a radical reformer, reducing the role of Gaelic and emphasizing the use of Latin, importing both Roman devotions and Roman art, imposing discipline on his clergy, and

---

[241] Quoted in Johnston, *Eastern Nova Scotia*, 2: 226.
[242] Walsh to Kirby, 2 August 1850, quoted in Ludlow, 'Disturbed by the Irish howl', 42.
[243] Walsh to Dollard, 4 December 1850, SJDA/DP/448.
[244] Walsh to Dollard, 22 March 1851, SJDA/DP/450.
[245] Kirby to Walsh, [January] and Kirby to Walsh, 31 May 1851, both AAH/WP.
[246] Kirby to Walsh, 31 May 1851, AAH/WP.
[247] John Cameron to Lachlan Cameron, 7 November 1851, ADA/JP/fons 8/series 4/sub series 1. Emphasis in original.

launching a diocesan newspaper.[248] He worked hard to build his diocese's long-neglected infrastructure, including St Ninian's Cathedral, for which he tried to order from Scotland two eighteen-foot columns of Aberdeen granite.[249] He also prioritized the creation of the diocesan seminary that eventually became St Francis Xavier University and imported a Prussian former student of the Propaganda to run it.[250] (This was not a happy choice, as the man ended his career as a Church of England minister in Ontario.)[251] In all of this MacKinnon proved to be exactly the thorough Roman that Walsh had hoped for. What Walsh did not realise, however, was that MacKinnon was also a Scot who had no intention of conforming to Walsh's will.

The flashpoint was the Irishman's ill-concealed hunger for Arichat's three mainland counties. He called it dividing the clans.[252] Walsh was furious when MacKinnon followed Fraser's example and continued to live in Antigonish, a 'totally rural place where there is not even a village'.[253] He thought a bishop should live in his cathedral city, in this case a small settlement on the Isle Madame. MacKinnon rightly suspected that this was a ploy to contain him on Cape Breton, and his riposte was sharp. There were more Catholics in just one of the mainland counties than there were in Halifax, he told Rome, and they were almost without exception 'Scottish or of Scottish origin'.[254] Any change in the boundaries would exacerbate the 'antipathy that exists between the Scots and the Irish' and result in 'disturbances and tumults in places where peace now reigns'.[255] Although MacKinnon soon gave up and moved to Arichat, he had made his point. He was also soon back in Antigonish. As Peter Ludlow put it, MacKinnon's goal was 'to form an ethnic rampart around his diocese, which would repel the Irish assault'.[256]

The conflict became increasingly rancorous. At a popular level, the *Halifax Catholic* (established by Walsh in 1854 as the successor to *The Cross*) and MacKinnon's *The Casket* competed to outdo the other with ethnic insults, regularly suggesting that the Irish were lazy or the Scots

---

[248] See Ludlow, 'Disturbed by the Irish howl', 43–5.

[249] MacKinnon to John Strain, 21 November 1868, SCACH/ED/106/8.

[250] See James D. Cameron, *For the People: A History of St Francis Xavier University* (Montréal and Kingston: McGill-Queen's University Press for St Francis Xavier University, 1996), 14–18.

[251] See Peter Ludlow, '"Pretend Catholics" and stampeders: The Romanization of the diocese of Arichat/Antigonish, 1851–1910', *Historical Papers 2014: Canadian Society of Church History*, 31–50, at 41.

[252] Ludlow, 'Romanization', 39–40.

[253] Quoted in Ludlow, 'Disturbed by the Irish howl', 45.   [254] Quoted in ibid., 46.

[255] MacKinnon to the Propaganda, 20 November 1854, quoted in ibid., 46.

[256] Ludlow, 'Disturbed by the Irish howl', 47.

subservient.[257] In 1856, MacKinnon took great pleasure in the bitter row between the leading Liberal Joseph Howe (then temporarily out of office) and his previously close allies among the Halifax Irish. Howe had grown increasingly exasperated at what he saw as a series of Irish Catholic provocations and, in particular, their attacks on his attempts to recruit Irish Americans to serve in the Crimean War. He finally exploded in a barrage of anti-Irish tirades after a gang of Irish navvies brutally assaulted a group of mostly Scots Presbyterian rail workers in what became known as the 'Gourlay Shanty Incident'. He accused the Irish clergy of fomenting 'a war of races and creeds'.[258] MacKinnon's brother, who was a member of the Liberal government, congratulated Howe on resisting the 'Irish Howl' and assured him that the 'Scotch and the French' of Arichat were his 'friends'. MacKinnon himself told Howe that his vitriolic letter to the *Halifax Catholic* had given 'great satisfaction in this quarter'.[259] It was only when Howe extended his attacks to Catholics as such that MacKinnon retreated and his brother resigned. 'Our creed and that of all Irish Catholics is identical,' he told Howe in early 1857, and 'we therefore consider and must consider all attacks made upon the Faith of Irish Catholics as leveled at ourselves.'[260] An infuriated Walsh saw only 'treachery in our own ranks'. As he complained to Cullen, it was a bitter pill to swallow coming 'from one upon whom for fifteen years past I have been showering all manner of benefits and substantial kindness'.[261]

Walsh had been right that MacKinnon would be an effective ultramontane bishop. What he had not realized was that his loyalty to Rome was not matched by any affinity or affection for the Irish. Once he was safely a bishop, they were simply a threat to be managed. Like Peter McIntyre in Prince Edward Island, he tended instead to look to Quebec and referred to Montreal as the 'Rome of North America'.[262] He also imported the Congrégation de Notre-Dame in 1856, albeit only after he had failed to secure a colony of Sisters of Charity from Archbishop Hughes of New York.[263] Like Montreal's Ignace Bourget he was (at

---

[257] Ibid., 47–8.
[258] J. Murray Beck, *Joseph Howe, Vol. 2, The Briton Becomes Canadian* (Montreal and Kingston: McGill-Queen's University Press, 1983), 108–10.
[259] Beck, *Briton Becomes Canadian*, 111; MacKinnon to Howe, 1 October 1856, Library and Archives Canada [LAC], Howe papers [HP], MG24 B29/vol. 2/pp. 774–777.
[260] MacKinnon to Howe, 20 February 1857, ADA, Mackinnon papers [MP]/fons 3, series 1, sub series 1.
[261] Walsh to Cullen, 16 February 1857, DDA/CP/339/5/II/4.
[262] MacKinnon to Thomas Chisholm, 23 March 1857, ADA/MP/fons 3/series 1/sub series 1.
[263] MacKinnon to Hughes, 30 March 1853, AANY/HP/Box 3/Folder 1.

least at first) as Roman as Cullen or Walsh, but he was also a Scot keen to preserve his people's ecclesiastical independence.

The desire for ecclesiastical independence also lay at the heart of Walsh's manoeuvrings: he knew that Bourget and his allies wanted to return the region to Canadian control, something both he and Fleming had long fiercely opposed. This fate had been narrowly avoided in 1844, when Rome finally approved the erection of a new ecclesiastical province consisting of Montreal, Kingston, Toronto, and Quebec itself. (Bytown – later Ottawa – was erected in 1847.) Walsh had been relieved that Rome had 'acted wisely in restricting the new Eccl Province to Canada itself'.[264] The issue re-emerged in 1847, when an appalled Fleming discovered that Newfoundland had been suddenly erected into a diocese and placed under Quebec (see Chapter 2.) At the same time, the Propaganda asked the Maritime bishops whether they would like to join him.[265]

This was a mortal threat: Walsh and Fleming remained opposed, but Fraser was firmly in favour and MacDonald was at least sympathetic. Much hinged on the attitude of William Dollard, who in 1842 had become the first bishop of New Brunswick. Dollard's own background gave few clues to his likely attitude: although Irish, he had emigrated to Quebec in 1816 in response to a call for Irish and Gaelic-speaking priests, completed his education there, and then served for several years as one of only two priests on Cape Breton. In 1823, he was assigned to New Brunswick, where he ministered to the growing Irish population in the Miramichi region, before moving to Charlottetown, where he helped to establish St Andrew's College, and then back to the New Brunswick capital Fredericton in 1836.[266] When the diocese was created, he was the obvious choice to lead it, despite the attempt of some fracophone clergy to promote Antoine Gagnon.[267] Fortunately for Walsh, however, Dollard took the view that it would likely be 'better or more convenient' for the Atlantic bishops to form their own province 'and let Canada form another'.[268]

Walsh thus began his campaign with a slim majority on his side. As he told Dollard in July 1847, 'A union of the Laity, clergy, and Bishops in N Brunswick, P.E. Island, N F Land, Cape Breton and Nova Scotia will add immensely to Catholic influence.' The best way to achieve this, he continued, was for the region's bishops 'to meet once a year as they do in

[264] Walsh to Dollard [?30] September 1844, SJDA/DP/416.
[265] See Fraser to Grant, 10 November 1847, SCR/16/91C.
[266] For Dollard, see P. M. Toner, 'The foundations of the Catholic Church in English-speaking New Brunswick', in Toner (ed.), *New Ireland*, 63–70, at 63–6.
[267] See LeBlanc, 109.
[268] Dollard to Walsh, 28 March 1844, PICRA/CUL/NC/4/1844/17.

Ireland'.[269] Two years later he '*most anxiously*' urged Dollard to join him at the seventh provincial council of Baltimore, partly to introduce him to friendly Irish-American bishops and partly to demonstrate the benefits of regular councils.[270] Here, Walsh was again following Cullen's lead. In 1844, Cullen had told Fleming that he, Walsh, and Dollard should 'hold a private meeting such as bishops hold in Ireland' in order to 'put down French and Scotch intriguing' and secure their own ecclesiastical province.[271] In Walsh's view, nothing else offered protection against present and future hostility from Canada, which he absurdly claimed had become the last refuge of 'Old Gallicanism'.[272]

By 1850, the situation again looked critical. The increasingly inert Archbishop Signay had finally given way to his coadjutor, the energetic Pierre-Flavien Turgeon. Almost immediately, he secured Roman permission to hold what would be the first council of the ecclesiastical province of Quebec. As Walsh put it darkly, 'I hope after all that has transpired for the last 7 years they will not have the *indecency* to revive' talk of annexing the Maritimes. If they did, he continued, 'I will act as before, and even with more determination.'[273] His fears were heightened when he received a suspiciously flattering letter from Turgeon appointing him honorary vicar general of Quebec. He sent a barely polite reply, telling Dollard it was all part of a campaign to 'pave the way for the renewal of their foolish project; the Metropolitan Union of all British North America'.[274]

It was through this lens that Walsh understood rumours that a new diocese would be carved out of northern New Brunswick to serve its rapidly growing Acadian population. This was one of the first manifestations of what would become a long-standing Acadian ambition, one that was not finally fulfilled until 1912. (Denying the Acadians ecclesiastical preferment was one of the very few things on which the Irish and Scots could be counted to agree.) If Dollard was amenable to such a division, Walsh wrote, it was imperative that the request came from him and 'no one else, and above all no one in Canada ought to be permitted to [meddle] in the matter'. He should also provide the candidates. If he was opposed, he could propose that a coadjutor of his choice be appointed to look after the Acadians. Either of these options, Walsh concluded, would be far better 'than if a stranger were sent in upon you by strangers'.[275] He was relieved to discover that Dollard was also 'fully alive to the disinterested intentions of

---

[269] Walsh to Dollard, 21 July 1847, SJDA/DP/431.
[270] Walsh to Dollard, 24 April 1849, SJDA/DP/434. Emphasis in original.
[271] Cullen to Fleming, 4 October 1844, ARCSJ/FP/103–10/3.
[272] Walsh to Cullen, [?10] September 1847, PICRA/CUL/NC/4/1847/41.
[273] Walsh to Dollard, 5 July 1850, SJDA/DP/446. Emphasis in original.
[274] Walsh to Dollard, 7 November 1850, SJDA/DP/443.   [275] Ibid.

our Canadian friends' and advised that, since New Brunswick only had some 50,000 Catholics, he should 'steadily resist every attempt at *dismemberment*'.[276]

The threat was to more than just New Brunswick. Walsh reminded Dollard of Upper Canada, where the bishop of Bytown was a French Oblate, the bishop of Toronto a French Sulpician, and the coadjutor bishop of Kingston an Irish one. 'If the present system be fully developed as at Toronto and Bytown', Walsh wrote, 'we may expect to have the present Bps of Fredericton, Arichat and Halifax, replaced by courtly and obsequious Prelates of another country who will no doubt be very obsequious to the British Government.' This prospect was particularly grotesque in the light of the No Popery agitation then roiling the United Kingdom; but, while the British threat was real, Walsh concluded, 'for the Independence of our Dioceses in this part of B. N. America I dread Canadians more than I do Lord John Russell'.[277]

Yet he was still hopeful. 'We have never had a better chance of getting an Eccl Province than now', he told Dollard, 'for it is the present policy of the Court of Rome to multiply them.'[278] Just to be sure he enlisted both Kirby and the visiting John Hughes in the cause and contemplated heading for Rome himself.[279] Although haste was important, Walsh also recognized that he had to be careful about seeming ambitious for himself. As he told Hughes in February 1851, 'I will be perfectly satisfied with any Metropolitan the Holy See provided it be not in Canada.'[280] He said much the same to Dollard.[281] This was sincere but disingenuous: Walsh knew that Halifax was the only plausible place.

The good news, he told Dollard in July 1851, was that Rome was 'fully prepared to grant' a new province once the situation in Arichat was resolved. He was still wary, however, urging his colleague to write to Cardinal Fransoni 'before any action be taken by Canada'.[282] In the meantime, Walsh was buoyed by what he took to be the failure of Quebec's provincial council. Both he and Dollard had refused to attend, and Mullock of Newfoundland had only gone because he thought he had to. (The letter exempting him had apparently been marooned for nearly a year on the French island of St Pierre.)[283] MacDonald of Prince Edward Island had attended but concluded that union with Quebec was a

[276] Walsh to Dollard, 4 December 1850, SJDA/DP/448. Emphasis in original.
[277] Walsh to Dollard, 22 March 1851, SJDA/DP/450.
[278] Walsh to Dollard, 22 March 1851, SJDA/DP/450.
[279] Kirby to Walsh [January] 1851, AAH/WP.
[280] Walsh to Hughes, 12 February 1851, AANY/HP/Box 3/Folder 9.
[281] Walsh to Dollard, 25 July 1851, SJDA/DP/453.
[282] Walsh to Dollard, 25 July 1851, SJDA/DP/453.
[283] Walsh to Dollard, 6 August 1851, SJDA/DP/454.

mistake. 'I hope', Walsh wrote in mid-August, 'there is now a reasonable prospect of our having the comfort and convenience of a Province amongst ourselves.'[284] The following month, Hughes reported from Rome that Fransoni and Alessandro Barnabò were supportive and some documents already appeared to assume the existence of a new province. What they did not contain, however, was the identity of the new archbishop. If the Maritime bishops could be prevailed upon collectively to write on the matter, Hughes reported, 'the appointment would be immediate – and then I should have the pleasure of addressing His Grace the Abp of Halifax'.[285]

While Walsh waited, however, the Irish faction suffered a sudden loss with the death of William Dollard in late August 1851. Despite long-standing ill health, Dollard's death came as an unwelcome surprise, but it also represented a useful opportunity to remake the Maritime hierarchy; Dollard was Irish, and had been an ally, but he was of the older, missionary generation that Walsh was determined to supplant. His preferred successor had apparently been a young Irish-born protégé, John Sweeny, but Walsh's enquiries suggested he was not universally popular, and he most likely never seriously considered recommending him.[286] Walsh was convinced that what was wanted was a 'stranger', but he was unwilling to make any suggestions himself on the grounds he was not yet an archbishop and had not yet been asked. Instead, he privately urged that the Irish College try and arrange that Cullen be asked 'to select *the best man he can get in the Irish Church* (with some knowledge of French) and he should be consecrated and sent forthwith'. A worried Walsh knew that 'any other plan will be attended with difficulty and delay, and delay in these countries is *death!*'[287] Throwing the appointment on Cullen was his best chance of avoiding Canadian interference.

Yet this was not how Rome worked. A formal consultation was required, multiple candidates offered, meetings held, and procedures followed. Cullen was often asked for suggestions, and those suggestions were very often followed, but appointments were never placed in his sole gift. Walsh's formal appointment as archbishop of Halifax in November 1851 rendered the problem moot, although as late as March 1852 he was still fretting about 'the ambitious intrigues of the Canadians who want to grasp the whole of British N. America, though they are hardly able to keep

---

[284] Walsh to Dollard, 15 August 1851, SJDA/DP/455.
[285] Hughes to Walsh, 25 September 1851, AAH/WP.
[286] For Sweeny, see K. Fay Trombley, *Thomas Louis Connolly (1815–1876): The Man and His Place in Secular and Ecclesiastical History* (Leuven: Katholieke Universiteit Leuven Faculty of Theology, 1983), 102.
[287] Walsh to Smith, 16 September 1851, quoted in Trombley, 103.

the faith amongst their people'.[288] In reality, however, Quebec was no longer relevant: Walsh now had the right to express his opinion, and the only other surviving bishop in the new province (which excluded Newfoundland) was the passive Bernard Donald MacDonald. He could recommend whomever he wished, and, in answer to the Propaganda's query, he named Colin MacKinnon and Thomas Louis Connolly. As MacKinnon was clearly destined for Arichat, his inclusion was presumably a means of meeting the congregation's long-standing requirement that it be given options. Connolly was his real and only choice. As Walsh put it when the appointment was confirmed in early 1852, 'If all America were ransacked a more fitting and capable person could not be selected.'[289]

New Brunswick was not an easy assignment. Irish migration to the province had been steady since at least 1816, and, as in Prince Edward Island, most had come before the Famine – in New Brunswick, they likely outnumbered Famine-era arrivals by around four to one.[290] Ireland was also the province's largest source of immigrants. Between 1840 and 1845, for example, some 90 per cent of the 33,000 migrants who landed had sailed from Irish ports.[291] Even more would have embarked from British ports such as Liverpool. Although many moved on, substantial Irish populations developed in Saint John, Fredericton, and the Miramichi region of the north-east; in the timber port of Saint John, for example, more than half the heads of household in 1851 were Irishmen.[292] As a result, New Brunswick became what Peter Toner has described as 'the most Irish province in British North America'.[293]

As was often the case in Canada, there was a significant Protestant element among the New Brunswick Irish. This was especially true for those who arrived before the Famine, although Catholic migration was always significant. By mid-century, however, Catholics were probably in a majority among the Irish, comprising around 60 per cent of those who had arrived and remained. Presbyterians and adherents of the Church of Ireland comprised some 15 per cent each, with smaller Protestant denominations making up the rest.[294] This resulted in significant Catholic strength across the province, and not simply in the Acadian heartlands in the north. In the Miramichi, for example, nearly 83 per

[288] Walsh to Bayley, 26 March 1852, AANY/HP/Box 4, Folder 5.
[289] Walsh to Smith, 29 April 1852, quoted in Trombley, 106.
[290] P. M. Toner, 'The 1851 census', in Toner, *New Ireland*, 110.
[291] See William A. Spray, 'Receptions of the Irish in New Brunswick', in Toner, *New Ireland*, 9–10.
[292] T. W. Acheson, *Saint John: The Making of a Colonial Urban Community* (Toronto: University of Toronto Press, 1985), 93.
[293] Toner, *New Ireland*, 3–4.   [294] Toner, '1851 census', 111.

cent of the Irish population was Catholic, as was around a third of the total population of Fredericton by the late 1850s.[295] The inevitable result was sectarian tension, especially as Protestants were a significant majority of the province as a whole.

The sectarian fracturing in the Irish community began to accelerate in the early 1840s. This was largely a consequence of the success Dollard and an energetic Irish priest called James Dunphy had enjoyed in rallying Irish Catholics around repeal of the union, loyalty to the bishop, and a more visible and politically assertive Catholicism.[296] Dunphy even founded a newspaper, *The St. John Liberator and Irish Advocate*, to pursue these causes. This in turn encouraged the rapid spread of the Orange Order: in 1844, there were 27 lodges across the province, many very recently established, but by 1850 that had grown to 123 lodges with perhaps 10,000 members.[297] The result was easily foreseeable: as early as July 1845, *The Liberator* warned young Catholics against carrying arms or responding to Orange provocations, and between 1847 and 1849 serial rioting claimed at least twenty lives.[298]

The Catholic Church in New Brunswick was not well placed to respond to this challenge. Before the creation of the diocese in 1842 it was dependent on Charlottetown or Quebec for resources, with predictable consequences. A handful of priests of various nationalities served at one time or another, but there were not many, they built little, and most made no enduring impression. Saint John in particular was roiled by internal conflicts, first in the mid-1820s and then again from the early 1840s. Dunphy's implacable opposition to what he saw as lay meddling provoked heated resistance, with competing petitions decrying 'his dictatorial sway over the parish' and demanding Dollard remove him, while others praised his 'unceasing assiduity and perhaps unparalleled industry' and begged that he be retained. Both were published in the newspapers.[299] Dollard finally moved to Saint John in an attempt to restore order, and once there refused demands to remove Dunphy, sanction the election of church wardens, or transfer church temporalities to lay control, arranging instead for a bill creating an episcopal corporation to be presented to the legislature. It passed in 1846 with the vociferous support of *The Liberator*, helpfully

---

[295] Ibid., 126; Scott W. See, *Riots in New Brunswick: Orange Nativism and Social Violence in the 1840s* (Toronto: University of Toronto Press, 1993), 35.

[296] Acheson, 102–6.

[297] Scott W. See, 'The fortunes of the Orange Order in 19th century New Brunswick', in Toner, *New Ireland*, 95–6.

[298] *The Liberator*, 19 July 1845. For the years of rioting, see See, *Riots in New Brunswick*.

[299] *New Brunswick Courier*, 18, 23 May 1844.

amplified by Dunphy's threat to excommunicate any Catholic bold enough to oppose it.[300]

By 1850, Dollard's assertion of episcopal authority and the unifying effect of sectarian violence had largely brought peace to the New Brunswick church. Difficulties remained, including the bitter political climate, a lack of resources, and an Acadian population whose growing size and confidence had already led to calls to divide the diocese. The shortage of personnel was a particular challenge: there were no nuns, and a steady supply of suitable priests remained frustratingly out of reach – among other problems, several of the students Dollard sent to the Séminaire de Québec complained bitterly that the staff there habitually 'wounded our feelings as Irishmen'.[301] Without clerical labour it would be impossible to build the sort of ecclesiastical infrastructure that Walsh was beginning to create in Halifax. Yet Dollard had still achieved an enormous amount: new parishes, more priests, even a cathedral of sorts in Fredericton. Shortly before his death there were some thirty-two priests and sixty-four churches serving a Catholic population of about 50,000.[302] Dollard was tireless, linguistically gifted (English, Irish, French, and some Mi'kmaq), and on good terms with the government.[303] When it became necessary to assert his authority in Saint John and elsewhere, he did not hesitate. He was the last and most effective of the region's missionary bishops.

Thomas Connolly was different. Born in Cork in 1814, he had entered the Capuchins in 1832 before being sent on to Rome to complete his studies. He was ordained in France in 1838, served for several years in Dublin, and accompanied Walsh to Halifax in 1842 where he served first as his chaplain and then as vicar general. He was confident, gregarious, and usefully multilingual; Archbishop Hughes, who was not really the best judge of such matters, thought he spoke 'Italian almost like a Roman'.[304] His consecration in Halifax became what amounted to a carnival of Hiberno-Maritime Catholicism: Hughes was invited both to preach and to dedicate the new parish church of St Patrick, the two convents put on 'exhibitions', some 1,500 children paraded through the streets behind 'religious banners', and seven new churches were blessed in seven weeks. As Walsh boasted to Cullen, 'For nearly a fortnight we had something new every day, and the result has been most satisfactory.'[305]

---

[300] Acheson, 102–5.
[301] Dennis Dunne to Dollard, 11 December 1846, SJDA/DP/656.   [302] Trombley, 113.
[303] Toner, 'Foundations', 64–5.
[304] Hughes to Smith, 29 December 1857, AANY/HP/A7.
[305] Walsh to Cullen, 26 August 1852, DDA/CP/325/1/II/144.

In New Brunswick, Connolly moved quickly. His immediate focus was on Saint John, where he promptly raised $25,000 to purchase land for a cemetery and a cathedral and established several schools.[306] He also gathered his clergy together, imposed order, and began a search for nuns. Within weeks of his consecration he visited the Sisters of Charity in New York, where he was refused on the grounds that they did not have women to spare.[307] He then appealed to Archbishop Hughes, telling him that 'I know you are all powerful if you only say yes.'[308] Thus motivated the sisters agreed to train New Brunswickers in New York, with three arriving in early 1854 before returning to Saint John later that year to care for the orphans created by a cholera epidemic. In 1855, Connolly turned his own house over to the community. Like Walsh, he also imported the Religious of the Sacred Heart directly from New York.[309] With all this activity it was little wonder that Walsh thought that 'Dr Connolly has opened his career in N. Brunswick in a very promising manner, and, thank God, every thing looks bright in that direction.'[310]

Connolly was also pleased with his progress. As he told Mullock of Newfoundland in May 1854, 'Our Catholics are every day growing more numerous and more influential and will in time please God be able to defend themselves.' His greatest worry was what he called the province's 'rampant North of Ireland Orangeism'. 'There is not a more bigoted & besotted den in the world', he wrote.[311] The Orange threat, however, did have its uses, especially as New Brunswick was transitioning to responsible government. As he explained to Nova Scotia's still-friendly Joseph Howe during the 1854 general election, he had 'succeeded in amalgamating the discordant elements of Catholicity in this province so as to present a bold and united front against our friends the Orangemen'. As a result, they had already 'gained five seats from the enemy' and were optimistic in four or five more.[312] Such unity had an immediate effect. In Saint John County, for example, the incumbent claimed that all but five of the some 500 Catholic electors had voted for his Liberal opponent, William Ritchie, whose margin of victory was six.[313] Ritchie then promptly became a leading figure in a new Liberal administration that, among

---

[306] Connolly to Hughes, 'New Year's day' [1853], AANY/HP/Box 2/Folder 18; Trombley, 114–15.

[307] Trombley, 117.

[308] Connolly to Hughes, 'New Year's Day' [1853], AANY/HP/Box 2/Folder 18.

[309] Trombley, 123–34.

[310] Walsh to Cullen, 12 November 1852, DDA/CP/325/1/II/145.

[311] Connolly to Mullock, 3 May 1854, ARCSJ/MP/104/1/8.

[312] Connolly to Howe, 10 June 1854, LAC/HP/MG24 B29/vol. 2/pp. 251–4.

[313] W. S. MacNutt, *New Brunswick, a History: 1784–1867* (Toronto: MacMillan of Canada, 1963), 378.

other things, lowered the franchise qualification and thus increased the number of Catholic electors. There was no doubting that Catholics had become a force to be reckoned with in provincial life.

The polarization brought about by the advent of responsible government in New Brunswick had already occurred in Nova Scotia. In 1847, the first election campaign under the new system had degenerated into bitter sectarianism, with the government and its allies warning against Catholic aggression and pointing out that the opposition Liberals relied on Catholic votes. Howe was even accused of converting to Catholicism after he attended Mass on St Patrick's Day in his capacity as president of the non-denominational Charitable Irish Society.[314] Walsh and *The Cross* entered the campaign with relish, defending Catholicism and Ireland with equal vigour against those they deemed guilty of the 'diabolical crime of stirring up religious feuds amongst a people who were disposed to live together in peace and good will'.[315] Walsh called this 'a chastising hand' and boasted of his 'castigation of the Nova Scotian bigots'.[316]

In the event, the Liberals won a convincing majority, including all four Halifax seats. The Protestant press complained that they had been defeated by the Irish 'Walshite' vote, noting that all but a handful of Catholics in the capital had plumped for the Liberals.[317] Walsh was understandably delighted, telling Hughes that 'Our Anti-Catholic and Tory government has been prostrated, and we now have in Office a Cabinet Council of Nine staunch Liberals.' These included several Catholics, including his long-standing allies Lawrence O'Connor Doyle and Michael Tobin. 'Toryism', he proclaimed, 'is at an end in British N. America.'[318] The alliance served both sides well: the Catholics gained access to power and patronage, as well as desiderata such as the creation of an episcopal corporation in Halifax, while the Liberals secured the political loyalty of a significant slice of the population. The result was that the party dominated provincial politics until Howe's outbursts almost a decade later.

That betrayal infuriated Walsh. As he explained to Cullen in early 1857, 'A most diabolical attempt was made here at Christmas to raise a No Popery Cry in Nova Scotia by an ungrateful wretch named Howe who owed all his political position for a quarter of a century to the Catholics.' He had 'grappled with the villain at once, and gave him a most unmerciful

---

[314] See J. Murray Beck, *Joseph Howe, Vol. 1, Conservative Reformer 1804–1848* (Montreal and Kingston: McGill-Queens University Press, 1982), 305.

[315] *The Cross*, 27 February 1847.   [316] Walsh to Dollard, 14 April 1857, SJDA/DP/430.

[317] Beck, *Conservative Reformer*, 309.

[318] Walsh to Hughes, 17 February 1848, CU/HBP/MS 1296/Series 1/Sub-series 1/Box 3/ Folder 5.

drubbing, so that all his apprentices were scared away, and he has been forced to eat his own words'. 'We are now', he continued, 'ensuring his total ejection from office, and the destruction of the government.'[319] For his part, Howe refused to bow his 'soul to the Priests and rowdies', attempted to set up a Protestant Association, and asked whether Nova Scotians should 'bend the knee to the Catholic Archbishop, now our political master and ruler'.[320] The inevitable result was an alliance between the Catholics and the more ideologically flexible Conservatives.

Politics was not Walsh's only or even primary concern. He continued to recruit nuns and priests, build the archdiocese's infrastructure, and erect as many schools, convents, and churches as his means would allow. Like all Hiberno-Roman bishops, he was also concerned to secure the Catholic population from proselytism and unnecessary mixing with Protestants. Among other things, he complained when Catholic children were forced to attend Protestant services in the poorhouse or the British government failed to provide adequate chaplaincy facilities to the Halifax garrison.[321] He was particularly exercised by the practice of fostering out the younger children of parents who had sought refuge in the poorhouse. It was cruel and unjust, he complained to Howe in 1854, to reduce 'poor Catholic Parents' to the 'dreadful alternative of being driven from the Poor House if they do not surrender their hapless offspring, and permit them to be boarded out in their tender age to those who are sure to rear them in a different religion'.[322]

From his own perspective, Walsh's greatest achievement came in September 1857, when he finally realized his long-standing goal of convening a provincial council for the ecclesiastical province of Halifax. That it had taken some five years was largely down to Walsh's own chronic ill health. Never strong, by the mid-1850s he was marooned in Europe trying to recover from an operation, and as early as 1856 Cullen feared for his life. 'You see', he told Kirby, 'the best go first' while 'old good for nothing fogies like me and you are spared'.[323] When Walsh finally felt well enough to gather the region's bishops in Halifax, he boasted to Cullen that it had all passed off 'with considerable éclat'. His only complaint was that Newfoundland's two bishops had refused to attend. They were, he grumbled, the only ones in 'all British N. America who stand apart from

---

[319] Walsh to Cullen, 16 February 1857, DDA/CP/339/5/II/4.
[320] Quoted in Beck, *Briton Becomes Canadian*, 119.
[321] Walsh to Howe, 22 March 1854, PANS/HP/vol. 2/247–50; Walsh to Thomas Grant, 10 February, 'Palm Sunday' 1857, AAS/GP.
[322] Walsh to Howe, 23 March 1854, PANS/HP/vol. 2/251–4.
[323] Cullen to Kirby, 17 December 1856, PICRA/NK/Carton II/Folder I/155.

their brothers'; but it didn't matter. 'I think', he told Cullen, 'you will be pleased with our decrees.'[324]

There was no risk that he would not be. Halifax was a typical Hiberno-Roman council, following closely on the model of Philadelphia, Thurles, and Baltimore and foreshadowing others such as Maynooth in 1875 and Sydney in 1886. Among other things, it decreed that the Roman liturgy would be used across the province, reiterated the already strict treatment of mixed marriages, and established procedures for the election of bishops.[325] There seems to have been little dissent, despite the province consisting of two Irish and two Scottish bishops; the Roman MacKinnon was unlikely to object to what were very Roman decrees, and Bernard Donald MacDonald was unlikely to object to anything at all. Connolly carried the draft to Rome, where Kirby reported that the 'celebrated act in the ecclesiastical annals of Halifax' had found favour.[326] The Propaganda and the pope duly gave their assent, and for many decades the council provided the ecclesiastical framework for the Catholic Church in the Maritimes.

The council was Walsh's swansong. By May 1858, his 'fits' had apparently become so frequent that thoughts were inevitably beginning to turn to the succession. 'If anything serious should happen in Halifax', Connolly told Hughes in New York, 'you will have the earliest information and to you and to you alone I will look for advice.'[327] There was no question that Connolly wanted the job. While Walsh was still on his deathbed, he wrote a lengthy letter to Dublin setting out his stall. The problem, Cullen learned, was that a small group of 'half-educated and inexperienced young men' were trying to influence the dying archbishop to recommend one of them. This would never do, and in fact there was 'not one in the whole Archdiocese that could be thought of for a single moment'. What was at stake was nothing less than continued Irish dominance. 'We have here', he wrote, 'two Scotch Bishops with a strong National bias', but there was no one 'in all Nova Scotia competent to represent Irish Catholic interests in Rome.' He did not know anyone, anywhere 'for whose appointment I would be conscientiously responsible', begged Cullen to help, and promised that 'whomsoever you recommend I will place first on the list when called on by the Propaganda'.

Connolly then did the one thing necessary for a man angling for ecclesiastical preferment: he denied in detail that he wanted it. Speaking in the third person, he admitted 'that both the Scotch bishops and the

[324] Walsh to Cullen, 27 November 1857, DDA/CP/339/5/II/45.   [325] Trombley, 157–8.
[326] Kirby to Walsh, 20 February 1858, HDA/WP.
[327] Connolly to Hughes, 25 May 1858, CU/BP/MS 1296/Series I/Sub-series 1/Box 2/ Folder 3.

majority of the Priests of Nova Scotia and the public at large both Catholic and Protestant would wish Dr Connolly to be the new Archbishop'; but, he continued, he could not possibly leave New Brunswick: it was a new diocese, riddled with debt, and far too challenging for a new man to come to grips with. He would resist his removal by all legitimate means. Yet he also admitted that he was 'conscientiously opposed to any other but an Irishman', could see no one in the archdiocese with even 'a tenth of the qualities required', and feared a 'disastrous appointment'. To avoid that calamity, he would reluctantly 'sacrifice natural feelings as dear to me as life' but only if he could name his own successor. To make sure Cullen got the message, he added a postscript: 'To prevent a Scotchman or a foreigner or any of the Nova Scotia Priests being foisted into such a position justice and gratitude and the honour of Religion and my love for the people of the country would exact from me any imaginable sacrifice.'[328] Walsh died two days later.

This was not especially subtle, but it was effective. Cullen did not know Connolly well, and had no special knowledge of Halifax, but he knew none of the local priests at all. He was also receptive to Connolly's appeal to Irish solidarity. This all mattered, as there appears to have been no significant domestic support for the Capuchin. The mostly Irish canons of the cathedral were opposed, partly from personal ambition, but so were at least some other priests otherwise opposed to the canons. As one told the French bishop of Toronto, Connolly lacked the 'sincerity – truthfulness – and honourable conduct' necessary in a bishop.[329] Even Archbishop Hughes, whom Connolly had approached in similarly faux reluctant terms, told Cullen that the Irishman would be unacceptable to both the clergy and the laity of Halifax.[330] Everybody thought Cullen should decide: Hughes appealed for him to recommend 'some suitable Irish priest', while the Halifax priest John Woods privately hoped that the 'great and good Archbishop' might 'have a salutary influence on the mind of the Propaganda'.[331] In the end, both Cullen and Rome took the obvious path, and Connolly was appointed in March 1859.[332]

Connolly's elevation allowed him to remake the region's hierarchy in a stroke. There was now a vacancy in Saint John, the ailing Bernard Donald MacDonald of Prince Edward Island needed a coadjutor, and Rome had

---

[328] Connolly to Cullen, 10 August 1858, DDA/CP/319/19/11/38. Emphasis in original.
[329] John Woods to Armand-François-Marie de Charbonnel, 4 August 1858, TAA/CAB1446.
[330] Connolly to Hughes, 30 August 1858, AANY/HP/Box 2/Folder 18; Hughes to Cullen, 17 December 1858, DDA/CP/319/1/II/56.
[331] Hughes to Cullen, 17 December 1858, DDA/CP/319/1/II/56; Woods to Charbonnel, 6 December 1858, TAA/CAB1482.
[332] Bernard Smith to Hughes, 8 March 1859, CU/BP/MS 1296/Series 1/Box 3/Folder 1.

agreed to erect a new diocese at Chatham in northern New Brunswick. As he boasted to Hughes in June, 'I will call a meeting of the suffragans in Halifax and our first act will be to nominate three Bishops!'[333] Prince Edward Island was still far too Scottish to attempt an Irish candidate, and Connolly seems not to have objected to Peter McIntyre's appointment. In New Brunswick, however, he had his way. His choice for Saint John was his Irish-born vicar general John Sweeny, while for Chatham he selected James Rogers, a thirty-three-year-old Irish-born Halifax priest.[334] Sweeny had once been Dollard's preferred successor, while Rogers had already served as a rural missionary, on Bermuda, and as Connolly's secretary.[335] Both men enjoyed long episcopates, with Sweeny living until 1901 and Rogers until 1903.

Yet Connolly, Rogers, and to a lesser extent Sweeny were not cut from the same cloth as Walsh, let alone Cullen's protégé Thomas Power in neighbouring Newfoundland. Nor were they as Roman as their Scottish episcopal neighbours, who had imbibed their ultramontanism at the Propaganda or in Quebec. Connolly's Roman experience had been that of a Capuchin, while Sweeny and Rogers had no Roman experience at all. Their formations were different and their loyalties lay elsewhere. Cullen had supported Connolly (and thus Sweeny and Rogers) because he trusted Walsh, not because he knew Connolly.

He realized his mistake in 1870, when all three of the Maritime Irish opposed the definition of papal infallibility at the Vatican Council. Connolly and Rogers were among the relative handful (88 of more than 600) brave enough to record their *non placet*, while Sweeny abstained.[336] They were the only Canadians to do so.[337] Nor was this a quiet dissent: Connolly worked closely with the Anglo-German layman Lord Acton (nephew of the late Cardinal Acton) to organize the opposition and boasted to him that he would become the council's most 'determined opponent' (*entschiedenste Gegner*) of infallibility.[338] Not even a threatening late-night meeting with Cardinal Barnabò could deter him.[339] As the council's most recent historian put it, Connolly became 'an impressive

[333] Connolly to Hughes, 15 June 1859, AANY/HP/Box 2/Folder 18.   [334] Ibid.

[335] See Laurie C. C. Stanley, 'ROGERS, James', in *DCB*.

[336] Cuthbert Butler, *The Vatican Council: The Story Told from Inside in Archbishop Ullathorne's letters*, 2 vols. (London: Longmans, Green and Co., 1930), 2: 150–1.

[337] Acton to Döllinger, 20 May 1870, in *Döllinger Briefwechsel*, 2: 361. Original in German.

[338] Acton met with Connolly regularly, and Connolly relied on Acton for intelligence about developments in the council. See Connolly to Acton, 'Monday morning', 'Monday evening', CUL/Add. MS. 8119(1)/C193, 194; Acton to Döllinger, 16 January 1870, *Döllinger Briefwechsel*, 2: 95. Original in German.

[339] Acton to Döllinger, 22 January 1870, *Döllinger Briefwechsel*, 2: 106. Original in German.

and persuasive voice for the minority position'.[340] Cullen unsurprisingly had a different view, remarking after Connolly's speech against the final definition in June 1870 that he had 'made a most foolish and offensive speech' and become 'a laughing stock for all'.[341] Even sympathetic observers admitted that he had failed to produce 'the impression expected by his friends'.[342] Connolly submitted when the doctrine was defined and later declined Acton's request to publish his speeches, but he and his protégés had made their divergence from orthodox Hiberno-Romanism crystal clear.[343]

At home, Connolly took a leading part in public affairs, from welcoming the Prince of Wales to excoriating the Fenians as 'wretched, deluded and godless'.[344] He continued Walsh's building programme, erecting among other things several schools, a convent, and an orphanage to his own architectural designs.[345] He also began work on what is now St Mary's basilica. He encouraged the expansion of the Sisters of Charity, welcomed the Irish Christian Brothers in 1862, and continued to patronize Irish associations and encourage displays of Irish identity. He was conscious enough of his own Irishness to refuse to call on Cardinal Wiseman when he visited London, something he admitted was motivated by 'petty national spite'.[346] More appealingly, he was famously relaxed with the Sisters of Charity, and there is a probably apocryphal story that when bored he hoisted a flag from his country house as a signal for the women at the nearby convent to come over for an evening of music and singing.[347]

Naturally, not everything went well. The Sisters of Charity, for example, were forced to close their home for female delinquents after only a year after failing to control the inmates, while the Christian Brothers left the diocese in high dudgeon in 1876.[348] Nor were his relations with his episcopal neighbours entirely smooth. Rogers was unfailingly loyal, but he came to despair of Sweeny's more

---

[340] John W. O'Malley, *Vatican I: The Council and the Making of the Ultramontane Church* (Cambridge, MA: The Belknap Press of Harvard University Press, 2018), 147.

[341] Cullen to Edward McCabe, 23 June 1870, DDA/CP/40/4.

[342] Odo Russell to Lord Clarendon, 24 June 1870, in Noel Blakiston (ed.), *The Roman question: Extracts from the Despatches of Odo Russell from Rome 1858–1870*, new ed. (Wilmington, DE: Michael Glazier, Inc., 1980), 448.

[343] Connolly to Acton, 30 June 1872, CUL/Add. MS. 8119(1)/C192.

[344] Quoted in Trombley, 252.   [345] Trombley, 461.

[346] Connolly to Cullen, 28 May 1866, DDA/CP/327/5/III/10.

[347] See P. B. Waite, *The Man from Halifax: Sir John Thompson, Prime Minister* (Toronto: University of Toronto Press, 1985), 61.

[348] For the failure of the Charity's House of Mercy, which Connolly housed in his summer retreat, see Judith Fingard, *The Dark Side of Life in Victorian Halifax* (Porters Lake, NS: Pottersfield Press, 1989), 137–8.

confrontational political style and continued to spar with MacKinnon, who once told him that something he had written had in 'true Hibernian style' contained 'almost as many inaccuracies as words'.[349] He also took little interest in non-Irish Catholics, something he had in common with his peers across Greater Ireland, and even sympathetic scholars have noted his programmatic neglect of the Acadians and Mi'kmaq.[350]

In politics, Connolly was an enthusiastic conservative who delighted in the sectarian divisions of Nova Scotia politics. As he explained to Sweeny in 1861, it was 'an unfortunate thing for Catholicity in the province that your Politicians are not in two hostile camps as here'.[351] He understood that the Conservative's dependence on the large Catholic vote gave him leverage and position, and he cultivated a mutually beneficial relationship with their leader Charles Tupper. After confederation, he was similarly supportive of the federal leader Sir John A. Macdonald, who in 1867 became Canada's first prime minister. Not all of Connolly's causes were well chosen. His support for the Confederacy in the American civil war, for example, was so extreme that one smitten southern lady declared she would 'vote for him for pope tomorrow', while in late 1865 he presented the exiled daughter of Jefferson Davis with 'a gold cross with amethysts and surrounded with emeralds'.[352]

Connolly's modern reputation rests largely on his support for Canadian confederation. He publicly endorsed it, privately lobbied for it, and visited London three times to secure its terms. Although he believed in the case on its own merits – among other things, he feared American economic and political power – his stated interest was in securing Catholic educational rights across the new country. He wanted guarantees that religious minorities in every province would receive aid similar to that offered to the Protestants of Lower Canada, and he lobbied both provincial delegates and the Colonial Office to include such guarantees in the new federal constitution. He failed: education would remain a provincial matter, although the final text did include an ultimately ineffectual right of appeal if religious minorities were being treated unjustly.

Failure did not cool Connolly's ardour, nor did the fact that confederation was wildly unpopular in Nova Scotia. In the first federal election, for example, he issued a pastoral letter declaring he would be voting for pro-union candidates and asked his flock to do the same. The result was that

---

[349] MacKinnon to Connolly, n.d. [probably 1864], ADA/MP/fonds 3/series 1/sub series 1.
[350] Trombley, 287–91.   [351] Connolly to Sweeny, 1 March 1861, SJDA/SP/1424.
[352] For the southern lady, see Greg Marquis, *In Armageddon's Shadow: The Civil War and Canada's Maritime Provinces* (Montréal and Kingston: McGill-Queen's University Press, 1988), 92. For Miss Davis' gift, see *The True Witness & Catholic Chronicle* (Montreal), 3 November 1865, 5.

the Catholic vote split, and anti-confederates led by Joseph Howe secured eighteen of the nineteen federal ridings and thirty-six of the thirty-eight seats in the provincial legislature.[353] Connolly was undaunted by the rebuke and promptly offered Sir John A. Macdonald his assistance in managing the new parliamentarians. Among other things, he suggested that peace could be restored if Howe were offered suitably juicy inducements.[354] Macdonald listened, Howe responded, and Connolly delightedly told the prime minister that he could now safely return to 'my beads and my sanctuary ... until some extraordinary and unforeseen emergency will call me forth again'.[355] Connolly's contribution to Canadian confederation was undeniably important, but it had very little to do with religion.

Indeed, it is difficult to escape the impression that Connolly was often prepared to put his own political interests above what his peers would have considered the interests of his flock. This was most obviously the case with the invariable flashpoint of education. He was undeniably committed to Catholic education, and worked hard to obtain it, but he never pressed Catholic claims so far as to compromise his political alliances. In 1865, for example, Charles Tupper assured him that his proposed system of free schools was safe on the novel grounds that simple demography ensured that Catholics would always be represented in the provincial cabinet, the provincial cabinet would always be ultimately responsible for the schools, and therefore Connolly had 'a permanent guarantee of justice to your people'.[356] Connolly agreed, and the Catholic schools in Halifax entered the public system under what amounted to a 'gentlemen's agreement' that their interests would be protected.[357] In 1867, he backed down when Tupper refused to consider a new bid for separate schools before the first federal election, and by 1874 he was prepared to tell Rogers that Nova Scotia's system was far superior to the separate schools for which Catholics were then campaigning in New Brunswick.[358]

This informal system slowly spread from Halifax to other areas of the province with significant Catholic populations, and by the end of the century one of Connolly's successors could boast that fully

---

[353] Trombley, 354.

[354] Trombley, 357–8; for the negotiations between Macdonald and Howe, see Beck, *Briton Becomes Canadian*: chaps. 10–11.

[355] Connolly to Macdonald, 6 October 1869, quoted in Trombley, 359.

[356] Quoted in E. M. Saunders, *The Life and Letters of the Right Hon. Sir Charles Tupper Bart., K.C.M.G.*, 2 vols. (London: Cassell and Company, 1916), 1: 95–6.

[357] See Sr. Francis Xavier, 'Educational legislation in Nova Scotia and the Catholics', *CCHA: Report*, 24 (1957), 63–74 at 71.

[358] Saunders, 1: 150–2; Connolly to Rogers, 23 January 1874, ADDB/1/20.

'nine-elevenths of the Catholic children are attending schools which, whilst not Catholic separate schools, are nevertheless Catholic in tone and free from all possible danger to the Faith'.[359] It was largely down to Connolly that Nova Scotia sidestepped the grinding controversy associated with the issue almost everywhere else in Greater Ireland; even the otherwise unsympathetic MacKinnon attributed the province's relative 'freedom of Education' to the combination of Scottish Catholic electoral might and 'the powerful influence and great popularity of our brave Archbishop in Halifax'.[360] It is difficult, however, to think of another Irish colonial bishop who would have been anything like as flexible, or as trusting.

This policy continued under Connolly's successor, the Limerick-born Michael Hannan. When news of Connolly's death reached Dublin in mid-1876, Cullen inevitably remarked that the 'people are nearly all Irish, and an Irish bishop ought to be appointed'; but, he continued, 'the cannie Scotch will know how to get possession of that see on the plea that the country is called Nova Scotia'.[361] In fact, Hannan was the obvious choice, having served for many years both as vicar general and as an emollient member of Halifax's school commission before Connolly finally sacked him for being beastly to the Sisters of Charity.[362] He had also once been Walsh's confidant and had been placed third on the bishops' *terna* after his death.[363] This time he came top with some Scottish support, largely because they did not think he would 'be inclined to boss his suffragans'.[364] Delays in Rome, however, led to rumours that Cullen was manoeuvring to install his protégé Thomas Power of Newfoundland. Although he flatly denied it, Peter McIntyre of Prince Edward Island was worried enough that he went to Europe to make sure.[365]

Like Connolly, Hannan was an active Conservative and close to Tupper, but unlike Connolly he preferred to operate behind the scenes. He was also a strict disciplinarian and seems to have disapproved of Connolly's social ease, but their differences were largely temperamental. As archbishop, he was relatively ineffectual: among other failings, he

---

[359] Cornelius O'Brien to Falcone, n.d. [c. 1899], quoted in Terrence Murphy, 'Emancipation vs. equity: Civic inclusion of Halifax Catholics, 1830-1865', *CCHA Historical Studies*, forthcoming. I am grateful to Professor Murphy for sharing the typescript of his article with me.
[360] MacKinnon to Rogers, 6 March 1872, ADDB/1/16.
[361] Cullen to Kirby, 31 July 1876, PICRA/KP/1876/31/7.   [362] Trombley, 242.
[363] See, for example, Walsh to Hannan, 14 February 1857, DDA/CP/339/5/II/3. For the *terna*, see the Memorandum dated 4 October 1858, APF/SC/AS/vol. 7/ff. 89–90.
[364] McIntyre to Rogers, 17 April 1877, ADDB/1/27.
[365] McIntyre to MacKinnon, 17 January 1877, CDA/MP; Cullen to Rogers, 6 February 1877, ADDB/1/27.

pursued his vendetta against the Sisters of Charity until Rome humiliatingly transferred jurisdiction over the women to the Propaganda-trained
John Cameron of Antigonish.[366] He died in 1882. Hannan's successor
was the Propaganda-educated Cornelius O'Brien, who largely followed
the approach of his two immediate predecessors. O'Brien was a prolific
builder, erecting a wide range of schools, asylums, hospitals, and reformatories. He also successfully resisted an attempt by the Board of School
Commissioners to take ownership of a school intended for Catholics,
forcing the concession that, while the commission could indeed own the
schools themselves, they would only hire Catholic teachers to teach in
Catholic-majority schools.[367] The result was that Halifax had de facto
separate schools into the early 1970s.[368] O'Brien died in 1906.

Under Connolly the church in Halifax was just as Irish as it had been in
Walsh's time, but Irish Catholics were increasingly well integrated into
provincial life at every level. Sectarian tensions remained – and under
O'Brien education was again briefly a flashpoint – but they were relatively
well contained. This was largely Connolly's doing, and it accounts for the
comparative acceptance in Halifax of what Mark McGowan called 'the
political, cultural, and imperial norms embraced by the charter Protestant
groups'.[369] This was also the case in Toronto and Kingston, which not
coincidentally acquired similar Irish bishops at a similar time.

The comparison with neighbouring New Brunswick is instructive. In
the north, Rogers loyally followed Connolly, regarded the 'British
Constitution as the most perfect form of Civil Government that can be
devised in our present state of human affairs', hammered the Fenians, and
was an enthusiast for confederation;[370] but his attention was increasingly
consumed by crushing debts and the challenge of managing (and latterly
thwarting) the energies unleashed by the Acadian renaissance. In Saint
John, Sweeny was much more assertive, not least in his active opposition
to confederation and later in his persistence in resisting the province's
anti-Catholic school legislation. Like Walsh, he emphasized the creation
of a thick web of Catholic devotional and social associations ranging from
the Father Mathew Association to the Irish Literary and Benevolent
Society to the Sodality of the Sacred Heart of Jesus. He was particularly
keen on a scheme to populate rural New Brunswick with Irish Catholic
migrants, and the settlement named after him at Johnville survives to the
present day.[371]

---

[366] Waite, 61–5.   [367] See Terrence Murphy, 'O'BRIEN, Cornelius', in *DCB*.
[368] Murphy, 'Emancipation vs. equity'.   [369] McGowan, *Imperial Irish*, 50.
[370] Rogers to John M. Johnston, 22 May 1866, ADDB/1/8.
[371] See Terrence Murphy, 'SWEENY, John', in *DCB*.

The primary difference with Nova Scotia (and Prince Edward Island), however, was the presence of a powerful Irish Catholic political leader, Timothy Warren Anglin. Unlike the more accommodating (from 1847) Edward Whelan, his fellow Irish Catholic politician and newspaper proprietor on Prince Edward Island, both Anglin and his newspaper the *Saint John Weekly Freeman* (later *Morning Freeman*) delighted in their uncompromising advocacy of Irish Catholic interests. Born and educated in Ireland, Anglin had migrated to New Brunswick in 1849 where he founded the *Freeman*, entered politics, won a provincial and then a federal seat, and ultimately became speaker of the Canadian House of Commons in 1874. By the late 1850s, he was the leading lay Catholic in Saint John. In 1865, Anglin opposed confederation so vociferously that many of its supporters claimed that he, Sweeny, and the clergy had so overawed Catholic voters as to crush their electoral chances.[372] The fact that Connolly had noisily supported confederation and Rogers had thought opposing it would turn his region into 'a perpetual wilderness' was ignored.[373] It was then alleged that Anglin and the anti-confederates were sympathetic to the Fenians, a point that was amplified by their *opéra bouffe* 'invasion' of New Brunswick in April 1866. As David A. Wilson put it, in New Brunswick the debate over confederation 'became a stand up fight between loyalty and Fenianism'.[374] The resulting anti-Catholic and anti-Irish backlash saw the anti-confederate landslide of 1865 almost exactly reversed in a new election, and the province duly entered confederation with Ontario, Quebec, and Nova Scotia in 1867.

Education was also a flashpoint. In 1871, New Brunswick passed the aggressively secular Common Schools Act, which removed all aid from denominational schools, banned both religious teaching and religious symbolism in state-supported schools, erected barriers to clerical teachers, and made school attendance compulsory. It also levied a special tax to pay for it all. Furious protests only increased tensions, and the government won the 1872 general election on the cry of 'Vote for the Queen against the Pope'.[375] Anglin, Sweeny, and others unsuccessfully appealed to Ottawa and to the Privy Council, and many Catholics had their property seized for non-payment of taxes, including Sweeny. The situation became untenable in 1875 when two men died in rioting

---

[372] William M. Baker, *Timothy Warren Anglin 1822–96: Irish Catholic Canadian* (Toronto: University of Toronto Press, 1977), 76–7.

[373] Rogers to F. Burns, 9 May 1872, ADDB/1/16. Rogers was explaining why he was now endorsing Anglin, despite thinking that his policy on confederation had been madness.

[374] Wilson, *McGee*, 2: 258.

[375] See George G. F. Stanley, 'The Caraquet riots of 1875', in P. A. Buckner and David Frank (eds.), *The Acadiensis Reader, Vol. 2: Atlantic Canada after Confederation* (Fredericton, NB: Acadiensis Press, 1985), 78–95, at 79.

triggered by local Protestants trying to impose the school tax on their Acadian neighbours. The result was a hasty compromise that maintained the principles of the Act while granting some practical concessions. The 'crushed and exhausted' Catholics were left with little alternative but to accept that they could not afford both the school taxes and their own schools. They also feared renewed rioting. It was, Rogers lamented, an 'utter defeat'.[376]

What these debates demonstrated is that sectarianism and ethnicity mattered in New Brunswick (and Prince Edward Island) in a way they no longer did in Nova Scotia. It is hard to imagine either province producing a figure such as the Conservative politician John Thompson, a Catholic convert whose career included stints on the Halifax Board of School Commissioners (1873–7), as provincial premier (1882), justice of the Supreme Court (1882–5), federal minister of justice (1885–92), and finally Canada's fourth prime minister (1892–4).[377] There were many reasons for this, including Nova Scotia's comparatively small *Irish* Catholic population and even smaller Irish *Protestant* population, but the significance of the more worldly, more emollient, and more pragmatic approach of Connolly and his successors should not be underestimated; it was no coincidence that the politician's eldest son was named John Thomas Connolly Thompson.

It is among the more pleasing ironies of Canadian Catholic history that William Walsh's true heir was not a fellow Irishman but a Scot. This was John Cameron, born in Nova Scotia to Scottish parents, educated in MacKinnon's grammar school, and then sent to the Propaganda in 1844 at the age of seventeen. He remained for more than a decade, finishing with excellent Italian, a doctorate, and a spell as Alessandro Barnabò's secretary.[378] He was close to Cullen, who likely saw his own younger self in the clever and linguistically gifted young man from the provinces. The Irishman gave Cameron access to his personal library, gifted him part of it, and sent him the decrees of the Synod of Thurles 'beautifully bound, and directed to me in a most honourable manner in his Grace's handwriting'.[379] When he was finally consecrated coadjutor bishop of Arichat in 1870, it was Cullen who did the honours.[380] Cullen described him to others as 'a great friend of mine' (an almost

---

[376] Rogers to Anglin, 8 May 1877, ADDB/1/28.

[377] Sir John A. Macdonald formed two distinct ministries, and as such Thompson appears in some lists as Canada's fifth prime minister.

[378] R. A. MacLean, *Bishop John Cameron: Piety and Politics* (Antigonish, NS: The Casket Printing Company, 1991), 20.

[379] Cameron to Lachlan Cameron, 2 May 1851, ADA/JP/fonds 8/series 4/sub series 1.

[380] MacKinnon had first suggested that Cameron should be his coadjutor in the early 1860s, pushed hard for it, and then changed his mind on the cusp of successes.

unprecedented formulation in the vast Cullen correspondence), while Cameron later recalled that he owed more to Cullen 'than to any other man living or dead'.[381]

Cameron also learned Cullen's mastery of ecclesiastical politics, ruthlessly retiring the faltering MacKinnon 1877, for example, and adjudicating disputes on Rome's behalf in Newfoundland, Halifax, and Quebec. His closest personal friend was his fellow Propagandist and Cullen protégé George Conroy, who became the first apostolic delegate to Canada in 1877. Cameron's Roman links made him fearless in challenging even senior colleagues such as Archbishop Hannan of Halifax or Archbishop Lynch of Toronto. As he explained to John Thompson in 1880, 'Rome is my country; and it so happens that it would be a dangerous undertaking for even an Archbishop to challenge me there.'[382]

Cameron was also adamantine on the subject of education. In 1872, for example, he told Sweeny that he envied his ability to openly fight New Brunswick's Common School Act. The system Connolly had agreed in Nova Scotia was 'virtually as bad as yours', he wrote, but 'such has been and is our apathy that we seem to be satisfied with it – so satisfied, that we never can, without inconsistency, publicly endeavour to obtain its repeal.'[383] In the mid-1890s, he was the only Maritime bishop to publicly campaign for what he saw as the restoration of Catholic educational rights in Manitoba, and his consequent edict to vote for the Conservatives prompted an outbound 'stampede' in one rural parish church.[384] Cameron was a disciplinarian, a builder, and a thorough ultramontane utterly committed, as Peter Ludlow has pointed out, to the 'Romanization' of his diocese.[385] In all of this, he was more like Walsh or Cullen than Connolly, Hannan, or O'Brien.

The Ontario Irish

The situation was different further west, where Quebec's influence was deeper and lasted longer. Since 1774, the Catholic Church in Canada was protected under the terms of the Quebec Act, and it had never lost its commanding place in society. It was socially dominant and politically quiescent in almost equal measure. Men such as Joseph-Octave Plessis

---

[381] Cullen to Charles Russell, 26 March 1873, MCA/RP/10/18/39; quoted in Ludlow, 'Romanization', 42.
[382] Cameron to Thompson, 28 February, 1880, quoted in Waite, 65.
[383] Cameron to Sweeny, 21 February 1872, ADDB/1/16. Sweeny passed the letter to Rogers.
[384] See R. A. MacLean, 'CAMERON, John', in *DCB*.
[385] See Ludlow, 'Romanization'.

and Joseph Signay, both bishops of Quebec, were content to defer to the government, work with Protestants, and minister to their flock. By the 1830s, however, leadership was passing to an increasingly self-confident, assertive, and passionately ultramontane generation exemplified by the first two bishops of Montreal, Jean-Jacques Lartigue and Ignace Bourget. They had little interest in deferring to the state in matters strictly spiritual and sought to build a church that would be as Roman as it was already French. The steady loss of ecclesiastical responsibility for the Maritimes and Upper Canada – which Bourget strove to reverse – also had the effect of rendering the church in Lower Canada ever more French, leaving the residual population of anglophone and indigenous Catholics a relatively small although by no means insignificant minority.

That is not to say they were ignored. Successive bishops of Quebec had recruited both Irish and Scottish priests to serve anglophone populations not only in the Maritimes and Upper Canada but also in Lower Canada itself. In 1844, for example, Bourget secured two priests from Daniel Murray of Dublin.[386] Suitably Francophile, Irish and Irish-descended figures such as the Sulpicians Patrick Phelan and John Larkin enjoyed rapid promotion. Phelan, for example, was instrumental in cooling Irish tempers after some twenty strikers were killed by troops at Beauharnois in 1843, and later that year he was appointed coadjutor bishop of Kingston.[387] The Irish were a particularly significant presence in Montreal: the city launched Thomas D'Arcy McGee's political career in the late 1850s, hosted numerous Irish societies, some Catholic and some secular, and supported a long-lived English-language Catholic newspaper, *The True Witness and Catholic Chronicle*. Irish visitors drew vast crowds, whether for Charles Stewart Parnell in 1880 or the poet-priest (and southern apologist) Abram J. Ryan in 1883.[388] Numbers did not translate to ecclesiastical influence, however, and in a nice irony Bourget eventually borrowed the Irish-American strategy of creating ethnic parishes in which to contain his Irish flock.

This would have been impossible in Upper Canada, which was created as a separate colony in 1791. There, the Irish comprised the single largest ethnic group for most of the nineteenth century and, as in the Maritimes, much of the migration occurred before the Famine. Donald Akenson has estimated that by 1842 approximately 25 per cent of the province's

[386] Bourget to Murray, 17 October 1843, 24 April 1844, PICRA/NC/4/1843/51.
[387] *Transcript* (Montreal), 11 March 1843, quoted in Brian Young, *In Its Corporate Capacity: The Seminary of Montréal as a Business Institution, 1816–1876* (Montreal and Kingston: McGill-Queen's University Press, 1986), 150.
[388] Abram J. Ryan to 'My Very Dear Friend', 4 February 1883, Archives of the Dominican Sisters of Peace, New Orleans.

population had either been born in Ireland or had parents who had been. Of these, some two-thirds were Protestants of one denomination or another, making the province one of only a handful of jurisdictions outside of the United States where Irish Protestants and their descendants significantly outnumbered Irish Catholics for more than a short time. Among Catholics, the Irish were probably the largest group by at least 1842, comprising by one reckoning some 44,000 of the perhaps 65,000 Catholics in the province.[389] By 1847, they were probably a quarter of the population of Toronto.[390]

Their first bishop, however, was a Scot. Alexander MacDonnell's 1819 appointment as vicar general for Upper Canada with episcopal rank had been a boon to the Scots concentrated in the region between Montreal and what would become Ottawa. MacDonnell was the obvious choice: not only was he a Gaelic-speaker but by 1809 he was the only Scottish priest in Upper Canada.[391] Nor was there any serious call for an Irish appointment: there were as yet relatively few Irish in the colony and most were relatively recent arrivals. They had few claims on ecclesiastical attention or preferment. MacDonnell himself was educated, efficient, and congenial to the government. He was also well known in Quebec (if not always well liked) and increasingly well connected in Rome. In 1826, he succeeded in securing appointment as bishop of the newly created diocese of Kingston by replicating Edmund Burke of Nova Scotia's strategy of going to Rome behind Quebec's back.[392] Like MacEachern or Fraser, he was a Scottish bishop among a largely Scottish people.

Increasing Irish migration, however, soon forced MacDonnell to contend with a widely dispersed, restless, and potentially disloyal population. His own loyalty to the British state was unquestionable. As a young priest in Scotland, for example, he had been instrumental in raising the Glengarry Fencibles, the British Army's first regiment of highland Catholics, and later defended their role in suppressing the Irish rebellion of 1798.[393] In 1802, he had helped many of the demobilized soldiers settle in Upper Canada, joined them himself in 1804, and then helped to raise the Glengarry Light Infantry to fight the War of 1812. In 1830, his loyalty was recognized with an appointment to Upper Canada's legislative council, and in 1836 he even formed an electoral alliance with the Orange Order.

MacDonnell also effectively leveraged British fears of Irish unrest, as Laura J. Smith has demonstrated in an important recent doctoral

---

[389] See Akenson, *Irish in Ontario*, chap. 1.   [390] McGowan, *Michael Power*, 201.
[391] J. M. Bumsted, 'Scottish Catholicism in Canada', in Murphy and Stortz, *Creed and Culture*, 79–99, at 89.
[392] Murphy, 'Language, ethnicity, and region'.   [393] Bumsted, 84–5.

thesis.[394] In 1824, for example, he exploited anxiety over Daniel O'Connell's Catholic Association to extort money from the Colonial Office. If adequate funds were provided to support Catholic schools, priests, and churches, he told Lord Bathurst, it would 'preclude the necessity of any application from the Irish Catholics of [Upper Canada] to the Catholic Association of Ireland'. An alarmed Bathurst gave £50 personally and suggested asking the Canada Company for more. Two years later, he successfully used the same tactic on the lieutenant governor.[395] MacDonnell appears to have been as good as his word: the O'Connell supporting Society of Friends of Ireland, for example, managed only one branch in Upper Canada, at Bytown, despite being ubiquitous elsewhere in British North America and despite there being significant Irish Catholic populations at Kingston and what was then York.[396] Several years later, the Irish of what had since become Toronto responded to the Upper Canada rebellion of 1837 not only by noisily proclaiming their loyalty, which was obviously prudent, but also by insisting that their own individual attachments to Ireland had 'been broken off, beyond all hope of renewal'.[397] They were happy Upper Canadians and loyal subjects of the British Empire.

This quiescence extended to the migrants' religious practices, which Smith suggests were essentially communal, 'local in orientation, subject to the environment, and not particularly Irish'.[398] Upper Canada was an important example of the 'earlier and alternative ways in which Irish religion was exported abroad' which, she argued, has been largely ignored by scholars such as myself who have been too focussed on Cullen and his network.[399] At all events, Alexander MacDonnell was simply the first in a long line of Upper Canadian bishops who neither came from nor owed their loyalty to that network.

In Kingston, MacDonnell had immediately secured as his coadjutor the aristocratic Englishman Thomas Weld, but family business and an unexpected elevation to the cardinalate kept him in Rome. He then unsuccessfully approached a series of leading Quebec priests, including the Irish-descended opponent of the Sulpicians, Thomas Maguire, and two Sulpicians, the Irish-descended John Larkin and Joseph-Vincent Quiblier. In 1832, he tried again, now insisting on a French Canadian in preference to an Irishman or a Scot. This was presented as a means of avoiding friction within the diocese but more likely reflected the lack of a plausible Scottish candidate. He finally settled on Rémi Gaulin, an

---

[394] Laura J. Smith, 'Unsettled settlers: Irish Catholics, Irish Catholicism, and British loyalty in Upper Canada, 1819–1840, unpublished PhD diss., University of Toronto, 2017.
[395] Ibid., 70–1.   [396] Ibid., 73.   [397] Quoted in ibid., 1.   [398] Ibid., 14.   [399] Ibid., 11.

English-speaker who had once served as his curate, then in Nova Scotia, and finally in Quebec.[400] He succeeded MacDonnell in 1840, soon began to struggle with his mental health, and in 1843 the Irish-born Sulpician Patrick Phelan was appointed his coadjutor and given full charge of the diocese.

In Toronto, the first bishop was Michael Power, who, although born in Nova Scotia to Irish parents, had spent his entire career in Lower Canada. In 1835, he had been selected to petition Gregory XVI to erect Montreal into a diocese over the opposition of the Sulpicians, and by the late 1830s he was the recognized leader of the anglophone clergy in the province.[401] Like MacDonnell, his allegiance to the crown was unquestioned: in 1837–8, for example, he had been horrified by what he called the 'insubordination and fierce democratic spirit' represented by the *patriote* risings that had wreaked havoc on his parish.[402] Most importantly, however, Power had become a protégé of Ignace Bourget and shared his goal of erecting a new and suitably ultramontane ecclesiastical province for the whole of British North America. In 1840, Bourget had even sent him to the Maritimes in a fruitless attempt to sell this vision. The following year, Bourget took him on a European tour that had among its goals the division of Kingston and the appointment of Power to the new diocese, which he told Rome required an English-speaking bishop familiar with Irish culture. Power duly became the first bishop of Toronto in late 1841.

The city was a blank canvas upon which he could build an ultramontane church on the model of Montreal, or rather Montreal as Bourget wished it to be. Power stressed internal unity and outward loyalty for the laity and imposed liturgical, financial, sexual, and sartorial discipline on the clergy. He imported French Jesuits, sent his own seminarians to Montreal, and instituted French-inspired lay groups such as the Holy Child Association and the Confraternity of the Immaculate Heart of Mary. He habitually wrote to the Propaganda in French. He also assiduously travelled his vast diocese, supported Hamilton's *Catholic* newspaper until it folded for lack of funds, and strained to impose episcopal authority on the laity. On the all-important question of marriage, Power was both a stickler for protocol and a realist: he insisted the required forms be followed, but counselled tolerance and regularly granted the required dispensations. He was also an assiduous clerical recruiter, securing the services of thirty-three priests of whom fifteen were mostly francophone Jesuits.[403] In 1847, he convinced the Loreto Sisters to send four women

---

[400] J. E. Robert Choquette, 'GAULIN, Rémi', in *DCB*.
[401] McGowan, *Michael Power*, 89–92.   [402] Quoted in ibid., 105.
[403] The information for Power's episcopate in the preceding paragraphs is drawn from McGowan, *Michael Power*, chaps. 6–9.

from Dublin to open both a day and 'common' school for girls in Toronto. Although he warned Teresa Ball that the mostly Irish population of the city 'are not rich', and he could not predict how many could afford fees, he was confident that 'many Protestants will feel happy in being able to avail themselves of the opportunity of giving to their daughters a good sound education'.[404] This last was typical: Power always got on exceptionally well with Protestants, while still naturally hoping for their eventual conversion.

Power also walked a fine line between demanding separate schools and accommodating himself to the public system. He was not only recommended by the Anglican bishop for a seat on Canada West's first public board of education, for example, but then served as its emollient chairman.[405] Nor did he oppose amendments that placed urban Catholics at the mercy of largely Protestant local school boards, while in Kingston his colleague Patrick Phelan took a full ten months to object. Although Mark McGowan has convincingly argued that both men were distracted by the sudden arrival of the Famine Irish (some 38,000 in Toronto alone), it remains the case that neither William Walsh nor any other Hiberno-Roman would have been anything like as accommodating.

Throughout Greater Ireland, non-Irish priests and bishops adapted themselves to their Irish surroundings and in time became indistinguishable from them. This is how Archbishop Vaughan of Sydney, Archbishop Redwood of Wellington, and even Cardinal Manning of Westminster sought to manage their often overwhelmingly Irish flocks. Michael Power did much the same thing in reverse, except he was not feigning. He was in every sense a product of the Quebec church, politically, culturally, and theologically. The fact that he had Irish parents and spoke English was irrelevant. As Rémi Gaulin of Kingston put it when recommending him for Toronto, 'This gentleman is sufficiently Irish to be well thought of here and sufficiently Canadian to live up to all we might expect of him.'[406] After his death in October 1847, the Methodist minister and education reformer Egerton Ryerson eulogized Power as 'virtually a Canadian'.[407]

It took nearly a year for the bishops of Quebec to settle on the Sulpician-turned-Jesuit John Larkin as Power's successor. Their aim seems to have been to avoid an Irishman by appointing a broadly acceptable Irish Canadian. Unfortunately, nobody had thought to ask Larkin,

---

[404] Power to Ball, 25 June 1847, LAD/TB/CAN/1/1.
[405] McGowan, *Michael Power*, 223–4.
[406] Quoted in Terence J. Fay, *A History of Canadian Catholics* (Montreal and Kingston: McGill-Queen's University Press, 2002), 88.
[407] Quoted in McGowan, *Michael Power*, 201.

and his horrified resistance caused further delays and some concern among the watching Irish. As Walsh observed in April 1849, 'We are all out of patience with good Father Larkin and fear that a Canadian will be thrust onto that unfortunate Toronto.'[408] He was almost right: the bishops' second choice was Armand-François-Marie de Charbonnel, a French Sulpician who had pursued a largely academic career in Lyons, Versailles, Bordeaux, Montreal, and Baltimore. From his arrival in September 1850, nearly three years after Power's death, he insisted on regular devotions, grand liturgies, clerical discipline, and separate schools. He abandoned Power's policy of accommodation, and in 1856 declared that Catholic electors 'who do not use their electoral power on behalf of Separate Schools are also guilty of *mortal* sin'.[409] He also imported numerous but mostly French priests and religious.

Charbonnel never impressed the Irish, who thought him both incompetent and hostile. Teresa Ball, for example, had to make it clear that no bishop had the right to appoint superiors or to vary the community's rules.[410] As Thomas Connolly put it in 1855, 'God help the poor Irish Congregations of his Diocese whose destinies are dependent on him.'[411] Charbonnel's difficulties were further compounded by his inability to master English, and as early as 1854 he admitted to Rome that his priests disliked him.[412] He knew he needed help, tried to resign in 1856, and when that failed sought the transfer of the Halifax priest John Woods, who promised the Propaganda that he would 'endeavour to allay the national prejudices of my countrymen, to make them *more Catholic than Irish*'.[413] Just a few months later, a number of Toronto parishes petitioned the pope 'to remove the present French clergy and give us those of our country who will be able to instruct and direct us', while another group urged 'All who wish to see the French Clergy out of Toronto' to gather at Charbonnel's house every night 'until we put them away'.[414]

It was little wonder that Charbonnel wanted out. His long-standing request for a coadjutor was finally granted in 1859, and he resigned and

---

[408] Walsh to Hughes, 3 April 1849, AANY/HP/Box 3/Folder 9.

[409] Quoted in Franklin A. Walker, *Catholic Education and Politics in Upper Canada* (Toronto: J. M. Dent & Sons, 1955), 181. Emphasis in original.

[410] Ball to Teresa Dease, 26 February 1852, LDA/TB/CAN/3/9.

[411] Connolly to Mullock, 25 September 1855, ARCSJ/MP/104/1/9.

[412] Murray W. Nicholson and John S. Moir, 'CHARBONNEL, Armand-François-Marie de', in *DCB*.

[413] Woods to Barnabò, 8 September 1858, APF/SC/AS/vol. 7/ff. 71–2. Emphasis in original.

[414] Congregation of the church of St Paul's in the city and diocese of Toronto to Pius IX, [probably January 1859], APF/SC/AS/vol. 7/ff. 111–179. Several other parishes sent similar appeals. The printed slip urging the protest at the bishop's house is in the same file, at f. 102.

returned to France the following year. His successor was John Joseph Lynch, a pioneer Irish Vincentian who had been in the United States since 1846 and had established the congregation's seminary at Niagara a decade later. He must have seemed ideal to the hard-pressed Frenchman: he was a gifted preacher and a competent administrator whose Irishness had been tempered by four years at Saint-Lazare in Paris. These characteristics would prove useful in a diocese that still lacked adequate clergy, something that was primarily due to Charbonnel's perceived hostility towards the Irish.

As bishop of Toronto (archbishop from 1870), Lynch was largely *sui generis*. He was neither a Hiberno-Roman like William Walsh nor a French ultramontane like Charbonnel. In politics he was probably closest to the pragmatic and accommodative approach of Dublin's Daniel Murray, although he was personally much more assertive, authoritarian, and nationalistic. Lynch supported separate schools, for example, and worked hard to protect them, but he also joined the Council of Public Instruction and later consented to Bible readings in the public schools. He consistently resisted pressure to take a more aggressive approach, including from fellow bishops, relying instead on his close relationship with Oliver Mowat's provincial Liberals to secure incremental improvements. He was relatively relaxed about social mixing, although not mixed marriages, but was an enthusiastic supporter of a wide variety of Catholic devotional and social organizations; however, he was also hostile towards any sign of lay initiative or independence. In the late 1870s, for example, he crushed an attempt to break his power over Toronto's Separate Schools Board.

Lynch also took a close interest in Irish affairs, famously writing to the bishops of Ireland in 1864 to discourage further Irish migration on the grounds that too many who had come to North American had lost their faith and found misery. The letter was a gift to the Fenians, who used it as yet another stick with which to beat Cardinal Cullen.[415] Lynch made amends two years later when he arranged for a petition to be sent to London condemning both the Fenians and the wickedness of English rule. As he privately admitted to Cullen, 'I cannot stop short when I speak of poor Ireland.'[416] Typically, he tolerated the Fenian-linked Hibernian Benevolent Society until they challenged clerical authority, at which point he condemned them fulsomely.[417] Yet Lynch was also careful to avoid overt disloyalty. One of his first episcopal acts, for example, was to beg

[415] See Sarah Roddy, 'Spiritual imperialism and the mission of the Irish race: The Catholic church and emigration from nineteenth-century Ireland', *Irish Historical Studies*, vol. 38, no. 152 (Nov 2013), 600–19, at 612.
[416] Lynch to Cullen, 24 March 1866, DDA/CP/327/5/III/6(1).   [417] Clarke, 190–2.

John Hughes to ensure a friendly reception from New York's Irish when the Prince of Wales visited the city, while in 1862 his tacit permission to resume St Patrick's Day parades came with the caveat that the guests at the subsequent banquet include leading Orangemen. There were also toasts to the Queen and to the British Army in Canada.[418]

Wariness of sectarian strife informed the whole of Lynch's episcopate. As he put it in 1866, 'We are in a very critical position, between Fenians on the one side, and blood thirsty Orangemen on the other.'[419] Demographic and political realities meant that Catholic gains could at any time be swept away, and violence was always a possibility. Far better, he thought, to work within the system and eschew overt displays of Catholic power or Irish nationalism. When Charles Stewart Parnell made his great tour of Canada in 1880, for example, Lynch unsuccessfully tried to discourage him from visiting Toronto, and he was similarly hostile to the Land League.[420] In 1887, he did his best to deter William O'Brien on the grounds that only 'grievous evils' would come from his appearance in the city. After the Fenian panic of the mid-1860s, he explained to an Irish bishop, thousands of Irish had fled Toronto either because 'they could not stand the taunts of their Orange fellow-workmen' or because they had been sacked by Protestant employers. Now he feared thousands more would have to move to America. 'It is a pity to disturb the Irish Catholics of this country who are on the high road to doing well.'[421]

In ecclesiastical terms, Lynch had few allies, little experience of Rome, and no influence outside of Ontario. In 1880, for example, John Cameron and the Halifax Sisters of Charity had easily outmanoeuvred 'the poor old man of Toronto'.[422] He was largely content with building his own regional powerbase, especially after Toronto was made an archdiocese in 1870; but even for this he needed help. In 1874, for example, he sent the newly appointed Peter Francis Crinnon of Hamilton to solicit Cullen's help in securing a suitable replacement for the ailing Edward John Horan of Kingston.[423] Cullen made several suggestions, including the future Archbishop Thomas Croke of Cashel, who was then manoeuvring to escape New Zealand, and the Waterford priest James Vincent Cleary, who was eventually sent to Kingston in 1880 and became its first archbishop in 1889.[424] Unluckily for Lynch, however, he had

---

[418] Lynch to Hughes, 11 September 1860, CU/BP/MS1296/1/1/2/13; Wilson, 2: 151–2.
[419] Lynch to Cullen, 24 March 1866.   [420] Clarke, 225–6.
[421] Lynch to Edward Thomas O'Dwyer, 27 May 1887, Limerick diocesan archives [LDA], O'Dwyer papers.
[422] Quoted in Waite, 64.
[423] Crinnon to Lynch, 27 June 1874, TAA, Lynch papers [LP], L.AD02.56.
[424] Crinnon to Lynch, 22 July 1874, TAA/LP/L.AD02.58.

picked the exact moment when Cullen's Roman power had come to an abrupt end.

Trouble had been brewing for some time, with the first blow falling in late 1869 with the death of Cardinal Karl August von Reisach of Munich. The men had known each other since the late 1820s when they were both protégés of the future Pope Gregory XVI, and Reisach had long been an important ally on the Propaganda.[425] His loss was keenly felt. Then, in the spring of 1871, it became apparent that Cardinal Barnabò's health was also beginning to fail: they had noticed in Dublin that he was no longer signing documents coming from Rome.[426] By 1873, he was effectively blind and had to have papers read to him.[427] Although Barnabò remained in post until his death in early 1874, his control slowly loosened as the cardinals and *minutanti* looked to the succession. To men like Reisach and Barnabò, Cullen was a friend, ally, or protégé, but to the other cardinals he was just a potential rival. This became painfully apparent when the papal diplomat Alessandro Franchi became cardinal prefect (see Chapter 2).

Not yet sensing a threat, Cullen made an atypical mistake: he asked Kirby to confirm whether Horan had really resigned, telling his friend to telegraph the cardinal's answer. 'You need not mention the see', he wrote, 'but you can say *send or don't send names*.'[428] Franchi reacted immediately, warning Kirby that any interference was unwelcome.[429] He then bluntly informed Lynch that Cullen's involvement was 'not pleasing'. On such a 'matter of the highest importance', Franchi wrote, it was necessary to be perfectly clear: nominations were solely the responsibility of the bishops of the relevant province. He conceded that it was legitimate to ask Cullen 'to indicate some worthy and proper person' for their consideration but then closed that door by insisting that, if there were qualified local candidates, 'it would not be becoming to ignore them and place over them priests strangers to the same province'.[430] The message could not have been clearer, and a local priest named John O'Brien was duly appointed.

By 1877, Franchi had largely made his point, and early that year he permitted the appointment of Cullen's protégé George Conroy as the first

---

[425] After advanced study at the German College in Rome, in 1830 Reisach was appointed prefect of studies in the Propaganda College while Cullen was still in residence there, and he stayed in contact with Reisach after his appointment as bishop of Eichstätt in 1836.
[426] Forde to Moran of Dunedin, 'Ascension Day' 1871, ADD, Moran papers [MP].
[427] Dowd, *Rome in Australia*, 2: 428.
[428] Cullen to Kirby, 27 June 1874, PICRA/NK/4/2/74. Emphasis in original.
[429] Crinnon to Lynch, 22 July 1874. Crinnon is quoting Cullen quoting Kirby.
[430] Franchi to Lynch, 9 September 1874, TAA/LP/L.AD01.87. Original in Italian.

apostolic delegate to Canada. His task was to investigate, arbitrate, and impose order. It was a typically Cullenite performance: in Quebec, he criticized the poor quality of clerical education, insisted on erudition as a criterion for promotion, complained of infirm ecclesiastical authority, and decried excessive episcopal partisanship.[431] In Ontario, he tried to impose the Irish-born bishop of London, John Walsh, as Lynch's coadjutor with full authority over the archdiocese. Lynch and the other bishops preferred someone else, Conroy persisted, and Walsh finally refused in order to spare Lynch's feelings.[432] The Irish were likely attracted by Walsh's very public enthusiasm for papal infallibility, and his more private hostility to the French. In early 1877, for example, he had told Cullen's nephew Patrick Francis Moran that they 'wd sooner vote for an English Orangeman than an Irish Catholic' and were opposed 'in every way' to Irish immigration.[433] In the event, Lynch was sent the disgraced Australian Cullenite Timothy O'Mahony as an auxiliary instead (see Chapter 6), thus ensuring at least some Hiberno-Roman influence in the affairs of Toronto. Walsh himself was eventually appointed archbishop in his own right in 1889.

Under Lynch, Ontario turned steadily greener, and after Franchi died in 1878 he again looked to Ireland for candidates. In Kingston, for example, he supported the appointment of James Vincent Cleary, whom Cullen had first recommended in 1874, and, when Hamilton came vacant in 1883, he sought the advice of Cullen's successor Edward McCabe on the grounds that 'Our last gift from Ireland ... encourages us to apply for another.'[434] Their choice was the Irish Dominican James Joseph Carbery, who was succeeded by the Irish-born Thomas Dowling three years later. Like Lynch, Dowling was both passionate about Ireland and a suitably temperate enthusiast for separate education.[435] He died in 1924. Irish or Irish-descended bishops were also appointed in London, where Bourget's Sulpician protégé Pierre-Adolphe Pinsoneault finally gave up and resigned in 1866. John Walsh's successor there, the disciplinarian Denis O'Connor, also replaced him in Toronto in 1899. Only Ottawa evaded the Irish.

James Lynch's legacy in Toronto was complex. As Mark McGowan has pointed out, he had an 'innate talent for sending out mixed messages to

---

[431] Perin, 75–7.
[432] See John P. Comiskey, *In My Heart's Best Wishes for You: A Biography of Archbishop John Walsh* (Montreal and Kingston: McGill-Queen's University Press, 2012), 136–8.
[433] Moran diaries, 21 February 1877, AAS/MP.
[434] Lynch to McCabe, 4 January 1883, DDA, McCabe papers. This collection is as yet uncatalogued.
[435] Gerald J. Stortz, 'DOWLING, Thomas Joseph', in *DCB*.

the community'.[436] He could simultaneously advocate social segregation and communal collaboration, while his practical and rhetorical appeals for toleration were often belied by equally fiery rhetoric. Yet he was a successful builder, an effective clerical recruiter, and in his prime the largely unquestioned leader of the city's Catholics; but he was also singularly unsuccessful in securing his own legacy in Toronto.

This was because John Walsh proved to be the antithesis of a Hiberno-Roman bishop. He did not simply tolerate social mixing but positively encouraged it, and even mixed marriages became commonplace. He went out of his way to work with Protestants, publicly praised them, and earned their respect in return. As McGowan put it, Walsh 'provided the bridge between the assertive Irish leadership of his predecessor and the profound attachment to Canada espoused by his episcopal successors'.[437] Not even Robert Dunne of Brisbane, otherwise the most liberal of the global Irish, went quite so far (see Chapter 6). Denis O'Connor tried valiantly to change things, but he soon gave up in frustration leaving Walsh's policies to be deepened by Fergus McEvay and then Neil McNeil.[438] Although Kingston under James Vincent Cleary was for a time much more conformist, the pattern had been set and the Catholic Church in Canada's largest province developed differently from the Maritimes, or indeed from Greater Ireland as a whole.

By 1900, the Irish largely dominated the Canadian church outwith Quebec. Attention soon turned, however, to the rapidly opening west, and language became the proxy for the ongoing struggle between French Canada and 'les Irlandais'. The question was simple but important: in which language should the hundreds of thousands of migrant Catholics experience Canadian Catholicism? As many spoke neither English nor French, it was not self-evident to francophones that that language should be English, especially in places such as Manitoba. The Irish disagreed, as did Roman figures such as the influential cardinal secretary of state Merry del Val. They believed that English was the language of the future in North America and that this required that every diocese west of Quebec be brought under Irish control.[439] French should be limited to Quebec itself and perhaps Acadia. In 1912, the Irish bishops in Ontario even went so far as to support a regulation that effectively prohibited the use of French in schools beyond the second grade, even in francophone

---

[436] McGowan, *Waning of the Green*, 58–9.   [437] Ibid., 62.   [438] Ibid., 57.

[439] Mark McGowan, 'The tale and trials of a "double minority": The Irish and French Catholic engagement for the soul of the Canadian church, 1815–1947', in Colin Barr and Hilary M. Carey (eds.), *Religion and Greater Ireland: Christianity and Irish Global Networks, 1750–1950* (Montreal and Kingston: McGill-Queen's University Press, 2015), 97–123, at 106–7.

areas.[440] The campaign was ruthlessly effective, and it is little wonder that the Oblate Archbishop Adélard Langevin of St Boniface, Manitoba, accused the Irish of spreading their 'anti-French rage and Francophobia' across the west.[441] Although St Boniface itself remained in French hands (but only after the loss of Winnipeg), the Irish victory was largely complete by 1920. It was capped in 1946 with the appointment of James McGuigan of Toronto as the first anglophone cardinal.

Catholicism in Ontario and western Canada developed along a path that emphasized patriotism, accommodation, and comparative flexibility. By 1914, it was undeniably the church of John Walsh. Explicit Irishness faded relatively rapidly, in a process Mark McGowan has described as 'the waning of the green', and certainly much faster than in Australia, America, Newfoundland, or New Zealand. Catholicism in central and western Canada was Irish but a different kind of Irish, and by the mid-twentieth century it was hardly Irish at all.

The Maritime provinces were different, both more Irish and more Roman, although still relatively accommodating; but it remains the case that William Walsh was the last true Hiberno-Roman in the region. John Cameron was a Scot, and Walsh's successors in Halifax were certainly Irish but rarely as Roman as he would have wished. It was both symbolic and appropriate that his dying wish was that his episcopal ring should be sent to Cardinal Cullen, who wore it until his own death in 1878.[442] It was even more appropriate that it then passed to Cullen's nephew Patrick Francis Moran, who took it with him to Australia.[443]

---

[440] Ibid., 111.   [441] Quoted in ibid., 109.

[442] William Hannigan to Cullen, 12 August 1858, DDA/CP/319/1/II/39.

[443] Moran to 'Canon Murphy', 15 September 1908, Archives of the Callan Sisters of Mercy [ACRSM]. How this letter wound up in Callan is a mystery.

6 Australia

At around 9 a.m. on 5 October 1947, a young Australian of Irish descent arrived at Rome's Termini station. He travelled with several companions, all Australians, all carefully selected for their academic prowess, and all sent to study for the priesthood at the Urban College of the Propaganda Fide.[1] Twenty-two years later, and no longer a priest, John Molony published *The Roman Mould of the Australian Catholic Church*. It was a groundbreaking book. As Manning Clark pointed out in a foreword, there had long been a 'lively debate on the characteristics of the Catholic Church in Australia'; but that debate, he continued, had focussed on the legacy of the early Irish priests and bishops, their clericalism, and their decades-long struggle with the English Benedictines of New South Wales.[2] As Molony himself put it in the first line of his introduction, 'The essential Irishness of the Catholic Church in Australia has long been a commonplace of Australian historical writing.'[3] Molony rejected this. 'When the accents of Ireland were most loudly heard in the Australian Church', he wrote, 'the ideas and attitudes they conveyed were not Irish but Roman, through and through.' The Irish bishops who had ruled and shaped Australian Catholicism from the mid-nineteenth century onwards 'were themselves products of an Irish Church undergoing a thorough-going Romanization at the hands of prelates trained in Rome, oriented to Rome, and consciously seeking to shape the Church both in Ireland and Australia in the Roman mould'.[4] Australia in 1968 was, Molony wrote, 'as firmly Roman orientated' as it had been 'in 1868 when Paul Cullen had almost completed his work of binding the Church here to Rome'.[5]

The emphasis on Ireland, and on an Irish struggle with the Benedictines, has long been embedded in Australian historiography, beginning as early as 1895 with Patrick Francis Moran's massive documentary compendium of Australian church history. Even the casual

---

[1] John Molony, *Luther's Pine: An Autobiography* (Canberra: Pandanus Books, 2004), 165.
[2] Manning Clark, 'Foreword', in John Molony, *The Roman Mould of the Australian Catholic Church* (Melbourne: Melbourne University Press, 1969), vii–viii, at vii.
[3] Molony, *Mould*, 1.   [4] Ibid.   [5] Ibid., 5.

reader would have been in no doubt of the essential, and essentially heroic, contribution of the Irish. It was influential enough to require a Benedictine response, with Henry Norbert Birt's two-volume *Benedictine Pioneers in Australia* appearing in 1911. As K. S. Inglis memorably put it, Birt had 'hardly picked up his pen before he is impaling the Cardinal on it'.[6] Writing largely from Benedictine sources, and at the behest of his Benedictine superiors, he unapologetically celebrated the order's contribution to Australian Catholicism. Birt in turn provoked Eris O'Brien (later the archbishop of Canberra-Goulburn), who from 1922 produced four well-researched but uncritical volumes that sought to restore the reputation of the pioneering Irish priests who had preceded the English monks. As Manning Clark remarked in 1969, the historiography had been reduced to competing claims that Australian Catholicism had been 'fashioned for good or evil by the early Irish priests' or 'saved from early Irish influences by English Benedictines'.[7]

By the 1960s, the Benedictines had unquestionably gained the upper hand. As Edmund Campion pointed out, both T. L. Suttor and C. J. Duffy (the influential Sydney archdiocesan archivist) revered John Bede Polding, the first of the Benedictine bishops.[8] They in turn strongly influenced Patrick O'Farrell, for whom Polding 'became a hero', and whose *Catholic Church in Australia* was deeply sympathetic to the Benedictines.[9] As O'Farrell boasted to his friend and fellow historian Tony Cahill not long after that book was published, the English Benedictines were 'delighted' with what he called 'this blow from Australia'.[10] The suspicion must be that the cultivated monks were both naturally more appealing to academic writers and conveniently long gone; by the 1960s, many Australian Catholics had had quite enough of authoritarian Irish bishops. The ex-Dominican Suttor, for example, suggested that the some fifty years of Benedictine rule in Sydney had given Australia a chance to absorb what he called 'the Christian school of thought in all its power'; but, he continued, 'it was an opportunity it neither seized nor appreciated nor deserved, preferring ... a tendentious and factitious proletarianism'.[11] It was an open question, he thought,

---

[6] K. S. Inglis, 'Catholic historiography in Australia', *Historical Studies: Australia and New Zealand*, vol. 8 (November 1958), 233–53, at 235.

[7] Clark, vii.

[8] Edmund Campion, 'Patrick O'Farrell: An expanded memory', *Journal of Religious History*, vol. 31, no. 1 (March 2007), 18–23, at 19.

[9] Ibid., 19–20.

[10] O'Farrell to Cahill, 28 October 1969, A. E. (Tony) Cahill papers, Mitchell Library, State Library of New South Wales, 1/9.

[11] T. L. Suttor, *Hierarchy and Democracy in Australia, 1788–1870* (Melbourne: Melbourne University Press, 1965), 21–2.

whether 'the Irish Way' was any more than 'a lot of emotional talk covering an inner lack of Christian purpose, of consistency, of seriousness'.[12]
Molony's book represented a chance to break this cycle.

It was not taken. There were several reasons for this. First, it was little
read outside Australia and even today remains relatively unknown. John
Silke, who was aware of the 'lively' Australian debates, mentioned it only
in passing in his exhaustive 1975 global survey of Irish Catholic
historiography.[13] The meticulous Emmet Larkin appears to have missed
it entirely, as did *Irish Historical Studies*, and it does not seem to have been
reviewed in America until 1972, and then only briefly by a lukewarm
Australian.[14] This was unfortunate, as Molony was among the first scholars anywhere in the world to demonstrate the absolute importance of
Rome to the global Cullenite network.

In Australia, where his book certainly was read, it seems to have had
little influence. This was partly because Molony broke so completely with
the established narrative of Irish vs Benedictine, but it also reflected
genuine problems with his thesis.[15] As S. J. Boland noted in his tardy
American review, while the Roman element in Australian Catholicism
had undoubtedly been 'overlooked' by scholars, it was overemphasized by
Molony. 'A really worthwhile point could have been made', he wrote,
'without allowing preoccupation with the theme to become
oversimplification.'[16] This was both fair and perceptive. As Molony
himself later recalled, an education in the Propaganda was intended to
emphasize the universality of the church and efface national attachments.
'For good and for ill', he wrote, 'I became a Roman.'[17] Yet even in Rome
Molony seems to have been repelled by the foreign binaries he saw in the
Australian church. Archbishop Justin Simonds of Melbourne, for example, impressed the young seminarian precisely because he was 'neither
Irish nor Roman, but thoroughly Australian'.[18]

The emphasis Molony placed on the power of Rome in nineteenth-
century Australia, and the hostility with which he described it, can make
The Roman Mould of the Australian Catholic Church read as a reaction
against the author's own clerical formation and as an assertion of his
developing sense of Australian identity. This was excusable in a man
without as yet any formal historical training (Manning Clark famously

[12] Ibid., 84.
[13] John J. Silke, 'The Roman Catholic Church in Ireland 1800–1922', *Studia Hibernica*, no.
15 (1975), 103.
[14] S. J. Boland, 'Review of *The Roman Mould of the Australian Catholic Church* by John N.
Molony', *Catholic Historical Review*, vol. 58, no. 2 (1972), 248–9.
[15] Walter Phillips, 'Australian Catholic historiography: Some recent issues', *Historical
Studies*, vol. 14 (1971), 600–11, at 601.
[16] Boland, 'Review', 248–9.   [17] Molony, *Luther's Pine*, 169.   [18] Ibid., 284.

rescued Molony from employment in a Heinz Tomato factory), but the special pleading and consequent overstatement undoubtedly minimized the book's impact.[19] Patrick O'Farrell's response was particularly robust. In the 1977 edition of his history, he flatly insisted that 'the agencies for transforming the laity were to be Irish episcopal authority and church discipline, Irish priests and religious teachers, Irish devotional practices'. Molony's question as to whether Irish or Roman influence was the stronger was 'false and misleading'. O'Farrell accepted that the two 'were blended, but it was an Irish blend'.[20]

Inevitably, it was O'Farrell's interpretation that was widely accepted. Indeed, his influence in Australia has been overwhelming, partly through sheer strength of personality and partly through great scholarly productivity. O'Farrell's writing was invariably punchy and often compulsively readable. Many of his judgements were sound and remain unchallenged. He undoubtedly knew more about his chosen topic than any historian before or since. But O'Farrell's hegemony came at a price. He made a fetish of his eschewal of footnotes, for example, leaving readers to guess at the sources of his information and the solidity of his interpretations. In fact he missed important archives and leaned more heavily on the early writings of Moran, Birt, and O'Brien than he would perhaps have liked to admit. The further he got from Sydney the more his grip slackened. His robust rhetorical style was also allied to an intellectual confidence that could border on hubris – as Hilary Carey pointed out, a 'scholar who could entitle one of his articles: "Irish Australia: My Role in Its History," was clearly not much troubled by doubts about the significance of his contribution to this field'.[21] After his death in 2003, *The Journal of Religious History* memorialized his career (and that of the influential but less productive A. E. Cahill) with a special issue. Challenging him was daunting.

O'Farrell was also keen to dispel what he called the 'fog of the obvious created by my name and Catholicism'. He had never seen himself as Irish, or Irish-Australian, and as a child had learned nothing 'of Irish history or culture, save that it was a joke'.[22] He claimed not to have heard of Sinn

[19] See Mark McKenna, *An Eye for Eternity: The Life of Manning Clark* (Melbourne: Miegunyah Press, 2011), 505.

[20] Quoted in Campion, 21–2.

[21] Hilary M. Carey, 'Introduction: Remembering the religious history of A. E. (Tony) Cahill (1933–2004) and Patrick O'Farrell (1933–2003)', *Journal of Religious History*, vol. 31, no. 1 (March 2007), 4.

[22] Patrick O'Farrell, 'Writing the history of Irish Australia', in Oliver MacDonagh & W. F. Mandle (eds.), *Ireland and Irish-Australia: Studies in Cultural and Political History* (London: Croom Helm), 218–28, at 218–19.

Féin until well after he had finished his doctoral studies.[23] Irish-American 'sentimentality' embarrassed him. Even his faith was that of 'Maritain, Mauriac, Chesterton' and the French Marists of his New Zealand youth, and he despised the uncultured All Hallows priests that had plagued his parents.[24] Above all, he wanted to 'deny the obvious but spurious equation: Irish Catholic Historian O'Farrell equals a History of the Irish in Australia'.[25] There is the hint here of the Player Queen: even setting aside his work on Australian Catholic history, which was necessarily much concerned with the Irish, O'Farrell produced at least six books and more than fifty articles, reviews, reflections, or commentaries directly concerned with the history of Ireland, Irish identity, or the Irish in Australia and New Zealand.

Of course Patrick O'Farrell was not the only scholar drawn to the subject. As early as 1958, K. S. Inglis observed that the history of Australian Catholicism was significantly 'richer' and more professional than that of any other denomination.[26] Ten years later, Walter Phillips was struck by how much had been added.[27] The 1970s saw the publication of, among others, Mary Shanahan's study of the controversial Benedictine Henry Gregory, John Hosie's bracing reassessment of Polding, James Waldersee's pioneering examination of lay society, and K. T. Livingston's *The Emergence of an Australian Catholic Priesthood*. Nor was it only New South Wales: the Irish foundress of the Brisbane Sisters of Mercy, Mother Vincent Whitty, received a biography in 1972, seven years before her authoritarian Irish bishop, James Quinn, and nineteen years before his more emollient Irish successor, Robert Dunne; Frances O'Kane's study of the early years of the church in Victoria (published in 1976) was followed in the early 1980s by Margaret Pawsey's two volumes on the church and church–state relations in the 1850s and 1860s, and more recently by Patrick Morgan's timely refocussing *Melbourne before Mannix*.

There do remain significant lacunae: most obviously, there is still no scholarly study of Polding, while his successor Archbishop Vaughan has not yet been treated at book length.[28] South Australia, Western Australia, and Tasmania remain underexplored, and there is a dearth of professional diocesan histories. Yet it is beyond question that in its depth, breadth, and

---

[23] Patrick O'Farrell, 'Explaining oneself: Labor, Catholic, Irish, UNSW', Specialist Papers from the 1998 Australian Academy of the Humanities Symposium, 99. Available at www .patrickofarrell.com, accessed 4 May 2017.
[24] O'Farrell, 'Writing', 218–19.   [25] Ibid., 220.   [26] Inglis, 234.
[27] Phillips, 'Australian Catholic historiography'.
[28] Vaughan is the subject of an important essay by Peter Cunich, '"Archbishop Vaughan and the empires of religion in colonial New South Wales', in Hilary M. Carey (ed.), *Empires of Religion* (Basingstoke: Palgrave Macmillan, 2006), 137–60.

sophistication the historiography of Australian Catholicism outpaces by a great distance that of every other English-speaking jurisdiction. Yet, for all its strengths, it remains beset by an enduring politicization. Catholic history has not been immune from Australia's history wars, and where else would a prominent Marxist complain of the marginalization of nineteenth-century Irish Catholicism by 'right-wing historians', as the Sydney bookseller and political activist Bob Gould regularly did?[29]

Consider Patrick Francis Moran and Daniel Mannix, both powerful Irish bishops, both central to the secular as well as the ecclesiastical history of Australia, both even now without a wholly satisfactory biography. In Moran's case, the problem was primarily one of stamina: at least four attempts were abandoned, beginning with that projected by his own controversial secretary, Denis O'Haran. Two more faltered in the decades that followed. From at least the late 1960s, however, it was assumed that Tony Cahill would produce the definitive life. Partly this was because he intermittently, but steadily and insightfully, published on Moran and partly because Patrick O'Farrell said he would. Certainly no one else could: Cahill retained a significant fraction of Moran's papers in his personal possession, and there is a perhaps apocryphal story that he lost some on a railway platform. Many were only returned to the Sydney archdiocesan archives after his death. Moran's life consequently remained unwritten until the appearance in 2007 of Philip Ayres' *Prince of the Church*, commissioned by Cardinal George Pell, the then archbishop of Sydney. The choice of Ayres was controversial, partly because he was not a subject specialist, partly because it came from Pell, partly because neither Pell nor Ayres came from Sydney, and partly because he wasn't Cahill. Gerard Windsor complained about all four in the *Sydney Morning Herald*.[30] The book was also limited by the tight deadline of three years' research and writing imposed by the terms of the archdiocese's commission. In fact, *Prince of the Church* was an excellent first sketch of a crucial figure in Australian history, but it is suggestive that it had to be commissioned by a cardinal from a scholar outwith the field.

Mannix has been even less well served, despite being the recipient of at least nine more or less biographical studies. The reason again was politics, and in particular the politics of the Australian Labor Party (ALP). In Moran's case, his early support for ALP and late 'radicalization' (as Tony Cahill put it) made democratic socialism safe for Catholics, and this in

---

[29] See a number of Gould's self-published pamphlets and, in particular, 'Race, nationality and religion in Australia: The Irish Catholics, the labour movement and the working class in the 19th and 20th centuries' (2000). Gould's work is available at www.marxists.org/archive/gould, accessed 12 May 2017.

[30] *Sydney Morning Herald*, 18 August 2007.

turn made him relatively congenial to left-leaning historians.[31] Mannix was more complicated. The Melbourne archbishop had also been an enthusiastic supporter of the ALP, until his perception of growing communist influence led him to back B. A. Santamaria and the Democratic Labor Party. The resulting split shut the ALP out of power for well over a decade. This infuriated those who continued to support the party, especially Catholics, and many on the left today detect a direct line of descent from Mannix to Santamaria to the modern Catholic conservatism of Tony Abbott.[32] Mannix's biographies inevitably reflect this.

Santamaria himself published the most influential in 1984. It was inevitably reverent, and it is unsurprising that it was welcomed by the then Father George Pell as 'far and away the best thing written on Mannix.'[33] The two most recent biographies have been no more helpful. The first, published in 2012, was written by James Griffin and completed after his death by Paul Ormonde. Both were critics of Santamaria's Catholic Social Movement and both had been involved with Melbourne's *Catholic Worker* newspaper. Indeed, Ormonde had published a hostile study of 'The Movement' as early as 1972.[34] The result was a muddled hatchet job that plumbed a new low in Australian historical writing with Griffin's speculation that Mannix's mother could not possibly have enjoyed conceiving him.[35] Brenda Niall's 2015 *Mannix*, on the other hand, could hardly be accused of hostility to its subject. She described a man who was personally daunting, even foreboding, but hardly sinister, often in the right, and surprisingly liberal in all the right ways. Niall even speculated that Mannix would never have tolerated clerical cover-ups of sexual abuse.[36]

Nineteenth-century Catholicism also remains trapped in old battles. As Anne Cunningham has pointed out, by 2002 there were at least twenty books and theses specifically concerned with the core years of Irish–Benedictine rivalry between 1865 and 1885.[37] Most took one side or another, and Cunningham herself wanted to move away from a Suttor

---

[31] A. E. Cahill, 'Moran, Patrick Francis', in *Australian Dictionary of Biography* [*ADB*].

[32] See Gerard Henderson, 'Bob Santamaria: A most unusual man', *The Australian*, 1 August 2015.

[33] B. A. Santamaria, *Daniel Mannix: A Biography* (Melbourne: Melbourne University Press, 1984); George Pell, 'The Mannix story told, and told well', *Advocate*, 15 November 1984.

[34] Paul Ormonde, *The Movement* (Melbourne: Thomas Nelson, 1972).

[35] James Griffin, *Daniel Mannix: Beyond the Myths* (Mulgrave, VIC: Garratt Publishing, 2012), 85.

[36] See the interview with Susan Wyndham, 'Brenda Niall wins National Biography Prize for Mannix', *Sydney Morning Herald*, 8 August 2016.

[37] Anne Cunningham, *The Rome Connection: Australia, Ireland and the Empire 1865–1885* (Darlinghurst, NSW: Crossing Press, 2002), xiii.

and O'Farrell–inspired emphasis on 'goodies versus baddies' towards a renewed focus on what she called (without reference to Molony) the 'path to Rome.'[38] This was welcome, although Cunningham's intemperate prose, hostility to denominational education, and unconcealed animosity towards the Benedictine archbishops undermined her aim of transcending the traditional debate.

The definitive treatment of the Benedictine period finally appeared in 2008, with the publication of the Dominican historian Christopher Dowd's two-volume *Rome in Australia*. Following Molony, Dowd recognized that what he called the 'Roman factor' was the key to understanding the development of Australian Catholicism. He differed from Molony in his emphasis, however, writing that 'his concern was Australian attitudes towards Rome whereas I am interested in Roman attitudes towards Australia'. He also agreed with O'Farrell that the 'Hibernianism of the Irish bishops was well to the foreground in their thinking', particularly towards the end of the Benedictine period. He drew particular attention to the Propaganda's bureaucratic character and sought, where the sources permitted, to describe and analyse the behaviour of the *minutanti* who managed it. By the end of the nineteenth century, Dowd rightly argued, the structure and leadership of the Catholic Church in Australia had been 'basically shaped by a series of Roman judgments'.[39]

From Beginnings to Benedictines, 1800–1867

Whatever it became, the continent was at the beginning an Irish mission. Most of its first Catholics – convicts, soldiers, a handful of settlers – were Irishmen. So were the early priests, the first three of whom were themselves convicts transported in the wake of the 1798 Rising. One, James Dixon, was briefly judged reliable enough to be granted a salary of £60 and permitted to say Mass publicly in Sydney, a privilege that was revoked within a year in the wake of a convict rebellion.[40] He was allowed to continue ministering in private and returned to Ireland in 1808. Of the other two, Peter O'Neil was pardoned and left in 1803 while James Harold found himself sent first to Norfolk Island and then Van Diemen's Land before briefly replacing Dixon in Sydney. He too returned home in 1810. For the next seven years, free Catholics had no religious provision at all, while the soldiers and convicts were compelled to attend Protestant services.

---

[38] Ibid., xvi–xvii.   [39] Dowd, *Rome in Australia*, 1: 1–3.
[40] Patrick O'Farrell, *The Catholic Church in Australia: A Short History, 1788–1967* (London: Geoffrey Chapman, 1969), 4.

This eventually attracted the attention of Jeremiah O'Flynn, an Irish member of the English Trappists who had joined a French mission to establish an abbey in America. He had fallen out with his new abbot en route, settled in Martinique from which he was subsequently expelled by the British, and then from Saint Croix, where he was suspended after a dispute with the archbishop of Baltimore. He appealed in person to Rome, where with local Irish assistance he managed to rehabilitate himself. While there, he met the clerical brother of a transported Irish convict, sensed an opportunity, and secured an appointment as prefect apostolic of New Holland. Entry to the colony required the consent of the colonial secretary, Lord Bathurst, who refused on the grounds that O'Flynn was only semi-literate in English. He went anyway, landed in Sydney in late 1817, lied to the governor about his lack of credentials, avoided immediate deportation by a promise not to act as a priest (which he promptly broke), and was expelled in May 1818 despite entreaties from the Catholic population that he be allowed to stay. O'Flynn went back to the Caribbean, was expelled from Santo Domingo by the Haitian government, contributed to the rebellion against Henry Conwell in Philadelphia, was thrown out, returned to Santo Domingo, was expelled again, and ultimately died in Pennsylvania not long after Francis Kenrick's appointment there. Despite pious attempts to recover the Irishman as a hero of Australian Catholicism, he was in reality a prototypical *vagabondi* who managed, as his modern biographer put it, 'to conflict with authority wherever he went'.[41]

O'Flynn's adventure foreshadowed the Anglo-Irish conflict that shaped Australian Catholicism. When he was proposed for New South Wales, Bathurst had sought the advice of William Poynter, the vicar apostolic of the London district. Poynter was discouraging, not least because he had not been consulted by Rome and understood O'Flynn's appointment as a snub by an anti-English faction within the Propaganda.[42] In fact, neither the English nor the Irish bishops had much interest in Australia: at every stage it was Rome that took the initiative, although figures such as John England (still a parish priest in Cork) were pushing the convicts' case at home.[43] It was the Propaganda that suggested that two Irish priests, Philip Connolly and John Joseph Therry, might replace O'Flynn. Archbishop Troy of Dublin simply remarked that he had 'never heard' of them, while Poynter seems to have considered it an Irish issue. He blandly recommended the men to Bathurst, whose anxieties were doubtless eased by Connolly's helpful

[41] Vivienne Parsons, 'O'Flynn, Jeremiah Francis (1788–1831)', in *ADB*.
[42] O'Farrell, *Short History*, 12.   [43] Suttor, 18.

provision of testimonials from several Church of Ireland ministers.[44] The men were duly appointed as chaplains on a salary of £100 per annum.

Travelling in 1820 with a fresh consignment of convicts, they arrived in a colony that already had some 6,000 Catholics. Connolly soon moved to Van Diemen's Land, where he remained until his death in 1839. Therry stayed in Sydney, the only Catholic priest on mainland Australia for the next five years. He worked hard, founded several schools, formed a good working relationship with successive governors, and secured government support for a chapel on the site of the present St Mary's Cathedral. Collaboration collapsed after the 1824 appointment of an Anglican archdeacon with a salary of £2,000 a year, official rank, and an *ex officio* seat on the legislative council. The 1825 creation of the Church and School Corporation further cemented Anglican hegemony by allocating one-seventh of the sums obtained through land grants to Anglican schools. Therry complained of the injustice, ignored rules he disliked, and was suspended from his chaplaincy in 1826 by the incoming governor Sir Ralph Darling. He continued his ministry without official support and in the face of much official hostility. Legend has him scaling the walls of the state orphanage to baptize a dying child.[45] Therry also fell out with the men sent to replace him: he assaulted his immediate successor at an execution and dragged the second out of the pulpit while he preached on the theme of fraternal charity.[46] He continued to row with the latter, the Irish Dominican Christopher Dowling, well in to the 1830s.

This was unsustainable in a colony that had by 1833 grown to some 18,000 Catholics, perhaps one-third of the total population.[47] Change tracked developments at home. First, in April 1829 the Irish Catholic Roger Therry (apparently no relation) was appointed commissioner of the court of requests of New South Wales, just days after the Roman Catholic Relief Act received the royal assent. A political ally of O'Connell, biographer of Canning, and a committed Catholic, Therry went on to serve as attorney general in the early 1840s. He was the first free Catholic of substance to arrive in Australia and the only layman with the standing to challenge Fr Therry. He was followed in 1832 by John Hubert Plunkett, another barrister and O'Connellite, who, for what appears to

---

[44] Troy to Poynter, n.d. [1818], in Eris O'Brien, *The Dawn of Catholicism in Australia*, 2 vols. (Sydney: Angus & Robertson, 1928), 1: 148–9; Patrick Francis Moran, *History of the Catholic Church in Australasia, from Authentic Sources* (Sydney: The Oceanic Publishing Company, n.d.), 78.

[45] Moran, *Australasia*, 105.

[46] Eris O'Brien, *The Foundation of Catholicism in Australia: Life and Letters of Archpriest John Therry*, 2 vols. (Sydney: Angus & Robertson, 1922), 1: 122–3; O'Farrell, *Short History*, 26.

[47] O'Farrell, *Short History*, 20.

have been personal reasons, had requested an overseas appointment and accepted that of solicitor-general of New South Wales.[48] He too would enjoy a long colonial career, now remembered primarily for his determined efforts to hang the white perpetrators of the Myall Creek Massacre.

With Plunkett came a priest, the Irishman John McEncroe. The Maynooth-educated McEncroe had already spent several years in South Carolina, where he had been John England's deputy in Charleston and an editor of the *United States Catholic Miscellany* before ill health (his critics said alcoholism, which he later overcame) drove him home against England's wishes.[49] Years later, he explained his decision to go to Australia as the result of a chance observation of the sentencing of some prisoners to transportation. He made enquiries about religious provision in New South Wales, was told there was only one 'half-cracked' priest, and resolved to apply to be a chaplain. The government – which thought Therry 'stark, staring mad' – was delighted to accept.[50] Despite his later portrayal by Michael Roe as the intransigent leader of the Irish rabble, McEncroe was a natural conciliator.[51] He even managed to work with Therry, whose authority he did not directly challenge, and his close relationship with Plunkett ensured access to elite circles. The Catholic Church in Sydney was beginning to take shape.

This process was accelerated by the 1832 appointment of William Bernard Ullathorne as vicar general of New Holland, as Rome continued to refer to mainland Australia. In theory, the colony had since 1818 been under the ecclesiastical authority of the English Benedictine vicar apostolic of Mauritius, Edward Bede Slater. His vicariate extended across the Indian Ocean from the Cape to New Zealand, and Slater seems to have paid little attention to Australia. Certainly Therry never noticed his authority. Slater's appointment nevertheless established the Benedictines' involvement in the region, and when local conflict in Mauritius necessitated the appointment of a coadjutor in 1831, Rome duly looked to England. Their first choice was Slater's cousin John Bede Polding, a monk of Downside Abbey in Somerset. Polding declined on health grounds and another Benedictine, William Placid Morris, was appointed instead.[52] He in turn recruited Ullathorne, then a young

[48] John Molony, *An Architect of Freedom: John Hubert Plunkett in New South Wales, 1832–1869* (Canberra: Australian National University Press, 1973), 5–7.

[49] Guilday, 1: 336, 372; Delia Birchley, *John McEncroe: Colonial Democrat* (Blackburn, VIC: Collins Dove, 1986), 25–7.

[50] Quoted in Birchley, 32–3.

[51] Michael Roe, *Quest for Authority in Eastern Australia* (Melbourne: Melbourne University Press, 1965), 121–2.

[52] William Bernard Ullathorne, *The Autobiography of Archbishop Ullathorne, with Selections from His Letters* (London: Burns & Oates, n.d.), 52.

monk at Downside, to join him in Mauritius. Before they could depart, an official despatch arrived from New South Wales begging for somebody to come and replace Therry. (McEncroe had not yet arrived in Sydney.) Morris was summoned to the Colonial Office, where he secured Ullathorne's appointment as 'His Majesty's Chaplain in New South Wales' on a salary of £200 a year plus £1 a day travel money. He then appointed him vicar general with authority over the entirety of mainland Australia. Ullathorne set sail in September 1832.

His first stop was Van Diemen's Land, where, with one brief exception in the mid-1820s, Philip Connolly had been the solitary priest since 1821. The people, Ullathorne recalled, were 'all of Irish origin'. Both Connolly and his chapel were unkempt, and Ullathorne was horrified to discover that the chalice was 'tarnished as black as ink' and the aisles strewn with rubbish. Despite lacking authority on the island, he cleaned up the chapel, preached to the people, and enjoyed several cordial conversations about religion with the reforming lieutenant governor Sir George Arthur.[53] In Sydney, he quickly established his authority, secured public funds to complete Therry's church, and erected a further six schools (bringing the total to nine). He also rejected Therry's attempt to draw him into the dispute between what the Irishman called the 'two parties' in Australian Catholicism. Ullathorne's response would be that of his Benedictine successors for another fifty years: there were no parties, only Catholics.[54]

Yet Ullathorne was still only in his twenties, and it was obvious that a more direct ecclesiastical authority was necessary. McEncroe had already appealed to Archbishop Murray of Dublin for a bishop before he arrived, and Ullathorne himself quickly agreed.[55] Rome again approached Polding. Despite having already refused Mauritius and then Madras (see Chapter 3), the Englishman was known to be fixated on Australia and there was reason to hope he would accept. There was also no one else suitable. He duly agreed, and the government was delighted when his appointment as vicar apostolic was made in June 1834. They awarded the new bishop a salary of £150 (soon increased to £500) and instructed the governor to allow him to exercise a 'salutary influence' over the colony's chaplains.[56] Thus fortified, Polding set out with two priests and six clerical students, three of whom were fellow Benedictines. These last were central to his mission: as he told the English father president shortly after his appointment, 'let me be considered only as a Deputy of our Congregation'.[57]

---

[53] Ibid., 62–4.   [54] Ibid., 66.
[55] McEncroe to Murray, 2 November 1832, in Moran, *Australasia*, 142–3; Suttor, 28.
[56] Quoted in Bede Nairn, 'Polding, John Bede (1794–1877)', in *ADB*.
[57] Polding to Birdsall, 29 June 1834, *PL*, 1: 32.

Polding landed first at Hobart in August 1835, left a priest and a student there to assist Connolly, and arrived in Sydney in mid-September. His first years in Australia were relatively successful. Ullathorne had been his protégé at Downside and was now an efficient assistant, McEncroe was astute and supportive, Therry was effectively if temporarily contained at Campbelltown to the south-west, and his adversary Dowling was far to the north first in Windsor and then Maitland. The government was delighted to be dealing with a cultured Englishman, and he had influential allies, most importantly the tolerant and sympathetic Irish Anglican governor, Sir Richard Bourke.[58] Prospects were bright.

Not all was smooth sailing, and in particular Polding found it difficult to secure enough clergy. Nor were all the ones he had suitable. Philip Connolly in Van Diemen's Land, for example, flatly denied the bishop's authority and declined to account for what he had done with collections 'obtained for religious purposes and not yet carried into effect'.[59] He was suspended in May 1836 and promptly sued Polding for £1,000.[60] The tumultuous John Therry was sent to replace him. Nor were the Benedictines themselves entirely satisfactory. Of the three who had accompanied Polding to Sydney, Ullathorne thought one was a worthless 'clog', while the second was publicly rebuked and eventually sent home for spreading unspecified rumours about the third.[61]

That third Benedictine was Henry Gregory, who had quickly emerged as Polding's favourite. Almost from the beginning Gregory's influence was widely felt to be excessive, and perhaps sinister. It was certainly enduring. Writing in 1867, for example, the Benedictine bishop of Newport, Thomas Brown, reported his observations of the reunion between the now elderly Polding and his protégé. The experience convinced him 'of the wisdom of the Holy See in separating them' several years earlier, when Gregory had been ordered back to England. Gregory, Brown wrote, 'possesses almost irresistible influence over the Archbishop and insists upon submission'. Polding had even wept when Gregory 'compelled' him to change his schedule and abandon a planned retreat 'but seemed unable to resist'. It was, he thought, 'exactly what many of the Clergy of Sydney complained of'.[62] Although Brown was by then a fierce critic of Polding, he seems to have been genuinely unsettled by what

---

[58] For Bourke's Irish background and liberalism, see Jennifer Ridden, 'The forgotten history of the Protestant Crusade: Religious liberalism in Ireland', *Journal of Religious History*, vol. 31, no. 1, March 2007, 82.

[59] Polding to Connolly, 25 May 1836, *PL*, 1: 62.

[60] Polding to Birdsall, 7 June 1836, *PL*, 1: 65.

[61] Mary Shanahan, *Out of Time, Out of Place: Henry Gregory and the Benedictine Order in Colonial Australia* (Canberra: Australian National University Press, 1970), 30–1.

[62] Brown to Talbot, 21 January 1867, AVCAU, Talbot papers [TP], 80.

he saw. So were others, and complaints were made regularly from the late 1830s onwards. Even Pius IX sensed something was amiss, responding with fury when he (probably wrongly) thought that Polding had 'embraced' Gregory during a catastrophic joint audience in 1854. Gregory himself attributed this misunderstanding to the pope's unfamiliarity 'with English manners', but Polding knew that it had served 'to crown and corroborate the complaints that had ... at many times and from various quarters reached the Holy See'.[63] Unfortunately the surviving evidence does not now allow us to recover the exact nature of the bond between Polding and Gregory, but it clearly ran very deep.

What is clear is that Henry Gregory was a bully. Like Polding himself, but much more aggressively, he sought to force the Australian church into a model of Benedictine spirituality and monastic obedience. Reluctance was interpreted as resistance to ecclesiastical authority and crushed. He took a dim view of the Irish, noting on one occasion the 'somewhat lesser mental and social habits of the clergy of Irish extraction'.[64] The Irish Sisters of Charity found him unbearably dictatorial, while he was furious that New South Wales Catholicism had reached such a nadir that 'even women' were prepared to challenge his authority.[65] In the late 1840s, he drove the Irish Christian Brothers out of Australia entirely, leaving a corporate memory so bitter that they refused to return to Sydney so long as it had a Benedictine bishop.[66]

Polding himself was warm, ferociously hardworking, and dedicated to his mission. He travelled thousands of miles on foot or on horseback. For a Catholic bishop of his era, he was remarkably flexible and accommodating and, at least in public, had little of the sectarianism of his Irish successors. He was interested in the Aboriginal population, hoped to evangelize them, and spoke up for what he conceived to be their interests. It is unsurprising that later historians have admired him. Yet he was badly out of his depth as a bishop, let alone colonial archbishop. He was a poor judge of character, bad with money, indecisive, and a weak administrator. He was also sensitive to slights, could be vindictive, and was widely perceived as duplicitous. At one time or another, almost every Australian bishop was convinced Polding had lied to him.

---

[63] Gregory to Talbot, 27 May 1862, and Polding to Talbot, 20 September 1862, AVCAU/TP/378, 590.

[64] Quoted in Suttor, 77.

[65] See M. M. K. O'Sullivan, 'A Cause of Trouble'?: Irish Nuns and English Clerics (Sydney: Crossing Press, 1995), 111.

[66] Ronald Fogarty, Catholic Education in Australia 1806–1950, 2 vols. (Melbourne: Melbourne University Press, 1957), 1: 245.

Polding's problems were amplified by the refusal of the English Benedictines to staff his mission, partly because they were hard-pressed at home and partly because some resented his insistence that they support Australia at the expense of England. The English vicars apostolic were no more helpful. From at least 1838, Ullathorne understood that the consequence of 'all this failure in England' was that the colony would become an 'Irish Mission' – New South Wales, he wrote, would be 'Hibernicized'. He also understood, as Polding did not, that what he called 'Benedictinizing the Colony' would consequently fail, 'all the superiors being English, and all the subjects, nearly, Irish'.[67]

On his European recruiting trip, Ullathorne had consequently turned to Ireland for help, returning to Sydney with two Irish priests, including a future bishop of Adelaide, the Franciscan Patrick Geoghegan, a group of Irish lay teachers, and a party of Irish Sisters of Charity. He had already recruited the Irishmen James Goold and John Brady in Rome, and Francis Murphy in Ireland. All three would soon be bishops. When he arrived in mid-1838, Murphy brought with him five priests and two seminarians, mostly from Maynooth.[68] As Ullathorne told the Irish bishops, 'Our Mission is but an appendage to the Church of Ireland.'[69]

Polding resisted this. His lifelong hope was that national differences could be subsumed under a common Benedictine identity: there would be no Irish or English, only Australians, Catholics, and Benedictines. As he wrote in 1861, when pressure for Irish episcopal appointments was intensifying, the church should encourage a 'national spirit' and 'favour not English, not Irish but Australian, and if the Irish or the English or any other do not wish to be considered Australian, but obstinately claim for themselves some altogether different origin, they will destroy unity, social harmony, and fidelity towards the Holy See as happened in America'.[70] Benedictinism was Polding's vehicle for creating Australians, and, like Gregory, he was unable or unwilling to accept those that refused to conform, especially religious. This had consequences not only for the Sisters of Charity and Christian Brothers but also for the Italian Passionists he imported in 1843 in the hope of evangelizing the Aborigines in what is now Queensland.[71]

Yet Polding also knew that he could not run the entire continent from Sydney with a handful of English monks. This was brought home to him when he made his own European trip in 1841–2. The outcome was the same as Ullathorne's: indifference in England, enthusiasm in Ireland. By

---

[67] Quoted in Butler, *Ullathorne*, 1: 62–3.   [68] Moran, *Australasia*, 237.
[69] Butler, *Ullathorne*, 1: 63.   [70] Polding to Barnabò, 22 December 1861, *PL*, 3: 54.
[71] O'Farrell, *Short History*, 90.

late 1841, he had secured the services of nine Irish priests and six semi-narians and had petitioned the pope to send Irish Christian Brothers.[72] Polding also knew that it was necessary to create new dioceses. The size of the country made this inevitable, but it would also allow him to concentrate his own resources on New South Wales. He secured the Propaganda's approval to erect two, at Adelaide and Hobart, while Sydney would become the metropolitan see.

Inevitably, he looked to England for his suffragans, nominating Ullathorne for South Australia and the Nottingham priest Robert Willson for Van Diemen's Land.[73] Both refused, Ullathorne on unconvincing health grounds and Willson because he did not want to leave his mission. Polding then suggested for Hobart the prior of Downside, Joseph Peter Wilson, who declined after being warned by a fellow Benedictine that the clergy and people were 'almost all Irish'.[74] Polding appealed again to Willson, who reluctantly agreed after extracting several assurances about the condition of the new diocese.[75]

South Australia was more difficult: with no suitable or willing candidate in England, Polding nominated his own vicar general Francis Murphy. This was not a compliment: he had only made Murphy vicar general because the Irishman had been threatening to leave Australia, and when Polding returned he was appalled at Murphy's too Irish and too 'lenient' administration of the diocese.[76] In particular, Murphy had clashed with the Scottish convert W. A. Duncan, the editor of the Catholic *Australasian Chronicle*. As Michael Roe put it, Duncan 'disliked the parvenu ex-convict Irish who dominated the Sydney laity and financed the *Chronicle*' and had backed the absent Polding in the struggle that was already developing between them.[77] At Murphy's behest, he was sacked shortly before Polding's return.[78] Distant, hot, and impoverished Adelaide was the Irishman's punishment. As he told a friend, 'To go there is one of the most painful sacrifices that I have been ever compelled as yet to offer.'[79]

---

[72] Polding to Fransoni, 21 November 1841, Polding to Gregory XVI, June 1841, *PL*, 1: 189, 176–7.
[73] Polding to Heptonstall, 7 March 1842, *PL*, 1: 197.
[74] Quoted in W. T. Southerwood, *The Convicts' Friend (Bishop R. W. Willson)* (George Town, TAS: Stella Maris Books, 1989), 29.
[75] Moran, *Australasia*, 266.
[76] Polding to Brady, 7 December 1840, *PL*, 1: 172; O'Farrell, *Short History*, 60; Polding to Heptonstall, 9 June 1843, *PL*, 1: 224.
[77] Michael Roe, 'Duncan, William Augustine (1811–1885)', in *ADB*.   [78] Suttor, 55.
[79] Murphy to Geoghegan, 4 May 1843, ACAA, Murphy papers [MP], Series 27/Box 1/ Folder 2.

Most importantly, the provision of bishops to Van Diemen's Land and South Australia freed Polding to concentrate on his idiosyncratic abbey-diocese in New South Wales. He had several years before secured the approval of the English Benedictines for a monastery in Sydney with himself as its superior, and in 1843 he obtained Gregory XVI's permission to erect on the same basis further monastic establishments across the archdiocese.[80] As he explained to Archbishop Murray of Dublin, each new mission would be a mini-monastery, with two Benedictine priests and a lay brother. He hoped this would avoid 'the grievous inconvenience' of clashes between the regular and secular clergy.[81] Although Polding hoped for a steady 'supply of Benedictine [missionaries] for the Aboriginal and Colonial service', he knew that this was unlikely to come from England.[82] His solution was to send Irish recruits to All Hallows on the understanding they would join the Benedictines on their arrival in Australia. Polding and Gregory would then teach them how to be monks.[83] Local candidates for the priesthood would become Benedictines, whether or not they were aware of a monastic vocation. The serial scandals and ultimate failure of Polding's monastic establishment can be traced to these decisions.

With Sydney apparently secured, Polding seems to have hoped that the Irish seculars would drift away. He had already sent Murphy to Adelaide in company with another Irishman, Patrick Geoghegan was posted to the Port Phillip District (later Victoria) as its first priest, and John Brady was despatched to distant Western Australia as Polding's vicar general and then as bishop. John Therry was left in Hobart, much to Willson's disgust. Yet there were never enough Benedictines to entirely dispense with the Irish, and influential figures such as John McEncroe remained in Sydney. The Augustinian James Goold continued to minister in Campbelltown to Sydney's west until his appointment as the first bishop of Melbourne in 1847. Others continued to arrive. In Sydney itself, however, Polding was enjoying the process of building a monastery, recruiting new members, and training those who arrived from elsewhere. Yet, even at this early stage, there were problems: in late 1843, for example, he was forced to send home yet another monk who was bothering the community 'with his imaginations about Gregory and myself'.[84]

While Polding built his abbey-diocese in Sydney, Willson had the inevitable difficulties in finding willing priests to accompany him to Van

[80] Polding to Gregory XVI, 21 March 1843, *PL*, 1: 222.
[81] Polding to Murray, 19 October 1843, *PL*, 1: 227.
[82] Polding to Heptonstall, 9 June 1843, *PL*, 1: 223.
[83] Polding to Heptonstall, 16 November 1843, *PL*, 1: 229.
[84] Polding to Heptonstall, 23 October 1843, *PL*, 1: 228.

Diemen's Land. It was a measure of his desperation that he approached the Cistercians, not the most obvious of missionary orders, and ultimately secured the services of a handful. Meanwhile, the Colonial Office stubbornly resisted paying for more than one chaplain until Willson dropped a heavy hint that their parsimony would force him to recruit in Ireland.[85] That concentrated minds and a second was authorized. The final travelling party consisted of the bishop himself, two priests, and several clerical students, all English. It did not take Willson long to realize his mistake. Arriving at Hobart on 11 May 1844, he found no welcome, no house, and no money. 'Alas! Alas!', he recalled years later, 'We were English!'[86]

The history of the Irish in Tasmania has long been overshadowed by the fleeting presence of the transported leaders of 1848's failed Young Ireland rebellion. Romantic but unrepresentative figures such as William Smith O'Brien and John Mitchel have absorbed the bulk of the limited scholarly attention given to colonial Tasmania, or at least that paid to the Irish. It is also the case that in both absolute and relative terms the colony had a significantly smaller population of the Irish-born than New South Wales and consequently a smaller number of Catholics. This was primarily due to the vagaries of the transportation system: before 1840, only 13 per cent of male and 29 per cent of female convicts arriving in the colony were Irish and obviously not all would have been Catholic.[87] As a result, there were, by the late 1830s, only some 5,000 Catholics (almost all Irish) in a population of around 45,000, or just over 10 per cent.[88] The figure in New South Wales hovered around one-third, again mostly Irish. By the time Willson landed, this was already changing, as the closure of transportation to New South Wales in the early 1840s saw nearly 15,000 Irish convicts arrive in Van Diemen's Land.[89] By the late 1860s, the Catholic population was around 20 per cent.[90] Although the island's Catholic (or Irish) population never reached the size or importance of the eastern mainland colonies, it was nevertheless substantial.

It was Willson's misfortune that the unquestioned leader of the island's Catholics was John Therry. The new bishop had also been deceived: Polding had promised that the diocese was debt-free and that he would recall Therry to Sydney. In fact, the debts amounted to more than £3,000, mostly for the new parish church in Hobart, and it seems that

[85] Ibid., 38.   [86] Willson to Cullen, 23 June 1862, DDA/Australia.

[87] Richard Davis, *Irish Traces on Tasmanian History 1803–2004* (Hobart: Sassafras Books, 2005), 9.

[88] Richard Davis, 'Preface', *Bulletin of the Centre for Tasmanian Historical Studies: Irish edition*, vol. 2, no. 3 (1989), i.

[89] Ibid., ii.

[90] Richard Davis, *State Aid and Tasmanian Politics, 1868–1920*, rev. ed. (Hobart: University of Tasmania, 1980), 21.

Therry had planned to pay from his future income as vicar general and thus did not count it as a real debt. As the clerical historian of Tasmanian Catholicism delicately put it, 'evidently Father Therry looked on money in sight as money in hand'.[91] When Willson sacked him in favour of one of his English companions, Therry decided that this relieved him from financial responsibility. That left several lay trustees apparently liable for the debt, although Therry's financial management had been so chaotic it was unclear who owed what, or even exactly how much was due. When Willson declined to assume the liabilities, the trustees and Therry refused to surrender the titles to the church's property in the colony. Polding meanwhile flatly refused to recall Therry.[92]

The consequent breakdown in relations between Willson and Polding was near terminal. In 1845, the archbishop despatched Gregory to Hobart, where he ordered Willson to obey Polding or resign his see. Willson refused on the incontrovertible grounds that Polding (let alone Gregory) had no authority to demand this, and by 1846 Polding was in Rome complaining of Willson's defiance. Therry meanwhile whipped up opposition and directed a steady stream of complaints to Sydney and Rome. When he returned from Europe in 1848, Willson later recalled, everything was 'misery [and] violence'.[93] The following year, Therry unavailingly asked Ullathorne to 'make through the Very Rev Dr Cullen a communication on my behalf to the Holy See'.[94] The dispute rumbled on for many years, and both Polding and Willson made serial appeals to Rome against the other. Meanwhile, with the exception of a short sojourn on the mainland in 1846–7, Therry remained in the colony causing trouble until his final departure for New South Wales in 1857.

With Therry hovering, Willson struggled to assert his authority. In 1850, for example, the editor of *The Irish Exile and Freedom's Advocate* published a scathing denunciation of Willson's supposed persecution of him for the 'crime of friendship with Father Therry'. Things could become unpleasant, he continued, 'when a small community such as the Irish in Hobart Town are so divided in to petty factions'.[95] Despite these problems, Willson did what he could to endear himself to his Irish flock. One strategy was to recruit more tractable Irish priests: in 1854–5, for example, his diary records visits to Maynooth, All Hallows, and

---

[91] John H. Cullen, *The Catholic Church in Tasmania* (Hobart: The Examiner Press, [1949]), 100.

[92] Moran, *Australasia*, 266–7.   [93] Willson to Cullen, 23 June 1862, DDA/Australia.

[94] Therry to Ullathorne, 17 August 1849, Archives of the Archdiocese of Birmingham [BAA], Ullathorne papers [UP], B1667(1).

[95] Patrick O'Donohoe, 'To the Irish inhabitants of Sydney', *The Irish Exile and Freedom's Advocate*, 16 March 1850.

Carlow College.[96] By 1858, he had four students in Ireland and one in Rome and was appealing for funds to support them.[97] He was delighted to accept the Irish Sisters of Charity fleeing Gregory's attentions in Sydney. Willson also worked hard for the Catholic convicts, most of whom were Irish, and seems to have done much to better their condition. Yet Willson knew that, as an Englishman, he was out of place in Tasmania. From at least 1859, he urged the necessity of an Irish successor, remarking that it 'would be an act of folly to appoint other than Irish Bishops for priests and people who were Irish'.[98]

On the face of it, Adelaide seemed more promising. Despite its isolation, climate, and relative youth, South Australia appeared to enjoy one great advantage over the other colonies: religious equality was a foundational principle in what Douglas Pike famously called the 'paradise of dissent'. There was no church establishment, no religious preferences, and no state support. Catholics were broadly welcomed and by the standards of the day there was relatively little sectarianism. It even had a liberal lieutenant governor in the form of the ubiquitous George Grey (see Chapters 4 and 7). Equality brought its own problems, however. So did the fact that South Australia was a free colony with a policy, at least in the early years, of rejecting the destitute: without convicts or paupers there were comparatively few Irish, without Irish there were very few Catholics, and without Catholics there was no one to support priests, churches, or schools in a purely voluntarist system. Indeed, in 1844 there were only 1,055 Catholics in all of South Australia, of whom 347 were in the capital. This represented around 6 per cent of the population.[99] There was only one church, a converted storehouse in Adelaide, with an average Sunday attendance of some 300.[100]

South Australia thus had few Catholics, no infrastructure, and hardly any clergy. Ullathorne had visited briefly in 1840, and he was followed by another transient Benedictine and then an elderly English priest whose mark on the historical record is limited to memories of his carpentry skills, sectarianism, inability to ride a horse, and row with the government over the protocol for registering marriages.[101] Murphy's assessment was that he was deranged, quarrelled with everyone, and left the Catholic children

---

[96] Willson diary for 1854–5, Archives of the Archdiocese of Hobart [HAA], Robert Willson papers [WP].

[97] See Willson's letter in the *Hobart Town Daily Mercury*, 2 August 1858.

[98] Quoted in Moran, *Australasia*, 276.

[99] Douglas Pike, *Paradise of Dissent: South Australia, 1829–1857*, 2nd ed. (Melbourne: Melbourne University Press, 1967), 274.

[100] Ibid., 264.

[101] Margaret M. Press, *From Our Broken Toil: South Australian Catholics, 1836–1906* (Adelaide: Archdiocese of Adelaide, 1986), 35–40.

to grow up 'in profound ignorance of their faith'.[102] In early 1844, he was relieved by an Irish priest, Edmund Mahoney, and returned to Sydney. Mahoney was more active, visited much of the vast colony, founded a school, and promptly settled the marriage dispute through the simple expedient of asking Grey nicely.[103] He also wrecked his health, leaving South Australia when Murphy arrived and dying the following year.

Murphy brought with him one priest, two clerical students, and two lay schoolmasters, all apparently Irish. For money, he was dependent on an annual subsidy of £490 from the Propagation of the Faith and the generosity of his parishioners, who were mostly unskilled Irish labourers.[104] Murphy nevertheless moved quickly, and by late 1845 he had secured some land for a cemetery and opened a school, an episcopal residence, a more suitable chapel in Adelaide (which he called St Patrick's), and an entirely new one some 25 kilometres to the south at Morphett Vale. He sought to alleviate unease at all this activity with explanations of the Catholic faith so apparently liberal that Protestants as far afield as Singapore eagerly anticipated his conversion.[105] This entirely false impression was only amplified when one of his clerical students publicly apostatized.[106]

After 1846, a change in government policy meant that limited state aid became available for religious purposes, and by 1847 Murphy had received grants of some 80 acres to house churches, schools, glebes, or cemeteries and had gratefully accepted his church's roughly proportional share of the modest funds set aside for clerical salaries, church and school buildings, and teachers' salaries. He even obtained money for his choir.[107] Yet, despite this relatively benign environment, sectarianism was not absent in South Australia: complaints about the quality and morality of the large number of single women sent out in the late 1840s, for example, were often expressed in anti-Irish and anti-Catholic terms despite the majority being neither. One newspaper complained that Irish Catholic 'servant girls' simply did not understand the 'vice' involved in abandoning their employers, and hoped 'their Priests may take cognizance of the matter'.[108] Meanwhile, the newly arrived Anglican bishop was horrified to find Murphy given protocol precedence and addressed by the governor as the 'Catholic bishop' of Adelaide. He wrote pained letters to the

---

[102] Murphy to Geoghegan, 14 November 1843, ACAA/MP/Series 27/Box 1/Folder 2.
[103] Press, 43–4.
[104] Murphy to Geoghegan, 20 June 1844, ACAA/MP/Series 27/Box 1/ Folder 2.
[105] Pike, 354.
[106] This was P. A. Lackay. See *The South Australian Register*, 'The Bishop and his Lackay', 30 July 1845.
[107] Pike, 369.   [108] *South Australian*, 2 June 1848.

newspapers, to the governor, and to London but was still careful to note that he had dined peaceably with Murphy and addressed him as My Lord.[109] Less genteel Anglicans expressed their prejudices by preventing Catholics from joining the police, and there were the usual complaints about popery.[110] Yet, by and large, Murphy worked well with Protestants, and vice versa. This was particularly true of the numerous dissenting congregations, especially after Murphy made a virtue of being denied further unconditional state aid by proclaiming his conversion to the voluntary principle.

For priests, Murphy inevitably looked to Ireland. In 1846–7, he visited various seminaries there with limited success, although he did find two students to take up his free places at the Propaganda.[111] In 1852, he asked Cullen to identify two more.[112] He failed outright to lure the Christian Brothers and returned disheartened with only a seminarian, a newly ordained priest, and a consignment of Roman paintings gifted to him by Cullen as a kind of consolation present.[113] Things improved en route when a disgruntled Sydney Benedictine offered himself as a clerical student, and in Adelaide Murphy found another gift from New South Wales: three Italian Passionists fleeing poverty and Polding and notionally bound for Perth. Also in flight from Sydney was the Propaganda-trained German Henry Backhaus, late of Calcutta. He too had fallen out with Gregory not long after arriving in Australia and had decided to minister to South Australia's growing community of German-speaking Catholics.[114] He remained for several years before moving again, this time to Victoria. In late 1848, two Austrian Jesuits arrived with another party of German migrants who ultimately settled in the Clare Valley some 150 kilometres to the north of Adelaide. Although one soon returned to Europe, more arrived, and the society opened first a winery (1851) and then a college (1856) at Sevenhill.[115] By 1851, Bishop Willson's Tasmanian Cistercians had appeared, giving the diocese a compliment of twelve priests.[116] Adelaide may have resembled a polyglot clerical refuge but it now boasted a ratio of priests to people of 1:500. The contemporaneous ratio in Ireland was around 1:3,300.

On balance, Murphy did well: his emollient style eased tensions in what was already a tolerant environment, he recruited successfully and

---

[109] Judith M. Brown, *Augustus Short, D.D., Bishop of Adelaide* (Adelaide: Hodge Publishing, 1973), 185–6.
[110] Pike, 380.   [111] Press, 79.
[112] Murphy to Cullen, 13 December 1852, DDA/Australia.   [113] Press, 81.
[114] Nolan, 31.
[115] Ursula M. L. Bygott, *With Pen and Tongue: The Jesuits in Australia, 1865–1939* (Melbourne: Melbourne University Press, 1980), 20.
[116] Press, 87, 106.

imaginatively (although not without mistakes), and he significantly increased the diocese's infrastructure. By 1851, there were five churches, four country chapels, and three schools serving a community of nearly 6,000 Catholics. He had begun to build a cathedral.[117] Yet money remained tight: the sudden depopulation associated with the Victorian gold rush, for example, nearly crippled both colony and diocese and four priests had to leave for lack of support.[118] In a desperate effort to clear his debts, Murphy managed to raise more than £2,000, including £400 from just four donors in Victoria, all Irish, and another £370 from Sydney.[119] He even entered into a trading relationship with Archbishop Carew of Calcutta and a group of Bengal merchants.[120] The crisis passed as money and then men returned from the goldfields, but the experience was a reminder of the diocese's inherent fragility.

Francis Murphy's health had long been brittle, and it began to break down completely in the mid-1850s. He died in April 1858. At the time of his death, there were some 14,000 Catholics in South Australia, about 10 per cent of the population, and a vast increase on what he had found in 1844.[121] And, despite the influx of Germans, most were still of Irish birth or descent: indeed, those born in Ireland of whatever denomination also comprised about 10 per cent of the colonial population in the late 1850s.[122] The primary charge against his rule appears to have been a relative lack of Catholic schools; his successor complained that he had found none in Adelaide and that 'my saintly predecessor is continually quoted against me' when he condemned the state schools. His weak response was that those schools had become materially worse since Murphy had entered his final illness.[123] In reality, Murphy seems not to have prioritized spending his limited resources on separate schools.

The challenges of South Australia and Tasmania, however, were nothing compared to those of Western Australia. The distant colony was isolated, poor, small, and had very few Catholics: in 1848, the first year for which solid numbers exist, there were only 337 in a European population of some 4,600.[124] In 1842, there may have been as many as 150 or as few 30.[125] From its foundation as the Swan River Colony in 1829, no priest had ever visited. In early 1842, however, an appeal from 'the Catholics of Perth' arrived in Sydney. Many Catholics had apostatized,

[117] Ibid., 106–7.   [118] Ibid., 109.
[119] Murphy to M. Ryan, 6 June 1852, ACAA/MP/Series 27/Box 1/Folder 1.
[120] Press, 114.   [121] Press, 106.   [122] Pike, 106.
[123] Geoghegan to Goold, 17 December 1859, Melbourne Diocesan Historical Commission [MDHC], James Goold papers [GP].
[124] D. F. Bourke, *The History of the Catholic Church in Western Australia* (Perth: Archdiocese of Perth, 1979), 1.
[125] Dowd, *Rome in Australia*, 1: 126.

Robert D'Arcy wrote on their behalf, and the numerous Protestant ministers were evangelizing the Aborigines. They wanted a priest and promised to support him.[126] Already in Rome when the letter arrived, Polding diffidently suggested to the Propaganda that Perth be created a diocese along with Adelaide and Hobart. The Propaganda was willing in principle but the scheme was dependent on the financial support of the Propagation of the Faith in Lyons. When this was not forthcoming, Polding dropped the matter and on his return to Sydney decided instead to send a vicar general.

His choice was John Brady, an Irishman based at Windsor some 60 kilometres to the north-west of Sydney. Brady had trained in France and served for a dozen years on what is now Réunion Island, and he was by all accounts more French than Irish. Indeed, his imperfect English attracted Protestant mockery.[127] He was also a spectacularly unsuitable choice for Western Australia, and Polding almost certainly knew it. In 1840, for example, Brady appears to have had some kind of crisis when Polding chose to take Gregory instead of him to Europe as his 'confidential friend and advisor'; the bishop had to write a long and emotional letter to soothe him.[128] When he returned, Polding noticed that something had changed, remarking that 'Mr. Brady has become very queer piously.'[129] The next day he appointed him vicar general of Western Australia.[130] He had his reasons: in Polding's absence, Brady seems to have built something of a personality cult at Windsor, meddled in politics, and sparked controversy by peremptorily seizing and then refusing to vacate a government building when flooding inundated his orphan school.[131] Western Australia was as surely Brady's punishment as South Australia had been Murphy's.

At least Brady was keen. He was interested in native languages, had opened what Patrick Moran later described as a 'native college' at Windsor, and he appears to have seen the appointment as an opportunity to evangelize what was widely assumed to be vast numbers of Aboriginals in the west.[132] He set off in October 1843, his companions an Irish clerical student and an elderly Dutchman who had served as a chaplain

---

[126] Robert D'Arcy to Ullathorne, 12 December 1841, quoted in *The Salvado Memoirs*, edited and translated by E. J. Stormon (Perth: University of Western Australia Press, 1977), 15–16.

[127] For example, 'The March of Intellect; Or, The Rev. Father "Jo. Brady"', *Sydney Gazette and New South Wales Advertiser*, 1 September 1838.

[128] Polding to Brady, 7 December 1840, *PL*, 1: 171–3.

[129] Polding to Heptonstall, 30 July 1843, *PL*, 1: 225.

[130] Polding to Brady, 1 September 1843, *PL*, 1: 226.

[131] For Windsor, see Suttor, 52–3; for the political activism, *Australasian Chronicle*, 14, 21 January 1843; for the flood, *Australasian Chronicle* 31 May, 18 June 1842.

[132] Moran, *Australasia*, 555.

in the armies of Napoleonic France.[133] They arrived in Perth in mid-December. The lieutenant governor granted several parcels of land, a school was quickly opened, and construction was begun on a church. Everything seemed very hopeful, but then, after just four months in the colony, Brady set off for Rome without bothering to inform Polding.

His aim was to convince the Holy See to erect Perth into a diocese, and he set about it with a breathtaking mixture of bureaucratic skill and outright fantasy. He gave the impression that Polding had approved of his trip, arranged for at least one Irish bishop to support 'the best interests of Religion in Australia' with a letter of introduction to Cullen, and represented Polding's letter appointing him vicar general as a testimonial of archiepiscopal favour.[134] He told the Propaganda that Western Australia had some 8,000 white inhabitants, 3,000 of them in Perth, 1,500 of whom were Catholic.[135] There were also at least two million Aborigines of a type 'far superior to those of New South Wales'.[136] This was more than enough to justify a new diocese. It was also wildly untrue. Brady's overestimate of the native population might be excused as what Christopher Dowd called 'an extravagant guess' but even Brady cannot have believed that Perth's 150 Catholics were actually 1,500.[137]

Brady was also careful to pose as an expert on the Aborigines. In 1845, for example, he used the Propaganda's press to publish in separate Italian and English editions a fifty-page 'descriptive vocabulary of the native language of W. Australia', which he dedicated to Cardinal Fransoni. It consisted of hundreds of words and their definitions, many with detailed glosses. This was an impressive exhibition of linguistic facility for a man who had spent only a few months in the colony, presumably not all of them in native company. It was especially impressive for a man who, in his long years in France and the French empire, had so forgotten how to speak English that four years in Sydney had apparently not fully restored the ability. The Propaganda was completely taken in, as was the pope, who created Brady a doctor of divinity. The Propaganda even acceded to his suggestion that Polding not be consulted about the proposed new diocese or its boundaries. Sydney, he told them earnestly, was too far away and the situation in Western Australia was too urgent to waste months in correspondence. On 4 May 1845, Perth was duly created a diocese, and two weeks later John Brady was consecrated as its first bishop. It was only in early 1846 that a horrified Polding discovered

---

[133] Ibid.   [134] See Higgins to Cullen, 21 September 1844, PICRA/CUL/947.
[135] Dowd, *Rome in Australia*, 1: 126.   [136] Moran, *Australasia*, 557.
[137] Dowd, *Rome in Australia*, 1: 126.

that his vicar general had become a bishop and he himself had just lost a huge slice of his archdiocese. Brady had repaid him with interest.

Whether Brady was a liar or a fantasist is now impossible to recover. Probably he was both. Yet he was undoubtedly convincing: the Propagation of the Faith allocated him some £1,600 and he returned to Australia with a party of twenty-eight. He did well in Ireland, where his passionate appeals secured one priest and seven clerical students. In Carlow, he recruited three professed Sisters of Mercy, three novices, and a lay sister under the leadership of M. Ursula Frayne, late of Newfoundland (see Chapter 2). Brady found volunteers everywhere, however, including five members of the French Society of the Immaculate Heart of Mary and two Spanish Benedictines, Joseph Serra and Rosendo Salvado, who had left their increasingly anti-clerical homeland for Naples in the mid-1830s. In 1844, they had jointly resolved on a foreign mission, put themselves in the hands of the Propaganda, and were assigned first to Sydney and then Perth.[138] Brady subsequently recruited two more monks, a novice in Paris and a subdeacon at Downside. The whole party finally arrived in Perth in January 1846.

Of course everything went wrong. Brady's plan was to despatch three missions into the interior. The 'northern mission' was shipwrecked, and the two Irish students accompanying it drowned. Only Fr Angelo Confalonieri survived, and he died of fever less than two years later. Of the Frenchmen assigned to the 'southern mission', one lost his mind on the voyage and died within days of arrival in Perth, while the others nearly starved to death in the bush before giving up and leaving for Mauritius.[139] Only the Benedictine 'central mission' succeeded, and then only through sheer force of will. The five men survived on lizards, grubs, and what they could shoot until Salvado walked back to Perth to beg for support. Neither Brady nor the Catholic population had any money, and the musical Spaniard was compelled to raise funds through a public recital. He had to borrow a piano from the Sisters of Mercy, his shoes no longer had soles, and his beard 'needed more than a touch of the comb'. 'Altogether', he recalled, 'I cut a comical and pitiful figure.' It was typical of the comic-opera nature of the mission that soon afterwards one member of their party accidently shot another. He in turn became mentally unbalanced and left.[140] Eventually the three remaining Benedictines settled some 130 kilometres north of Perth, at a place they called New Norcia. There, the community stabilized and grew and survives today as what is billed as 'Australia's only monastic town'.[141]

[138] *Salvado Memoirs*, 17–20.   [139] Ibid., 31–2.   [140] Ibid., 37–44.
[141] See www.newnorcia.wa.edu.au, accessed 28 June 2017.

In Perth, Brady himself lived in a jury-rigged shelter so small he supposedly had to sleep upright in his chair.[142] He began to persecute the Sisters of Mercy, cut their allowance, interfered in their affairs, and bitterly criticized them for not treating him with what he thought was due respect.[143] Meanwhile, the only other English-speaking priest fell ill and left. Brady's debts mounted, reaching an astonishing £10,000 by 1849. At first he told the Propaganda that everything was fine, and, when he eventually admitted otherwise, he insisted that it was not his fault.[144] Rome finally intervened, dividing Perth and creating a new diocese in the north called Port Victoria. Serra, who was in Europe on a successful begging tour, was appointed its bishop. The Propaganda soon decided to make him coadjutor bishop and economic administrator of Perth instead. Salvado meanwhile succeeded him at Port Victoria, a place that never actually existed.

When Serra arrived, Brady accepted his money but not his authority, sued him for various offences including 'the unlawful castration of 18 rams', and called a diocesan council to excommunicate him.[145] He then left for Europe to complain about his own ill-treatment. He tried to play the Irish card, telling Cullen it was all a conspiracy got up by Alessandro Barnabò and the Spanish and that what Western Australia really needed was 'an Irish coadjutor and clergy who will be one with us'.[146] In other circumstances this might have worked, although the once bureaucratically astute Brady had not reckoned on Cullen's relationship with Barnabò; but his reputation was already shattered, Cullen refused to help, and he was ordered to remain in Rome. To the Propaganda's consternation, he snuck out, could not be found, and ultimately set sail for Australia. In Perth, he insisted that the pope had ordered his return, claimed full authority, and encouraged an assault on Serra's residence.[147] Letters from Rome announcing his suspension were denounced as forgeries, despite at least one being opened and then hand delivered by the governor.[148] Nothing could be done until Polding appeared in Perth with incontrovertible documentation. Only then did Brady submit.

He returned to Europe, where the Propaganda treated him leniently, allowed him a pension, and consigned him to Ireland under Cullen's

[142] Moran, *Australasia*, 558.

[143] Frayne to M. Cecilia Marmion, November 1846, in Geraldine Byrne, *Valiant Women: Letters from the Foundation Sisters of Mercy in Western Australia, 1845–1849* (Melbourne: Polding Press, 1981), 45–53.

[144] Dowd, *Rome in Australia*, 1: 131–2.

[145] *The Perth Gazette and Independent Journal of Politics and News*, 17 May 1850.

[146] Brady to Cullen, 15 August 1850, DDA/Australia.

[147] Dowd, *Rome in Australia*, 1: 154.

[148] *The Perth Gazette and Independent Journal of Politics and News*, 16 April 1852.

strict supervision.[149] He died in 1871, still bishop of Perth. John Brady's disastrous reign might have been forgotten if he had not raised the ethnic issue, but, by framing his struggle with Serra as one between Irish and Spanish, he ensured it would continue long after his departure. As Serra himself complained to Polding, 'all my crime is not to be an Irish'.[150] Although there is no evidence that Serra was hostile to the Irish, he had left himself open to the charge – and not only because of his shaky English. He was, for example, an excellent recruiter of clergy and religious, but only in Spain. That relatively few spoke English mattered little at New Norcia, which was focussed on the native mission, but it mattered a great deal around Perth, especially as Irish Catholic numbers began to grow with the beginning of transportation in 1850.

Serra's reputation for hostility towards the Irish was cast back at him from surprising directions. When he complained to London of official hostility towards Catholics, for example, the governor defended himself by pointing out that of Serra's 'eight priests seven are Spanish monks little educated & scarcely able to make themselves understood by the resident Catholics chiefly Irish'. The only Catholic school 'worthy of the name', he continued, was 'kept by Irish Sisters of Mercy who receive little encouragement from the Bishop'.[151] Serra understood the problem but lamented in 1857 that, despite a letter of support from Cullen, he could not find a single priest in Ireland who was willing to go to Western Australia.[152] Irish priests wanted an Irish bishop, while the British government made it clear that it would be 'both graceful & politic' if Serra could be sacked and a 'British subject' sent 'to a colony containing an exclusively British population'.[153] Neither got their wish: in 1859, Serra appointed the Catalan Martin Griver as administrator while he was in Europe trying to resolve an unrelated row with Salvado. He resigned in 1862, and Griver's appointment was made permanent despite Cullenite hopes that 'some Dublin man will be sent out'.[154] He became bishop of Perth on Brady's death in 1871 and died himself in 1886. The Irish only regained control with Griver's successor, Matthew Gibney. One of the relatively few products of All Hallows to become a bishop, Gibney's primary claim to fame is that he administered the last rites to Ned Kelly.

Sydney seemed, by comparison, a haven of peace and tranquillity. Polding's visit to Rome in the early 1840s had realized all of his hopes, and he had even arranged for Gregory to be granted a papal doctorate and

---

[149] Dowd, *Rome in Australia*, 1: 160.   [150] Quoted in Bourke, 45.
[151] John Ball to Grant, 11 November 1856, SAA/GP.
[152] Serra to Grant, 12 August 1857, SAA/GP.
[153] See Ball to Grant, 18, 30 September, 4 October 1858, SAA/GP.
[154] Grimley to Moran, 13 July 1862, PEDA/MP/TG/PM.245/PM/1.

he soon appointed him abbot. Throughout the decade, he secured further Roman concessions: St Mary's became a monastic church, the Benedictine breviary was made standard for all clergy, as was the English Benedictine liturgical calendar.[155] He imposed what amounted to a tax on the secular clergy to support the monastery, which was also the sole diocesan seminary. In 1848, he secured a Benedictine coadjutor (and notional bishop of Maitland), the prior of Downside Charles Henry Davis. In 1849, a Benedictine convent was established at Parramatta, and in 1850 the community at St Mary's peaked at around forty-five members.[156] Excepting Brady and Western Australia, every new diocese and every new bishop was made at his suggestion.

The reality was something different. Polding's problems were consistent, escalating, and largely self-made. Most flowed from his refusal to treat non-Benedictines as equals. This lay behind his disagreements not only with the Irish secular clergy and every religious community that attempted (often at his invitation) to establish itself there but also with lay figures as diverse as his erstwhile Scottish ally W. A. Duncan and the English social reformer Caroline Chisholm. Gregory magnified these problems but he did not create them. To make matters worse, Polding invariably behaved with a combination of prickliness and dissimulation that infuriated his opponents and ultimately undermined his standing in Rome. He concealed a Roman document transferring control of the Sisters of Charity to Sydney for four years, for example, and the nuns only learned of it when Gregory suddenly produced it as part of his campaign to turn them into Benedictines. Nor was it just nuns: Polding systematically misrepresented the behaviour of the French Marists who were using Sydney as a logistical base for their missions in the Pacific, while Gregory harassed them, seized their property, and ordered them to close their chapel.[157] The Marist general fumed that he was not going to send men just for Polding 'to make them into Benedictines'.[158] Even the sympathetic Suttor regretted Polding's 'blindness' towards Chisholm and his generally 'too aristocratic' approach to the laity.[159] Under Polding it was not Benedictine vs Irish but Benedictine vs everybody else.

Naturally he was convinced that things were going splendidly. The only lingering cloud was Rome's continuing reluctance to decree that the mission should be Benedictine in perpetuity, and in 1850 he sent Gregory to secure that final ambition. His case was a mixture of fantasy, mendacity, and special pleading: perpetual English governance of the

---

[155] Dowd, *Rome in Australia*, 1: 94.   [156] Ibid., 1: 95.   [157] Ibid., 1: 105–16.
[158] Quoted in John Hosie, *Challenge: The Marists in Colonial Australia* (Sydney: Allen & Unwin, 1987), 50–2.
[159] Suttor, 49.

diocese was appropriate because the Irish Catholic migrants would soon be replaced with English, Scots, or Germans; things were going splendidly in New South Wales, and religion was thriving; it was all thanks to the monks; monastic discipline protected against avarice and scandal; only Benedictine bishops could ensure this happy state continued.[160] Gregory's speculations on future migration patterns might be excused as an overly optimistic guess but his rosy picture of the state of religion in the colony was simply false. In August 1850, for example, Polding's Benedictine coadjutor privately remarked that Catholic educational provision was so poor that 'we have hundreds of children growing up in a state almost of barbarity'. More priests were urgently needed, he continued, but it would be 'some years before we shall be able to supply the wants of the mission from the monastery'.[161] Even while Gregory was in Rome, Polding himself admitted that 'no part of the world is in such spiritual poverty as we are'. 'The harvest is great', he sighed, 'the labourers few.'[162] He was right: between 1841 and 1851, the Catholic population had increased by some 66 per cent (almost all of it Irish), whereas the already inadequate number of priests had only grown by around 40 per cent.[163] That left the ratio of priests to people to worsen from 1:1,320 in 1841 to 1:1,500 in 1851.[164] Even that flattered: the concentration of clergy in Sydney, which admittedly had the largest number of Catholics, left many rural areas effectively unattended.

Gregory might still have got away with it had John McEncroe not anticipated him by writing a long, detailed, and devastating letter directly to the pope. Easily the most influential secular priest in the diocese, the Irishman had served the archbishop loyally, if at times warily. Polding had even made him archdeacon. By 1851, however, he had had enough: the situation was deteriorating; apostasy and indifference were up; attendance at Mass was down; so was religious observance more widely and especially so outside of Sydney. The problem was simple but overwhelming: there were not enough priests and the Benedictines could not supply them. The church must instead look to Ireland, McEncroe wrote, as '95 out of every 100 Catholics in all these colonies are Irish, or of Irish descent'. Yet Irish priests would not come to Sydney, he continued, 'because they have heard that the Archbishop intends to supply his

---

[160] Dowd, *Rome in Australia*, 1: 164.

[161] Davis to Heptonstall, 22 August 1850, in Henry Norbert Birt, *Benedictine Pioneers in Australia*, 2 vols. (London: Herbert and Daniel, 1911), 2: 166.

[162] Polding to Serra, 10 September 1851, *PL*, 2: 165.

[163] James Waldersee, *Catholic Society in New South Wales, 1788–1860* (Sydney: Sydney University Press, 1974), 201.

[164] Ibid., 213.

mission with Benedictine monks, and that Irish clergy will be employed only as assistants to the English Benedictines'. Polding's attempt to tax the secular clergy had only solidified this impression. The 'Irish and English characters are very different in their natures', McEncroe insisted, 'and when any difference takes place between an English Bishop and an Irish priest, then national antipathies and mutual distrust spring up'. He pointed to the dioceses of Adelaide and Melbourne, the latter established in 1847 under the Irish Augustinian James Goold, which easily recruited in Ireland 'because they are governed by Irish Bishops'. The only option was to divide Sydney, create new dioceses at Goulburn and Brisbane, and appoint Irishmen to each.[165]

It was very bold for a mere priest to write in this way to the pope. It was undoubtedly disloyal to Polding. Yet it was also true in almost every particular. As James Waldersee put it, 'Someone had to bell the cat.'[166] The Propaganda found McEncroe's clear, careful, and respectfully expressed argument compelling. By contrast, Gregory did not impress, not least because years of complaints from varied sources had taken their toll on the credibility of his master. The Propaganda duly decided on 10 May 1852 that Sydney would not be a Benedictine fief and that future bishops would be selected on merit from among both the religious and the secular clergy. All of the Australian bishops were enjoined to open seminaries for the training of diocesan clergy. McEncroe was awarded an honorary doctorate in theology. The only concession was to postpone a decision about new dioceses until the rest of the Australian episcopate could be consulted.[167]

Polding's problems mounted. Not long after McEncroe's victory, a Sydney Benedictine named Peter Farrelly appeared in Rome. He claimed that Polding had forced his monastic vocation and asked to be made a secular priest. Like McEncroe, Farrelly denounced Polding's administration, Gregory's sinister influence, and the impossibility of the Benedictines ever providing enough priests. To Polding's astonishment, the Propaganda released Farrelly from his vows, although they insisted that this was merely a kindness to the Irishman and not a rebuke to the archbishop. Two years later, and almost certainly encouraged by Farrelly, seven mostly Irish Sydney Benedictines sent a letter to the Propaganda questioning the validity of their vows and complaining of arbitrary rule. Polding sensed the danger and set out for Europe with Gregory in tow.

Over several months, Polding rowed with the Propaganda, threatened resignation, and offended the pope with his supposed 'embrace' of

[165] McEncroe to Pius IX, 7 March 1851, quoted in Birchley, 141–2.
[166] Waldersee, 202.   [167] Dowd, *Rome in Australia*, 1: 166–7.

Gregory at their ill-fated joint audience. He did, however, finally secure a ruling that the monks' vows were valid; the men were forced to recant and do penance. Yet this was not really a victory: the Propaganda was prepared to sustain Polding's authority against rebellious clergy, and even offer him symbolic marks of favour, but they no longer fully believed what he told them. This was not solely the fault of the Irish. Bishop Willson of Tasmania, for example, was also in Rome attacking Gregory's credibility over issues as diverse as his treatment of the Sisters of Charity and the ongoing dispute with Therry. To make matters worse, Polding's Benedictine coadjutor Charles Davis died in Sydney in May 1854. Now he had no successor. Davis' death also left John McEncroe in charge until Polding returned.

There were other pressures. In 1850, McEncroe had founded the *Freeman's Journal* as the voice of New South Wales Catholicism. McEncroe understood the importance of the press from his time in America, and in Sydney he had supported and ultimately edited the *Australasian Chronicle*. He was thrilled when his political opponents complained of being defeated 'by a "popish" press', and, when it folded in 1848, he retained its press and types.[168] The *Freeman*, McEncroe wrote, would be 'soundly Catholic and at the same time liberal in its general views and Irish in its sympathies'.[169] Domestically, it pledged itself to democracy, temperance, and 'complete Political and Religious Emancipation'; but its focus was on Ireland and the Irish: the inaugural front page consisted of a lament for 'poor but faithful Ireland' and a lengthy account of a speech by John Bright condemning the government's Irish policy.[170] Thomas Meagher was an early and well-paid contributor, and there were the usual stories about the consecration of a new bishop of Charleston or the dedication of a cathedral in Dubuque.[171] Even its name pointed to Catholicism's Greater Ireland: the Dublin *Freeman's Journal* was the oldest nationalist newspaper in Ireland, while the New York *Freeman's Journal and Catholic Register* had begun publication just a year before.

The *Freeman's* democratic politics and unapologetic Irishness undoubtedly annoyed colonial elites. Not long after he was appointed governor general in 1855, for example, Sir William Denison privately wrote that McEncroe was 'too ultra in his opinions – too Irish'.[172] The paper regularly exchanged insults with Protestants and political conservatives, but under McEncroe's ownership it normally eschewed direct

---

[168] McEncroe to Geoghegan, 24 July 1866, ACAA/GP/Series 20/Box 1/Folder 3.
[169] Quoted in Birchley, 134.   [170] *Freeman's Journal* [*FJ*], 27 June 1850.
[171] Birchley, 137; both in the *FJ*, 14 July 1858.
[172] Denison to Willson, 19 March 1855, HAA/ CA.6/WIL.380.

criticism of the Benedictines. This was not always enough: under the editorship of Michael D'Arcy (whom McEncroe appointed in 1853), the newspaper became so militant that Polding advertised in the Protestant press that he was not responsible for its contents. He also issued a pastoral letter decrying ethnic identifications: 'we are', he wrote, 'no longer Irishmen and Frenchmen and Englishmen and Scotchmen but Australians; and the man who seeks by word or writing to perpetuate invidious distinctions is an enemy to our peace and prosperity.' The *Freeman's* riposte was that it was 'a journal solely devoted to the cause of Ireland in Australia' and would continue to be so regardless of whether that upset the 'delicate English susceptibilities' of Polding and Gregory.[173] D'Arcy then compounded the offence by transferring the editorship to an ex-Benedictine. Polding was enraged, and McEncroe was forced into a lengthy legal struggle to reassert his control as proprietor.[174] With Polding's permission, he then transferred ownership to the English convert Jabez King Heydon.

This made matters worse: with Polding's former ally W. A. Duncan, Heydon promptly launched an assault on all things Benedictine. The complaints were the usual ones – Gregory, Polding's disdain for the laity – but they were now conflated with ethnic rivalries and often expressed in ethnic terms. This was inevitable: an Englishman and a Scot could only sustain a war on the hierarchy if the newspaper's Irish Catholic readership understood their campaign as being pro-Irish and not anti-Catholic. As Willson explained to a Roman correspondent in late 1858, the *Freeman's* was now simultaneously 'a violent Irish paper' and a 'medium for any dissatisfied Priest or layman, to say what he pleases about the Abp. or any other Bishop'.[175] Polding blamed McEncroe, whom he thought had become 'infatuated' with a 'licentious press' in America, and firmly believed that the Irishman still controlled the newspaper despite repeated denials.[176]

As a result, Polding demanded that the Propaganda denounce both the *Freeman's Journal* and McEncroe on the grounds that he could not do so himself without sparking 'the prejudices and bitterness of nationality'.[177] Rome was unmoved. This was partly because the Propaganda was now in the hands of Alessandro Barnabò, partly because Polding's credibility was

---

[173] Polding's letters, and the *Freeman's* response, both 'The Archbishop and the *Freeman's Journal*', *FJ*, 26 April 1856.

[174] Birchley, 138–9.   [175] Willson to Talbot, 11 December 1858, AVCAU/TP/752.

[176] Polding to McEncroe, 6 May 1858, *PL*, 2: 254–5; for example, *FJ*, 19 June 1858. Willson wrote in late 1858 that he had 'reason to suppose' that McEncroe was still the proprietor: Willson to Talbot, 11 December 1858, AVCAU/TP/752.

[177] Polding to Barnabò, 10 June 1858, *PL*, 2: 259–60.

shot, and partly because McEncroe chose to defend himself in person.[178] It was likely only James Goold of Melbourne's on-the-spot advocacy that secured the congregation's tepid condemnation, which focussed on the *Freeman's* tone and a handful of objectionable items.

As the pressure on Polding mounted, attention turned to the creation of new dioceses and the provision of bishops to fill them. McEncroe's long-standing plea that there be many and that they be Irish was widely known. As early as 1853, for example, an Irish Franciscan in New South Wales reported to the Irish Franciscan bishop of Newfoundland rumours that the colony would soon have three new Bishops. 'I hope', he wrote, 'they will be Irish men [as] there is a feeling of that sort getting up amongst both Clergy and People.'[179] More importantly, Cullen was undoubtedly aware of McEncroe's 1851 appeal to the pope. McEncroe himself was careful to cultivate the link; when he raised some £470 for the widows and orphans of Catholic soldiers killed in the Crimean War, for example, he sent it directly to Dublin.[180] It was Cullen's letter of thanks for this 'magnificent contribution' that gave McEncroe his opportunity to enlist the archbishop's direct support.[181]

Writing in April 1856, McEncroe begged for Cullen's help in addressing 'the inadequate supply of Prelates and priests for the daily increasing Catholic population of New South Wales'. In the five years since he had first written to the pope, Cullen learned, the Catholic population had doubled while the number of priests had remained the same. Although Australia was 'an English colony', McEncroe continued, 'it should be considered an affiliation from the Church of Ireland, as the great mass of the Catholics, both clergy and laity, are from that Island of Saints'. He therefore hoped that Cullen would 'bring the case before the Propaganda and get additional Bishops appointed for Australia'. Without his intervention 'the same evils will arise in Australia that did in America from the want of appointing in time a greater number of Bishops'. John England, he reminded Cullen, had made this point as early as 1826.[182] McEncroe's letter was again carefully phrased, respectful, and calculated to appeal to its recipient. It was also true: if anything, the situation had actually deteriorated since 1851; by 1857, even prominent English secular priests were begging to go home, and by 1860

---

[178] For example, see Polding to Barnabò, 24 June 1854, *PL*, 2: 201.
[179] B. Coffey to Mullock, 4 November 1853, ARCSJ/MP/104/1/7.
[180] McEncroe to Cullen, 22 February 1855, DDA/Australia.
[181] Cullen to McEncroe, 21 February 1856, DDA/1856/21/2.
[182] McEncroe to Cullen, 11 April 1856, in Moran, *Australasia*, 781–2.

the ratio of priests to people had collapsed to 1:2,000 in Sydney itself.[183]

Despite this, there is no evidence that Cullen answered McEncroe's letter or that he took any steps in Rome. The most likely explanation is simply that he did not know anybody in Australia. McEncroe was essentially a stranger, and his relations with Murphy and Goold were polite but distant. He had already resisted the temptation to intervene in the affairs of Western Australia. In fact, Cullen had hitherto only involved himself in colonial affairs when he was asked to do so by the Propaganda or somebody he knew. This had been the case with Francis Kenrick and John England in America, William Walsh in Halifax, and those for whom assistance had been solicited by Archbishop Daniel Murray. Perhaps more importantly, Barnabò only became cardinal prefect of the Propaganda in mid-1856 and was only beginning to habitually consult Cullen on missionary affairs.

Yet Cullen was still interested in Australia. He appears, for example, to have encouraged the Irish Franciscan Peter O'Farrell to write back on his experiences there. O'Farrell had been Cullen's agent in the archbishop's attempts to impose order on the Franciscans, but they had resented his manner and ultimately removed him from his position as guardian of the convent in Drogheda. With Cullen's permission he then went to Australia with the notional plan of raising funds to establish a Franciscan community there.[184] His first report was written not long after he arrived and not long after McEncroe's own letter. McEncroe, O'Farrell wrote, had governed well while Polding and Gregory were in Europe but on their return they had set about unpicking all his good work. Gregory, who wanted 'to make it appear that [McEncroe] was unfit to govern the Archdiocese in their absence', deliberately reversed every clerical appointment and on an apparently random basis; in a single week, O'Farrell was assigned to four different missions hundreds of miles apart. Gregory 'seemed not to care where I went – and told me so'. Three secular priests had consequently left 'for home' and another two for Melbourne.

O'Farrell believed that this exodus, and Polding's rule in general, had resulted in a significant 'falling off from the faith of their Fathers among the Irish in this colony': 'flesh meat' was eaten 'every day of the week'; people were 'getting married in Protestant conventicles' and to both Protestants and other Catholics; increasingly they did not go to Mass,

---

[183] J. Donovan to Grant, 20 June 1857, SAA/GP: Donovan was the president of St Mary's College in Sydney; Waldersee, 213.

[184] See Patrick Conlon, 'Reforming and seeking an identity, 1829–1918', in Edel Bhreathnach, Joseph MacMahon, and John McCafferty (eds.), *The Irish Franciscans, 1534–1990* (Dublin: Four Courts Press, 2009), 108–9.

and did not send their children; and the 'state of religious observance in some parts of this country is wretched indeed'. It was exactly as McEncroe had said: Polding could not recruit priests in Ireland 'owing to his well known prejudices against every thing Irish', and it would 'be a very great act of charity on the part of the Irish Bishops' if they could secure Irish prelates for Australia. 'English bishops', he concluded, 'will never govern a body of Irish priests satisfactorily – their prejudices are, I might say, antagonistic.'[185] He sent a similar letter to Pius IX, telling him that 'very few Englishmen know how to guide or govern Irishmen'.[186]

Cullen's well-known power inevitably tempted the disgruntled across Australia to take their complaints to Dublin. In July 1856, for example, a Victorian priest named Patrick Dunne wrote to his friend Thomas Grimley, then still a parish priest in Dublin, to complain about conditions in Victoria. Despite its wealth, Dunne wrote, most of the diocese's Irish secular priests were preparing to leave, either for home or elsewhere in Australia. The problem was not English monks, as in New South Wales, but Irish friars. Dunne carefully acknowledged that, 'although a friar', the Augustinian James Goold was a great man, but his vicar general, the Franciscan Patrick Geoghegan, was 'an ambitious little man who is pushing for a mitre'. He would do anything to further this goal, Dunne continued, and consequently 'the poor secular priests who are really the working men are kicked about & particularly those who are in the little Doctors way'. The Irishman's solution was predictable: a new diocese should be created with an Irish secular bishop.[187]

Dunne had to be careful in a letter he clearly intended would be shown to Cullen. This was especially true not only because the dispute was much more complicated than he had suggested but because the real problem was not Geoghegan but Goold himself. Dunne had first fallen foul of his bishop when he and two other Irish priests, Patrick Bermingham and Michael McAlroy, had proved too independent-minded in Geelong, a substantial town some 75 kilometres from Melbourne. They were promptly despatched to separate missions, and McAlroy and Bermingham soon left the diocese entirely. The men saw overreaction, which they thought driven by hostility to the secular clergy. Goold saw defiance in need of a rebuke, which he was happy to administer.

Goold's personality made such misunderstandings all too easy, which is one reason he had not been the obvious choice for Melbourne in 1847. Most observers had in fact expected that the position would go to Patrick

[185] O'Farrell to Cullen, 14 May 1856, DDA/Australia.
[186] O'Farrell to Pius IX, n.d. [?1856], FLK/Australia(I). This is a draft.
[187] Dunne to Grimley, 1 July 1856, DDA/Australia.

Geoghegan, who had been in the Port Phillip district since 1839. This was certainly the view of bishops like Murphy and prominent laymen such as Roger Therry. According to Murphy, however, a 'very close minded' Polding had declined to consult the other bishops.[188] Appointing Geoghegan would mean foregoing the opportunity to dispose of another strong-willed Irishman, and Polding's carefully constructed list for the Propaganda consequently omitted the Franciscan.[189] McEncroe was too old and (ironically) too timid, Polding wrote, and he had only met the English Benedictine Placid Burchall once, and had no reason to suppose he would accept, while Henry Gregory was very well qualified indeed but would never agree 'to be separated from me by a great distance'. That left Goold, who, despite limited theology and 'impatience of character', was a good organizer and had done well in Campbelltown.[190] It was hardly a ringing endorsement.

James Goold was in fact very much like John Hughes of New York or Thomas Connolly of Halifax: independent; politically astute; intolerant of dissent and of real or perceived encroachments on his authority; very Irish, but no Cullenite. He was master in his own house and pointedly rebuked any bishop who showed the slightest 'inclination to meddle' in his affairs.[191] Like Hughes, he was also something of a martinet, with a view of episcopal dignity extraordinary even for the time. He seems to have fully trusted only Geoghegan, his episcopal uncle J. T. Hynes, his vicar general John Fitzpatrick, the politicians Sir John O'Shanassy and W. H. Archer, and perhaps one or two others. Although he dominated the Victorian church, his influence on the laity was less sure, especially among those of lower social status, and many openly flouted his authority. In 1854, for example, he was ineffectual in his attempts to cool the tensions that led to the Eureka Stockade, despite making a dramatic personal appeal.[192] Goold has nevertheless been generously treated by historians, perhaps because relatively little is known about him. Even the formidably well-informed Geoffrey Serle found his abilities 'difficult to judge in the absence of much information', while Patrick O'Farrell thought him a less colourful version of Polding, albeit energetic, organized, and possessed of 'stability and sense'.[193] Frances O'Kane saw him as essentially heroic.

[188] Murphy to Geoghegan, 20 September 1847, ACAA/MP/Box 1/Series 27/Folder 2.
[189] Roger Therry blamed Gregory for Geoghegan's omission: Therry to Geoghegan, 15 October 1847, ACCA/GP/Series 20/Box 1.
[190] Polding to Fransoni, 22 February 1847, *PL*, 2: 76–7.
[191] Goold to Vaughan, 3 September 1878, AAS, Vaughan papers [VP], U1521/6.23.
[192] Geoffrey Serle, *The Golden Age: A History of the Colony of Victoria, 1851–1861* (Melbourne: Melbourne University Press), 166; James Goold diary, MDHC, 29 November 1854.
[193] Serle, 340; O'Farrell, *Short History*, 85.

The reality was more complicated. The proximate cause of the dispute with Dunne, for example, was the fate of some £1,000 subscribed to build a new church in Belfast (modern Port Fairy). At issue was whether Goold had the right to dispose of the monies for his own purposes without consulting the laity or Dunne, in this case to pay the previous incumbent for repairs he claimed to have made on the presbytery. A relatively mild dissent from Dunne elicited an icy response from Fitzpatrick: 'Anyone reading your note', he grumbled, 'would think you wished to encourage the lay people to interfere in church matters against the Bishop'.[194] Surely he did not want his predecessor to be forced to live in a noisy public house for want of funds? Dunne responded that he could not imagine why the laity should not inspect the accounts, something he claimed was normal in Ireland, and pointed out that he had himself once been forced to lodge in a public house less than two miles from Goold's own spacious home.[195] Even Polding thought that his subsequent suspension was a bit unreasonable.[196]

Dunne's sally was well chosen: Goold was already becoming notorious in Melbourne for his handling of money and his determination to live in a grand style. He took a particular interest in his own accommodation, which was costly, frequently upgraded, and luxurious. He also quietly built an extraordinarily large collection of paintings and prints, mostly baroque and mostly copies but containing at least one masterpiece by Jacques Stella and several other significant works.[197] Some were destined for churches and some were later loaned or given to public galleries but many remained in his private collection. On being shown that collection, one Irish nun recorded her astonishment at the presence of 'so many beautiful things'. 'Oh sister', M. Gonzaga Barry was told by the priest conducting the tour, 'if you stop to look at half the things here, we shall not be out of this today!'[198] Such acquisitiveness was not unusual among colonial bishops – many imported Roman pictures for their churches and several had excellent libraries – but Goold purchased on an unprecedented scale. He was also, as Jaynie Anderson has pointed out, extremely discreet about his

---

[194] Fitzpatrick to Dunne, 6 May 1856. Quoted in Margaret Pawsey, *The Demon of Discord: Tensions in the Catholic Church in Victoria 1853–1864* (Melbourne: Melbourne University Press, 1982), 8.

[195] Dunne to Fitzpatrick, 12 May 1856. Quoted in ibid., 9.

[196] Dowd, *Rome in Australia*, 1: 243–4.

[197] For Goold as a cultural patron and art collector, see Jaynie Anderson, Max Vodola, and Shane Carmody (eds.), *The Invention of Melbourne: A Baroque Archbishop and a Gothic Architect* (Melbourne: The Miegunyah Press, 2019).

[198] Diary of M. Gonzaga Barry, 19 July 1875, Loreto Archives, Ballarat [LAB], SER17/002.

collecting.[199] That it remains unclear where he got the money to pay for it suggests the habitual financial opacity that was at the heart of Dunne's allegations.

Dunne had meanwhile arrived in Ireland, and by late 1857 he was confident enough to write to Cullen directly, not only to provide more information but also to secure his assistance in Rome.[200] He even published a summary of events in Melbourne.[201] Cullen obliged, telling Tobias Kirby that Dunne had 'a great deal of information' about Australia which 'perhaps the Propaganda will be able to avail itself of'.[202] Goold's uncle, J. T. Hynes, who was in Rome on other business, was appalled at Cullen's 'very improper' meddling, lamented his own lack of Italian, and urged his nephew to come to Rome as soon as possible.[203] He even enlisted the Augustinian general.[204] In reality there was little to fear: the Propaganda was unwilling to intervene and Dunne left after a few months. Hynes was delighted, not least because it seemed that Cullen had done little more than facilitate the 'reprobate priest's' access to the Propaganda. 'Dr Cullen', he optimistically wrote, 'is far too cautious a man to allow his name to be used against you or any other Bishop.'[205]

Goold himself was taking no chances, and he arrived in Rome on 7 November 1858. This was probably wise: although Dunne had left, complaints from Melbourne had continued to arrive, McEncroe was en route, and Cullen appeared to be stirring.[206] Goold was also a shrewd politician, and before leaving Australia he had carefully secured the support of Polding and Willson for a common line against the lay and clerical dissidents who troubled each man, thus guaranteeing that the Propaganda heard only one episcopal voice. Goold and Willson consequently overlooked their long-standing doubts to champion Polding against the *Freeman's Journal* and McEncroe, while Polding reversed his qualified support for Dunne and assured the Propaganda that Goold was popular and Melbourne well governed.[207] The archbishop also made his peace with Willson, acknowledged that the 'long delay' in resolving the

[199] Jaynie Anderson, 'Visible and invisible: Jacques Stella in Melbourne', *Burlington Magazine*, CLVIII (April 2016), 245–50, at 246. I am grateful to Professor Anderson for drawing my attention to her work.
[200] Dunne to Cullen, 3 November 1857, DDA/Australia.
[201] *Extracts from the Victorian Press in Reference to the General State of Catholic Affairs in Victoria and to the Case of the Rev. P. Dunne in Particular* (Dublin: James Duffy, 1857).
[202] Cullen to Kirby, 12 December 1857, PICRA/NKP/2/2/54.
[203] Hynes to Goold, 13 [January] 1858, MDHC/GP.
[204] Diary of J. T. Hynes, from a transcript prepared by the MDHC, 13, 20 February 1858.
[205] Hynes to Goold, 20 November 1858, MDHC/GP.
[206] For the complaints from Melbourne, Dowd, *Rome in Australia*, 1: 249–50.
[207] Polding to Barnabò, 10 June 1858, *PL*, 2: 257–8.

situation with Therry had not been his fault, and copied the letter to the Propaganda.[208]

It helped that Goold had good Italian.[209] This allowed him to go anywhere and speak to anybody, and he did so with great assiduity. He haunted the Propaganda, dined regularly in the Irish College, and cultivated the powerful Englishman George Talbot, who had previously encouraged Dunne. He even went on long walks with Cullen.[210] Soon he was confident enough to challenge Cullen and Kirby on their support for Dunne and other turbulent Australians, apparently securing from a flustered archbishop the admission that they were a 'nuisance'.[211] He convinced Barnabò to show him the complaints that had been arriving from Melbourne, denouncing the petitioners as drunks, apostates, and criminals, and submitted a lengthy defence of his own record, which he declared successful, popular, and fiscally prudent.[212] By early 1859, he had secured a complete vindication; the only shadow was that the Propaganda did not also condemn Dunne. He even secured Geoghegan's promotion to Adelaide without significant opposition.

Goold had effectively demonstrated that only a determined intervention could be successful, and only at a very high cost in time, effort, and political capital. Cullen continued to protect Dunne – much to Goold's fury – but otherwise left Victoria strictly alone. As a result, the colony remained largely outside the Hiberno-Roman orbit until after Goold's death in 1886, long after Tasmania, Queensland, and most of New South Wales had acquired Cullenite bishops. Nor was it an accident that the diocese was not divided until 1874, exactly when Cullen's power was at its weakest in a generation.

This did not mean that Goold had a perfectly free hand: wherever possible, he avoided drawing Hiberno-Roman attention and stayed neutral as the situation in New South Wales deteriorated. He also cultivated Cullen, asked his advice, and sought his help with the recruitment of nuns, priests, and seminarians. In 1869, he advanced the Hiberno-Roman agenda by advocating the appointment of Irish bishops to New Zealand while leaving their nomination to Cullen. The Irish Franciscans Geoghegan and Laurence Sheil pursued a similar strategy in Adelaide. In 1862, for example, Geoghegan sent Cullen a solid gold chain as a

---

[208] Polding to Willson, 10 June 1858, *PL*, 2: 258–9.
[209] Hynes to Goold, 27 September 1851, MDHC/GP.
[210] Diary of James Alipius Goold, OSA 1812–1886, 8 February 1859. A transcript of the diary was prepared in 1997 by Brian Condon on behalf of the Melbourne Diocesan Historical Commission.
[211] Goold to Geoghegan, 3 December 1858, quoted in Dowd, *Rome in Australia*, 1: 252.
[212] Dowd, *Rome in Australia*, 1: 253.

personal gift and £571 for the pope.[213] He also imported Roman practices such as the Forty Hours' Devotion, which he had first seen in Melbourne, and waged a high-profile battle against secular education.[214] Yet the men also kept Cullen at arm's-length; among other things, they preferred the English Benedictine Thomas Heptonstall as their European agent, not Kirby and the Irish College. They governed their dioceses largely as they saw fit but along broadly Hiberno-Roman lines.

Goold was less successful as Polding's agent. This is unsurprising: the archbishop's reputation was compromised and McEncroe was a greater threat than Dunne could ever be; on balance, Goold did well to secure even the limited condemnation of the *Freeman's Journal*. Nor did Polding help himself, especially when it came to the division of Sydney. He knew that 'a good choice of Bishops' was the 'hinge on which the spiritual prosperity of our Province depends', but he could not decide on how many dioceses there should be nor who should lead them.[215] In just the first few months of 1859, for example, he suggested the creation of at least six different sees with sixteen possible candidates. Nine of these were English and seven Irish, but the rough ethnic balance was deceptive: two of the Irish were Sydney Benedictines; four had first been recommended by Goold, three of them for Adelaide; and one was Bartholomew Woodlock of All Hallows, who wasn't available. In fact, Polding's overriding concern was to avoid non-Benedictine Irish appointments. He was keen to stress that this was not because he was anti-Irish. To the allegation that he was driving good Irish priests away, for example, Polding informed the Propaganda that twenty of the thirty-one priests who had left the mission over the years were indeed Irish but eleven of them were drunks, mostly habitual, and two of these were also unchaste, or 'unchaste to a scandalous degree'. Others were mad, violent, 'very foolish', quarrelsome, had been the subject of 'very serious allegations', or were 'known already in Rome'. One had left when his 'contract' ended, one had left without permission, and two more were in Europe for health reasons.[216] He had a point: bishops around the world had long used Sydney as a dumping ground. In 1844, for example, William Walsh of Halifax suggested that an Irish priest who had given scandal in Boston and Detroit be sent to

---

[213] Cullen to Geoghegan, 29 October 1862, AAS, Geoghegan papers [GP], U1419.
[214] Geoghegan to Michael Ryan, 17 January 1860, ACAA/GP/Series 20/Box 1/Folder 10. For education, see the lengthy report in the *FJ*, 17 October 1860.
[215] Polding to Willson, 10 March 1859, HAA/CA.6/WIL.395.
[216] Polding to the Propaganda, n.d. [mid-May] 1859, *PL*, 2: 294–5.

Polding, who was usefully 'on the other side of the Globe far away from America'.[217]

The reality was that Polding was overwhelmed. In despair, he wished that the 'Holy See would take into its own hands the entire management and completion of this most important business'.[218] This left Goold to represent the archbishop's interests as he saw fit, and in early January 1859 he duly presented the Propaganda with Polding's most recent preferences. He also worked hard to block the possibility of McEncroe's elevation (he had been suggested for Adelaide) and diffidently agreed that Gregory could be appointed to Maitland, which Polding had requested, although certainly not as the archbishop's coadjutor.[219] Other appointments in New South Wales should await a provincial council. Yet Goold also wrecked Polding's plans for a Benedictine in Queensland by suggesting two Irish candidates, the Dublin secular priest James Quinn and the Melbourne Augustinian James Hayes.

It is easy to explain the inclusion of Hayes, but Quinn is more of a mystery: he had no apparent links to Goold, and it is unclear if they had even met; he seems to have had no idea he was a candidate; and, while Polding had already mentioned him for Adelaide, he had done so only at Goold's suggestion. Yet Quinn was close to Cullen, which Goold would have known, and the archbishop of Dublin was delighted when the Propaganda asked his opinion on the appointment.[220] It is unlikely to be a coincidence that shortly afterwards Cullen permitted a party of Dublin Mercy Sisters to depart for Victoria.[221] A message had been sent, received, and answered. Polding meanwhile had no grounds for complaint when a candidate he had recommended for Adelaide was appointed to Brisbane instead. For Polding, however, there was much worse: Pius IX vetoed Gregory's proposed appointment to Maitland. He had not forgotten the 'embrace'.

Polding found this unbearable and instantly told Rome that Gregory had been the victim of disgruntled laity, 'some bad priests', and all the 'hatred there is in the spirit of faction'. This opposition was not the result of Gregory's own behaviour, or his relationship with Polding, or any other reason except that he was 'the rod of Discipline in my Diocese'. Otherwise, he continued, 'nobody ever enjoyed a popularity more cordial

---

[217] Walsh to Cullen, 29 August 1844, PICRA/CUL/935. The nature of the scandal was not specified.
[218] Polding to Willson, 20 February 1859, HAA/CA.6/WIL.392.
[219] Dowd, *Rome in Australia*, 1: 273–4.   [220] Ibid., 1: 273.
[221] See Hynes to Goold, 13, 15 June, 15 July 1859, MDHC/GP; Goold diary, MDHC, 9, 15 June 1859.

or more widespread'.[222] Gregory himself wrote the same day to demand that Barnabò reveal the nature and source of the allegations against him. This did him no favours in Rome, but it reflected the hurt and anger felt by both men.[223] Indeed, Polding was so upset that he forgot for a week to congratulate Patrick Geoghegan on his elevation to Adelaide.[224] He had been too 'overwhelmed, trouble coming on trouble, that I am almost out of heart to think of anything else'.[225]

Polding knew the source of his troubles. For some time, he had been warning against the meddling of 'Irish prelates' who 'are not sufficiently conscious of what is for the good of the Church in these regions'.[226] He soon had more cause for complaint. In mid-1859, a prominent Sister of Charity, M. Baptist De Lacy, announced her intention to return to Ireland. One of the pioneer Irish sisters, De Lacy had supported Polding and remained in Sydney when the rest fled to Tasmania. She soon became mother superior, but after several placid years tensions rose in the mid-1850s over the provision of a permanent convent: the sisters had been living in rented accommodation, and De Lacy wanted something that could also be used as a hospital. With Polding and Gregory in Europe and Charles Davis in his grave, the women raised some £2,600 by public subscription towards the £10,000 purchase price of a substantial house that could be used for both purposes. The title was held by J. H. Plunkett as the leading Catholic layman, John McEncroe as vicar general, and De Lacy as the director of the hospital, now called St Vincent's. When Polding and Gregory returned, they did not approve of the location, the mortgage, the hospital, or the involvement of Plunkett and McEncroe. It was all too independent, too expensive, too Irish. They soon found a pretext to sack De Lacy, who threw up her hands and announced her return to Ireland, while Plunkett and her supporters used allegations of Benedictine tyranny to rally the Irish Catholic vote in a forthcoming election.[227] It was all lovingly reported in the newspapers.[228]

In one sense the affair was simply another skirmish in the escalating war between Polding and the laity; there were also near contemporary rows over Gregory's attempt to stack the fellowship of St John's College in the University of Sydney and his nomination of a Protestant to the board of the state-funded Catholic orphanage in Parramatta. The *Freeman's Journal* called the latter 'Treason against the Holy Church and the

[222] Polding to Barnabò, c. 14 June 1859, *PL*, 2: 298–9.
[223] Dowd, *Rome in Australia*, 1: 213.   [224] Polding to Barnabò, c. 14 June 1859.
[225] Polding to Geoghegan, 21 June 1859, *PL*, 2: 299.
[226] Polding to Barnabò, 12 June 1859, *PL*, 2: 297.   [227] Molony, *Architect*, 264–5.
[228] For example, *FJ*, 1 June 1859.

lambs of her flock!', criticized the implication that no suitable Catholic was available, and speculated on Gregory's sanity.[229] It all culminated in a group of prominent laymen denouncing Polding's 'mal-administration' to the Holy See.[230] Yet these were local disputes. As Polding explained to Rome, through 'malicious cunning' a rebellious lay faction had sought to make 'dupes' of the easily excitable Irish.[231] De Lacy was different because she had friends in Ireland.

Polding thus set out to discredit her in what was probably the longest letter he ever wrote to Paul Cullen. His tone was carefully calibrated: De Lacy was temperamental, chose her advisors poorly, listened too much to Plunkett, and was generally 'infatuated' with lay advice; she was too close to the hospital's Protestant doctor, who often conversed with her 'far longer than duty required' and may have tampered with her faith; although trained in Ireland, she belonged to the Australian community and had no right to leave; if she did appear, she should be sent home. He had already banned her from the sacraments. There was no mention of McEncroe, the Irish, or Gregory.[232]

He was right to worry. In late August, Cullen had answered McEncroe's 'anxious' request for a suitable first rector of St John's College with the name of an Irish College–trained Dublin priest, John Forrest.[233] He would have known that the letter would be shown to the college's fellows, who included Gregory, and he even subscribed himself with almost unprecedented 'great esteem'.[234] Polding could only construe this as an endorsement of McEncroe, against whom he had complained directly to Cullen in March 1859.[235] There were other warning signs too. In September, Cullen asked Kirby to introduce Roger Therry to Barnabò; the diplomatic Therry was no danger to Polding himself but he was a long-standing public critic of Gregory.[236] Polding and his supporters later blamed him particularly for Gregory's fate.[237] The following month, Cullen intervened directly, explaining to Barnabò that De Lacy was the victim of Polding's meddling with the constitutions of the Sisters of Charity, that he had given her refuge in Dublin, and that he did not

---

[229] *FJ*, 23 February 1859.

[230] Published in the *FJ*, 24 September 1859. The appeal itself was sent in April.

[231] Polding to Barnabò, 15 November 1859, *PL*, 2: 311–12.

[232] Polding to Cullen, 14 July 1859, *PL*, 2: 302–4.

[233] Robert Lehane, *Forever Carnival: A Story of Priests, Professors & Politics in 19th Century Sydney* (Charnwood, ACT: Ginninderra Books, 2004), 17–18.

[234] Cullen to McEncroe, 20 August 1859, St John's College, University of Sydney, College Archives, Box 1, Item 13. This form is exceptionally rare in Cullen's correspondence.

[235] Polding to Cullen, 14 March 1859, *PL*, 2: 273.

[236] Cullen to Kirby, 7 September 1859, PICRA/NKP/II/II/136a; Shanahan, 120.

[237] Polding to Goold, 17 April 1860, *PL* 2: 321; Thomas Makinson to Gregory, 20 June 1861, Downside Abbey Archives [DAA], Birt, N. 329.

think she should be sent back to Australia. There was no mention of Protestant doctors or rebellious laity.[238]

The Propaganda now needed to establish the facts. Was Polding incompetent and Gregory malevolent, as the Irish alleged? Or were their problems the result of a defiant national faction? Polding's opponents had a solution: send a Roman investigator. They even offered to pay his expenses. McEncroe made the same suggestion to Cullen and Kirby and they in turn made the case to Barnabò, who quickly agreed.[239] The Propaganda then approached W. B. Ullathorne, since 1850 the bishop of Birmingham and perhaps the only man anywhere who was trusted by both sides. Ullathorne, however, had spent nearly twenty years avoiding Australia, claimed that a visitation would compromise episcopal authority, and offered to write a report instead. The result was an attempt at even-handedness that nevertheless struck at the heart of Polding's regime in Sydney. The archbishop was indeed the author of much of his own misfortune, Ullathorne wrote, and Gregory was an arrogant and unsuitable administrator but they were being unfairly persecuted. There was no justification for the behaviour of the *Freeman's Journal* and complaints of anti-Irish prejudice were unfounded. He made several recommendations, the most important of which was that Gregory be removed from Australia for the sake of peace.[240] Rome accepted them all.

Polding was heartbroken. He would spend the next year fighting to prevent Gregory's departure and several more campaigning for his return. He could focus on little else; as his secretary wrote in September 1861, the archbishop was 'evidently lonely and has less confidence I think than ever in his own decisions'.[241] Within weeks, he was pointing the finger at Cullen, confiding to Bernard Smith that 'lying' had become common even in 'high places', and that meddlers in Ireland and England should look to their own affairs.[242] To Barnabò he remarked how 'bitter' it was to learn that Cullen had been the 'promoter of Sister De Lacy's idle tales', despite Polding having advised him of the 'Truth'. The archbishop of Dublin, he reported sadly, had not even 'deigned to reply'.[243] He knew that Gregory's removal had been Cullen's work, he told Goold, but could not fathom why he 'should interfere so much in our affairs'.[244]

This became a recurring theme. In late 1861, for example, he begged Barnabò 'with the most respectful importunity' that 'no Prelate, whether Bishop or Archbishop, of a country as distant as Ireland, be allowed to

[238] Dowd, *Rome in Australia*, 1: 208.   [239] Ibid., 1: 214–15.   [240] Ibid., 1: 214–17.
[241] Makinson to Gregory, 22 September 1861, DAA/Birt/N.337.
[242] Polding to Smith, 16 April 1860, DAA/Birt/N.256.
[243] Polding to Barnabò, 16 April 1860, *PL*, 2: 317.
[244] Polding to Goold, 17, 21 April 1860, *PL*, 2: 321–2.

intervene in the affairs of this country'.[245] If, he continued in a separate letter the next day, 'prelates in Ireland continue to involve themselves in the ecclesiastical affairs of this province, they give too little thought to the good of the Church in these regions'.[246] Two years later, he remarked to Geoghegan that it was 'pretty cool' for 'Bps in Ireland to recommend Priests in Australia to the Episcopacy, not to Dioceses in Ireland but in Australia!' 'How', he lamented, 'is it possible for us to govern the Church, with an *imperium in imperio?*'[247]

Neither Polding's anger nor his grief abated. In late 1863, for example, he wrote that he was 'sick sick sick' of being 'slapped and spit upon' by the Propaganda and anonymous accusers.[248] A few months later, his secretary told Gregory that the archbishop was 'often very sad, and in want of the support and sympathy you used to give him'.[249] There was nothing he could do except persevere and try to get Gregory back. Yet, although this remained his overriding priority, Polding knew that the creation of new dioceses could not be postponed forever. He also knew that the choice of their bishops would be crucial. As he admitted to Geoghegan in mid-1861, 'We must have an encrease [*sic*] in the Episcopacy.' This could have been managed years before, he continued, if only there had been local candidates 'whom with a safe conscience we could recommend to the Holy See'; but leaving the choice to Rome had resulted in the appointment of men who were 'cold and reserved – who value our experience as naught'.[250] He undoubtedly had Dublin's James Quinn in mind.

The Irishman had finally arrived in Australia in early May 1861, more than two years after his appointment. To Polding's relief, rumours that he would come with the authority of an apostolic delegate proved unfounded, as did reports that De Lacy would accompany him.[251] Polding, however, was still 'much disappointed' by their first meeting. He had hoped for 'free, unreserved intercourse' but 'could get nothing out of him'. Under questioning, Quinn simply 'affected ignorance' about the status of Gregory and De Lacy. He also revealed nothing about his plans for Queensland.[252] It must have been an awkward encounter: even Polding's secretary thought that the archbishop had been 'rather cold and on the defensive toward Dr. Quinn'.[253]

---

[245] Polding to Barnabò, 21 December 1861, *PL*, 3: 53.
[246] Polding to Barnabò, 22 December 1861, *PL*, 3: 54.
[247] Polding to Geoghegan, 17 December 1863, *PL*, 3: 132–3.   [248] Ibid., 3: 133.
[249] Makinson to Gregory, 22 October 1864, DAA/Birt/N.341.
[250] Polding to Geoghegan, 17 August 1861, *PL*, 3: 30.
[251] Polding to Geoghegan, 17 August 1861; Polding to Gregory, 14 February 1861, *PL*, 3: 11.
[252] Polding to Gregory, 21 May 1861, *PL*, 3: 24.
[253] Makinson to Gregory, 21 May 1861, DAA/Birt/N.326.

His mood cannot have been improved by the St Benedict's Young Men's Society's reception for the new arrival. The crowd then greeted with 'loud cheers' Quinn's remark that 'in so large an assemblage of true and loyal Catholics he thought he could detect many generous and warm-hearted Irishmen' and followed it with songs including 'The Harp that once through Tara's halls'. All that was left for Polding was to make a pointed observation that all present were 'children of the same loving mother, who cast her mantle over all alike'.[254] Yet, despite the grand reception in Sydney, and another a few days later in Brisbane, Quinn's mission was not off to a good start. It had escaped no one's notice that he had secured very few companions; Polding cheerfully informed Gregory of the 'queer lot of Clergy he has brought – Four French, *one Irish*, and one Italian!'[255] This was embarrassing, not least because McEncroe and others had long maintained that it was only Benedictinism that prevented the easy recruitment of Irish priests.

The problem was Quinn himself. One of three clerical brothers educated at the Irish College, he was shaped by his more than decade-long experience of papal Rome. Like many Hiberno-Roman bishops, he excelled academically, and back home he soon founded a secondary school and minor seminary named after Dublin's patron, St Laurence O'Toole. He did not lack for ambition: Archbishop Murray suggested a modest rural location, Quinn leased grand buildings off St Stephen's Green; he promised Cullen an affordable day school, but dreamed of a Catholic Rugby and charged accordingly.[256] In 1854, St Laurence's became a collegiate house of John Henry Newman's Catholic University of Ireland, while retaining its role as Dublin's leading Catholic secondary school.[257] Quinn employed there a small group of Irish College–trained clerics, including his brother Matthew, their cousin James Murray, and his eventual successor in Brisbane, Robert Dunne. The regime was strict – certainly stricter than Newman's house nearby – and resolutely nationalistic. Although the school was a success, in part due to lack of competition, the university struggled and Quinn quarrelled with Newman over discipline, authority, and money. In both 1856 and 1858, he threatened to withdraw his students entirely. He also threw himself into the

---

[254] *FJ*, 8 May 1861.
[255] Polding to Gregory, 19 April 1861, *PL*, 3: 20. Emphasis in original.
[256] Neil J. Byrne, *Robert Dunne, Archbishop of Brisbane* (St Lucia: University of Queensland Press, 1991), 36–7.
[257] See Donal Kerr, 'Dr. Quinn's school and the Catholic University, 1850–67', *Irish Ecclesiastical Record*, 5th series, 108 (1967): 89–101.

confusion surrounding Newman's prolonged departure and appears to have harboured hopes of succeeding him.[258]

By late 1858, Quinn was worried: he had failed to become Newman's successor, fallen out with most of his university colleagues, and knew St Laurence's would suffer when its clerical students moved to the new Holy Cross College in Clonliffe. (He unsuccessfully recommended Matthew as its first president.) His clumsy plotting had also drawn Cullen's wrath.[259] He made an abject apology, but it is not hard to believe that both Cullen and Quinn himself were glad to see him out of Dublin. Indeed, Quinn's career in Ireland foreshadowed both the strengths and the weaknesses of his episcopate: he was profligate and prickly, trusted only a small circle, and was temperamentally incapable of collaboration; but he was also ambitious, organized, and absolutely committed to Catholic education.

Quinn's one great success occurred before he left Ireland: he convinced M. Vincent Whitty to accompany him to Australia. Whitty had joined the nascent Sisters of Mercy in 1839, 'a soft, young girl apparently just out of her teens'.[260] Ten years later, she was elected the fourth reverend mother of their 'Head House' in Dublin's Baggot Street. She proved a confident and astute leader, willing to assert herself against meddling or unsatisfactory clerics but also taking care to build a powerful network of supporters. Her brother Robert was a confidant of Cardinal Wiseman, for example, and she cultivated her own links with the wider Maher family and by extension their Cullen and Moran relatives.[261] In 1852, she oversaw the foundation of what would become the Mater hospital, and in 1854 she despatched a party of Mercy Sisters to the Crimea. As James Quinn's elder brother Andrew put it, not only had she filled 'Baggot St. with real nuns, [and] Dublin with Hospitals and Reformatories', but 'throughout the five continents of the world including the two Americas' she had planted 'numerous foundations of Sisters of Mercy'.[262] She was also among the handful of people to whose judgement Cullen deferred. It is unlikely that any Irish woman at the time enjoyed more power, influence, or responsibility.

There appear to have been several reasons for Quinn's success in luring her to Brisbane. The first was pure chance: the pioneer priest James Dixon had been a family friend, and she grew up hearing his stories of

---

[258] Anne McLay, *James Quinn: First Catholic bishop of Brisbane*, Rev. ed. (Toowoomba, QLD: Church Archivist' Society, 1989), 24.

[259] Ibid., 26.

[260] Andrew Quinn to Cullen, 27 December 1861, Mercy International Centre Archives, Dublin, FI8.

[261] Mary Xaverius O'Donoghue, *Mother Vincent Whitty: Women and Education in a Masculine Society* (Melbourne: Melbourne University Press, 1972), 21.

[262] Andrew Quinn to Cullen, 27 December 1861.

Australia.[263] So was the second: the new bishop was the long-standing confessor to the Baggot Street community. The last was more practical: her tenure as reverend mother had ended in May 1858, and it seems that her successor felt threatened by her continuing presence. Although the truth of the matter is hard to judge, not least because Mary Xaverius O'Donoghue's biography and Whitty's own published correspondence for this period are conspicuously silent, what is clear is that by early 1860 she had decided to leave Ireland. As she explained in July, she wanted 'to go on the next Mission leaving Baggot Street'. If this was Queensland, all well and good, although she wasn't sure 'if Dr Quinn *even* likes me'. She did, however, prefer Brisbane to Melbourne or Geelong because she relished starting from scratch. 'Going to a new settlement', she wrote, 'seems to me like taking the *children*, rather than the grown girls from the Work House.'[264] She could also be in charge again. After lengthy negotiations, Whitty was permitted to take two professed sisters (both sickly and uneducated, according to Andrew Quinn) and two postulants with her, and collected a third professed sister in Liverpool.[265]

They were all in for a shock. On landing, Quinn famously asked 'Where is the city of Brisbane?'[266] The nuns found that the house designated for them was unfurnished 'and in such an exposed position' that Quinn insisted they take the one prepared for him, gave theirs to his priests, and slept himself in what Whitty described as 'a sort of outdoor verandah'.[267] It was all very primitive. The vast whole of Queensland then had a European population of about 30,000, a quarter of whom (7,676) were Catholic.[268] Until Quinn's arrival, there had been only two priests: one at Brisbane, which had 1,429 Catholics, the other at Ipswich, which had 1,255.[269] Significant populations at Maryborough, Toowoomba, and Warwick had no provision at all, while even Brisbane was left without for weeks at a time while the resident priest travelled in the bush.[270] There were four schools, none of any size, and a handful of modest churches.[271]

As elsewhere in Australia, Queensland's Catholic population was overwhelmingly Irish. Indeed, the only significant 'foreign' group in the colony were some 2,100 Germans, mostly single men.[272] Of the Irish, 5,537 had migrated directly and more arrived after first spending time in

---

[263] O'Donoghue, *Whitty*, 5.
[264] Whitty to MM of Mercy Norris, 14 July 1860, *WL*, 116. Emphasis in original.
[265] James Quinn to Norris, 19 November 1860, *WL*, 120; Andrew Quinn to Cullen, 27 December 1861; O'Donoghue, *Whitty*, 28–9.
[266] O'Farrell, *Short History*, 96.   [267] Whitty to Norris, 13 May 1861, *WL*, 132.
[268] *Census of the Colony of Queensland, taken the 7th April, 1861*, xv.
[269] *Queensland Census*, table 5.   [270] Whitty to Norris, 13 May 1861, *WL*, 135.
[271] McLay, *Quinn*, 47.   [272] *Queensland Census*, xiv.

another Australian colony. Others had Irish parents; and, although the census did not cross-reference religion and place of birth, it is reasonable to assume that most were Catholic. In Brisbane, for example, Whitty described her charges as largely 'good but poor Irish', although the booming economy meant 'they all have enough work and they are no longer poor'.[273] Queensland was 'a fine place for immigration just now', she wrote, and 'particularly for working people'.[274] The problem was how to educate them.

This was no small task: in 1861, some 60 per cent of those between the ages of five and fourteen were 'to all good purposes uneducated'.[275] Whitty knew schools were 'the want of the day' but did not know how she was to provide them. Unfortunately the new and strictly secular primary education system in Queensland was much worse than that of Ireland, she reported to Baggot Street, and Quinn would need 'ten sets of nuns' if he was to provide adequate schools across the colony. She pleaded for a 'School Sister or two', pointedly reminding her successor that none of the women with her were capable of passing a teacher training examination.[276] She made the same request to Cullen, telling him that 'the poor parents cry when they look at us, saying we remind them of the "Ould Country" and the good nuns in Cork or Tralee or Carlow'.[277] Baggot Street was adamantine: no one could be spared, not even for Cullen, and Whitty should stop asking.[278] Even so, she soon managed to open several 'Poor Schools', which quickly had more than 150 students.[279]

Quinn was also busy with schools. Based on a similar policy in New South Wales, the Queensland Grammar Schools Act of 1860 provided for government matching funds where there was tangible local support. A deposit of £1,000 would secure £2,000, for example, while a guarantee of £250 in fee income for three years would be matched by a similar sum from the government. In exchange, they would appoint four of the prospective school's seven trustees. Any interested group could apply. Yet the Act also mandated that the education provided should be secular and open to all. This did not deter Quinn, and within six weeks of arrival he had lodged a deposit of £3,000 towards a school in Brisbane and £2,000 for one in Ipswich.

---

[273] Whitty to Norris, 13 May 1861, *WL*, 134.
[274] Whitty to Norris, 9 June 1861, *WL*, 139.   [275] *Queensland Census*, xii.
[276] Whitty to Norris, 13 May 1861. Emphasis in original.
[277] Whitty to Cullen, 19 July 1861, *WL*, 141. Emphasis in original.
[278] Norris to Cullen, 27 March [1862], *WL*, 129. This is dated March 1861 in the Whitty correspondence but from the context must surely be from the following year.
[279] Whitty to Norris, 9 June 1861; Whitty to Cullen, 19 July 1861.

How he achieved this is a mystery. In his study of secondary education in Queensland, Rupert Goodman suggested that the monies had already been raised locally on the grounds that Quinn just had not had enough time to do the job himself.[280] This is possible, but the colony's Catholics had not hitherto shown such fundraising prowess while a forceful new bishop might have been able to raise all or most of the money quickly. Either way, Quinn had presented the government with a dilemma: funding Catholic schools was political poison but the Act did not specifically prohibit it. At first they tried to refuse on the grounds that any school must be 'strictly unsectarian', but, when Quinn gave assurances that his would be 'open to all classes of denomination', the government reversed itself and insisted on collaborative applications from more than one denomination. An attempt to achieve this in Ipswich ended in brawling, sectarian passions were inflamed throughout the colony, and no funding was ultimately provided.[281]

The experience taught Quinn the importance of politics: without sympathetic parliamentarians, Catholic grievances would never be answered. This could be achieved in several ways. One was to establish a public voice, and the *North Australian* duly began publication in late 1861 under what Anne McLay called 'de facto Quinn management'.[282] Another was to form alliances wherever possible, in particular with the high church Anglican bishop Edward Tufnell. The men even toured the colony together in 1864–5 to demand state-funded denominational education. At least one rally ended in violence and what a disapproving newspaper called 'victory for the Irish party', while the Irish Protestant governor came to see Tufnell as 'an instrument of Irish Romanists and demagogues'.[283] Although unusual, such alliances were not entirely unknown; in New South Wales, for example, James Murray of Maitland gave electoral support to what he called 'a few respectable Church of England men who entertain to some extent our views on the question of education'.[284]

Quinn's tolerance did not extend to the government. As the more emollient Polding quickly noticed, he had a 'strange desire to do what we have always avoided – to put the Government in the wrong'.[285] His *North Australian* was a persistent critic, and he privately campaigned to

[280] Robert Goodman, *Secondary Education in Queensland 1860–1960* (Canberra: Australian National University Press, 1968), 31–2.

[281] Ibid., 31–4.   [282] McLay, *Quinn*, 116.

[283] See E. R Wyeth, *Education in Queensland: A History of Education in Queensland and in the Moreton Bay District of New South Wales* (Melbourne: Australian Council for Educational Research, n.d.), 102–3; quoted in McLay, *Quinn*, 118.

[284] Murray to Cullen, 3 December 1869, DDA/Australia.

[285] Polding to Gregory, 11 November 1861, *PL*, 3: 43.

have the governor sacked for bigotry.[286] Quinn was also prepared to engage in electoral politics. In the 1863 general election, for example, he tried to help the prominent layman Patrick O'Sullivan win the seat of Robert Herbert, the colony's premier, despite having threatened to excommunicate O'Sullivan just the year before.[287] In another seat, Herbert complained, Quinn rode through the streets with 'a swindler from Ireland, to show he was a proper person for all good R. Catholics to vote for'. Quinn's candidates didn't win – Herbert thought that the 'Pope must feel very small' – but the election established him as a force in Queensland politics.[288]

Yet the simplest way of increasing Catholic influence was to increase the number of Catholics. Queensland's hunger for migrants provided the opportunity. Passed in 1860, the Alienation of Crown Lands Act provided that land orders to the eventual value of £30 would be awarded to any European migrant who stayed in the colony for at least two years, including children. Quinn raised £3,500 to begin what he told the government would be a 'succession of vessels' filled with migrants eager to avail themselves of this largess. In early 1862, he created the Queensland Immigration Society to put his plans into effect. He assured the government that it would not solicit only Irish or Catholic migrants but would look everywhere and take anyone.[289] This was a polite fiction: it worked solely with Irish Catholic clergy under the supervision of Matthew Quinn in Dublin.

The model was simple: prospective migrants or their benefactors would pay for their passage either with cash or by signing over their land orders. This resulted in an average profit of around £15 per migrant, which was to then subsidize the next group. One shipload paid for the next. The first consignment was organized by the rebellious Patrick Dunne of Victoria, who was now running a minor seminary at Tullamore in the King's County. He convinced some 400 people recently displaced from the nearby Geashill estate that their future lay in Queensland, collected money for their passage, and organized their voyage on the grossly unsuitable *Erin-go-Bragh*. They arrived in Brisbane after twenty-five weeks' sailing and fifty-one deaths.[290]

[286] McLay, *Quinn*, 118–19.

[287] H. J. Gibbney, 'O'Sullivan, Patrick (1818–1904)', in *ADB*.

[288] Herbert to an unknown correspondent, 18 June [1863], in *The Queensland Letters of Robert Herbert, Premier: Letters and Papers*, edited by Bruce Knox (St Lucia: University of Queensland Press, 1977), 65.

[289] Quinn to Herbert, 6 February 1862, published in *The Courier*, 10 October 1862.

[290] See T. P. Boland, 'The Queensland Immigration Society: A notable experiment in Irish settlement'. The text of this 1963 lecture may be consulted online at http://fliphtml5 .com/kjno/wsjl/basic, accessed 7 September 2019.

Opposition grew as the scale of Quinn's ambitions became apparent. Although complaints were made on various grounds, including the alleged 'extortion' of the migrants, the poor condition of the ships, and Patrick Dunne's predictably impolitic behaviour, the real problem was that Quinn had been too successful.[291] Herbert later admitted as much.[292] In late 1862, the government decreed that land orders would henceforth be available only to those who applied via official channels. By the summer of 1863, the last migrants had arrived, Quinn had exhausted his personal and political appeals, and the society was finished. In a mere eighteen months, it had succeeded in bringing more than 4,000 Irish Catholic migrants to Queensland, increasing the Catholic population by about 50 per cent. Quinn was not the only colonial bishop to systematically organize Irish Catholic migration in this way – John Sweeny of New Brunswick's settlement scheme was begun in 1861 and the first settlers arrived in 'Johnville' the following year – but his efforts had been uniquely ambitious in their scale.

James Quinn's virtues were outward facing: he was ambitious, entrepreneurial, and efficient. Few of his contemporaries achieved so much in so little time. He was also remarkably tolerant and consistently eschewed sectarianism. Yet he had an overriding weakness: he had a conception of the episcopal state that would have made John Hughes or James Goold blush. 'I am', he declared, 'a sacred person; I have been ordained and received the Holy Ghost; anyone attacking my character commits a most gross and sacrilegious act.' Or, as he put it near the end of his life, as a bishop he was always 'in a state of perfection'.[293] Quinn was a liberal outside his church and a tyrant within.

In 1862, for example, he fell out with one of the priests who had preceded him in the colony, William McGinty of Ipswich. McGinty had raised money for his church, Quinn claimed the right to it, McGinty refused, and Quinn suspended and replaced him. McGinty rallied lay support, refused to hand over the keys, and sued Quinn in the civil courts. (This was the case that nearly saw Patrick O'Sullivan excommunicated.) McGinty was only the first of many priests to fall foul of Quinn: in 1867, six young Irishmen, mostly trained in All Hallows, left in a single group; in the early 1870s, their Italian successors bitterly complained that among other things Quinn was 'starving' them.[294] He was equally high-handed with his fellow bishops: he ignored Goold's fury at his employment of Patrick Dunne, for example, despite the fact that Dunne was still working

[291] For claims of extortion, e.g., *The Courier*, 18 October 1862; for Dunne, e.g., *The Courier*, 22 May 1863.

[292] Boland, 'Immigration Society'.   [293] Both quoted in McLay, *Quinn*, 54.

[294] Cullen to Murray, 8 October 1872, MNDA/MP/A.1.36.

to get Goold sacked as bishop of Melbourne.[295] High-profile laymen who did not toe the line found themselves excommunicated, while the lay secretary of the Queensland Immigration Society claimed that Quinn had concealed its profits and appealed to Cullen for justice.[296] Quinn even sacked Mother Whitty. Tellingly, her offence was insufficient rigidity. Also tellingly, Quinn himself temporarily took her place.[297] Some years later, he threatened to excommunicate Mary MacKillop. Quinn's flaws ultimately overwhelmed his episcopate. As Cullen privately admitted in 1870, he was 'ungracious *e senza discrezione*'.[298] These flaws were apparent from the beginning: as Polding observed to Gregory in 1862, Quinn had 'already made more and deeper administrative blunders in his five months career than you – than we – made in 25 years'.[299]

Quinn was equally unimpressed with Polding. The archbishop had suspected as much, telling Goold in March 1862 of his 'conviction' that the 'Bp of Brisbane has some *arrière pensée*'. Although he did not think Quinn had a formal commission 'to examine and report', Polding continued, he was still certain that 'the result of his observations will be communicated'.[300] He was right. On 19 May 1862, Quinn set those observations out in a long letter to Cullen, who he had promised to keep 'regularly informed' of the situation in Australia. 'Such information', he knew, would enable Cullen 'to use with advantage to the whole Church of Australia the influence at Rome which you derive from your position, and the high opinion of you entertained there.'

Quinn's case was straightforward: Polding was damaging religion, and only carefully chosen new bishops could retrieve the situation. He inevitably stressed the importance of an immediate provincial council. Before he had left Rome, Quinn recalled, Barnabò had informed him that the Australian bishops should meet as soon as possible. Quinn was delighted, the other bishops were supportive, and prominent laypeople such as John O'Shanassy and Charles Gavan Duffy were eager. Yet Polding did not agree with 'Cardinal Barnabò, or the Bishops, Clergy and zealous laity of this country'. This was deplorable, partly because of 'the present state of education and other questions in relation to the Australian governments', and partly because the church itself was 'in a state of disorganisation which is very detrimental to religion'. 'Flagrant abuses', he continued,

---

[295] See Dunne to Talbot, 19 August 1862, AVCAU/TP/1507.
[296] McLay, *Quinn*, 62; C. B. Lyons to Cullen, 18 June, 19 October 1863, DDA/Australia. Lyons had been Cullen's secretary.
[297] O'Donoghue, *Whitty*, chap. 4.   [298] Cullen to Conroy, 14 June 1870, ACDA.
[299] Polding to Gregory, 10 October 1861, *PL*, 3: 40.
[300] Polding to Goold, 12 March 1862, *PL*, 3: 68.

'and scandals of a gross and degrading kind have, and are still taking place.' Regular synodical councils, Quinn concluded, 'would put an end' to such abuses and 'establish the salutary reforms so much required for the progress of religion in these Colonies'.

He knew Cullen would agree. After all, 'You are better aware than perhaps any one out of America of the immense good that has accrued to the American Church from Synods.' At home, Quinn continued, the councils instituted by Cullen had 'united and strengthened the hierarchy of Ireland, placed ecclesiastical affairs on a proper footing, and been productive of most beneficial results to the Irish Church, and consequently to every part of the world in which Irish Priests and people are to be found'.[301] This was not just flattery: an insistence on regular synodical meetings was a repeating tactic across Greater Ireland, and with Roman approval a majority could bind Polding to whatever policies it chose.

Polding's defence against this threat was simple: call a meeting when nobody but his ally Patrick Geoghegan and Quinn himself were able to attend. Quinn duly journeyed to Sydney in February 1862, but with only three bishops present the gathering could not constitute a synod and any decisions the men took would not be binding. It was in any event a set-up: Polding and Geoghegan had agreed a line in advance, and in nearly four weeks they met only four times, Quinn complained, always briefly and rarely substantively. Soon, even these meetings stopped. When he protested, Polding offered only 'the most frivolous pretexts'.

The archbishop also left the question of new dioceses to the afternoon of Quinn's departure. To the Irishman's surprise, Polding readily agreed that New South Wales should be further divided. He and Geoghegan even had a list of candidates, including Geoghegan himself (he was ill and found Adelaide difficult) and Polding's Benedictine vicar general Austin Sheehy. They pushed hard to secure his agreement – Polding even tried to bribe him with a second-hand buggy – but Quinn was adamant. Courtesy prevented him opposing Geoghegan's translation, but otherwise he would not comment on the suitability of people he had never met. Quinn's own conclusions were clear: it was absolutely necessary to insist on regular councils, new bishops should be appointed by Rome, and under no circumstances should any of them be a Benedictine.[302] At least the meeting was not an entire waste: they agreed that Armidale and Goulburn should be erected into dioceses and that Geoghegan should be appointed to the latter.

[301] J. Quinn to Cullen, 19 May 1862, DDA/Australia.   [302] Ibid.

Quinn wasn't the only threat. Although a change in ownership had tamed the *Freeman's Journal*, the disgruntled Irish had not gone away. Polding's latest problem was Patrick Bermingham, one of the three Victorian priests expelled by Goold in 1857. Polding had given both him and Michael McAlroy refuge, and by March 1858 Bermingham had charge of the mission at Yass, some 60 kilometres north of modern-day Canberra.[303] Polding had ignored Goold's complaints, pretending that it was an open question whether *his* Patrick Bermingham was the same one who had assailed the bishop with what he admitted were 'foul lies and calumnies'.[304] Goold was predictably furious, and his episcopal uncle J. T. Hynes wistfully hoped that those Polding 'now uses as his tools may void their slime upon himself'.[305] He did not have to wait long.

Although Bermingham had been complaining to Cullen privately since mid-1859, the inevitable public break came over education.[306] The only Catholic secondary school in New South Wales was St Mary's College, Lyndhurst, which Polding had opened in 1852. This allowed him to both concentrate resources and ensure that any vocations were steered towards the Benedictines. He was very proud of it. In early 1861, however, it emerged that Bermingham planned to accompany ten young men to Ireland. There they would enrol in the ubiquitous Patrick Dunne's seminary in Tullamore, which Dunne hoped would become a 'preparatory school' for the Australian mission.[307] Polding was incandescent. Bermingham had betrayed his trust and deceitfully alienated the 'affections and the interests of the people of his district from me'. He should never have employed him, regretted it bitterly, and withdrew anything nice he had ever said. 'Treachery and underhandedness cancel every title to regard.'[308]

It soon got worse: Bermingham appeared in Rome to complain of Polding's anti-Irish prejudices. And worse again: with Cullen's support, he made such a good impression that Barnabò asked his advice on Australian affairs.[309] Yet worst of all was the potentially catastrophic effect on Gregory's appeal, and Polding promptly reminded Barnabò that the Propaganda itself had once reprimanded Bermingham for his part in the plots against Goold. He even admitted his own fault in welcoming him to Sydney, which he blamed on misplaced charity.[310]

---

[303] *Empire*, 13 March 1858.   [304] Polding to Bermingham 4 February 1861, *PL*, 3: 6.

[305] Hynes to Goold, 15 August 1860, MDHC/GP.

[306] Dowd, *Rome in Australia*, 1: 227.

[307] Dunne to Grimley, 16 February 1861, AACT/Box 13.

[308] Polding to James Walshe, 19 February 1861, *PL*, 3: 13–14. Walshe was the bishop of Kildare and Leighlin.

[309] Dowd, *Rome in Australia*, 1: 227.

[310] Polding to Barnabò, 21 December 1861, *PL*: 3: 52–3.

That Polding was anti-Irish had become a commonplace in Rome. It had been repeated for more than a decade and from many quarters. Nor was it entirely unfair. Yet now this reputation had put everything at risk. His response was twofold: to correct the impression that New South Wales was an extension of Ireland and to deny that he was biased. The first was very bold, although Gregory had trialled a similar argument as early as 1850. For evidence, Polding pointed to the 1861 census, which had revealed that only one-seventh of the population had been, as he rather archly phrased it, 'brought here from Ireland'. He also stressed that native-born Catholics, 'so Australians in national custom and feeling', significantly outnumbered those born in Ireland.[311] Polding's figures were correct: in 1861, there were 54,829 Irish-born in New South Wales, comprising 15.6 per cent of the European population. By contrast, 47 per cent were native-born.[312] Even if every last Irish migrant to New South Wales was Catholic, they could represent only slightly more than half the Catholic population. Allow for Irish Protestant migration, which Polding estimated at one in six, and it would be much less.[313]

Nationality was at the heart of Polding's case. Those 'who are trying to make this colony of ours Irish or English or anything else except Australian', he wrote, provoked the hostility of all true Australians. Every year, he continued, 'the number of the faithful Australians surpasses in greater proportion the number of those who have come here from Ireland and from other parts of Europe'.[314] As he explained to Geoghegan in late 1863, 'The Catholic Irish pop. [in Australia] is about one-twelfth. The native pop. is more than one half – and it is there that our Catholic strength lies.' Nothing, he continued, 'would sooner alienate the native pop. from the Church' than that the 'Irish element should hold rule in all things'. In America, where 'this very doctrine' had been acted upon 'by some hot headed Emigrants', it had given rise to the Know Nothings and might even have led to a 'social and religious war of extermination' had civil war not intervened. 'And this is the state of things', he concluded, 'to wh. Bermingham, the grand oracle, and his tools, the Irish Bps, are to bring us.'[315]

Polding's understanding of nationality left no room for hybrid identities. In emphasizing that less than half of Australian Catholics had been born in Ireland, he ignored the fact that almost all of them had Irish

[311] Polding to Barnabò, 22 December 1861, *PL*, 3: 53–5.
[312] *Census of the Colony of New South Wales, Taken on the 7th of April 1861* (Sydney: Thomas Richards, 1862), 13–15.
[313] Polding to Geoghegan, 17 December 1863.
[314] Polding to Barnabò, 22 December 1861.
[315] Polding to Geoghegan, 17 December 1861.

parents or grandparents. One was either Irish or Australian. He did not understand why the children or grandchildren of Irish migrants (or even the migrants themselves) should continue to identify with their ancestral homeland. Why should they take an interest in Irish affairs, Irish concerns, Irish rivalries? Why should they still be considered Irish? Why did they need Irish priests, Irish nuns, or Irish bishops? Surely Catholics were simply Catholics and those born in Australia were simply Australians. Patrick O'Farrell, Manning Clark, or John Molony would have understood this argument perfectly.

Polding was on stronger ground on the matter of his own supposed bias. To the charge that he preferred English priests, for example, he pointed out that the administrators he had appointed to Goulburn and Armidale were both Irish, as were four of the five deans, as was Archdeacon McEncroe. He even boasted that 'no Bishop ever in the whole world' was as well loved by his flock.[316] Nor was Polding without support among the secular clergy: the Irishman Richard Walsh, for example, published a pamphlet insisting that he had always found Polding and Gregory to be fair. But even he tellingly addressed himself to Cullen, on the rather off-message grounds that the archbishop took 'so much interest in the Catholic Religion all over the world, and particularly in Missions where all are Irish Catholics, or the descendants of the Irish'.[317]

Although Rome accepted Polding's denials, it did not matter, not least because complaints continued to arrive, both from humble priests and from more substantial figures like McEncroe.[318] As before, the Irishman was Polding's most effective critic. Writing to Cullen in early 1863, for example, McEncroe pointed out that, while there were indeed now 100,000 Catholics in New South Wales, there were also '*fewer* efficient Priests' than even five or six years before when there had only been 56,000. Many never saw a priest or received the sacraments, and children were growing up ignorant of the Christian faith. This clerical shortfall was entirely Polding's fault, McEncroe insisted, and was the predictable consequence of his ill-concealed prejudices.[319] This was the sort of complaint Rome listened to.

Soon, even the Englishman's allies began to desert him. Despite having been key to the campaign to restore Gregory, the Benedictine Bishop

---

[316] Polding to Barnabò, 22 December 1861.

[317] [Richard Walsh], *A Letter on the State of Religion & Education in the Archdiocese of Sydney and the Colony of New South Wales, Addressed to His Grace the Most Rev. Dr. Cullen, Archbishop of Ireland, Apostolic Delegate, &c &c &c.*, by the Very Rev. Dean Walsh, New South Wales (Waterford: Printed at 'The News' office, 1862), 1.

[318] D. J. D'Arcy to Cullen, 20 July 1862, DDA/Australia; Dowd, *Rome in Australia*, 1: 230, 286.

[319] McEncroe to Cullen, 19 February 1863, DDA/Australia. Emphasis in original.

Thomas Brown was appalled when, in late 1864, Polding requested an English Benedictine as his coadjutor. 'Australia is almost an Irish colony, so far as Catholics are concerned', he told the influential George Talbot in Rome, '& nearly every priest is Irish.' Given 'how the Irish lower Class hate the Saxon', and given that the 'Irish party' would sooner or later win anyway, how could it be right to 'doom a poor Benedictine to the misery he must have to endure in Sydney'? Irish bishops, he concluded, 'will work by far the best in Australia with an Irish Clergy'.[320]

The death of Patrick Geoghegan in May 1864, just two months after his translation to the newly created diocese of Goulburn, proved to be an important catalyst. There were now vacancies at Adelaide, Armidale, and Goulburn, Perth was thought to require a new apostolic administrator, Polding still wanted a coadjutor for himself, and there were long-standing proposals to erect Bathurst and to regularize Maitland. (The latter had been created for the convenience of Polding's late coadjutor, Charles Davis, and had remained vacant since his death in 1855.) Then, in early January 1865, Robert Willson suffered a massive stroke en route to England, leaving Hobart also in need of a coadjutor. In a hierarchy of eleven (including the putative Bathurst and the illusory Port Victoria), Rome needed to find up to eight new bishops.

Cullen's manipulation of this process was a masterpiece of the bureaucratic arts. He was wary of direct involvement, partly because as archbishop of Dublin he lacked standing in the matter and partly because Polding had complained bitterly of his previous meddling. He could of course reply to any questions the cardinals might have, but what if they did not ask the right ones, or did not ask at all? His solution was elegant in its simplicity. Through Barnabò, he advised the Propaganda to consult two young Irish priests who had recently returned from Australia on the grounds that they could provide the up-to-date information necessary to make an informed decision. No one could object to that. Naturally Cullen already knew what they would say, having been advised of their return to Ireland by John McEncroe.[321] This would not have been significant if the congregation had consulted widely, but it did not. As Christopher Dowd has pointed out, their internal report on the situation in Australia was effectively an anonymized restatement of the Irishmen's testimony. This was not a coincidence: its author was Cullen's friend and ally Cardinal Karl August von Reisach, who unsurprisingly assured the assembled cardinals that the young priests had impeccable references.

---

[320] Brown to Talbot, 25 November 1864 AVCAU/TP/58.
[321] McEncroe to Cullen, 19 February 1863.

Reisach's report was damning. There were not enough bishops and not enough priests for such a vast country. It was impossible to provide an adequate level of spiritual care, and many areas went without. Many secular priests had fallen or given scandal or enriched themselves. The Benedictines were no better: shallow or forced vocations had resulted in everything from concubinage to apostasy. Polding's favouritism made things worse. The people were falling away, many children were in secular or Protestant schools, and mixed marriages were common, even to 'pagan Chinese'. Polding had defied orders to hold a synod, Reisach reported, and an apostolic visitor would struggle to understand the country. The only solution was to further divide Sydney.[322]

The Propaganda's first attempt in May 1865 aimed for balance. Bathurst and Maitland went to the Dublin priests Matthew Quinn and James Murray, although Pius IX decided to substitute Perth for Maitland. Australian observers had long expected Quinn to be made a bishop, and Murray was both Cullen's long-standing secretary and a distant cousin.[323] The Franciscan Laurence Sheil and the Augustinian James Hayes, both favourites of Goold, were appointed to Adelaide and Armidale respectively. Of Polding's candidates, only James Hanly, who was appointed to Goulburn, was successful. The result was thus two bishops for Cullen, two for Goold, and just one for Polding. There were no Benedictines. All were Irish-born.

This outcome reflected the position of the congregation as a whole, as distinct from that of Barnabò or Reisach personally: Cullen was in the ascendant but not yet dominant; Goold remained influential; and, while the cardinals despaired of Polding, they were wary of pushing him too far. The Irish College was nevertheless delighted. The Propaganda, Patrick Moran told Murray, had inaugurated an 'important era in the history of the Australian Church'. The Holy See would now have bishops it could trust, and 'the united representatives of Brisbane, Bathurst and Perth will render impossible the continuance of former abuses'.[324] It was telling that Polding knew none of this: as late as September, he had heard only rumours – always, he pointedly remarked, via Brisbane.[325]

Yet Cullen was not satisfied with a partial victory. His first task was to return James Murray to Maitland; on hearing the pope's decision, his reaction had been that there were 'already 3 or 4 Bishops of Perth'. 'It must', he told Kirby, 'be hard to manage the place.'[326] To Barnabò he

---

[322] See the summary of Reisach's report in Dowd, *Rome in Australia*, 1: 293–4.
[323] For example, Goold to Hynes, 25 July 1862, MDHC/GP.
[324] Moran to Murray, 4 July 1865, MNDA/MP/D.3.1.
[325] Polding to Brown, 20 January 1866, *PL*, 3: 201.
[326] Cullen to Kirby, 27 June 1865, PICRA/KP/K-65–140.

remarked that tumultuous Perth was no place for an inexperienced bishop. Murray himself did everything he could to escape, including claiming ill health. The real problem for both men was that Western Australia was dominated by the Spanish Benedictines and would likely remain so.[327] Barnabò soon agreed to ask the pope if Murray could be restored to Maitland so as to 'be close to his Irish friends'.[328]

That was the easy part. Blocking Hayes, Hanly, and perhaps Sheil would be far harder. Cullen needed a pretext. Fortunately, complaints began as soon as the nominations became public, with Patrick Bermingham predictably to the fore. It seemed that Hayes was fond of parties, while Hanly was ignorant, lazy, and overly keen on shooting kangaroo. The allegations quickly found their way to Barnabò, most likely via the Irish College. He then asked Cullen to investigate, his letter crossing in the post with Cullen's own detailed summary of the charges. In his subsequent formal reply, Cullen admitted that Bermingham could be imprudent but vouched for his honesty and added the testimony of Roger Therry that neither Hayes nor Hanly was a safe choice.[329] Cullen was particularly fierce against Hanly, telling Moran that his appointment 'wd. be a disgrace and a calamity'.[330] In mid-September, the Propaganda advised the pope to put the appointments on hold.

Hobart was also complicated. There was a view in England that Robert Willson's successor should also be English, which made a contested succession likely. Unfortunately, however, nobody asked the paralysed bishop for his opinion, and he was annoyed by rumours that Ullathorne had approached several candidates. Willson immediately dictated a letter to the Propaganda telling them that it was 'very important' that his coadjutor should be an Irishman. Both priests and people were almost entirely Irish, and appointing an Englishman would create 'unnecessary difficulties'. Above all, he concluded, an Irish bishop would 'conduce to the good of religion in Tasmania'.[331]

This effectively eliminated the prospect of an English appointee. As a result, Cullen's nomination of the Irish College–trained Daniel Murphy, late of Hyderabad, was approved with little controversy, and he was duly translated in time to help Cullen consecrate Matthew Quinn and Murray in mid-November. At the dinner afterwards, Cullen reported, 'We drank the Pope's health with enthusiasm and we had a spectacular display of

---

[327] Beverly Zimmerman, *The Making of a Diocese: Maitland, Its Bishop, Priests, and People, 1866–1909* (Melbourne: Melbourne University Press, 2000), 19–20.

[328] Quoted in Dowd, *Rome in Australia*, 1: 298.

[329] Dowd, *Rome in Australia*, 1: 297–8.

[330] Cullen to Moran, 28 July 1865, PICRA/NK/3/1/116.

[331] John Morris to Smith, 29 June 1865, copy in SAA/01735/8.1.

ultramontanism.'[332] Murphy set sail in early 1866, taking with him a clerical nephew. They were soon joined by another, as well as his own sister at the head of a party of Irish Presentation nuns.[333] Willson's death in June 1866 simply finalized the Irish takeover in Tasmania, and for the rest of Murphy's long episcopate he continued to look to Ireland for personnel. In 1890, for example, he returned from a trip home with four new priests and three postulants for the Presentation Sisters.[334]

Polding soon sensed something was wrong. As he put it to Bernard Smith in August 1865, he knew Barnabò 'had a multitude of counsellors about our Australian matters' but 'whether there has been amongst them an abundance of wisdom is another affair'.[335] He also worried about Bermingham's 'intrigues and machinations'.[336] His fears were confirmed when he received first the news of the appointment of Hayes and Hanly and shortly afterwards instructions not to publish it. Then, in October, Hayes revealed that he had asked to decline Armidale. If anything were to be salvaged, Polding would have to go to Rome, which he did in late November.

His appearance surprised everyone. In September, the Propaganda had excused him on grounds of age from making his *ad limina* visit and was not expecting him. Neither were the Irish; Quinn and Murray were in Rome preparing to leave for Australia but decided to remain and monitor their archbishop. Polding was appalled to discover the Irishmen already consecrated and Hayes definitively set aside. As he told Thomas Brown, with 'two Br[other]s and a Cousin in a Hierarchy of seven or so' there was now 'too much "Quinnine" for my taste'. It was, he admitted, 'a bitter pun'. Yet at least in Rome he would have to be consulted and perhaps could 'prevent that intensely Irish party from having all things their own way'.[337]

The results were not encouraging. In February, Hanly's nomination was revoked by the pope, largely on the strength of a letter from James Quinn reporting that he wished to be spared elevation to the episcopate.[338] It was probably no accident that within weeks Polding was alleging (not incorrectly) that the situation in Brisbane was 'deplorable' and Quinn had lost the confidence of both priests and people.[339] He also mounted an

---

[332] Cullen to Kirby, 15 November 1865, PICRA/KP/K-65–260. There was just the hint of irony in this, as Cullen disliked the word ultramontane and occasionally mocked his critics' use of it.

[333] Davis, *Irish Traces*, 57.

[334] Murphy to Murray, 25 November 1892, MNDA/MP/3/1/1810/2/8.

[335] Polding to Smith, 20 August 1865, *PL*, 3: 191.

[336] Polding to Smith, 17 October 1865, *PL*, 3: 195.

[337] Polding to Brown, 20 January 1866.   [338] Dowd, *Rome in Australia*, 2: 307.

[339] Polding to Barnabò, 14 March 1866, *PL*, 3: 207.

impassioned retrospective defence of Hayes and Hanly.[340] More importantly, he submitted a lengthy rebuttal of the allegations proffered by
Reisach: no priests were enriching themselves, except for a handful of
rogues, most of whom were Irish; the Benedictines were hardworking,
disciplined, and a boon to religion; Polding himself was both impartial
and beloved. He also pointed to the growing number of schools and
convents and insisted that his priests were everywhere 'most attentive in
advising the People to frequent the Sacraments and their zeal is rewarded
by the most consoling results'. As for those 'who consider Australia as a sort
of feudal possession of Ireland' and insisted that an Irish people required
Irish bishops and Irish priests, he remarked that 'no greater fallacy than this
can be invented'. 'The people of Australia are Australians', he insisted,
'they are neither English nor Irish nor Scottish.'[341]

Fortunately for the Irish, Reisach was again in charge of explaining
things to the congregation. This was, Murray dryly remarked to Cullen, 'a
great advantage'. They would be able to make use of the Irish College's
carefully gathered collection of books, maps, and gazettes to explain the
situation to the cardinal, a task made easier by the fact that 'he under-
stands English so very well'.[342] On 20 March, Reisach duly proposed the
diocesan boundaries Quinn and Murray preferred, suggested that the
fiasco of Hayes and Hanly proved the necessity of sourcing bishops
from Ireland, and recommended that in future they be selected through
the American system of ranked lists provided by each bishop privately and
then by the assembled hierarchy collectively. Rome would then make the
final decision. As a result Armidale and Goulburn should not be filled
until the Australian bishops could meet. The cardinals agreed.[343]

This was a disaster for Polding. The four Cullenites could recommend
whomever they wished and present their choice as that of the hierarchy. It
is unlikely his mood was improved when Barnabò and Reisach subsequently mocked him during a chance encounter a few days after the
congregation. His frustration boiled over soon after during a meeting
with Quinn and Murray, where his complaints against Cullen became
so violent that Murray threatened to walk out.[344] News of how bad things
were going had already reached Australia; Polding's secretary was 'quite
sure that the horrid spirit of nationality is at the bottom of it'.[345] The only

---

[340] Polding to Barnabò, 23 April 1866, *PL*, 3: 212–13.
[341] For the entire report, see Polding to Barnabò, 19 August 1866, *PL*, 3: 225–49.
[342] Murray to Cullen, 2 March 1866; Moran had gathered a selection of Australian books at
the Irish College, which he left behind when he returned to Dublin with instructions that
they be kept together: Moran to Murray, 21 March 1866, MNDA/MP/D.3.2.
[343] Dowd, *Rome in Australia*, 2: 310–11.
[344] Murray to Cullen, 28 March 1866, DDA/Australia.
[345] Mackinson to Polding, 21 April 1866, DAA/Birt/O.153.

consolation was that Irish allegations about Sheil's supposed alcoholism arrived too late to derail his appointment to Adelaide.[346]

Murray and Quinn soon left Rome, first for Ireland to look for priests and nuns and then for Australia. They were confident nothing would happen in their absence. As Kirby put it, 'of course there will be no appointments made till they hear from you in Australia'.[347] Cullen's elevation to the cardinalate and assignment to the Propaganda can only have reassured them; almost his first act was to promise Murray that 'If I can do any thing for Australia, you may count on my exertions'.[348] The Irish however did not reckon on Polding's persistence. His immediate strategy was to convince the Propaganda to overlook its own instructions on the nomination of bishops; he wanted to suggest candidates for Goulburn and Armidale immediately and not wait until the Australian bishops could be assembled. With magnificent inconsistency, Polding also announced that Englishmen should be nominated alongside the Irish, and he would 'go straight away to England to consult on this proposition'.[349] Shortly afterwards, and to universal astonishment, he obtained papal permission for Gregory's return. It turned out that after years of trying all he had to do was ask.

This was not quite the triumph it appeared: Pius IX left the details to the Propaganda, and Gregory himself seems to have been unwilling to return to Australia without a mitre. Almost no one except Polding thought that that was a good idea. The Benedictine Thomas Brown, for example, now opposed Gregory's restoration in any capacity. If he were in Polding's position, he told Talbot, he would give up and resign.[350] Polding was undaunted: as Cullen heard in late July from 'Mario the priest who used to translate for us', he was preparing an application for Gregory to be his coadjutor, and the Englishman duly appeared on every list of prospective Australian bishops.[351] Of course this was hopeless: Barnabò would never countenance the appointment, the pope had no intention of making him, and Gregory remained in England. Despite Irish fears and Polding's hopes, it was an anticlimactic end to a long and emotionally draining campaign.

Polding stood a better chance with the vacant dioceses, largely because in late July the pope had unexpectedly agreed that the new procedures could be suspended. This was partly a tribute to Polding's persistence,

---

[346] See Cullen to Murray, 3 January 1866, MNDA/MP/A.1.8.
[347] Kirby to Murray, 19 May 1866, MNDA/MP/A.3.3.
[348] Cullen to Murray, 2 July 1866, MNDA/MP/A.1.11.
[349] Polding to Barnabò, 12 May 1866, PL, 3: 214.
[350] Brown to Talbot, 11 May 1866, AVCAU/TP/77.
[351] Cullen to Moran, 26 July 1866, DDA/CP/40/4; Dowd, Rome in Australia, 2: 316.

partly an attempt to placate an old man, and partly a recognition that the matter had already dragged on far too long. It was a notable triumph. With Murray and Quinn gone and Cullen home in Ireland, the appointments would be in Polding's gift. If he picked wisely, he could ensure a majority in the hierarchy. He might even secure a coadjutor of his own choosing.

Inevitably he botched it. His first mistake was to add the name of William Lanigan to what was ultimately a list of ten possible candidates. Quite why he did so is a mystery. After Maynooth and eleven years as a priest in Cashel, Lanigan had arrived in New South Wales in 1859 and thereafter had served quietly in several rural missions.[352] He had taken no part in the various controversies, and his only apparent distinction was an endorsement from the archbishop of Cashel, an ally of Cullen but hardly his creature.[353] Polding presumably thought that by recommending the inoffensive Lanigan he could insulate himself against charges of anti-Irish prejudice. It does not seem to have occurred to him that Rome might actually pick the Irishman.

His attention was anyway focussed on England. His first thought was of the gifted and aristocratic Vaughan brothers, Herbert and Roger. Herbert, who was the elder of the two, was in the process of founding what became the Mill Hill Missionary Society, would soon buy *The Tablet*, and was appointed bishop of Salford in 1872. He ended his career as cardinal archbishop of Westminster. He was not remotely interested in Sydney, although he carefully told Talbot that he would leave the entire matter in the hands of the pope before providing a long list of reasons why he could not possibly leave Mill Hill.[354] To Ullathorne, he declared flatly that it was the more important work.[355] His brother Roger was also still wanted in England, where he was prior of Belmont Abbey and an important figure in the internal battles of the English Benedictine congregation. There was also significant doubt in England that he would be a prudent choice. Thomas Brown, for example, told Talbot that the arguments against Gregory's return also applied to Vaughan. 'Extreme nationality', he wrote, would excite 'antagonistic feelings', especially if Polding's coadjutor was 'not only an Englishman – but a Benedictine'.[356]

---

[352] Diary of William Lanigan, Archives of the Archdiocese of Canberra-Goulburn [ACGA], MS. 3718/2/4.

[353] This was Patrick Leahy. Polding to Lanigan, 31 January [1867], ACGA/MS3718/1/5. Polding misdated this letter 1866.

[354] Herbert Vaughan to Talbot, 12 July 1866, AVCAU/TP/705.

[355] Herbert Vaughan to Ullathorne, 24 June 1866, BAA/UP/B4424.

[356] Brown to Talbot, 9 September 1866, AVCAU/TP/78.

From Polding's changing lists the Propaganda finally selected three names: Lanigan, the English secular John Crookhall, and Polding's own vicar general, the Benedictine Austin Sheehy. Gregory was excluded and Sheehy was to be an auxiliary bishop, not coadjutor. Again the Propaganda had tried for balance. In September, for example, they had asked Polding for the relative number of English and Irish Catholics in Armidale and Goulburn, presumably in order to appoint Lanigan and Crookhall to the most suitable diocese. His reply was heroically disingenuous: he did not know the exact numbers, but Australia's Catholics were a mixture of English, Scots, Irish, and Australians. Neither the government nor 'the ecclesiastical authority' made such national distinctions and had in fact 'taken special care to avoid it at all costs'.[357] In reality, Polding knew perfectly well that there were hardly any English Catholics in either place.

Nobody was happy: Polding got neither Gregory nor a coadjutor, while the Irish were lumbered with an Englishman, a Benedictine, and an Irishman none of them knew. Their reaction was predictable. James Quinn begged Cullen to block the appointments outright, telling him without irony that 'if *bad men* or men having no other qualification than their partisanship be appointed the progress of Religion in Australia will be impeded'.[358] Nor were the Cullenites impressed by Lanigan. He was a 'very good man', Murray reported to Cullen, but everyone, 'including himself poor man, says that his attainments and talents are moderate'. At least he was Irish, Murray concluded, and 'in the absence of a better let him be appointed'. As for Crookhall, it was 'simply absurd to appoint him or any Englishman to any place here'.[359] He might as well be sent to a diocese in Connaught.[360]

In fact, both men were quickly dealt with, with Quinn and Murray immediately moving to co-opt Lanigan.[361] They need not have worried: it turned out that Lanigan was a bitter critic of the Benedictines. Of the twelve monks he had met in his seven years in Australia, he told Quinn in February 1867, at least five were 'living notoriously scandalous' lives.[362] Quinn soon reported that Lanigan was 'much more intelligent than I had been at first led to believe', while Murray described his consecration as 'a

---

[357] Polding to Capalti, 28 September 1866, *PL*, 3: 251.
[358] James Quinn to Cullen, 25 January 1867, DDA/Australia. Emphasis in original.
[359] Murray to Cullen, 22 January 1867, DDA/Australia.
[360] Murray to Moran, 21 January 1867, DDA/Australia.
[361] Matthew Quinn to Lanigan, 27 December 1866, ACGA/MS. 3718/2/5.
[362] Lanigan to Matthew Quinn, 14 February 1867, Bathurst diocesan archives [BDA], Quinn papers [QP], 2/67.

great triumph of the Church in Australia'.[363] They had every reason to be pleased. As Anne Player has noted, Lanigan drew his ecclesiology entirely from Irish and Roman sources.[364] He even gave Patrick Bermingham a job. Polding had accidently recommended a fifth Cullenite.

He compounded the error by failing to ensure that Crookhall would take an Australian see if one were offered. In fact, the Englishman was horrified and refused on the grounds that he was ill, his father was old, and he couldn't ride a horse.[365] When he learned that the pope had excused him, he told Talbot that in 'getting me off you are really doing good for Australia'.[366] Polding's inevitable attempt to substitute Gregory was inevitably unsuccessful, despite his belief that Barnabò had promised to allow it.[367] He was instead ordered to consult the Australian bishops. When they duly met in August 1868 the Cullenites recommended Michael McAlroy, the last of the three Victorian priests who had so infuriated Goold in the late 1850s. This was an error, as Goold was predictably opposed and the Propaganda was unwilling to upset both Sydney and Melbourne.[368] The setback was minor, however, as they still got their second choice, the Irish College–trained Dublin priest Timothy O'Mahony. In a hierarchy of eleven, there were now six Hiberno-Romans, including the adopted Lanigan. Five were products of Cullen's Irish College. As Goold observed even before the appointment of Lanigan and O'Mahony, Rome's choices all had had 'something of haste & greenness about them'.[369]

Far more bitter was the battle over Polding's proposed auxiliary bishop, the Benedictine Austin Sheehy. Irish opposition was predicated on long-standing complaints about St Mary's College, Lyndhurst, where he had been president since 1861. In early 1864, for example, John Forrest reported to Cullen that a monk there had moved to Melbourne with the college's housekeeper.[370] In 1867, Murray added the allegation that Sheehy had known of the affair for at least eight months but had done nothing.[371] These complaints were tangled up with those against the Benedictines as a whole. Lanigan, for example, maintained that the order suffered from 'some radical cause of decay'.[372] He reported that

[363] Matthew Quinn to Kirby, 23 June 1867, BDA/QP/49/67; Murray to Barnabò, 22 June 1867, quoted in Dowd, Rome in Australia, 2: 322.
[364] Anne V. Player, 'Bishop William Lanigan of Goulburn and the making of a Catholic people', unpublished PhD thesis, Australian National University, 2004, 1.
[365] Crookhall to Talbot, 24 October 1866, AVCAU/TP/1514.
[366] Crookhall to Talbot, 12 November 1866, AVCAU/TP/1516.
[367] Dowd, Rome in Australia, 2: 321.   [368] Ibid., 363.
[369] Goold to Heptonstall, 25 December 1865.
[370] Forrest to Cullen, 20 February 1864.   [371] Murray to Moran, 21 January 1867.
[372] Lanigan to Murray, 26 February 1867, MNDA/MP/A.6.74.

elite parents distrusted Lyndhurst because of the 'gravest scandals [that] have come from that place'. Sheehy's predecessor was a public drunk, as was the present prior, as was another resident Benedictine who at times was too inebriated to say Mass.[373] Sheehy himself was in the habit of taking carriage rides with a nun at 'all hours from early dawn to late at night'.[374] She had even been seen emerging from his room in the middle of the night.[375] There were also more practical concerns: as Moran pointed out, if Sheehy were given a vote at the projected provincial council it might tilt the balance of power.[376]

The Irish turned to Cullen. If the cardinal thought his detailed protest to the Propaganda was 'alright', Murray wrote, 'please forward it, if not all right, please not to send it'. 'In a word', he continued, 'whatever your Eminence wishes in the matter, is just what I wish'.[377] Matthew Quinn wrote in similar terms and added a collection of documents illustrating Benedictine iniquities.[378] He knew Cullen would 'make the very best use of them that can be made for the benefit of religion in this Colony'.[379] Cullen assured them that their letters were fine and forwarded them to the Propaganda. He then gave his protégés a tutorial. 'Write frequently to Rome', he told Murray, and 'give them facts and statistics.' General complaints were useless, he continued, as there were problems everywhere and 'unless particular grievances of a serious nature can be established, general charges will produce no effect'. As an example, he noted that Quinn had 'made serious charges against some of the Benedictines individually'. 'If these charges be not contradicted', Cullen concluded, 'they will produce the desired effect.'[380]

The campaign against Sheehy was typically brutal. In Sydney, it was widely reported that his consecration had been postponed because 'a charge of gross immorality has been preferred against him'.[381] It is impossible now to assess whether these claims were accurate. Probably they were not, although they were widely believed. The suggestion of an affair, for example, seems unlikely. Even Murray eventually admitted as

---

[373] Lanigan to Matthew Quinn, 14 February 1867, BDA/QP/2/67.

[374] Lanigan to Matthew Quinn, 24 February 1867, DDA/Australia. This letter was forwarded to Cullen, and the information about Sheehy's nocturnal activities came in a postscript in Quinn's hand.

[375] Dowd, *Rome in Australia*, 2: 331.

[376] Moran to Murray, 21 April 1867, MNDA/MP/D.3.8.

[377] Murray to Cullen, 19 February 1867, DDA/Australia.

[378] Matthew Quinn to Cullen, 21 March 1867, BDA/QP/26/67.

[379] Matthew Quinn to Cullen, 21 March 1867 (second letter), BDA/QP/29/67.

[380] Cullen to Murray, 16 June 1867, MNDA/MP/A.1.16.

[381] F. F. Turville to Talbot, 10 October 1867, AVCAU/TP/669. Turville, who was English, was on the governor's staff.

much.[382] As one prominent lay supporter wrote indignantly, 'No one who knows that man can believe in the possibility of such an accusation having any foundation.'[383] The allegations against the Benedictines as a whole were much better founded, as Polding's own Benedictine successor recognized when he closed Lyndhurst and suppressed the order in Australia. The Irish were not making this up. As for Sheehy, his fate was sealed when Barnabò commissioned Murray himself to investigate the situation. Polding fought hard, but Sheehy was unwilling to endure the attacks on his character and Rome gratefully accepted his resignation in June 1868.

The Irish had won. The appointments of Murray, Quinn, Murphy, Lanigan, and O'Mahony, together with James Quinn in Brisbane, introduced undiluted Hiberno-Roman Catholicism to Australia. Even Goold and Sheil outwardly conformed to their vision. Only Polding and Western Australia stood aloof. Murray and Matthew Quinn especially were totally devoted to Cullen. When they landed in Sydney, for example, Murray assured the reception committee that Cullen was 'my great patron, my best friend', while Quinn declared him to be 'great in talent, great in knowledge, and great in the vigour with which he pursues what he knows is good'.[384] Quinn later remarked that 'the greatest object of my life has been to emulate [Cullen] at an humble distance'.[385] James Quinn, Murphy, and O'Mahony were cut from the same cloth. This is what T. L. Suttor meant by 'Cullen Catholicism'.[386] It is also why Cullen merited an entry in the *Australian Dictionary of Biography* despite never having set foot on the continent.

Building the Irish Church, 1867–1883

The first task of the victorious Cullenites was to secure adequate priests, brothers, and nuns to erect and run the parishes, convents, schools, hospitals, orphanages, and asylums integral to Hiberno-Roman Catholicism. In many places, the situation was acute. In 1868, for example, an Irish Jesuit in Victoria reported that even in the 'chief towns' Mass was said only once a month and in smaller places only every three to six months.[387] The problem was exacerbated by the fact that Ireland had

[382] Dowd, *Rome in Australia*, 2: 342.   [383] Turville to Talbot, 10 October 1867.
[384] *Empire*, 23 October 1866.
[385] James Murray, 'Welcome Address', n.d., MNDA/MP; *FJ*, 22 January 1870, quoted in Michael Potts, '"We Never Sink": Matthew Quinn as bishop of Bathurst', unpublished BA (Hons.) thesis, University of Sydney (1971), 3.
[386] Suttor, *Hierarchy*, 5.
[387] Edward Nolan to Provincial, 'Feast of the Sacred Heart', 1868, Irish Jesuit Archives [IJA], MSSN/AUST/237.

long since become a seller's market for colonial clergy and especially for missions with a hard climate or a poor reputation. In 1863, for example, Patrick Geoghegan of Adelaide had bemoaned 'the impossibility of getting Priests in Ireland'.[388] He wound up recruiting Belgians who couldn't speak English.[389] In mid-1866, the much better connected Murray remarked that 'the want of Priests will be fearful for a few years'.[390]

The Irish faced a significant problem: reputation was vitally important and James Quinn's was so bad that Cullen worried his 'severity' might compromise recruiting for the whole of Australia.[391] In 1870, for example, Quinn had 'failed signally' to find priests or students, and 'the Dublin clergy all avoided him'.[392] He was forced to try England and then the continent, ultimately finding what Cullen dubiously called a 'cargo' of some sixteen Italians.[393] They too promptly rebelled. Things were so bad that Murray was told in 1873 that the students in All Hallows 'did not care for the Australian mission'.[394] The shortage of recruits was exacerbated by the imposition of tight controls on those already in post. Quinn was of course an extreme case, but, as K. T. Livingston has pointed out, the others pursued similar policies – Lanigan insisted his clergy live in common presbyteries, avoid pubs, abstain from drink, and never visit nuns without permission.[395] Many left for Polding's more accommodating regime in Sydney.

Despite these challenges, Ireland remained Australia's leading provider of priests, not least because its Catholics demanded them. Recruiting at Carlow College, for example, Lanigan remarked that his people were principally Irish and consequently wanted Irish priests.[396] The bishops agreed. As Sheil's successor in Adelaide explained in 1881, perhaps with Quinn in mind, 'A bad Irishman is a great affliction, but a bad Italian-!'[397] As a result, and despite the reputational difficulties, by 1891 All Hallows alone had provided 426 priests to the Australian mission, while Carlow sent another 170 by 1922.[398]

---

[388] Geoghegan to Smyth, 24 July 1863, ACAA/GP/Series 20, Box 1/Folder 11.
[389] Geoghegan to Smyth, 24 December 1863, ACAA/GP/Series 20/Box 1/Folder 11.
[390] Murray to Cullen, 18 July 1866, DDA/Australia.
[391] Cullen to Edward McCabe, 2 June 1870, DDA/CP/40/4.
[392] Conroy to Cullen, 20 June 1870, DDA/CP/321/7/4/52.
[393] Cullen to Murray, 19 January 1871, MNDA/MP/A.1.31.
[394] Murray to Cullen, 'Easter Sunday', [?1873], DDA/Australia.
[395] K. T. Livingston, *The Emergence of an Australian Catholic Priesthood, 1835–1915* (Sydney: Catholic Theological Faculty, 1977), 62–3.
[396] Lanigan to an Irish bishop, 2 October 1869, ACGA/MS 3718/1/2.
[397] Christopher Reynolds to Joseph Byrne, 26 January 1881, ACAA/RP/Series 32/Box 1/Folder 4.
[398] Carmichael, 'Analysis'.

The pre-eminence of All Hallows was not universally welcomed. Goold, for example, complained in late 1865 that its products were too often 'a most ill-mannered set' whose 'roughness reflects upon us all the greatest amount of discredit'.[399] Although he wished that the college authorities would try and recruit a better class of students, Melbourne still took 127 priests from there by 1891. He had little choice: in early 1861, for example, Goold bitterly complained about an Irish Augustinian who soon after his arrival had had 'a charge of a nature not fit to be mentioned' brought against him. As a result he instructed his agent not to accept Irish religious who volunteered for Melbourne. 'Those who offer themselves', he wrote, 'are for the most part the refuse of their respective communities.'[400] It was the same in Sydney, where they regretted that All Hallows graduates were not 'better furnished with a little ordinary refinement, and accomplishment, and knowledge of the world' but still welcomed at least 101 over the same period, almost all under Polding or Vaughan.[401]

Ironically, it was the Cullenites who were the most hostile to All Hallows. Like all bishops, they wanted obedient and well-trained priests, but like Cullen himself they also emphasized educational attainment. As a result, Armidale, Maitland, and Bathurst admitted only seven, eighteen, and fourteen All Hallows graduates respectively, despite being desperately short of priests for much of the period.[402] Even tiny Perth took twenty.[403] The Cullenites sought to foster domestic vocations instead. In 1875, for example, Matthew Quinn opened St Charles Seminary in Bathurst to serve all the Hiberno-Roman bishops. His explicit model was the Irish College in Rome; he copied its rules and ensured that the first rector had been trained there.[404] He even recruited ten of the original twelve students in Ireland.[405] Patrick Moran later opened St Patrick's College in Manly along the same lines but on a much grander scale. The Cullenites could not do entirely without All Hallows (or Carlow), but they strove to form as many of their priests as possible in their own Roman image. For most, this meant Bathurst or later Manly. For the brightest, it could mean Clonliffe or Rome itself. The Australian-born Patrick Dwyer, for example, was sponsored by Murray to attend St Charles' before being sent onwards to Clonliffe, where he impressed Cullen with his examination results – the cardinal thought

[399] Goold to Heptonstall, 25 December 1865.
[400] Goold to Heptonstall, 21 January 1861, DDA/Birt/N.303.
[401] Carmichael, 'Analysis'.   [402] Ibid.
[403] In 1890, there were only about 44,000 Europeans in all of Western Australia.
[404] Livingston, 92.   [405] Ibid., 90.

he had 'more the appearance of a stout Irishman than an Australian'.[406] Next came the Propaganda and the Irish College, where Cullen's nephew Michael Verdon marked Dwyer out as a 'first rate' future bishop, before ordination and a return to Maitland.[407] Dwyer was appointed Murray's coadjutor in 1897, succeeded in 1909, and died in 1931.

Yet above all the bishops needed women religious. A handful of priests could manage even a large mission, but many more nuns were required to run a school, hospital, orphanage, or asylum. Unfortunately historians have too often seen these women as an undifferentiated mass, undeniably important yet curiously anonymous. Yet Ursula Frayne, Baptist De Lacy, or Vincent Whitty were not merely the passive transmitters of male ideas or initiatives. They controlled important and often complex organizations with a significant degree of autonomy and did so while navigating environments that were often hostile to female agency. This was particularly true in Australia, where the two most important Irish communities, the Sisters of Mercy and the Cabra Dominicans, were fully integrated into the global Cullenite network and often enjoyed mutually respectful relationships with their Cullenite bishops. This is hardly a surprise: many of their leading members were themselves part of the Cullen–Maher–Moran ecclesiastical cousinage.

Although the Sisters of Charity had arrived in Sydney in the late 1830s, and the Sisters of Mercy in Perth in the mid-1840s (before moving to Melbourne in the mid-1850s), there was no systematic attempt to secure Irish women religious for Australia before 1859, when both James Goold and James Quinn obtained communities from Baggot Street. That same year, John McEncroe approached the Sisters of Mercy in Westport, Co. Mayo, where Cullen's cousin Paula Cullen was the mother superior.[408] He convinced six sisters to accompany him to Goulburn, where they soon opened a poor school and admitted their first local postulant.[409] By 1862, they had built a convent costing some £3,000 paid for by local subscription and dedicated to St Patrick.[410] Under Lanigan they expanded to Albury in 1868, founding St Bridget's convent, and in 1875 Lanigan and Michael McAlroy convinced seven women from the Rochfortbridge convent in Co. Westmeath to establish a new community in Yass. Goulburn

---

[406] Cullen to Murray, 27 September 1877, MNDA/MP/A.1.54.

[407] Verdon to Murray, 24 July [?1882], MNDA/MP/A.3.80.

[408] Kathleen Healy, *Frances Warde: American Founder of the Sisters of Mercy* (New York: Seabury Press, 1973), 141.

[409] Eileen M. Casey, *Held in Our Hearts: The Story of the Sisters of Mercy of the Goulburn Congregation* (Fyshwick, ACT: Panther Publishing, 2009), 16; *FJ*, 11 August 1860.

[410] *FJ*, 22 March 1862.

and Yass between them ultimately founded some twenty-one convents, mostly in south-eastern New South Wales.[411]

In 1866, the newly appointed Matthew Quinn convinced a party of Sisters of Mercy from Charleville, Co. Cork, to join him in Bathurst. En route, their ship received so much snow that Murray and Quinn organized a snowball fight, with the Mercies arming their bishop while the Presentation nuns bound for Tasmania seconded Murray.[412] This was typical of the relaxed relationship Cullen and his protégés (James Quinn excepted) enjoyed with women religious. The Cullenites were grateful to the nuns and expected their flocks to be as well: as Murray later told those attending the ceremonial laying of the Mercy convent's cornerstone in Bathurst town, the women had 'abandoned friends, country, home, and their endearing associations, to devote all their energies for the education of your daughters'.[413] Between 1868 and 1875, at least thirty-eight women travelled from Charleville to Bathurst, a relationship that was facilitated by the fact that M. Joseph Croke was the mother superior in Cork while her sister M. Ignatius Croke held the same position in New South Wales.[414] Their brother Thomas was Matthew Quinn's agent in Ireland, and would soon become the second bishop of Auckland, New Zealand (see Chapter 7).[415] By 1914, Bathurst had made eleven foundations, including at Mudgee, Orange, and Dubbo.[416]

James Murray meanwhile approached the Cabra Dominicans, whose mother superior Catherine de Ricci Maher was another of Cullen's cousins. By the mid-1860s, she had already overseen deployments to Cape Town, New Orleans, and Lisbon. Murray promised passage money, a debt-free convent, and the expulsion of Polding's Good Shepherd Sisters (later known as the Sisters of the Good Samaritan).[417] As he told Cullen, 'I fear they have not got the religious spirit and many of them have got not education.'[418] He left everything to Maher, telling her to 'do what you think best and you may rest assured that I will be perfectly

---

[411] [Nancy Clarke and Claudia Hyles], *Walking Nuns: Sisters of Mercy Goulburn Congregation Sesquicentenary* (Goulburn, NSW: Sisters of Mercy Goulburn Congregation, 2009), 9.

[412] M. R. MacGinley, *Ancient Tradition, New World: Dominican Sisters in Eastern Australia, 1867–1958* (Strathfield, NSW: St Paul's Publications, 2009), 24.

[413] *FJ*, 22 February 1868.

[414] See the obituary for M. Ignatius Croke in the *Bathurst Convent Annual* (December 1905).

[415] Quinn to Croke, 30 March 1867, BDA/QP/32/67.

[416] [Anonymous], *Sisters of Mercy – Bathurst – 100 years – 1866–1966* (Bathurst, NSW: The Sisters of Mercy Bathurst, 1967), unpaginated.

[417] Annals of the Dominican Convent Maitland, Dominican Archives Strathfield [DAS].

[418] Murray to Cullen, 19 March 1868, DDA/Australia.

satisfied'.[419] She selected six choir and two lay sisters, all volunteers, including Cullen's cousin Mary Kate Molloy.[420] Like many of the elite Dominicans, she was well educated (in Molloy's case on the continent) and was multilingual, musical, and a talented artist. Cullen called her 'the best nun they have', while she carefully preserved a volume of Italian libretti that he had given her.[421] For their journey to Australia, Murray prescribed sherry, brandy, and the 'very best' champagne to deter seasickness.[422]

The women finally arrived in Maitland on 10 September 1867, and six days later they opened a combination day and boarding school.[423] They were reinforced from Ireland in 1868, 1871, 1873, and 1875, founded a branch house at Newcastle in 1873 (at a cost of £6,500), and accepted their first local postulant in 1872. Within weeks of opening, their high school in Newcastle had seventeen day students, eight of whom were Protestant.[424] Women from the convent also successfully restored order to the community at Adelaide, which had been planted from Cabra in 1868 but had fallen into serious disorder after the death of Bishop Sheil.[425] Sheil himself had been lucky to get them after having 'travelled from one end of Ireland to the other in search of nuns'. He also secured four Sisters of Mercy from Paula Cullen's Westport convent.[426]

In 1875, Murray recruited a party of seven Mercy Sisters and three postulants from the convent at Ennis, Co. Clare. This was only one of Ennis' foundations in the period: between 1872 and 1884, at least fifty women travelled from Clare to Hertford, Connecticut, Hokitika in New Zealand, and Murray's new convent at Singleton, some 45 kilometres north-west of Maitland.[427] There, they promptly opened a school welcoming 'Young ladies of all religious denominations'.[428] By 1900, Singleton had founded eleven convents elsewhere in Australia and two in New Zealand.

---

[419] Murray to Maher, 21 November 1866, DACI/K/DL/G1/2.

[420] The institutional memory at Strathfield has Molloy as Cullen's niece. While this is possible, I can find no direct proof of it. A cousin is much more likely.

[421] Cullen to Murray, 25 April 1867, MNDA/MP/A.1.14. The volume – *Opera Sacra di Pietro Metastasio* (Milan, 1826) – is preserved in the Dominican convent at Strathfield, Sydney. For Molloy, see the obituary published on www.opeast.org.au, consulted 3 August 2017.

[422] Murray to 'Rev. Mother', 21 December 1866, DACI/K/DL/G1/3.

[423] 'Annals', DAS.   [424] Murray to Cullen, 11 July 1873, DDA/Australia.

[425] Murray to M. M. De Sales, 22 November 1873, Dominican Archives Dún Laoghaire [DADL], K/DL/G1/20; MacGinley, 104–6.

[426] Sheil to Smyth, 24 December 1867, ACAA/SP/Series 36/Box 1/Folder 1.

[427] Colleen Kelly, *A Journey through Light and Shadow: Sisters of Mercy Singleton, 1875–1995* (Singleton: Sisters of Mercy, 1997), 4–5.

[428] See the advertisement in *The Singleton Argus and Upper Hunter General Advocate*, 22 September 1875.

The Irish did not rely solely on the Sisters of Mercy and the Dominicans. In Tasmania, for example, the nine Presentation Sisters led by Bishop Murphy's own sister also immediately opened schools, first in Richmond and then Launceston, devoted to the 'moral and religious education of the Catholic children'.[429] As elsewhere, these schools fused religion, politics, and Irish identity. At a school prize ceremony in 1868, for example, the hall was decorated with banners proclaiming 'God save the Queen', 'Long Live Pius IX', 'Free Education', and 'Religion Welcome'. Guests entered via a triumphal arch emblazoned *'Cead Mille Failthe'*.[430] In 1869, the women held their first local professions in a service attended by Murphy, Murray, and both Quinns.[431] In 1875, McAlroy and Bermingham convinced five Presentation Sisters from Kildare to establish a convent and school at Wagga Wagga, and they in turned founded a further three convents (all with schools) by 1900. In 1886, a party of eleven left Lucan in Co. Dublin for Lismore in north-east New South Wales, while in 1891 nine women from various Irish convents settled in Geraldton in Western Australia. In Victoria, meanwhile, the first bishop of Ballarat secured ten Irish Loreto Sisters under the leadership of M. Gonzaga Barry. When they arrived at Ballarat station in July 1875, an excited crowd rushed their carriage before the women were conveyed in a great procession to the site of their new convent and school.[432] They too soon expanded across Australia.[433]

Demand nevertheless continued to outstrip supply. This was addressed in a variety of ways, including continued recruitment in Ireland, the development of local vocations, and the establishment of domestic religious communities. Local women were the most obvious source, and as convent schools spread they rapidly produced vocations among their students. In May 1878, for example, two of the three women who joined the Sisters of Mercy in Fitzroy, Melbourne, had been educated there.[434] The demographics of Catholic Australia ensured that most if not all were of Irish birth or descent. Another option was to found an entirely new community, as Julian Tenison-Woods (an Englishman) and Mary MacKillop (an Australian born to Scottish parents) did in South Australia in 1866. Their Sisters of St Joseph spread rapidly but controversially: the founders fell out, MacKillop was briefly excommunicated by Bishop Sheil, and the sisters were at one time or another expelled from

---

[429] *Tasmanian Morning Herald*, 31 October 1866.   [430] *The Mercury*, 4 January 1869.
[431] *The Mercury*, 19 May 1869.   [432] Barry Diary, LAB/SER17/002.
[433] See Mary Rylls Clark, *Loreto in Australia* (Sydney: University of New South Wales Press, 2009).
[434] *Advocate*, 4 May 1878.

Brisbane, Bathurst, and Adelaide. The issue was not ethnicity but authority: MacKillop wanted to retain central control, something both the Cullenites and some other bishops resisted. In 1876, Matthew Quinn consequently founded the Diocesan Sisters of St Joseph to ensure episcopal supervision, causing a split that was not finally healed until 2014. Mary MacKillop became Australia's first saint in 2010.

The greatest barrier to female recruitment was money. In many communities, prospective nuns were expected to provide a dowry. Others required the sort of good secondary education that was still largely limited to the more prosperous classes. Those without either could hope only to become lay sisters, the powerless and understudied servant class of convent life. The Dominicans, for example, normally required a dowry of £1,000, and none of the first twenty in New South Wales paid less than £300. As a result, bishops like James Murray regularly received appeals from Ireland to help women who wanted to become nuns in Australia but lacked the means.[435] The solution to this apparently intractable problem came from an unexpected quarter, the Sisters of Mercy in Callan, Co. Kilkenny.

The community in Callan was at the heart of the Cullenite cousinage. It had been founded from Athy, Co. Kildare in 1872 at the request of Patrick Francis Moran, who, as bishop of Ossory, was trying to suppress a complicated clerical revolt in the town and thought the nuns might help.[436] The mother superior in Athy, M. Teresa Maher, was Cullen's cousin, as was the first mother superior in Callan, M. Michael Maher. Among the other pioneer sisters was Moran's niece M. Berchmans Commins, who became mother superior in due course. Over time, other nieces and cousins also found their way to the convent. As M. Michael Maher remarked shortly after Moran was created the family's second cardinal, 'what fine old stock [our grandparents] were to spread their seed so far & wide over the new as well as the old world in the shape of Cardinals, Priests and Nuns'.[437]

In 1881, Maher, Moran, and James Murray agreed to establish what they called a 'preparatory school for aspirants to the religious life in Australia'.[438] It would follow the model of All Hallows, matching women who could not afford a dowry or an education with bishops or congregations abroad who required subjects. Crucially, what became

---

[435] MacGinley, 83; for example, Mary Paul Cahill to Murray, 22 October 1872, MNDA/MP/3/1/1810/2/5.

[436] See Barr, *Culture Wars*.

[437] Michael Maher to Moran, 17 September 1885, Sisters of Mercy Archive, Parramatta [ARSMP], Box 60.

[438] Moran to 'Rev. Mother' (Michael Maher), 31 January 1882, ARSMP.

St Brigid's Missionary College was not tied to the Sisters of Mercy but rather was open to all religious communities. By the time the college closed in the early 1950s, it had supplied some 1,500 women to more than twenty-two congregations in at least sixteen countries.[439]

Yet St Brigid's early clients were all Australian. Murray took the first five aspirants, giving them a choice between the Sisters of Mercy in Singleton and the Dominican Sisters in Maitland. He was soon asking for more. 'We will want them all', he told Callan.[440] The college gained an even more powerful patron when Moran was promoted to Sydney, and soon St Brigid's graduates found themselves in almost every Australian diocese. In the early 1890s, for example, James Moore of Ballarat commissioned the college to supply the local Sisters of St Joseph.[441] In the 1880s and 1890s, the first bishop of Wilcannia in extreme western New South Wales imported at least twenty-two women to staff the Mercy convent at Broken Hill.[442] By 1914, some 150 women had left Callan for Australia.[443]

Tuition was kept low, at around £25 a year, of which the receiving bishop or community was expected to pay at least £15. As Rose Luminiello has demonstrated, this allowed women from all backgrounds and ages to become choir sisters. In one instance, both the inmate of a workhouse and the daughter of its governor joined.[444] To make ends meet, Murray held bazaars in Maitland while Moran sent a gold nugget to be raffled in Callan and assigned the college the copyright to his many books.[445] They even marketed his *The Writings of Cardinal Cullen* at a guinea for the three-volume set. James Murray bought ten.[446] St Brigid's was thus able to provide access to an overseas career to women for whom it would otherwise have been beyond reach. Just as importantly, and just like the young priests who emerged from the Irish College in Rome or its

---

[439] See Colin Barr and Rose Luminiello, '"The leader of the virgin choirs of Erin": St. Brigid's Missionary College, 1883–1914', in *Ireland's Imperial Cultures*, edited by Michael DeNie, Timothy McMahon and Paul Townend (London: Palgrave Macmillan, 2017), 155–178.

[440] Murray to 'Mother Michael' (Michael Maher), 14 April 1884, ACRSM.

[441] Berchmans to Moran, 16 November 1898, ARSMP/Box 60.

[442] 'Register of Aspirants, St. Brigid's Missionary College', ACRSM. Although the register is extant into the 1950s, the Callan Sisters of Mercy only permit scholars to report specific information up to 1914.

[443] Register of Aspirants, ACRSM.

[444] For a detailed analysis of the social composition of St Brigid's aspirants, see Rose Luminiello, 'St. Brigid's Missionary College and the effects of Irish Catholic religious sisters in the Irish spiritual empire and diaspora', unpublished MSc dissertation, University of Edinburgh, 2014.

[445] Barr and Luminiello, 162.

[446] Moran to Murray, 27 June 1883, MNDA/MP/D.3.152.

clones, St Brigid's aspirants were inculcated in Cullenite Hiberno-Roman Catholicism at the most important point of their religious formation.

Women religious filled a wide range of needs across Australia. The most obvious and widespread was education but also included caring for the sick, as at St Vincent's hospital in Sydney, or for the marginalized, poor, or vulnerable. In Newcastle, for example, a deaf mute Dominican named M. Gabriel Hogan opened a Deaf and Dumb Institution at Waratah in 1876. In its first fourteen years, it educated thirty-nine pupils at a cost of nearly £12,000.[447] In Goulburn, the Sisters of Mercy gave 'unremitting' attention to the condemned in the town's jail, both male and female, often staying with them until their execution.[448] Nuns also provided services specifically for women. In 1866, for example, an Irish Jesuit reported that 'four young women' with whom he had sailed to Melbourne had discovered on arrival that the person who had sent for them was dead. They were 'taken in to the house of Mercy', he wrote, and 'would be lost only for the nuns'.[449]

Yet education was always the primary focus. As James Quinn put it in 1862, 'Religion in this colony must depend on the education of the female children & consequently on Nuns.'[450] Five years later, Cullen told Murray that your 'mixed system of education will be very dangerous. The nuns will help put it down.'[451] This reliance on women religious became particularly acute as the Australian colonies moved away from direct public funding of denominational schools towards more aggressively secular systems. As a result, even small and isolated communities needed Catholic schools and thus nuns. The ability of the Australian Catholic Church to provide them must count as its greatest success. It was also distinctive within Greater Ireland: as James Murray remarked during a visit to the United States in 1889, 'my American friends were quite astonished' by the widespread distribution of convent schools. 'The idea of having Nuns in places where we have only 30 children', he continued, 'never crossed their minds.'[452]

In the Australian colonies, the pace of educational secularization differed but its course was relentless. After a brief experiment, South Australia abandoned explicit denominationalism first, in 1852, then Van Diemen's Land in 1853, Western Australia in 1856, Queensland in

---

[447] Statement of Accounts, 1876–1889, Deaf and Dumb Institute Waratah, Newcastle University Cultural Collections, A5 696(v).
[448] For example, *Goulburn Herald*, 9 May 1860, 7 May 1862.
[449] Joseph Lentgaine to Daniel Jones, 24 September 1866, IJA/MSSN/AUST/9.
[450] Quinn to Cullen, 17 May 1862, DDA/Australia.
[451] Cullen to Murray, 14 May 1867, MNDA/MP/A.1.15.
[452] Murray to Patrick Hand, 1 April 1889, MNDA/MP/E.1.45.

1860, Victoria in 1862, and finally New South Wales in 1866.[453] In every case, the end of unconditional state aid represented a crisis for the church. In South Australia, for example, the emollient Francis Murphy had complained about the loss of funding but did little to create a Catholic alternative. His successor Patrick Geoghegan, on the other hand, launched a campaign to demand that Catholics receive a proportionate share of educational funds 'to be employed according to the Faith & discipline of the Church'.[454] Without it he could not even pay for teachers.[455] In 1866, his successor Laurence Sheil announced that he would 'have nothing to do' with the educational system 'unless they give us control of our own schools'.[456] He had little hope of this, telling his vicar general that 'South Australian bigotry is ineradicable'.[457] He instead encouraged the nascent Sisters of St Joseph to provide independent Catholic schools, especially for the poor. Indeed, most of the women themselves were from the poorer strata of society, and even servants could become sisters. This was controversial, but it was the only way to provide education across the vast colony. The appetite was certainly substantial: under Julian Tenison-Woods' idiosyncratic leadership the number of schools increased in only five years from twenty-three to sixty-five, educating some 3,500 children. Meanwhile Mary MacKillop's community grew from nothing to 127 in the same period, eighty-one of whom (65 per cent) had been born in Ireland.[458] Despite personality clashes and chronic instability, especially in the wake of Sheil's death in 1872, South Australia demonstrated what could be achieved even with exceptionally limited resources.

In the eastern colonies, the situation was slightly different. From 1847 in Van Diemen's Land, and 1848 in New South Wales, educational provision was overseen by separate 'national' (i.e. secular) and denominational boards. Grants were provided for land, buildings, and teachers' salaries in exchange for an agreed curriculum and the right of inspection, while religious instruction was largely left to the sponsoring denomination. Van Diemen's Land abandoned the system in 1854 as did Queensland shortly after separation, in each case for a single central board, but both colonies continued to provide limited funding for denominational schools under stricter conditions. Catholic responses varied: Bishop Willson accepted the system as the best obtainable in

---

[453] See Fogarty, 1: 47.   [454] Geoghegan to Goold, 17 December 1859, MDHC/GP.
[455] Geoghegan to Michael Ryan, 17 January 1860, ACAA/GP/Series 20/Box 1/ Folder 10.
[456] Sheil to Goold, 12 September 1866, MDHC/GP.
[457] Sheil to Smyth, 15 January 1870, ACAA/SP/Series 36/Box 1/Folder 1.
[458] See Marie Therese Foale, *The Josephite Story: Mary MacKillop and the Sisters of St. Joseph, 1866–1893* (Sydney: St Joseph's Generalate, 1989), 21–37.

Tasmanian conditions, while Bishop Quinn joined his Anglican counter-part in a crusade against godless education.[459] Victoria, which had inher-ited the New South Wales legislation, followed suit in 1862, although its system remained practically denominational.[460] In New South Wales itself, a similar attempt had faltered in 1859 in the face of Catholic opposition to what amounted to ministerial control of their schools.[461]

The next wave of reforms coincided with the arrival of the Cullenite bishops in the mid-1860s. In Tasmania, Murphy immediately renounced Willson's accommodations and demanded the 'complete separation' of Catholic and Protestant students, while his clerical nephew scandalized Protestants and secularists alike by bursting into a national school to prevent Catholic students receiving a scripture lesson, despite their par-ents having given permission.[462] By early 1868, Murphy boasted that the Presentation Sisters had already 'rescued' some 300 children 'from the dangers of Protestant schools'.[463] The same year, he heatedly opposed a further reform that, in Richard Davis' phrase, left Tasmania with 'an education system which was mildly compulsive, ambiguously secular, and not entirely free'.[464] In Victoria, Goold refused even to testify to an 1866 Royal Commission investigating the educational system, while the two lay Catholics nominated to it declined because the government had not first consulted Goold.[465] The subsequent bill was lost in the face of united Catholic and Anglican opposition. The result was an appreciable increase in sectarian rancour.

The fighting was particularly bitter in New South Wales. In 1866, the introduction of the Public School Act signalled what its author Henry Parkes called 'an ecclesiastical storm'.[466] The Act abolished the denomi-national board but allowed denominational schools to continue receiving public funds, provided they agreed to regular inspections, a common curriculum, prescribed texts, and state-trained teachers. Parkes put par-ticular emphasis on the last, later recalling that the 'golden provision of the Bill was that no person, man or woman, should be allowed to enter any school as a teacher who had not been trained for the work of

---

[459] Davis, *State Aid*, 20; Wyeth, chap. 5.

[460] Stuart Macintyre, *A Colonial Liberalism: The Lost World of Three Victorian Visionaries* (Melbourne: Oxford University Press Australia, 1991), 133.

[461] Alan Powell, *Patrician Democrat: The Political Life of Charles Cowper 1843–1870* (Melbourne: Melbourne University Press, 1977), 106.

[462] Quoted in Davis, *State Aid*, 20; *The Mercury*, 8 March 1867.

[463] Murphy to Cullen, 27 March 1868, DDA/Australia.   [464] Davis, *State Aid*, 27.

[465] See Gwyneth M. Dow, *George Higinbotham: Church and State* (Melbourne: Sir Isaac Pitman & Sons, 1964), 58–62.

[466] Henry Parkes, *Fifty Years in the Making of Australian History*, 2 vols. (London: Longmans, Green, & Co., 1892), 1: 198.

teaching'.[467] This was aimed squarely at Catholic schools, which often employed untrained nuns, brothers, priests, or laity.[468] Polding thought the 'effect of it will be to shut up almost all our Schools'.[469]

The Cullenites were appalled. Quinn thought the new arrangement 'far worse' than the Irish national system, while Murray called it 'this shadow or phantom of education which is a mere sham'.[470] Lanigan compared the position of Catholic children in the public schools to Catholic servants in a Protestant home.[471] Even Polding thought 'we must reject it in toto'.[472] In June 1867, Quinn, Lanigan, and Sheehy (as vicar general) presented Parkes with a list of demands: free establishment of new Catholic schools; the right to dismiss teachers; a guarantee that Catholics and Protestants be separated for religious instruction, 'moral or doctrinal', and should never receive it from a teacher of another faith; fair representation on the education board of which Parkes was the president; aid to train their teachers; the right to use Catholic books, meaning in practice those prepared by the Christian Brothers. They were sure that 'a liberal Government' would agree. It didn't. The only way to change the Act, Parkes told them, was to change the government.[473]

The resulting sectarianism has often been attributed to the Cullenites, while Polding blamed them and Parkes equally.[474] In reality, their intervention was inevitable: education was the single most important political and social issue across Catholicism's Greater Ireland, and mixed education was anathema – the 'curse of our age & country', as one Victorian bishop put it.[475] By contrast, the Catholic *beau idéal* was, in James Murray's words, a 'high literary education, but always subject to ecclesiastical authority and control'.[476] If this could only be secured through political action, then most bishops were prepared to engage in politics. Thus James Quinn rode around town with his preferred candidate, his brother Matthew worked 'actively at the electoral roll', and their cousin

---

[467] Ibid., 1: 196.
[468] For Parkes' intentions and anti-clericalism, see A. W. Martin, *Henry Parkes: A Biography* (Melbourne: Melbourne University Press, 1980), 224–8.
[469] Polding to Lanigan, 30 July [?1867], ACGA/MS. 3718/1/5.
[470] Matthew Quinn to Cullen, 21 November 1866, DDA/Australia; Murray to Maher, 21 November 1866, DACI/K/DL/G1/2.
[471] See Lanigan's open letter to the clergy and laity of Goulburn, *Southern Argus*, 17 July 1867.
[472] Polding to Lanigan, 30 July [?1867].
[473] For a lengthy account of the interview, see the *Sydney Mail*, 29 June 1867.
[474] For example Martin, 226; O'Farrell, *Short History*, 109.
[475] O'Connor to Murray, 25 December 1874, MNDA/MP/B.3.41.
[476] 'Appeal of the Right Rev. Dr. Murray to the Catholics of the Diocese of Maitland', 17 February 1867. A copy of this printed appeal may be consulted in the Dominican Archives, Strathfield.

James Murray sought sympathetic Anglicans willing to stand in Maitland.[477]

The church would remain engaged so long as the question remained unresolved. As the first bishop of Ballarat remarked in 1875, 'We are keeping up a perpetual agitation on the Education question.'[478] Two years later, he boasted to Cullen that 'we are doing all we can in every quarter to return members who are disposed to modify the existing education law'.[479] The uproar surrounding Henry Parkes' Public Instruction Act of 1880, which fully secularized New South Wales education, gave the Irish a useful rallying cry, and in that year's general election Matthew Quinn noted that 'more Catholics are standing for parliament than ever, and with a fair chance of election'.[480] He was delighted when what he called the 'Catholic party' pushed Parkes into the final seat in East Sydney behind the prominent Irish Catholic politician Daniel O'Connor, who finished second, and 'a new man named Reid, a free-trader and an anti Public Schools man' who headed the poll.[481] (This was the future Sir George Reid, who in 1904 became Australia's third prime minister.) Two years later, the bishops had the satisfaction of seeing Parkes and a number of his allies actually if temporarily unseated. As one complained, 'I met with most ferocious opposition from the *Romans*, who were canvassed to a man by the Priests of this and adjoining districts.' The cry of these 'black-coated gentry', he continued, was 'Down with Parkes, *the bitter foe of our religion and our race*'.[482]

The education question often overshadowed everything else. In Victoria, for example, Sir John O'Shanassy and his allies felt the need to seek Goold's permission in 1880 to join a ministry not explicitly pledged to overturning the colony's secular system. Goold agreed on the condition that they did not accept the education portfolio and did everything possible to 'secure the rights of Catholics'.[483] In 1885, he encouraged the foundation of the Education Union League to agitate for public payment of Catholic teachers under the slogan 'For God and the Country'.[484] As Goold wrote not long before his death, 'This education question is everything to us. The future of the Church in Australia

---

[477] Quinn to Lanigan, 'Feast of the Epiphany', 1869, ACGA/MS. 3718/2/5.

[478] O'Connor to Murray, 8 August 1875, MNDA/MP/B.3.42.

[479] O'Connor to Cullen, 21 February 1877, DDA/Australia.

[480] Matthew Quinn to Murray, 23 October 1880, MNDA/MP/A.4.20.

[481] Matthew Quinn to Murray, 23 November 1880, MNDA/MP/A.4.22.

[482] James Torphy, who was defeated in Orange in Quinn's Bathurst diocese. Quoted in Martin, 333. Emphasis in original.

[483] Minutes of a meeting with Archbishop Goold, 24 July 1880, Melbourne University Library [MUL], W. H. Archer papers [AP].

[484] Minute book of the Education Union League, MUL/AP/15.2.

depends on it.'[485] The issue continued to shape Catholic political behaviour for many years, despite (or because of) the fact that, by 1880, every colony except Western Australia had ceased to fund denominational schools. As Patrick Francis Moran remarked in 1889, Australian Catholics were 'free to take whatever side they liked in politics'. No one, he continued, knew how he voted, and he told no one how to vote. He did not even know himself whether he was a free-trader or a protectionist; but 'there is one species of freetrade I have always clamoured for, and that is freetrade in education'.[486]

The education debate and its concomitant sectarianism in fact served both sides. On the one hand, it gave politicians such as Parkes, Victoria's James Francis, or the young Alfred Deakin a potent electoral weapon.[487] As the *Freeman's Journal* pointed out, the 1869–70 New South Wales election was fought largely on the cry 'Public Schools Act in Danger!', while two years later Charles Gavan Duffy attributed the defeat of his short-lived Victorian ministry to his own vulnerability 'to the cry of No Popery'.[488] An avowedly secular education act immediately followed his ouster, doubtlessly helped along by Goold's announcement that any Catholic who supported a proponent of 'Godless education' in the subsequent ministerial by-elections placed 'himself at once in opposition to the church and conscience'.[489] Across Australia, anti-Catholicism remained a reliable vote winner well into the 1920s.[490]

Yet perceived persecution also brought Catholics together. Resisting bigotry, petitioning governments, fighting elections, and struggling to create, fund, and maintain a separate school system simultaneously increased communal identity and bound it to the institutional church. Henry Parkes later claimed to have feared exactly that, recalling his anxiety 'that those who were taught and religiously coerced by their spiritual guides to withold their children' from the state schools would 'create for themselves a standing grievance, and by brooding over their self-imposed hardships, work themselves into a morbid belief that they

---

[485] Goold to Murray, 12 February 1887, MNDA/MP/A.4.207.

[486] 'Cardinal Moran and politics', *Goulburn Evening Penny Post*, 9 April 1889.

[487] A pledge to keep 'priestcraft, dogma and intolerance' out of the schools was a key plank of Deakin's first parliamentary campaign in 1880. See Judith Brett, *The Enigmatic Mr Deakin* (Melbourne: The Text Publishing Company, 2017), 62–3.

[488] *FJ*, 18 June 1870; for the text of Duffy's remarks at a banquet shortly after his electoral defeat, see the *Bendigo Advertiser*, 4 July 1872.

[489] Quoted in Michael Linehan, 'Archbishop Carr and Catholic education: The attitude and response to the Registration of Teachers and Schools Act 1905', unpublished M. Ed. dissertation, University of Melbourne (n.d.), 9–10.

[490] See Jeff Kildea, '"A veritable hurricane of sectarianism": The year 1920 and ethno-religious conflict in Australia', in Barr and Carey (eds.), *Religion and Greater Ireland*, 363–82.

were an oppressed class'.[491] Parkes' regret was disingenuous but his analysis was correct, and throughout Australia Catholic bishops used this sense of grievance to help their campaigns against social mixing.

Not mixing too freely with Protestants was in any event a core aspiration of Hiberno-Roman Catholicism. To achieve this, a full range of social controls were necessary, not simply separate schooling. In Tasmania, for example, Murphy insisted that Catholic orphans be looked after by the Sisters of Charity at public expense. This was preferable, he told the government, both to the existing state orphanage where their faith was at risk and to a foster system reliant on the 'cold charity of strangers'.[492] When his requests were denied, he began fundraising for a private orphanage and industrial school.[493] In Adelaide, Sheil bemoaned the lack of 'justice or decency' in the treatment of orphans by the government, while in New South Wales Murray regularly tried to place children in the state-funded Catholic orphanage after the death of the Catholic partner of a mixed marriage.[494] In 1871, for example, he sought admission for two children whose mother was intending to 'hand them over' to Protestants.[495]

It did not take long for the Cullenites to identify mixed marriages as their primary domestic challenge; but, whereas schools and orphanages were negotiated with the state, mixed marriages could only be addressed internally. Yet they were intimately linked, and the Cullenites were appalled to learn that many of these unions were celebrated by priests. It had, Murray wrote, 'produced an impression that there is no harm in them'.[496] Matthew Quinn heard much the same from his priests. 'Protestants & Catholics have been married here without the least distinction', Philip Ryan reported from Carcoar near Bathurst, and 'this is what leaves them in infidelity as they are.' He knew many families where half the children were Protestant and the other half Catholic. The people thought Polding was a great holy man for tolerating this, Ryan continued, and he warned Quinn not to press the issue. They were not afraid of priests as they were in Ireland, he wrote, and it was impossible to 'persuade them to do things here if they don't like'.[497] Quinn promptly forwarded the letter to Cullen.

---

[491] Parkes, 2: 2–3.
[492] Murphy to Colonial Secretary, 12 May 1874, Tasmanian Archive Service, CSD7/1/63/1553.
[493] See Murphy to Murray, 13 August 1878, MNDA/3/1/1810/2/2.
[494] Sheil to Smyth, 15 January 1870, ACAA/SP/Series 36/Box 1, Folder 1.
[495] Murray to Mackinson, 10 January 1871, MNDA/MP/3/1/1810/2/4.
[496] Murray to Moran, 21 January 1867, DDA/Australia.
[497] Philip Ryan to M. Quinn, 12 January 1867, DDA/Australia.

It was undoubtedly in the Cullenites' interest to emphasize lax practices. The long-standing justification for Irish bishops had after all been the paucity of religious supervision through much of the country.[498] Yet this did not mean that it was untrue: in 1866, for example, the clerical son of the Anglican bishop of Tasmania found himself baptizing the child of a mixed marriage: the boys were raised Catholic, the girls Protestant. It was 'a compromise very popular I find'. A few weeks later, a woman told him that, unlike in 'Ould Ireland', where she 'would sooner have departed this life than meet the priest's displeasure', in Tasmania things 'were very different' and the clergy were openly defied.[499] Indeed, the available evidence suggests that mixed marriages were widely accepted throughout Australia. Although more prevalent in rural areas and among the poor, they were by no means limited to either. This was largely a by-product of the shortage of clergy, but it also reflected a greater tolerance (or resignation) among the older generation of bishops and priests.

The Cullenites were determined to change this at the provincial council mandated by Rome. Polding, however, did everything possible to avoid calling a meeting where he knew he would be systematically outvoted. He tried a variety of excuses: too many bishops were away; there was no suitable place to meet; it should wait until the results of the First Vatican Council were known. Under pressure from the Propaganda, Polding finally called a meeting for April 1869, although as late as mid-March Matthew Quinn was convinced he would find yet another reason to delay.[500] Although other issues were discussed, not least education, it was mixed marriages that 'engaged our attention very much'.[501] Many of the older priests were prepared to defend the practice, Murray reported, 'but it is high time to check them if we are to have a religious people free from Indifferentism'. Only in Sydney, he continued, were mixed marriages 'allowed without much difficulty' and, among the bishops, only Polding resisted change. Murray consequently 'drew up one or two of the decrees having in my mind the practice in Sydney'.[502]

Those decrees were uncompromising. As the disapproving Jesuit provincial remarked privately, the bishops were 'terribly severe about mixed marriages'.[503] Such unions, they wrote, were 'strictly forbidden by the

---

[498] For this recurring trope see, for example, Gavin Brown, '"The evil state of tepidity": Mass-going and absenteeism in nineteenth-century Australia ecclesiastical discourse', *Journal of Religious History*, vol. 33, no. 1 (March 2009), 28–48.

[499] J. H. B. Mace, *Henry Bodley Bromby, A Memoir* (London: Longmans, Green, and Co., 1913), 31, 41.

[500] Matthew Quinn to Lanigan, 16 March 1869, ACGA/MS. 3718/2/5.

[501] Murray to Cullen, 24 April 1869, DDA/Australia.

[502] Murray to Cullen, 11 July 1869, DDA/Australia.

[503] Edward Nolan to Irish provincial, 19 May [1868], IJA/MSSN/AUST/237.

ancient law of the Church' and confirmed by successive popes; they were the occasion of 'great evils', including 'domestic broils', 'the perversion of the Catholic party', or 'what frequently happens in this country', the infection of children with 'indifferentism'. Priests were obliged to explain 'the evils arising' from these marriages and always 'labour to prevent' them. Those who persisted had to promise to raise all their children as Catholics and strive to convert their non-Catholic partner. Only the local bishop could give permission, and the wedding could only take place outside the church and without ceremony. It could not happen at all if the priest knew or suspected that the couple also intended to appear before a Protestant minister or a civil registrar. If they did, they were guilty of a 'grievous sin' that only the bishop could absolve. If two Catholics chose to marry in front of a 'heterodox minister or a Registrar' they were automatically excommunicated.[504]

Outside observers were inevitably hostile. Melbourne's reliably anti-clerical *The Age*, for example, deplored the bishops' attempt to link infidelity 'to mixed schools and mixed marriages' and urged the 'Australian prelates ... to abstain from any attempt to import into Australia the intolerance of liberty' that disgraced Catholic Europe.[505] Under the heading 'Ultra Sectarianism', the *Goulburn Herald* compared the council's attempt to 'interfere with young lady's lovers' with the campaign of a censorious Presbyterian minister in Adelaide to dictate how they dressed.[506] *Melbourne Punch* even produced a full-page cartoon of Polding as a shepherd, declaring to his flock 'We will have no more (mixed) marriages.' Its heading was 'The Pastoral Letter – Black Sheep and White.'[507] In fact, Polding had no intention of enforcing the decrees, partly because he lacked the energy and partly because strict social segregation had never been a part of his agenda. The Cullenites were predictably furious. In early 1870, for example, Murray heard rumours of a marriage that had been celebrated in St Mary's Cathedral in Sydney before the wedding party processed to a nearby Anglican church. If it was true, he told Moran, 'then there is no point in legislating against mixed marriages'.[508]

Other issues were more easily resolved. In Adelaide, Sheil was succeeded by the Irish-born but Benedictine and Jesuit-trained Christopher Reynolds. His appointment was by no means inevitable: all concerned

---

[504] *Translation of the Decrees Regarding Education, Mixed Marriages, and Other Subjects, Adopted by the Archbishop and Bishops Assembled in Provincial Council, at Melbourne, in April, 1869* (West Maitland, NSW: Henry Thomas, 1873).
[505] *The Age*, 27 April 1869.   [506] *Goulburn Herald*, 2 June 1869.
[507] *Melbourne Punch*, 6 May 1869.
[508] Murray to Moran, 18 April 1870, DDA/Australia.

claimed to want a 'stranger' and Reynolds had been in South Australia since 1860.[509] The Cullenites preferred McAlroy or an appointee direct from Ireland, Goold was in Europe, and Polding had no suggestions at all. With Adelaide in chaos, however, a decision had to be made quickly and Reynolds was a universally acceptable compromise; Murphy and Matthew Quinn regarded him highly and Polding had appointed him administrator on Sheil's death.[510] His record was mixed: over a long episcopate, Reynolds increased the number of Catholic schools and imported the Irish Christian Brothers, but he also incurred vast debts and fell out with Mary MacKillop. He slowly drew closer to the Cullenites, placing his better students in the Irish College, soliciting Irish Presentation Sisters with the promise that Adelaide would soon be a 'New Dublin', and even reaching for a Cullen quotation when times were tough.[511] When he heard that Patrick Moran had been appointed to Sydney he declared that 'the Blessed Virgin has indeed *very specially* interceded for our Australia'.[512]

It was Victoria that finally demonstrated the limits of Cullenite power. James Goold had watched while Polding was surrounded by the cardinal's appointees, and he had no desire to experience the process himself. As a result, he had long resisted proposals to divide Melbourne. This could not, however, be postponed indefinitely – by 1870, neighbouring New South Wales already had five dioceses, despite what was now a smaller population. In 1869, Goold proposed the erection of one new see at Ballarat while the Cullenites pushed for a more extensive division in the hopes of further augmenting their numbers. They wanted three or four (Lanigan suggested six) and Goold reluctantly countered with a maximum of two. Goold, however, was a more formidable opponent than Polding, retained his influence in Rome, and was careful to be on the spot when decisions were made. The combination of conflicting advice from Australia and the final collapse of the Papal States postponed a final decision until mid-1874.[513]

The delay meant that Victoria's fate would be determined just as Cullen's influence in the Propaganda reached its nadir. In early 1873, for example, he had received a stark warning through Kirby: the *minutante* responsible for Australian affairs, Achille Rinaldini, had told him that it

---

[509] Matthew Quinn to Polding, 1 April 1872, BDA/QP/16/72; Cullen to Murray 22 March 1872, MNDA/MP/A.1.35; Polding to Barnabò, 20 April 1872, *PL*, 3: 357–8.

[510] Matthew Quinn to Polding, 1 April 1872, BDA/QP/16/72.

[511] Reynolds to Byrne, 4 June 1880, ACAA, Reynolds papers [RP], Series 32, Box 1, Folder 4; M. Agatha to Reynolds, 12 July 1881, ACAA/RP/Series 32/Box 1/Folder 3; Reynolds to Murray, 6 November 1882, MNDA/MP/A.4.16.

[512] Reynolds to Murray, 22 January 1884, MNDA/MP/A.4.48. Emphasis in original.

[513] See Dowd, *Rome in Australia*, chap. 14.

would be better if in future Cullen transmitted his views on the selection
of colonial bishops indirectly. Letters sent to the Propaganda 'must pass
through different hands', and Rinaldini claimed to be worried that this
could allow internal critics to argue that the appointments were being
fixed in Dublin.[514] This could be avoided, Rinaldini advised, by 'com-
municating the same things to them not directly in your own name when
it is a question of elections'.[515] Rinaldini may not have been entirely
sincere in his concern – he was close to Polding's secretary, a fellow
Italian – but his warning was nevertheless suggestive of the changing
climate in the Propaganda.

Barnabò's final illness and subsequent death in February 1874 further
complicated the situation. We have already seen the consequences in
Newfoundland and Canada. It also gave Goold his opportunity. In
November 1873, he returned to Rome, intensively lobbied *minutanti*,
cardinals, and pope, and in March 1874 secured his preferred outcome:
there would be only two new dioceses, at Ballarat and Sandhurst
(Bendigo), and Melbourne would be elevated to an archdiocese. He did
almost as well with his nominees. The Cullenites again recommended
McAlroy and added Robert Dunne, James Quinn's eventual successor in
Brisbane.[516] Goold was so enraged by the former that he warned the
Cullenites not to even call on him if they happened to visit Melbourne.[517]
Yet he too produced a largely Irish list, although it also included the
German Henry Backhaus. A determined Cullenite counter-attack saw
Goold's first choice for Ballarat set aside for supposed personal and
familial drunkenness. As Murray put it, James Moore's 'own weakness
and his brother's fall put his promotion out of the question'.[518] In his
place, the Propaganda substituted another name on Goold's list, the
Dublin priest Michael O'Connor. For Sandhurst, they chose William
Fortune, the president of All Hallows, who declined on health grounds,
as did the next choice, a Cork Augustinian.[519] The Propaganda finally
settled on another Irish Augustinian, Martin Crane.[520]

Goold had preserved his independence through a combination of
political skill and good fortune. It was a signal triumph. Yet the implications should not be exaggerated: Goold was fiercely opposed to Cullenite
interference, not to Hiberno-Romanism. He was equally firm with

---

[514] Kirby passed along Rinaldini's advice in Italian: '*Che tutto pesse fatto per mezzo di* ...'
[515] Kirby to Cullen, 'Epiphany' 1873, DDA/CP/45/I/1/116/1.
[516] Dowd, *Rome in Australia*, 2: 383.
[517] Murray to Lanigan, 13 October 1873, ACGA/MS. 3718/2/5.
[518] Murray to Lanigan, 13 October 1873.
[519] Fortune apparently suffered a kidney complaint that was thought to worsen in hot
climates. See Cullen to Kirby, 5 May 1874, PICRA/NK/4/2/64.
[520] Dowd, *Rome in Australia*, 2: 387–91.

Polding's English Benedictine successor, pointedly reminding him that they each had enough to do without meddling 'with what does not concern us'. 'It has been the rule of my life', he concluded, 'not to mix myself up with the affairs of others.'[521] In fact, Goold's own long experience of Italy had made him a reliable ultramontane, and his choice of suffragans reflected this. Michael O'Connor, for example, had had an important parish in Dublin and was highly regarded by Cullen, with whom he continued to correspond. In Ballarat, he immediately launched himself against mixed education, telling Murray that there was 'no one who is more thoroughly opposed to the mixed system root & branch'.[522] In only eight years, he imported the Irish Christian Brothers, the Irish Loreto nuns, and the Sisters of Mercy and built more than forty churches and a magnificent episcopal palace. He also spent some £67,000 on education, almost all of it raised locally. He died in early 1883.[523] His successor was the alleged drunkard Moore, who continued O'Connor's building campaign. By his death in 1904, the diocese had eleven boarding schools, thirteen high schools, and some sixty primary schools across thirty-five parishes. He also recruited heavily in Ireland. In late 1888, for example, he returned to Ballarat with what a watching Irish bishop described as 'a whole army of religious'.[524] Like Goold himself, these men were effectively Hiberno-Romans without necessarily being Cullenites.

Polding also hoped to avail himself of the changing climate in Rome. From mid-1868, he had been systematically petitioning the Propaganda to appoint Roger Bede Vaughan as his coadjutor.[525] He was open about his reasons: it was 'not appropriate for the Coadjutor to be Irish', he told Barnabò, and 'some Englishman' should be appointed, preferably Vaughan.[526] For several years, he got nowhere: Vaughan was still required in England, and Barnabò essentially told him that if he wanted a coadjutor he should pick somebody who was available after consulting the other bishops.

By mid-1871, however, Polding's unrelenting appeals had softened Barnabò enough that he sought advice in England about possible non-Benedictine candidates, although the Irish only learned of the threat in early 1872.[527] By November, the politics of the English Benedictines had rendered Vaughan both expendable and willing to go, and in late January

---

[521] Goold to Vaughan, 3 September 1878, SAA/VP/U1521/6.23.

[522] O'Connor to Murray, 22 December 1874.

[523] James Griffin, 'O'Connor, Michael (1829–1883)', in *ADB*.

[524] Carr to Murray, 15 November 1888, MNDA/MP/A.4.157.

[525] Dowd, *Rome in Australia*, 2: 402.

[526] Polding to Barnabò, 6 September 1868, *PL*, 3: 304–5.

[527] Murray to Cullen, 'Easter Sunday' [1872], DDA/Australia.

1873 the Propaganda met to finally decide the matter. Barnabò was present but ailing, the summary was provided by the scholarly Benedictine Jean Baptiste Pitra, and of the eleven cardinals in attendance only two or three were close to Cullen.[528] Times had changed, and Polding was an old man who needed help.[529] As he told Lanigan, 'God has at length answered my long, long prayer.'[530]

The Irish were predictably furious. Matthew Quinn thought the appointment 'calculated' to materially injure the Australian church.[531] His brother was amazed that the cardinals had believed 'it to be for the advancement of Religion to send *"Un Signore Inglese"* as coadjutor'. He even compared Sydney to the Kingdom of Italy.[532] In May, the Quinns, Lanigan, and O'Mahony sent Cullen an astonishingly intemperate protest. Among other things, they rehearsed the failures and scandals of the Benedictines, denounced Polding's deceitfulness, and pointed out that in the entire diocese 'the Catholics not Irish could be accommodated in *one small church*'. 'British statesmen', they complained, 'are more fortunate in finding Irish Governors for British Colonies than Propaganda in finding Irish bishops.' In short, Vaughan's appointment 'gives unqualified offence'.[533] Only Murray struck a note of caution, telling Matthew Quinn that 'he would be guided exclusively by Cardinal Cullen's advice'.[534] That advice was predictable: what's done is done and, as the pope's choice, Vaughan deserved respect. 'Some times things look badly', he consoled Murray, 'but in the end they turn out well especially when they are done by one like the Pope under the guidance of heaven.'[535] He did not forward their letter to Rome.

Vaughan knew what he was facing. He immediately decided against taking Gregory with him, for example, telling Bernard Smith that 'it would be the gravest blunder for me to go out there with the suspicion of being a party man'.[536] While the Cullenites were writing their protest, Vaughan was in Dublin to support Cullen himself at his high-profile trial for criminal libel.[537] Once in Sydney, he sent gently ironic letters to each

---

[528] See Dowd, *Rome in Australia*, 2: 406–11.

[529] This was essentially Kirby's summary: see Kirby to Murray, 18 February 1873, MNDA/MP/A.3.24.

[530] Polding to Lanigan, 17 April 1873, ACGA/MS. 3718/1/5.

[531] Matthew Quinn to Lanigan, 24 April 183, ACGA/MS. 3718/2/5.

[532] James Quinn to Murray, 29 September 1873, MNDA/A.4.4b. Emphasis in original.

[533] Letter to Cullen, 17 May 1873, DDA/Australia. Emphasis in original.

[534] Matthew Quinn to James Quinn, 24 April 1873, BDA/QP/23/73.

[535] See Cullen to Murray, 8, 30 October, 29 December 1873, MNDA/MP/A.1.39, 41, 44.

[536] Vaughan to Smith, [?6] March 1873, ASSP/SP/10/10.

[537] Moran to Kirby, 19 May 1873, PICRA/K/73/205. For the libel trial see Barr, *Culture Wars*, chap. 4.

thanking them for their 'kind and encouraging' welcome.[538] It worked: Murray's first impression was that he was a 'magnificent man' who understood that Benedictinism had failed in Australia.[539] He soon thought the Englishman was 'getting on wonderfully well' and was likely to 'do an immense deal of good'. Matthew Quinn also liked him. The new coadjutor was 'a man that we can talk to'.[540] Vaughan himself reported to Bernard Smith that the 'Irish Suffragans' were 'very zealous and earnest men' with whom he could work. Their objection, he continued, 'was not so much my being an Englishman as being a Benedictine'. This was unsurprising given the order's 'many gross scandals' and consequent collapse in public esteem.[541] By late 1874, he claimed to be getting on 'first class' with his Irish colleagues.[542]

There were several reasons for this apparent amity. First, Vaughan understood that in the short term his own success depended on his ability to collaborate with the Cullenites. He solicited their opinions and preached what he called 'united action' on issues such as education.[543] Second, he abandoned Polding's open hostility towards Irish secular clergy, did not immediately attempt to import Englishmen, and suppressed the Benedictines. Third, he went out of his way to express sympathy with Ireland and encourage expressions of Irish identity while still insisting on loyalty to the Empire.[544] In early 1874, for example, he thanked the Hibernian Australasian Catholic Benefit Society for its welcome by praising the 'culture and genius' of the Irish. They were a 'heroic people', he remarked, 'whose generosity and devotedness have only been eclipsed by the sufferings which they have sustained with unbending fortitude in the cause of common justice and religion'.[545] As he put it privately in 1877, 'I have written, spoken, and published more in favour of the Irish people than all the Irish Bishops in Australia put together.'[546] Vaughan framed his own Englishness – which he neither hid nor downplayed – in the context of a shared Catholicism, but, unlike Polding, he did not overtly try to dissolve national identities in an Australian melting pot. Although this strategy did not silence Irish criticism, it did help to minimize it.

---

[538] For example, Vaughan to Lanigan, 18 December 1873, ACGA/MS. 3718/4/2, and Vaughan to Murray, 18 December 1873, MNDA/MP/B.1.5.
[539] Murray to Cullen, 7 February 1874, DDA/Australia.
[540] Murray to Cullen, 10 April 1874, DDA/Australia.
[541] Vaughan to Smith, 8 May 1874, ASSP/SP/10/10.
[542] Vaughan to Smith, 4 September 1874, ASSP/SP/10/10.
[543] Vaughan to Murray, 17 July 1874, MNDA/MP/B.1.6.
[544] See, for example, 'Archbishop Vaughan on Loyalty', *Empire*, 26 January 1875.
[545] *FJ*, 10 January 1874.   [546] Vaughan to Smith, 3 August 1877, ASSP/SP/10/10.

Vaughan also shared the Cullenites' ecclesiastical agenda. Like them, he was an unabashed supporter of the papacy (his first pastoral letter after Polding's death was titled *Pius IX and the Revolution*), and his hostility to mixed education was beyond even James Quinn's reproach. In 1879, for example, he joined his Irish suffragans in a trenchant pastoral letter denouncing New South Wales' educational system as the cause of indifferentism and the tool of infidels. All this inevitably polarized opinion. In the approving formulation of the *Freeman's Journal*, it 'divided men in to two opposing camps', Catholics and 'all who have firm religious principles' and 'Ultra-Protestants and worldly-hearted men'.[547]

Yet, for all their ideological sympathy, the alliance between Vaughan and the Cullenites was always doomed. The primary reason for this was the purely tactical nature of the archbishop's Hibernophilia. In private, he held the Irish in contempt, telling a Roman correspondent in 1878, for example, that they had a 'slave mentality' and loved drink, intrigue, and loose women. His own suffragans preferred gold and nationalism to the salvation of souls.[548] Such sentiments were a regular feature of his private correspondence and seem to have been heartfelt. The reality was that Vaughan was a much better politician than Polding, and had fewer illusions, but he was ultimately no more willing than his predecessor to see New South Wales become an Irish outpost.

This first manifested in the peculiar case of Armidale's Timothy O'Mahony. In early 1874, an allegation was made that two years previously O'Mahony had fathered a child with a then fifteen-year-old girl named Ellen Nugent. Nugent claimed she had been seduced in the confessional, while O'Mahony's version was that she had appealed to him after being sexually assaulted by a commercial traveller and that he had immediately informed her mother. In fact, things were even more complicated: Nugent later claimed that the father was really her employer, a surveyor named W. A. B. Greaves, who had put her up to blaming the bishop to distract attention from himself. Local belief was that she was a prostitute and she made her initial allegation from jail where she had been committed for theft; her brother thought that neither Greaves nor O'Mahony was the father and hinted strongly that his sister had returned to a life of prostitution in America.[549]

---

[547] *FJ*, 30 August 1879.   [548] Quoted in Dowd, *Rome in Australia*, 2: 493.

[549] Statement of Ellen Nugent, 16 November 1874, TAA, Timothy O'Mahony papers [OP], AM01.07; John Nugent to O'Mahony, 1 May 1880, TAA/OP/AM01.23. O'Mahony retained a small group of papers related to his case after his translation to Toronto. Although marked 'strictly private' and requiring special permission to access, they are open to researchers.

The charges were spread, if not actually solicited, by a group of disgruntled clergy led by the long-serving resident priest John Lynch and a newly arrived Irishman, Martin Kelly. Even before Nugent's allegations emerged, they had been secretly retailing stories of O'Mahony's supposedly excessive drinking. Neither was a particularly reliable source: Lynch appears to have been irritated at being overlooked for preferment, while Kelly had fled Ireland after having himself fathered a child there, a circumstance of which O'Mahony was then unaware.[550] Yet, whatever the reasons, opposition seems to have been widespread within the diocese: in October 1874, for example, O'Mahony learned that all but one of his priests had been plotting to denounce him to Vaughan in an effort to have him removed.[551]

O'Mahony also badly miscalculated the situation. His first mistake was to accept Kelly's advice to give Nugent's mother £200 so the family could leave Australia. The Irishman implied that Vaughan had suggested the idea and undertook to make the arrangements himself. With breathtaking hypocrisy he then spread the word that O'Mahony had paid hush money to rid himself of his embarrassment. When the news reached Vaughan, he took the view that O'Mahony's situation was untenable, a position with which the Cullenites at first agreed.[552] That changed, however, when it emerged in mid-November 1874 that both Nugent and her mother had recanted their allegations in the presence of Sir John O'Shanassy in Melbourne. They admitted that it had all been an attempt to extort money and conceal the child's true parentage.[553] Before this became clear, however, Vaughan had already written to Rome to report the charges and his own opinion that whatever their truth the scandal alone necessitated O'Mahony's departure. The Propaganda, now under Cardinal Franchi, promptly commissioned him to investigate.

To this point, the Irish had had little to complain of: the charges were grave, Vaughan had consulted them at every turn, and Rome had not unreasonably demanded an investigation. It was Vaughan's methods that were extraordinary. He prepared a set of questions about the bishop's moral character which he then distributed to a group of clergy and laity nominated by Kelly. This of course had the effect of making the charges public. It also made the outcome predictable: O'Mahony was reported to be a drunkard and a seducer. That there was relatively little tangible evidence for the former and none at all for the latter did not matter, and

---

[550] Dowd, *Rome in Australia*, 2: 431–2.
[551] J. O'Sullivan to O'Mahony, 5 October 1874, TAA/OP/AM01.06.
[552] Dowd, *Rome in Australia*, 2: 433–4.
[553] Statement of Ellen and Ann Nugent, 16 November 1874.

Vaughan reported that his opinion had been confirmed and O'Mahony had to go.[554]

The Irish were apoplectic. The combination of Nugent's recantation and Vaughan's investigatory methods convinced them that their colleague was the victim of a conspiracy. This was undoubtedly true of O'Mahony's local opponents, but Vaughan's motivations are harder to gauge. It seems that he never believed the charge of seduction, although he did accept that there was at least some evidence of intemperance. Even the Irish were worried about that. His conviction that the damage to O'Mahony's reputation was terminal was also reasonable; but that does not explain his curiously careless investigation, nor his adamantine and at times duplicitous refusal to reconsider in light of new evidence. It is also worth noting that O'Mahony's eventual successor was the jovial Italian Elzear Torreggiani, who was a personal friend of Vaughan. As Matthew Quinn put it, 'however well inclined [he] is only a tool in the hands of the Archbishop'.[555] Torreggiani's arrival in 1879 with a party of Capuchin monks effectively ended Irish influence in Armidale for a generation. On balance, the safest conclusion is that Vaughan was repaying the Irish in their own coin.

That was certainly the Cullenites' view. Intemperately led by James Quinn, but with the more subtle assistance of Kirby and Moran, they launched a campaign in Rome every bit as consuming as Polding's had once been to recover Henry Gregory. For six years, the affair absorbed their energies and dominated their correspondence. They secured some significant victories, including a ruling that O'Mahony was innocent of the most serious charges. Rome even suggested he might like an Irish diocese. So long as the Propaganda was under Cardinal Franchi, however, there was no hope of his returning to Australia. By the time Franchi died in 1878, the congregation was too committed to reverse itself, and O'Mahony eventually became an auxiliary bishop in Toronto where he died in 1892.[556]

Vaughan had meanwhile turned his attention to James Quinn's Brisbane, securing a Roman commission to investigate charges ranging from poor financial controls to sexual immorality to being beastly to Italians. He reprised his tactic of sending loaded questionnaires to carefully selected critics and even tried to recruit Sir John O'Shanassy as an informant. The two bishops traded bitter insults in Rome, and by 1878 Quinn was complaining to O'Mahony that they were now in the same

---

[554] Dowd, *Rome in Australia*, 2: 435.
[555] Matthew Quinn to [?] Kirby, 30 November 1881, BDA/QP/27/81.
[556] The best account of the O'Mahony affair is Dowd, *Rome in Australia*, 2: chap. 17.

boat.[557] Matthew Quinn thought their treatment proved that successive 'English Archbishops of Sydney' had conspired against 'the Irish in general'.[558] Only Quinn's death in August 1881 brought their battle to a halt.

His successor was Robert Dunne, Quinn's one time protégé in Dublin, who emerged only after a long and ethnically charged struggle; Murray, Matthew Quinn, and Lanigan hoped for another bishop in their own image, while Vaughan preferred an Italian or a German Benedictine.[559] Dunne was ultimately acceptable only because he was both Irish *and* had fallen out with Quinn. Moran thought his appointment was perhaps 'the very best under all the circumstances', while Vaughan was consoled by the knowledge that Dunne was an Anglophile who had come to share the archbishop's distaste for the Cullenites.[560] Vaughan's judgement was shrewd: Dunne would develop into the sole significant Australian opponent of Hiberno-Roman Catholicism.

Such a ruthless and bureaucratically skilful opponent was an unsettling experience for the Irish. As Matthew Quinn put it, Vaughan's 'intrigues have already done irreparable harm to religion in these Provinces, and God only knows where it will end'. The archbishop had 'persecuted' his brother 'to the day of his death' and 'no lie was too base or too gross for him'.[561] Given time there was every chance that he would erase the Cullenites from New South Wales and Queensland, and he was evidently committed to trying. It is important however to remember that these disagreements were personal and national, not ideological. There were no material differences in policy. By 1883, for example, fully 12,500 of Sydney's some 15,200 Catholic children were enrolled in Catholic schools.[562] Yet, while Vaughan would undoubtedly have continued to flatter his Irish flock, he would not have encouraged the intergenerational transmission of their identity. He preferred the Jesuits, French Marist Brothers, and the Sisters of St Joseph to the Irish communities favoured by the Cullenites, and it seems likely that he would have reduced recruiting from All Hallows and other Irish seminaries as quickly as possible. When he died unexpectedly in England on 18 August 1883, he was on mission to recruit further priests and orders both there and in continental Europe.

[557] Dowd, *Rome in Australia*, 2: 491–3.
[558] Matthew Quinn to Murray, 30 August 1881, MNDA/MP/A.4.27.
[559] Dowd, *Rome in Australia*, 2: 510–1.
[560] Moran to Murray, 31 December 1881, MNDA/MP/D.3.144; Dowd, *Rome in Australia*, 2: 511.
[561] Quinn to [?] Kirby, 30 November 1881, BDA/QP/27/81.
[562] A. E. Cahill, 'Vaughan, Roger William Bede (1834–1883)', in *ADB*.

The Irish Ascendancy, 1884–1914

Vaughan's death changed everything. For the first time since Barnabò's decline, one eager parish priest told James Murray, there was a chance to 'appoint an Irishman to Sydney' and thus 'put an end to the unnatural state of things that has prevailed there so long'.[563] Matthew Quinn thought that 'there is no part of the world in which any action could be of more importance to the Church than the selection of a suitable Archbishop for Sydney'.[564] Murray hurriedly called the surviving bishops together in Australia, while Quinn installed himself at the Irish College and haunted the Propaganda. They were taking no chances. With a safe Cullenite majority the provincial bishops recommended William Walsh, then president of Maynooth, Patrick Moran, since 1872 the bishop of Ossory, and Murray himself.

Murray immediately demurred on grounds of health, age, and the probable hostility of the Sydney clergy. Walsh, who would likely have been Rome's first choice, wasn't interested despite Matthew Quinn's insistence that his 'accepting the see of Sydney would be the salvation of religion in New South Wales and above all would keep the church in the hands of the Irish'.[565] Lanigan made a similar appeal.[566] Walsh was unmoved, and even if they had convinced him Cardinal McCabe of Dublin flatly told Rome that he was too valuable in Ireland.[567] That left Moran, who appears to have been genuinely surprised by his nomination despite being first mentioned for an Australian diocese in the early 1860s.[568] He assumed that he had been included simply to make the point 'that Australia must be regarded as an Irish Church & that Sydney is an Irish see'. Still, if he were chosen, he would 'not hesitate for a moment about accepting in order to put an end to the English doings in Australia'.[569]

A fear of 'English doings' pervaded the Irish campaign for Sydney. As Moran himself put it not long after Vaughan's death, 'there will be a great agitation among the English Benedictines to secure the See'.[570] Quinn reported rumours that 'the English are moving heaven and earth for the appointment of another Benedictine or at any rate an Englishman in some

---

[563] Phelan to Murray, 28 November 1883, MNDA/MP/E.2.10.
[564] Quinn to Kirby, 6 September 1863, quoted in Dowd, *Rome in Australia*, 2: 527.
[565] Quinn to Walsh, 22 November 1883, DDA/Australia.
[566] Lanigan to Walsh, 3 October 1883, DDA/Australia.
[567] Quinn to Murray, 22 March 1884, MNDA/MP/A.4.53.
[568] Hynes to Goold, 24 September 1863, MDHC/GP.
[569] Moran to Murray, 14 December 1883, MNDA/MP/D.3.156.
[570] Moran to Murray, 18 September 1883, MNDA/MP/D.3.154.

shape'.[571] There were indeed some such efforts: Vaughan's Benedictine secretary submitted a lengthy report criticizing the Irish faction in New South Wales; Cardinal Manning observed that finding a qualified Irishman was impossible and suggested the late archbishop's uncle instead, an idea that was echoed by the influential curial cardinal Edward Henry Howard; from Armidale, Torreggiani recommended either a German Benedictine or several protégés of Manning; even Austin Sheehy was mentioned.[572] It did not matter: without Franchi, there was no appetite in the Propaganda to impose an Englishman on what was now widely agreed to be a predominately Irish church, and it was no surprise when Patrick Francis Moran was finally appointed in March 1884.[573] Nevertheless, the Irish were ecstatic: Quinn, who would die in early 1885, 'was quite beside himself with joy', while Kirby declared it to be 'the greatest victory the *Irish* church has gained for the last fifty years'.[574]

Their enthusiasm was justified. Nearly a half-century of English Benedictinism had been swept aside in favour of Paul Cullen's literal and ecclesiastical heir. As Patrick O'Farrell put it, Moran was 'a Cullen out of place and out of time, with Cullen his model, with many of Cullen's attitudes and policies, and with something, perhaps much of Cullen's power and stature'.[575] To the Australian Cullenites, Moran was a relative, friend, former classmate, or agent. As Moran himself wrote, there was now 'no danger of there being a want of union among the Bishops of New South Wales. Indeed with the sole exception of Dr Torreggiani, all the Bishops are my old & dearest friends.'[576] Others in Queensland, Victoria, South Australia, and Tasmania were similarly well disposed, and as a result Moran's appointment set the course of Australian Catholicism as a whole well into the twentieth century. As Tobias Kirby gloated, there was now 'good reason to hope for some bright & prosperous times for the Australian offshoot of the Island of Saints'.[577]

Moran moved quickly. By mid-June, he had recruited ten Irish priests and Denis O'Haran, the vice rector of the Irish College.[578] He also collected the first batch of aspirants from St Brigid's. In late July, he visited London, calling on the New South Wales' representative, the colonial secretary, the chancellor of the exchequer (the former Victorian

---

[571] Quinn to Murray, 30 November 1883, MNDA/MP/A.4.45.
[572] See Dowd, *Rome in Australia*, 2: 533–7.
[573] Quinn to Murray, 1 April 1884, MNDA/MP/A.4.54.
[574] Quinn to Murray, 1 April 1884; Moran to Murray, 25 March 1884, MNDA/MP/D.3.159. Emphasis in original.
[575] O'Farrell, *Short History*, 150.   [576] Moran to Murray, 25 March 1884.
[577] Kirby to Murray, 15 July 1884, MNDA/MP/A.3.52.
[578] Moran to Murray, 17 June 1884, MNDA/MP/D.3/160.

politician Hugh Childers), and William Gladstone. They were welcoming and at least 'appeared to enter into my views on the matter of Education'.[579] In early September, he landed in Adelaide, where he was met by Reynolds, Murphy, Murray, and Moore of Ballarat. The whole country, Reynolds told a banquet the night before Moran's arrival, should be 'grateful' that the pope had appointed 'a man who will be the Saint Patrick of the Church in Australia'.[580]

In Sydney, an estimated 100,000 people turned out to welcome him. He sailed through a flotilla of boats, several with bands playing 'Irish songs and patriotic melodies', and was met at the quay by a representative of the governor who placed his carriage at the new archbishop's disposal. He was then formally welcomed in a grand ceremony at St Mary's, with each diocese and several Catholic associations reading out tributes. Bathurst's was particularly blunt, recalling the people's 'cherished desire that a son of St. Patrick' should be appointed and their delight when the 'Holy See, being rightly informed of our case', responded by sending such a distinguished bishop, scholar, and patriot.[581] In his own remarks, Moran immediately reasserted Vaughan's rejection of mixed education, observing that everywhere there was an attempt to 'introduce secularism and infidelity in to the educational systems of the present day', fetter the church, and 'obscure the mind and corrupt the heart of our Catholic youth'. He warned the laity against supporting such a system, promised to use every 'legitimate means to resist such tyranny', and insisted that it was 'free education' that had built the institutions that were the 'glory and pride' of the Empire.[582]

Within days, Moran had launched a comprehensive visitation, inspecting schools, churches, and religious orders in a burst of energy that impressed even outside observers.[583] By early October, he had visited more than seventy schools as well as every church and religious house, begun the construction of an episcopal residence, and commissioned architectural drawings for a seminary.[584] He was uncompromising, boasting in late October that he had been 'getting a good deal of abuse during the past few days from the Protestant newspapers'. He had, he told Lanigan, probed 'the wound of infidelity & freemasonry, & the patient's roar showed that I had touched a sore point'.[585] Moran was determined to establish that power in the archdiocese now lay exclusively with him. At St Vincent's hospital, for example, he took the opportunity of a vacancy to

[579] Moran to Phelan, 25 July 1884, ARSMP.   [580] FJ, 6 September 1884.
[581] Sydney Morning Herald, 9 September 1884.   [582] FJ, 13 September 1884.
[583] Sydney Morning Herald, 10 September 1884.
[584] Moran to Murray, 7 October 1884, MNDA/MP/D.3.162.
[585] Moran to Lanigan, 28 October 1884, ACGA/MS. 3718/2/5.

make his own appointments and force the resignation of almost the entire medical staff, many of whom were Protestants. He called them a 'Freemason Ring' and celebrated his cleansing of the 'Augean Stables'. Public criticism was dismissed as simple 'prejudice & falsehood'.[586] Within a year, he began construction of a new wing to the hospital at a cost of some £8,000.[587] This all represented a departure from Vaughan's more diplomatic and incremental approach to achieving the same goals. As a delighted Kirby observed in early 1885, 'But what a change ... in Sydney in so short a time!'[588]

There were also more substantive differences. Despite his own claim to have become 'an Australian among Australians', and Murray's description of him as a 'full-grown Australian', Moran rejected the assimilationist hopes of Polding and Vaughan.[589] As he told the *Boston Pilot* shortly before his departure from Rome, he was setting out not 'to a land of strangers' but rather 'to the faithful Irish people in Australia who had brought the Catholic faith to that country'. The church's remarkable growth, he insisted, was 'chiefly, if not wholly, owing to the Irish'. 'As in England, and in Scotland, and the United States', he concluded, 'the very great bulk of the Catholic population is Irish or descended from the Irish people.'[590]

Moran did not believe that one ceased to be Irish simply because one's parents or grandparents had moved to a foreign country. The image he chose was transplantation, remarking in 1888 that 'It would seem as if a fruitful branch of a fruitful tree had been wafted to a genial soil and was soon clothed with blossoms & fruit' in what he called 'that new Ireland under the Southern Cross.'[591] Where Polding and to a lesser extent Vaughan had encouraged an Australian identity that stood alone, supplanting or replacing pre-existing national (but not imperial) loyalties, Moran embraced hybridity. He saw no contradiction in being a proud Australian and a patriotic Irishman. Had he been sent to the United States, he would have become a proud American. He was determined that Sydney would conform to this vision and he had nearly thirty years in which to ensure that it did, not least through the ongoing importation of Irish clergy. This is the antithesis of what Peter Cunich claimed was Moran's passive acceptance of 'an Australian church neither Irish nor

---

[586] Moran to Lanigan, 13 December 1884, ACGA/MS. 3718/2/5.
[587] Philip Ayres, *Prince of the Church: Patrick Francis Moran, 1830–1911* (Melbourne: The Miegunyah Press, 2007), 155.
[588] Kirby to Murray, 12 January 1885, MNDA/MP/A.3.53.
[589] *FJ*, 13 September 1884; Murray to Maher, 5 January 1885, ARSMC.
[590] The interview was reproduced in the *FJ*, 12 July 1884.
[591] Manuscript copy of the address of Cardinal Moran on the occasion of his visit to Kilkenny in 1888, SAA, Moran papers [MP].

Roman', an argument that has been repeated by scholars such as John Luttrell.[592] In fact, the Australian church after Moran differed only slightly from those elsewhere in Greater Ireland, with the conspicuous exception of Brisbane. Very little about Australian Catholicism was distinctively Australian until well into the twentieth century.

Moran's power was augmented by his appointment as Australia's first cardinal. Although there had been rumours of such a promotion when he was first named to Sydney, the speculation had largely ceased after he arrived.[593] Yet, not long after Dublin's Cardinal Edward McCabe died in February 1885, Moran was urgently summoned to Rome. Although even privately he claimed to 'have no idea as to what may be the business for which my presence is required', it was widely believed that he would be McCabe's successor.[594] This prospect caused consternation in Australia. As Lanigan told him, 'I look on the danger of your being taken from us as a great calamity.'[595] Fortunately, the idea was equally upsetting in Ireland, where, after nearly thirty years of domination by Cullen, there was little appetite for his nephew. The well-informed Murray had no doubt that Moran would return, reassuring Lanigan that 'under present circumstances he will not be welcome to the clergy of Dublin or to the Irish Bishops'.[596] He was right: Leo XIII chose William Walsh for Dublin and honoured Moran with the red hat, membership of the Propaganda, the status of apostolic delegate, and instructions to convene a plenary council for the whole of Australasia. He returned to Australia in October 1885 with six Irish nuns, all from the Sisters of the Little Company of Mary, a nursing order, two Irish Vincentians, and seven Irish secular priests.[597] His welcome in Sydney was even grander than before – as the ageing William Bernard Ullathorne remarked when he read the accounts, 'What a change since my time in that country!'[598]

Moran was now as ascendant in Australia as his uncle had been in Ireland. As a delighted Kirby put it, 'Let us hope that the appointment of an Irishman as first Cardinal in Australia will tend to the greater good of religion in that vast Continent.'[599] Moran was inevitably pleased by the prospect of a national council, having already planned a provincial gathering for New South Wales before being called to Rome.[600] It met in

[592] Cunich, 156; John Luttrell, '"Australianizing" the local Catholic Church: Polding to Gilroy', *Journal of Religious History*, vol. 36, no. 3, 342.
[593] Thomas Carr to Walsh, 22 January 1884, DDA/Australia.
[594] Moran diary, 1 May 1885, SAA/MP; Ayres, 140–3.
[595] Lanigan to Moran, 10 June 1885, SAA/MP/2/44/Australian bishops.
[596] Murray to Lanigan, 19 June 1885, ACGA/MS. 3718/2/5.   [597] *FJ*, 3 October 1885.
[598] Ullathorne to 'Philomena', 27 December 1885, BAA/UP/B9595.
[599] Kirby to Lanigan, 15 November 1885, ACGA/MS. 3718/4/1.
[600] Moran to Murray, 7 October 1884, MNDA/MP/D.3.162.

Sydney on 14 November 1885, with some sixteen bishops in attendance from across Australia and New Zealand, including the late Matthew Quinn's successor Joseph Byrne, who had been his vicar general and president of St Charles' seminary.[601] Moran carefully managed proceedings, placing his fellow Cullenites in charge of all but one of the committees responsible for drafting the decrees, while silencing the potentially wayward Robert Dunne of Brisbane through the expedient of making him the council's secretary.[602]

Following the precedents of Philadelphia in 1832, Thurles in 1850, Baltimore in 1852, Halifax in 1857, and Maynooth in 1875, the council emphasized the centrality of the parish through the introduction of a parochial system with its accompanying canonical protections for parish priests, while also insisting on clerical discipline, meticulous record-keeping, regular access to the sacraments, and the creation of sodalities, confraternities, and lay associations ranging from Catholic subscription libraries to mutual aid societies. The Irish catechism was adopted for the whole of Australasia and special celebrations were ordered for the feasts of St Patrick and St Brigid. There were also urgent appeals to eschew drink, support Catholic schools, and avoid mixed marriages and godless education. The evils of the latter two were delineated at great length in the accompanying pastoral letter.[603]

Moran also took the opportunity to remake the Australian hierarchy. In addition to appointments in New Zealand (see Chapter 7), the council recommended that Adelaide and Brisbane should become archdioceses, despite being in the hands of the spendthrift Reynolds and the renegade Cullenite Dunne, respectively, and that there should be four new dioceses, two in New South Wales and one each in Victoria and South Australia. It also recommended that Perth and Melbourne should have coadjutors, the latter over the ageing and absent Goold's fierce objections.

The new bishops were all Irish: John Dunne (nephew of the tempestuous Patrick Dunne) for Wilcannia in extreme western New South Wales, the Armidale priest and O'Mahony loyalist Jeremiah Doyle for Grafton (later Lismore) on the north coast of New South Wales, John O'Reily for Port Augusta in South Australia, and the long-serving Matthew Gibney for Perth. Goold's sensitivities were acknowledged by the appointment of his Limerick-born protégé James Francis Corbett to the new Victorian diocese of Sale. None of these men were Cullenites in

---

[601] Also in attendance were the vicar apostolic of North Queensland and a procurator acting for Archbishop Goold of Melbourne.
[602] Byrne, *Dunne*, 145.   [603] For the full text, see Moran, *Australasia*, 684–701.

the sense that Moran, Murray, the Quinns, Murphy, or O'Mahony had been. None, for example, was Roman-trained: Corbett, Doyle, Gibney, and O'Reily had been formed at All Hallows and Dunne at Carlow. It did not matter: like William Lanigan, they took the policies of their patrons and predecessors for granted as orthodox best practice.

They also proved to be committed builders. In Grafton, for example, Doyle increased the number of schools from nine to twenty-three in little more than twenty years, largely by importing the Sisters of Mercy, who ultimately had seven convents, and the Presentation Sisters.[604] Corbett, who had made his reputation as a fierce critic of mixed education, was similarly industrious in importing religious orders to Sale, including the Christian Brothers, while in Wilcannia Dunne was an early and enthusiastic customer of St Brigid's.[605] He ultimately spent some £16,000 on the Mercy convent, schools, and orphanage at Broken Hill, and even quite small towns in his vast rural diocese soon boasted Mercy convents.[606] At Deniliquin, for example, their school had some 180 students within a year of its foundation in 1877.[607] In Perth, the profligate Gibney not only increased the number of churches from twelve to thirty-one, the number of primary schools from eleven to forty-three, and the number of higher schools from three to twenty-one but also built two hospitals, a monastery, and an asylum for women.[608] Throughout rural Australia, the church now followed almost without exception a distinctively Hiberno-Roman pattern of rapid growth, institutional consolidation, and social, sexual, and educational separation overseen by Irish priests, nuns, and bishops.

The most important change was in Melbourne. Under Goold it had remained semi-detached from the rest of the Australian church even as it developed along roughly parallel lines, and as he aged he became ever more unwilling to tolerate meddling. He particularly resisted the idea of a coadjutor. While Vaughan lived he might have hoped to name his own replacement, but after Moran arrived that chance was gone. Already deeply suspicious of Cullenite intrigue, Goold consequently snubbed the new cardinal on his triumphal return from Rome.[609] His fury was unbounded when he learned that the council had decided to recommend an appointment anyway. When Adelaide's Christopher Reynolds passed through Melbourne on his way home, Goold sent word that 'there is

[604] Gregory Haines, 'Doyle, Jeremiah Joseph (1849–1909)', in *ADB*.

[605] Monica Starke, 'Corbett, James Francis (1834–1912)', in *ADB*.

[606] Obituary, *Barrier Miner*, 26 December 1916.

[607] Dunne to Murray, 22 May 1888, MNDA/MP/A.4.126.

[608] V. E. Callaghan, 'Gibney, Matthew (1835–1925)', in *ADB*.   [609] Boland, *Carr*, 121.

neither a bed nor hospitality for you here'. Reynolds only managed to avoid what he called 'great scandal' through the expedient of showing up at Goold's house and refusing to leave until the archbishop received him.[610]

The succession was crucial to the future of Australian Catholicism. Of the four existing or newly created archdioceses, Sydney was now safely under Moran, but Brisbane was departing ever further from Cullenite orthodoxy under Dunne, and Adelaide was mired in debt under Reynolds. Without Melbourne, undiluted Hiberno-Roman Catholicism might yet have been limited to New South Wales and rural Australia. As Moran put it, such an important city required 'a very active & intelligent man'. There were 'few places in the whole Church', he told William Walsh of Dublin, 'where greater good can be expected than in the See of Melbourne'.[611] Moran had reason to worry: the province's two Cullenites, Reynolds and Murphy of Hobart, wanted James Murray to be translated from Maitland, while Moore of Ballarat joined the Irish Augustinians Martin Crane and his coadjutor Stephen Reville in preferring Thomas Carr, since 1883 the bishop of Galway. The balance fell to the ailing Martin Griver of Perth, who apparently decided to support Carr solely on the grounds he would be 'more agreeable' to Goold. Moran sensed which way the wind was blowing, asked for a short postponement in the proceedings, and then delivered a unanimous vote for Carr the following day.[612] It was a setback but not a major one: Moran was perfectly content with the outcome. It was, he told Walsh in Dublin, 'the only case in which we have been obliged to call on our home friends'.[613] Despite a last-ditch protest from Goold, Rome agreed to the recommendation.

Moran had reason to be pleased: Carr was cultured, intellectually gifted, and a favourite of John MacEvilly, a Cullen protégé who had been the bishop of Galway since 1857. More importantly, he was close to Paula Cullen and the Sisters of Mercy in Westport, Co. Mayo, where he was first posted as a curate. He became their confessor in 1867, three of his own sisters joined the community between 1868 and 1874, and, when Cullen visited the convent, it was Carr who accompanied him up nearby Croagh Patrick.[614] All this helped to overcome his otherwise unpropitious (to a Cullenite) background as a product of St Jarlath's College,

---

[610] Reynolds to Moran, 19 December 1885, MDHC, Carr papers [CP], B.154.
[611] Moran to Walsh, 20 September 1885, DDA/Australia.
[612] See Martin Crane to 'Dr Glynn', 23 December 1886, Sandhurst diocesan archives, Crane papers. This is a photocopy of an original held in an unknown archive, most likely that of the Irish Augustinians in Rome.
[613] Moran to Walsh, 20 September 1885, DDA/Australia.   [614] Boland, *Carr*, 28–9.

Tuam, and then Maynooth. Although he had no desire to go to Australia and tried to avoid the promotion, he was appointed archbishop in his own right (Goold having died in the interim) in September 1886.[615] As he told a confidant, 'In leaving Ireland I shall have much indeed to lose, and I fear those to whom I go will not have much to gain.'[616]

When Carr arrived at Melbourne's Spencer Street Station in June 1887, he was greeted by local worthies, a massed rank of men from the St Patrick's and Hibernian Societies, and some 6,000 Catholic school children, all wearing a 'Celtic cross, bearing the inscription *Cead mille failthe*'. It was a very Irish affair, with the subsequent procession halting briefly at St Patrick's Hall before passing St Patrick's College and finally arriving at St Patrick's Cathedral. There the assembled clergy welcomed Carr's appointment as 'another proof' of the pope's 'paternal and affectionate solicitude towards the Irish race', the St Patrick's Society greeted him 'in the name of the Irishmen of Victoria', and the Confraternity of the Holy Family assured him that he would find the Australian Irish no less pious than those born in Ireland. Everybody stressed the iniquities of the educational system and the importance of supporting the Catholic schools.[617] Like Moran, Carr too immediately set out on a comprehensive visitation of his diocese.[618]

Moran was delighted. 'All the Australian bishops', he gloated, 'will now be thoroughly united!'[619] He was right: for nearly a quarter of a century, Moran habitually consulted Carr on every aspect of church governance and public policy, while Carr in turn deferred to Moran as the leader of Australian Catholicism.[620] They had their disagreements, all relatively minor and never pressed, but their devotional, administrative, political, and educational preferences were effectively identical. The primary difference was that Carr was more temperate and more emollient than the strident Moran and more willing to work across confessional boundaries outside the narrow bounds of politics. In 1900, for example, he gave powerful encouragement to the high-profile campaign of the Irish Protestant Alexander Leeper, later an intemperate opponent of Irish Home Rule, to protect the University of Melbourne from what Carr called 'infidelity and immorality'.[621]

---

[615] Carr to Walsh, 22 January 1884, DDA/Australia.
[616] Carr to E. T. O'Dwyer, 2 October 1886, LDA.   [617] *Advocate*, 18 June 1887.
[618] Boland, *Carr*, 150.
[619] Quoted in John N. Molony, 'Carr, Thomas Joseph (1839–1917)', in *ADB*.
[620] Boland, *Carr*, 150–1.
[621] Quoted in John Poynter, *Doubts and Certainties: A life of Alexander Leeper* (Melbourne: Melbourne University Press, 1997), 284. The issue was whether the controversial G. W. L. Marshall-Hall should be re-appointed to the Ormond Chair of Music.

Carr's appointment meant that Australia's two most important cities were now firmly under Hiberno-Roman leadership. Indeed, with the death of Martin Griver in November 1886, the Australian church as a whole was now almost entirely in Irish hands. The only exceptions were Salvado in the far west and the Italians Elzear Torreggiani and John Cani, both Vaughan appointees, in the peripheral eastern dioceses of Armidale and Rockhampton. Ideologically too there was agreement, with one glaring exception. As Moran put it in late 1888, 'we must insist on uniformity'. 'Otherwise', he told Murray, 'there will be no end of changes introduced very soon.'[622] Almost certainly he had Robert Dunne's Brisbane in mind.

Dunne's resistance to the Cullenites was programmatic and determined. Among other things, he slowed the growth of Catholic education and limited it to urban areas; in a nearly thirty-year episcopate, he added a mere ten schools to the thirty-nine he had inherited from Quinn, despite Queensland's population more than doubling over the period, and built none at all during his first decade in Brisbane.[623] Dunne's priority was to ensure that Catholic schools compared well to the public system and were seen by Protestants to do so. To achieve this, he favoured fewer, better schools, took a close interest in their pedagogy and management, and insisted that they follow the state curriculum and be open to state inspection despite receiving no state support.[624] He was largely content to leave primary education to the state, especially in rural areas. Dunne's emphasis on elite secondary education did yield some successes, such as the Irish Christian Brothers boarding school at Nudgee which opened in 1891 with forty students, but it came with a cost: by 1894, only some 1,300 of the archdiocese's 8,000 school-age boys were receiving a Catholic education and the proportion that did so continued to fall into the early 1900s.[625]

Dunne thought that Catholic interests were best advanced by economic progress, social integration, land ownership, and temperance. He cared little for ecclesiastical infrastructure, eschewed Irish symbolism, and urged political accommodation. He also tolerated mixed marriages. This was not accommodation for its own sake, however, or not entirely. Like all the bishops, for example, Dunne saw the restoration of state aid as a matter of natural justice. Yet he also recognized that Queensland's widely scattered (and thus electorally weak) Catholic population could only achieve the political influence necessary to secure it with Protestant support. Any hint of triumphalism or Irish nationalism would make an

[622] Moran to Murray, 8 December 1888, MNDA/MP/3/1/1810/2/6.
[623] Byrne, *Dunne*, 149.   [624] Ibid., 150.
[625] Goodman, 152–3; Byrne, *Dunne*, 174; see Roland Lawson, *Brisbane in the 1890s: A Study of Australian Urban Society* (St Lucia: University of Queensland Press, 1973), 267.

already difficult task impossible in what remained an intensely sectarian political landscape.[626] When one of his priests denounced a candidate in the 1898 election, for example, both Dunne and the colony's leading Catholic politician immediately disavowed him as a threat to 'liberty of conscience'.[627] This emollience undoubtedly helped Catholics rise to positions of power, including Thomas Byrnes, the colony's short-lived first Catholic premier, but only at the price of their disclaiming any attempt to restore state aid.[628] What they could do was agitate for state scholarships tenable at Catholic secondary schools, something Dunne had been pushing since at least 1889. The measure's eventual success ten years later marked both a partial vindication of Dunne's strategy and the beginning of an enduring Catholic alliance with the local Labor Party.[629]

Although Dunne deviated from Cullenite practice in almost every particular, the significance of his opposition should not be overemphasized. Much of his reluctance to build, for instance, was simply temperamental – even as a parish priest he had had a reputation for parsimony, particularly with nuns, and he died with £90,000 in the bank.[630] His distaste for Irish nationalism was also of long-standing. In 1857, for example, he had been appalled when the Quinn brothers had gloated over the fall of Delhi.[631] Yet Dunne was also content to 'fish' for his clergy in Ireland and send his high-flyers to Rome.[632] He maintained close if occasionally fractious relations with the Sisters of Mercy and the Christian Brothers, who together dominated Catholic educational provision in Queensland, and agreed with his Hiberno-Roman brethren as to the importance of Catholic education. He just disagreed about the sacrifices worth making to secure it. Indeed, many of their differences came down to tone or temperament, although real disagreements did exist over such issues as mixed marriages and social separation.

Yet ultimately Robert Dunne had little influence on the development of Australian Catholicism. This was partly because he did not build a party and was consequently largely ignored by Moran and Carr and partly because his comparative inertia allowed the church in Brisbane to drift until his death in 1917. It is telling that he remains without an entry in the *Australian Dictionary of Biography*, which is normally exhaustive in its coverage of Catholic bishops. The contrast with his successor is stark. Over a lengthy episcopate, the Limerick-born and Irish College–educated James Duhig, who had first been promoted to the episcopate at Moran's

---

[626] Lawson, 253.
[627] *Maryborough Chronicle, Wide Bay and Burnett Advertiser*, 19 May 1898.
[628] Lawson, 255.   [629] Ibid., 257.   [630] O'Donoghue, *Whitty*, 66; Lawson, 267.
[631] Byrne, *Dunne*, 39.   [632] Kirby to Murray, 17 July 1890, MNDA/MP/A.3.66.

suggestion, managed to open more than fifty parishes and spend some three million pounds on more than 400 major ecclesiastical structures.[633] Duhig died only in 1965, six years after he became the first Australian Catholic prelate to accept a knighthood.

Brisbane was not Moran's only problem. In Adelaide, Christopher Reynolds' always heavy debts had slowly become unmanageable – by 1888, they had reached at least £57,000 and even that was a guess.[634] In what remained a poor diocese, Reynolds spent freely on everything from schools to a new cathedral to a splendid private art collection. Fundraising was neglected and interest payments consumed what revenue there was. Reynolds tried hard and did have some successes, including securing the Christian Brothers in 1878 after a long courtship. Indeed, he was so committed to obtaining the brothers that he wept when they delayed their arrival.[635] Typically, he toasted their eventual appearance with the 'best champagne'.[636] Also typically, they had to find the funds (some £8,000) themselves.[637] In 1880, he also welcomed a party of Irish Sisters of Mercy fleeing anti-clericalism in Argentina. Within months, the twenty-four women had purchased a convent (with their own money) and opened a school and a refuge for 'girls of unblemished reputation'.[638] Many more schools, convents, and refuges followed. At Reynolds' death in 1893, the diocese and its debts passed to John O'Reily, the Kilkenny-born and All Hallows–educated bishop of nearby Port Augusta.

O'Reily proved to be a prudent manager and emollient public figure. In 1896, for example, he plotted with the Anglican bishop of Adelaide J. R. Harmer to restore state aid and even entertained him at home.[639] In 1902, he worked behind the scenes with the then acting governor general of Australia, Lord Tennyson, to find a compromise that would permit Bible reading in South Australian public schools.[640] His support was welcomed by Tennyson but provoked a sharp rebuke from Archbishop Carr: 'If Catholic children are present', he wrote, 'and say a Wesleyan

---

[633] Duhig was appointed to Rockhampton in 1905. Moran to Joseph Higgins, 20 June 1905, Archives of the Diocese of Ballarat [BDAV], Joseph Higgins papers [HP], 63/5/4; T. P. Boland, 'Duhig, Sir James (1871–1965)', in *ADB*.

[634] Ayres, 160.

[635] K. K. O'Donoghue, *P. A. Treacy and the Christian Brothers in Australia and New Zealand* (Melbourne: Polding Press, 1983), 117,120.

[636] Quoted in Press, 203.   [637] O'Donoghue, *Treacy*, 117,120.

[638] Quoted in Anne McLay, *Women on the Move: Mercy's Triple Spiral: A History of the Adelaide Sisters of Mercy, Ireland to Argentina 1856–1880 to South Australia 1880* (Adelaide: Sisters of Mercy, 1996), 37.

[639] See Harmer to O'Reily, 11 January 1896, O'Reily to Harmer, 18 January 1896, and Harmer to O'Reily, 22 January 1896, ACAA, O'Reily papers [OR], Series 144, Box 1, Folder 2.

[640] See Tennyson to O'Reily, 20 June, ACAA/OR/Series 144/Box 1/Folder 9.

Teacher is giving instruction, it is morally certain that he will use the opportunity to misrepresent Catholic doctrine.'[641] O'Reily retreated.[642] Unlike Robert Dunne, he was not ideologically opposed to Hiberno-Romanism and remained a champion of Catholic education and a forthright critic of any attempt to curtail what he saw as Catholic rights. By O'Reily's death in 1915, the archdiocese had stabilized and even begun to grow again, but Reynolds' profligacy had cast a long shadow.

The situation in Perth was even worse. It began well enough: the All Hallows–educated Matthew Gibney was committed to Catholic education and keen to preserve state support. He also took an active interest in politics. In 1888, for example, he successfully rallied the Catholic vote behind John Horgan, a radical firebrand who also served as the bishop's solicitor. One local newspaper framed the choice as 'between the capitalist and the working man'.[643] Yet Horgan soon lost his seat in a conservative backlash, and when responsible government was granted in 1890 the franchise was structured to exclude radicals by disenfranchising as much of the Irish population as possible through stringent property qualifications. Gibney protested the 'injustice' but was ignored.[644] Without a significant Catholic vote the final withdrawal of state aid was inevitable, and when it passed in 1895 Gibney was able to secure only £15,000 in compensation. As a result, he turned to property speculation, buying among other things shops, houses, and a hotel.[645] As early as 1898, Moran and O'Reily were fretting that his debts of some £50,000 were unsustainable.[646] Ten years later, they learned that the total now exceeded £150,000. Much of the increase came from Gibney's desperate attempts to keep his newspaper afloat after its circulation had collapsed, reputedly because he had forbidden the reporting of racing news. An investigation by Maitland's Patrick Dwyer revealed that the real figure was closer to £216,000.[647] Dwyer recommended that Gibney be sacked, Moran agreed, and Rome formally requested his resignation in 1910.[648] He was replaced the following year by the Irish Redemptorist Patrick Clune.[649]

---

[641] Tennyson to O'Reily, 10 July 1902, ACAA/OR/Series 144/Box 1/Folder 9; Carr to O'Reily, 16 July 1902, ACAA/OR/Series 144/Box 1/Folder 9.
[642] Carr to O'Reily, 25 July 1902, ACAA/OR/Series 144/Box 1/Folder 9.
[643] *Eastern Districts Chronicle*, 26 May 1888.
[644] *Daily News* (Perth), 27 November 1890.
[645] V. E. Callaghan, 'Gibney, Matthew (1835–1925)', in *ADB*.
[646] Moran to O'Reily, 2 December 1898, ACAA/OR/Series 144/Box 2/Moran letters.
[647] Ayres, 264–6.   [648] Bourke, 161–4.
[649] Christopher Dowd, *Faith, Ireland, and Empire: The Life of Patrick Joseph Clune CSSR 1864–1935, Archbishop of Perth, Western Australia* (Strathfield, NSW: St Paul's Publications, 2014).

Despite these problems, Moran's appointment to Sydney inaugurated a period of relative stability and Hiberno-Roman consolidation in the Australian church. One of his first steps was to deepen popular piety (and thus social controls) through the establishment of parish missions. This had been the primary mechanism through which Cullen had sparked Ireland's devotional revolution in the 1850s, and as ever Moran had his uncle's example in view. As a result, he had brought with him two Irish Vincentians when he returned from Rome in 1885.[650] Within weeks, they were in the Sydney suburb of Petersham, where they drew many 'negligent and cold Catholics' to a fortnight of lectures, preaching, and confessions. The mission culminated with Moran administering confirmation, before a branch of the confraternity of the Sacred Heart of Jesus was established to 'make the great good brought about by the missioners permanent'. They then moved on to James Murray's Maitland.[651] The following year, the Irish congregation formally accepted a permanent mission in Australia.[652] By 1887, two of its missioners were in Western Australia, evangelizing 'all the churches and convents of the vast diocese of Perth'.[653] In rural New South Wales, Bishop Dunne planned to travel his diocese with the Vincentians after their 'very effective mission' at Deniliquin in May 1888.[654] Early the next year, Archbishop Carr closed a mission at Williamstown with confirmation, a papal blessing, and the inauguration of the local Temperance League of the Cross.[655] By the mid-1890s, even the most remote parishes had hosted a mission.

The Redemptorists also owed their presence in Australia to the Cullenites. After declining requests from Polding in 1848 and again in 1867, and from James Quinn in 1859 and 1865, in 1881 they finally agreed to a joint appeal from Murray and Moran. Six Redemptorists duly arrived in the New South Wales town of Singleton the following year.[656] They, too, soon began to conduct missions across the country. In 1885, the Redemptorists gave their first mission in Victoria, and in 1889 they arrived in Queensland. Their energy was astonishing. In 1890, for example, the small community in Ballarat managed fifty-two missions, rising to at least seventy-three four years later.[657]

---

[650] 'The Vincentian Fathers at the Cathedral', *FJ*, 21 November 1885.
[651] *FJ*, 19 December 1885.   [652] Moran diary, 10 August 1886, AAS.
[653] *FJ*, 3 March 1888.   [654] Dunne to Murray, 22 May 1888, MNDA/MP/A.4.126.
[655] *Williamstown Chronicle*, 23 February 1889.
[656] S. J. Boland, *Faith of Our Fathers: The Redemptorists in Australia, 1882–1982* (n.p.: Redemptorist Fathers, 1982), 23–5.
[657] Ibid., 64.

Yet the Redemptorists had a significant flaw in Cullenite eyes: although many of the priests and brothers were Irish, the first superior was Edmund Vaughan, uncle of the late archbishop, and the community was dependent on a province that was dominated by Englishmen. Cardinal Manning and other leading English Catholics had even recommended Vaughan for Sydney ahead of Moran. The inevitable tensions finally came to a head in 1894, when the pioneer Redemptorist Thomas O'Farrell solicited Moran's help in securing an Irish province under which Australia could be placed. He called it 'Home Rule'.[658] Moran agreed with alacrity, telling O'Farrell that, while he had the 'greatest veneration for several English fathers of your order', they were simply ineffective in a diocese where 'only a handful' were not Irish or of Irish descent. He pointed to a mission they had recently given at St Mary's Cathedral: three of the four missioners were English, he wrote, and although 'all most excellent & eloquent men' the 'mission was a complete failure'. The problem, Moran concluded, was that the 'ideas & manners & sympathy of Englishmen are cast in a different mould from those of our Irish people'. Until the community in Australia was placed under Irish control, as the Jesuits and the Vincentians already were, they would be incapable of reaching their full potential.[659] In 1898, an Irish province was duly erected, Australia was placed under it, and O'Farrell became the community's third superior. All but one of the English priests was recalled and no new ones were sent.[660]

Moran's devotional revolution also required suitably Hiberno-Roman nuns, and almost as soon as he was appointed he requested 'devoted Sisters to come out and give a helping hand to the little children of St. Patrick at the Antipodes'.[661] In early 1887, he formally asked the Callan Sisters of Mercy to establish a colony in New South Wales, a prospect that 'delighted' the women.[662] He wanted a 'numerous battalion', and from a number of volunteers nine were selected.[663] From the moment of their arrival, Moran enjoyed a relaxed, almost intimate relationship with the community. Among other things, he repeatedly offered to buy them a cow, gave them money for a proper kitchen, warned them against excessive fasting, helped them displace the Sisters of Charity from part of the

---

[658] O'Farrell to Joseph Higgins, 13 January 1894, SAA/MP. Higgins was Moran's auxiliary bishop, and O'Farrell was asking him to intercede with the cardinal.

[659] Moran to O'Farrell, 12 February 1894, SAA/MP.

[660] Boland, *Faith of Our Fathers*, 75–6.

[661] Quoted in Madeleine Sophie McGrath, *These Women? Women Religious in the History of Australia, the Sisters of Mercy Parramatta 1888–1988* (Kensington: New South Wales University Press, n.d.), 14.

[662] M. Berchmans to Moran, 'Feast of the Holy Name' 1887, ARSMP/Box 60.

[663] Moran to 'Rev. Mother', 16 June 1888, ACRSM; McGrath, 15–16.

site of their Parramatta convent, and teased them for their 'American style of advertising' when that convent suffered a fire.[664] As a result, he is still remembered as the 'domestic prelate'. Within a year, the sisters had opened two schools with a combined enrolment of 234.[665] They also established a convent and school in Surry Hills, displacing the Sisters of the Good Samaritan.[666] It soon had some 400 students.[667] Moran continued to take a close interest in the community, whether chiding them when their students fell short, urging the creation of a vegetable garden for the orphaned children, or celebrating good exam results.[668] He also continued to encourage their expansion, again often at the expense of other groups. In 1897, for example, he arranged for the sisters to take over a villa in Ryde belonging to the Patrician Brothers.[669] Despite this attentiveness, however, he rarely intervened in how the women managed their affairs.

Moran was similarly encouraging of the other quintessentially Cullenite community of women religious, the Cabra Dominicans. In 1890, he convinced the community at Maitland to found a convent and boarding school at Moss Vale, some 130 kilometres south-west of Sydney in what he called the 'thoroughly anti-Catholic' southern highlands. Moran boasted that it would become a 'citadel in a hostile territory'.[670] Two years later, the women borrowed £5,000 to purchase a property in Sydney and then spent another £4,200 to build a convent and school, both of which opened in 1894.[671] By 1936, the Dominicans had nine convents in New South Wales overseeing sixteen schools with a combined enrolment of 2,292.[672] Even the older communities steadily greened. In 1898, for example, Moran was delighted when Polding's Sisters of the Good Samaritan elected an Irishwomen as mother superior.[673] Six weeks later, Murray invited them to return to Maitland.[674]

Yet Moran undoubtedly thought that his most important project was his great seminary at Manly, on Sydney Harbour's North Head. Within months of his arrival, he had signed contracts for both the seminary and an episcopal residence on the site. (In a nice irony, much of the some

---

[664] Moran to M. Clare Dunphy, 13 December 1888, 3 January 1889, 20 December 1889, ARSMP.

[665] Moran to M. Berchmans, 14 November 1889, ARSMP/Box 60.

[666] Moran to Rev. Mother, 4 July 1889, ARSMP.

[667] Moran to M. Berchmans, 14 November 1889, ARSMP/Box 60.

[668] Moran to Rev. Mother, 8 January 1894, 2 September 1901, ARSMP; Moran to M. Alphonsus, 23 November 1896, ARSMP.

[669] Moran to M. Alphonsus, 26 October 1897, ARSMP.

[670] Moran to M. Berchmans, 13 April 1891, ARSMP/Box 60.   [671] MacGinley, 150–1.

[672] From a note in the Dominican Archives at Strathfield.

[673] Moran to Murray, 30 December 1898, MNDA/MP/3/1/1810/2/8.

[674] Moran to Murray, 14 February 1899, MNDA/MP/3/1/1810/2/8.

£60,000 the buildings were projected to cost came from the estate of the late Archbishop Vaughan.) Moran's ambition was clear: the initial plans called for space for up to 200 clerical students and ten resident staff.[675] This was vastly more than Sydney could require – a seminary on such a scale could only be intended to serve the entire continent. He even hoped that in time it might form the nucleus of a Catholic university for a newly united Australia.[676]

From the beginning Moran's intention was to replicate Dublin's Holy Cross College, Clonliffe, which Cullen had opened in 1859 as a counterweight to the nearby national seminary at Maynooth. Holy Cross was in turn modelled on the Irish College in Rome and the *Collegio Urbano*. Moran was clear that the education, ethos, and clerical formation it provided were to be unambiguously Roman. To ensure this he appointed his cousin Michael Verdon as the first rector of what he had named St Patrick's College. Verdon's career arc was prototypically Cullenite: born in Liverpool, the son of Cullen's sister, educated by the Vincentians at Castleknock and then in Rome under Tobias Kirby, president of Clonliffe from 1870, and then vice rector of the Irish College from 1879. After seven years at Manly, he was appointed the second bishop of Dunedin in New Zealand, where he soon opened Holy Cross College in Mosgiel (see Chapter 7). Moran wanted no surprises in his model Hiberno-Roman seminary, and, as K. J. Walsh has pointed out, Manly was and remained 'in thrall' to its founder. The college adopted Moran's coat of arms, his bust was prominently displayed in its hall, and his intentions had for generations the status of 'holy writ'.[677]

Under Verdon the college was an immediate success, admitting some ninety students during his relatively brief rectorship. Most came from Melbourne or Sydney, but all except four Australasian dioceses sent at least one. Even Robert Dunne's Brisbane was a regular customer. By 1904, at least forty-eight had been ordained, and by 1914 that number exceeded 150.[678] Some of the bishops, however, continued to prefer sourcing their clergy from Ireland, often for financial reasons. In later years, this came to be seen in some quarters as anti-Australian prejudice, and in 1914 a group of alumni formed the 'Manly Union' to campaign for the advancement of locally trained clergy. They had a point: it was not until 1930 that the first graduates reached the Australian episcopate. It is also the case that frustration at what might be called Irish-Irish domination eventually came to be expressed in national or nationalist terms.[679]

[675] K. J. Walsh, *Yesterday's Seminary: A History of St. Patrick's Manly* (St Leonards, NSW: Allen & Unwin, 1998), 61.
[676] Ibid., 68.   [677] Ibid., 66–7.   [678] Livingston, 124, 250.
[679] See O'Farrell, *Short History*, 248–50.

Yet in one very important sense none of this mattered: Moran had ensured that the products of St Patrick's were as surely Hiberno-Roman as were their Irish-trained rivals, if not more so. Although it took much longer than expected, the rise of Manly ultimately marked both the eclipse of the Irish and the apotheosis of the Hiberno-Romans.

Yet Moran's secular reputation now rests on the outsized role he played in Australian society. From the beginning he embraced his position as the leader of the continent's Catholics. He clearly enjoyed his access to power, and his private diary is full of meetings with colonial and imperial worthies. He also took a close interest in the minutiae of politics and served as an advisor to a generation of politicians, not all of them Catholic. The contrast with his successor Michael Kelly is striking: as the Labor politician William Arthur Holman recalled, with Kelly the 'perplexed party leader who called in upon him was much more likely to get wholesome counsel as to the state of his soul' than the practical political advice previously dispensed by Moran.[680]

Moran was particularly associated with two undeniably secular causes, federation and the Australian Labor Party (ALP). Indeed, his enthusiasm for the latter was crucial to its eventual success. In New South Wales, for example, leading figures in the state party attributed the formation of their first government in 1910 to Moran's 'politic mind'. He was, Holman recalled, 'one of the first to foresee in Australia the possibilities of the rising Labor Party'. By urging both rich and poor Catholics to support the party, Holman continued, Moran had assured 'a rational and successful future' for both state and commonwealth.[681] Moran's interest was of long standing. As early as 1889, for example, he had addressed a mass meeting in support of the London dock strikers.[682] The following year, he had sought to mediate in the great Australian maritime strike, itself a foundational event in the history of the ALP. He was, he informed the New South Wales Labour Defence Committee, 'heart & soul with the welfare of the people'.[683] When he finally urged a settlement, it was on the entirely typical grounds that the country risked anarchy if the intransigence of the 'Capitalists' was met by similar behaviour from the unions. He praised them for their achievements and urged them to look to the

---

[680] William Arthur Holman, 'My political life', in *The First New South Wales Labor Government 1910–1916, Two Memoirs: William Holman and John Osborne*, edited by Michael Hogan (Sydney: University of New South Wales Press, 2005), 56.

[681] Holman, 'My political life', 5.

[682] See Bede Nairn, *Civilising Capitalism: The Labor Movement in New South Wales 1870–1900* (Canberra: Australian National University Press, 1973), 28.

[683] Moran to Labour Defence Committee [draft], 9 September 1890, AAS/MP. This letter is part of a small group that was extracted from the archdiocesan archives by the late Tony Cahill and then returned after his death. They are not yet numbered.

legislature for 'fair play and justice'.[684] In return, Moran was one of the few churchmen of any denomination that the committee exempted from its denunciations of 'sacerdotal clap-trap'.[685]

The next year, Moran decided to elucidate his views on what he called the 'rights and duties of labour'. Although the pretext for his intervention was the appearance earlier in the year of Leo XIII's great social encyclical *Rerum Novarum*, Moran had been developing his ideas for some time.[686] As he wrote privately in 1890, among other things workers were entitled to a 'Fair day's toil', 'fair wages', and the ability to provide for their family in 'frugal comfort' while putting something aside for a 'rainy day'. A workingman also had the right to 'contract for a fair share of the fruits of his industry', a 'comfortable home', and representation in parliament.[687] In his 1891 lecture, he added to these rights a bitter attack on the rhetoric of freedom of contract, which he described as having 'been turned into an engine of robbery', and mounted a spirited defence of the right to organize trades unions. He also urged the election of workers' representatives and congratulated Australia for being the 'first to add the strength and vigour of a labour party to her Parliamentary representation'.[688]

Moran's lecture was, and was intended to be, a political act. In his diary, he boasted of the presence of '4 Members of the Upper House & 14 Members of the House of Assembly on the Platform' and a week later gave copies of both his own text and *Rerum Novarum* to the governor.[689] His intervention had several purposes. First, he was concerned to channel growing working-class radicalism in safe directions.[690] In his defence of trades unions, for example, he urged the unions themselves to 'combine with the benign influence of religion' to serve both the moral and the economic needs of their members.[691] Like the pope, his model was the medieval guilds. He also anathematized the use of force, insisted that strikes were only to be undertaken as a last resort, and defended the rights of capitalists to enjoy their property unmolested. In all of this, he echoed Leo XIII.

[684] Moran to Labour Defence Committee, 21 October 1890, AAS.
[685] Walter Phillips, *Defending 'A Christian Country': Churchmen and Society in New South Wales in the 1880s and After* (St Lucia: University of Queensland Press, 1981), 163.
[686] Patrick Francis Moran, *Lecture on the Rights and Duties of Labour, Sydney 17 August 1891* (Sydney: Fine Brothers & Co., 1891), 3–4.
[687] Memoranda on the rights of labour and the responsibilities of trades unions, 1890, AAS/MP.
[688] Moran, *Rights and Duties*, 7, 17.   [689] Moran diary, 17, 25 August 1891, AAS.
[690] See Mark Hearn, 'Containing "contamination": Cardinal Moran and *fin de siècle* Australian national identity, 1888–1911', *Journal of Religious History*, vol. 34. no. 1, March 2010, 20–35, at 25.
[691] Moran, *Rights and Duties*, 14.

Yet Moran also drew on the long tradition of Irish Catholic criticism of British capitalism, of which he had ample experience in his own family. As early as 1830, for example, Cullen had noted that, despite the extreme poverty of peasants in the Roman Campagna, they were still not in 'such a deplorable state as the poor Irish', largely because the papal government ensured that they never 'should die of hunger or want'.[692] Twelve years later, he observed the clearance of beggars in Liverpool 'lest the eyes of the rich should be offended by such sights'. The English, he concluded, were 'the most uncharitable people on the face of the earth'.[693] To the end of his life, Cullen believed that British capitalism was cruel, heartless, and degrading. As he remarked in 1857, the 'over anxiety of England to make money will some day or other bring on gt ruin'.[694] There is every indication that his nephew agreed, and this should qualify A. E. Cahill's claim that after 1895 Moran experienced a 'radicalization of his political and social attitudes'.[695] In reality, he was once again following in his uncle's footsteps.

Moran's other concern was to ensure Catholic political influence, and he was among the first to recognize that the ALP could become the means to advance both Catholics and Catholic interests. This is not to say that Moran ignored more established Catholic figures. Among others, he worked closely with Sir Patrick Jennings, a leading free-trader who was briefly premier of New South Wales in 1886–7, and more fractiously with R. E. O'Connor, a protectionist who served as government leader in the first post-federation senate before joining the high court. Yet, while men like this could be useful, they were too politically diverse, too independent, and often too wealthy to form the basis of a political party that could command Catholic support and deliver desiderata such as state aid. By contrast, the ALP needed the votes of the poor Irish if it was to have any hope of success.

Yet first it was necessary to make Labor safe for Catholics. To do this, Moran needed to challenge the more radical strain of socialism that had come to dominate the party in the early 1890s. His opportunity came in 1897, when Labor nominated avowed socialists for nine of the ten New South Wales' seats in the forthcoming federal convention. Moran denounced them as 'wild theorists and mere experimentalists' and decided to stand for election himself.[696] Although he was a long-standing

---

[692] Cullen to Margaret Cullen, 11 October 1830, DDA/CP.
[693] Cullen to Kirby, 25 June 1842, PICRA/KP/98.
[694] Cullen to Kirby, 6 December 1857, PICRA/NK/II/II/52.
[695] Cahill, 'Moran', in *ADB*.
[696] Patrick Ford, *Cardinal Moran and the A.L.P.: A Study of the Encounter between Moran and Socialism, 1890–1907, Its Effects upon the Australian Labor Party, the Foundation of*

champion of federation, his primary purpose was to teach Labor a lesson. As Patrick Ford put it, Moran wanted to demonstrate to the party 'that it could expect the Catholic suffrage only if it renounced Socialism'.[697] The entry of a Catholic cardinal inevitably produced a sectarian backlash, which complicated the situation for everyone but also strengthened his hand among Catholic voters. As he wrote privately, 'for six weeks I was the best abused man in Australia'.[698] The result was a catastrophe for Labor, which was shut out completely while Moran himself came four-teenth on a respectable 43,583 votes. He was delighted with the outcome, telling the Callan Sisters of Mercy that, as a direct result of his candidacy, 'ten excellent representatives were elected, not one of whom is hostile to Catholics'.[699] Labor meanwhile concluded that extreme socialism was electoral poison, many socialists left the party, and within a year more moderate members were firmly back in charge.[700]

The impact was soon apparent. Moran was pleased with the Labor's 'excellent candidates' in the 1901 New South Wales election, noting in his diary that it was 'the first time they put forward Catholic representatives'.[701] The election itself returned as many as twenty-four Catholics, seven of whom sat for Labor, and the party used its strength to prop up Sir John See's minority Progressive ministry.[702] Four years later, Moran intervened decisively to defend the party against renewed charges of socialism. The catalyst was an article in *The Catholic Press* that sought to use *Rerum Novarum* to disqualify the ALP from Catholic support. This set off a storm of controversy as everyone from labour activists to the secular press parsed the encyclical's text and waited for Moran's reaction.[703] This was not as curious as it might seem: as Rose Luminiello has pointed out, Leo's ambiguous language and dense reasoning made its interpretation politically charged from Ireland to Prussian Poland.[704]

Moran's response was unequivocal: socialism was indeed and rightly condemned, but what the pope had had in mind was European socialism. Australia was different, as was its 'socialism', and the ALP was now a perfectly safe repository for Catholic votes.[705] As he explained privately,

---

Catholic Social Thought and Action in Modern Australia (Melbourne: Melbourne University Press, 1966), 202.

[697] Ibid., 205.   [698] Moran to M. M. Maher, 28 June 1897, ARSMP/Box 60.   [699] Ibid.
[700] Ford, 213–21.   [701] Moran diary, 24 June 1901, AAS.
[702] Moran diary, 8 July 1901, AAS.
[703] See A. E. Cahill, 'Catholicism and socialism: The 1905 controversy in Australia', *Journal of Religious History*, vol. 1, no. 2 (December 1960), 88–101, at 92.
[704] See Rose Luminiello, 'Confronting modernity: Pope Leo XIII, *Rerum Novarum*, and the Catholic Church in Ireland and Poland, 1878–1914', unpublished PhD diss., University of Aberdeen, 2019.
[705] Cahill, 94–6.

the party was a bulwark against an 'Orangeism & sectarianism that wd renew the persecution of Catholics if they had the power'. He admitted some in the ALP 'assume the name of Socialists' but insisted that they had repudiated 'the perverse theories of those who in Europe are known as Socialists'. So long as the 'anti-Catholic party' was raising an anti-socialist cry, he concluded, he was happy to 'rally all genuine patriots as our friends no matter what name they assume'.[706]

The effect of Moran's support was plain. As William Arthur Holman recalled some years later, he 'swept something like nine-tenths of his congregation into our camp'.[707] In Melbourne, Carr agreed with Moran's analysis of Australian 'socialism' but remained wary of the ALP until the advent of Hugh Mahon to Victorian politics in 1906, and even then he preferred to exert pressure through the Catholic Federation (founded in 1911) rather than to cast his lot directly with Labor.[708] His coadjutor and successor Daniel Mannix extended this policy in an attempt to force the party to bid for Catholic votes rather than take them for granted; he hoped to secure state aid for education as the price. The resulting conflict between the Federation and the ALP resulted in a clear victory for the latter at the 1914 election.[709] In reality, of course, each needed the other: Labor could not win power without the support of most Catholics, and most Catholics had no one to vote for except Labor. Mannix recognized his error, and the subsequent reconciliation survived largely intact until it was destroyed many years later by the combination of B. A. Santamaria and Mannix himself. Although demography and self-interest made such an alliance inevitable, it was Moran who saw it first, shaped it, and worked hard to ensure its success.

Yet Moran was not interested in politics for its own sake. His overriding concern was to secure his church's place in society and consolidate its control over its flock. Support for the ALP was a necessary means to these ends but was not in itself sufficient. He also needed to ensure ecclesiastical control over Irish Australia. In 1896, for example, he seized the management of Sydney's St Patrick's Day festivities from its increasingly chaotic lay organizers. He was concerned, as the *Freeman's Journal* put it, that the celebrations should be edifying and 'worthy of Irishmen', but also to establish it as a specifically Catholic occasion.[710] A High Mass was celebrated in the cathedral in the presence of the governor and local

---

[706] Moran to Hagan, 20 December 1905, PICRA/Hagan papers/HAG1/1905/53.
[707] Holman, 'My political life', 56.   [708] Boland, *Carr*, 290, 296.
[709] Santamaria, 63–4.
[710] *FJ*, 15 February 1896; see also Malcolm Campbell, *Ireland's New Worlds: Immigrants, Politics, and Society in the United States and Australia, 1815–1922* (Madison: University of Wisconsin Press, 2008), 153.

worthies, and at the luncheon afterwards Moran toasted the 'wonderful spread' of Britain's colonial empire which had 'given many a happy home to the sons of St. Patrick'. The working classes were meanwhile entertained with carefully organized sporting events on Sydney's Association Grounds.[711]

The fusion of Irish, Catholic, and Australian was reinforced the following year in Melbourne, where the governor and much of Victoria's political establishment gathered to watch Moran, Carr, and all but one of the Australian bishops consecrate St Patrick's Cathedral. In his lengthy sermon, Moran returned to his favourite botanical metaphor for Australian Catholicism. 'The tree of faith', he told his listeners, 'transplanted from Erin to these shores, found here a deep root'; and it was not just Australia, he continued, for now, at the end of the nineteenth century, 'the sun never sets on the spiritual empire which exults in St. Patrick's apostolate'.[712]

Moran's attempt to bring all expressions of Irish identity under ecclesiastical control did not go entirely unresisted. In 1898, for example, he was forced by public pressure to permit a lay initiative to disinter two Australian-buried exiles from the rebellion of 1798. Moran allowed their coffins to rest in the cathedral, but he only provided a tepid eulogy, did not accompany the remains to their new resting place, and failed to attend the subsequent unveiling of a 1798 memorial at the graves. Yet he did stage an unambiguous riposte, as Richard Reid has pointed out. For the 1901 St Patrick's Day festivities, Moran arranged for the remains of Archbishop Polding and three pioneer Irish priests, John Therry, Daniel Power, and John McEncroe, to be paraded through Sydney to St Mary's Cathedral, where they rested in the Chapel of the Irish Saints before reburial in the crypt. The magnificent display far outdid that given to the erstwhile rebels, drawing perhaps 250,000 spectators, and Moran thought it was 'probably the most successful celebration of St. Patrick's Day ever witnessed in Australia'.[713] He doubtless had had in mind his uncle's response to a similar provocation, the 1861 Dublin funeral of the Young Ireland rebel Terence Bellew McManus. The following year, Moran had helped Cullen organize an even more massive public celebration for the laying of the foundation stone of the Catholic University of Ireland.

To the end of his life, Moran was interested in Irish history and Irish culture and was determined to identify the Australian Catholic Church

---

[711] *The Sydney Mail and New South Wales Advertiser*, 21 March 1896.
[712] *The Advocate*, 6 November 1897.
[713] See Richard Reid, '"Dark and rude and strange ... " Cardinal Patrick Francis Moran and the St. Mary's 1904 Fair', unpublished paper, by courtesy of the author; Moran diary, 18 March 1901, AAS.

with Ireland. This took various forms, from placing a specially commissioned 5.8-metre-high replica of a tenth-century Irish high cross at the heart of the 1904 St Mary's Fair, to amassing a private collection of Irish books, art, and manuscripts, to his advice to the Parramatta Sisters of Mercy on the best Irish history textbooks to use in their schools.[714] In 1906, he worked with Murray's coadjutor Patrick Dwyer to prepare material for a statewide 'Irish History competition', and one of the last entries in his private diary recorded his delight at receiving a telegram from Dublin with the news that Irish would soon be compulsory for matriculation in the National University of Ireland. It was, he wrote, 'a grand step towards "Ireland a nation"'.[715]

Moran's rule was transformative. Within a quarter-century, he had stabilized a church that had been habitually divided against itself, ensured its Irish identity, and done much to embed it into Australian life. Through force of personality, he had raised its profile and status and ensured it an enduring political voice. Internally, he and his fellow Hiberno-Romans successfully imposed devotional uniformity and social conformity. By the time of his death, the bulk of Australia's Catholics habitually deferred to their church's wishes, participated in its sacraments, sent their children to its schools, and married other Catholics. They also paid for the massive infrastructure that made this possible. When Moran died in 1911, Australia's some 850,000 Catholics were served by 1,487 churches, 1,002 priests, 5,552 nuns, 505 brothers, and 1,441 schools educating 116,243 children.[716] The vast majority of bishops, priests, nuns, and brothers were Irish-born or Irish-descended, as were the men, women, and children they served, nursed, married, buried, or educated. Their institutions and community identity were saturated in Irish imagery even as they took their place in Australian life and defined themselves as Australians.

None of this would have been possible without the continuing Hiberno-Roman domination of the Australian episcopate. The surviving Cullenites were aware of the need to ensure their succession and consequently paid close attention to actual or potential vacancies. In 1891, for example, Moran urged Murray to travel to Tasmania, ostensibly to attend the opening of a new church in Launceston but in reality to ensure a satisfactory outcome in the election of Daniel

---

[714] For the cross, see Reid, '"Dark, rude, and strange"'; for an outsider's account of Moran's collection, see 'Cardinal Moran at home', *The Australasian*, 1 August 1896; for Irish history texts, Moran to M. M. Alphonsus, 19 January 1903, ARSMP.

[715] Moran to Dwyer, 27 August 1906, MNDA, Dwyer papers [DP], Box 4; 'Special Religious Events, 1910', Moran diary, AAS.

[716] *Australasian Catholic Directory for 1911*.

Murphy's coadjutor.[717] Eight years later, Murray in turn urged Moran to obtain 'some clever Irish Ecclesiastic' as his own coadjutor. There 'were parties in both Rome and in England', he warned, 'who were most anxiously looking for an opportunity of having an English man appointed to Sydney'.[718]

Moran eventually settled on the unworldly and accident-prone rector of the Irish College in Rome, Michael Kelly. It was an unhappy choice that Carr deplored and Moran came to regret, but Kelly did not die until 1940 after a very long and very Irish episcopate. His successor was the Australian-born Norman Gilroy, who had been appointed as Kelly's coadjutor in 1937 after the surprise resignation of the Irishman Michael Sheehan. Gilroy opened up the higher reaches of the archdiocese to native-born clerics, although he seems to have managed the process slowly, tactfully retaining a rough balance between Irish and Australian appointments for many years.[719] For the Propaganda-educated and Irish-descended Gilroy, this was in any case more a matter of equity and demographic reality than ideological change or incipient nationalism; his frequent clashes with the unapologetically Irish Daniel Mannix, for example, were largely driven by differences in temperament and judge-ment, not ethnicity. A meticulous administrator and emollient public figure, Gilroy became Australia's second cardinal in 1946, was knighted in 1969, and finally retired in 1971. He died in 1977.

The pattern was the same across Australia. In Maitland, Murray arranged for the appointment of Patrick Dwyer, who was simultaneously the first Australian-born bishop and a confirmed Hiberno-Roman, edu-cated at Bathurst, Clonliffe, and Rome. He was also intensely Irish: in his papers, for example, there is a lengthy manuscript booklet in his hand containing the lyrics of dozens of Irish songs.[720] Dwyer was in turn succeeded by the Irish-born Redemptorist Edmund Gleeson, who died in 1957. In Tasmania, Murphy's successor was the Irish-born and All Hallows–educated Patrick Delany. He died in 1926 and was succeeded by the Cork-born and All Hallows–educated William Barry (d. 1929) and then the Kilkenny-born and Propaganda-educated William Hayden, who died in 1936. In Perth, the Kerry-born and Wexford-educated Redmond Prendiville succeeded Patrick Clune in 1935 and only died himself in 1968, while Adelaide's John O'Reily was succeeded by Robert Spence, an Irish Dominican who had led the first party of friars to Australia in 1898. On his death in 1934, he was succeeded by the Offaly-born and Carlow-

---

[717] Moran to Murray, 16 January 1891, MNDA/MP/3/1/1810/2/7.
[718] Murray to Moran, 28 June 1899, MNDA/MP/3/1/1810/2/8.   [719] Luttrell, 345–6.
[720] See MNDA/DP, BOX 1912.

educated Andrew Killian and then in 1940 by the Croatian-descended Matthew Beovich, the first Australian archbishop since Vaughan who was neither Irish nor of Irish descent; but even Beovich had been educated by the Irish Christian Brothers in Melbourne and then at the Propaganda, where he had overlapped with Gilroy. He died in 1981.

Yet by far the most significant Irish succession was in Melbourne. In 1908, the now seventy-year-old Carr had embarked on his *ad limina* visit to Rome, followed by a lengthy sojourn in Ireland. He had good reason to be pleased: since 1898, he told the Propaganda, the number of diocesan priests had doubled to 104, the number of nuns had nearly trebled, from 192 to 761, while the number of Catholic school students had increased by 11,661 to nearly 25,000.[721] He intended to ask for a coadjutor, something he had first requested the year before, but in the event he decided to delay. By 1911, he could wait no longer, and the Melbourne clergy duly gathered to duly elect his preferred choice, the president of Maynooth, Daniel Mannix. Carr seems to have wanted his energy and his forthright commitment to Catholic education and perhaps did not expect that Mannix would also prove to be a provocative politician, charismatic orator, and noisy Irish patriot. Almost from the beginning Mannix dominated Victorian Catholicism, and his campaigns against conscription and for Irish independence made him a national figure, which he remained until his death in 1963 at the age of ninety-nine. His legacy still divides Catholic Australia.

Yet, in a very real sense, Mannix was an outlier in Australia. He had little or no experience of Rome and was a constant worry for the Propaganda. His background, formation, and preferences were entirely Irish and shaped by Maynooth, Cullen's bête noire. Above all, his aggressive nationalism and confrontational political style would have shocked Moran, let alone Cullen. Mannix often pushed far beyond what his peers thought were the limits of prudence; his opposition to conscription, for example, was widely (but not universally) shared by Australia's bishops but not his emphatic support of the republican cause in the Irish civil war. In Australia, Mannix's denunciations of British tyranny must be weighted against Carr's patriotic exhortations, (Sir) Norman Gilroy's enlistment in the Australian navy, or (Sir) James Duhig's condemnation of the Easter Rising.[722] So too his later patronage of Santamaria and 'The Movement' should be set against the continued support of Gilroy and others for the ALP. Daniel Mannix was undeniably an Irishman, but he was not a Hiberno-Roman. By contrast, Gilroy, Duhig, or even Beovich were all bishops in the 'Roman mould' and were thus more truly Moran's heirs.

---

[721] Boland, *Carr*, 360.   [722] Ibid., 404.

Mannix was in any event the last of the great Irish bishops in Australia. Within a decade of his death, only three Irish-born prelates remained, all in rural dioceses. But it no longer mattered. Hiberno-Romanism had long since gone native, and Australian Catholicism was indelibly associated with Ireland. Later waves of Catholic migrants found themselves absorbed into a church that was overwhelmingly Irish in personnel, structure, and ethos. Yet Australia was also associated with a particular variant of Irish Catholicism, one forged in the papal Rome of Paul Cullen's youth, seasoned in post-Famine Ireland, and transmitted by his ecclesiastical heirs across the English-speaking world. Its success in Australia was Patrick Moran's achievement and Paul Cullen's most enduring legacy.

Early in his prize-winning novel *Plumb*, Maurice Gee's eponymous character recalls from old age his early days at Kumara on the west coast of New Zealand's South Island. 'The friendliness between the churches was something I came across in no other place', the young Presbyterian minister remembered, 'We had our social and picnics together and even the Catholics joined in.' The Catholic priest, a 'Father O'Halloran', was a 'good chap' and a keen cricketer, although 'of course' a bit too prone to drink. The other ministers looked out for him. As Gee makes a Church of England priest tell the callow Plumb, 'If you see him fall off of his bicycle you must tell any children standing about that he's had a heart attack. He has frequent heart attacks.'[1] It is obviously unreasonable to put much weight on Gee's fictional portrait of ecumenism and ethnic prejudice in early twentieth-century New Zealand: the book is after all a novel, written in the 1970s, and Gee himself was an active secularist who based the character Plumb on the life of his grandfather J. H. G. Chapple, whose career ranged from the Salvation Army through the Presbyterian ministry to Unitarianism, pacifism, and socialism. But its narrative echoes a long-standing tradition in New Zealand to minimize if not actually deny the presence and power of religious feeling and its concomitant sectarianism. It fits well with what John Stenhouse called 'This loud silence in New Zealand historical writing.'[2]

What Stenhouse and others have identified is an enduring disposition among scholars and public intellectuals to marginalize religious belief, underestimate its importance, and ignore its historical adherents. 'Many New Zealand historians', Stenhouse wrote, 'consigned Christianity to oblivion because they considered it not only irrelevant but pernicious, a Bad Thing.'[3] The problem for historians is that colonial New Zealand

---

[1] Maurice Gee, *Plumb* (Auckland: Oxford University Press, 1979), 40. The novel, the first of a trilogy, won the James Tait Black memorial prize.

[2] John Stenhouse, 'God's own silence: Secular nationalism, Christianity, and the writing of New Zealand history', *New Zealand Journal of History*, 38, 1 (2004), 52–71, at 52.

[3] Ibid., 58.

was and remained an intensely religious society. As late as the first quarter of the twentieth century, as James Belich has pointed out, the country was 'the very opposite of irreligious'.[4] Historians have begun to notice, and in recent years scholars such as Judith Binney have explored the rich tapestry of Māori Christianity, while others have begun to examine the intense religiosity and significant sectarianism of nineteenth- and early twentieth-century Pākehā society. Still, it is indicative that the index to Philippa Mein Smith's high-profile *A Concise History of New Zealand* (2005) contains no entry at all for religion but nine for 'Rogernomics'.

The Roman Catholic Church is particularly vulnerable to this historical elision, with the consequence that New Zealand Catholicism has until recently been particularly badly served, with only South Africa among the English-speaking lands having a less developed or professional historiography. The field has largely been left to confessional scholars, with the inevitable result that reverence has too often substituted for rigour. This has been amplified by the curiously poor survival of Catholic archival records; only Newfoundland and India have less from the nineteenth century.

The Irish have had more attention, although they are still often lost in a historians' binary of Māori and Pākehā.[5] It is striking, for example, that the first substantive account of the Irish in New Zealand did not appear until 1990. (Richard P. Davis' 1974 *Irish Issues in New Zealand Politics, 1868–1922* had a much narrower focus.) Also striking is that it was written not by a New Zealander but by the Canadian historian Donald Akenson. As Lyndon Fraser noted in 1994, 'Irish Catholics and other white ethnics have received little note from New Zealand historians, despite the visibility and longevity of the institutional organizations and social networks they created and sustained in New Zealand during the colonial period.'[6] Fraser's own groundbreaking doctoral thesis and subsequent books on the Christchurch and west coast Irish demonstrated both the importance of ethnicity and the centrality of the Roman Catholic Church in creating and maintaining it.[7] Following Akenson and Fraser, there has been a surge in the study of English, Scottish, Irish, and Irish Protestant

---

[4] James Belich, *Paradise Reforged: A History of the New Zealanders from the 1880s to the Year 2000* (Auckland: Allen Lane, 2001), 164.

[5] Donald Harman Akenson, *Half the World from Home: Perspectives on the Irish in New Zealand 1860–1950* (Wellington: Victoria University Press, 1990), 6.

[6] Lyndon Fraser, 'Community, continuity and change: Irish Catholic immigrants in nineteenth-century Christchurch', unpublished PhD thesis, University of Canterbury, 1994, 20.

[7] Lyndon Fraser, *To Tara via Holyhead: Irish Catholic Immigrants in Nineteenth-Century Christchurch* (Auckland: Auckland University Press, 1997), and *Castles of Gold: A History of New Zealand's West Coast Irish* (Dunedin: Otago University Press, 2007).

migration and settlement, and the Irish in particular are coming into sharper focus as a distinct ethnic group.[8] Despite this, the most important institutional, educational, moral, political, and social force in the lives of Irish Catholic New Zealanders remains significantly understudied in its own terms and not at all in its global context.

From French to Irish, 1838–1874

New Zealand's Catholic history began with the arrival of Bishop Jean Baptiste Pompallier on 10 January 1838. His mission, which encompassed the entire western Pacific, was the first to be undertaken by the French Society of Mary. Founded in Lyon in 1816, the Marists never planned on foreign missions, and the idea of sending them to the Pacific seems to have arisen in the Propaganda. The congregation was having difficulties convincing a religious order to accept the vast and difficult mission and effectively traded Oceania for the papal recognition that the Marists craved.[9] The vicariate of the western Pacific was duly erected on 10 January 1836, the Society of Mary became a pontifical institute on 29 April, Pompallier was appointed vicar apostolic on 13 May, the first Marists made their solemn vows on 24 September, and Pompallier set sail with several companions on 24 December. What he found was an increasingly unstable amalgam of rival European powers, competing missionaries, settlers, and itinerant whalers, and a complex, sophisticated, and occasionally combative indigenous population.

The signing of the Treaty of Waitangi on 6 February 1840 marked the end of France's territorial ambitions, although a handful of French settlers lingered on in places such as Akaroa. Although Pompallier himself played a minor role in the negotiations, insisting on the insertion of what amounted to a clause guaranteeing religious freedom, he was hardly pleased with the outcome. He chose to persevere, however, and continued to pursue what he saw as his primary mission of evangelizing the Māori. Yet despite quickly learning the language and working hard, conversions came slowly: after three years, there were perhaps 1,000 Māori prepared to describe themselves as Catholic.[10]

[8] For example, the essays in Lyndon Fraser (ed.), *A Distant Shore: Irish Migration and New Zealand Settlement* (Dunedin: Otago University Press, 2000).

[9] Carlo-Maria Schianchi, 'Colin and the congregation of Propaganda Fide in Rome', in Alois Greiler (ed.), *Catholics Beginnings in Oceania: Marist Missionary Perspectives* (Hindmarsh, NSW: ATF Press, 2009), 29.

[10] E. R. Simmons, *Pompallier: Prince of Bishops* (Auckland: CPC Publishing, 1984), 33.

Of Pākehā Catholics, there were also as yet very few, perhaps 750 in 1841.[11] This number too grew slowly through the 1840s and into the 1850s. In the South Island, Canterbury was planned as an Anglican colony and Otago a Presbyterian one; Catholics were admitted but not encouraged. In the North Island, most of the interior and much else remained contested or under Māori control, while in the towns there were a smattering of Catholics of varying classes and nationalities. Auckland was unusual in hosting relatively early a small but well-established and influential group of prosperous Irish Catholics.[12] A more typical elite Catholic was Frederick Weld, an Englishman related both to the late curial cardinal Thomas Weld and to the aristocratic Clifford family. Resident in New Zealand since 1844, he was the early colony's most prominent lay Catholic, serving briefly as premier in 1864–5.[13]

Pompallier and the Marists worked hard. Soon they were joined by a handful of secular priests, some satisfactory, many not. Most were Irish. All the Marists were French. From the beginning Pompallier's administration was fraught with difficulties, some unavoidable but most self-made. Among the former were the vast scale of his territory – all of New Zealand and much of the south Pacific – and the challenge of securing enough Marists to service it. These difficulties were amplified by Pompallier's grand manner and administrative incompetence, and by 1842 he had fallen out with the society, which removed his authority as provincial and refused to honour his debts.[14] Soon they were demanding his resignation. By 1849, relations had reached the point that New Zealand was divided into two dioceses, Auckland and Wellington. The latter was given to Philippe Viard, Pompallier's coadjutor since 1846. He promptly moved the entire Marist establishment south, leaving Pompallier with whatever secular clergy he could cobble together. Viard had a reputation for holiness but not for competence: the Marists had been surprised when he was made Auckland's coadjutor and astonished when he was appointed to Wellington. They had not thought him suitable and were not consulted.[15]

Under Viard and Pompallier alike the church's growth was hobbled by debt and maladministration, and both men were subject to regular complaints to Rome and Lyon. Yet that is not to say that there was no growth

---

[11] Ibid., 34.

[12] See Gabrielle A. Fortune, 'Hugh Coolahan and the prosperous Irish of Auckland, 1840-1870', unpublished MA thesis, University of Auckland, 1987, 2.

[13] See Jeanine Graham, *Frederick Weld* (Auckland: Auckland University Press, 1983).

[14] Simmons, *Pompallier*, 69.

[15] Forest to Moran [Dunedin], 1 January 1873, Wellington Archdiocesan Archives [WAA].

at all. In 1849, for example, Pompallier visited Ireland as part of a four-year-long European recruitment trip. He found a few priests and seminarians and also secured the services of a group of Sisters of Mercy led by Cecilia Maher, a cousin to both Cardinal Cullen and Frances Warde, the foundress of the Sisters of Mercy in the United States. The local bishop only permitted Maher to go after reflecting on the 'immense good' the Mercies had done in Pittsburgh. Cullen's uncle and mentor, James Maher, also approved.[16] In Auckland, they assumed control of a small orphanage and a school with about sixty students. The local Irish were delighted, although some did wonder if the nuns might feel 'lonely after Ireland'.[17] Over the next twenty years, the community slowly expanded, opening both day and boarding schools and receiving a handful of new members from home and a small number of local professions. They remained devoted to Pompallier, although not unaware of his faults.

Also devoted to Pompallier was Suzanne Aubert, a strong-willed Frenchwoman from Lyons who had responded to the bishop's appeal on another of his European recruiting trips. In 1860, she boarded a ship for Auckland with Pompallier, his niece, three other Frenchwomen, an Irish priest, a seminarian from All Hallows, five French seminarians, and eight Italian Franciscans.[18] The women were intended for the Sisters of Mercy but had trouble integrating. In 1863, Pompallier consequently created a new diocesan congregation for them and made his niece the superior. Their task was the education of the children of Catholic Māori, many of them orphans, and from the beginning they had Māori members. The creation of the Holy Family Sisters allowed the Sisters of Mercy to concentrate their efforts on the largely Irish Pākehā, and the two communities enjoyed tetchy relations which left the Holy Family Sisters and their Nazareth Institute entirely dependent on Pompallier. When he finally left New Zealand for good, he took his niece with him, leaving Aubert in sole charge.

Viard also recruited in Europe when he could. He needed all the help he could get: the Marists were spread thinly across the vast diocese, which encompassed almost half the North Island and all of the South. Their focus was also on the Māori, although they by no means ignored Europeans. For some years, this was unproblematic: the South Island contained only a handful of Pākehā Catholics, mostly in Christchurch and Dunedin, while in Wellington itself Viard could rely on the long-

[16] Maher to Warde, 4 August 1849, copy in Archives of the Sisters of Mercy, Auckland [ASMA] from an original in the Sisters of Mercy Archives, Pittsburgh.
[17] Maher to 'Rev. Mother', 3 May 1850, ASMA.
[18] Jessie Munro, *The Story of Suzanne Aubert* (Auckland: Auckland University Press, 1996), 53–9.

serving Irish Capuchin Jeremiah O'Reily. When O'Reily first landed in 1843, he had been 'delighted to find some of my countrymen from Erin's most distant shores', although they had no chapel and he had to celebrate Mass on the beach.[19] From Wellington, O'Reily could also serve the smattering of Catholics in nearby Nelson and Marlborough. It all worked reasonably well.

The discovery of gold changed that. First in Otago in 1861 and then on the west coast from 1864, migrants of all nationalities arrived on the diggings. Most had already chanced their luck elsewhere, with some following the gold strikes from California to Victoria and then New Zealand. Many were Irish. In 1864, for example, so many Irish Catholics left the Cape for the gold fields that Bishop Grimley feared for the fate of his mission (see Chapter 4). The Marists were numerically, culturally, and linguistically unprepared to cope with this sudden surge in Catholic numbers, although they did their best to minister to the miners both in the camps and in boom towns such as Hokitika. With the Irish migrants came Irish priests, and, although Viard was in most cases pleased to have the help, he did little to establish their suitability. Drink was a recurring problem, as were politics.

In Hokitika, for example, the Irish priest William Larkin helped organize a March 1868 commemoration of the so-called Manchester Martyrs, Fenians who had been executed for the murder of a policeman. This was one of several that occurred in the region, almost always with the close involvement of an Irish priest and always in defiance of Viard's explicit instructions. Observers sensed Fenianism and tensions rose along the entire coast. The failed assassination of Prince Alfred in Sydney, supposedly at the hands of a Fenian sympathizer, led the provincial government to arrest Larkin and several others and charge them with seditious libel. The resulting civil disorder took on an unsettling Orange-Green hue, and Larkin ultimately pled guilty and was sentenced to a £20 fine and a month in the Hokitika jail.[20] Viard had already suspended him.[21]

Hokitika was just a passing skirmish, but it raised tensions between the Irish and their French bishop and priests. Writing many years later, the Marist Nicolas Binsfield recalled being assigned to replace Larkin. The miners, he remembered, considered the Irishman's behaviour 'a matter of pardonable patriotism' and petitioned Viard to reinstate him. When he refused, they boycotted Binsfield. The boycott spread, and Binsfield recalled arriving at Notown where he was met by some 300 miners who demanded to know 'Are you an Irish priest or a French

[19] Quoted in Simmons, *Pompallier*, 106.   [20] Fraser, *Castles*, 133–40.
[21] Keys, *Viard*, 207.

priest?' His reply that he was 'neither' but rather a Catholic priest sent by the Catholic bishop of Wellington to be their parish priest did not impress: 'If you are not one of ours, we shall have nothing to do with you.'[22]

Tempers soon cooled, and French Marists continued to serve on the west coast for many years, but the affair gave Viard a reputation as anti-Irish and ensured that complaints would find their way to Dublin. They were amplified by the situation in Dunedin, where the French Marist Delphin Moreau had been assigned since 1861 after Viard had tried and failed to secure a Scottish priest.[23] In 1864, Moreau was joined by two Irish priests, although one soon left for the coast. The other, J. G. Williams, regularly clashed with the Frenchman, who thought him a drunkard. In 1867, Williams helped to organize a public meeting to demand 'British priests', and the offended Moreau promptly suspended him.[24] Viard intervened, reminding Moreau that it was 'quite natural' that Dunedin's Catholics would 'want to have priests of their own nationality'. It didn't matter: further meetings reiterated the demand for 'British priests' and added one for a 'British bishop'.[25] As in India, 'British' was most likely code for 'Irish', although the not insignificant number of Scottish Catholics in Dunedin may have contributed to the imprecision.

Viard was also fighting an internal battle. The Marists had always been uneasy about his competence, and these concerns had reached a peak in the mid-1860s. Regular reports reached Lyon complaining of everything from Viard's refusal to permit female housekeepers to his reluctance to visit mission stations or attend clerical retreats. Finally, the society had had enough, bluntly telling Cardinal Barnabò that Viard did 'not possess the qualities of a bishop'.[26] They wanted him recalled and sacked.

Viard instead sent his confidant Jeremiah O'Reily to Europe in the spring of 1867. His task was to both recruit priests and represent Viard against Marist attacks. In Dublin, he approached Cullen for help, giving him a letter from the Frenchman describing conditions in Wellington. An unsuspecting Cullen consequently wrote to the Propaganda in early January 1868 'repeating just what the Bishop said'.[27] He then seems to have forgotten about the matter and was surprised when, a few months

---

[22] 'Memoirs of Dean Binsfield, SM, St. Mary's, Napier, July 1904', Christchurch Diocesan Archives [CHDA], Clergy.

[23] See Seán Brosnahan, 'Being Scottish in an Irish Catholic church in a Scottish Presbyterian settlement: Otago's Scottish Catholics, 1848-1895', *Immigrants & Minorities*, vol. 30, no. 1 (March 2012), 22–42, at 31–2.

[24] N. P. Vaney, 'The dual tradition: Irish Catholics and French priests in New Zealand: The west coast experience, 1865–1910', unpublished MA thesis, University of Canterbury, 1976, 122. Vaney was the Catholic chaplain at the University of Canterbury.

[25] Keys, *Viard*, 205–6.   [26] Quoted in ibid., 211.

[27] Cullen to Kirby, 15 September 1868, PICRA/K/68/325.

later, a leading Marist appeared in Dublin to give 'a very bad account' of both Viard and O'Reily. The latter, it seemed, 'had filled the diocese of Wellington with drunken priests' and 'inflicted severe wounds on religion'. This was the first Cullen had heard of it, and he wondered if the Marists were well informed even 'though the Bishop belonged to their congregation'. Cullen of course was always prepared to believe the worst of missionary friars, and he quickly warned Tobias Kirby against letting O'Reily stay in the Irish College.[28]

In the meantime, however, O'Reily had impressed both Kirby and Barnabò with his piety, and Kirby suspected that the Marists were prejudiced against the Irish. Would they, he asked Cullen, 'wish to exclude all Irish priests ... when Irishmen form the great majority of the Catholic population?'[29] This unwonted confusion was the result of Cullen's previous lack of curiosity about New Zealand. Beyond a handful of passing mentions in correspondence dating back to the 1850s, there is no evidence of any interest in events there before O'Reily's appearance in Dublin. Had the situation not disintegrated in the late 1860s, it is unlikely that Cullen would have involved himself. Once again, it was the disgruntled Irish who drew him in.

As early as December 1868, Cullen had passed to Barnabò descriptions of the 'deplorabile dello stato d'immoralità e d'irreligione' in New Zealand. His source was an Irish laywoman in Christchurch, who had written in February 1868 to ask that Irish priests be supplied to the mission. Cullen offered no opinion on the cause of the situation, and his letter also addressed the failure of the Oblate mission on Vancouver Island, the hundreds of Irish Catholics soldiers posted to the newly acquired American territory of Alaska, and the spiritual problems of the numerous but widely scattered Irish of Argentina.[30] New Zealand had become a concern but not yet a pressing one.

That changed as more complaints arrived. Writing directly to Cullen in late 1868, for example, a layman named Alexander McBride noted that it had been nearly a year since a priest had been resident at Queenstown in central Otago, the previous one having left for a richer mission on the coast. Viard, he continued, had 'never inquired into the loss that stripped us of all that is as dear as his life to an Irishman I mean his holy religion.' There was no prospect of access to the sacraments or religious

[28] Ibid.
[29] Kirby to Cullen, 15 October 1868, quoted in Rory Sweetman, 'Paul Cullen and the remaking of Catholicism in the Antipodes', in Dáire Keogh and Albert McDonnell (eds.), *Cardinal Paul Cullen and His World* (Dublin: Four Courts Press, 2011), 377–400, at 387.
[30] Cullen to Barnabò, 30 December 1868, APF/SOGC/vol. 996/fols. 840rv.

instruction, and 'since I came to the colony I did not see a catechism put into any children's hands'. McBride was clear about the cause: 'the French mission is a failure in this country.' The Marists did not speak English, he continued, and the people, who were mostly Irish, did not understand French. He wanted Cullen to ask the pope to 'establish an Irish mission here or at least grant us one bishop along with some of his clergy'.[31]

McBride was promptly echoed by William Hickie, an Irish priest on an Antipodean fundraising tour for the Catholic University of Ireland. Hickie had at first liked Viard, whom he thought a 'good old man', and at the bishop's request he had given missions wherever he went, helped to mediate the dispute in Hokitika, and raised more than £1,000 for the university on the North Island. New Zealand impressed him as a worthy 'field for good Irish priests', although he lamented that those Irishmen who had 'hitherto been on the mission here were such sources of scandal.'[32] The longer he stayed and the further south he travelled, however, the more his opinion soured. Writing from Dunedin on Christmas Eve, Hickie complained of the 'spiritual desolation' faced by what he described as a 'fine well disposed and to a great extent Irish population'. The Marists, he continued, were 'very pious' but not suitable for an English-speaking colony. Nor were there enough of them, and he claimed to be regularly implored for help in securing good priests who could be understood. As for 'Poor Bishop Viard', he was 'a regular saint' but an inadequate bishop. Writing to Bartholomew Woodlock, Hickie could be blunt: it would be a 'great act of charity' if he would urge Cullen 'to have Irish bishops' appointed for the whole of New Zealand and especially the South Island.[33] Woodlock did as he was asked, and Cullen translated the more incendiary portions of Hickie's letter for the Propaganda.[34]

Yet it was the catastrophic state of Auckland that made Cullen's intervention inevitable. Pompallier had left for Europe in the spring of 1868, arriving at Paris in late July. He almost certainly intended to resign on reaching Rome, although this might not have been as clear in Auckland as his biographer assumed.[35] The newspapers reported the trip as merely 'the customary decennial visit to the Holy See', and both Suzanne Aubert and the Sisters of Mercy expected he would return.[36] Once in Europe, he

[31] McBride to Cullen, 22 December 1868, DDA/CP/341/3/I/70.
[32] Hickie to Bartholomew Woodlock, 5 September 1868, DDA/CP/45/5/IV/39.
[33] Hickie to Woodlock, 24 December 1868, DDA/CP/Australia.
[34] Cullen to Barnabò, 10 April 1869, APF/SOCG/vol.996/fols 844rv.
[35] Simmons, *Pompallier*, 182.
[36] See *Daily Southern Cross*, 2 March 1868; 'The pupils of Nazareth Institution' to James McDonald, 11 December 1868, in *Letters on the Go: The Correspondence of Suzanne*

took his time, calling on the Propagation of the Faith and issuing various appeals for financial support, including directly to Napoleon III. He also travelled to London and at least intended to 'pay a visit also to dear Ireland'.[37] Without a resident bishop the diocese began to collapse. The Sisters of Mercy, for example, felt it necessary to ask Pius IX to personally adjudicate a dispute with a wayward member.[38] The already fragile financial position was also worsening, and in late September the bishop's creditors forced the sale by auction of his personal possessions.[39] By November, an embarrassed Pompallier had approached the French government for financial support in his retirement.[40]

Yet Pompallier was not without friends. He secured support from Frederick Weld, for example, who wrote at length to the Propaganda in late 1868. Although Weld had left New Zealand for good the year before, his lineage commanded respect in Rome. He blamed the parlous state of Auckland's finances not on Pompallier but on the wider economic climate following nearly a decade of conflict with the Māori. He advised that the colony should be divided into four dioceses, Auckland, Wellington (to include Marlborough and Nelson on the South Island), Canterbury and the west coast, and Otago and Southland. Pompallier should remain as bishop of Auckland but be granted a coadjutor. Although Weld noted that the 'Catholics of New Zealand are almost all poor chiefly Irish immigrants', he did not recommend Irish appointees and offered no solution to the financial crisis.[41] This was New Zealand as seen through Pompallier's eyes.

Pompallier himself did not appear in Rome until mid-February 1869, more than six months after he had arrived in Europe. He promptly entered into discussions about his future, although he did not submit his formal resignation until 23 March. Barnabò had already told Cullen a few days before that they planned to appoint a coadjutor for Auckland and divide Wellington.[42] A few weeks later, Pompallier submitted a lengthy report reiterating his own recommendations for Auckland. Given his difficulties with the Irish laity, and his awareness of events in New South Wales, it is unsurprising that he did not recommend an Irish successor despite his earlier admission to the

---

Aubert, edited by Jesse Munro (Wellington: Bridget Williams Books, 2009), 27, hereafter *AC*; M. Cecilia Maher to M. M. Catherine, 27 August 1869, ASMA.

[37] Pompallier to James McDonald, 7 September 1868, Archives of the Catholic Diocese of Auckland [ACDA], Pompallier papers [PP], 22–5/3.

[38] M. Paul Ennis to Pius IX, 29 September 1869, Segreteria di Stato, Sezione per I rapporti con gli stati, fondo Affari Ecclesiastici Straordinari, periodo II, Inghilterra I, positione 76, f. 32.

[39] *Daily Southern Cross*, 21 September 1868.   [40] Simmons, *Pompallier*, 184.

[41] Quoted in ibid., 185.   [42] Barnabò to Cullen, 18 March 1869, DDA/CP/326/4/93.

Propaganda that what Auckland needed was an energetic Irishman.[43] He instead recommended Roger Bede Vaughan, possibly at the suggestion of Weld. Pompallier also urged the erection of a separate vicariate for the Māori, with his vicar general James McDonald as bishop. He himself should remain in charge of Auckland for a year from France until Vaughan assumed full control.[44]

Pompallier's report muddied the waters. Although years of complaints had taken their toll on his credibility, his advice could not be arbitrarily dismissed; but neither could the accounts arriving from New Zealand and now Dublin about the inadequacies of both Pompallier and Viard. In late May, Barnabò asked Cullen for more information: Rome simply did not understand what was going on.[45] By June, he reported that Pompallier had definitively resigned. He also told Cullen that Viard was not up to the job in Wellington and asked him to suggest outright replacements for both.[46] This was his second request for names: he had asked first in March, on the grounds that most New Zealand Catholics were Irish or English.[47] Cullen had duly begun a somewhat leisurely process of identifying suitable candidates to act as 'missionari o vescovi nella Nuova Zelanda'.[48] In a lengthy letter to Patrick Moran in South Africa, Cullen's vicar general Laurence Forde explained how matters stood in Dublin that spring. 'New Zealand', he wrote, 'is at present without a Bishop' as Pompallier had resigned and Viard was 'about to leave'. 'As usual', he continued, Rome was 'looking to Ireland' for their successors.

This presented Forde with a dilemma. It was his job to keep Dublin running, and there simply were not enough 'capable' priests to meet local needs. As he pondered the problem, he thought of Moran, who had not been silent about the frustrations of the Eastern Cape. Perhaps Auckland might provide a 'more expansive field for your labours', he wrote, although Pompallier had 'managed to sink it in debt'. There was great work to do there for a bishop 'of learning, prudence, and a knowledge of colonial life'. On this basis, he had suggested his friend's name to Cullen, whose 'only reply was to ask whether I thought you would accept'.[49]

Moran's reply is not recorded, and, when Barnabò's second request for names arrived in Dublin, there was no time to wait on one. On 14 June, Cullen's secretary George Conroy informally offered Auckland to

[43] Pompallier to Barnabò, 27 January 1869, cited in Sweetman, 'Antipodes', 383.
[44] Simmons, *Pompallier*, 187.   [45] Barnabò to Cullen, 25 May 1869, DDA/CP/326/4/101.
[46] Barnabò to Cullen, 8 June 1869, DDA/CP/326/4/104.
[47] Barnabò to Cullen, 18 March 1869, DDA/CP/326/4/93.
[48] Cullen to Barnabò, 10 April 1869, APF/SOCG/vol. 996/ff. 844rv.
[49] Forde to Moran, 23 May [1869], PEDA/MP/FO/PM/307.

Thomas Power, who swithered. Power soon apologized for his indecision, confessing to Cullen that he knew so little about New Zealand that he had at first thought that Conroy was being 'playful, as he had already made some jokes about Newfoundland'. He was horrified when he realized that the offer was serious. He had 'never seriously entertained' the idea of the foreign missions, had not trained for them, and was not physically or mentally prepared. He begged Cullen's forgiveness.[50] This was more than pro forma reluctance, and it is striking that Power remained in consideration for New Zealand and was ultimately sent to Newfoundland. In part, this was likely the result of the need to create a vacancy at Clonliffe for Michael Verdon (see Chapter 2) and in part a reflection of how shallow the episcopal talent pool had become in Dublin.

With Power temporarily out of the running, Forde again recommended Moran for Auckland, telling Cullen that his experience would be invaluable in helping 'his brother Prelates (practically) to found a new church' in New Zealand. He also suggested that the parish priest of Ballybrack, George Harold, could be sent to Wellington.[51] A few weeks later, the other Patrick Moran told James Murray in New South Wales that 'You will be getting very soon an Irish bp in New Zealand'. The candidates were now the South African Moran, Power, and James Hickey, a curate in Dundrum. Moran also favoured his namesake, as his 'experience will enable him to set things right'. He seems to have been less sure that a bishop would now be required for Wellington itself but still expected that the diocese would be divided and thus a 'second Irish Bp. will be appointed', most likely Power or Hickey. 'All this', he told Murray, 'is to be kept secret.'[52]

In the meantime, the diocese of Auckland was slowly collapsing. Its already extensive debts had grown by some £2,000 since Pompallier's departure and, by the middle of 1869, stood at an eye-watering £7,400. In late August, a devastating memorandum on Pompallier's financial mismanagement had been drafted by leading lay Catholics there and sent to the Propaganda. They began by claiming that, since 1850, the diocese had received more than £80,000 from the government and the laity. This amounted to nearly half of Auckland's income, the rest being provided by the Propagation of the Faith. Despite this, the laity had had no part in its financial administration and had been kept in the dark as to the scale of its debts. The situation was bleak: the clergy were not being

[50] Power to Cullen, 17 June 1869, DDA/CP/321/1/I/64.
[51] Forde to Cullen, 15 June 1869, DDA/CP/341/8/V/4.
[52] Moran to Murray, 8 July 1869, MNDA/MP/D.3.36.

paid, two churches were shortly to be foreclosed on and sold, and the bishop's effects had been publicly auctioned to great scandal. Pompallier himself had signed a promissory note for £400 shortly before leaving New Zealand, but, because his credit was so poor, he had 'induced a Protestant gentleman to endorse it'. With Pompallier gone and the debt unpaid, the man had had to mortgage his own property to meet the obligation. All that was left were a 'few churches and church sites, and one or two small properties acquired by purchase or bequest'.

This had serious consequences, not least for education. Owing to a lack of resources, they wrote, 'For many years our schools have ceased to provide anything more than the simple rudiments of education.' To provide enough skills for Catholic children to be 'something more than hewers of wood and drawers of water, the Catholics of the Diocese have been reluctantly compelled to send them to the better managed schools of other denominations'.[53] The signatories were drawn from the middle-class Catholic elite of Auckland documented by Gabrielle Fortune, men such as Charles Canning, a prosperous baker and restaurateur born in Scotland to Irish parents, and John Sheehan, a New Zealander with Irish parents who became the first native-born member of parliament.[54] Many of the rest had obviously Irish names such as Leahy, Shanagan, and Brophy.

The scale of the collapse gave Rome pause: a new bishop could not be sent without first establishing the facts of the situation. The obvious solution was to send an Australian bishop on a visitation, and the Propaganda settled on James Goold of Melbourne. It is difficult to read anything into the choice other than that neither James Murray nor Matthew Quinn were then planning to attend the Vatican Council, whereas Goold was and could stop on the way. He arrived in New Zealand on 25 October, after first calling at Sydney to confer with Murray and Quinn.[55] The situation was bleak: the land which held the bishop's house, Aubert's Nazareth Institute, the Holy Family convent, and the Church of the Immaculate Conception had been foreclosed and sold earlier in the month.[56] In Auckland, he found thirty girls in their poor school, forty in the fee-paying, eighteen boarders, and thirty-two orphans. At Onehunga, he visited both the Mercy school and one for boys run by

---

[53] 'To his eminence Alexander, Cardinal Barnabò, Prefect of the Sacred Congregation of Propaganda Fide, and to the Central Council for the Propagation of the Faith, Auckland, 28 August 1869', ACDA/INTI/1–5/2.
[54] For Canning, see Fortune, 'Hugh Coolahan', 172.
[55] Goold diary, 18 October 1869, MDHC.
[56] E. R. Simmons, *In Cruce Salus: A History of the Diocese of Auckland* (Auckland: Catholic Publications Centre, 1982), 98.

the Catholic Young Men's Society.[57] He was less impressed with what he called 'the public schools in connection with the Church' and especially with the quality of religious instruction provided in the boys' schools.[58] On 7 November, he examined some sixty children gathered in the cathedral. They did a bit better, with Goold noting that the girls had been instructed in Christian doctrine by the Mercy Sisters and the boys 'by some good soldiers belonging to the Royal Irish'.

Goold was particularly attentive to Pompallier's lay critics. He appears to have been especially struck by the 'most important information about the Bishop' provided over two interviews by the registrar of the Supreme Court (and later judge in the native land court), the Dublin-born Loughlin O'Brien.[59] He also received copious and scurrilous accusations from Suzanne Aubert, who seems to have been hurt at being abandoned by her former protector. Aubert also had more than a little to say about the Sisters of Mercy, whom she believed looked down on her, and it was from her that Goold probably obtained the primary allegations of immorality against Pompallier. Such complaints had a long pedigree: the Marists had alleged alcoholism as early as 1847, a charge that was renewed in the early 1850s. In 1854, Rome had asked Viard to investigate the allegation as well as rumours of improprieties with the Sisters of Mercy. He exonerated Pompallier from the charge of drunkenness but accepted he had been too familiar with the sisters, sometimes hearing their confessions in his rooms or staying in the convent until 8 p.m.[60] By 1869, this had evolved into lurid claims that the aged bishop had had a sexual relationship with Cecilia Maher and had solicited sex from other nuns in the confessional. Although Aubert was neither the originator nor the only source of these accusations, she was among their most enthusiastic vendors. As she put it to her Marist confidant, 'The Sisters of Mercy impudently denied my statements but to their confusion he did not lack other crushing evidence.'[61] The charges were so outlandish, so implausible, and so cruel, and Aubert's motivation so petty, that the attempts of both E. R. Simmons and Jessie Munro to explain or minimize her behaviour seem like special pleading for 'New Zealand's saint in the making'.[62] That Goold at least partly believed her reveals the nadir to which Pompallier's reputation had fallen.

Yet the Frenchman did not lack defenders. The Sisters of Mercy remained loyal to their 'beloved Bishop', and Maher wrote to her cousin

---

[57] Goold diary, 25 October 1869, MDHC.   [58] Ibid., 28 October 1869.

[59] Ibid., 4 November 1869.   [60] Simmons, *Pompallier*, 135–8.

[61] Aubert to Poupinel, 20 December 1869, quoted in Simmons, *Pompallier*, 190.

[62] Simmons, *Pompallier*, 189–90; Munro, *Aubert*, 99. See the website www
    .suzanneaubert.co.nz, which campaigns for Aubert's sanctification.

to warn him against listening to gossip from Auckland. Many of the people there were Irish, she told Cullen, 'but alas very different from those in Ireland, inquisitive, prying into what does not concern them', overly judgemental of the clergy, and 'so addicted to misrepresentations that one cannot rely on their statements though quite plausibly made'.[63] The Kilkenny-born clerical brothers Walter and James McDonald, who had arrived in Auckland in the 1850s, continued to mount a spirited defence of his tenure and conduct, although Walter at least was forced to admit that 'things were in a very sad state in Auckland'.[64] It did not matter: Goold had made up his mind, probably before he left Melbourne, and nothing he heard in New Zealand changed it.

When Goold arrived in Rome in early February, he found that the Propaganda 'already knew everything regarding Auckland.'[65] Over the next ten days, he drafted his report, reading correspondence in the Propaganda and meeting Viard (in Rome on his own business), who 'threw out a few hints about Auckland' and further condemned Pompallier's financial management.[66] He also received a personal visit from Cullen.[67] In rank-conscious Rome, it was customary for bishops to call on cardinals, not the other way around, and Cullen must have been very eager indeed to learn what Goold intended to say. Goold was open with him, reporting 'that things were very bad in Auckland – no French Bishop should be sent – all the Catholics are Irish'. A delighted Cullen thought that Goold's report would 'probably open the eyes of the Propaganda'.[68]

His verdict was damning and his advice clear. Pompallier was a failure and a scandal: he hardly ever visited outlying districts; his diocese was bankrupt; he slept with nuns. The only solution was the immediate appointment of a new bishop, who should be Irish.[69] It is unclear to what extent Goold believed what he wrote and the Propaganda what it read. The allegations against the Sisters of Mercy, for example, quickly melted away. This could be attributed to Maher's relationship to Cullen, but if there had been even the slightest shadow her June 1870 re-election as superior would have been impossible. The Mercies themselves detected no hostility from Goold despite being at least generally aware of the charges against Pompallier, and, when the new bishop arrived in Auckland, he worked

---

[63] M. Cecilia Maher to M. M. Catherine, 27 August 1869, ASMA; Maher to Cullen, 14 December 1869, DDA/CP/321/1/V/44.
[64] Goold diary, 10 February 1870, MDHC.   [65] Goold diary, 13 February 1870, MDHC.
[66] Ibid., 15 February 1870.   [67] Ibid., 15, 22 February 1870.
[68] Cullen to Conroy, ARDA/CP/1870/17/2.
[69] For the full report, APF/Acta/vol. 236/f. 370–2.

enthusiastically with them.[70] It is probable that there were simply so many accusations over so many years that Goold (and Rome) came to believe that some at least must be true and therefore the details of any one were irrelevant. That does not, however, make all of the charges against him untrue. Unlike the rumours of sexual impropriety, most of what was alleged about Pompallier's financial conduct was accurate. Even the sympathetic Simmons admitted that he 'did not understand money and its ramifications'.[71] It is also worth observing that the Sisters of Mercy had managed to stay solvent, boasting in late 1869 that 'we have five convents ... not one of them mortgaged'.[72]

The affairs of Wellington were also on the Propaganda's mind. Viard had followed O'Reily to Rome in late October 1868, a few months before Pompallier. His first task was to come to an understanding with the Marists, which he did by mid-December. He knew that he could not continue to fight them on one front and the Irish on the other. If the Propaganda approved it, their agreement effectively returned power in Wellington to the society and thus cleared the way for a campaign to protect Viard until the succession there could be assured. In early 1869, he followed Weld and Pompallier in recommending that the diocese be divided, although not as Weld had suggested: the new see should comprise only Otago and Southland; Canterbury and the west coast would remain with Wellington, as would Marlborough and Nelson. This was probably tactical: if the Marists wished to retain Wellington (especially with Canterbury and the coast attached), they needed to offer something in return. The pressure they were under became clear in early September when they learned that the Propaganda was blocking their agreement with Viard until he agreed to select an English-speaking coadjutor.[73]

In the meantime, Cullen was still looking for a bishop for the south. As Viard reported on 8 June, Barnabò had agreed to Wellington's division but was waiting for the names Cullen had 'promised to send to him' for Auckland and Dunedin. Until then, 'nothing can be concluded.'[74] With Auckland on hold until Goold reported, thoughts in Dublin turned again to Patrick Moran of Grahamstown. By September, Viard had informed Lyon that Moran had definitely been selected for Otago.[75] The other Moran confirmed the news in early November and also reported that it had been agreed that Viard would retain Wellington 'but is to have an

[70] M. Paula to M. M. Catherine, 18 November 1869, quoted in Simmons, *Pompallier*, 190.
[71] Simmons, *Pompallier*, 196.
[72] M. Cecilia Maher to M. M. Catherine, 'November' 1869, ASMA.
[73] See Yardin to Reignier, 10 September 1869, quoted in Keys, *Viard*, 218.
[74] Viard to Favre, 8 June 1869, quoted in ibid., 218.   [75] Ibid.

Irish Coadjutor'.[76] Again according to Moran, Viard had asked Power to accept this role, which he would have known to do only if prompted by Cullen or an intermediary. This was probably the source of the rumours that reached New Zealand in early 1870 about the imminent arrival of the 'celebrated Dr Power'.[77]

The Marists had long feared that Viard would seek the appointment of Jeremiah O'Reily as his coadjutor, which is why they had been so eager to denounce him to Cullen in 1868.[78] But the Capuchin friar was not a long-term threat, even in the unlikely event he was appointed. Power was different: the Marists knew that, once installed, the Cullenites rarely relinquished power and never without a fight. Fear of losing their last foothold in New Zealand and with it their Pacific base provoked them to bombard the Propaganda with letters explaining why the imposition of a diocesan priest of any ethnicity would be a disaster.[79] Cullen was aware of the pressure, writing in late December that 'I understand that [the] Marists insist that Dr. Viard must take one of their body as Coadjutor for Wellington, so all the surmises in Dublin will terminate un fiasco.'[80] By February, Cullen noticed Viard had fallen silent on the subject, and by the end of the month his secretary George Conroy described Power's appointment as 'doubtful'.[81] Cullen's own opinion was clear and had been strengthened by his conversations with Goold: 'all the Catholics are Irish', he told Conroy, and therefore the Propaganda 'must appoint all Irish Bishops' right across New Zealand.[82]

The Marists knew there was little point in resisting this. The proposition that an Irish flock required an Irish bishop had been accepted by the Propaganda for nearly forty years; Barnabò's insistence that Viard seek a coadjutor in Ireland simply drove this home. What the Marists could influence was what *sort* of Irish bishop should be appointed. They knew that Cullen and Barnabò invariably preferred diocesan priests but also that this could not be insisted on as a matter of policy. This is why the Marists stressed the unsuitability of a secular coadjutor in Wellington, not the unsuitability of an Irish one. The problem was that they did not yet have any suitable candidates to offer, and they consequently played for time. This was a dangerous game, as there was something approaching consensus in Rome that Viard was incompetent and an English-speaking

[76] Moran to Murray, 1 November 1869, MNDA/MP/D.3.38.
[77] *Wellington Independent*, 31 March 1870.   [78] Sweetman, 'Antipodes', 384.
[79] O'Meeghan, *Steadfast*, 102.
[80] Cullen to Conroy, 30 December 1869, ARDA/CP/1869/30/12.
[81] Cullen to Conroy, 17 February 1870, ARDA/CP/1870/17/2; Conroy to Cullen, 25 February 1870, DDA/CP/321/7/4/20.
[82] Cullen to Conroy, 17 February 1870, ARDA/CP/1870/17/2.

replacement vital. Certainly Barnabò took this view – at one point, he contemplated ordering the Marists to withdraw from New Zealand completely.[83] Even so, by July they had managed to secure the Propaganda's agreement to leave Viard in place and postpone a decision on a coadjutor but only on the understanding that they would 'little by little' send the products of their Irish novitiate to New Zealand.[84]

The most likely explanation for the Marists' success was simple arithmetic. Moran had already been appointed in Dunedin, and it was clear that Auckland would soon be supplied with an Irishman of Cullen's choosing. The other Patrick Moran had long hoped that New Zealand would either be erected into an ecclesiastical province in its own right or be attached to New South Wales. As he told Murray in November 1869, he looked forward to 'the annexation of the New Zealand Dioceses to your Australian Province'.[85] In either case, there would be a Hiberno-Roman majority – eight to six in a joint province or two to one in New Zealand alone.[86] It was no accident that, when Moran heard that Auckland had finally been filled, his first thought was that there should be immediately held in Rome 'a sort of Provincial council of New Zealand.'[87] If Viard resisted he could be systematically outvoted, and with the bishops on the spot the Propaganda could quickly review and approve any decrees. Barnabò was keen on the idea even before Auckland was settled.[88] Cullen did not fight the Marists in 1870 because he did not need to. Why expend the energy necessary to thwart the determined and well-regarded society when time was on his side and the balance of power in the New Zealand church secure?

The Marists in turn did not interfere with the other appointments. Dunedin of course had already been decided, although it is unclear when Patrick Moran definitively learned of the Propaganda's plans for him. His own successor in the Cape thought it might have been as late as December 1869, when a letter from Rome arrived in Grahamstown.[89] Moran was reluctant, telling Forde that he had no 'desire to exchange this mission poor and out of the way as it is for any Diocese in New Zealand'. He pled poverty but Barnabò was not deterred: 'I thought I had

[83] Barnabò to Cullen, 10 April 1870, DDA/CP/326/5/58.
[84] Yardin to Forest, 13 July 1870, quoted in Keys, *Viard*, 219.
[85] Moran to Murray, 1 November 1869, MNDA/MP/D.3.38.
[86] Six would be the highest possible total and assumes that Goold of Melbourne, Polding of Sydney, Sheil of Adelaide, Griver of Perth, and Salvado of Port Victoria would all vote with Viard. This would be profoundly unlikely.
[87] Moran to Conroy, 24 June 1870, from a transcript in the AAS/MP.
[88] Barnabò to Cullen, 10 April 1870, DDA/CP/326/5/58.   [89] Wilmot, 83.

succeeded in getting free of New Zealand', Moran wrote, 'but I now see how much mistaken I was.'[90]

The Propaganda moved quickly, with Bishop Grimley of Cape Town reporting on 1 February that 'Dr Moran's case has been settled at the Propaganda'.[91] Moran himself, however, still hoped as late as April that he might escape and in his diary recounted that he only finally resolved on such a 'very great undertaking' after receiving firm assurances from Viard that a former hotel had been bought in Dunedin for a convent, which was true, and a 'large sum of money had been collected for the new Bishop', which was not.[92] Moran was attracted by what he hoped was the greater material resources available in New Zealand. As he told J. D. Ricards, who had offered him £50, 'your mission is poor, and Dunedin they say is rich'. Although he did not wholly believe 'in Dunedin riches', Moran seems to have accepted the assurances of Viard and others that there would be adequate funds awaiting him. It was on this basis that he borrowed the Propagation of the Faith's grant to Grahamstown to pay for his passage, promising Ricards to repay it with interest as soon as he landed in New Zealand.[93]

With Dunedin decided and Wellington in limbo, attention reverted to Auckland. The submission of Goold's report in late February meant that an appointment could now be made, and there was no doubt that it would be an Irish one. The only question was who would accept what was widely regarded as a poisoned chalice. Goold flatly 'declined to send in names' on the grounds that 'Cardinal Cullen has done this'.[94] And, indeed, in mid-March the Propaganda again asked Cullen for suggestions.[95] Yet this was easier said than done: Power would soon be on his way to Newfoundland; Conroy was horrified when someone in Rome suggested him (he was hoping for the vacant archdiocese of Armagh) and insisted that Cullen get him off the hook; and it seemed that James Hickey wasn't ready to be a bishop after all.[96] Cullen finally settled on George Harold, the Dublin parish priest whom Forde had first recommended in the summer of 1869. He did not want to go either, telling Forde in early April that he could not accept because he was using a family legacy to

[90] Moran to Forde, n.d., DDA/Australia. This letter is badly damaged and the first page is missing entirely. It likely dates from December 1869 or January 1870.
[91] Grimley to McMahon, 1 February 1870, AACT/GP/Box 18.
[92] 'Diary of Bishop Moran', n.d., ADD, Moran papers [MP].
[93] Moran to Ricards, n.d., PEDA/MP/PM/2/213. The most likely date of this letter is late May or early June 1870.
[94] Goold to J. Dalton, 'April' 1870, MDHC/GP.
[95] Simeoni to Cullen, 15 March 1870, DDA/CP/326/4/127.
[96] Cullen to Conroy, 16 June 1870, ARDA/CP/1870/16/6; Forde to Cullen, 12 April 1870, DDA/CP/321/7/I/29.

rebuild his presbytery.[97] In the meantime, rumours swirled around Rome; in mid-April, Viard asked Grimley of Cape Town if *he* had been appointed to Auckland.[98]

Fortunately, Laurence Forde had a solution, Thomas Croke of the diocese of Cloyne. 'It strikes me', he told Cullen, 'that Dr Croke ... would be a good substitute.' Forde admitted that he did 'not know much of him', but he had heard that Croke bore 'a very high character' and, more importantly, he was already in Rome assisting his bishop at the Vatican Council.[99] Croke was in fact an excellent choice, and the reason it took so long to alight on him was the embedded Cullenite reluctance to entrust colonial appointments to priests from outwith Dublin. In the absence of a familial link to Cullen, it was prudent to have direct experience of a candidate's suitability, and Croke's was the only such appointment during Cullen's tenure.

Born in 1823, Thomas Croke was, in his biographer's phrase, 'a strange admixture of aristocrat and peasant'.[100] His father had had a varied career ranging from soldier to estate agent, while his mother was a wealthy Protestant related to the Knights of Glin. The Protestant influence must have been vestigial, however, as three of the five sons became priests and two daughters became nuns. In 1839, Thomas was sent to the Irish College in Paris after winning a diocesan scholarship. He loved France, embraced its language, and always wrote to the Roman authorities in French.[101] He moved to the Irish College, Rome, in 1845, where he promptly won several academic prizes and where the topic of his doctoral defence was 'The moral power of the pope'.[102] Cullen, who always admired academic success, thought him a 'good and talented' young man.[103] Although he briefly but seriously considered following Daniel Murphy to Hyderabad (see Chapter 3), Croke decided his future lay in Ireland. He returned in late 1847, despite Cullen's hope that he would stay at least another year in Rome.[104]

In Cloyne he enjoyed a stellar clerical career: founding president of St Colman's College in 1857 and then parish priest of Doneraile and vicar general of the diocese ten years later. He maintained a high public profile, particularly in the escalating campaign against the perceived dangers of

---

[97] Forde to Cullen, 12 April 1870, DDA/CP/321/7/I/29.

[98] Grimley diary, 14 April 1870, AACT/GP/Box 12.

[99] Forde to Cullen, 12 April 1870, DDA/CP/321/7/I/29.

[100] Mark Tierney, *Croke of Cashel: The Life of Archbishop Thomas William Croke, 1823–1902* (Dublin: Gill & Macmillan, 1976), 1.

[101] Ibid., 7.   [102] Ibid., 10.

[103] Cullen to Joseph Dixon, 18 April 1847, Cardinal Tomás Ó Fiaich Memorial Library and Archive, Armagh, Dixon papers, Irish College Rome file, Box 1.

[104] Cullen to Kirby, 17 October 1847, PICRA/NK/I/I/52.

the national system of education. Cullen thought one of his published attacks on the system 'went to the very bottom of the subject'.[105] Croke's education, confidence, and substantial personal wealth marked him out as an inevitable future bishop; he had no need to go to New Zealand to find a mitre. Although the final list Cullen provided to the Propaganda contained six names, Croke was undoubtedly the cardinal's choice. As he later boasted, Cullen had 'pressed' him on the congregation 'as about the only man who could put [Auckland] on its legs'.[106] Croke's Francophilia suited New Zealand, and his wealth was an attraction for bankrupt Auckland – Mark Tierney was probably right to suspect it played some part in the decision.[107]

The Propaganda duly made the appointment on 3 June, the pope confirmed it five days later, and Kirby wrote to tell an apparently surprised Croke. Although Barnabò ordered him to Rome 'without one moment's delay', he was uncertain whether to accept.[108] As he explained to his sister Issy, he could 'see pros and cons'. He knew nothing about New Zealand and had 'made no inquiries, have no books to consult, and no one to talk to'. This did not deter him, and he claimed not to 'mind a bit what kind of place it is'. 'The only question is – Am I to go *any* where. *If so*, no matter where it is.'[109] Although Croke was genuinely ignorant of New Zealand, he was familiar with the foreign missions in general and Australia in particular. His older sister Margaret was a Sister of Mercy in Bathurst, his younger brother David lived in Ballarat, and both Matthew Quinn and William Lanigan confided in him about the situation in New South Wales.[110] For their part, the Irish Australian bishops in Rome kept an eye on the progress of his nomination and were undoubtedly pleased by it.[111]

It did not take Croke long to decide, despite learning that Auckland's debts amounted to a sobering but still underestimated £5,000.[112] It remains unclear whether he accepted out of obligation to the Holy See, a genuine desire to go on the foreign mission, or as a stepping stone to greater things in Ireland. Whatever the case, Cullen promptly consecrated him at the Irish College with Murphy (now of Hobart) and

---

[105] Cullen to William Keane, 17 December 1859, Cloyne Diocesan archives, Keane papers, 1796.04/40/1859.

[106] Croke to Issy Croke, 3 July 1870, Archives of the Archdiocese of Cashel [CDA], Croke papers [CP], CR1870(2).

[107] Tierney, 41.   [108] Croke to Issy Croke, 22 June 1870, CDA/CP/CR1870(2).

[109] Croke to Issy Croke, 23 June 1870, National Library of New Zealand, Alexander Turnbull Library [NLNZ], MS. 2113(2). Emphasis in original.

[110] M. Quinn to Croke, 'August' 1867, BDA/QP/68/67.

[111] O'Mahony to Lanigan, 22 June [1870], ARCG/LP/3718/2/5.

[112] Croke to Issy Croke, 3 July 1870, CDA/CR1870(2).

Matthew Quinn assisting. On 11 July, Croke drafted a letter to the clergy and people of Auckland from the college's summer villa at Tivoli. It was brief, largely consisting of a lament that he had been forced by God's will to leave a happy life in Ireland for a 'strange land unknown to me except in name'. His focus was on the European population, with the Māori mentioned in passing as 'magnificent, but, I fear misguided men whose arms are raised in unequal contest against a civilization which they hopelessly strive to conquer'.[113]

On his arrival in mid-December 1870, Croke was greeted by a deputation of the 'laity of the Diocese of Auckland', all with Irish names. He promised to live on terms of friendship with all and expressed his 'unbounded confidence' in his flock, especially those 'of the Irish race' who could be relied upon to support the cause of 'rational progress and religion'.[114] He promptly began a punishing programme of visitations to what he privately called 'the outlying and savage portions of the Diocese'.[115] His first stop was the booming mining town of Thames, which he claimed as his mensal parish (displacing two Franciscans) and where he was greeted by the Hibernian Society, whose chaplain he agreed to become. Over five days, he preached four times and gave a lecture 'on the state of Ireland'.[116] Less than two weeks later, he was in Coromandel, where he was greeted by local worthies who hoped their new bishop would 'have no cause to regret leaving the dear old land [of] Saint Patrick – to which our thoughts so oft fly back'. They too were treated to a lecture on Ireland.[117] It is little wonder that Suzanne Aubert's first impression was that Croke was 'very Irish, always preaching to us the Faith of Patrick and the Gospel of Erin'.[118]

Throughout his visitation, Croke meticulously recorded the condition of every parish, from the number of children in school, to the state of the church, presbytery, and schoolhouse, to its debts and the quality of the pastor. In Otahuhu, for example, Croke found a 'parochial residence, four acres of prime land, convent, Boys school' and some land to which there appeared to be no clear title. 'All', he recorded in his journal, 'in fair condition – convent small, Church wants painting badly, and so indeed do all the other buildings.' The religious books and church furniture were '*passable* only'. There were 4,000 Catholics, and the parish was worth

---

[113] To the clergy and laity of Auckland, 11 July 1870, NLNZ/MS 2113(2).
[114] *New Zealand Herald*, 20 December 1870.
[115] Croke to Issy Croke, 6 April 1871, CD/CR1871(4).
[116] 'Record of Events Connected with My Administration of the Diocese of Auckland' [Auckland Journal], 5 January 1871, CDA/CR; *Daily Southern Cross*, 11 January 1871.
[117] *New Zealand Herald*, 31 January 1871.
[118] Aubert to Yardin, 20 January 1871, *AC*, 43.

about £115 a year. Less satisfactory was the school attendance, which was 'poor' with only twenty boys and thirty-five girls and 'no male teacher for the last 5 years'.[119]

Croke was particularly attentive to the quality of his clergy. In Otahuhu, that was the Franciscan Joseph Gregori. He had been in post since November 1869, and yet the paltry ten candidates who presented themselves for confirmation gave 'barely tolerable' answers to the bishop's questions.[120] At Rangiaowhia (the site of a battle and massacre in 1864), he found that the church was 'disgraceful'. That earned its French pastor Laurence Vinay 'a well merited castigation'. In a rare instance of concern for Māori evangelization, Croke noted that there had been 5,000 'Catholic natives' at Rangiaowhia in 1845, 1,500 in 1863, and '*ONE* at present!!'[121] This was unfair: as E. R. Simmons pointed out, most of the Māori in the district were out of reach in land closed to Europeans by Tāwhiao, the Māori king. Fair or not, Croke repeated the allegation in his correspondence with Rome and Vinay soon retired to France.[122]

To come to grips with Auckland itself, Croke ordered a census of its Catholic population in January 1871. A fascinating and perhaps unique document in Catholicism's Greater Ireland, it recorded the names, addresses, size, composition, marriage habits, and religious practices of households containing a total of 1,466 people. Marginal notations chronicled everything from skipping Mass to drunkenness to bigamy. An analysis made by Elizabeth Sullivan-Burton reveals the scale of Croke's challenge: 64 per cent of the population as a whole had not made their first communion, while some two-thirds of eligible children had not been confirmed, and more than half were not in school. Of the 294 who answered the question, only 65 per cent received the sacraments. (Presumably the very high number – 1,172 – that did not answer reflects some embarrassment at lax practice.) The only bright spot was that attendance at Mass was slightly more than 75 per cent of those willing to give an answer.[123] As E. R. Simmons admitted, the religious practice of at least half the Catholic population 'ranged from the bare minimum to the non-existent'.[124]

On 10 July, Croke compiled a comprehensive account for Patrick Moran, with an explicit request to pass it to Cullen. A similar document

---

[119] Auckland Journal, 5 March. Emphasis in original.   [120] Ibid.   [121] Ibid.
[122] Simmons, *In Cruce Sales*, 110.
[123] 'Census of the Catholics of Auckland City Commenced 30 January 1871', ACDA/CRO5-1. Elizabeth Sullivan-Burton undertook a tabulation and analysis of the census in 2009 as an assignment at Ave Maria University. I am grateful to Ms Sullivan-Burton for allowing me to use her research.
[124] Simmons, *In Cruce Salus*, 109.

went to Rome. Croke reported that his diocese contained perhaps 8,000 Catholics, or one in seven of the population, for whom he had seventeen priests, two French, five Italian (all Franciscan), one English, and nine Irish. The Frenchmen claimed that, as they had not been ordained for Auckland, they could leave whenever they liked, something Croke could not confirm 'as no diocesan records have been kept here'. The Italians were of 'of an exceedingly low type', the worst being their superior, who 'is far and away the most troublesome and intriguing of the lot'. What he wanted, but could not afford, was 'four good Irish priests' to replace them. As for Pompallier, he had 'left nothing after him here unsold'.

Incompetence had consequences: although the convent schools were 'good, and fairly attended', those for boys were 'generally shabby', 'attendance bad, and masters incapable'. There was 'no respectable School in the whole Diocese – except for Protestant ones' and no classical teacher available and no funds to pay for one. As a result, 'our children have no alternative but to go to Protestant schools'. There were barely ten 'comfortable' Catholics in the diocese and no leading public men; there was only one Catholic in the general assembly. The newspapers were mostly Protestant and all bigoted to a degree. All in all, the 'Protestants have it nearly all their own way'.[125] The only bright spot was the Sisters of Mercy. It is little wonder that he told Kirby that 'An Irish bishop was not sent here one day too soon. Had there been more of a delay, I fear the faith would have died out here altogether.'[126]

Croke made two recommendations. One was the by now conventional observation that bishops should not be permitted to accept priests without unambiguously good testimonials. The other was also predictable: 'No Bishop is fit for a British Colony, except an English speaking bishop – in fact, except an Irishman, for our flocks are *all* Irish.' This principle should be immediately extended to Wellington, where 'The Catholics are all Irish – the Bishop and priests almost exclusively foreigners – *and they do not "love or like" each other.*'[127]

The accusations unsurprisingly provoked the aged Pompallier, now living in retirement in France. In September 1871, he wrote Croke a lengthy letter denying his claims about Auckland's finances: they were not really that bad; he had not mortgaged everything; several valuable properties had been transferred intact. In short, they were 'not all grounded upon the reality of things'. Pompallier was not entirely wrong: he had not lost everything, primarily because land granted by the crown

---

[125] Croke to Moran [Dublin], 10 July 1871, DDA/CP/40/7/V/15. Emphasis in original.
[126] Croke to Kirby, 10 July 1871, PICRA/K/1871/147.
[127] Croke to Moran [Dublin], 10 July 1871, DDA/CP/40/7/V/15. Emphasis in original.

could not be mortgaged or sold.[128] Pompallier, however, did not content himself with correcting the record. Croke, he complained, had withheld the some £3,200 provided by the Propagation of the Faith in 1869 and 1870 (which Pompallier claimed as his own) and refused to pay £1,400 in compensation for the properties Pompallier had made over to him. He then tried to enlist the Irishman in his campaign to secure a British government pension.[129]

There were more serious criticisms to be made of Croke's rule. As Suzanne Aubert's biographer Jessie Munro wrote, 'From the outset Bishop Thomas Croke was prejudiced against anyone who was not Irish, anyone associated with the French Marists in New Zealand, and anyone who criticized the Sisters of Mercy.'[130] This was Aubert's own view, and it has been widely accepted in New Zealand. She had eagerly anticipated Croke's arrival and seems to have hoped that he would punish the Sisters of Mercy and patronize her.[131] Instead, the new bishop declined Aubert's services and ordered her to return the Māori children 'to their tribes'. Her assurances that she had both land and money in hand were brushed aside: 'I want only one establishment in Auckland and it's the Sisters of Mercy', she recalled him saying, and they 'neither wish nor are able to have the Māori children.' Aubert should give up pretending to be a nun and go back to France. She knew the source of her troubles, and, when Croke instructed her to seek advice from the Sisters of Mercy, she tartly declined on the grounds that she did not 'like Diocesan Councils in petticoats'.[132] As Munro put it, 'Erin prevailed in Auckland and Suzanne settled her affairs.'[133]

Aubert was a scandalmonger, hated the Mercies, and was prone to self-pity and falling out with bishops but that does not mean that she was wrong about Croke's attitude towards the Māori. Like most Hiberno-Romans, Croke's focus was on his largely Irish flock. He was neither hostile to the Māori nor much interested in them. He did allow James McDonald to continue his forays from his mission at Drury, but his attempt to assign a newly arrived Irish priest to the mission faltered when, according to Aubert, the Māori cooked him pigeons without first gutting them. She feared that they were consequently turning Protestant or reverting to 'their old superstitions'.[134] E. R. Simmons' conclusion is surely right: under Croke the church in Auckland became almost wholly

---

[128] Simmons, *In Cruce Salus*, 113.
[129] Pompallier to Croke, 7 September 1871, ACDA/CRO4-6(4).
[130] Munro, *Aubert*, 107.   [131] Aubert to Poupinel, 30 August 1870, *AC*, 41–2.
[132] Aubert to Yardin, 20 January 1871, *AC*, 47.   [133] Munro, *Aubert*, 110.
[134] Aubert to Poupinel, 29 May 1874, *AC*, 89.

one of 'Irish settlers and the missionary drive of its beginnings had come to a halt'.[135]

The Italian Franciscans fared little better, and they finally left New Zealand in 1873. They took the view, as their superior told Rome, that Croke was 'an enemy of the friars, and as he said, of foreign priests'.[136] This was true, although Mark Tierney thought the Franciscans were merely using Croke 'as a scapegoat or excuse' for a long-desired exit.[137] This was also true, but Croke's antipathy to 'foreign' clergy seems to have been the primary reason. When he heard that James Quinn of Brisbane had recruited a 'legion of Italian priests', for example, he did 'not envy him or them'. 'You must', he continued, 'have English speaking priests for English speaking people: and none but an Irish Bishop will do for an Irish flock.'[138] It is significant that when the Italians left the sole Irish Franciscan stayed behind. Their departure was a 'relief' to Croke, who thought they were 'unsuited' to New Zealand and consequently 'discontented, querulous, and troublesome'.[139]

Croke's public persona could be surprisingly emollient. This was particularly apparent in regards to education. Although he had made his name in Ireland as a biting critic of the national system, in Auckland he pursued a more pragmatic approach. He had not the personnel, resources, or support to do otherwise. Before his arrival, the city's Catholics had been divided: the leading layman, John Sheehan, actively supported secular public education in order to forestall Protestant calls for Bible reading; some went so far as to petition against denominationalism as such.[140] Croke himself was a keen advocate of Catholic education but not at all costs. While Moran was 'kindling up a terrible row about *Education*' in Otago, Croke saw 'no sense in cursing them who send their children to Protestant schools, unless I have a Catholic school in which to place them afterwards'.[141] Years later, he caused consternation by giving an interview in which he appeared to endorse New Zealand's secular education system. Although he quickly clarified his comments, the slip was suggestive.[142]

The genteel Croke also enjoyed his position as a leading member of colonial society. This was particularly true on issues such as temperance,

---

[135] Simmons, *In Cruce Salus*, 120.
[136] Galosi to the Franciscan Minister-General, 31 May 1871, quoted in Tierney, 49.
[137] Tierney, 49.
[138] Croke to Moran [Dublin], 'Holy Thursday' 1871, DDA/CP/40/7/V/3.
[139] Croke to Cullen, 28 August 1873, DDA/Australia.
[140] Richard P. Davis, *Irish Issues in New Zealand Politics, 1868–1922* (Dunedin: Otago University Press, 1974), 73.
[141] Croke to Lanigan, '10 June' [?1871], ACGA/LP/MS3718/4/2. Emphasis in original.
[142] Davis, *Irish Issues*, 73.

which often drew even the sternest Hiberno-Romans (although not Moran) into cross-denominational collaborations. Internally, he oversaw the creation of a Catholic Temperance Society and publicly endorsed its pledge.[143] Externally, he was happy to work with all comers in the cause: in 1871, for example, he joined the provincial superintendent, the Anglican bishop, and a leading Protestant minister in a 'demonstration of tea drinking' to celebrate the passage of restrictions on the licensed trade.[144] He also accepted one of Auckland's three seats on the council of the nascent University of New Zealand, the only Catholic on a body that included politicians, judges, Anglican bishops, and Protestant ministers.[145]

Accommodation still had its limits, and Croke was prepared to engage in public controversy when necessary. In 1872, for example, he attacked a history book used in the Auckland Grammar School as 'ill-written and bigoted'. *Collier's British History*, he complained, insisted on calling Catholics Romanists and their faith Romanism while praising the Reformation. Ireland was consigned to a handful of pages and the Anglo-Saxon church dismissed 'in one or two insulting sentences'. All this in a publicly endowed school that was 'said to be secular or unsectarian in its teaching, and a fit place for the education of our Roman Catholic youth'.[146] Yet, where possible, he preferred to work within the system: when it appeared that the Orange Order would be invited to participate in an official celebration, for example, Croke protested and the Orangemen were disinvited.[147]

By the summer of 1873, he felt able to declare victory. 'The difficulties of this mission', he told Cullen, 'exist no longer.' He did 'not owe a penny personally or officially', his credit was good, confidence in ecclesiastical administration had been 'completely restored', and he had bought back 'every bit of useful property alienated by Bishop Pompallier' and purchased more besides. He had paid £2,000 for a house, had £1,600 in the bank for a new cathedral, and the mission was 'abundantly supplied with suitable schools and Churches'. In Auckland alone, and despite 'uncompromising opposition from the government schools', some 638 children were in daily attendance in Catholic schools. The Sisters of Mercy were thriving, the 'confraternities of the Scapular and Holy Rosary are established in *every* parish', and the confraternity of the Christian Doctrine was operating in Auckland with 'encouraging results'.[148]

---

[143] *New Zealand Herald*, 23 December 1873.
[144] *Daily Southern Cross*, 10 February 1871.
[145] J. C. Beaglehole, *The University of New Zealand: An Historical Study* (Wellington: New Zealand Council for Educational Research, 1937), 48, 81.
[146] *Daily Southern Cross*, 9 March 1872.   [147] Simmons, *In Cruce Salus*, 117.
[148] Croke to Cullen, 28 August 1873, DDA/Australia. Emphasis in original. Similar letters went to Kirby and the Propaganda.

This picture of unrelieved triumph should not be taken entirely at face value. E. R. Simmons, for example, thought that Croke's statements were 'mostly true, but curiously misleading': he hadn't retrieved quite everything lost under Pompallier; some of the new land was worthless; and, while he had indeed built four new churches, he had lost two others 'through inaction'. Simmons nevertheless accepted that Croke had restored faith in the diocesan administration and stabilized Auckland's finances.[149] In his qualified praise, Simmons seems to have been drawing on the institutional memory of the diocese: the Italian Benedictine Felice Vaggioli, who arrived in Auckland in the late 1870s, gained the impression that Croke had not been 'a successful bishop' and 'was not suited' to the mission.[150]

Others were more impressed. Walter McDonald, for example, privately thought that 'Dr Croke is doing a great deal in this diocese in the interests of religion': he had built schools and churches, 'secured all the properties (valuable) that were in difficulty or embarrassed', and was well liked by his now almost entirely Irish clergy.[151] Given McDonald's dedication to Pompallier, his assessment carries weight. It is certainly true that Croke enjoyed good fortune, including ample revenues from the Thames goldfields, the financial support of the Propagation of the Faith (from 1872), and surging Irish immigration. It is also true that his effective abandonment of the Māori mission now looks like failure, although he would not have seen it that way. Yet he was also efficient, effective, and totally committed to his largely Irish flock, not only retiring Pompallier's debts but purchasing by his own estimation more than £4,000's worth of property between December 1870 and March 1873; at least some of that came from his private resources.[152] Under him, Auckland stabilized and began to grow, not only in material terms but also in religious practice. Mark Tierney plausibly claimed that Croke achieved 'a devotional revolution in the young colony'.[153] Or as Cecilia Maher put it, he was 'quick and clever' and 'improves very much on acquaintance'.[154]

There is a long-standing tradition that Croke had accepted Auckland on the condition that he was to remain only three or four years. His biographer went so far as to claim that 'All the evidence points to the fact that Croke accepted the appointment with some proviso or

---

[149] Simmons, *In Cruce Salus*, 119–20.
[150] Felice Vaggioli, *A Deserter's Adventures: The Autobiography of Dom Felice Vaggioli*, translated by John Crockett (Dunedin: Otago University Press, 2001), 18.
[151] McDonald to J. J. Horan, 24 April 1873, BDA/QP/2/73.
[152] 'List of properties acquired by me since my arrival in Auckland', ACDA/CRO/4–1(1).
[153] Tierney, 62.   [154] Maher to M. M. Catherine, 12 February 1874, ASMA.

reservations' which he made clear to the Propaganda.[155] This has been broadly accepted in New Zealand, with both E. R. Simmons and Rory Sweetman echoing Tierney, albeit more cautiously.[156] It is also almost certainly untrue. The Propaganda sent bishops for life, and, while resignation, recall, or translation were possible, fixed-term contracts were not. It is theoretically possible that, in their desperation to fill Auckland, the Propaganda made Croke a deal, but it is distinctly unlikely. Certainly there was no institutional memory of such an arrangement: when Croke arrived in Ireland in 1874, for example, Cullen commented that 'I do not know what brought him home. Probably he is come to look for missionaries.'[157] The Propaganda itself was surprised by his resignation and did not immediately accept it. Nor did Croke allude to any deal or understanding when he asked Cullen for help.[158] Even if the Propaganda had forgotten and Cullen had never known, Croke himself gave no hint before 1873 of a formal or informal arrangement, or indeed a private plan. In his goodbye letter to Issy, for example, he admitted his own nervousness and consoled his sister but did not suggest that their separation would be anything other than permanent.[159]

There were as many as four distinct but overlapping reasons for his change of heart: his health; the death of his uncle; general frustration with the mission; and, perhaps, a better job at home. Health was likely the most serious: within months Croke was complaining to his sister that a headache that had already lasted a fortnight had been aggravated by a serious 'derangement of the stomach'.[160] The summer heat and punishing programme of visitations continued to weigh on him, and by early 1873 medical complaints were a constant in his journal and his letters. In March, he became seriously ill; two doctors apparently told him it was 'absolutely necessary' that he resign and go home.[161] In August, he told Cullen flatly that 'My health is not good: and I shall very likely return to Europe next year.'[162] His uncle's death (which he learned of in June) and the business that fell to him as the sole executor also increased his desire to pay a visit home.

He was also growing tired of Auckland. In early 1873, he complained to Kirby that 'This is a miserable mission'.[163] A particular problem was the quality of clergy that it attracted: three of the Irish priests he had imported

---

[155] Tierney, 41. [156] Simmons, *In Cruce Salus*, 105; Sweetman, 'Antipodes', 384.
[157] Cullen to Kirby, 25 May 1874, PICRA/NK/4/2/69.
[158] Croke to Cullen, 20 August [1874], DDA/CP/342/3/II/32A.
[159] Croke to Issy Croke, 'Friday' 1870, CDA/CR1870(13).
[160] Croke to Issy Croke, 6 April 1871, CDA/CR1871(4). [161] Quoted in Tierney, 63.
[162] Croke to Cullen, 28 August 1873, DDA/Australia.
[163] Croke to Kirby, 23 January 1873, quoted in Tierney, 60.

turned out to be drunks and another was prone to bar fights.[164] There was also the running sore of the Franciscans: when Felice Vaggioli arrived in Auckland in the late 1870s, he was told that one of the frequent arguments between the friars and the Irish seculars had escalated to the point of them hitting one another with chalices. He was later shown a dented one that had been carefully preserved.[165] It is unsurprising that Croke was fed up and wanted to go home. The question was what he expected to find there.

Many years later, Vaggioli recorded what had become the accepted wisdom in Auckland: Croke had gone to New Zealand only 'as a stepping-stone to an appointment to an Irish bishopric'.[166] Although flatly dismissed by Mark Tierney, there is probably some truth to the idea. As early as October 1873, Croke had received letters from Ireland alerting him to an impending episcopal vacancy in his native diocese of Cloyne. Some there were speaking of him as a potential successor. 'But', his informant continued, 'whether owing to your absence or the idea you are already provided for, their number is not great.' If Croke were 'on the spot', however, 'I should hope that it would be sufficient to give you a respectable locus standi' in any election.[167] It was in this correspondence that the notion of a fixed term in New Zealand first appeared, and the inference must be that Croke invented it to make himself a more plausible candidate, excuse leaving New Zealand, or both. Whether he was lying is impossible to know, but it seems likely.

Croke left Auckland for good on 28 January 1874. If he had decided to resign, he kept it to himself: he told Barnabò only that he was visiting Ireland and would call in Rome; the Sisters of Mercy thought he was planning to return with new postulants for them; the newspapers thought he was raising funds for a new cathedral.[168] Once in Ireland, he made his intentions perfectly clear. He called on Cullen to inform him that under no circumstances would he return to New Zealand. He also discussed with the cardinal 'certain matters in which I feel an interest'.[169] This was almost certainly Cloyne, as a few days after their meeting Cullen advised Rome that Croke would make an excellent bishop in a diocese that wanted 'a stirring up'.[170] Apparently confident of success, Croke posted his resignation on 25 June.

---

[164] Simmons, *In Cruce Salus*, 115–116.   [165] Vaggioli, 18.   [166] Ibid., 18.

[167] John McCarthy to Croke, 25 August 1873, ACDA/CRO/4/3a. The letter would have arrived in Auckland some time in October or early November. As it turned out, McCarthy himself would be appointed bishop of Cloyne.

[168] Croke to Barnabò, 21 January 1874, quoted in Tierney, 65: Barnabò died in February, before the letter could have arrived; Maher to M. Catherine, 12 February 1874, AMSA; *Marlborough Express*, 31 January 1874.

[169] Croke to Kirby, 12 June 1874, quoted in Tierney, 66.

[170] Cullen to Franchi, 2 June 1874, quoted in ibid., 67.

Yet he had not placed all his hopes on Cloyne. As Peter Francis Crinnon of London, Ontario, wrote on 27 June, Cullen 'spoke highly' of Croke and recommended him for the vacant see of Kingston (see Chapter 5). Croke, Cullen apparently continued, 'hopes to get a diocese in Ireland – but if not, he would be willing to come to Canada'.[171] While Barnabò lived, Cullen's enthusiasm would have settled the matter. Under Franchi, it did not: eager to be seen to curtail the Irishman's influence, the new cardinal prefect ruled out any move and left Croke to twist; he ultimately had to formally deny that he had ever harboured even the slightest thought of Cloyne.[172]

Croke now scrambled to ensure that he would at least not be sent back to New Zealand. As he told Cullen, 'I want no pay, pension, or preferment. All I ask is to have my resignation accepted and thus be restored to home again.'[173] The Propaganda finally accepted on health grounds but offered no alternative employment until 1875, when it imposed him on the archdiocese of Cashel over the wishes of its priests. Although Croke eagerly welcomed the prospect, and Cullen supported it, its origins lay in Rome. Franchi had made his point, and, as Mark Tierney noted, the appointment relieved the Propaganda 'from the embarrassment of having an unattached, ex-colonial bishop on their hands'.[174] Croke's reputation now rests on his long tenure in Cashel, commemorated in the name of the national stadium for Gaelic games. His legacy in Auckland is more complex: he was an effective and efficient bishop so long as he remained bishop. Thomas Croke's greatest failure in New Zealand was his manner of leaving it.

Croke's flight left the Propaganda at a loss: how would they fill Auckland this time? Croke provided three names but no definite recommendation when he was appointed to Cashel. In response, Franchi asked Cullen's opinion.[175] This was almost certainly to further emphasize the Irishman's impotence by giving the Propaganda the opportunity to reject the entire list, despite Cullen's enthusiastic endorsement of one of Croke's suggestions.[176] In early 1876, Franchi asked Cullen to join the Marist Francis William Redwood of Wellington (Viard's successor) and Patrick Moran of Dunedin in providing a new list of three names.[177] This did not work either: Moran could suggest no one in New Zealand and in

---

[171] Crinnon to John Joseph Lynch, 27 June 1874, TAA/LP/L.AD02.56.
[172] Croke to Kirby, 9 October 1874, quoted in Tierney, 68.
[173] Croke to Cullen, 20 August [1874], DDA/CP/342/3/II/32A.   [174] Tierney, 73.
[175] Croke to Cullen, 17 February [1876], DDA/CP/322/3/1/18/C(1), Franchi to Cullen, 28 July 1875, DDA/CP/326/6/21.
[176] A Fr. Fitzgerald. See Cullen to Croke, 16 February 1876, DDA/64/21/4.
[177] Franchi to Cullen, 23 January 1876, DDA/CP/326/6/40.

fact doubted the wisdom of maintaining Auckland at all.[178] The prudent Redwood apparently told Moran he would agree in advance to whomever he and Cullen selected. With no suitable candidates in New Zealand, Moran was compelled to turn his 'attention to the dear old land'. He suggested the Irish Vincentian James Dixon and two other Irish priests and recommended that the Vincentians take over the Māori missions. Cullen translated this into Italian and added a renewed recommendation that New Zealand be reduced to two dioceses if no one could be found.[179]

The Propaganda decided instead to appoint a Christchurch-based French Marist, Peter Chareyre. Croke was astonished: the 'appointment will be most distasteful to the people of Auckland', he told Cullen, 'as they have already had too much of the French element'.[180] The Marists must have seen the danger and Chareyre declined. Rome then offered Auckland to the Irish Franciscans, who swithered and then refused.[181] Croke wondered what 'on earth they are doing at the Propaganda' and told Cullen that, as he did 'not see an Irish Bp' being appointed, he was going to give his property there to the Sisters of Mercy.[182]

Meanwhile, Auckland drifted. Croke had left his vicar general Henry Fynes (an Englishman) in charge, but his authority was thrown into doubt by Croke's appointment to Cashel. As the Dunedin Moran noted in April 1876, 'the priests have one and all repudiated his claim'.[183] Croke himself was receiving with 'every post' letters from both priests and laity 'begging of me to urge on the appointment of a Bishop at once'.[184] Failing that, both men thought it would be necessary to designate an administrator to stabilize the situation. Moran's subsequent appointment to that position helped, but he did not visit Auckland until early 1878 and seems to have made little impression beyond imposing Dunedin's strict regulations on mixed marriages.[185] As Cecilia Maher complained, 'large districts are left without clergy' and many were 'living without Mass, or Sacraments, no confirmation given, while heresy and infidelity abound'. The thirty-six Mercy nuns were doing their best, but they received little support and their schools were dilapidated and undersubscribed.[186] After visiting with Redwood and Quinn of Brisbane, Moran agreed: Auckland

---

[178] Moran to Cullen, 4 April 1876, DDA/Australia.
[179] Moran to Cullen, 2 May 1876, DDA/Australia. The draft of Cullen's Italian letter to the Propaganda is appended to this document.
[180] Croke to Cullen, 24 April [1877], DDA/CP/329/1/II/15.
[181] Simeoni to Cullen, 23 August 1878, DDA/CP/326/6/63.
[182] Croke to Cullen, 12 April [1878], DDA/CP/329/5/I/25.
[183] Moran to Cullen, 4 April 1876, DDA/Australia.
[184] Croke to Cullen, 17 February [1876], DDA/CP/322/3/I/18/C(1).
[185] Fynes to the Clergy of Auckland, 15 May 1878, ACDA.INTII/1–1(1).
[186] Maher to Cullen, 24 January 1878, DDA/CP/329/7/111/6.

was 'in a deplorable state' and would get even worse unless a bishop was appointed immediately.[187]

Franchi's death in July 1878 simplified matters – his successor Giovanni Simeoni did not share his policy of frustrating the Irish and promptly consulted Cullen about what to do.[188] Before his own sudden death in late October, Cullen again suggested three Irish secular priests, but it had become clear that only a religious order could properly staff the diocese. Although at least five were approached, only the Italian Benedictines were prepared to help. The ultimate solution was a compromise: in 1879, Walter Steins, the Dutch Jesuit vicar apostolic of Calcutta was appointed but joined by five Benedictines on a trial basis and with a view to the diocese being consigned to them. Steins was already ill, and his appointment was likely an attempt by his friend Henry Edward Manning to save him from the Bengal climate.[189] He died anyway after less than two years in New Zealand. After yet more delays that 'astonished' Moran, he was succeeded by a Benedictine from Kent's Ramsgate Abbey, John Edmund Luck.[190] Kirby was quick to assure James Murray of Maitland that, despite being an Englishman, he bore 'a high character for piety & prudence'.[191] Luck imported more Benedictines (who soon made up roughly half the clergy) and various religious orders, none of them Irish. He died in 1896 and was succeeded by another English-born Benedictine, George Lenihan, who enjoyed Redwood's enthusiastic support.[192] (Intriguingly, Luck himself appears to have favoured Maitland's Patrick Dwyer.)[193] It was only in 1910 with the appointment of Henry Cleary that the Irish regained what Croke had so carelessly ceded.

Stalemate, 1874–1914

Unlike the sojourning Croke, Patrick Moran committed himself to New Zealand. His influence was both more enduring and more deeply felt, and it was Moran who brought undiluted Hiberno-Roman Catholicism to at least parts of the country. He was determined to curb both Marist and secular influences alike wherever possible. To do so, he drew on his long tenure in the Eastern Cape, which had shaped him as an administrator,

---

[187] Quoted in Simmons, *In Cruce Salus*, 141.
[188] Simeoni to Cullen, 23 August 1878, DDA/CP/326/6/63.
[189] Simmons, *In Cruce Salus*, 142.
[190] Moran to Fynes, 3 May 1882, ACDA/INTIII/1–4/9.
[191] Kirby to Murray, 15 July 1882, MNDA/MP/A.3.46.
[192] Redwood to Grimes, 12 February 1896, CHDA, John Joseph Grimes papers [GP], Box 12b.
[193] Luck to Grimes, 10 January 1896, CHDA/GP/Box 12b.

a politician, and an unbending champion of what he saw as Catholic rights. As the late Hugh Laracy put it, 'South Africa saw a dress rehearsal of the thoroughness, and unwillingness to compromise with the secular state that marked the Bishop of Dunedin.'[194]

His first task was to find priests and nuns. The former proved problematic: a tour of the Irish seminaries proved fruitless, and he ultimately secured only one priest, a curate from Cork named William Coleman. Moran was more successful with nuns, turning as he had in South Africa to the Sion Hill Dominicans. Although they wondered if a cloistered order was suitable to Otago, the Dominicans accepted Moran's assurance that 'it would be better for the people to come to the Sisters rather than the Sisters come to the people'.[195] Ten women were chosen, eight choir and two lay, ranging in age from fifty-nine to twenty-one. In keeping with the socially elite Dominicans, it was an impressively well-connected group: M. Catherine Hughes was a late vocation after a career as a teacher and was a sister-in-law of the politician Charles Gavan Duffy; M. de Ricci was a niece of Tobias Kirby; and the new mother superior, M. M. Gabriel, was a wealthy debutant who had first appeared at Sion Hill in her ballgown after fleeing a dance. Moran guaranteed the sisters a suitable convent and school and the services of a chaplain and promised not to interfere in their community life.[196]

On 5 October 1870, Moran set sail for New Zealand, a sort of Cullenite chaperone escorting not only his own nuns but two for Hobart, three for Maitland, four priests for Bathurst, and a seminarian for Auckland.[197] After an eventful journey and near shipwreck, they landed in Sydney in February. Murray was waiting for them on the docks, arranged lodgings, and paid their bill. Moran woke the next day to find that Matthew Quinn had 'travelled all night 135 miles' to meet them. They must have briefed him on the situation in New South Wales, as Moran reported back to Grahamstown on Polding's incompetence and hostility towards the Irish. He was overwhelmed by the hospitality, telling Ricards 'I only hope our own people will give us half as hearty a welcome.'[198]

They did their best, greeting the party's arrival in Dunedin in mid-February with a 'cavalcade' lining the streets up from the port.[199] There were also the customary addresses from the laity and from the clergy led

[194] Hugh M. Laracy, 'The life and context of Bishop Patrick Moran', unpublished MA thesis, Victoria University of Wellington, 1964, 3.

[195] Quoted in Mary Augustine McCarthy, *Star in the South: The Centennial History of the New Zealand Dominican Sisters* (Dunedin: St Dominic's Priory, 1970), 16.

[196] Ibid., 18–22.   [197] 'Diary of Bishop Moran', ADD.

[198] Moran to Ricards, 13 February 1871, PEDA/RP/PM/JR/318/PM/2.

[199] *Otago Daily Times*, 20 February 1871.

by Delphin Moreau. Local legend recalled Moreau somewhat unfortunately describing the new diocese's financial position to Moran as 'I am
tight, you are tight, we are all tight together.'[200] Although Dunedin
impressed him as a prosperous and 'beautiful little city', Moran was
otherwise appalled by what he found.[201] With no convent prepared, the
nuns had to be lodged in the parochial house, which forced Moran to
board with a prominent layman. There was, he told Ricards, 'Plenty of
up-hill work here.'[202]

Within days, he launched a coruscating public attack on his own flock,
telling them 'how sad, how deplorable is the state of religion here'. He had
been lied to: 'We had been led to believe that there was a good Church in
Dunedin, and eleven other Churches and Chapels in the country districts – a fair episcopal residence – Schools – a large house for a Convent
for religious ladies, – all free from debt; and finally, funds in hand to start
us in the great work before us.' He invited them to imagine his disappointment on discovering 'that there was scarcely even the remotest appearance of the truth' in these claims. Things were so bad that he was
contemplating reporting that the diocese had been erected on a false
prospectus 'and that there is no provision here for a Bishop or religious
institutions'. It was up to the laity to prove him wrong, and they could
begin by providing for the Dominicans.[203]

After fifteen years, Moran had grown weary of the hardships and
limitations of the Eastern Cape, and it is easy to understand his fury
when he found he had been deceived. His temper did not cool, however.
Writing to Forde ten days later, he reported that some of his priests were
planning to leave, while others would need to be expelled for drinking;
'I should not be surprised', he wrote, 'if in less than three months the
entire clergy of this diocese consisted of myself and Father Coleman.'
The Marists, he continued, had been a catastrophe. Focussed solely
'on the interests of their Order', they had satisfied themselves 'with
saying their prayers' and administering the sacraments. They had squan-
dered the money provided by the faithful, which they had considered
'exclusively their own'. They had built almost nothing. Had there been an
Irish secular priest in Dunedin, he continued, 'there would be today in
this city, a noble church fit to be a cathedral, a good presbytery, excellent
schools and a large convent'. Moreau had had an 'income such as few
Irish bishops enjoy', he raged, and 'yet this good man, vowed to poverty,

---

[200] Mary Catherine Goulter, *Sons of France: A Forgotten Influence on New Zealand history*,
2nd ed. (Wellington: Whitcombe and Tombs, 1958), 146.
[201] Moran to Forde, 20 February 1871, DDA/Australia.
[202] Moran to Ricards, 13 February 1871, PEDA/RP/PM/JR/318/PM/2.
[203] Moran to the Catholics of Dunedin, 3 March 1871, printed circular, ADD/MP.

leaves his generous Irish people without a chalice, a vestment, an altar stone, etc.'. He was 'obliged to start as it were in the wilderness'.[204]

By May, Moran had completed his visitation of the diocese and prepared a detailed report for Dublin. His purpose was unusually bluntly expressed: knowing Cullen's 'interest' in Dunedin and the 'responsible part' he was 'called upon to assume in the regulation of our affairs', Moran wanted to put the cardinal 'fully in possession of the state of things ecclesiastical here'. It was dire: the Marists had all been recalled to Wellington, one secular priest had gone back to Auckland against his wishes, and another was a drunk who would have to leave. Moran consequently had only four priests to provide for some 6,500 widely dispersed Catholics. 'As to churches, schools and Catholic Institutions generally', he complained, 'this Diocese is in a lamentable state.' It did not have a single church worthy of the name, and of its fifteen chapels only one was made from stone and all were 'small and very poorly furnished'. Many lacked basic liturgical furniture or even chalices. Two were in debt, one for the full £300 it had cost to build, loaned at 10 per cent. Clerical accommodation was even worse, where it existed at all. One priest lived in a 'shanty'. There were only two schools, and 'these are not as they ought to be'.[205]

Even worse was Moreau's conduct on leaving Dunedin. According to Moran, the 'Marist Father who is personally a correct moral man seems very determined to fill the purse of his society'. Moreau refused to sell a piece of ground Moran hoped to use for a new convent, despite being offered what he had originally paid for it. He insisted Moran also buy the Robin Hood Hotel for the nuns, which he refused as a 'worthless house' unsuitable to a cloistered community; Mother Gabriel called it 'just a shed'.[206] This showed 'the way the Marists treat the people who gave them means to buy this ground', he grumbled, and no secular priest would have behaved in this way.[207] Moran's rage was unbounded when he discovered that Moreau had taken 'every thing with him ... even the very chalice and altar stone'. 'After having received such large sums of money he left the people', Moran continued, 'without the means of having the adorable sacrifice.' 'He was a Marist and all the Marists acted in a similar manner.'[208]

Although Lyon had had hints of dispute as early as November 1871, they were startled when some months later the Propaganda peremptorily

[204] Moran to Forde, 13 March 1871, PICRA/FP.
[205] Moran to Cullen, 12 May 1871, DDA/Australia.
[206] Moran to Forde, 27 September 1871, PICRA/FP; quoted in McCarthy, 37.
[207] Moran to Forde, 3 August 1871, PICRA/FP.
[208] Moran to Forde, 29 August 1871, PICRA/FP.

demanded an explanation. Cullen had of course passed along the gist of
Moran's letters, and Moran had written to Rome himself. The charges
jeopardized the society's entire position in New Zealand, and they consequently mounted a spirited defence: Moreau and the other Marists had
worked hard, sacrificed much, and lived frugally; they had taken nothing
that did not belong to them and left much behind that did. Moran had left
Europe without taking precautions or talking to them and then 'complained bitterly' (*plaint amèrement*) that he had been deceived.[209] The
implication was clear: Moran was reckless, unreasonable, and intemperate.

The Marists neither forgot nor forgave, and in 1887 the question re-
emerged in a bitter correspondence between Moran and the Marist
Archbishop Francis Redwood of Wellington. The pretext was an article
in Moran's *New Zealand Tablet* that repeated the claim that the bishop had
found 'mere shanties' in Dunedin and 'had not a roof that you could claim
as the property of the church to shelter you'. A 'perplexed' Redwood drew
attention to various buildings valued cumulatively at some £6,000 and
demanded to know how that was 'consistent' with Moran's allegations.[210]
Moran's reply was uncompromising: the diocese's total estate was worth
at best £2,000, and most of that was the sole property of a layman who
was acting in trust. He reiterated that when he left the church after his
installation 'I stood in the yard houseless and homeless; and, I may add
landless.'[211] He also had Moreau's debts to pay. Redwood was not
impressed: St Joseph's was a splendid building, and he had contemporary
photographs to prove it; Moran had had a house but chose to give it to the
nuns; and he had nobody to blame but himself for being surprised by
the state of Dunedin. Moran was a liar, although he did not quite use the
word.[212] For his part, Moran reiterated his claims and came very close to
calling Redwood a liar.[213]

Both men had a point. On the one hand, Dunedin was indeed a mess
and Moran had undoubtedly been deceived. The Marists' claim that he
had not taken the proper precautions nor spoken to them was disingenuous: Moran had asked Barnabò about the state of Dunedin, Barnabò
advised him to consult Viard, and, as Viard was a Marist, he had reasonably concluded that he had in fact consulted the society. Moran was
also on strong ground in pointing to the paucity of ecclesiastical

[209] [?Favre] to Barnabò, 3 May 1872, NLNZ/MS/Papers/3566. Original in French. The
      signature is unfortunately illegible on this copy, but it was most likely from Julien Favre,
      the Marist superior.
[210] Redwood to Moran, 5 July 1887, ADD/MP.
[211] Moran to Redwood, 11 July 1887, ADD/MP.
[212] Redwood to Moran, 12 July 1887, ADD/MP.
[213] Moran to Redwood, 15, 25 July 1887, ADD/MP.

infrastructure. If some of his specific claims were exaggerated, they were in the main correct: the Marists had built very little. In his unpublished history of the diocese, Basil Howard attempted to minimize this by observing that they 'had not pressed heavily on their people'. He also noted that Moreau had purchased properties amounting to some £3,000 over nine years.[214] This would be convincing, except that Moreau apparently admitted that his total receipts had exceeded £11,000 over the same period.[215] If Moran was lying about this, and about his other allegations, he was lying not only to Rome and later Redwood but also to Forde and Cullen. The safe conclusion is that the Marists' had had the resources to build but had chosen not to.

On the other hand, Moran was somewhat unfair to Moreau and the other Marists, although he invariably admitted their personal probity and dedication. As Redwood pointed out in 1887, there would have been little point in erecting 'permanent and expensive buildings' among the unsettled mining population of central Otago.[216] Nor could they fairly be held responsible for Viard misleading Moran in Rome. The underlying problem was one of differing priorities. As N. P. Vaney (himself a Marist) pointed out, 'in the eyes of Irish clerics, sound finance, good organization and completed church buildings were considered the indispensable basis for a strong and living parish'.[217] By contrast, the Marists saw themselves as itinerant pastors with a special mission to the Māori. Moran was undoubtedly correct that an Irish secular priest would have built more heavily and more enthusiastically challenged perceived injustices, particularly educational; but that was not the Marists' purpose or intent. As A. H. McLintock observed, Moreau's 'ministrations did little to disturb the provincial calm'.[218] His departure from Dunedin was publicly lamented only by local Protestants.[219]

Moran extended Moreau's failure to the Marists as a body. He took the view that the country could properly support only two bishops, one for each island. 'Were such an arrangement made', he told Cullen, it would be possible to build the colleges, convents, and schools 'which are absolutely necessary' but unforthcoming 'under the present arrangements'. The Marists should lose Wellington and 'be placed in the normal state of a religious community'. This was not the same as expulsion: they did

---

[214] Basil Howard, 'Church in Otago', undated, unpublished work, Marist Archives Wellington [MAW], 65.
[215] Moran to Forde, 3 August 1871, PICRA/FP.
[216] Redwood to Moran, 12 July 1887, ADD/MP.   [217] Vaney, 160.
[218] A. H. McLintock, *The History of Otago* (Dunedin: Otago Centennial Historical Publications, 1949), 518.
[219] Vaney, 118.

good work, 'deserve well of all New Zealand', and could live and minister in small communities under the bishops' watchful eyes. The main thing was that the 'permanent interests of the Church in the Dioceses should not be held subordinate to the interests of the Order'.[220] His solution to 'our religious and educational destitution' was predictable: Rome, he told Forde, ought 'to direct the Bishops to hold a Synod'.[221]

Moran was undeniably right about one thing: Wellington *was* drifting. Although Viard brought three Marists home with him from Europe, and promptly recalled those posted in the south, he had nothing like enough priests. Everything was crumbling: priests were overworked, missions unfilled, and the condition of the schools was 'pitiful'. In answer to his pleas for help, Lyon apparently told him to wait until the Irish novitiate could supply his needs.[222] Worse, Jeremiah O'Reily had recruited two Irish secular priests only for them to be rejected by the society. Even some of the local Marists were blaming Viard for that.[223] O'Reily himself changed sides and privately denounced Viard to Cullen for his 'erroneous' understanding of the Vatican Council.[224] He also made a point of inviting Moran up to Wellington to give a typically combative lecture on education.[225] The ailing Viard did not help himself by appointing an admitted 'muddler' as procurator of the Marists in New Zealand. When challenged, his explanation was simple: 'I do not like changes.'[226]

Cardinal Barnabò greeted the news of Viard's death in June 1872 coldly, observing that, while he hoped Viard had gone to heaven, he had freed the Propaganda from '*un grande imbarazzo*'. A delighted Kirby was confident that Rome would now do whatever Croke and Moran suggested, and Moran was immediately appointed to administer Wellington, apparently by Pius IX personally.[227] 'We will thus', Kirby gloated, 'know the true state of things there, and Dr Moran has in the mean time full powers to do whatever he deems necessary or useful there for the good of religion.'[228] The only limitation was that he lacked any direct authority over the Marists, although Forde hoped he would have 'influence enough'.[229]

The Marists were appalled. According to Moran, some 'went to the expense of telegraphing Rome' in a desperate effort to block his

[220] Moran to Cullen, 12 August 1871, DDA/Australia.
[221] Moran to Forde, 29 August 1871, DDA/Australia.   [222] Keys, *Viard*, 223.
[223] Ibid., 225.   [224] O'Reily to Cullen, 16 May 1871, DDA/Australia.
[225] *Wellington Independent*, 19 September 1871.   [226] Quoted in Keys, *Viard*, 225–6.
[227] Kirby to Murray, 'La Madonna della Neve' [5 August] 1872, MNDA/MP/A.3.14; Forde to Moran, 22 August 1872, ADD/MP.
[228] Kirby to Murray, 8 August 1872, MNDA/MP/A.3.15.
[229] Forde to Moran, 22 August 1872, ADD/MP.

appointment.[230] That was never going to work, and, within weeks of receiving his briefs, Moran set out for Wellington. As with Croke in Auckland, his first task was to undertake a systematic inventory of the diocese. In a typically energetic display, Moran completed his tour in three phases between December 1872 and April 1873. Each stop was modelled on the Vincentian parish missions he knew so well: several days of preaching, lectures, confessions, and liturgical celebrations. The condition of the diocese shocked him: there were not enough priests, not enough schools, and not enough spiritual instruction – almost everywhere he refused candidates for confirmation because they were 'so imperfectly instructed in the rudiments of the Christian faith'.[231]

The Marists' response was to deflect all blame to Viard. As a result, Moran's belief that a 'large number of the Marists are glad of my appointment' was less fantastical than it first appears; if they could not stop their new administrator, they had every interest in courting him. This approach was made crystal clear by the long-serving Jean Forest, a founder member of the society who had been based in New Zealand since 1842. Writing to Moran in early January 1873, Forest frankly admitted the many flaws he would find. Some were the result of a lack of resources and others could be attributed to clerical failings, but the 'fundamental cause of *many many miseries* in this diocese is the want of a proper head'.

For twenty-five years, he continued, the Marists had been 'like good soldiers but without a general or captain'. Viard was undoubtedly pious, but piety was not enough; he had not been 'a fit person' for the job. Forest reminded Moran that the society had had no part in Viard's appointment and had never thought him suitable. They had been 'driven' from Auckland by Pompallier, forced to begin again in Wellington under the incompetent Viard, and now 'our poor Society' was getting the blame 'for every neglect'. Forest welcomed the visitation, telling Moran that by 'knowing the real cause of our past and present miseries you may be able to appreciate the better the work that has been done in this diocese by priests alone, the priests left to themselves, and also in order that during your visits and in your report you may do justice to our poor priests and Society'.[232]

This was clever. Moran admired the piety and self-sacrifice of the Marist priests; he just thought they were incompetent administrators. The society also knew that the Irishman was an enthusiast for strong episcopal authority and blaming Viard for failing to provide it allowed them to evade corporate responsibility. Moran would never support the

---

[230] Moran to Forde, 15 November 1872, DDA/Australia.
[231] Quoted in O'Meeghan, *Steadfast*, 95–6.
[232] Forest to Moran, 1 January 1873, WAA. Emphasis in original.

continuation of what he called 'dual government' in Wellington, but he might not condemn the society so systematically as to make that result impossible. It worked: although Moran strove to prevent a Marist succession, he praised the missionaries themselves. As a delighted Marist observed to Forest in late 1873, Moran had made '*un grand eloge de nos missionaires*' to Rome.[233]

The Marists also had a plan. Since late 1869, they had intended that Francis William Redwood should be the next bishop of Wellington. Born in England but raised in New Zealand, Redwood had entered the Marists in 1854 and studied at their novitiate in France. He was then posted to Ireland, helping to establish the novitiate at Dundalk and then the society's Catholic University School in Dublin. In 1871, he drafted the address presented to Cullen on the school's prize day, singling out for praise his 'lifelong exertions to procure for all the Irish youth the blessings of a truly liberal and Catholic education'.[234] Redwood was the perfect candidate: English-speaking, nearly a native New Zealander, and well-regarded in Ireland. He was also every bit a Marist: as a child his vocation had been nurtured by the French priests, and as an adult he continued to keep his retreat notes and private diaries in French. There was only one problem: in 1869, he was only thirty years old and the canonical minimum age for a bishop was thirty-five.

This was not an insuperable bar – Moran was sent to the Cape at thirty-three – but it was generally observed. This is why the Marists consistently sought to delay any changes in Wellington. Moran knew this, reporting within months of his arrival that the Marists 'intend to propose one of their congregation' for Wellington on the death or resignation of Viard.[235] He 'vehemently' objected to this, commenting a bit later that the 'perpetuation of the state of things I condemn and despair is entirely owing to the Marists who are postponing the regulation of the ecclesiastical affairs of the Diocese of Wellington until they have a fit person prepared to recommend for that see'.[236] In early 1873, he complained that 'the Marists [are] still bent on having Mr Redwood appointed'.[237]

Yet there could be no decision until Moran's visitation had been completed. He took a predictable line: the Marists were good men, but it was unsustainable that twenty-five of Wellington's twenty-seven priests were French. At least fifteen English-speakers were needed urgently, or 'Catholicity will soon be but a name in very many places'. They should, if

[233] Poupinel to Forest, 25 December 1873, MAW/DNM 217.
[234] See Francis Redwood papers [RP], WAA/Box 211.
[235] Moran to Forde, 3 August 1871, PICRA/FP.
[236] Moran to Forde, 27 September 1871, PICRA/FP.
[237] Moran to Forde, 10 January 1873, DDA/Australia.

possible, be from Ireland, as the Irish 'sigh and petition for priests from their own dear land'. Moran thought it unlikely that the Marists could supply this number, and, even if they could, the church needed to encourage what he called an 'indigenous priesthood'. 'This could hardly be done', he wrote, 'if all the priests belong to a religious order or congregation.' Not all vocations would be 'for the Marist family', and there was a 'great danger of the interests of the order being placed before those of the diocese'.[238]

Some of this was uncontested. The Marists accepted that both bishop and clergy should be native English-speakers and if possible Irish, which is why they had opened their novitiate in Dundalk and chosen Redwood for Wellington. Moran's point about the inadvisability of entrusting a diocese to a religious community was dogma among the Cullenites but less so beyond their ranks. An order could provide clergy for missions that were otherwise difficult to staff, whereas the Irish bishops in New Zealand and elsewhere had ongoing problems with the recruitment of suitable priests. As Moran himself complained, 'It would appear as if all the drunken priests of Ireland, Australia and the United States had conspired to make a descent like harpies on the unfortunate Irish Catholics here'.[239] And, by blaming Viard, the Marists had a reasonable explanation for the undeniably poor condition of Wellington. They may also have concentrated minds by threatening to withdraw completely if a secular bishop was appointed.[240] Cumulatively, these amounted to a plausible case for retaining control.

For many years, that would not have mattered: Cullen's influence at the Propaganda would have ensured that Moran's advice was followed. With Cardinal Barnabò fading, however, things were different; we have already seen the effects in Newfoundland, Canada, and Australia, as well as Auckland. The early 1873 warning to Cullen to offer his advice on episcopal appointments only indirectly (see Chapter 6) was merely a symptom of this changing reality.[241] Redwood meanwhile waited in Lyon, telling a fellow Marist in September 1873 that 'I have had no news about my destiny in New Zealand for the last month.' He was suspicious that Moran was 'delaying to send in his report as long as possible, and that *for a purpose*'.[242] In fact, delay only aided the Marists; each passing month saw Barnabò weaken and Redwood creep ever closer to his thirty-fifth birthday. By the end of 1873, they were confident of success. Reporting

---

[238] Moran to Kirby, 6 April 1873, quoted in Sweetman, 'Antipodes', 395. This letter amounts to Moran's briefing notes on his formal report.
[239] Moran to Forde, 13 March 1871, PICRA/FP.   [240] Sweetman, 'Antipodes', 396.
[241] Kirby to Cullen, 'Epiphany' [6 January] 1873, DDA/CP/45/1/I/116/1.
[242] Redwood to Grimes, 9 September 1873, MAW/HD7/149–150. Emphasis in original.

on a congregation scheduled for early in the new year, one relieved Marist reported that '*enfin cette affaire va se terminer*'.[243] Redwood was duly appointed in January, Croke left Auckland that same month, and Barnabò finally died in February. Almost as importantly, the boundaries of Wellington were left unchanged. As Rory Sweetman has suggested, '1874 was the decisive turning point in New Zealand Catholic history'.[244]

The Marists had won a bitterly contested bureaucratic battle against Cullen's Irish. There has been a tendency in New Zealand to minimize this fact: writing in 1993, for example, Sweetman identified a tradition of portraying the Marists as 'holy innocents, unsoiled by grubby ecclesiastical politicking'.[245] This was nonsense, but it did not stop Michael O'Meeghan from dismissing as 'facile' any idea of a power struggle between French and Irish nor Jessie Munro from echoing him.[246] This confusion is an artefact of the late and still imperfect professionalization of New Zealand Catholic history; for many years, the late Hugh Laracy was the sole academic historian publishing on the subject, and then only intermittently. The situation was further complicated by the fact that the most complete Catholic archive in New Zealand is that of the Society of Mary. It is only more recently, with the work of Sweetman, Ciara Breathnach, Seán Brosnahan, and Lyndon Fraser, that a more nuanced portrait has emerged.

Although the Marists had won, their victory heralded significant changes for the society. Even before Redwood was appointed, Suzanne Aubert was fretting about the future of the French in New Zealand. Moran, she told a friend, was 'a pureblood Irishman' who had 'reached an agreement' with the society that everything 'was to become Irish'; no more French priests or nuns would be sent out, and the existing ones would be sent home – 'Apparently we're a nuisance and a plague.' 'Only the Irish', she continued, 'can renew the face of the Earth. They're the noble and zealous battalion who've sallied forth from the Isle of Saints and nothing will halt them in their path – they'll convert the whole world, provided they meet none but the sons of Erin.'[247]

Aubert's instincts were correct. The price of Marist survival was the greening of the society. This began with Redwood himself: he chose to be consecrated on St Patrick's Day, named the Marists' first college after

---

[243] Poupinel to Forest, 25 December 1873, MAW/DNM/217.
[244] Sweetman, 'Antipodes', 400.
[245] Rory Sweetman, Review of Patrick O'Farrell, *Vanished Kingdoms: Irish in Australia and New Zealand, a personal excursion*, in *The New Zealand Journal of History*, vol. 27, no. 1 (1993), 107–8.
[246] O'Meeghan, *Steadfast*, 102; Munro, *AC*, 90.
[247] Aubert to Outhwaite, 6 July 1873, *AC*, 86–7.

Ireland's patron, and invited Cardinal Moran to open it. Like Vaughan in Sydney, he went out of his way to demonstrate his Irish sympathies.[248] He encouraged the Sisters of Mercy, for example, and asked Cullen for help finding more in Ireland.[249] As he explained in 1881 to a priest who had asked if he should permit a meeting in support of the Irish Land League, discountenancing such an event would be both 'against my own deepest convictions' and 'too harsh an opposition to the vast majority of my flock'.[250] On a visit to Ireland, he joined the Land League himself and was an enthusiastic supporter of Home Rule and later Sinn Féin, organizing a collection for the party at the height of the Irish War of Independence.[251]

Much of this was sincere: Redwood had spent nearly a decade in Ireland and had imbibed its politics. Yet it was also tactical. When his fellow English Marist John Joseph Grimes was appointed the first bishop of Christchurch in 1886, Redwood advised him on how to avoid appearing 'anti-Hibernian'. The key was to say 'nothing against the Irish' but instead follow the lead of Cardinal Manning 'and always have some kind things to say in their favour, and if possible, express your sympathy with them in their exertions to obtain Home Rule'.[252] The Irish were not unaware of this strategy: as 'Paddy' wrote in the *New Zealand Tablet* in 1887, 'if his Grace is not Irish he is trying to be next thing to it'. Even so, 'the natural growth is always better than the manufactured article, and the native born Irish priest is preferable to the trained one'.[253] Although neither Redwood nor Grimes ever defused Irish demands for Irish bishops, they did over time manage to minimize tensions.

The Marists, meanwhile, continued to supply the mission from their now overflowing Irish novitiate, and, although the French priests remained, their influence was inexorably diluted. The result was an ecclesiastical culture that was neither Irish nor French but distinctively Marist. It was this that made possible N. P. Vaney's observation that, despite having Irish grandparents and graduating from St Patrick's College, Wellington, he was unable to identify any 'echo of Irish influence' in his own childhood or education; but he was also unable to 'detect any trace of French influence in either my training or my colleagues' when he joined the Marists.[254]

---

[248] Rory Sweetman, 'Introduction', in Felice Vaggioli, *A Deserter's Adventures: The Autobiography of Dom Felice Vaggioli*, translated by John Crockett (Dunedin: Otago University Press, 2001), xviii.
[249] Redwood to Cullen, 8 September 1876, DDA/Australia.
[250] Redwood to Edward Guiney, 22 July 1881, MAW.
[251] Davis, *Irish Issues*, 137, 201.
[252] Redwood to Grimes, 18 July 1887, quoted in Sweetman, 'Vaggioli', xviii–xix.
[253] *NZT*, 1 July 1887.   [254] Vaney, vi.

The comparison with Auckland is instructive. It had both the largest absolute number of Irish Catholics and one of the highest proportions of Irish Catholics in its population, yet it played little part in the Irish-inflected controversies that were so prevalent in pre-war New Zealand; as late as 1922, for example, Auckland's Catholics were still widely believed to be only lukewarm Irish patriots.[255] This can be attributed to the fact that between 1874 and 1929 its bishops were a Dutch Jesuit, successive English Benedictines, and (from 1910) an imperially minded Irishman. In 1883, for example, John Luck refused to countenance the Auckland leg of John and William Redmond's Australasian fundraising tour, although he was careful to quote Cardinal Cullen's views on Fenianism in justification.[256] He also made a point of stating publicly that 'the details of English rule in Ireland made him feel ashamed of his country'.[257] This qualification seems to have passed unnoticed, as the *Otago Daily Times* unhelpfully praised Luck as 'an Englishman first, a Catholic second'.[258] The Irish remembered: five years later, an anonymous letter appeared in a New York newspaper complaining that Luck not only had 'opposed the Redmonds' but had been 'heard lamenting the wickedness of Irish priests conniving in Ireland at murder and crime!'[259] In 1886, Cardinal Moran told Rome that Luck had lost the confidence of his wholly Irish flock.[260] Redwood also faced Irish attacks (especially in 1886), but his approach was significantly better at deflecting them.

This was particularly evident in those parts of the South Island that Wellington successfully retained in 1874. The turbulent Irish of the west coast had disrupted and ultimately discredited Viard's rule, and, despite the fading of the gold rush, they had not entirely gone away. Further east, there had always been Catholics in Christchurch and the fertile Canterbury plains, despite the area's origins as an Anglican settlement. Frederick Weld, for example, had been a favourite of the Anglo-Irish gentry who founded and then dominated Christchurch, but the Catholicism of Weld and his friends was offset by their social status and English nationality. Perhaps with his co-religionists in mind, Weld had himself fretted about what would happen when Christchurch's founding generation was replaced by what he called 'an inferior race'.[261]

---

[255] Ibid., 98; see Rory Sweetman, *Bishop in the Dock: The Sedition Trial of James Liston* (Auckland: Auckland University Press, 1997), 8.

[256] Davis, *Irish Issues*, 102.   [257] *NZT*, 23 March 1883.

[258] *Otago Daily Times*, 24 March 1883.

[259] An unsigned letter dated Sawyus Bay, Pt. Chalmers, Otago, New Zealand, *New York Tablet*, 18 September 1887. It is preserved in Redwood's papers in Wellington.

[260] Ayres, 151–2.

[261] Quoted in Edmund Bohan, *'Blest Madman': FitzGerald of Canterbury* (Christchurch: Canterbury University Press, 1998), 87–8.

Before 1860, there was no permanent church and no resident priest in Canterbury and only a handful of Irish Catholics; a mere fifteen were present when the first church was dedicated.[262] Dependent on Wellington, the clergy was largely French and Marist. According to Lyndon Fraser, there was little sense of a collective Irish identity – people were busy with their own concerns and faced little in the way of anti-Catholic prejudice. This changed in the early 1870s as the arrival of Irish priests coincided with the emergence of a substantial Catholic middle class, especially in Christchurch.[263]

Patrick Moran's 1873 tour of the region electrified the Irish population: at Ahaura in Nelson, his carriage joined children, congregation, and 'upwards of one hundred horseman' in processing through an arch of evergreens into the local school; the Arnold district met him with miners carrying green boughs and a triumphal arch inscribed 'Cead Mille Failthe'; Reefton welcomed his visit as lifting the 'dark chain of silence' that had hung over the west coast for many years; and the laity of Christchurch, whose 'members have been ever on the increase', were delighted to finally see a bishop in their town. It would have escaped no one's notice that he was hosted in Christchurch by Fathers Boibieux, Ecuyer, and Chareyre and in the Arnold district by Fathers Pertius and Belliard.[264]

For the Irish of Canterbury and the west coast, Moran was seen as the natural recipient of lay complaints about the Marists: they were too French; they were anti-Irish; they did not encourage lay organizations; they did not build or sustain adequate schools. When Redwood sought to build a new episcopal residence in Wellington, for example, Christchurch gave nothing.[265] For their part, the rapidly increasing Irish secular clergy sought to 'negate' the Marists by what Fraser called 'a more independent, combative stance to New Zealand Catholicism, asserting the primacy of Hibernian interests in matters of church policy'.[266]

By the early 1880s, it was obvious that a new diocese was needed on the South Island. Moran unsurprisingly thought the new bishop should be Irish and secular, while the Marists preferred the Englishman John Joseph Grimes. In 1885, Redwood thought that he had secured Grimes' appointment during a visit to Rome; but the news reached New Zealand before the matter could be finalized, prompting some twenty Irish secular priests to get up a petition denouncing the Marists and requesting a secular bishop for Christchurch. Redwood was sure that they were 'abetted' by

---

[262] A. G. Butchers, *A Centennial History of Education in Canterbury* (Christchurch: Centennial Committee of the Canterbury Education Board, [1950]), 86.
[263] Fraser, 'Community', 94.
[264] *Grey River Argus*, 21, 20, 24 February 1873; *The Press*, 1 February 1873.
[265] Fraser, 'Community', 125.   [266] Ibid., 121–2.

Moran. The Marists were now the victims of bad timing: the other Patrick Moran was in Rome to collect his red hat. Redwood was unsure whether Moran brought the priests' petition with him from Sydney or received it while in Rome, but either way 'he took it up warmly and got all negotiations broken off' until the first council of the Australasian church could be held later that year.[267]

This was a disaster for the Marists: the Cullenites were an overwhelming majority in the combined hierarchies. The erection of Christchurch was unanimously approved, and by a smaller margin it was stripped from the Marists, while Dunedin was recommended as the metropolitan see of a new ecclesiastical province.[268] Redwood was infuriated when the old stories of Marist incompetence were retold by one Moran and taken up by the other as a justification for these decisions. As soon as the news leaked, the Christchurch Irish organized an address calling for an Irish bishop and lamenting the fate of Irish Catholics 'cast on foreign lands without a shepherd of their own race'.[269] The Marists got up a counter-petition.[270] While Rome dithered, the newspapers reported every rumour, including Moran's nomination of J. D. Ricards of Grahamstown. Even Moran was mortified by the subsequent embarrassment.[271]

The final result stunned the Irish: Redwood would be New Zealand's first archbishop and Grimes the first bishop of Christchurch. It was a resounding endorsement of the Marists. Moran reacted with ill-concealed pique: he refused to invest Redwood with the archbishop's pallium and declined to attend or otherwise mark Grimes' arrival in Christchurch.[272] His *New Zealand Tablet* at first tried to spin the announcements as a triumph for the 'Irish Catholic element' who had built the church to the point it needed an archbishop; its correspondents saw an English takeover and an insult to Irish nationality.[273] The suspicion was that New Zealand had fallen victim to the same aristocratic lobby that had meddled in the recent appointment to Dublin, and this thesis was spelled out in a *Tablet* leader almost certainly written by Moran.[274]

---

[267] Redwood to Grimes, 29 January 1886, quoted in O'Meeghan, *Steadfast*, 129. This is Redwood's retrospective account to Grimes of what had gone wrong.

[268] O'Meeghan, *Steadfast*, 129.   [269] See Fraser, 'Community', 121.

[270] O'Meeghan, *Steadfast*, 130.

[271] Moran to Ricards, 6 September 1886, PEDA/RP/PM/JR/506/PM/2.

[272] Hugh Laracy, 'Bishop Moran: Irish politics and Catholicism in New Zealand', *The Journal of Religious History*, vol. 6, no. 1 (June 1970), 62–76, at 74.

[273] *NZT*, 27 May, 17 June 1887.

[274] Laracy, 'Bishop Patrick Moran', 71–2; the anonymous correspondent of the *New York Tablet* cited above claimed that it was an 'open secret' that the leader was written by Moran, and the style is certainly consistent with his.

'We have', it began, 'certain information that the leaders of the English Catholic Tories have exerted their influence in Rome in a way adverse to Irish ecclesiastics in this country.' They had convinced the Propaganda 'that only Englishmen, or Irishmen acting as Englishmen, were fit to rule over dioceses comprised almost exclusively of Irish Catholics'. Why had they involved themselves in the affairs of distant New Zealand? Because, as supporters of 'coercion for Ireland', they wished to avoid the appointment anywhere in the world of Home Rulers or 'patriots'; and, if they succeeded in New Zealand, they might then be able to 'secure the appointment of English priests and prelates to important Irish sees'. 'Is it not enough', the *Tablet* concluded, 'that our people have been driven from the homes of their fathers by these people and their cruel legislation, but is it to be also tolerated that they should be permitted to pursue us to the end of the earth in their effort to cast reproach on us and to continue to press the heel of tyranny and slander on our necks?'[275] Others were even blunter: the anonymous correspondent of the *New York Tablet* denounced the 'English Cawtholics' [*sic*] who sought to 'place English ecclesiastics in the chief Irish Sees throughout the British Empire, and through such men to denationalize the Irish people and so to break down their opposition to landlordism and Toryism!' Although it was too late for New Zealand, he urged the 'Irish press in Ireland, in Australia, and in America' to warn their people of the danger, inform Rome, and 'smash the conspiracy'.[276]

This was paranoid but not entirely absurd. Despite its Catholic population being overwhelmingly Irish, the recommendations of the Australasian council had been ignored and New Zealand now had three English bishops in a hierarchy of four, including the newly created archbishop; but it painted with too broad a brush. Redwood and Grimes were indeed Englishmen but they were Marists first. Both had spent substantial time in Ireland, and Redwood in particular pursued a determinedly pro-Irish policy. Luck's hostility to Irish nationalism gave some credence to the charge of 'denationalizing' and, indeed, it had for a time that effect in Auckland. Yet this seems to have been a personal preference and hard to construe as part of a conspiracy or even a considered policy. The allegation of English manipulation in Rome is more plausible, albeit ironic: there is no doubt that after Cullen's death Henry Edward Manning became increasingly influential in the Propaganda; he was behind Steins' appointment in Auckland, for example, and it is likely that Redwood sought his help in 1886. Ultimately, though, the elevation of

---

[275] *NZT*, 22 July 1887.   [276] *New York Tablet*, 18 September 1887.

Wellington (which was after all the capital) and Grimes' appointment in Christchurch are better understood as Marist victories not English ones. According to Marist legend, Cardinal Moran reacted to the news by exclaiming 'The Marists must be very powerful at Rome.'[277]

Grimes understood the threat of Irish disappointment, and he did his best to follow Redwood's advice. On his first St Patrick's Day, for example, he presided in a hall festooned with Irish flags and emblems. The toasts were to the pope, the queen, the governor, St Patrick himself, William Gladstone 'and his British Home Rule Sympathisers', and finally Charles Stewart Parnell.[278] This enthusiasm was not entirely disinterested: the following year, his Irish Marist vicar general organized a *'splendoribus'* feast to forestall a competing event hosted by the Hibernian Society.[279] As late as 1899, a French (but not Marist) priest complained that his newly appointed curate had come 'here to criticize me, ridicule me, insult me, and dare call me a liar, a liar that he is, and I have to accept this all like a lamb just because he is Irish!' Grimes, however, offered no support and the Frenchman returned to Europe.[280]

Grimes and his successors also pursued policies on mixed marriages and education that were above even Moran's reproach. In 1892, for example, one of the remaining French Marists sought advice about what to do with some sixteen families who persisted in sending their children to the public schools. Grimes' vicar general was prepared to make an exception for one small child who would have to walk six miles to the Catholic school but only on condition it was not considered a precedent. The priest should 'act peremptorily' with the rest so as to 'unflinchingly' stamp out any sign of resistance to parochial authority and any hint of cooperation with the public schools.[281] Partly as a result, by 1892 there were some 3,000 students in Christchurch's Catholic schools and 80 teachers, and some £150,000 had been spent on Catholic education in the region since 1875. By 1910, there were 16,700 children in the diocese's schools and it was ambitiously claimed that the total expense had amounted to nearly five million pounds over thirty-seven years.[282] Mixed marriages too were exceedingly rare. As in Wellington, Christchurch under the Marists conformed as nearly as possible to the Cullenite vision.

---

[277] Sauzeau to Hervier, 14 June 1887, quoted in Laracy, 'Bishop Patrick Moran', 75.
[278] *Press*, 21 March 1888.
[279] Stephen Cummings to Grimes, 4 March 1889, CHDA/GP/Clergy.
[280] Quoted in Vaney, 152.   [281] Cummings to Aubrey, 7 March 1891, CHDA/Box 3a.
[282] MS memorandum relating the Catholic Schools in New Zealand for 1892, CHDA/Box 3a. The information for 1910 was appended to this document.

That is not to say that there were not differences with the undiluted Hiberno-Romanism further south. This is particularly true of the west coast, which remained a Marist (and French) stronghold for much longer than almost anywhere else in New Zealand – of the fifty-four priests who served there between 1870 and 1910, twenty were French and thirty-four Irish.[283] Many of both were Marists, and Neil Vaney and Lyndon Fraser have both noted the enduring popularity of individual French Marists, including with the Irish, while Patrick O'Farrell recalled how many in the Irish population were sorry to see them replaced by heavy-handed Irish secular clergy.[284] This seems to have resulted in what Fraser called a 'relative harmony' in the community, something that is reflected both in O'Farrell's childhood memories of Greymouth and in the fiction of Maurice Gee.[285] This was possible not only because of the enduring Marist influence – and the absence of an Hiberno-Roman bishop before 1915 – but also because the post-gold west coast towns were largely small, struggling, and 'economically homogeneous' communities in which the Labour Party, at least in Patrick O'Farrell's memory, seems to have commanded greater loyalty than the several churches.[286]

Yet, even on the west coast, the Marist influence steadily declined, although it never vanished entirely. Their French priests were inexorably replaced with Irishmen or Irish-descended New Zealanders. More and more All Hallows priests arrived to torment the genteel. Catholic education meanwhile was largely in the hands of the Sisters of Mercy, many of whom came directly from Ireland. At least twenty-one were sent from the convent at Ennis between 1877 and 1921, for example.[287] Other women came from the unimpeachably Cullenite St Brigid's Missionary College, including James Joyce's sister Margaret and three companions who travelled from there to Greymouth in 1909. As Sister Mary Gertrude, she taught music in various South Island schools until shortly before her death in 1964.[288] On the west coast, the church greened just as surely as in the rest of New Zealand, just more slowly and, it seems, more peaceably.

At all events, the failures of 1874 and 1886 had left Patrick Moran the only true Hiberno-Roman in the country. Moran's fusion of Irish ethnicity and Catholic faith was total and the means of securing both was the provision of an authentically Catholic education. Until 1876, education

---

[283] Vaney, 158.

[284] Vaney; Fraser, *Castles of Gold*, 118; Patrick O'Farrell, *Vanished Kingdoms: Irish in Australia and New Zealand, a Personal Excursion* (Kensington: New South Wales University Press, 1990), 154–5.

[285] Fraser, *Castles of Gold*, 122.   [286] Quoted in Ibid., 122–3.   [287] Vaney, 104.

[288] See Barr and Luminiello.

in New Zealand was a provincial responsibility, and responsiveness to Catholic concerns varied widely, from liberal Nelson's state-funded 'separated schools' (in practice, all Catholic) to 'militantly secular' Wellington.[289] In Otago, as John Mackey noted, 'the Presbyterians determinedly resisted all efforts to loosen their hold upon the system'.[290] By the time Moran arrived, this control had become less explicit – although Bible reading remained required – but no less real.

Moran issued his inevitable ban on the provincial schools in April 1871, not long after arriving in New Zealand.[291] In Otago, he explained, the 'teachers were Presbyterian, the system was Presbyterian, the books were Presbyterian, and the whole temper of the school was against' Catholics.[292] This led unfailingly to 'indifferentism and infidelity'.[293] Moran soon boasted to Dublin that he had initiated a 'lively warfare on the question of Education', and had 'succeeded in withdrawing almost all our children from the government schools'.[294] In 1873, he reminded the Catholics of Dunedin and Wellington (where he was now the administrator) that they could not 'with safe consciences, permit your children to frequent the schools' of Otago, Canterbury, or Wellington as they were 'directly hostile to our religion'. Their educational ordinances amounted to a virtual repeal of the Emancipation Act and a 're-enactment of some of the provisions of the odious, impolitic, and cruel penal code'.[295]

The abolition of New Zealand's provinces in 1876 made education a national issue, and the following year the Irish Protestant C. C. Bowen introduced an effectively secular bill that made primary education compulsory while denying state aid to private schools.[296] The only concessions to religious sensibilities were mandated Bible readings (soon dropped) and the recitation of the Lord's Prayer at the beginning of the school day. No Catholic bishop could accept this, but Moran and Redwood had suggestively different responses. The Marist Redwood appealed to his opponents on their own terms, tempered his rhetoric, stressed the injustice of double taxation, and insisted on the philosophical point that secular and religious knowledge could not be separated. The

---

[289] John Mackey, *The Making of a State Education System: The Passing of the New Zealand Education Act, 1877* (London: Geoffrey Chapman, 1967), 99.

[290] Ibid., 118.

[291] It was later modified to exempt those living more than three miles from a Catholic school. See Hugh Laracy, 'Paranoid popery: Bishop Moran and Catholic education in New Zealand', *New Zealand Journal of History*, vol. 10, no. 1 (1976), 51–62, at 52.

[292] *Evening Star*, 20 April 1871.   [293] *Otago Witness*, 27 May 1871.

[294] Moran to Forde, 3 May 1871, PICRA/FP.

[295] 1873 Lenten Pastoral to the diocese of Wellington, annotated copy in the NLNZ, Richmond Family Papers, MS4298(63).

[296] Davis, *Irish Issues*, 76.

Hiberno-Roman Moran raged that the bill was designed to force Catholics 'to forswear their religion, abandon their faith, and apostatize'. It was a return to Ireland's penal laws, as bad as anything in contemporary Germany or Russia, and a 'more atrocious and tyrannical measure was never conceived in the mind of man'. If it passed, Catholics would be obliged either to withdraw at least two miles from the nearest state school (the most a student was obliged to travel) 'or to flee from the Colony as an accursed spot, blasted by the tyranny of a persecuting Government and Legislature'.[297]

Moran's rhetoric seemed unhinged to many contemporaries (and most historians), but it served a purpose. The compulsory element of the Education Act meant that he had to almost instantly create a comprehensive network of schools. If he did not, Catholic parents would have no choice but to send their children to the state schools – he knew they would not retreat to the hills or leave the country. Moran saw this as an existential threat to the church: he needed to prevent participation in the state system and secure the necessary funds for a Catholic alternative, and the angrier his people were the more likely this was to happen. Furthermore, as Richard Davis noted, 'appeals to ancient memories and suggestions of forthcoming anti-Catholic bigotry were usually effective in arousing the fighting spirit of an Irish community'.[298]

This had other benefits. Opposing the Education Act was necessarily political, and Moran was 'a born politician'.[299] As a child, he had reputedly entertained visitors by reciting Daniel O'Connell's speeches.[300] Indeed, Moran's interest in politics was extreme even among Hiberno-Romans, who, like Cullen himself, tended to limit their overt political activism to what they took to be church prerogatives such as education. (Cardinal Moran was another conspicuous exception.) Moran, however, was suspicious of state power in almost any guise and in southern Africa had involved himself in electoral politics on a wide range of issues. In Dunedin, he expressed opinions on subjects ranging from sweated labour to female suffrage, telling his flock that the latter could only be supported by 'unlovely loud-voiced' women.[301] A festering sore such as education gifted him a central role in the political life of New Zealand.

Yet this did not simply gratify Moran's own private interests. In New Zealand, as elsewhere, so long as Catholics believed themselves to be persecuted, religious identity would remain paramount in public life. Moran encouraged this, regularly urging his flock to vote as 'one man'

---

[297] *Otago Daily Times*, 13 August 1877.   [298] Davis, *Irish Issues*, 78.   [299] Wilmot, 85.
[300] Laracy, 'Bishop Patrick Moran', 11.
[301] See Stenhouse, 'Building "God's own country"', 358.

on educational issues.[302] Such intransigent political Catholicism triggered an atavistic response in both Protestants and secularists, hardened their resolve, prompted intemperate debate, and increased sectarian tensions. This in turn exacerbated Catholic feelings of persecution. For Moran, this was a virtuous circle: he cared little that many lay Catholics and some Protestants (including his old Cape sparring partner Sir George Grey) sought and continued to seek compromise. He did not want to make the system safe for Catholics but to destroy it entirely. The state, he told a parliamentary select committee in 1883, 'has no business being a schoolmaster'.[303] Moran wanted to keep Dunedin's Catholics spatially, socially, sexually, and politically separate from Protestants. Compulsory secular education was the perfect mechanism to achieve this. He just needed to keep fanning the flames. He needed a newspaper.

Moran understood the power of the press. In the Eastern Cape, he had used *The Colonist* to attack mixed education in uncompromising terms until financial exigency had forced him to sell it. In Dunedin, he established the *New Zealand Tablet* in 1873 and appointed himself editor. This time he succeeded: the paper survived as the distinctively Irish voice of New Zealand Catholicism until 1996. It also became a model for others in Catholicism's Greater Ireland. When Adelaide struggled to establish a Catholic newspaper in the late 1870s, for example, its bishop took heart from the fact that, while the *Tablet* had lost money for its first two years of operation, its subsequent profits had allowed Moran to 'support his schools & convents'.[304]

Yet Moran's purpose was not solely to make money or even to hammer the government. He also intended that the paper should deepen its readers' identification with Ireland. He published Irish news, denounced British rule, championed Home Rule, and looked with favour on the Land League. It is probably no accident that the *Tablet's* more measured (and less Irish) competitors quickly folded: Auckland's *Freeman's Journal* in 1887 after eight years of operation and Wellington's *Catholic Times* in 1894 after only six. As Richard Davis put it, the *Tablet* successfully used 'Irish patriotic enthusiasm to buttress the demand for Catholic education in New Zealand';[305] and, by the same token, as Donald Akenson has pointed out, the 'very act of fighting for Catholic separate education helped to crystallize the group identity of the Irish Catholics of New Zealand'.[306]

---

[302] *NZT*, 31 December 1875, quoted in Davis, *Irish Issues*, 164.
[303] Quoted in Laracy, 'Bishop Patrick Moran', 80.
[304] Reynolds to Byrne, 18 October 1879, ACCA/RP/Series 32.
[305] Davis, *Irish Politics*, 7.   [306] Akenson, *Half the World*, 159.

The New Zealand Tablet spoke with Moran's own strident voice. In its columns, he could denounce the government, anathematize backsliders, row with Marists, promulgate Lenten regulations, advertise missions, encourage devotion, discourage mixed marriages, raise money for schools, and urge ethnic solidarity. He could also indulge his passion for politics. In early 1883, for example, Moran took the extraordinary step of standing in a parliamentary by-election in Otago. His aim was to punish the Catholic candidate, Michael Donnelly, who had pledged to abandon demands for state aid for Catholic schools to focus on other issues. He threw himself into the campaign, telling one rally that the 'Irish people have for centuries stood upon these claims for justice', despite the offer of state schools and despite bribes to enter them. Did his opponents then think, he asked, that 'we their children, inheriting their principles, proud of their courage, loving their memories, are going to be driven into your schools by anything that you can do?'[307]

In the end, Moran received only 138 votes to Donnelly's 182, while William Larnach, a prominent businessman who favoured Bible reading in the public schools, won 667. But victory had not been the point: Moran had established that crossing him was lethal to the electoral hopes of any Catholic. *The Tablet* drove the point home, printing every week from August 1883 until 1897 an extract from one of Moran's educational speeches as a standing leader – public schools were merely 'tyranny, oppression and plunder'. This had an enduring effect. In 1893, for example, Moran's vicar general privately boasted that there would not be a single 'Catholic "rat"' in Dunedin at election time'. 'One of our prominent Labour Catholics', Patrick Lynch continued, 'told the Labour Committee the other day that until the Education injustice would be removed he [would] have nothing to do with their programme. A Catholic prohibitionist spoke in precisely the same terms.'[308] Even so, Lynch was worried that 'Catholics in other places are being got at'.[309]

He was right to worry: New Zealand's Catholics never voted entirely as a block, not even in Otago. In part this was because the 1877 settlement had gained widespread public acceptance despite (or because of) attempts to amend it in 1878, 1882, 1889, and 1891. Why should Catholics waste their vote in a hopeless cause? This was particularly true when some of the most prominent opponents of state aid were also assiduous in courting Irish Catholic support, and leading politicians such as William Pember Reeves, John Ballance, and Sir Robert Stout

---

[307] *Otago Daily Times*, 16 January 1883, quoted in Laracy, 'Bishop Patrick Moran', 99.
[308] Lynch to Grimes, 24 October 1893, CHDA/Clergy.
[309] Lynch to Grimes, 12 October 1893, CHDA/Clergy.

consistently tried to use Irish nationalism or progressive politics or both to separate Irish Catholics from their bishops. As Patrick Lynch admitted in 1893, the only thing he 'feared in Dunedin was the "labour" idea'.[310] The liberal Stout, for example, was a leading freethinker, educational secularist, connoisseur of Irish crime statistics, and sometime advocate of limiting Irish Catholic migration; in 1884, Moran privately described him as a deadly enemy and the 'worst' of the candidates standing for Dunedin, while the *Tablet* compared him to the evil Haman in the Book of Esther.[311] Yet Stout was also a noisy enthusiast for Home Rule and a committed labour reformer; when he was finally defeated in Dunedin in 1887, he soon returned to parliament for a west coast and then a Wellington constituency with significant Irish support.[312] He even received some kind words from the *Catholic Times* shortly before it went bankrupt. Although Moran's campaigning was conventionally ineffectual – the 1877 Act was never seriously threatened – it kept religious (and thus ethnic) identity in the foreground of public life.

Moran knew this would not matter if he were unable to provide adequate Catholic schools and doing so had been his priority almost from the moment he landed in Dunedin. Within weeks of their arrival, for example, the Dominicans had opened a primary school and then a high school, both for girls. In 1872, they added a boarding school. By 1875, they had 83 boarders and 216 day students on two sites.[313] Dunedin's boys were in the charge of two secular priests, and, in common with many of his brethren, Moran was desperate to secure Irish Christian Brothers. To entice them, he bought a residence for £1,350 and offered it free of debt. 'I hope', he told Cullen, 'they will send us a few good men, real men, able and willing to work and make sacrifices.'[314] In 1876, they obliged, opening their first New Zealand school with four brothers. Soon there were more than 250 students, all paying between one and two shillings a week depending on age, and all enrolled in the Society of the Sacred Heart.[315] Importing the brothers ultimately cost some £3,000, but Moran was delighted and grateful to Cullen for his help.[316] By Moran's death in 1895, the Dominicans and the Christian Brothers between them educated more than 2,000 children in two boarding schools, seven secondary day schools, and

---

[310] Ibid.

[311] Moran to Sr. Gertrude, n.d. [1884?], quoted in Lilian Keyes, 'Bishop Moran – 5 – Education question', *Zealandia*, 2 June 1966, 10; *NZT*, 2 January 1885.

[312] R. P. Davis, 'Sir Robert Stout and the Irish question, 1879–1921', *Historical Studies: Australia and New Zealand*, vol. 12, no. 47 (1966), 417–34.

[313] McCarthy, 56.   [314] Moran to Cullen, 4 May 1875, DDA/Australia.

[315] K. O'Donoghue, *P.A. Treacy*, 102–4.

[316] Moran to Cullen, 2 May 1876, DDA/Australia.

eighteen primary schools.[317] In New Zealand as a whole, there were in that year some 114 Catholic primary schools educating 10,458 students.[318] All this cost money: £42,966 was spent on buildings and land alone just between 1877 and 1883, for example.[319]

The combination of separate schools, perceived persecution, devotional enthusiasm, and social controls ensured that Dunedin's Catholics retained their religious and ethnic identity long after Moran's death. This was aided by a steady supply of priests from Ireland or, later, formed in Hiberno-Roman seminaries. Perhaps more importantly, Moran proved to be a particularly successful recruiter of nuns: by 1895, the initial group of ten Dominicans had ballooned to seventy-five. During Moran's lifetime, most (60 per cent) came directly from Ireland, although two local women, both students at the order's Dunedin school, were professed as early as 1878.[320] So urgent was the need, and so fixed the attention on home, that Moran and Mother Gabriel even attempted in the late 1880s to establish a novitiate in Dublin to supply women directly to New Zealand. Despite attracting a number of postulants, the project was soon abandoned as unworkable.[321] The community nevertheless continued to grow, with 120 women entering by 1914. After Moran's death, it also began to rely more on local recruits, with only six women coming directly from Ireland between 1895 and 1914.[322] This steady supply allowed the order to open new convents and schools first at Queenstown and then Omaru and then in smaller communities such as Milton, Lawrence, and Teschemakers.

The supply of priests, meanwhile, was assured through regular trips to Ireland. Moran was a careful and clever recruiter. As he explained to Forde in 1872, it was good to be seen as a liberal spender (Forde had bought a prospective priest's travelling outfit) as it would get Dunedin 'a good name in the Colleges'.[323] In 1889, he arranged a European trip around his need to be in Ireland 'before the colleges break up for the midsummer holidays as I am badly in want of three priests'.[324] Yet Moran was also picky: in the early 1870s, for example, he accepted two young priests from Scotland but kept them close in Dunedin for 'some time to train them in our ways'.[325] He also avoided All Hallows, accepting only two men from the college before 1891.[326] When William Coleman went

---

[317] Laracy, 'Bishop Patrick Moran', 39.   [318] Akenson, *Half the World*, 170.
[319] Davis, *Irish Issues*, 83–4.   [320] McCarthy, 64.   [321] Ibid., 100–6.
[322] See appendix B in McCarthy, 320–9.
[323] Moran to Forde, 15 November 1872, DDA/Australia.
[324] Moran to Murray, 11 January 1889, MNDA/MP/A.4.170.
[325] Moran to Forde, 10 January 1873, DDA/Australia.
[326] Carmichael, 'Matricula: 1842–91'.

on an Irish recruiting trip in 1875, for example, he placed only one of his prospects there, while sending two to the Propaganda, three to the Trappists at Mt Melleray, and one to St John's College in Waterford.[327] This was different from the rest of New Zealand, which relied heavily on All Hallows for non-Marist vocations; by 1891, Auckland had already received nine and Wellington sixteen.[328] The reason for Moran's aversion is not recorded, but it is likely that he shared the Cullenite prejudice that, while the college's clerical proletarians were an undeniably useful source of manpower, they were best avoided where possible.

Moran had achieved an enormous amount by the time of his death in 1895, but the task of securing and consolidating Dunedin's Hiberno-Romanism fell to his successor, Michael Verdon, then still the founding rector of St Patrick's, Manly. Although at the time of his appointment he was preparing to return to Rome as the agent of the Australian bishops, there seems to have been little doubt of his elevation.[329] Redwood and Grimes were not reckless enough to attempt a Marist candidate in Irish Dunedin, and the ailing Luck refused to express any opinion at all.[330] Verdon also appears to have been the local favourite.[331]

As a bishop, Verdon's most significant achievement was the establishment of New Zealand's national seminary. Redwood had first mooted the idea shortly before the Irishman's appointment, ironically as a means of retrieving local students from Manly, and, when the first provincial council of New Zealand in 1899 resolved to erect a college, the responsibility inevitably fell to Verdon. No one else was interested. Redwood in particular remained content to look to Ireland for whatever non-Marist personnel he required. As late as 1913, for example, he was begging the bishop of Limerick for the loan of any surplus priests, promising £20 for their outfit and a first-class ticket to Wellington.[332]

Holy Cross College duly opened in the Dunedin suburb of Mosgiel on 3 May 1900 with a staff of three local priests, all Irish, and eleven students. Neither Redwood nor Lenihan attended, although Grimes came down from Christchurch. Verdon served as president, overseeing everything from the design of the chapel (commissioned from a Roman architect) to what the students read, when they woke, and what games they played. He soon replaced the original faculty with young priests trained in Rome, and by 1906 a staff of five (including Verdon himself) oversaw twenty-six students. As elsewhere, particularly clever boys were

[327] McCarthy, 52.   [328] Carmichael, 'Matricula: 1842–91'.
[329] Moran [Sydney] to Murray, 8 April 1896, MNDA/MP/3/1/1810/2/7.
[330] Luck to Grimes, 1 June 1895, CHDA/Box 12b.
[331] See Lynch to Grimes, 23 December 1895, CHDA/Clergy.
[332] Redwood to O'Dwyer, 6 January 1913, LDA/OD.

sent on to the Propaganda or Dublin for finishing, and the first of these was ordained in Rome in 1906.

Holy Cross College was as significant as the Marist victories of 1874 to the development of New Zealand Catholicism. Prior to 1900, true Hiberno-Romanism was confined (excepting Croke's interlude in Auckland) to the far south. It is true that the other dioceses were greening rapidly, as were the Marists, but ethnically Irish priests (often from All Hallows or the Marist's Irish seminary) and an emphasis on Irish ethnicity, symbols, or even politics were not the same thing. At Mosgiel, the bulk of the nation's diocesan priests would be trained in an unambiguously Hiberno-Roman atmosphere and then dispersed across the country. Inevitably, many became bishops: the first, Hugh John O'Neill, was appointed coadjutor bishop of Dunedin in 1943. He was soon followed by Peter McKeefry, who was born in Greymouth in 1899 to Irish parents, educated (like O'Neill) by the Christian Brothers in Dunedin, and sent to Mosgiel in 1916 and then the Propaganda in 1922 before ordination in 1926. In 1947, he became coadjutor archbishop of Wellington (archbishop from 1954) and in 1969 New Zealand's first cardinal. McKeefry was 'intensely' interested in the careers of Moran and Croke and found the time to thoroughly research them in the Roman archives. He hoarded his knowledge, and his secretary recalled him gleefully boasting that '"No one knows I've got this."'[333]

The college's success can be demonstrated by the fact that in 1976 Dunedin had by far the lowest percentage of Irish-born clergy in New Zealand, only 10 per cent against more than a quarter elsewhere.[334] Thus the most obviously Irish and Hiberno-Roman of the four dioceses came to have the fewest native Irish; it had Hiberno-Romans instead. Verdon also imported Sisters of Mercy from Maitland, and by early 1907 they had 40 sisters in 5 convents educating 773 children and were about to open another convent in south Dunedin at a cost of some £4,000. They also ran a 'badly needed' orphanage.[335] By the time Verdon died in November 1918, his diocese had 35 priests in 65 churches ministering to a Catholic population of around 25,000. There were also 10 Christian Brothers and more than 200 nuns overseeing some 40 schools and 2,400 children, as well as at least 100 more in the orphanage.[336] Even so, Verdon's most important achievement was undoubtedly Mosgiel.

Further north, the Irish finally recovered Auckland with the 1910 appointment of Henry William Cleary, who became the second Irish-

[333] Patricia O'Connor to E. R. Simmons, 30 June 1982, WAA.   [334] Vaney, 3.
[335] Verdon to Murray, 18 January 1907, MNDA/MP/Box 1811.
[336] *Otago Witness*, 27 November 1918.

born bishop in the hierarchy. (He had the invitations to his consecration printed in Irish.)[337] Before being imported by Verdon to edit the *Tablet*, Cleary had built his career in Australia as an energetic public defender of Catholicism. In Auckland, he pursued a relatively emollient rhetorical strategy more akin to Redwood than Moran, although he heatedly opposed the renewed campaign to mandate Bible reading in the public schools. He also, and probably inevitably, rowed with Suzanne Aubert, who had been invited back to Auckland in the last years of Lenihan's regime. As Jessie Munro put it, 'Suzanne must have glimpsed more than once the shadowy presence, suspicious and disapproving, of Bishop Thomas Croke ... standing behind Cleary's shoulder.'[338]

Cleary also fell out with his own coadjutor, James Michael Liston. Born to prosperous Irish parents in Dunedin in 1881, Liston was educated by the Christian Brothers before being sent on to Manly at the age of eleven. There he met Verdon, still the president, who soon arranged for Liston to be despatched to Clonliffe. In 1900, he moved to the Irish College. He was ordained by Verdon in 1904, only the seventh New Zealand–born priest, and promptly assigned to Mosgiel.[339] Liston became rector in 1910, was overlooked as Verdon's successor in 1918, and was then appointed coadjutor to Cleary in 1920. As he worriedly explained to the rector of the Irish College, all he had to offer Auckland were 'good health, toughness, a stout heart, some faith (that comes from Clonliffe and Roman training) and deep respect and affection for Bishop Cleary'.[340]

Cleary was by then, however, a divisive figure, having enthusiastically backed the war effort to the point of serving as a battlefield chaplain in Flanders. He subsequently fell out with the advanced Irish nationalists clustered around the firebrand editor of the *Tablet*, James Kelly, banned the display of Sinn Féin and other patriotic banners, declared his loyalty to the Empire (while criticizing aspects of British rule in Ireland), and insisted that his priests eschew partisan politics.[341] In 1919, he accepted an OBE. Like Michael Howley in Newfoundland or Thomas Carr in Melbourne, Cleary was of the generation of colonial bishops who had grown up supporting both Home Rule and the Empire, and who remembered Cardinal Cullen's anathemas of violent nationalism.

Liston had no such qualms. On 17 March 1922, he told some 3,000 people gathered in Auckland's town hall that his own parents had been 'driven' from Ireland by their 'foreign masters', that the recent Anglo-Irish Treaty was only 'the first installment' of freedom and that Irishmen

---

[337] Akenson, *Half the World*, 180.   [338] Munro, *AC*, 284.
[339] See Nicholas Reid, *James Michael Liston, a Life* (Wellington: Victoria University Press, 2006), 23–47.
[340] Quoted in ibid., 83.   [341] Rory Sweetman, 'Cleary, Henry William', in *DNZB*.

were 'determined to have the whole of it', and that the 1916 rebels had been 'martyrs' 'murdered by foreign troops'.[342] The speech lost nothing in the retelling, there was a political outcry, and Liston was prosecuted for seditious libel. (He was ultimately acquitted by an all-Protestant jury.) He promptly compounded the offence by publicly celebrating the success of 'our friends' in the Labour Party in the 1922 general election.[343] The resulting rupture was permanent, and the two men traded allegations of mental instability until Cleary's death in 1929.[344]

Liston's dynamism, orthodoxy, and Irishness were unquestionable. In his first twenty-five years as bishop, he oversaw a doubling of priests, a near doubling of nuns, and the introduction of sixteen religious congregations. He also built some thirty new parishes, forty-three new churches, and twenty-nine new schools. He immediately imported both the Dominican sisters and the Christian Brothers from Dunedin and become a champion of the Sisters of Mercy.[345] He was an enthusiastic patron of social organizations ranging from the Knights of the Southern Cross, to the Catholic Basketball Association, to the Catholic Repertory Society. He often presided at the Thursday meetings of the Catholic Men's Luncheon Club.[346] Liston hammered mixed marriages and contraception (which he thought intimately related), championed Catholic schools, turned Cleary's publication *The Month* into the weekly *Zealandia*, and established Newman Hall at Auckland University. As late as 1937, nearly one-third of his 119 diocesan priests had been born in Ireland, and Liston actively recruited there into the 1950s and beyond. In 1976, 27.3 per cent of Auckland's priests were still Irish-born.[347] The Sisters of Mercy also mounted regular Irish recruiting trips – Mother Genevieve O'Donnell, for example, returned from one in 1949 with twenty-four postulants. Even the sisters who served as domestic staff in the minor seminary were imported directly from Ireland.[348] Liston was promoted to titular archbishop in 1954, retired in 1970, and only died in 1976, a year after New Zealand's Catholic schools were integrated into the state system on terms acceptable to the Catholic Church.[349]

James Michael Liston is perhaps the clearest example anywhere in the world of the transmissibility of Cullenite Catholicism. Although he was

---

[342] Sweetman, *Bishop in the Dock*, 9–11.

[343] Rory Sweetman. 'Liston, James Michael' in *DNZB*.

[344] For Cleary on Liston's supposed hereditary insanity, see Reid, 144. Liston's ally Matthew Brodie of Christchurch denied these allegations and made his own against Cleary: 'Statement by Bishop Brodie' to the Propaganda, n.d. [early 1920s?], CHDA/Box 11.

[345] Reid, 162–4.   [346] Ibid., 208.   [347] Vaney, 3.   [348] Reid, 187–8.

[349] See Rory Sweetman, *'A Fair and Just Solution?' A History of the Integration of Private Schools in New Zealand* (Palmerston North: Dunmore Press, 2002).

born three years after the cardinal's death and nearly 20,000 kilometres from Dublin, he governed Auckland as a self-conscious Hiberno-Roman and Cullenite. As Nicholas Reid has pointed out, Liston's lineage was clear – from 1803 to 1976: 'Cullen. Moran. Verdon. Liston.'[350] He kept a photograph of Michael Verdon on his desk and prayed for his intercession.[351] As Reid also noted, the Catholicism that Liston embedded in Auckland owed its origins entirely to Cullen's fusion of Ireland and Rome and the seminaries that reproduced it.[352] It was also from Liston in turn that later bishops such as McKeefry (who had been Liston's student and later his secretary) learned their churchmanship. As a cardinal, McKeefry still subscribed his letters to Liston 'your devoted child'.[353]

Marist influence continued to wane. In Christchurch, for example, the Auckland priest Matthew Brodie succeeded Grimes in 1915. The appointment was a rebuke to the Marists, who had hoped to simply nominate one of their own. Instead, Rome demanded candidates from the entire clergy, both Marist and secular, and appointed first the Dublin priest Michael Sheehan (later coadjutor archbishop of Sydney), who declined, and then Brodie.[354] Born in 1871 to Irish parents and educated by the Auckland Sisters of Mercy, he was the first native New Zealander and the first graduate of St Patrick's, Manly, to become a bishop.[355] He swiftly curtailed Marist influence in Christchurch, to the delight of the largely Irish secular clergy.[356] He also pointedly invited the (Italian) apostolic delegate to consecrate him in place of Archbishop Redwood, much to the latter's fury.[357] Brodie was a typical Hiberno-Roman and was soon denouncing the state schools as 'a most efficacious way of banishing Christianity from the country' at a meeting that paired renditions of 'God Save the King' with 'Let Erin Remember' and 'God Defend New Zealand' with 'The Harp that Once through Tara's Halls'.[358] He was succeeded in 1944 by Patrick Francis Lyons, who moved to Sydney in

---

[350] Reid, 35.
[351] See Liston's essay 'Bishop Verdon – Founder' in B. Mannes (ed.), *Golden Jubilee, Holy Cross College, Mosgiel, New Zealand, 1900–1950* (Auckland: Whitcombe and Tombs, 1949), 5; Reid, 35.
[352] Reid, 35–6.   [353] Ibid., 181.
[354] See Michael O'Meeghan, *Held Firm by Faith: A History of the Catholic Diocese of Christchurch, 1840–1987* (Christchurch: Catholic Diocese of Christchurch, 1988), 247–8.
[355] 'Address to the Right. Rev. Monsignor Brodie, Bishop Elect of Christchurch, from the Sisters of Mercy, Auckland', n.d., CHDA/Box 11; *FJ*, 2 March 1916.
[356] Unknown to Brodie, 6 January 1916, CHDA/Box 11. The writers were two secular priests but the signatures are illegible.
[357] O'Shea to Brodie, 27 December 1915, CHDA/Box 11.
[358] 'Catholic Congress, Colosseum, Christchurch, 9 November 1916', CHDA/Box 3a.

1950 and then Sale a few years later, and then by Edward Michael Joyce, who died in 1964.

In Wellington, Redwood had begun the hunt for a coadjutor as early as 1912, approaching an Irish-American Marist in Mississippi before settling on his own vicar general, Thomas O'Shea. The secular clergy were not consulted and the appointment was announced as a fait accompli. The Marists were taking no chances.[359] (It was the furious reaction to O'Shea's appointment that led Rome to abandon the practice of Marist direct nomination when Christchurch fell vacant two years later.) Born to Irish parents in California, O'Shea had been educated first by the Marist Brothers in Napier and then at St Patrick's in Wellington before entering the society's New Zealand seminary at Meeanee in 1890. As coadjutor archbishop (archbishop from 1935), O'Shea continued Redwood's relatively accommodative approach to public life; in the early 1930s, for example, his negotiations with the Bible in State Schools League resulted in an agreement that was humiliatingly repudiated first by the Hiberno-Romans and then by Redwood himself.[360] Brodie denounced it as truckling to Protestant bigotry.[361] The isolated O'Shea never abandoned his taste for compromise but it did not matter. Senility began to overtake him in the early 1940s, and he was already incapacitated by the time McKeefry was appointed in 1947.[362] McKeefry himself died in 1973.

Of the eighteen bishops appointed to New Zealand between 1869 and 1950, fifteen were Irish-born or Irish-descended.[363] All three of the non-Irish (Redwood, Grimes, Luck) were appointed before 1890. The last Marist (and the last religious) appointed before 1950 was O'Shea, in 1913. In many ways, this simply tracked the country's demography: into the 1950s, the Irish-born or Irish-descended comprised at least 90 per cent of the Catholic population.[364] As a result, nearly every aspect of twentieth-century New Zealand Catholicism was coloured green, while its French history was effaced or even erased. The cover of the Christchurch Marist Brothers' 1938 'Jubilee Journal', for example, was adorned with green shamrocks despite the fact that the brothers themselves had come directly from France at the invitation of the Englishman Grimes. By 1938, almost all of their students had Irish surnames: of the

---

[359] O'Meeghan, *Steadfast*, 193–4.
[360] See *Bible-in-Schools: Negotiations with Roman Catholics: Official Statement 13 November 1931* (n.p., n.d) – a copy is available in CHDA/'Bible-in-Schools' Box. For Redwood, *Evening Post*, 14 October 1932.
[361] See 'Minutes of the Meeting of the Hierarchy', 28 April 1930, CHDA/Box 19.
[362] Christopher van der Krogt, 'O'Shea, Thomas', in *DNZB*.
[363] Akenson gives fourteen, presumably counting Lenihan, who had Irish parents, as English. See *Half the World*, 162.
[364] Ibid.

fourteen clerical graduates, three were named Cullen and two called Mannix.[365] As late as 1976, Irish-born priests still comprised at least a quarter of the total in every diocese except Dunedin.[366]

On every metric, the story of New Zealand Catholicism to the middle of the twentieth century is one of steady growth and deepening control. In 1874, for example, only some 27 per cent of Catholics attended Mass on census day. By 1926 (the last year the statistic was recorded nationally), it was above 50 per cent. In 1949, around 75 per cent of Auckland's Catholics were in attendance. They were served by a steadily growing clergy: 146 priests and 691 other religious in 1900 had become 533 priests and 2,094 other religious by 1950. More importantly, the ratio of priests to people (a crucial measure of the ability to maintain social controls) improved over the same period from 1:752 to 1:487, and of religious to people from 1:131 to 1:99. By 1950, there were some 250,000 Catholics in New Zealand, representing about 12 per cent of the population, and at least 75 per cent of their children were in a Catholic school.[367]

In addition to schooling and spiritual support, the Catholic Church in New Zealand provided its adherents with hospitals, asylums, orphanages, old-age homes, libraries, newspapers, social clubs, luncheon clubs, confraternities, sodalities, theatre groups, insurance schemes, and sports teams, all reliant upon the enthusiasm or generosity of the faithful. Every Sunday, its ministers enjoyed the opportunity to remind Catholics how to behave, how to vote, where to educate their children, and who to marry, and these strictures were ruthlessly enforced.

This social, spatial, political, and sexual separatism continued to provoke a sectarianism which could erupt over anything from marriage policy to school rugby. When *Ne Temere* was promulgated in 1908, for example, it set off what Bishop Cleary of Auckland described as 'a cycle of sectarian epilepsy'.[368] In 1920, the Protestant Political Association capped several years of crude sectarian agitation by obtaining legislation that notionally banned the decree itself.[369] A year earlier, they had helped to defenestrate the former prime minister Sir Joseph Ward, a Catholic of Irish descent.[370] In Dunedin, the Christian Brothers' schools were banned from playing rugby against the state schools in 1922, a prohibition that was soon extended to all Catholic schools and to all sports from rugby to netball.

---

[365] A copy is available in Christchurch.   [366] Vaney, 3.

[367] The statistics in this paragraph are all drawn from Akenson, *Half the World*, 166–72.

[368] Quoted in O'Meeghan, *Held Firm*, 257.

[369] Jock Phillips and Terry Hearn, *Settlers: New Zealand Immigrants from England, Ireland and Scotland, 1800–1945* (Auckland: Auckland University Press, 2008),187

[370] Michael Bassett, *Sir Joseph Ward: A Political Biography* (Auckland: Auckland University Press, 1993), 248–9.

It lasted until 1977. Catholics in turn become passionate supporters of their school and club teams, almost invariably known as 'The Greens' or, later, by the prefix 'Marist'. (As Seán Brosnahan has pointed out, by the mid-twentieth century that term had been 'symbolically hibernicised'.) There remain today some twenty-eight 'Marist' clubs supported by a loyal 'Vatican Army'.[371] It is unsurprising that New Zealand's Catholics retained both their faith and their self-identification as Irish.

Some historians, however, have suggested that this phenomenon was primarily limited to the far south, or at least disproportionately centred there. Neil Vaney and Lyndon Fraser, for example, have both stressed the relative tolerance of the Marists and identified a concomitant absence of sectarianism (after around 1870) on the west coast, while Vaney has also criticized Richard Davis for focussing too much on an unrepresentative Dunedin. Patrick O'Farrell agreed, insisting that 'there has been no single Irish Catholic experience in New Zealand history' and pointing out that Moran's Otago and Southland were quite different from his own Greymouth or south Canterbury, or indeed from Wellington or Auckland.[372] These differences undoubtedly existed; but they were more a question of pace, or perhaps of tone. Different parts of New Zealand moved at different speeds. Dunedin was far out in front. The west coast was farther behind. Auckland was long a laggard and then raced ahead. Yet the destination was the same, and it was the Dunedin of Moran, Verdon, and Liston that pointed the way.

---

[371] Seán Brosnahan, '"Taking off the gloves": Sectarianism in New Zealand rugby in the 1920s', unpublished paper, by courtesy of the author.

[372] Vaney, 12; O'Farrell made the comment first in a 1976 review and then repeated it in 2000: Patrick O'Farrell, 'Varieties of Irishness', 25–6.

Conclusion

Old Conn Docherty was confused. It was bad enough that his son had married a Protestant, but now he was sending their children to the 'Protestant schil' on the unconvincing grounds that it was 'nearer'. He wondered if he should ever have left Ireland for the west coast of Scotland and dropped heavy hints that it was all the fault of his daughter-in-law. His son was furious: the old man thought only what 'Father Rankin' told him to think. 'They confiscated yer bloody brains at birth', he raged, 'An' stuffed their stinkin' catechism in their place.' Reflecting on the argument later, Tam Docherty wondered if he was even still a Catholic. Yet it was not that simple. 'His father and mother had done their work well. Woven into the whole texture of his boyhood were formative memories of the crucifix on the wall, family pilgrimages to nine o'clock Mass, priests whose casual opinions became proverbial wisdom for his parents.' Tam never resolved his relationship with the Catholic Church, and his own and his children's lives were marked by his mixed marriage, his defiance of clerical authority, and his refusal to send his sons to the Catholic schools.[1]

The world of William McIlvanney's *Docherty* is fiction, but it was also to some degree autobiographical. Tam's Graithnock was McIlvanney's Kilmarnock, and there seems much of William in Tam's son young Conn. Nor are the experiences it relates in any way unusual: the New Zealand historian Edmund Bohan, for example, recalled that in 1940s Invercargill his sisters had suffered 'casual malevolence' from Irish nuns who disapproved of their mother's Presbyterian background, and that his father was denied communion when the family moved to Christchurch and placed him in a series of non-Catholic schools.[2] I have heard of many similar experiences from elderly men and women wherever I have spoken

---

[1] William McIlvanney, *Docherty* (Edinburgh: Canongate, 2014 [1975]), 36–8, 40–1.
[2] Edmund Bohan, *The Singing Historian: A Memoir* (Christchurch: Canterbury University Press, 2012), 14.

about Ireland's spiritual empire: they each have a story to tell about the social pressures experienced by their parents, and sometimes by themselves.

In the nineteenth and much of the twentieth century, the Catholic Church's attitude towards its members was that they should be seen but not heard. They were expected both to support their clergy and to defer to them, to be at once active and docile. Above everything stood the local bishop, the master in his own house, and behind him the pope. As the emphatically ultramontane Ignace Bourget of Montreal famously instructed his flock, 'Let each declare in his heart, I hear my *curé*, my *curé* hears the bishop, the bishop hears the Pope, and the Pope hears Our Lord Jesus Christ.'[3] No Hiberno-Roman bishop anywhere in the world would have disagreed. To these men it was self-evident that God had created a hierarchical universe and that the laity was on its bottommost human rung, above only Protestants, heretics, infidels, and pagans. Yet this would have been just an idle boast if the faithful chose to disagree: a leader without followers or a parish without people soon becomes conspicuous.

It is therefore important to stress that the Catholic Church in Greater Ireland was an entirely voluntary society, lacking even the vestige of formal, legal, or physical coercive power. Its members could do what they wished, ignore what they wished, and leave when they wished. That relatively few did is attributable to the complex web of social controls created by Hiberno-Roman bishops, priests, nuns, and brothers across the English-speaking world. Men like Tam Docherty could check out, but they could never leave. Yet most stayed because they believed what their church taught and found comfort in its embrace. Social controls were important, but without faith they would have ultimately proved futile.

The clergy's most important task was therefore to maintain that faith. This primarily meant ensuring that Catholics regularly approached the sacraments, and their failure to do so was a recurring complaint of the first generation of Hiberno-Romans. This was true both in urban areas and on Greater Ireland's remotest frontier. In Auckland, for example, the newly arrived Thomas Croke complained in 1871 that the people had 'long since given up all the practices, as in some instances, even the profession of our holy faith', while ten years later the first Irish priest in the Falkland Islands grumbled that few in his flock were willing to go to confession, receive communion, join his rosary society, or become 'practical Catholics'.[4] In Ireland, Paul Cullen himself was horrified by the situation

---

[3] Quoted in Clarke, *Piety and Nationalism*, 3.
[4] Croke to Kirby, 10 July 1871, PICRA/K/1871/147; James Foran to Caroline D'Arcy, 15 April 1881, St Mary's Parish Archives, Stanley [SMFI], FC 8-D2/39.

not only in Armagh, where he became archbishop in 1850, but across the country. He knew that regular Mass attendance, confession, Lenten observance, and communion habituated Catholics to deference and discipline, and he set out to instil them in his famous 'devotional revolution'.

The most important mechanism for achieving this was the parish mission, which modelled orthodox doctrine, liturgy, and behaviour for the laity, while building communal solidarity and centring Catholic life on the parish. The style, structure, and effect of these missions varied little from place to place. Over a week in the Western Cape town of George in November 1865, for example, two Irish missioners gave expository lectures on scripture and Catholic doctrine and celebrated Mass during the day, while each evening concluded with a rosary, a hymn, 'instruction on some point of morality', another hymn, 'a dogmatic discourse', and finally 'the benediction of the Most Holy Sacrament'. The mission culminated on the Sunday night with the large congregation, all holding lighted candles, renewing their baptismal vows, followed by communion, including some eighteen first communions, a *Te Deum*, and finally benediction. Following Irish practice, the missioners then instituted a Sodality of the Holy Rosary to maintain piety after they had gone.[5]

A similar scene played out nearly twenty years later in the Sydney parish of St Patrick's, where two newly arrived Redemptorists held a carefully structured mission. The first few days focussed on the parish's children and culminated in a 'general communion and the renewal of Baptismal vows', followed by a week entirely directed towards adult women, again culminating with some 800 receiving communion, and finally a week solely for the men, who were taught basic hymns, offered confession, and treated to sermons on topics ranging from 'Human Respect' to the 'Transfiguration of Our Lord'. The mission ended with some 500 men receiving communion, many for the first time in years, and renewing their baptismal vows, all 'holding lighted candles in their hands, and reverently repeating the solemn words after the good priest'.[6] The secular press called it a 'Roman Catholic Revival'.[7]

Missions often fused ultramontane piety, social controls, and Irish ethnicity. At a Redemptorist mission held in Invercargill in March 1887, for example, two weeks of preaching by the two missionaries drew crowds from outlying communities to see the lavishly decorated church, with the high altar 'lit up' so as to appear 'a perfect pyramid of light and flowers'. As at every mission, large numbers made their confession, some 750 people received communion, including 45 children who

---

[5] *George Town Advertiser*, 9 November 1865, printed in O'Haire, 246–8.
[6] *FJ*, 24 May 1884.   [7] *The Daily Telegraph* (Sydney), 5 May 1884.

made their first. Yet there was also an 'energetic crusade' against the state schools, with the missionaries returning to the subject 'again and again until there could be no shadow of doubt on the minds of anyone present as to the evils of sending Catholic children to godless schools'. This preaching was so effective, the *New Zealand Tablet* boasted, that several 'children were withdrawn from the state schools during the mission'. On St Patrick's Day itself, after two morning masses, some 450 people took what was described as an 'excursion train' to a nearby beach for a sports day organized by the local Catholic literary society. On their return home, they were treated to an 'eloquent panegyric on St. Patrick' and the 'piety and worth of the Irish people'.[8]

Yet missions were not enough. As everyone from Cardinal Cullen to Old Conn Docherty understood, marriage was the key to preserving Catholic practice and ensuring its transmission to the next generation. If Catholics married other Catholics, they were sure to raise Catholic children and likely to educate them in Catholic schools. Those schools could then serve to define and maintain what Donald Akenson (speaking of New Zealand) described as the 'border' between Irish Catholics and the rest of society.[9] It is this that accounts for Irish ferocity against mixed marriages, which far predated the promulgation of *Ne Temere* in 1908. Indeed, for many years many Hiberno-Roman bishops were far more severe than Rome thought prudent. The Propaganda's only objection to William Walsh's 1857 synod in Halifax, for example, was its strict regulations on mixed marriages.[10] When it came to marriage, Rome followed where Ireland led.

The assault on mixed marriages was both enduring and brutally consistent. Walsh, for example, wanted to ensure that no concession took from the 'disobedient child of the Church all the horror of his sin and folly with which he ought to be inspired'.[11] In South Africa, James O'Haire boasted of refusing to administer the sacraments to a Catholic widow who had had seven children with her Protestant husband 'until she first tried to snatch her children from heresy', while Bishop John Leonard of Cape Town ordered the marriage of a woman who had married in an Anglican church denounced from the altar as 'illicit, sinful, and sacrilegious'.[12] Nearly seventy years later, Bishop Matthew Brodie of Christchurch took a similarly hard line. In 1942, for example, he personally insisted that the children of a mixed marriage be instantly removed from an Anglican school near their home. Their Protestant father agreed but asked to wait

---

[8] *NZT*, 8 April 1887.   [9] Akenson, *Half the World*, 190.
[10] I am grateful to Professor Terrence Murphy for drawing my attention to this.
[11] Walsh to Cullen, 'Feast of St. Celestine' [27 July] 1851, DDA/CP/39/2/II/18.
[12] O'Haire, 309; Brown, 94.

until the end of term, explaining that he had just been invalided home after being badly wounded in the Second World War, had already paid the tuition, and wanted to keep his children close. The Catholic school, Noel Newton told the bishop, was far away and the children would have to board. Brodie was unmoved: every day they remained in the school constituted 'a public proclamation and proof that the sacred contract entered into between you & Mrs Newton, as the indispensable contract on which your marriage was sanctioned, is being overlooked or disregarded'.[13]

Preventing mixed marriages and dealing with their consequences often led bishops and priests deep into their parishioners' lives. In 1870, for example, James Murray made the 130-kilometre journey to Sydney solely to confirm a rumour that a mixed marriage he had forbidden in Maitland had been performed in St Mary's Cathedral. When he discovered that it had been, he bitterly complained to Archbishop John Bede Polding that the precedent would encourage other couples to 'evade the wise laws of the Church'.[14] The following year, Archbishop John Joseph Lynch of Toronto wrote a detailed letter on the subject of the Keith family to the vicar apostolic of the Eastern District of Scotland. Mrs Keith was a good Catholic, he wrote, but her Protestant husband had fled with their children and was rumoured to be working as a plumber in the coastal town of Arbroath. Lynch wanted his colleague to ask the parish priest there to discreetly check a series of addresses and, if possible, 'speak to the children to encourage them to remain firm in their mother's faith'.[15]

The danger was particularly acute when the children of mixed marriages lost their Catholic parent or were orphaned. When the widowed father of Henry and Elizabeth Goat announced his intention to move to Sydney in 1870, for example, James Murray panicked. The children, who were aged three and four, had been living with nuns but might now be consigned to Protestants. This had left them, he wrote, 'in great distress and what is of more importance their faith is in danger'. He tried to get them sent to the state-supported Catholic orphanage at Parramatta instead.[16] Nearly ten years later, J. D. Ricards of the Eastern Cape tried to secure control over three children whose Catholic father had died at the Battle of Isandlwana on the grounds that their grandfather had put them

[13] See Mabella Newtown to Brodie, Noel Newton to Brodie, and Brodie to Noel Newton, 3, 4, 9 February 1942, CHDA/3a.
[14] Murray to Polding, 7 September 1870, MNDA/MP/3/1/1810/2/3.
[15] Lynch to John Strain, SCACH/ED/106/7.
[16] Murray to Mackinson, 30 May 1870, MNDA/MP/3/1/1810/2/3.

in the care of Protestants.[17] In 1871, Cardinal Cullen demanded that the
lord lieutenant order the transfer of two brothers from Dublin's Royal
Hibernian Military School to a Catholic orphanage, collected the boys
himself, and then carefully 'examined the little fellows about their
religion'.[18] Everywhere there were fierce objections to any scheme that
might see a Catholic orphan educated outside the faith: in Dunedin, the
intemperate Patrick Moran accused the local orphanage of 'kidnapping
Catholic children for the purpose of making Protestants of them', while
forty-three years later the emollient John O'Reily of Adelaide denounced
a plan to lodge otherwise impossible-to-place Catholic orphans with
Protestant families as 'the most barefaced and most shameless attempt
at official proselytism that I have ever come across in Australia'.[19]

By no means all bishops or priests agreed on the toxicity of mixed
marriages, and relative leniency became a significant marker of difference across Greater Ireland. In Brisbane, for example, Robert
Dunne not only ignored the decrees that effectively banned them in
Australia but celebrated such unions in his own home, while in
New York 'careless Catholics' continued to flock to several priests
who were known to 'marry indiscriminately', despite neighbouring
bishops pleading with John Hughes to 'take some stringent
measures'.[20] In Quebec, Irish Catholics were especially prone to
marry across linguistic and religious lines, while by the late 1890s
fully one in five Catholic marriages in Toronto was mixed.[21] No
bishop positively encouraged such unions, not even Toronto's John
Walsh, but many despaired of preventing them. The Sulpician-
trained David Bacon of Portland, for example, could have spoken
for many when he argued for greater flexibility on the grounds that
mixed marriages were 'a great evil, but, I fear, an inevitable one in
this country'.[22]

To the Hiberno-Romans this was defeatism. As William Walsh told
Cullen, the near-blanket prohibition kept 'our Catholics together, like
a wall of brass, and almost every week in the year recruits [to] our ranks of

[17] See John Fagan to Ricards, 19 May, 14 July, 6 August 1879, PEDA/RP/JF/JR/278, 279, 280/JR1. Fagan was the priest responsible for the mission at King William's Town.
[18] Cullen to Leonard, 16 July 1871, AACT/LP/Box 30.
[19] 'Dr Moran's discourse', 30 April [1871], ADD/MP; O'Reily to Secretary of State of the South Australia State Children's Department, 7 February 1914, ACAA/OR/Series 114/Box 3/Folder 7.
[20] Byrne, Dunne, 143, 148; James Roosevelt Bayley to Hughes, 29 January 1859, AANY/HP/Box 2/Folder 14.
[21] Danielle Gauvreau and Patricia Thornton, 'Marrying "the Other": Trends and determinants of culturally mixed marriages in Québec, 1880–1940', Canadian Ethnic Studies, vol. 47, no. 3 (2015), 111–41; McGowan, Waning of the Green, 107.
[22] Bacon to Hughes, 20 December 1855, AANY/HP/Box 2/Folder 14.

converts both men and women'.[23] To advocate the toleration of sexual or educational mixing was to align with evil – in Gibraltar, Henry Hughes actually preferred a spell in the provost's gaol. As Laurence Sheil of Adelaide put it, mixed marriages were a conspiracy of the 'powers of darkness' to stifle Catholicity, while James Murray declared that 'Mixed Education and Mixed Marriages are the curse of this country.'[24] Although some couples left the church, and others braved its disapproval and its restrictions, when pressed most Catholics seem to have obeyed. In Waimate in South Canterbury, for example, only 4 of the 136 people found on the parish marriage register between 1881 and 1899 were non-Catholic, while in religiously mixed St John's, Newfoundland, only 108 mixed marriages occurred between 1904 and 1913 in the vast cathedral parish.[25] In some smaller parishes, such as St Mary's on the southern Avalon Peninsula, no mixed marriages were 'attempted or occurred' over the same period.[26]

Yet stopping mixed marriages was meaningless if the subsequent children did not attend Catholic schools. As one New Zealand priest put it in 1875, 'teaching is one of the special ways for taking hold of the youth of the country; and if priests do not make an effort to take hold of the youth of this country, very soon they will have no congregations'.[27] Without Catholic schools it was impossible to maintain the disciplined devotional life desired by all Hiberno-Romans. As James Foran complained from the Falkland Islands, 'I have great difficulties in bringing children to preparation for first communion and after that I see no more of them at the sacraments.' 'All this', he wrote, 'is readily traced to education.'[28] Nearly thirty years later, a government inspector urged that the grant to Stanley's 'farcical' Catholic school be withdrawn on the grounds its students would better off 'if they were running about in the fresh air than sitting hour after hour doing nothing and learning nothing'.[29] 'In our day', Thomas Grimley of Cape Town wrote in the 1860s, 'the battle of the Church is to be fought in the School Room.'[30]

[23] Walsh to Cullen, [27 July] 1851.
[24] Sheil to Murray, 6 April 1871, MNDA/MP/3/1/1/1810/2/4; Murray to Cullen, 11 July 1869, DDA/Australia.
[25] Brosnahan, 'Battle of the Borough', 53–4; 'Report of the cathedral parish of St. John the Baptist', ARCSJ/HP/106/24/8.
[26] S. O'Driscoll to 'Chancellor of the diocese', 25 November 1913, ARCSJ/HP/24/8.
[27] Quoted in Davis, *Irish Issues*, 75.   [28] Foran to D'Arcy, 15 April 1881.
[29] See H. E. W. Grant to Fr Migone, 15 January 1907, SMFI/FC B-D2-42. Grant was the colonial secretary and enclosed with this letter extracts from the report of the inspector, an H. M. Richards.
[30] Autobiography of Thomas Grimley, AACT/GP/Box 20A.

The nature of that battle depended on local circumstance. It was relatively easy to attract students in such places such as Newfoundland or Nova Scotia, where there was de jure or de facto state support for Catholic schools, but much harder in jurisdictions where those schools were costly, crumbling, distant, or just not as good. As Foran put it, 'I have often told the parents that they can never make their children Catholics as long as they attended the Government School & they all agreed with me and said they would be glad if they had a Catholic school'; but, he continued, despite providing a master, building a schoolhouse, and importing books at his own expense the people all 'doggedly refused to take their children from the Government school'.[31] To build and sustain a separate system, the church had to convince, not simply compel.

To do so, many bishops appealed directly to Irish pride and to Irish memories of persecution and proselytism. Patrick Moran of Dunedin, for example, reminded an audience in rural New South Wales that the Irish 'in the United States of America, in Canada, in Australia, and in South Africa, in New Zealand and South America, even in the burning Indies, East and West' had 'established the church, and were it not for them in many of these countries the Catholic church would have no existence'. They should be proud of this, he continued, but also wary: 'Having failed by brute force and penal enactments to rob you of your faith, the enemies of that faith now endeavour to effect its ruin by an unchristian education.' Irish Catholics, he concluded, must be sure to 'resist all these mixed and godless systems, and to leave nothing undone to secure for your children a thoroughly Catholic education'.[32] The laity often echoed these themes. A few days before Moran's address, for example, a speaker at a meeting thousands of kilometres away in Geraldton, Western Australia, remarked that the colony's refusal to fully support Catholic education 'reminded him once more of the tithe and taxation, tyranny and spoliation which were the laws of the land of Ireland, before he expatriated himself from her shores'. Until justice was done in Australia, he concluded, 'his watchword would be that of the great O'Connell, Agitate! Agitate! Agitate!'[33]

It was of course not only the Irish who demanded Catholic schools. Peter McIntyre of Prince Edward Island, for example, insisted that 'the State has no right to control Education ... its direction belongs to the spiritual Kingdom of Christ upon earth, that is, the Church', while at

---

[31] Foran to D'Arcy, 15 April 1881.   [32] *Otago Witness*, 18 March 1871.
[33] *The Inquirer and Commercial News* (Perth), 22 March 1871.

a confirmation Roger Bede Vaughan of Sydney asked for a show of hands and then excluded any child still 'receiving a godless education'.[34] Catholic bishops everywhere sought to provide Catholic education with or without state support. The question was one of degrees and of what was deemed possible. Thus Archbishop Daniel Murray of Dublin supported both the Irish national schools and the non-denominational Queen's Colleges, Archbishop Richard Smith of Trinidad agreed to exclude religious instruction from his schools in exchange for state support, and Archbishop Robert Dunne of Brisbane was largely content to leave primary education to the state. Such flexibility was transient, however: Murray was succeeded by Cullen, in Trinidad the church's position changed 'from a practical acquiescence to a most uncompromising opposition', and in Brisbane Archbishop James Duhig was an avid builder of schools.[35] No Hiberno-Roman was ever anything other than totally committed to denominational schooling.

By 1914, most Catholics in most parts of the English-speaking world were educated in Catholic schools, whether state-supported or dependent on the generosity of the faithful. Those schools in turn were almost invariably ultramontane in ideology and in most places Irish in identity. Many celebrated the pope and Daniel O'Connell with equal fervour. This was not inevitable: universal public schooling, of course, would over time have blurred or replaced pre-existing ethnic or religious identities. Its advocates often saw its purpose as exactly that, and this is why almost all Catholics everywhere opposed it. Yet Catholic schools as such did not guarantee the perseverance of a specifically Irish identity. If Archbishops Polding or Vaughan of Sydney had had their way, for example, the Catholic schools of New South Wales would have continued to inculcate an Australian identity, not in parallel with pre-existing national loyalties but in place of them. One of the most important consequences of Hiberno-Roman ecclesiastical success was thus the resulting saturation of Catholic schools in Irish symbolism, Irish history, and Irish culture. These schools did strive to make their students proud Australians, Americans, or Newfoundlanders, but they also ensured that they would see themselves as Irish-Australian, Irish-American, or Irish-Newfoundlander. It is this more than anything else that accounts for the endurance of a coherent diasporic Irish Catholic identity long after significant Irish migration had ceased.

---

[34] Pastoral letter to the clergy and laity of the diocese of Charlottetown, 22 December 1873, CDA; *FJ*, 2 August 1879.

[35] For Trinidad, see J. M. Feheney, *Catholic Education in Trinidad in the Nineteenth Century* (Dublin: Four Courts Press, 2001), 89.

Yet it was not enough to keep your people separate if you could not control their behaviour. This was true for every level of society, but the need was particularly acute for the large number of poor Irish living in temptation-ridden urban areas. Thus, in the Eastern Cape, Patrick Moran denounced dancing as a 'mortal sin', while 'Houses of Mercy' and similar institutions were established everywhere to institutionalize women who were vulnerable or who had transgressed social or sexual norms.[36] The Adelaide suburb of Walkerville, for instance, hosted a 'Retreat for women who have fallen but had previously led a respectable life'. Like its Irish counterparts it had strict rules, including that inmates remain in residence for at least a year, attend morning and evening prayers, and eschew 'improper language' and talking at night. It even supported itself through the operation of a commercial laundry.[37] Margaret Anna Cusack, the prolific 'Nun of Kenmare', not only wrote an advice book for Irish women living in America but also established a religious order in New Jersey where she opened a holiday home for Irish servant girls on the cliffs overlooking Manhattan.[38] She called them 'Bridgets' and looked both to their physical and to their moral health.[39] Further north in Nova Scotia, the Sisters of Charity's first attempt in the early 1860s to create a refuge for delinquent women faltered in the face of the inmates' irreverence and the nuns' inexperience. In 1886, they tried again with a home for unwed mothers, while in 1890 the Sisters of the Good Shepherd opened a facility that accepted both women prepared to 'forsake the paths of shame' and those serving a criminal sentence.[40]

It was, however, alcohol that inevitably consumed the most attention, and its abuse was widely understood to be a peculiarly Irish problem: as one Hiberno-Roman bishop observed, 'no Irishman who loved sobriety' had ever failed to achieve success overseas, while 'no Irishman addicted to drink' ever did.[41] In Ireland, this had led to Father Theobald Mathew's wildly popular abstinence campaigns, and by 1843 about half of the adult population had taken the pledge. Admiring Hiberno-Roman bishops (and others) tried to replicate this success, albeit with a greater emphasis on clerical oversight and control. Not only was sobriety good in itself, they thought, but it could improve the reputation of Irish Catholic

---

[36] Moran to Grimley, 11 December 1865, AACT/GP/Box 13.

[37] 'Adelaide Retreat for Women', printed copy of the rules [1904], ACAA.

[38] [Margaret Anna Cusack] 'The Nun of Kenmare', *Advice to Irish Girls in America* (New York: J. A. McGee, 1872). Her community was known as the Sisters of Peace, later changed to the Sisters of St Joseph of Peace.

[39] See the Cusack papers held by the Sisters of St Joseph of Peace, Englewood Cliffs, New Jersey.

[40] Fingard, 137–8, 124, 146–7.

[41] Thomas Croke to Patrick Francis Moran, Moran diaries, 4 November 1874, AAS.

communities and aid their social and material advancement.[42] It would also strengthen the church. As Thomas Connolly of Halifax remarked in 1868, 'temperance institutions ought to be considered the handmaid of religion'.[43] Thus one of the first things Thomas Grimley did after being appointed to Cape Town was to launch a temperance society, while in Madras John Fennelly was an enthusiastic champion of the Irish Total Abstinence Society.[44] His local Catholic press was full of temperance meetings, such as the 'Grand Teetotal Festival' attended by more than 300 people at Kamptee. It was organized by the Irish military chaplain, had the full support of the local commander, and the toasts were to the Queen, the Royal Family, and Fr Theobald Mathew.[45]

Despite being supported by clergy of all nationalities, temperance campaigns often served as a means of reinforcing Irish identity. As early as 1842, for example, the travelling Charles Dickens was 'particularly pleased' to spot a distinct Irish contingent at a 'temperance convention' in Cincinnati. They 'mustered very strong with their green scarves', he wrote, 'carrying their national Harp and their portrait of Father Mathew, high above the people's heads'.[46] Twenty years later, the St Patrick's Temperance Society participated in Ottawa's St Patrick's Day parade wearing a badge of green and white silk emblazoned with the 'Harp of Erin', while carrying a life-size portrait of Fr Mathew and marching behind St Patrick's Band.[47] Organized temperance bound Irish Catholics to their church, to each other, and to Ireland.

Social and spatial separation also extended beyond the grave, and deciding who could be buried in a Catholic cemetery became another mechanism of social control. Thus William Walsh established his authority in Halifax through the erection of Holy Cross Cemetery, and one of Thomas Connolly's first acts in Saint John was to purchase the land that would become St Mary's Cemetery. Its rules insisted that it would receive only Catholics and that only the bishop could decide who had been one.[48] The exclusion of the defiant was often met with fury. In Gibraltar, for example, a hostile crowd gathered when Bishop Hughes declined to proceed with the funeral of a man whose coffin bore a Masonic symbol.

---

[42] Clarke, *Piety and Nationalism*, 137–8.   [43] Quoted in Fingard, 28.   [44] O'Haire, 88.

[45] *Madras Catholic Expositor*, vol. 4, no. 1, March 1844.

[46] Charles Dickens, *American Notes & Pictures from Italy* (London: Chapman & Hall, 1907), 161.

[47] *Ottawa Tribune*, 21 March 1862, quoted in Mike McLoughlin, 'Catholicism, masculinity, and middle-class respectability in the Irish Catholic temperance movement in nineteenth-century Canada', in Barr and Carey, *Religion and Greater Ireland*, 178.

[48] Mary Kilfoil McDevitt, *"We hardly knew ye": St. Mary's Cemetery, an Enduring Presence* (Saint John, NB: Irish Canadian Cultural Association, 1992), 20–1.

The police tried to compel the burial 'as the weather was very warm', there were cries of 'burn the church', and Hughes pressed some off-duty Irish soldiers into protecting him from the ensuing violence.[49] Nearly fifty years later, Archbishop Michael Corrigan of New York was sued after he refused to bury a man who had joined a proscribed society shortly before his death.[50] The matter, he told an Australian colleague, was only decided when the Supreme Court vindicated 'the absolute right of the churches to say who should be interred in consecrated ground'.[51] Like any news of interest to Irish Catholics, the affair was reported in detail from San Francisco to Wanganui.[52]

Like the orb lines of a spider's web, the newspapers of Greater Ireland reprinted one another's articles, reported one another's news, and inculcated a common identity that bound together the Catholic Irish from Boston to Ballarat. Even the smallest details were of interest. The 1843 departure for India of a handful of Irish priests, for example, was reported in the United States, while in India itself the *Madras Catholic Expositor* published over many issues Bishop Fleming of Newfoundland's long description of his diocese and apologia for his rule.[53] Everywhere, Irish news was reported as home news, and the opening of a church in Dubuque was considered of interest to people in Dunedin. By 1914, almost every city and many smaller communities in the English-speaking world had at least one newspaper that was avowedly Catholic in its ethos and Irish in its loyalties. Some were beholden to the church and others were in lay hands, but such details rarely mattered: collectively, they first gave Greater Ireland its coherence and then helped to maintain it. As Cian T. McMahon has pointed out, 'By reading, writing, and physically transmitting individual copies of the weekly rag to friends and families overseas, the Irish created what one editor called an "empire of the press" where, though physically apart, they could virtually assemble once a week to debate and define information and identity.'[54]

Although the Irish press could be used to whip up nationalist fervour, raise money for visiting Home Rule politicians, or simply encourage campaigns for state aid, it could also help augment social controls. In 1881, for example, the *New Zealand Tablet* reported on the sad story of

[49] Hughes to Murray, 1 October 1840, DDA/MP/38/10/5/1.
[50] See Anthony D. Andreassi, '"The cunning leader of a dangerous clique?": The Burstell affair and Archbishop Michael Augustine Corrigan', *The Catholic Historical Review*, vol. 86, no. 4 (October 2000), 620–39.
[51] Corrigan to Murray, 8 November 1889, MNDA/MP/A.4.175.
[52] See 'An interesting case', in *Daily Alta California*, 29 February 1888, and 'Broadbrim's letter', in the *Wanganui Chronicle*, 2 June 1888.
[53] *The United States Catholic Magazine*, vol. 2 (1843), 754.
[54] McMahon, *Irish Identity*, 2.

Frank and Gertrude Adamson, aged sixteen and six, who had been caught at Newark station trying to flee their Protestant father in the hope of joining their Catholic mother in Washington, DC. Despite brutally beating his son on the platform, brandishing a pistol, and later fighting with the police, the father was released with a small fine and given custody of his daughter. The *Tablet's* unsubtle headline was 'A Mixed Marriage'.[55] A few years later, it quoted the New York *Freeman's Journal* and the Erie *Lake Shore Visitor* to the effect that such unions were invariably unhappy for everybody except Satan.[56] More prosaically, Irish Catholic newspapers published everything from Lenten regulations to pastoral letters, alerted their readers to missions or special devotions, and advertised suitably Catholic literature.

The global Irish press was matched by a global trade in Irish books. The appetite was substantial. As early as 1837, for instance, a branch of the Catholic Book Society of Ireland had been established in Calcutta, while in Sydney John Bede Polding had begun importing devotional books from 1835 and established a lending library five years later.[57] The demand was met by firms such as Patrick Donohoe in Boston, D & J Sadlier & Co. in Montreal, P. J. Kennedy & Co and Louis Benziger in New York, and the Dublin-based publishers James Duffy and M. H. Gill. All of their lists were a mixture of religious titles and what Kevin Molloy calls 'Irish national literature', albeit heavily weighted towards the devotional.[58] These publishers were in turn supported by a network of importers, wholesalers, and booksellers who advertised their books in the Irish Catholic press to largely Irish Catholic readers. Nor was this trade purely commercial: in the first six months of 1906, for example, the 'Catholic Book Depot' operated by Cardinal Moran of Sydney distributed 120,000 catechisms across Australia, as well as stocking a 'vast supply' of Irish Catholic Truth Society pamphlets.[59] Collectively, all of this made possible what Molloy described as a 'global Irish reading community' that lay 'at the heart of the ethnic cohesion found in many nineteenth-century Irish Catholic settlements'.[60]

The representative figure of this community was the Irish-Canadian-American novelist Mary Anne Sadlier. Born in Co. Cavan in 1820, Sadlier migrated to Quebec in 1844, where she met her publisher husband, also an Irishman. She was fantastically prolific, writing more than

[55] *NZT*, 30 September 1881.   [56] *NZT*, 12 September 1884.
[57] See the *Bengal Catholic Expositor*, 6 July 1839, 11 January 1840; Kevin Molloy, 'Religious texts for the Catholic migrant: International print networks and the Irish-Australian book trade', in Barr and Carey, *Religion and Greater Ireland*, 71–93, at 74.
[58] Molloy, 82–3.   [59] Moran to Higgins, 16 July 1906, BDAV/HP/63/5/4.
[60] Molloy, 72.

sixty novels, as well as devotional works, translations, and a catechism. In the 1860s, she effectively ran the firm's New York office while editing its newspaper, the *New York Tablet*. In all of her work, Sadlier fused ortho-dox piety with Irish history and culture while modelling appropriate Catholic behaviour for her readers. In her 1855 novel *The Blakes and Flanagans*, for example, she contrasted the fates of two Irish migrant families in New York City. On the one hand, the Flanagans were 'good old fashioned Catholics' for whom 'religion was the sun of their solar system, giving life and warmth to themselves and all around them'. They were happy, pious, and sent their children to Catholic schools. The Blakes, on the other hand, 'professed to be good Catholics' but were mostly interested in making money, approached the sacraments irregu-larly, and sent their children to the public schools.[61] Their respective fates were entirely predictable. Sadlier's unapologetically didactic work was carefully targeted at different segments of Irish migrant society. Thus *The Blakes and Flanagans* was first published in Thomas D'Arcy McGee's *American Celt* and pitched at middle-class readers, while *Bessy Conway, or the Irish girl in America* (1861) was aimed at preserving the faith and virtue of Irish domestic servants.[62] Both were global bestsellers.

Like newspapers, novels, and devotional literature, school texts were also created and shared across Greater Ireland. The Christian Brothers, for example, produced them on subjects ranging from *The Elements of Arithmetic* to *The Catechist's Manual*. Their globally popular *Irish History Reader* hewed to an emphatically Catholic and nationalist narrative that was designed to 'keep brightly flaming the torch of love of country kindled at the hearth of every Irish home'.[63] As a result of these books, one Newfoundland-based brother boasted in 1898, 'our boys are as Irish as any by the Shannon or the Lee'.[64] Yet the Christian Brothers did not have a monopoly. In Australia, for example, Cardinal Moran commissioned a modified version of the Catholic readers sold in the United States by Benziger Brothers, and proofs and instructions passed back and forth between New York and Sydney. Moran, Archbishop Carr of Melbourne, and Bishop Higgins of Ballarat all took a detailed interest in the final text, and the first twenty-seven cases arrived in 1898 at a cost of $2,337.[65] A few years later, Moran bought the entire Australian stock of

---

[61] Mary Anne Sadlier, *The Blakes and Flanagans: A Tale, Illustrative of Irish Life in the United States* (New York: D. J. Sadlier & Co., 1855), 11–12.

[62] See Eileen P. Sullivan, *The Shamrock and the Cross: Irish American Novelists Shape American Catholicism* (Notre Dame, IN: University of Notre Dame Press, 2016), 30.

[63] The Christian Brothers, *Irish History Reader* (Dublin: M. H. Gill & Son, 1905), v.

[64] Quoted in Lambert, 'Far from the home of our fathers', 161.

[65] The correspondence is held in the Joseph Higgins papers in the Ballarat diocesan archives, file 63/1/11.

P. W. Joyce's *Social History of Ancient Ireland* (some 700 copies) and offered to buy 1,000 more in exchange for its author making specific changes and bringing his coverage up to the nineteenth century. He was confident that the newly created 'Hibernian Competition in Irish History' would stimulate demand across Australia.[66]

The success of these missions, schools, books, newspapers, and social controls is difficult to overstate but something of it can be glimpsed in the New Zealander Dan Davin's 1947 collection of short stories *The Gorse Blooms Pale*. Recalling his own Southland childhood through the eyes of a young boy, Mick, Davin writes of a world saturated in religion and tinged with sectarianism. Mick's family takes the 'Catholic weekly', he learns about Drogheda and Cromwell from Brother Athanasius, Johnny Nolan is judged for stepping out with a 'black North of Ireland Presbyterian', and Protestant and Catholic schoolboys trade insults and stones on the way home from their separate schools. Irish and Catholic are perfectly fused; Protestants exist but are to be suspected, fought, or pitied, and young Mick 'knew that God was green and Irish and a Catholic'.[67] This was the world as Paul Cullen, Francis Patrick Kenrick, and Patrick Francis Moran had dreamed it should be, and in most places it survived well into the twentieth century.

Throughout the English-speaking world, Irish Catholics and their descendants were born in Catholic hospitals, educated in Catholic schools, married other Catholics, read Catholic books and newspapers, joined Catholic societies, and were buried in Catholic cemeteries. The regularity and content of their religious practice were carefully structured and then enforced through the intimacy of the confessional and the power of social conformity. Those who deviated were chastised, shamed, or punished but never willingly abandoned to another faith or none. The walls around their community were self-built, very high, and thickened by a shared sense of threat and persecution. Behind those walls, Catholic society was and remained very Irish, even as time passed, distance from the island grew, and others began to arrive, sometimes in great numbers. This was the deliberate policy of the Hiberno-Roman bishops who had so meticulously seized the commanding heights of a hierarchical church. As William Walsh of Halifax put it in 1852, it was important to encourage Catholics to identify with Ireland 'for the associations and memories of their

[66] Moran to Joseph Higgins, 21 June 1905, 17 July, 6 October 1906, BDAV/HPA63/5/4.
[67] Dan Davin, *The Gorse Blooms Pale: Dan Davin's Southland Stories*, edited by Janet Wilson (Dunedin: University of Otago Press, 2007), 65, 93, 79, 58.

country bind them more and more to their religion'.[68] Ireland, Catholicism, and Rome became impossibly tangled and then fused together in a distinctively diasporic Hiberno-Roman amalgam. Over time, the overt Irishness of the church inevitably began to fade, and in some places largely vanished. Yet almost everywhere Hiberno-Romanism endured and became normative. The Roman Catholic Church is thus the solution to the problem posed by the American novelist Peter Quinn: the real question, he wrote, was not how the Irish became white but how they stayed Irish.[69] The answer is that the Irish made the church and the church kept them Irish. This was Ireland's empire.

[68] Walsh to Bayley, 26 March 1852, AANY/HP/Box 4/Folder 5.
[69] Peter Quinn, 'The future of Irish America', in Lee and Casey, 680–5, at 682.

Bibliography

Primary Sources

(I)   *Manuscripts*

Australia

Archives of the Archdiocese of Adelaide: Patrick Bonaventure
    Geoghegan papers; Laurence Sheil papers; Christopher Reynolds
    papers; John O'Reily papers
Archives of the Archdiocese of Canberra-Goulburn, National Library of
    Australia, Canberra: William Lanigan papers
Archives of the Archdiocese of Hobart: Robert Willson papers
Archives of the Archdiocese of Perth: Matthew Gibney papers
Archives of the Archdiocese of Sydney: Roger Bede Vaughan papers;
    Patrick Bonaventure Geoghegan papers; Patrick Francis Moran
    papers
Archives of the Diocese of Ballarat, VIC: Joseph Higgins papers
Archives of the Diocese of Bathurst, NSW: Matthew Quinn papers
Archives of the Diocese of Sandhurst, Bendigo, VIC: Henry Backhaus
    papers; Martin Crane papers
Archives of the Sisters of Mercy, Parramatta, NSW: Community archives
Brigidine Sisters' Archive, Coogee, NSW: Community archives
Dominican Sisters of Eastern Australia and the Solomon Islands,
    Strathfield, NSW: Community archives
Institute of the Sisters of Mercy of Australia and Papua New Guinea,
    Alphington, VIC: Community archives
Institute of the Sisters of Mercy of Australia and Papua New Guinea,
    Bathurst, NSW: Community archives
Loreto College Ballarat, Loreto Archive Centre: Community
    archives
Maitland-Newcastle Diocesan Archives, Newcastle: James Murray
    papers; Patrick Dwyer papers
Melbourne Diocesan Historical Commission: James Goold papers;
    Thomas Carr papers
Melbourne University Library: W. H. Archer Papers
St John's College, University of Sydney: College archives

State Library of New South Wales, Sydney: A. E. (Tony) Cahill papers; Sir Patrick Jennings papers

Tasmanian Archive Service, Hobart: Colonial Secretary registered papers

University of Newcastle, Auchmuty Library: Cultural collections

Canada

Antigonish Diocesan Archives, Nova Scotia: Colin MacKinnon papers; John Cameron papers

Archives of the Archdiocese of Halifax: William Walsh papers; John Loughnan papers

Archives of the Archdiocese of St John's, Newfoundland: Michael Anthony Fleming papers; J. T. Mullock papers; Thomas Power papers; Michael Howley papers

Archives de l'Archevêché de Québec: Nova Scotia letters

Archives Diocésaines de Bathurst, New Brunswick: James Rogers papers

Archives of the Diocese of Charlottetown, Prince Edward Island: Bernard Donald MacDonald papers; Peter McIntyre papers; James Charles MacDonald papers; James Morrison papers

Library and Archives Canada, Ottawa: Joseph Howe papers

Memorial University of Newfoundland, Archives and Special Collections, Queen Elizabeth II Library, St John's: Robert Bond papers

Nova Scotia Archives, Halifax

Presentation Congregation, St John's, Newfoundland: Community archives

Saint John Diocesan Archives, New Brunswick: William Dollard papers; James Sweeny papers

Toronto Archdiocesan Archives: William McDonald papers; John Joseph Lynch papers; Timothy O'Mahony papers

England

Archives of the Archdiocese of Birmingham: William Bernard Ullathorne papers

Archives of the Archdiocese of Southwark, London: Thomas Grant papers

Archivum Britannicum Societatis Iesu, London: India papers; Zambesi Mission papers

Bodleian Library, University of Oxford: Clarendon deposit

British Library, London: India Office Records; Sir Robert Peel papers

Cambridge University Library: Acton papers

Downside Abbey, Stratton-on-the-Fosse: H. N. Birt papers

The National Archives, Kew: Colonial Office papers

University of Nottingham, Manuscripts and Special Collections: Portland Wellbeck Collection

Westminster Diocesan Archives, London: Nicholas Wiseman papers

Falkland Islands

St Mary's Church, Stanley: Parish archives

Gibraltar

Cathedral of St Mary the Crowned: Cathedral archives
National Archives of Gibraltar

Italy

Archivio Storico dell'Istituto della Carità, Stresa: Antonio Rosmini papers
Archivium Venerabilis Collegii Anglorum de Urbe (Venerable English College), Rome: Rectors' papers; George Talbot papers
Pontifical Irish College, Rome: Paul Cullen papers; Tobias Kirby papers; Michael O'Riordan papers; John Hagan papers
Pontifical Scots College, Rome: Rectors' papers

New Zealand

Archives of the Catholic Diocese of Auckland: Jean-Baptiste Pompallier papers; Interregnum papers; Thomas Croke papers
Archives of the Diocese of Dunedin: Patrick Francis Moran papers; Michael Verdon papers
Christchurch Diocesan Archives: John Joseph Grimes papers; Matthew Brodie papers
Marist Archives, Wellington: Community archives
National Library of New Zealand, Alexander Turnbull Library: Thomas Croke papers; Richmond Family papers
Sisters of Mercy, Auckland: Community archives
Wellington Archdiocesan Archives: Francis Mary Redwood papers

Northern Ireland

Cardinal Tomás Ó Fiaich Memorial Library and Archive, Armagh: Joseph Dixon papers

Republic of Ireland

All Hallows College Archive, Dublin (now at Maynooth College)
Archives of the Archdiocese of Cashel: Thomas Croke papers
Archives of the Discalced Carmelites, Dublin: John Francis Whelan papers
Ardagh & Clonmacnois Diocesan Archives, Longford: George Conroy papers; Bartholomew Woodlock papers
Cloyne Diocesan Archives, Cobh: William Keane papers
Dominican Archives Dún Laoghaire: Community archives
Dominican Archives, Cabra, Dublin: Community archives
Dublin Diocesan Archives: Daniel Murray papers; William Hamilton papers; Paul Cullen papers; Laurence Forde papers; Australia papers; Edward McCabe papers

Franciscan Archives, Dún Mhuire, Killiney, Co. Dublin: Community archives
Irish Jesuit Archives, Dublin: Australia Papers
Irish Province of the Order of Carmelites, Gort Muire, Dublin: Carmelite archives
Limerick Diocesan Archives: Edward O'Dwyer papers
Loreto Archives, Dublin: Teresa Ball papers
Mercy International Centre, Dublin: Mercy archives
National Library of Ireland, Dublin: William Monsell papers
Presentation Convent, Galway: Community archives
Russell Library, St Patrick's College, Maynooth: Laurence Renehan papers; Charles Russell papers
St Mary's Convent, Callan, Co. Kilkenny: Community archives; St Brigid's Missionary College papers

Scotland
Archives of the Archdiocese of Glasgow: Western District papers
Scottish Catholic Archives, Columba House, Edinburgh: Eastern District papers
University of Aberdeen, Sir Duncan Rice Library, Scottish Catholic Archives Historic Collection: Oban letters

Spain
Royal Scots College, Salamanca: Rectors' papers

South Africa
Archives of the Archdiocese of Cape Town: Thomas Grimley papers; John Leonard papers
Cory Library for Historical Research, Rhodes University, Grahamstown
Port Elizabeth Diocesan Archives: Patrick Francis Moran papers; J. D. Ricards papers

The United States
Archives of the Archdiocese of Boston: Benedict Joseph Fenwick papers
Archives of the Archdiocese of New York: John Hughes papers
Archives of the Archdiocese of St Louis: Peter Kenrick papers
Archives of the Archdiocese of San Francisco: Joseph Sadoc Alemany papers
Archives of the Diocese of Charleston: John England papers
Archives of the Diocese of Sacramento: Eugene O'Connell papers
Archives of the Dominican Sisters of Peace, New Orleans: Community archives
Associated Archives, St Mary's Seminary and University, Baltimore: James Whitfield papers; Samuel Eccleston papers; Baltimore Visitation Monastery Collection; Francis Patrick Kenrick papers; Martin J. Spalding papers

The Catholic University of America, American Catholic Research Center and University Archives, Washington, DC: Francis Patrick Kenrick papers

Columbia University, Rare Books and Manuscript Library, New York: Henry Joseph Browne papers

Filson Historical Society, Louisville, KY: Catholic diocese of Bardstown papers

Philadelphia Archdiocesan Historical Research Center: St Mary's Church papers

Pittsburgh Diocesan Archives: Monsignor A. A. Lambing Manuscript Collection; Michael O'Connor papers

Seton Hall University Library, Monsignor Field Archives and Special Collections Center, South Orange, NJ: James Roosevelt Bayley papers

Sisters of St Joseph of Peace, Englewood Cliffs, NJ: Margaret Anna Cusack papers

University of Notre Dame Archives, South Bend, IN: Archdiocese of Cincinnati papers; Archdiocese of New Orleans papers

Villanova University, Philadelphia: University Archives

Vatican City

Archivio della Congregazione degli Affari Ecclesiastici Straordinari

Archivio Segreto Vaticano: Charles Acton papers

Archivio Storico di Propaganda Fide, Sacred Congregation for the Evangelisation of the Peoples

Archivio Storico di San Paolo fuori le Mura: Bernard Smith papers

(II)   *Periodicals*

The Advocate (Melbourne)

The Age (Melbourne)

The Australasian (Sydney)

Australasian Chronicle (Sydney)

The Barrier Miner (Broken Hill, NSW)

Bathurst Convent Annual

Bendigo Advertiser

Bengal Catholic Expositor (Calcutta)

The Bombay Catholic Standard and Military Chronicle

The Boston Pilot

The Calcutta Christian Observer

Catholic World (New York)

The Colonist (Grahamstown, Eastern Cape)

The Colonist (Sydney)

Cornwall Chronicle (Launceston, Tasmania)

The Courier (Brisbane)

The Cross (Halifax)

Daily Alta California (San Francisco)
Daily News (Perth)
Daily Southern Cross (Auckland)
The Daily Telegraph (Sydney)
Eastern Districts Chronicle (York, Western Australia)
Empire (Sydney)
The Evening Herald (St John's, NL)
Evening Star (Dunedin)
Freeman's Journal (Sydney)
Gibraltar Chronicle
Goulburn Evening Penny Post
Goulburn Herald
Great Eastern (Grahamstown, Eastern Cape)
Grey River Argus (Greymouth, New Zealand)
Hobart Town Daily Mercury
The Inquirer and Commercial News (Perth)
The Irish Exile and Freedom's Advocate (Hobart)
The Irish Harp and Farmers' Herald (Adelaide)
The Journal (Grahamstown, Eastern Cape)
The Liberator (Saint John, NB)
The Mercury (Hobart)
The Morning Chronicle (St John's, NL)
Madras Catholic Expositor
Madras Examiner
Marlborough Express (New Zealand)
Maryborough Chronicle, Wide Bay and Burnett Advertiser (New South Wales)
Melbourne Punch
New Brunswick Courier
New York Tablet
New Zealand Herald
New Zealand Tablet (Dunedin)
Newfoundlander (St John's, NL)
The North Australian (Brisbane)
Otago Daily Times (Dunedin)
Otago Witness (Dunedin)
The Perth Gazette and Independent Journal of Politics and News
The Press (Christchurch)
The Record (St John's, NL)
The Singleton Argus and Upper Hunter General Advocate
The South Australian (Adelaide)
The South Australian Register (Adelaide)
Southern Argus (Port Eliot, South Australia)
The Standard & Mail (Cape Town)
Sydney Gazette and New South Wales Advertiser
Sydney Herald
Sydney Mail

The Sydney Mail and New South Wales Advertiser
Sydney Morning Herald
The Tablet (Dublin and London)
Tasmanian Morning Herald (Hobart)
The Times (London)
The True Witness & Catholic Chronicle (Montreal)
The United States Catholic Magazine
Wanganui Chronicle
Wellington Independent
Williamstown Chronicle (Victoria)
Woodville Examiner (New Zealand)

(III)   Printed

Address of the Right Rev. Daniel O'Connor, D.D. Vicar Apostolic of Madras to the Clergy and People of the See of Meliapore (Madras: Printed at the Courier Press, 1838)

Annals of the Propagation of the Faith, vols. 1–9 (London, 1840–49)

Anonymous, *The Centenary of the Congregation of the Poor Sisters of Nazareth, Cape Town, 1882–1982* (Cape Town: Salesian Institute, 1982)

Anonymous, *Sisters of Mercy – Bathurst – 100 years – 1866–1966* (Bathurst: The Sisters of Mercy Bathurst, 1967)

'Fr Agathangelus' (ed.), *The Catholic Church and Southern Africa: A Series of Essays Published to Commemorate the Establishment of the Hierarchy in South Africa* (Cape Town: The Catholic Archdiocese of Cape Town, 1951)

Aubert, Suzanne, *Letters on the Go: The Correspondence of Suzanne Aubert*, edited by Jessie Munro (Wellington: Bridget Williams Books, 2009)

Australasian Catholic Directory for 1911

Bateman, Josiah, *The Life of the Right. Rev. Daniel Wilson, D.D., Late Lord Bishop of Calcutta and Metropolitan of India*, 2 vols. (London: John Murray, 1860)

Birt, Henry Norbert, *Benedictine Pioneers in Australia*, 2 vols. (London: Herbert and Daniel, 1911)

Blakiston, Noel (ed.), *The Roman Question: Extracts from the Despatches of Odo Russell from Rome 1858–1870*, new ed. (Wilmington, DE: Michael Glazier, 1980)

Bohan, Edmund, *The Singing Historian: A Memoir* (Christchurch: Canterbury University Press, 2012)

Bryce, James, *Impressions of South Africa* (London: Macmillan & Co., 1897)

Byrne, Geraldine, *Valiant Women: Letters from the Foundation Sisters of Mercy in Western Australia, 1845–1849* (Melbourne: Polding Press, 1981)

Cape of Good Hope, Debates in the Legislative Council, vol. 1

Carew, P. J., *An Ecclesiastical History of Ireland, from the Introduction of Christianity into that Country to the Commencement of the Thirteenth Century* (Dublin: John Coyne, 1835)

Census of the Colony of New South Wales, Taken on the 7th of April 1861 (Sydney: Thomas Richards, 1862)

Census of the Colony of Queensland, taken the 7th April, 1861

Centenary Volume: Benevolent Irish Society, St. John's Newfoundland (Cork: n.p., 1906)

The Christian Brothers, *Irish History Reader* (Dublin: M. H. Gill & Son, 1905)

[Clarke, Nancy and Hyles, Claudia], *Walking Nuns: Sisters of Mercy Goulburn Congregation Sesquicentenary* (Goulburn: Sisters of Mercy Goulburn Congregation, 2009)

Cole, Alfred W., *The Cape and the Kaffirs: Notes of Five Years' Residence in South Africa* (London: Richard Bentley, 1852)

Conzemius, Victor (ed.), *Ignaz v Döllinger Briefwechsel mit Lord Acton, Band 2: 1869–1870* (Munich: C. H. Beck'sche Verlagsbuchhandlung, 1965)

The Correspondence of Mother Vincent Whitty, 1839–1892, compiled by Anne Hetherington and Pauline Smoothy (St Lucia: University of Queensland Press, 2011)

Cullen, Paul, *Publicam Disputationem de Theologia Universa et Historia Ecclesiastica* (Roma: Congregazione de Propagande Fide, 1828)

[Cusack, Margaret Anna], 'The Nun of Kenmare', *Advice to Irish girls in America* (New York: J. A. McGee, 1872)

Davin, Dan, *The Gorse Blooms Pale: Dan Davin's Southland Stories*, edited by Janet Wilson (Dunedin: University of Otago Press, 2007)

Dickens, Charles, *American Notes & Pictures from Italy* (London: Chapman & Hall, 1907)

Dilke, Charles Wentworth, *Greater Britain: A Record of Travel in English-Speaking Countries during 1866 and 1867*, 2nd ed. (London: Macmillan and Co., 1869)

'The diocese of Baltimore in 1818. Archbishop Maréchal's account to Propaganda October 16, 1818', *The Catholic Historical Review*, vol. 1, no. 4 (January 1916), 439–53

Duffy, Charles Gavan, *My Life in Two Hemispheres*, 2 vols. (New York: Macmillan, 1898)

Extracts from the Victorian Press in Reference to the General State of Catholic Affairs in Victoria and to the Case of the Rev. P. Dunne in Particular (Dublin: James Duffy, 1857)

Fennelly, Stephen, *Relations of the Catholic Church in India with the Honourable the East India Company's Government* (Dublin: James Duffy, 1857)

'F. E. T.', *The Kenrick-Frenaye Correspondence: Letters Chiefly of Francis Patrick Kenrick and Marc Antony Frenaye, Selected from the Cathedral Archives Philadelphia, 1830–1862* (Philadelphia: N.P., 1920)

Gosse, Edmund, *The Naturalist of the Sea-Shore: The Life of Philip Henry Gosse* (London: William Heinemann, 1896)

Griffin, Martin I. J., 'The life of Bishop Conwell of Philadelphia', *Records of the American Catholic Historical Society*, vols. 24(1913)–29(1918) at 29 no. 2, pp. 181–2 and 24 no. 3, at pp. 251–4

Griffith, Patrick, *The Cape Diary of Bishop Griffith, 1837–1839*, edited by J. B. Brain (Cape Town: South African Catholic Bishops Conference, 1988)

Henningsen, Amelia de, *The Reminiscences of Amelia de Henningsen (Notre Mère)*, edited by Margaret Young (Cape Town: Maskew Miller Longman for Rhodes University, 1989)

Herbert, Robert, *The Queensland Letters of Robert Herbert, Premier: Letters and Papers*, edited by Bruce Knox (St Lucia: University of Queensland Press, 1977)

Holman, William Arthur, 'My political life', in *The First New South Wales Labor Government 1910–1916, Two Memoirs: William Holman and John Osborne*, edited by Michael Hogan (Sydney: University of New South Wales Press, 2005)

Howley, M. F., *Sermon Preached by the Rev. Doctor Howley in the Cathedral, St. John's, on the Feast of St. Patrick, 1869* (St John's: n.p., 1869)

Howley, M. F., *The Ecclesiastical History of Newfoundland* (Boston: Doyle and Whittle, 1888)

Howley, R. V., 'Cardinal Barnabò: A reminiscence', *Catholic World*, April 1903

Hughes, John, *A Sermon Preached in the Church of St. Augustine, in Philadelphia, on the 31st of May, 1829, at a Solemn, Religious Thanksgiving to Almighty God for the Emancipation of the Catholics of Great Britain and Ireland* (Philadelphia: Garden & Thompson, 1829)

Hughes, John, *The Catholic Chapter in the History of the United States, a Lecture: Delivered in the Metropolitan Hall, before the Catholic Institute, on Monday Evening, March 8, 1852, for the Benefit of the House of Protection, under the Charge of the Sisters of Mercy* (New York: Edward Dunigan & Brother, 1852)

Hughes, John, *The Church and the World, a Lecture: Delivered at the Chinese Museum, Philadelphia, on Thursday Evening, January 31, 1850* (New York: Edward Dunigan & Brother, 1850)

Joyce, James, *A Portrait of the Artist as a Young Man*, edited by Kevin J. H. Demar (New York: Barnes and Noble, 2004)

Joyce, James, *Ulysses*, Oxford World's Classics (Oxford: Oxford University Press, 1998)

Keegan, William, *An Account of the Begum Sombre and Her Family* (Sirdhana: 1889)

Kenny, John, *A History of the Commencement and Progress of Catholicity in Australia, up to the Year 1840* (Sydney: F. Cunningham & Co., 1886)

Kenrick, Francis Patrick, *Diary and Visitation Record of the Rt. Rev. Francis Patrick Kenrick, Administrator and Bishop of Philadelphia, 1830–1851* (Philadelphia: Archdiocese of Philadelphia, 1916)

Kenrick, Peter Richard, *The Validity of Anglican Ordinations Examined; Or, a Review of Certain Facts Regarding the Consecration of Matthew Parker, First Protestant Archbishop of Canterbury* (Philadelphia: Eugene Cumminskey, 1841)

Laheen, Kevin, 'The Letters of an Irish Brother, Edward Sinnott, S.J., from Calcutta, 1834–37', *Collectanea Hibernica*, nos. 46 & 47 (2004–5), 155–97

Macaulay, James, *Ireland in 1872: A Tour of Observation with Remarks on Irish Public Questions* (London: H. S. King and Co., 1873)

Mace, J. H. B., *Henry Bodley Bromby, A Memoir* (London: Longmans, Green, and Co., 1913)

McCourt, Peter, *Biographical Sketch of the Honorable Edward Whelan, Together with a Compilation of His Principal Speeches* (Charlottetown: The Author, 1888)

Medlycott, A. E., 'Catholic Army Chaplains – An Historical Statement of their Case', *The Tablet*, 17 February 1883

Molony, John, *Luther's Pine: An Autobiography* (Canberra: Pandanus Books, 2004)

Moran, Patrick Francis, *History of the Catholic Church in Australasia, from Authentic Sources* (Sydney: The Oceanic Publishing Company, n.d.)

Moran, Patrick Francis, *Lecture on the Rights and Duties of Labour, Sydney 17 August 1891* (Sydney: Fine Brothers & Co., 1891)

Moran, Patrick Francis, *The Writings of Cardinal Cullen*, 3 vols. (Dublin: Browne & Nolan, 1882)

Mullock, J. T., *The History of Heresies, Their Refutation, and the Triumph of the Church, Translated from the Italian of St. Alphonsus M. Liguori*, 2 vols. (Dublin: James Duffy, 1847)

Mullock, J. T., *Two Lectures on Newfoundland, Delivered at St. Bonaventure's College, January 25, and February 1, 1860* (St John's: John Mullaly, at the Office of the Metropolitan Record, 1860)

Newman, John Henry, *The Letters and Diaries of John Henry Newman*, edited by Charles Stephen Dessain et al., 32 vols. (Edinburgh and Oxford: Thomas Nelson and Oxford University Press, 1961–2008)

O'Connor, Michael, *Archbishop Kenrick and His Work: A Lecture* (Philadelphia: Catholic Standard, 1867)

O'Haire, James, *Recollections of Twelve Years' Residence (as a Missionary Priest) Viz: From July 1863 to June 1875 in the Western District of the Cape of Good Hope, South Africa, Selected Chiefly from His Diary* (Dublin: Cooke, Keating & Co., [1876])

O'Leary, John, *Recollections of Fenians and Fenianism*, 2 vols. (London: Downey and Co., 1896)

O'Reilly, Bernard, *John MacHale, Archbishop of Tuam: His Life, Times, and Correspondence*, 2 vols. (New York: Fr. Pustet & Co., 1890)

[O'Reilly, Hugh], *The Letters of Hibernicus, Extracts from the Pamphlet Entitled "A Report on the Committee of St. Mary's Parish, Halifax, N.S.", and a Review of the Same* (Pictou: n.p., 1842)

O'Riley, Alban, *Notre Mère: A Record of the Life of Sœur M. Gertrude du S. Sacrement, Foundress of the First Community of Nuns in South Africa* (London: Burns Oates & Washbourne, 1922)

Parkes, Henry, *Fifty Years in the Making of Australian History*, 2 vols. (London: Longmans, Green, & Co., 1892)

Prowse, D. W., *The History of Newfoundland, from the English, Colonial, and Foreign Records* (London: Macmillan & Co., 1895)

Report from the House of Commons Select Committee on Indian Territories (1853)

Ricards, J. D., 'Popular education: A lecture delivered by the Right Rev. Dr. Ricards, R.C. bishop, and vicar apostolic of the Eastern Province of the Cape Colony, in St. Augustine's Hall, Port Elizabeth, and in the Albany Hall, Graham's Town, June, 1872' (Port Elizabeth: Richards, Impey & Co., 1872)

Ricards, J. D., *The Catholic Church and the Kaffir: A Brief Sketch of the Progress of Catholicity in South Africa, and the Prospects of Extensive Catholic Missions on the Point of Being Founded for the Natives of British Kaffraria* (London: Burns & Oates, [1879])

Rule, W. H., *Memoir of a Mission to Gibraltar and Spain, with Collateral Notices of Events Favouring Religious Liberty, and of the Decline of Romish Power in that*

Country, from the Beginning of This Century, to the Year 1842 (London: John Mason, 1844)

'Rules and constitutions of St. Joseph's Catholic Institute' (*Newfoundlander* Office, 1872)

'Rules of the Grahamstown St. Patrick's Catholic Mutual Benefit Society' (Grahamstown: Journal Office, 1890)

Russell, Matthew, 'Another batch of letters', *The Irish Ecclesiastical Record*, 4th series, vol. 3 (January–June 1898)

Ryan, J. Tighe, *The Attitude of the Catholic Church: A Special Interview with His Eminence Cardinal Moran* (Sydney: George Robertson & Co., 1894)

Sadlier, Mary Anne, *The Blakes and Flanagans: A Tale, Illustrative of Irish Life in the United States* (New York: D. J. Sadlier & Co., 1855)

The Salvado Memoirs, edited and translated by E. J. Stormon (Perth: University of Western Australia Press, 1977)

'Sister Maura', *The Sisters of Charity of Halifax* (Toronto: Ryerson Press, 1956)

Sisters of the Good Samaritan (eds.), *The Letters of John Bede Polding*, 3 vols. (Sydney: Sisters of the Good Samaritan, 1994)

Statutes of the Cape of Good Hope, 1872–1886

Therry, Roger, *Reminiscences of Thirty Years' Residence in New South Wales and Victoria* (Sydney: Sydney University Press, 1974 [1863])

Translation of the Decrees Regarding Education, Mixed Marriages, and Other Subjects, Adopted by the Archbishop and Bishops Assembled in Provincial Council, at Melbourne, in April, 1869 (West Maitland, NSW: Henry Thomas, 1873)

Trevelyan, George Otto, *The Life and Letters of Lord Macaulay*, 2 vols., new ed. (London: Longmans, Green, & Co., 1878)

Ullathorne, William Bernard, *The Autobiography of Archbishop Ullathorne, with Selections from His Letters* (London: Burns & Oates, n.d.)

Vaggioli, Felice, *A Deserter's Adventures: The Autobiography of Dom Felice Vaggioli*, translated by John Crockett (Dunedin: Otago University Press, 2001)

[Walsh, Richard], *A Letter on the State of Religion & Education in the Archdiocese of Sydney and the Colony of New South Wales, Addressed to His Grace the Most Rev. Dr. Cullen, Archbishop of Ireland, Apostolic Delegate, &c &c &c., by the Very Rev. Dean Walsh, New South Wales* (Waterford: Printed at "The News" office, 1862)

Ward, Harriet, *Five Years in Kaffirland; with Sketches of the Late War in That Country, to the Conclusion of the Peace. Written on the Spot*, 2nd ed., 2 vols. (London: Henry Colburn, 1848)

Wilmot, Alexander, *The Life and Times of the Right Rev. James David Ricards, Bishop of Retimo, in partibus infidelium, and Vicar-Apostolic of the Eastern Districts of the Cape Colony* (Cape Town: The Salesian Institute, 1908)

Secondary Sources

(I)   Printed

Acheson, T. W., *Saint John: The Making of a Colonial Urban Community* (Toronto: University of Toronto Press, 1985)

Akenson, Donald Harman, *Occasional Papers on the Irish in South Africa* (Grahamstown: Institute of Social and Economic Research, Rhodes University, 1991)

Akenson, Donald Harman, *Half the World from Home: Perspectives on the Irish in New Zealand 1860–1950* (Wellington: Victoria University Press, 1990)

Akenson, Donald Harman, *The Irish in Ontario: A Study in Rural History* (Montreal and Kingston: McGill-Queen's University Press, 1984)

Anchukandam, Thomas, *Catholic Revival in India in the 19th Century: Role of Mgr. Clément Bonnard (1796–1861), Vol. 1: Up to the General Division of the Indian Missions (1845)* (Bangalore: Kristu Jyoti Publications, 1996)

Anchukandam, Thomas, *Catholic Revival in India in the 19th Century: Role of Mgr. Clément Bonnard (1796–1861), Vol. 2: From the General Division of the Indian Missions to the Death of Mgr. Bonnard* (Bangalore: Kristu Jyoti Publications, 2006)

Anchukandam, Thomas, *The First Synod of Pondicherry 1844: A Study Based on Archival Sources* (Bangalore: Kristu Jyoti Publications, 1994)

Anderson, Jaynie, 'Visible and invisible: Jacques Stella in Melbourne', *Burlington Magazine*, CLVIII (April 2016), 245–50

Anderson, Jaynie, Vodola, Max, and Carmody, Shane (eds.), *The Invention of Melbourne: A Baroque Archbishop and a Gothic Architect* (Melbourne: The Miegunyah Press, 2019)

Andreassi, Anthony D., '"The cunning leader of a dangerous clique?": The Burstell affair and Archbishop Michael Augustine Corrigan', *The Catholic Historical Review*, vol. 86, no. 4 (October 2000), 620–39

Archer, E. G. and Traverso, A. A., *Education in Gibraltar, 1704–2004* (Gibraltar: Gibraltar Books, n.d.)

Ashley, John B., 'The consecration of the cathedral in 1855', in John F. Wallis, Francis Puddister, Gary J. Walsh, and John A. O'Mara (eds.), *The Basilica-Cathedral of St. John the Baptist, St. John's, Newfoundland, 1855–1980* (St John's: The basilica parish, 1980)

Ayres, Philip, *Prince of the Church: Patrick Francis Moran, 1830–1911* (Melbourne: The Miegunyah Press, 2007)

Baker, D. W. A., *Preacher, Politician, Patriot: A Life of John Dunmore Lang* (Melbourne: Melbourne University Press, 1998)

Baker, William M., *Timothy Warren Anglin 1822–96: Irish Catholic Canadian* (Toronto: University of Toronto Press, 1977)

Ballantyne, Tony, *Webs of Empire: Locating New Zealand's Colonial Past* (Wellington: Bridget Williams Books, 2012)

Ballhatchet, Kenneth, *Caste, Class and Catholicism in India 1789–1914* (Richmond: Curzon, 1998)

Bannister, Jerry, 'Whigs and nationalists: The legacy of Judge Prowse's History of Newfoundland', *Acadiensis*, vol. 32, no. 1 (Autumn 2002)

Barr, Colin, '"An ambiguous awe": Paul Cullen and the historians', in Dáire Keogh and Albert McDonnell (eds.), *Cardinal Paul Cullen and His World* (Dublin: Four Courts Press, 2011), 414–34

Barr, Colin, *The European Culture Wars in Ireland: The Callan Schools Affair, 1868–81* (Dublin: University College Dublin Press, 2010)

Barr, Colin, "'Imperium in Imperio": Irish Episcopal Imperialism in the Nineteenth-Century', *The English Historical Review*, vol. 123, no. 502 (2008), 611–50

Barr, Colin, 'Paul Cullen, Italy, and the Irish Catholic imagination, 1826–70', in Colin Barr, Michele Finelli, and Anne O'Connor (eds.), *Nation/Nazione: Irish Nationalism and the Italian Risorgimento* (Dublin: University College Dublin Press, 2014), 133–56

Barr, Colin, *Paul Cullen, John Henry Newman, and the Catholic University of Ireland, 1845–65* (Notre Dame, IN: University of Notre Dame Press, 2003)

Barr, Colin and Luminiello, Rose, "'The leader of the virgin choirs of Erin": St. Brigid's Missionary College, 1883–1914', in Michael DeNie, Timothy McMahon, and Paul Townend (eds.), *Ireland's Imperial Cultures* (London: Palgrave Macmillan, 2017), 155–78

Bartlett, Thomas, 'The Irish soldier in India, 1750–1947', in Michael Holmes and Denis Holman (eds.), *Ireland and India: Connections, Comparisons, Contrasts* (Dublin: Folens, 1997), 12–28

Bassett, Michael, *Sir Joseph Ward: A Political Biography* (Auckland: Auckland University Press, 1993)

Bayley, C. C., *Mercenaries for the Crimea: The German, Swiss, and Italian Legions in British Service, 1854–1856* (Montreal and Kingston: McGill-Queen's University Press, 1977)

Bayly, C. A., *The Birth of the Modern World, 1780–1914: Global Connections and Comparisons* (London: Wiley-Blackwells, 2004)

Bayor, Ronald H. and Meagher, Timothy J. (eds.), *The New York Irish* (Baltimore: Johns Hopkins University Press, 1996)

Beaglehole, J. C., *The University of New Zealand: An Historical Study* (Wellington: New Zealand Council for Educational Research, 1937)

Beck, J. Murray, *Joseph Howe, Vol. 1: Conservative Reformer 1804–1848* (Montreal and Kingston: McGill-Queen's University Press, 1982)

Beck, J. Murray, *Joseph Howe, Vol. 2: The Briton Becomes Canadian* (Montreal and Kingston: McGill-Queen's University Press, 1983)

Becker, Christopher, *Early History of the Catholic Missions in Northeast India (1598–1890)* (Shillong: Vendrame Institute, 1980)

Becker, Christopher, *History of the Catholic Missions in Northeast India (1890–1915)* (Shillong: Vendrame Institue, 1989)

Belich, James, *Paradise Reforged: A History of the New Zealanders from the 1880s to the Year 2000* (Auckland: Allen Lane, 2001)

Bellamy, Kathrine E., *Weavers of the Tapestry* (St John's: Flanker Press, 2006)

Bickford-Smith, Vivian, *Ethnic Pride and Racial Prejudice in Victorian Cape Town: Group Identity and Social Practice, 1875–1902* (Cambridge: Cambridge University Press, 1995)

Birchley, Delia, *John McEncroe: Colonial Democrat* (Blackburn, Vic: Collins Dove, 1986)

Bohan, Edmund, *'Blest Madman': FitzGerald of Canterbury* (Christchurch: Canterbury University Press, 1998)

Boland, S. J., *Faith of Our Fathers: The Redemptorists in Australia, 1882–1982* (N.P.: Redemptorist Fathers, 1982)

Boland, S. J., 'Review of The Roman Mould of the Australian Catholic Church by John N. Molony', *Catholic Historical Review*, vol. 58, no. 2 (1972), 248–9

Boland, T. P., 'The Queensland Immigration Society: A notable experiment in Irish settlement', University of Queensland Library, n.d.

Boland, T. P., *Thomas Carr: Archbishop of Melbourne* (St Lucia: Queensland University Press, 1997)

Bolger, Francis W. P., *Prince Edward Island and Confederation, 1863–1873* (Charlottetown: St Dunstan's University Press, 1964)

Boner, Kathleen, *Dominican Women: A Time to Speak* (Pietermaritzburg: Cluster Publications, 2000)

Bourke, D. F., *The History of the Catholic Church in Western Australia* (Perth: Archdiocese of Perth, 1979)

Bowen, Desmond, *Paul Cardinal Cullen and the Shaping of Modern Irish Catholicism* (Dublin: Gill & Macmillan, 1983)

Brain, J. B., *Catholic Beginnings in Natal and Beyond* (Durban: T. W. Griggs & Co., 1975)

Brain, J. B., *The Catholic Church in the Transvaal* (Johannesburg: Missionary Oblates of Mary Immaculate, 1991)

Brain, J. B., *Catholics in Natal II* (Durban: Archdiocese of Durban, 1982)

Brain, J. B., 'The Irish influence on the Roman Catholic Church in South Africa', in D. McCracken (ed.), *The Irish in Southern Africa, 1795–1910*, vol. 2 (Durban: Irish in Southern Africa Project, 1992), 121–31

Brett, Judith, *The Enigmatic Mr Deakin* (Melbourne: The Text Publishing Company, 2017)

Brosnahan, Seán, 'The "Battle of the borough" and the "Saige of Timaru": Sectarian riot in colonial Canterbury', *The New Zealand Journal of History*, vol. 28 no. 1 (April 1994), 41–59

Brosnahan, Seán, 'Being Scottish in an Irish Catholic church in a Scottish Presbyterian settlement: Otago's Scottish Catholics, 1848–1895', *Immigrants & Minorities*, vol. 30, no. 1 (March 2012), 22–42

Brosnahan, Seán, '"Taking off the gloves": Sectarianism in New Zealand rugby in the 1920s', unpublished paper, by courtesy of the author

Brown, Gavin, '"The evil state of tepidity": Mass-going and absenteeism in nineteenth-century Australian ecclesiastical discourse', *Journal of Religious History*, vol. 33, no. 1 (March 2009), 28–48

Brown, Judith M., *Augustus Short, D.D., Bishop of Adelaide* (Adelaide: Hodge Publishing, 1973)

Brown, L. W., *The Indian Christians of St. Thomas: An Account of the Ancient Syrian Church of Malabar* (Cambridge: Cambridge University Press, 1956)

Brown, W. E., *The Catholic Church in South Africa*, edited by Michael Derrick (New York: P. J. Kennedy & Sons, 1960)

Bumsted, J. M., 'Scottish Catholicism in Canada', in Terrence Murphy and Gerald Stortz (eds.), *Creed and Culture: The Place of English-Speaking Catholics in Canadian Society, 1750–1930* (Montreal and Kingston: McGill-Queen's University Press, 1993), 79–99

Burns, Robert E., *Being Catholic, Being American: The Notre Dame Story, 1842–1934* (Notre Dame, IN: University of Notre Dame Press, 1999)

Butchers, A. G., *A Centennial History of Education in Canterbury* (Christchurch: Centennial Committee of the Canterbury Education Board, [1950])

Butler, Cuthbert, *The Life and Times of Bishop Ullathorne 1806–1889*, 2 vols. (London: Burns Oates and Washbourne, 1926)

Butler, Cuthbert, *The Vatican Council: The Story Told from Inside in Archbishop Ullathorne's Letters*, 2 vols. (London: Longmans, Green and Co., 1930)

Bygott, Ursula M. L., *With Pen and Tongue: The Jesuits in Australia, 1865–1939* (Melbourne: Melbourne University Press, 1980)

Byrne, Cyril J., *Gentlemen-Bishops and Faction Fighters* (St John's: Jesperson Press, 1984)

Byrne, Neil J., *Robert Dunne, Archbishop of Brisbane* (St Lucia: University of Queensland Press, 1991)

Cadigan, Sean, *Newfoundland and Labrador: A History* (Toronto: University of Toronto Press, 2009)

Cahill, A. E., 'Catholicism and socialism: The 1905 controversy in Australia', *Journal of Religious History*, vol. 1, no. 2 (December 1960), 88–101

Cameron, James D., *For the People: A History of St Francis Xavier University* (Montreal and Kingston: McGill-Queen's University Press for St Francis Xavier University, 1996)

Campanini, Giorgio, 'Antonio Rosmini and representative institutions', *Parliaments, Estates and Representation*, vol. 17, no. 1 (2010), 129–37

Campbell, Malcolm, *Ireland's New Worlds: Immigrants, Politics, and Society in the United States and Australia, 1815–1922* (Madison: University of Wisconsin Press, 2008)

Campion, Edmund, 'Patrick O'Farrell: An expanded memory', *Journal of Religious History*, vol. 31, no. 1 (March 2007), 18–23

Carey, Hilary M., 'Introduction: Remembering the religious history of A. E. (Tony) Cahill (1933–2004) and Patrick O'Farrell (1933–2003)', *Journal of Religious History*, vol. 31, no. 1 (March 2007), 1–17

Carey, Hilary M. and Colin Barr, 'Introduction', in Colin Barr and Hilary M. Carey (eds.), *Religion and Greater Ireland: Christianity and Irish Global Networks, 1750–1850* (Montreal and Kingston: McGill-Queen's University Press, 2015), 3–29

Carey, Patrick W., *An Immigrant Bishop: John England's Adaptation of Irish Catholicism to American Republicanism* (New York: United States Catholic Historical Society, 1982)

Carey, Patrick W., *People, Priests and Prelates: Ecclesiastical Democracy and the Tensions of Trusteeism* (Notre Dame, IN: University of Notre Dame Press, 1987)

Carson, Penelope, *The East India Company and Religion, 1698–1858* (Woodbridge: The Boydell Press, 2012)

Caruana, Charles, *The Rock under a Cloud* (Cambridge: Silent Books, 1989)

Casey, Eileen M., *Held in Our hearts: The Story of the Sisters of Mercy of the Goulburn Congregation* (Fyshwick, ACT: Panther Publishing, 2009)

Clark, Manning, 'Foreword', in John Molony, *The Roman Mould of the Australian Catholic Church* (Melbourne: Melbourne University Press, 1969), vii–viii

Clark, Mary Rylls, *Loreto in Australia* (Sydney: University of New South Wales Press, 2009)

Clarke, Brian P., *Piety and Nationalism: Lay Voluntary Associations and the Creation of an Irish-Catholic Community in Toronto, 1850–1895* (Montreal and Kingston: McGill-Queen's University Press, 1993)

Clifton, Michael, *The Quiet Negotiator: Bishop Grant of Southwark* (The Author: n.p., n.d.)

Codignola, Luca, *The Coldest Harbour of the Land: Simon Stock and Lord Baltimore's Colony in Newfoundland, 1621–1649* (Montreal and Kingston: McGill-Queen's University Press, 1988)

Codignola, Luca, 'The policy of Rome towards the English-speaking Catholics in British North America, 1750–1830', in Terrence Murphy and Gerald Stortz (eds.), *Creed and Culture: The Place of English-Speaking Catholics in Canadian Society, 1750–1930* (Montreal and Kingston: McGill-Queen's University Press, 1993), 100–25

Coffey, Leigh-Ann, 'Drawing strength from past migratory experiences: The *Church of Ireland Gazette* and southern Protestant migration in the post-independence period', in Colin Barr and Hilary M. Carey (eds.), *Religion and Greater Ireland: Christianity and Irish Global Networks, 1750–1950* (Montreal and Kingston: McGill-Queen's University Press, 2015), 52–70

Coleman, Francis L. with Farnell, Tony, *St. Aidan's College Grahamstown* (Grahamstown: Institute of Social and Economic Research, Rhodes University, 1980)

Comiskey, John P., *In My Heart's Best Wishes for You: A Biography of Archbishop John Walsh* (Montreal and Kingston: McGill-Queen's University Press, 2012)

Condon, Kevin, *The Missionary College of All Hallows, 1842–1891* (Dublin: All Hallows College, 1986)

Conlon, Patrick, 'Reforming and seeking an identity, 1829–1918', in Edel Bhreathnach, Joseph MacMahon, and John McCafferty (eds.), *The Irish Franciscans, 1534–1990* (Dublin: Four Courts Press, 2009), 102–31

Connolly, R. J., *A History of the Roman Catholic Church in Harbour Grace* (St John's: Creative Publishers, 1986)

Cook, S. B., *Imperial Affinities: Nineteenth Century Analogies and Exchanges between India and Ireland* (New Delhi: Sage Publications, 1993)

Corish, Patrick J. *Maynooth College, 1795–1995* (Dublin: Gill & Macmillan, 1995)

Crosbie, Barry, *Irish Imperial Networks: Migration, Social Communication and Exchange in Nineteenth-Century India* (Cambridge: Cambridge University Press, 2012)

Crunican, Paul, *Priests and Politicians: Manitoba Schools and the Election of 1896* (Toronto: University of Toronto Press, 1974)

Cullen, John H., *The Catholic Church in Tasmania* (Hobart: The Examiner Press, [1949])

Cunich, Peter, 'Archbishop Vaughan and the empires of religion in colonial New South Wales', in Hilary M. Carey (ed.), *Empires of Religion* (Basingstoke: Palgrave Macmillan, 2006), 137–60

Cunningham, Anne, *The Rome Connection: Australia, Ireland and the Empire 1865–1885* (Darlinghurst, NSW: Crossing Press, 2002)

Curran, Charles E., *The Origins of Moral Theology in the United States: Three Different Approaches* (Washington, DC: Georgetown University Press, 1997)

Cuthbertson, Brian, *Johnny Bluenose at the Polls: Early Nova Scotian Election Battles 1758–1848* (Halifax: Formac Publishing, 1994)

D'Agostino, Peter R., *Rome in America: Transnational Catholic Ideology from the Risorgimento to Fascism* (Chapel Hill: University of North Carolina Press, 2004)

D'Arcy, Fergus, *Terenure College 1860–2010: A History* (Dublin: Terenure College, 2009)

Darcy, J. B., *Noble to Our View: The Saga of St. Bonaventure's College, St. John's: The First 150 Years, 1856–2006* (St John's: Creative Publishers, 2007)

Davis, Richard P., 'Sir Robert Stout and the Irish question, 1879–1921', *Historical Studies: Australia and New Zealand*, vol. 12, no. 47 (1966), 417–34

Davis, Richard P., *Irish Issues in New Zealand Politics, 1868–1922* (Dunedin: Otago University Press, 1974)

Davis, Richard, *Irish Traces on Tasmanian History 1803–2004* (Hobart: Sassafras Books, 2005)

Davis, Richard, 'Preface', *Bulletin of the Centre for Tasmanian Historical Studies: Irish Edition*, vol. 2, no. 3 (1989)

Davis, Richard, *State Aid and Tasmanian Politics, 1868–1920*, rev. ed. (Hobart: University of Tasmania, 1980)

de Kiewiet, C. W., *A History of South Africa: Social and Economic* (Oxford: Oxford University Press, 1975 [1941])

Denis, Philippe, *The Dominican Friars in Southern Africa: A Social History (1577–1990)* (Leiden: Brill, 1998)

Diner, Hasia R., '"The most Irish city in the Union": The era of the Great Migration, 1844–1877', in Ronald H. Bayor and Timothy J. Meagher (eds.), *The New York Irish* (Baltimore: Johns Hopkins University Press, 1996), 87–106

Dinn, Mary James, *Foundation of the Presentation Congregation in Newfoundland* (St John's: n.p., 1975)

Dischl, Marcel, *Transkei for Christ: A History of the Catholic Church in the Transkeian Territories* (N.P.: The Author, 1982)

Dolan, Jay P., *The American Catholic Experience: A History from Colonial Times to the Present* (New York: Doubleday, 1985)

Dolan, Jay P., *The Immigrant Church: New York's Irish and German Catholics, 1815–1865* (Baltimore: Johns Hopkins University Press, 1975)

Dow, Gwyneth M., *George Higinbotham: Church and State* (Melbourne: Sir Isaac Pitman & Sons, 1964)

Dowd, Christopher, *Faith, Ireland, and Empire: The Life of Patrick Joseph Clune CSSR 1864–1935, Archbishop of Perth, Western Australia* (Strathfield, NSW: St Paul's Publications, 2014)

Dowd, Christopher, *Rome in Australia: The Papacy and Conflict in the Australian Catholic Missions, 1834–1884*, 2 vols. (Leiden: Brill, 2008)

Doyle, D. N., 'The Irish in North America, 1776–1845', in W. E. Vaughan (ed.), *A New History of Ireland, Vol. 5: Ireland under the Union, 1801–1870* (Oxford: Oxford University Press, 1989), 682–725

Doyle, Francis B., 'South Africa', in Patrick J. Corish (ed.), *A History of Irish Catholicism*, vol. 6, fascicle 4 (Dublin: Gill & Macmillan, 1971), 1–27

Doyle, Marjorie, *Reels, Rock and Rosaries: Confessions of a Newfoundland Musician* (Lawrencetown Beach, NS: Pottersfield Press, 2005)

Dubow, Saul, *A Commonwealth of Knowledge: Science, Sensibility, and White South Africa 1820–2000* (Oxford: Oxford University Press, 2006)

Dwyer, John T., *Condemned to the Mines: The Life of Eugene O'Connell, 1815–1891: Pioneer Bishop of Northern California and Nevada* (New York: Vantage Press, 1976)

Farragher, Seán P., *Edward Barron, 1801–1854: Unsung Hero of the Mission to Africa* (Dublin: Paraclete Press, 2004)

Fay, Terence J., *A History of Canadian Catholics* (Montreal and Kingston: McGill-Queen's University Press, 2002)

Feheney, J. M., *Catholic Education in Trinidad in the Nineteenth Century* (Dublin: Four Courts Press, 2001)

Fingard, Judith, *The Dark Side of Life in Victorian Halifax* (Porters Lake, NS: Pottersfield Press, 1989)

Finlayson, T. J., *Gibraltar, Military Fortress or Commercial Colony* (Gibraltar: Gibraltar Books, 2011)

Fisher, Michael H., *The Inordinately Strange Life of Dyce Sombre: Victorian Anglo-Indian MP and Chancery 'Lunatic'* (London: C. Hurst & Co., 2010)

Foale, Marie Therese, *The Josephite Story: Mary MacKillop and the Sisters of St. Joseph, 1866–1893* (Sydney: St Joseph's Generalate, 1989)

Fogarty, Gerald P., *Commonwealth Catholicism: A History of the Catholic Church in Virginia* (Notre Dame, IN: University of Notre Dame Press, 2001)

Fogarty, Ronald, *Catholic Education in Australia 1806–1950*, 2 vols. (Melbourne: Melbourne University Press, 1957)

Ford, Patrick, *Cardinal Moran and the A.L.P.: A Study of the Encounter between Moran and Socialism, 1890–1907, Its Effects upon the Australian Labor Party, the Foundation of Catholic Social Thought and Action in Modern Australia* (Melbourne: Melbourne University Press, 1966)

Frantz, Christian, 'A history of St. Mary's Cathedral Parish' [Cape Town], available online at www.stmaryscathedral.org.za/cathedralhistory.pdf. (Accessed November 2011)

Fraser, Lyndon, *Castles of Gold: A History of New Zealand's West Coast Irish* (Dunedin: Otago University Press, 2007)

Fraser, Lyndon (ed.), *A Distant Shore: Irish Migration and New Zealand Settlement* (Dunedin: Otago University Press, 2000)

Fraser, Lyndon, *To Tara via Holyhead: Irish Catholic Immigrants in Nineteenth-Century Christchurch* (Auckland: Auckland University Press, 1997)

Galbraith, Alasdair, 'Re-discovering Irish Protestant traditions in colonial New Zealand', in Brad Patterson (ed.), *Ulster-New Zealand Migration and Cultural Transfers* (Dublin: Four Courts Press, 2006), 31–54

Gardella, Peter, *Innocent Ecstasy: How Christianity Gave America an Ethic of Sexual Pleasure* (Oxford: Oxford University Press, 1985)

Gauvreau, Danielle and Thornton, Patricia, 'Marrying "the Other": Trends and determinants of culturally mixed marriages in Québec, 1880–1940', *Canadian Ethnic Studies*, vol. 47 no. 3 (2015), 111–41

Gee, Maurice, *Plumb* (Auckland: Oxford University Press, 1979)

Glanville, Helena, *Growing in Faith: A Historical Sketch of the Diocese of Port Elizabeth 1847–2007* (Port Elizabeth: n.p., n.d.)

Gleeson, David T., *The Irish in the South, 1815–1877* (Chapel Hill: University of North Carolina Press, 2001)

Goodman, Robert, *Secondary Education in Queensland 1860–1960* (Canberra: Australian National University Press, 1968)

Goulter, Mary Catherine, *Sons of France: A Forgotten Influence on New Zealand History*, 2nd ed. (Wellington: Whitcombe and Tombs, 1958)

Graham, Jeanine, *Frederick Weld* (Auckland: Auckland University Press, 1983)

Greene, John P., *Between Damnation and Starvation: Priests and Merchants in Newfoundland Politics, 1745–1855* (Montreal and Kingston: McGill-Queen's University Press, 1999)

Griffin, James, *Daniel Mannix: Beyond the Myths* (Mulgrave, VIC: Garratt Publishing, 2012)

Guilday, Peter, *The Life and Times of John England, First Bishop of Charleston (1786–1842)*, 2 vols. (New York: The America Press, 1927)

Gunn, Gertrude, *The Political History of Newfoundland, 1832–1864* (Toronto: University of Toronto Press, 1966)

Hale, Frederick, 'A Catholic voice against British imperialism: F C Kolbe's opposition to the Second Anglo-Boer War', *Religion and Theology*, vol. 4, no1–3 (1997), 94–108

Halpin, Paddy, 'A Skerries bishop', Time & Tide: Skerries Historical Society, vol. 1 (1998)

Hastings, Adrian, *The Church in Africa, 1450–1950* (Oxford: Oxford University Press, 1994)

Healy, Kathleen, *Frances Warde: American Founder of the Sisters of Mercy* (New York: Seabury Press, 1973)

Hearn, Mark, 'Containing "contamination": Cardinal Moran and *fin de siècle* Australian national identity, 1888–1911', *Journal of Religious History*, vol. 34, no. 1 (March 2010), 20–35

Heisser, David C. R. and White, Sr., Stephen J., *Patrick N. Lynch: Third Catholic Bishop of Charleston* (Columbia: University of South Carolina Press, 2015)

Henderson, Gerard, 'Bob Santamaria: A most unusual man', *The Australian*, 1 August 2015

Hennesey, James, *American Catholics: A History of the Roman Catholic Community in the United States* (New York: Oxford University Press, 1981)

Hosie, John, *Challenge: The Marists in Colonial Australia* (Sydney: Allen & Unwin, 1987)

Howard, Basil, 'Church in Otago', undated, unpublished work, Marist Archives Wellington

Inglis, K. S., 'Catholic historiography in Australia', *Historical Studies: Australia and New Zealand*, vol. 8 (November 1958), 233–53

Jennings, John, *Bishop Joseph-Octave Plessis and Roman Catholics in Early 19th Century New Brunswick* (Saint John: Diocese of Saint John, 1998)

Johnston, Angus Anthony, *A History of the Catholic Church in Eastern Nova Scotia*, 2 vols. (Antigonish, NS: St Francis Xavier University Press, 1971)

Johnston, Angus Anthony, 'A Scottish bishop in New Scotland: The right reverend William Fraser, second vicar apostolic of Nova Scotia, first bishop of Halifax and first bishop of Arichat', *The Innes Review*, vol. 6, no. 2 (1955), 107–24

Johnston, Wayne, *The Colony of Unrequited Dreams* (Toronto: Knopf Canada, 1998)

Jupp, James, *The English in Australia* (Cambridge: Cambridge University Press, 2004)

Kavanagh, J. P., 'The Most Rev. Dr Michael Verdon: Bishop of Dunedin, 1896–1918' [n.p., 1982]

Kealy, Máire M., *Dominican Education in Ireland 1820–1930* (Dublin: Irish Academic Press, 2007)

Kearney, Paddy, *Guardian of the Light: Denis Hurley: Renewing the Church, Opposing Apartheid* (New York: Continuum, 2009)

Keay, Susan, *Farazana: The Woman Who Saved an Empire* (London: I.B.Tauris, 2014)

Kelly, Colleen, *A Journey through Light and Shadow: Sisters of Mercy Singleton, 1875–1995* (Singleton, NSW: Sisters of Mercy, 1997)

Kerr, Donal, 'Dr. Quinn's school and the Catholic University, 1850–67', *Irish Ecclesiastical Record*, 5th series, vol. 108 (1967)

Kerr, Donal, 'Dublin's forgotten archbishop: Daniel Murray, 1768–1852', in James Kelly and Dáire Keogh (eds.), *History of the Catholic Diocese of Dublin* (Dublin: Four Courts Press, 2000), 247–67

Kerr, Donal, *Peel, Priests, and Politics: Sir Robert Peel's Administration and the Roman Catholic Church in Ireland, 1841–46* (Oxford: Oxford University Press, 1984)

Keys, Lilian, 'Bishop Moran – 5 – Education question', *Zealandia*, 2 June 1966

Keys, Lillian G., *Philip Viard: Bishop of Wellington* (Christchurch: Pegasus Press, 1968)

Kildea, Jeff, '"A veritable hurricane of sectarianism": The year 1920 and ethnoreligious conflict in Australia', in Colin Barr and Hilary M. Carey (eds.), *Religion and Greater Ireland: Christianity and Irish Global Networks, 1750–1950* (Montreal and Kingston: McGill-Queen's University Press, 2015)

Killerby, Catherine Kovesi, *Ursula Frayne, a Biography* (Fremantle, WA: The University of Notre Dame Australia, 1996)

Kinnear, A. Muriel, 'The Trappist monks at Tracadie, Nova Scotia', *Report of the Annual Meeting, Canadian Catholic Historical Association*, vol. 9, no. 1 (1930), 97–105

Körner, Axel, *America in Italy: The United States in the Political Thought and Imagination of the Risorgimento, 1763–1865* (Princeton: Princeton University Press, 2017)

Korten, Christopher, 'Converging worlds: Paul Cullen in the world of Mauro Cappellari', in Dáire Keogh and Albert McDonnell (eds.), *Cardinal Paul Cullen and His World* (Dublin: Four Courts Press, 2011), 34–46

Kottuppallil, George, *The History of the Catholic Missions in Central Bengal, 1855–1886* (Shillong: Vendrame Institute, 1988)

Kowalsky, Nikolaus, '*Die Errichtung der Apostolischen Vikariate in Indien 1834–1838 nach den Akten des Propaganda Archivs*' (Rome: Pontifica Universitá Urbaniana, 1950)

Lahey, Raymond J., 'Catholicism and colonial policy in Newfoundland, 1779–1845' in Terrence Murphy and Gerald Stortz (eds.), *Creed and Culture: The Place of English-Speaking Catholics in Canadian Society, 1750–1930* (Montreal and Kingston: McGill-Queen's University Press, 1993), 49–78

Lambert, Carolyn, 'This sacred feeling: Patriotism, nation-building and the Catholic Church in Newfoundland, 1850–1914', in Colin Barr and Hilary M. Carey (eds.), *Religion and Greater Ireland: Christianity and Irish Global Networks, 1750–1950* (Montreal and Kingston: McGill-Queen's University Press, 2015), 124–42

Laracy, Hugh, 'Bishop Moran: Irish politics and Catholicism in New Zealand', *The Journal of Religious History*, vol. 6, no. 1 (June 1970), 62–76

Laracy, Hugh, 'Paranoid popery: Bishop Moran and Catholic education in New Zealand', *New Zealand Journal of History*, vol. 10, no. 1 (1976), 51–62

Larkin, Emmet, *The Historical Dimensions of Irish Catholicism* (Washington, DC: The Catholic University of America Press, 1987)

Larkin, Emmet, *The Making of the Roman Catholic Church in Ireland, 1850–1860* (Chapel Hill: University of North Carolina Press, 1980)

Larkin, Emmet, 'Paul Cullen: The great ultramontane', in Dáire Keogh and Albert McDonnell (eds.) *Cardinal Paul Cullen and His World* (Dublin: Four Courts Press, 2011), 15–33

Lawson, Roland, *Brisbane in the 1890s: A Study of Australian Urban Society* (St Lucia: University of Queensland Press, 1973)

Le Cordeur, Basil A., *The Politics of Eastern Cape Separatism 1820–1854* (Cape Town: Oxford University Press, 1981)

LeBlanc, Ronnie Gilles, 'Antoine Gagnon and the mitre: A model of relations between *Candien*, Scottish and Irish clergy in the early Maritime church', in Terrence Murphy and Cyril J. Byrne (eds.), *Religion and Identity: The Experience of Irish and Scottish Catholics in Atlantic Canada* (St John's: Jesperson Press, 1987), 98–113

Lee, J. J. and Casey, Marion R. (eds.), *Making the Irish American: History and Heritage of the Irish in the United States* (New York: New York University Press, 2006)

Lee, Joseph, *The Modernisation of Irish Society, 1848–1918* (Dublin: Gill & Macmillan, 1989 [1973])

Lehane, Robert, *Forever Carnival: A Story of Priests, Professors & Politics in 19th Century Sydney* (Charnwood, ACT: Ginninderra Books, 2004)

Lennon, Joseph, *Irish Orientalism: A Literary and Intellectual History* (Syracuse, NY: Syracuse University Press, 2004)

Light, Dale B., *Rome and the New Republic: Conflict and Community in Philadelphia Catholicism between the Revolution and the Civil War* (Notre Dame: University of Notre Dame Press, 1996)

Livingston, K. T., *The Emergence of an Australian Catholic Priesthood, 1835–1915* (Sydney: Catholic Theological Faculty, 1977)

Loughery, John, *Dagger John: Archbishop John Hughes and the Making of Irish America* (Ithaca, NY: Three Hills – Cornell University Press, 2018)

Lubienecki, Paul E., 'John Timon – Buffalo's first bishop: His forgotten struggle to assimilate Catholics in western New York', *New York History Review* (August, 2010)

Ludlow, Peter, *The Canny Scot: Archbishop James Morrison of Antigonish* (Montreal and Kingston: McGill-Queen's University Press, 2015)

Ludlow, Peter, '"Disturbed by the Irish howl": Irish and Scottish Roman Catholics in Nova Scotia, 1844–1860', *Historical Studies*, vol. 81 (2015), 32–55

Ludlow, Peter, '"Pretend Catholics" and stampeders: The Romanization of the diocese of Arichat/Antigonish, 1851–190', *Historical Papers* 2014: *Canadian Society of Church History*, 31–50

Lupol, Manoly R., *The Roman Catholic Church and the North-West School Question* (Toronto: University of Toronto Press, 1974)

Luttrell, John, '"Australianizing" the local Catholic Church: Polding to Gilroy', *Journal of Religious History*, vol. 36, no. 3 (2012), 335–50

Macaulay, Ambrose, *Dr Russell of Maynooth* (London: Darton, Longman and Todd, 1983)

MacDonald, Carmel, 'An era of consolidation', in Michael F. Hennessey (ed.) *The Catholic Church in Prince Edward Island, 1720–1979* (Charlottetown: The Roman Catholic Episcopal Corporation, 1979), 58–70

MacDonald, Edward, *The History of St. Dunstan's University, 1855–1956* (Charlottetown: Board of Governors of St Dunstan's University and Prince Edward Island Museum and Historical Foundation, 1989)

MacDonald, Edward, 'Who's afraid of the Fenians? The Fenian scare on Prince Edward Island, 1865–1867', *Acadiensis*, vol. 38, no. 1 (Winter/Spring 2009), 33–51

MacDonald, Heidi, 'Developing a strong Roman Catholic social order in the late nineteenth-century Prince Edward Island', *Canadian Catholic Historical Association, Historical Studies*, 69, (2003), 34–51

MacGinley, M. R., *Ancient Tradition, New World: Dominican Sisters in Eastern Australia, 1867–1958* (Strathfield, NSW: St Paul's Publications, 2009)

Macintyre, Stuart, *A Colonial Liberalism: The Lost World of Three Victorian Visionaries* (Melbourne: Oxford University Press Australia, 1991)

Mackenzie, John M. with Dalziel, Nigel R., *The Scots in South Africa: Ethnicity, Identity, Gender and Race, 1772–1914* (Manchester: Manchester University Press, 2007)

Mackey, John, *The Making of a State Education System: The Passing of the New Zealand Education Act, 1877* (London: Geoffrey Chapman, 1967)

MacLean, R. A., *Bishop John Cameron: Piety and Politics* (Antigonish, NS: The Casket Printing Company, 1991)

MacNutt, W. S., *New Brunswick, a History: 1784–1867* (Toronto: MacMillan of Canada, 1963)

Malherbe, Ernst G., *Education in South Africa (1652–1922)* (Cape Town: Juta & Co., 1925)

Mannes, B. (ed.), *Golden Jubilee, Holy Cross College, Mosgiel, New Zealand, 1900–1950* (Auckland: Whitcombe and Tombs, 1949)

Mannion, John, 'Tracing the Irish: A geographical guide', *Newfoundland Ancestor*, vol. 9, no. 1 (May 1993), 4–18

Mannion, Patrick, *A Land of Dreams: Ethnicity, Nationalism and the Irish in Newfoundland, Nova Scotia, and Maine, 1880–1923* (Montreal and Kingston: McGill-Queen's University Press, 2018)

Marquis, Greg, *In Armageddon's Shadow: The Civil War and Canada's Maritime Provinces* (Montreal and Kingston: McGill-Queen's University Press, 1988)

Marsala, Rosanna, 'Catholics in the Irish parliament: Daniel O'Connell and his influence in Italy', *Parliaments, Estates, and Representation*, vol. 34, no. 2 (2014), 167–81

Martin, A. W., *Henry Parkes: A Biography* (Melbourne: Melbourne University Press, 1980)

Marwick, Donna, *Boston Priests, 1848–1910: A Study of Social and Intellectual Change* (Cambridge, MA: Harvard University Press, 1973)

McCann, M. A., *Archbishop Purcell and the Archdiocese of Cincinnati* (Washington, DC: Catholic University of America, 1918)

McCann, Philip, 'Bishop Fleming and the politicization of Irish Roman Catholic in Newfoundland, 1830–1850', in Terrence Murphy and Cyril J. Byrne (eds.), *Religion and Identity: The Experience of Irish and Scottish Catholics in Atlantic Canada* (St John's: Jesperson Press, 1987)

McCann, Philip, 'The politics of denominational education in nineteenth century Newfoundland', in William A. McKim (ed.), *The Vexed Question: Denominational Education in a Secular Age* (St John's: Breakwaters Books, 1998)

McCarthy, Mary Augustine, *Star in the South: The Centennial History of the New Zealand Dominican Sisters* (Dunedin: St Dominic's Priory, 1970)

McCracken, Donal P., *The Irish Pro-Boers, 1877–1902* (Johannesburg: Perskor, 1989)

McCracken, Donal P., 'Irish settlement and identity in South Africa before 1910', *Irish Historical Studies*, vol. 28, no. 110 (November 1992), 134–49

McCracken, Donal P., 'Preface', in Donal P. McCracken (ed.), *The Irish in Southern Africa*, vol. 2 (Durban: Ireland and Southern Africa Project, 1992)

McDevitt, Mary Kilfoil, *"We hardly knew ye": St. Mary's Cemetery, an Enduring Presence* (Saint John, NB: Irish Canadian Cultural Association, 1992)

McGloin, John B., *California's First Archbishop: The Life of Joseph Sadoc Alemany, 1814–1888* (New York: Herder & Herder, 1966)

McGowan, Mark G., '"Pregnant with perils": Canadian Catholicism and its relation to the Catholic Churches of Newfoundland, 1840–1949', *Newfoundland and Labrador Studies*, vol. 28, no. 2 (Fall 2013), 193–218

McGowan, Mark G., *Michael Power: The Struggle to Build the Catholic Church on the Canadian Frontier* (Montreal and Kingston: McGill-Queen's University Press, 2005)

McGowan, Mark G., *The Imperial Irish: Canada's Irish Catholics Fight the Great War* (Montreal and Kingston: McGill-Queen's University Press, 2017)

McGowan, Mark G., *The Waning of the Green: Catholics, the Irish, and Identity in Toronto, 1887–1922* (Montreal and Kingston: McGill-Queen's University Press, 1999)

McGowan, Mark G., 'The tale and trials of a "double minority": The Irish and French Catholic engagement for the soul of the Canadian church, 1815–1947', in Colin Barr and Hilary M. Carey (eds.), *Religion and Greater Ireland: Christianity and Irish Global Networks, 1750–1950* (Montreal and Kingston: McGill-Queen's University Press, 2015), 97–123

McGrath, Madeleine Sophie, *These Women? Women Religious in the History of Australia, the Sisters of Mercy Parramatta 1888–1988* (Kensington: New South Wales University Press, n.d.)

McGreevy, John T., *Catholicism and American Freedom: A History* (New York: W. W. Norton, 2003)

McGuigan, Peter, 'From Wexford and Monaghan: The Lot 22 Irish', *The Abegweit Review* (Winter 1985), 61–84

McIlvanney, William, *Docherty* (Edinburgh: Canongate, 2014 [1975])

McKenna, Mark, *An Eye for Eternity: The Life of Manning Clark* (Melbourne: The Miegunyah Press, 2011)

McLaughlin, Robert, *Irish Canadian Conflict and the Struggle for Irish Independence, 1912–1925* (Toronto: University of Toronto Press, 2013)

McLay, Anne, *James Quinn: First Catholic Bishop of Brisbane*, rev. ed. (Toowoomba, QLD: Church Archivist' Society, 1989)

McLay, Anne, *Women on the Move: Mercy's Triple Spiral: A History of the Adelaide Sisters of Mercy, Ireland to Argentina 1856–1880 to South Australia 1880* (Adelaide: Sisters of Mercy, 1996)

McLay, Anne, *Women Out of Their Sphere: A History of the Sisters of Mercy in Western Australia* (Northbridge, WA: Vanguard Press, 1992)

McLintock, A. H., *The History of Otago* (Dunedin: Otago Centennial Historical Publications, 1949)

McLoughlin, Mike, 'Catholicism, masculinity, and middle-class respectability in the Irish Catholic temperance movement in nineteenth-century Canada', in Colin Barr and Hilary M. Carey (eds.), *Religion and Greater Ireland: Christianity and Irish Global Networks, 1750–1950* (Montreal and Kingston: McGill-Queen's University Press, 2015)

McMahon, Cian T., *The Global Dimensions of Irish Identity: Race, Nation, and the Popular Press, 1840–1880* (Chapel Hill: University of North Carolina Press, 2015)

McNally, Vincent J., *The Lord's Distant Vineyard: A History of the Oblates and the Catholic Community in British Columbia* (Edmonton: University of Alberta Press, 2000)

McNamara, Robert F., *The American College in Rome, 1856–1955* (Rochester, NY: The Christopher Press, 1956)

Metcalf, Thomas R., *Imperial Connections: India in the Indian Ocean Area, 1860–1920* (Berkley: University of California Press, 2007)

Meyer, Paul Michael (ed.), *The Roman Catholic Church in South Africa, A Select Bibliography* (Cape Town: University of Cape Town Libraries, 1979)

Millar, Anthony Kendal, *Plantagenet in South Africa: Lord Charles Somerset* (Cape Town: Oxford University Press, 1965)

Miller, Kerby A., *Emigrants and Exiles: Ireland and the Irish Exodus to North America* (New York: Oxford University Press, 1985)

Moffitt, Miriam, *The Society for Irish Church Missions to the Roman Catholics, 1849–1950* (Manchester: Manchester University Press, 2010)

Moir, John S., 'The problem of a double minority: Some reflections on the development of the English-speaking Catholic Church in Canada in the nineteenth century', *Histoire sociale/Social History*, vol. 7 (1971), 53–67

Molloy, Kevin, 'Religious texts for the Catholic migrant: International print networks and the Irish-Australian book trade', in Colin Barr and Hilary M. Carey (eds.), *Religion and Greater Ireland: Christianity and Irish Global Networks, 1750–1950* (Montreal and Kingston: McGill-Queens University Press, 2015), 71–93

Molony, John, *An Architect of Freedom: John Hubert Plunkett in New South Wales, 1832–1869* (Canberra: Australian National University Press, 1973)

Molony, John, *The Roman Mould of the Australian Catholic Church* (Melbourne: Melbourne University Press, 1969)

Mullane, George, 'A sketch of Lawrence O'Connor Doyle, a member of the house of assembly in the thirties and forties', *Collections of the Nova Scotia Historical Society*, vol. 17 (1913), 151–95

Munro, Jessie, *The Story of Suzanne Aubert* (Auckland: Auckland University Press, 1996)

Murphy, Angela F., *American Slavery, Irish Freedom: Abolition, Immigrant Citizenship, and the Transatlantic Movement for Irish Repeal* (Baton Rouge: Louisiana State University Press, 2010)

Murphy, James H., '"Nursery of Saints": St. Vincent's ecclesiastical seminary, 1835–60', in James H. Murphy (ed.), *Nos Autem: Castleknock College & Its Contribution* (Dublin: Gill & Macmillan, n.d.)

Murphy, Terrence, 'Emancipation vs. equity: Civic inclusion of Halifax Catholics, 1830–1865', *CCHA Historical Studies*, vol. 83 (2017), 7–24

Murphy, Terrence, 'The emergence of Maritime Catholicism', *Acadiensis*, vol. 13, no. 2 (Spring, 1984), 29–40

Murphy, Terrence, 'James Jones and the establishment of Roman Catholic church government in the Maritime provinces', *CCHA Study Sessions*, vol. 48 (1981), 26–42

Murphy, Terrence, 'Language, ethnicity, and region: Rome and the struggle for dominance of the Canadian Catholic Church, 1785–1930', in Matteo Binasco (ed.), *Rome and Irish Catholicism in the Atlantic World, 1622–1908* (London: Palgrave Macmillan, 2019), 73–91

Murphy, Terrence, 'Priests, people and polity: Trusteeism in the first Catholic congregation at Halifax, 1785–1801', in Terrence Murphy and Cyril J. Byrne (eds.), *Religion and Identity: The Experience of Irish and Scottish Catholics in Atlantic Canada* (St John's: Jesperson Press, 1987), 68–80

Murphy, Terrence, '"Religion walked forth in all her majesty": The opening of Holy Cross Cemetery and the transformation of Halifax Catholicism', *Journal of the Royal Nova Scotia Historical Society*, vol. 18 (2015), 77–88

Murphy, Terrence, 'Transformation and triumphalism: The Irish Catholics of Halifax, 1839–1858', *Historical Studies*, vol. 81 (2015), 56–81

Murphy, Terrence, 'Trusteeism in Atlantic Canada: The struggle for leadership among the Irish Catholics of Halifax, St. John's, and St. John, 1750–1850', in

Terrence Murphy and Gerald Stortz (eds.), *Creed and Culture: The Place of English-Speaking Catholics in Canadian Society, 1750–1930* (Montreal and Kingston: McGill-Queen's University Press, 1993), 126–51

Murphy, Terrence and Byrne, Cyril J. (eds.), *Religion and Identity: The Experience of Irish and Scottish Catholics in Atlantic Canada* (St John's: Jesperson Press, 1987)

Murphy, Terrence and Stortz, Gerald (eds.), *Creed and Culture: The Place of English-Speaking Catholics in Canadian Society, 1750–1930* (Montreal and Kingston: McGill-Queen's University Press, 1993)

Murray, John Courtney, *We Hold These Truths: Reflections on the American Proposition* (New York: Sheed & Ward, 1960)

Nairn, Bede, *Civilising Capitalism: The Labor Movement in New South Wales 1870–1900* (Canberra: Australian National University Press, 1973)

Neill, Stephen, *A History of Christianity in India, 1707–1858* (Cambridge: Cambridge University Press, 1985)

Niall, Brenda, *Mannix* (Melbourne: Text Publishing, 2015)

Noel, S. J. R. *Politics in Newfoundland* (Toronto: University of Toronto Press, 1971)

Nolan, Hugh J., *The Most Reverend Patrick Kenrick Third Bishop of Philadelphia 1830–1851* (Philadelphia: American Catholic Historical Society of Philadelphia, 1948)

Nolan, M. J., *The Enterprising Life of Dr Henry Backhaus: Bendigo Pioneer* (Bendigo: The Author, 2008)

O'Brien, Eris, *The Dawn of Catholicism in Australia*, 2 vols. (Sydney: Angus & Robertson, 1928)

O'Brien, Eris, *The Foundation of Catholicism in Australia: Life and Letters of Archpriest John Therry*, 2 vols. (Sydney: Angus & Robertson, 1922)

O'Connor, Anne, *Translation and Language in Nineteenth-Century Ireland: A European Perspective* (London: Palgrave Macmillan, 2017)

O'Connor, Thomas H., *Fitzpatrick's Boston, 1846–1866: John Bernard Fitzpatrick, Third Bishop of Boston* (Boston: Northeastern University Press, 1984)

O'Donnell, George E., *St. Charles Seminary, Philadelphia: A History of the Theological Seminary of Saint Charles Borromeo, Overbrook, Philadelphia, Pennsylvania, 1832–1964, with a Chronological Record of Ordinations and Pictures of the Living Alumni* (Philadelphia, PA: American Catholic Historical Society, 1964)

O'Donoghue, K. K., *P. A. Treacy and the Christian Brothers in Australia and New Zealand* (Melbourne: Polding Press, 1983)

O'Donoghue, Mary Xaverius, *Mother Vincent Whitty: Women and Education in a Masculine Society* (Melbourne: Melbourne University Press, 1972)

O'Donoghue, Tom, *Catholic Teaching Brothers: Their Life in the English-Speaking World* (New York: Palgrave Macmillan, 2010)

O'Farrell, Patrick, *The Catholic Church in Australia: A Short History, 1788–1967* (London: Geoffrey Chapman, 1969)

O'Farrell, Patrick, 'Explaining oneself: Labor, Catholic, Irish, UNSW', Specialist Papers from the 1998 Australian Academy of the Humanities Symposium. Available at www.patrickofarrell.com, accessed 4 May 2017.

O'Farrell, Patrick, *Vanished Kingdoms: Irish in Australia and New Zealand, a Personal Excursion* (Kensington: New South Wales University Press, 1990)

O'Farrell, Patrick, 'Writing the history of Irish Australia', in Oliver MacDonagh and W. F. Mandle (eds.), *Ireland and Irish-Australia: Studies in Cultural and Political History* (London: Croom Helm, 1986), 218–28

O'Flaherty, Patrick, *Lost Country: The Rise and Fall of Newfoundland 1843–1933* (St John's: Long Beach Press, 2005)

O'Gallagher, Marianna, 'The Sisters of Charity of Halifax – the early and middle years', *CCHA Study Sessions*, vol. 47 (1980), 57–68

O'Grady, Brendan, *Exiles and Islanders: The Irish Settlers of Prince Edward Island* (Montreal and Kingston: McGill-Queen's University Press, 2004)

O'Malley, John W., *Vatican I: The Council and the Making of the Ultramontane Church* (Cambridge, MA: The Belknap Press of Harvard University Press, 2018)

O'Meeghan, Michael, *Held Firm by Faith: A History of the Catholic Diocese of Christchurch, 1840–1987* (Christchurch: Catholic Diocese of Christchurch, 1988)

O'Meeghan, Michael, *Steadfast in Hope: The Story of the Catholic Archdiocese of Wellington, 1850–2000* (Palmerston North: Dunmore Press, 2003)

O'Shea, Art, *A Century Plus Forty: An Historical Review of the Diocese of Charlottetown, 1829–1969* (The Author, 2009)

O'Shea, Art, *Priests and Bishops Who Served in the Diocese of Charlottetown, 1829–1996* (The Author, 1996)

O'Sullivan, M. M. K., *'A Cause of Trouble'? Irish Nuns and English Clerics* (Sydney: Crossing Press, 1995)

O'Toole, James M., *Militant and Triumphant: William Henry O'Connell and the Catholic Church in Boston, 1859–1944* (Notre Dame, IN: University of Notre Dame Press, 1992)

Ormonde, Paul, *The Movement* (Melbourne: Thomas Nelson, 1972)

Parker, Kenneth L. and Handschy, Daniel, 'Eucharistic sacrifice, American polemics, the Oxford Movement, and *Apostolicae Curae*', *Journal of Ecclesiastical History*, vol. 62, no. 3 (July 2011), 515–42

Pasquier, Michael, *Fathers on the Frontier: French Missionaries and the Roman Catholic Priesthood in the United States, 1789–1870* (Oxford: Oxford University Press, 2010)

Pawsey, Margaret, *The Demon of Discord: Tensions in the Catholic Church in Victoria 1853–1864* (Melbourne: Melbourne University Press, 1982)

Pell, George, 'The Mannix story told, and told well', *The Advocate*, 15 November 1984

Perin, Roberto, *Rome in Canada: The Vatican and Canadian Affairs in the Late Victorian Age* (Toronto: University of Toronto Press, 1990)

Phillips, Jock and Hearn, Terry, *Settlers: New Zealand Immigrants from England, Ireland and Scotland, 1800–1945* (Auckland: Auckland University Press, 2008)

Phillips, Walter, 'Australian Catholic historiography: Some recent issues', *Historical Studies*, vol. 14 (1971), 600–11

Phillips, Walter, *Defending 'A Christian Country': Churchmen and Society in New South Wales in the 1880s and After* (St Lucia: University of Queensland Press, 1981)

Pike, Douglas, *Paradise of Dissent: South Australia, 1829–1857*, 2nd ed. (Melbourne: Melbourne University Press, 1967)

Powell, Alan, *Patrician Democrat: The Political Life of Charles Cowper 1843–1870* (Melbourne: Melbourne University Press, 1977)

Poynter, John, *Doubts and Certainties: A Life of Alexander Leeper* (Melbourne: Melbourne University Press, 1997)

Press, Margaret M., *From Our Broken Toil: South Australian Catholics, 1836–1906* (Adelaide: Archdiocese of Adelaide, 1986)

Price, Richard, *Making Empire: Colonial Encounters and the Creation of Imperial Rule in Nineteenth-Century Africa* (Cambridge: Cambridge University Press, 2008)

Quinn, Peter, 'The future of Irish America', in Lee, J. J. and Casey, Marion R. (eds.), *Making the Irish American: History and Heritage of the Irish in the United States* (New York: New York University Press, 2006), 680–5

Rafferty, Oliver, *Violence, Politics and Catholicism in Ireland* (Dublin: Four Courts Press, 2016)

Reid, Nicholas, *James Michael Liston, a Life* (Wellington: Victoria University Press, 2006)

Reinerman, Alan J., *Austria and the Papacy in the Age of Metternich, Vol. 2: Revolution and Reaction, 1830–1838* (Washington, DC: Catholic University of America Press, 1989)

Restano, John, *Justice So Requiring: The Emergence and Development of a Legal System in Gibraltar* (Gibraltar: Calpe Press, 2012)

Ridden, Jennifer, 'The forgotten history of the Protestant Crusade: Religious liberalism in Ireland', *Journal of Religious History*, vol. 31, no. 1 (March 2007), 78–102

Robertson, Ian Ross, 'The Bible question in Prince Edward Island from 1856 to 1860', in P. A. Buckner and David Frank (eds.), *The Acadiensis Reader, Vol. 1: Atlantic Canada before Confederation* (Fredericton, NB: Acadiensis Press, 1985), 261–83

Robertson, Ian Ross, *The Tenant League of Prince Edward Island: Leasehold Tenure in the New World* (Toronto: University of Toronto Press, 1996)

Roddy, Sarah, 'Spiritual imperialism and the mission of the Irish race: The Catholic church and emigration from nineteenth-century Ireland', *Irish Historical Studies*, vol. 38, no. 152 (November 2013), 600–19

Roe, Michael, *Quest for Authority in Eastern Australia* (Melbourne: Melbourne University Press, 1965)

Ross, Robert, *Status and Respectability in the Cape Colony, 1750–1870: A Tragedy of Manners* (Cambridge: Cambridge University Press, 1999)

Rotberg, Robert I., *The Founder: Cecil Rhodes and the Pursuit of Power* (New York: Oxford University Press, 1988)

Rowe, Frederick W., *The Development of Education in Newfoundland* (Toronto: The Ryerson Press, 1964)

Santamaria, B. A., *Daniel Mannix: A Biography* (Melbourne: Melbourne University Press, 1984)

Saunders, E. M., *The Life and Letters of the Right Hon. Sir Charles Tupper Bart., K. C.M.G.*, 2 vols. (London: Cassell and Company, 1916)

Schianchi, Carlo-Maria, 'Colin and the congregation of Propaganda Fide in Rome', in Alois Greiler (ed.), *Catholics Beginnings in Oceania: Marist Missionary Perspectives* (Hindmarsh, NSW: ATF Press, 2009), 27–51

See, Scott W., 'The fortunes of the Orange Order in 19th century New Brunswick', in P. M. Toner (ed.), *New Ireland Remembered: Historical Essays on the Irish in New Brunswick* (Fredericton, NB: New Ireland Press, 1988), 90–105

See, Scott W., *Riots in New Brunswick: Orange Nativism and Social Violence in the 1840s* (Toronto: University of Toronto Press, 1993)

Serle, Geoffrey, *The Golden Age: A History of the Colony of Victoria, 1851–1861* (Melbourne: Melbourne University Press)

Shanahan, Mary, *Out of Time, Out of Place: Henry Gregory and the Benedictine Order in Colonial Australia* (Canberra: Australian National University Press, 1970)

Shaw, G. P., *Patriarch and Patriot: William Grant Broughton 1788–1853, Colonial Statesman and Ecclesiastic* (Melbourne: Melbourne University Press, 1978)

Shaw, Gerald, *Some Beginnings: The* Cape Times *1876–1910* (Oxford: Oxford University Press, 1975)

Shea, C. Michael, *Newman's Early Roman Catholic Legacy, 1845–1854* (Oxford: Oxford University Press, 2017)

Sherry, Richard, *Holy Cross College, Clonliffe, Dublin, 1859–1959* (Dublin: Holy Cross College, 1959)

Silke, John J., 'The Roman Catholic Church in Ireland 1800–1922', *Studia Hibernica*, no. 15 (1975), 61–104

Simmons, E. R., *In Cruce Salus: A History of the Diocese of Auckland* (Auckland: Catholic Publications Centre, 1982)

Simmons, E. R., *Pompallier: Prince of Bishops* (Auckland: CPC Publishing, 1984)

Sinclair, Keith, *William Pember Reeves: New Zealand Fabian* (Oxford: Clarendon Press, 1965)

Smith, Ken, *Alfred Aylward: The Tireless Agitator* (Johannesburg: AD. Donker, 1983)

Smith, Philippa Mein, *A Concise History of New Zealand* (Cambridge: Cambridge University Press, 2005)

Solomon, W. E. G., *Saul Solomon, The Member for Cape Town* (Cape Town: Oxford University Press, 1948)

Southerwood, W. T., *The Convicts' Friend (Bishop R. W. Willson)* (George Town, TAS: Stella Maris Books, 1989)

Sparks, Randy J., *Religion in Mississippi* (Jackson: Mississippi Historical Society, 2001)

Spray, William A., 'Receptions of the Irish in New Brunswick', in P. M. Toner (ed.), *New Ireland Remembered: Historical Essays on the Irish in New Brunswick* (Fredericton, NB: New Ireland Press, 1988), 9–26

Sprows Cummings, Kathleen, *New Women of the Old Faith: Gender and American Catholicism in the Progressive Era* (Chapel Hill: University of North Carolina Press, 2009)

Stanley, George G. F., 'The Caraquet riots of 1875', in P. A. Buckner and David Frank (eds.), *The Acadiensis Reader, Vol. 2: Atlantic Canada after Confederation* (Fredericton: Acadiensis Press, 1985), 78–95

Stenhouse, John, 'God's own silence: Secular nationalism, Christianity, and the writing of New Zealand history', *New Zealand Journal of History*, vol. 38, no. 1 (2004), 52–71

Stern, William J., 'How Dagger John saved New York's Irish', *City Journal* (Spring 1997)

Stoneman, David, 'Richard Bourke: For the honour of god and the good of man', *Journal of Religious History*, vol. 38, no. 3 (September 2014), 341–55

Story, G. M., '"A tune beyond us as we are": Reflections on Newfoundland song and ballad', *Newfoundland Studies*, vol. 4, no. 2 (1998), 129–44

Sullivan, Eileen P., *The Shamrock and the Cross: Irish American Novelists Shape American Catholicism* (Notre Dame, IN: University of Notre Dame Press, 2016)

Suttor, T. L., *Hierarchy and Democracy in Australia, 1788–1870* (Melbourne: Melbourne University Press, 1965)

Sweetman, Rory, *Bishop in the Dock: The Sedition Trial of James Liston* (Auckland: Auckland University Press, 1997)

Sweetman, Rory, *'A Fair and Just Solution?' A History of the Integration of Private Schools in New Zealand* (Palmerston North: Dunmore Press, 2002)

Sweetman, Rory, 'Introduction', in Felice Vaggioli, *A Deserter's Adventures: The Autobiography of Dom Felice Vaggioli*, translated by John Crockett (Dunedin: Otago University Press, 2001)

Sweetman, Rory, 'Paul Cullen and the remaking of Catholicism in the Antipodes', in Dáire Keogh and Albert McDonnell (eds.), *Cardinal Paul Cullen and His World* (Dublin: Four Courts Press, 2011), 377–400

Sweetman, Rory, 'Review of Patrick O'Farrell, *Vanished Kingdoms: Irish in Australia and New Zealand, a personal excursion*', *The New Zealand Journal of History*, vol. 27, no. 1 (1993), 107–8

Sweetman, Rory, 'Towards a history of Orangeism in New Zealand', in Brad Patterson (ed.) *Ulster-New Zealand Migration and Cultural Transfers* (Dublin: Four Courts Press, 2006), 154–64

Szarnicki, Henry A., *Michael O'Connor: First Catholic Bishop of Pittsburgh, 1843–1860* (Pittsburgh: Wolfson Publishing, 1975)

Thompson, Frederic F., *The French Shore Problem in Newfoundland* (Toronto: University of Toronto Press, 1961)

Tierney, Mark, *Croke of Cashel: The Life of Archbishop Thomas William Croke, 1823–1902* (Dublin: Gill & Macmillan, 1976)

Toner, P. M., 'The 1851 census', in P. M. Toner (ed.), *New Ireland Remembered: Historical Essays on the Irish in New Brunswick* (Fredericton, NB: New Ireland Press, 1988), 106–32

Toner, P. M., 'The foundations of the Catholic Church in English-speaking New Brunswick', in P. M. Toner (ed.), *New Ireland Remembered: Historical Essays on the Irish in New Brunswick* (Fredericton, NB: New Ireland Press, 1988), 63–70

Toner, P. M. (ed.), *New Ireland Remembered: Historical Essays on the Irish in New Brunswick* (Fredericton, NB: New Ireland Press, 1988)

Trombley, K. Fay, *Thomas Louis Connolly (1815–1876): The Man and His Place in Secular and Ecclesiastical History* (Leuven: Katholieke Universiteit Leuven Faculty of Theology, 1983)

Van Onselen, Charles, *Masked Raiders: Irish Banditry in Southern Africa, 1880–1899* (Cape Town: Zebra Press, 2010)

Viaene, Vincent, *Belgium and the Holy See from Gregory XVI to Pius IX (1831–1859), Catholic Revival, Society and Politics in 19th-Century Europe* (Leuven: Leuven University Press, 2001)

Waite, P. B., *The Man from Halifax: Sir John Thompson, Prime Minister* (Toronto: University of Toronto Press, 1985)

Waldersee, James, *Catholic Society in New South Wales, 1788–1860* (Sydney: Sydney University Press, 1974)

Walker, Eric A., *A History of South Africa* (London: Longmans, Green & Co., 1935[1928])

Walker, Eric A., *The South African College and the University of Cape Town* (Cape Town: Cape Times, 1929)

Walker, Franklin A., *Catholic Education and Politics in Upper Canada* (Toronto: J. M. Dent & Sons, 1955)

Walsh, K. J., *Yesterday's Seminary: A History of St. Patrick's Manly* (St Leonards, NSW: Allen & Unwin, 1998)

Whelan, Irene, 'Religious rivalry and the making of Irish-American identity', in J. J. Lee and Marion R. Casey (eds.), *Making the Irish American: History and Heritage of the Irish in the United States* (New York: New York University Press, 2006), 271–85

Wilson, Catherine Anne, *A New Lease on Life: Landlords, Tenants, and Immigrants in Ireland and Canada* (Montreal and Kingston: McGill-Queen's University Press, 1994)

Wilson, David A., *Thomas D'Arcy McGee, Vol. 1: Passion, Reason, and Politics, 1825–1857* (Montreal and Kingston: McGill-Queen's University Press, 2008)

Wilson, David A., *Thomas D'Arcy McGee, Vol. 2: The Extreme Moderate, 1857–1868* (Montreal and Kingston: McGill-Queen's University Press, 2011)

Wilson, David A. (ed.), *The Orange Order in Canada* (Dublin: Four Courts Press, 2007)

Wilson, David A. (ed.), *Irish Nationalism in Canada* (Montreal and Kingston: McGill-Queen's University Press, 2009)

Wyeth, E. R, *Education in Queensland: A History of Education in Queensland and in the Moreton Bay District of New South Wales* (Melbourne: Australian Council for Educational Research, n.d.)

Wyndham, Susan, 'Brenda Niall wins National Biography Prize for Mannix', *Sydney Morning Herald*, 8 August 2016

Xavier, Francis, 'Educational legislation in Nova Scotia and the Catholics', *CCHA: Report*, 24 (1957), 63–74

Young, Brian, *In Its Corporate Capacity: The Seminary of Montreal as a Business Institution, 1816–1876* (Montreal and Kingston: McGill-Queen's University Press, 1986)

Zimmerman, Beverly, *The Making of a Diocese: Maitland, Its Bishop, Priests, and People, 1866–1909* (Melbourne: Melbourne University Press, 2000)

(II)   Theses and Dissertations

Boner, Kathleen, 'The Irish Dominicans and education in the Western Cape (1863–1892)', unpublished MA thesis, University of South Africa, 1976

Carmichael, Mary S., 'Analysis of All Hallows "Matriculata 1842–1891"', unpublished BA project, Ave Maria University, 2010

Doyle, Francis B., 'The Irish contribution to the Catholic Church in South Africa, 1820–1900', unpublished MA thesis, National University of Ireland, 1963

FitzGerald, John Edward, 'Conflict and culture in Irish-Newfoundland Roman Catholicism, 1829–1850', unpublished PhD diss., University of Ottawa, 1997

Fortune, Gabrielle A., 'Hugh Coolahan and the prosperous Irish of Auckland, 1840–1870', unpublished MA thesis, University of Auckland, 1987

Fraser, Lyndon, 'Community, continuity and change: Irish Catholic immigrants in nineteenth-century Christchurch', unpublished PhD diss., University of Canterbury, 1994

Horn, Gerard, '"A loyal united and happy people": Irish Protestant migration to Wellington province, 1840–1930: Aspects of migration, settlement, and community', unpublished PhD diss., Victoria University of Wellington, 2010

Lambert, Carolyn, 'Far from the homes of their fathers: Irish Catholics in St. John's, Newfoundland, 1840–86', unpublished PhD diss., Memorial University of Newfoundland, 2010

Laracy, Hugh, 'The life and context of Bishop Patrick Moran', unpublished MA thesis, Victoria University of Wellington, 1964

Linehan, Michael, 'Archbishop Carr and Catholic education: The attitude and response to the Registration of Teachers and Schools Act 1905', unpublished M.Ed. diss., University of Melbourne (n.d.)

Lipscomb, Oscar H., 'The administration of Michael Portier, vicar apostolic of Alabama and the Floridas, 1825–1829 and the first bishop of Mobile, 1829–1859', unpublished PhD diss., Catholic University of America, 1963

Luminiello, Rose, 'Confronting modernity: Pope Leo XIII, *Rerum Novarum*, and the Catholic Church in Ireland and Poland, 1878–1914', unpublished PhD diss., University of Aberdeen, 2019

Luminiello, Rose, 'St. Brigid's Missionary College and the effects of Irish Catholic religious sisters in the Irish spiritual empire and diaspora', unpublished MSc diss., University of Edinburgh, 2014

Mannion, Patrick, 'The Irish diaspora in comparative perspective: St. John's, Newfoundland, Halifax, Nova Scotia, and Portland, Maine, 1880–1923', unpublished PhD diss., University of Toronto, 2013

Player, Anne V., 'Bishop William Lanigan of Goulburn and the making of a Catholic people', unpublished PhD diss., Australian National University, 2004

Potts, Michael, '"We Never Sink": Matthew Quinn as bishop of Bathurst', unpublished BA (Hons.) thesis, University of Sydney, 1971

Smith, Laura J., 'Unsettled settlers: Irish Catholics, Irish Catholicism, and British loyalty in Upper Canada, 1819–1840', unpublished PhD diss., University of Toronto, 2017

Vaney, N. P., 'The dual tradition: Irish Catholics and French priests in New Zealand: The west coast experience, 1865–1910', unpublished MA thesis, University of Canterbury, 1976

Veitch, Noel A., 'The contribution of the Benevolent Irish Society to education in Newfoundland from 1823 to 1875', unpublished M.Ed. thesis, St Francis Xavier University, 1965

(III)   *Works of Reference*

Australian Dictionary of Biography
Dictionary of Canadian Biography
Dictionary of Irish Biography
Dictionary of New Zealand Biography; Te Ara – the Encyclopaedia of New Zealand
Oxford Dictionary of National Biography

Index